Human Resource Management

Second Canadian Edition

Sandra L. Steen
University of Regina

Raymond A. Noe
Ohio State University

John R. Hollenbeck
Michigan State University

Barry Gerhart
University of Wisconsin–Madison

Patrick M. Wright
Cornell University

McGraw-Hill Ryerson

Toronto   Montréal   Boston   Burr Ridge, IL   Dubuque, IA   Madison, WI   New York
San Francisco   St. Louis   Bangkok   Bogotá   Caracas   Kuala Lumpur   Lisbon   London
Madrid   Mexico City   Milan   New Delhi   Santiago   Seoul   Singapore   Sydney   Taipei

McGraw-Hill Ryerson

HUMAN RESOURCE MANAGEMENT
Second Canadian Edition

Copyright © 2009, 2006 by McGraw-Hill Ryerson Limited, a Subsidiary of The McGraw-Hill Companies. Previous editions copyright © 2007, 2004 by The McGraw-Hill Companies, Inc. All rights reserved. No part of this publication may be reproduced or transmitted in any form or by any means, or stored in a data base or retrieval system, without the prior written permission of McGraw-Hill Ryerson Limited, or in the case of photocopying or other reprographic copying, a licence from The Canadian Copyright Licensing Agency (Access Copyright). For an Access Copyright licence, visit www.accesscopyright.ca or call toll free to 1-800-893-5777.

Statistics Canada information is used with the permission of Statistics Canada. Users are forbidden to copy this material and/or redisseminate the data, in an original or modified form, for commercial purposes, without the expressed permission of Statistics Canada. Information on the availability of the wide range of data from Statistics Canada can be obtained from Statistics Canada's Regional Offices, its World Wide Web site at http://www.statcan.ca and its toll-free access number 1-800-263-1136.

ISBN-13: 978-0-07-097986-4
ISBN-10: 0-07-097986-3

1 2 3 4 5 6 7 8 9 10 TCP 0 9

Printed and bound in Canada

Care has been taken to trace ownership of copyright material contained in this text; however, the publisher will welcome any information that enables it to rectify any reference or credit for subsequent editions.

Vice-President and Editor-in-Chief: Joanna Cotton
Senior Sponsoring Editor: Kim Brewster
Managing Editor, Development: Kelly Dickson
Developmental Editor: Tracey Haggert
Executive Marketing Manager: Joy Armitage Taylor
Permissions Editor: Christine Lomas
Marketing Manager: Cathie Lefebvre
Manager, Editorial Services: Margaret Henderson
Supervising Editor: Cathy Biribauer
Copy Editor: Rodney Rawlings
Production Coordinator: Lena Mastromarco
Page Layout: Laserwords Private Limited
Cover Design: Brett Miller, BJM Graphic Design & Communications
Cover Photo: First Light
Inside Design: Brett Miller, BJM Graphic Design & Communications
Printer: Transcontinental Printing Group

Library and Archives Canada Cataloguing in Publication Data

Human resource management/Steen

... [et al.].—2nd Canadian ed.

ISBN 978-0-07-097986-4

1. Personnel management—Textbooks. I. Steen, Sandra

HF5549.F848 2009   658.3   C2008-906318-X

In tribute to the lives of Walter and Alice Yung, and to
my husband, Aaron, and my children, Matt and Jess
—S.L.S.

In tribute to the lives of Raymond and Mildred Noe
—R.A.N.

To my parents, Harold and Elizabeth, my wife, Patty,
and my children, Jennifer, Marie, Timothy, and Jeffrey
—J.R.H.

To my parents, Robert and Shirley, my wife, Heather,
and my children, Chris and Annie
—B.G.

To my parents, Patricia and Paul, my wife, Mary,
and my sons, Michael and Matthew
—P.M.W.

About the Authors

Sandra L. Steen is a faculty member of the Paul J. Hill School of Business and the Kenneth Levene Graduate School of Business at the University of Regina. Sandra has an integrated education and background in both Human Resource Management and Organizational Behaviour. She has enjoyed more than 25 years of leading, managing, training, teaching, and consulting across a wide range of organizations in the private, public, and not-for-profit sectors. Her knowledge base combines theory gained from an MBA focusing on human resource management and organizational behaviour from the University of Regina as well as practitioner and consultant perspectives. Sandra teaches in the undergraduate, MBA, and Executive MBA programs at the University of Regina. Sandra holds the designation of Certified Human Resources Professional (CHRP) and she is a member of the Saskatchewan Association of Human Resource Professionals. Recent accomplishments include recognition as "Inspiring Teacher Award—Business Administration" and the publication of *Canadian Organizational Behaviour—Seventh Edition* which she co-authored with Steven McShane. In her leisure time, Sandra enjoys spending time at the lake with her husband, Aaron, and their children, Matt and Jess.

Raymond A. Noe is the Robert and Anne Hoyt Professor of Management at Ohio State University. He was previously a professor in the Department of Management at Michigan State University and the Industrial Relations Center of the Carlson School of Management, University of Minnesota. He received his B.S. in psychology from Ohio State University and his M.A. and Ph.D. in psychology from Michigan State University. Professor Noe conducts research and teaches undergraduate as well as MBA and Ph.D. students in human resource management, managerial skills, quantitative methods, human resource information systems, training, employee development, and organizational behavior. He has published articles in the *Academy of Management Journal, Academy of Management Review, Journal of Applied Psychology, Journal of Vocational Behavior,* and *Personnel Psychology.* Professor Noe is currently on the editorial boards of several journals including *Personnel Psychology, Journal of Applied Psychology,* and *Journal of Organizational Behavior.* Professor Noe has received awards for his teaching and research excellence, including the Herbert G. Heneman Distinguished Teaching Award in 1991 and the Ernest J. McCormick Award for Distinguished Early Career Contribution from the Society for Industrial and Organizational Psychology in 1993. He is also a fellow of the Society for Industrial and Organizational Psychology.

John R. Hollenbeck is currently the Eli Broad Professor of Management at the Eli Broad Graduate School of Business Administration at Michigan State University. He received his Ph.D. in Management from New York University in 1984 and joined the Michigan State faculty that year. Dr. Hollenbeck has published over 60 articles and book chapters, with more than 35 of these appearing in the most highly cited refereed outlets (*Journal of Applied Psychology, Academy of Management Journal, Personnel Psychology,* and *Organizational Behavior and Human Decision Processes*). Dr. Hollenbeck was the acting editor at *Organizational Behavior and Human Decision Processes* in 1995, the associate editor at *Decision Sciences* from 1999 to 2004, and the editor of *Personnel Psychology* between 1996 and 2002. Prior to serving as editor, he served on the editorial board of these journals, as well as the boards of the *Academy of Management Journal, Academy of Management Review, Journal of Applied Psychology,* and *Journal of Management.* Dr. Hollenbeck was the first recipient of the Ernest J. McCormick Award for Early Contributions to the field of Industrial and Organizational Psychology in 1992, and is a Fellow of the American Psychological Association.

Barry Gerhart is Professor of Management and Human Resources, the Bruce R. Ellig Distinguished Chair in Pay and Organizational Effectiveness, and Director of the Strategic Human Resources Program, School of Business, University of Wisconsin–Madison. His previous faculty appointments include serving as Area Coordinator of the Organization Studies area at Vanderbilt University's Owen Graduate School of Management and as Chair of the Department of Human Resource Studies, Cornell University. His major fields of interest are human resource management and strategy, compensation, and business performance. Professor Gerhart received his B.S. in Psychology from Bowling Green State University and his Ph.D. in Industrial Relations from the University of Wisconsin–Madison. Current and past editorial board appointments include the *Academy of Management Journal, Administration Science Quarterly, Industrial and Labor Relations Review,* the *International Journal of Human Resource Management,* the *Journal of Applied Psychology,* and *Personnel Psychology.* In 1991, Professor Gerhart received the Scholarly Achievement Award from the Human Resources Division, Academy of Management. He is also a Fellow of the American Psychological Association and of the Society for Industrial and Organizational Psychology. Professor Gerhard is co-author of the book, *Compensation: Theory, Evidence, and Strategic Implications,* as well as co-editor of *Compensation in Organizations.*

Patrick M. Wright is Professor of Human Resource Studies and Director of the Center for Advanced Human Resource Studies in the School of Industrial and Labor Relations, Cornell University. He holds a B.A. in Psychology from Wheaton College, and an MBA and Ph.D. in Organizational Behavior/Human Resource Management from Michigan State University. Professor Wright teaches, conducts research, and consults in the area of Strategic Human Resource Management (SHRM), particularly focusing on how firms use people as a source of competitive advantage. He has published over 50 articles in journals such as *Academy of Management Journal, Academy of Management Review, Strategic Management Journal, Organizational Behavior and Human Decision Processes, Journal of Applied Psychology, Personnel Psychology,* and *Journal of Management,* as well as over 20 chapters in books and edited volumes such as *Research in P/HRM* and *Handbook of I/O Psychology.* He currently serves on the editorial boards of *Personnel Psychology, Human Resource Management Journal, Human Resource Management Review, Journal of Management, Human Resource Planning, Management and Organization Review, Journal of Management Studies,* and *Journal of Managerial Issues.* He has co-authored two textbooks, and has co-edited a number of special issues of journals dealing with the future of Strategic HRM as well as Corporate Social Responsibility. He has taught in Executive Development programs, and conducted programs and/or consulted for a number of large public- and private-sector organizations. Dr. Wright served as Chair of the HR Division of the Academy of Management, and on the Board of Directors for SHRM Foundation, World at Work, and Human Resource Planning Society.

Brief Contents

Contents

Preface

Welcome to the second Canadian edition of *Human Resource Management*. This is a fully Canadianized text, created to give students, supervisors, managers, entrepreneurs, and leaders a focused introduction to HRM in Canada that is rich in content and relevant in its strategic application. This text comprises 12 chapters that balance theory and application, and present the material in a manner that is engaging to both students and instructors.

We've made this second edition even easier to study the lessons you'll need to know to gain a competitive advantage in Human Resource Management. With **Learning Objectives** clearly outlined in the chapter opening pages, and then re-emphasized within the chapter, students are sure to grasp the key learning outcomes. The **Summary, Key Terms, Review and Discussion Questions**, and **Cases** at the end of each chapter solidify the lessons learned. For those who may be pursuing the Certified Human Resources Professional designation, we have identified the **Required Professional Capabilities** linked to applicable content areas with the RPC icon shown here in the margin. A full list of these RPCs can be found on the inside front cover of the text.

Also new to this edition are a wealth of tools designed to bring real-world relevance that help students better prepare for challenges they may face on the job. Look for the new part-opening feature **Real People in HR** (highlighting insights from human resource professionals) and the **Thinking Ethically exercises** (designed to challenge your thinking about topics ranging from "greenwashing" to aggressive recruiting practices). This second edition also brings enhanced coverage of workplace safety, engaging work environments, and global human resource management.

Emphasis on the Whole Picture

Human resource management affects every aspect of the workforce: management/labour, employer/employee, student/professional—we all have a vested interest in effective human resource management. This book provides coverage of all the expected HRM topics such as analyzing jobs; planning; recruiting, selecting, training, developing, and compensating employees; managing performance; and handling labour relations. In addition, we have strived to give you more of what you may need to understand, facilitate, and contribute to achieving extraordinary results in organizations of all types and sizes. We have rounded out our discussion of HRM in Canada by including topics that we feel represent the additional expectations of the proactive human resource professional and leader, such as managing human resources globally, adopting a total rewards approach to compensating and rewarding employees, and creating a high-performance work environment where employees' hearts and minds are engaged.

Real and Relevant Examples

You will find a broad range of Canadian examples featuring organizations from coast to coast that are leading the way in proactive human resource management. Following graduation, most students will find themselves working in businesses, government, or not-for-profit organizations. Regardless of their position or career aspirations, their role in either directly managing other employees or understanding human resource management practices is critical for ensuring both company and personal success. As a result, *Human Resource Management* focuses on human resource issues and how HR is used at work in Canada. An important feature of this book is that it is rich with examples and engages the student with practical applications. Students not only learn about best human resource practices but also are actively engaged in learning about human resources through cases, ethical discussions, and decision making. This is critical for helping students learn how to find, develop, and nurture talent, which is one of the most important tasks in organizations; but it is sometimes woefully performed. For example, as described in detail in the guided tour of the book, each chapter includes a section called **Thinking Ethically** that presents students with ethical issues regarding managing human resources and asks them to make and justify their decisions. Several different cases are included in each chapter that look at events of real companies and encourage students to critically evaluate each situation and apply the chapter concepts.

While other books may have similar coverage of HR topics, the author team believes that three characteristics distinguish this book from the rest:

- Timely coverage of important HR issues
- Easy to read
- Features that grab students' attention and get them actively involved in learning

We thank those who adopted the first edition, and hope you will continue to use the second! For those considering *Human Resource Management* for adoption, we hope you agree that the book's features make it your text of choice.

Organization of the Second Canadian Edition

We have made some changes to the structure of the second Canadian edition—changes which we feel organize the key HRM topics more effectively and logically. The text consists of 12 chapters in five parts as follows:

- **Part 1** discusses several aspects of the human resource environment. To be effective, human resource management must begin with an awareness of the trends and challenges shaping this field, including changes in the workforce, technology, and society as well as the profession of HR itself. Such trends and issues are the topic of *Chapter 1*. On a more detailed level, human resource management must also ensure that the organization's actions comply with legal requirements, the topic of *Chapter 2*. *Chapter 3* addresses how organizations provide safe and engaging work environments.
- **Part 2** explores the responsibilities involved in preparing for and acquiring human resources. *Chapter 4* covers the topics of analyzing work and designing jobs. *Chapter 5* explains how to plan for human resource needs and recruit candidates to meet those needs. *Chapter 6* discusses the selection of employees and their placement into jobs or teams.

- In **Part 3**, the discussion turns to the development of human resources. *Chapter 7* addresses various ways organizations train and develop their employees to perform their jobs, prepare for future jobs and help establish career paths that take into account work interests, goals, values, and other career issues. *Chapter 8* describes the various activities involved in managing performance, including regular performance appraisals.
- An important element of attracting, retaining, and engaging human resources is the employee's belief that he or she is being fairly rewarded for the work performed. **Part 4** addresses several topics related to compensation and rewards. *Chapter 9* explores decisions related to the organization's overall pay structure, discusses ways organizations can use pay to recognize individual and group contributions to the organization's performance, considers benefits—forms of total compensation other than pay—and looks at how to create a total rewards culture.
- **Part 5** addresses a number of special topics that human resource managers face today. *Chapter 10* discusses responsibilities of human resource management in organizations where employees have or are seeking union representation. *Chapter 11* explores issues that arise when the organization has human resources working in more than one country. And *Chapter 12*, the last chapter, returns to the topic of high-performance organizations, taking a closer look at how human resource management can foster high performance.

Instructors' Resources

Instructors can access all of the resources associated with the text, create custom presentations, exam questions, and Microsoft PowerPoint® lecture slides, by downloading from the Instructor's Resource Centre of the Online Learning Centre (OLC) at www.mcgrawhill.ca/olc/steen. This valuable set of resources was developed by the text author, Sandra Steen, to ensure accuracy and tight alignment with text content.

Instructor's Manual

The Instructor's Manual includes a wealth of information to assist instructors in presenting this text and their course to its best advantage. It includes lecture notes, answers to end-of-chapter questions, and other valuable aids.

EZ Test Computerized Test Bank

McGraw-Hill's EZ Test is a flexible and easy-to-use electronic testing program. The program allows instructors to create tests from book-specific items. It accommodates a wide range of question types and instructors may add their own questions. Multiple versions of the test can be created and any test can be exported to use with course management systems such as WebCT, Blackboard, or PageOut. The program is available for both Windows and Macintosh environments.

Microsoft PowerPoint® Presentations

A complete set of PowerPoint® slides for each chapter is provided, including graphics and key chapter material to aid in illustrating and explaining concepts.

Human Resource Management Video Package

The video package contains carefully selected segments from current CBC programming as well as segments from the McGraw-Hill Management Video Library. It is an excellent supplement to lectures and useful for generating in-class discussions.

WebCT/Blackboard

This text is available in two of the most popular course-delivery platforms—WebCT and Blackboard—for more user-friendly and enhanced features. Contact your McGraw-Hill *i*Learning Sales Specialist for more information.

Instructor Online Learning Centre (www.mcgrawhill.ca/olc/steen)

Along with the Student OLC (see below), *Human Resource Management* includes a password-protected website for instructors. The site offers downloadable supplements and a wealth of other resources.

Manager's Hot Seat Online (www.mhhe.com/mhs)

In today's workplace, managers are confronted daily with issues such as diversity, working in teams, and the virtual workplace. The Manager's Hot Seat Online is an interactive website (available as an instructor supplement or for packaging with texts) that allows students to watch as 15 real managers apply their years of experience to confront these issues. New segments available in January 2009.

Group-Video Resource Manual (www.mhhe.com/mobmanual)

Available through this website with hotlinked exercises, this instructor supplement offers additional exercises, teaching notes, and instructor PowerPoint® presentations linked to the Manager's Hot Seat Online, as well as group exercises and lecture supplements. The resource conveniently hotlinks to additional self-assessment exercises, Test Your knowledge exercises, group exercises, and the Hot Seat segments, grouped in a resource matrix sorted by topics.

Integrated Learning System

Great care was used in the creation of the supplemental materials to accompany *Human Resource Management*. Whether you are a seasoned faculty member or a newly minted instructor, you will find the support materials to be comprehensive and practical.

*i*Learning Sales Specialist

Your Integrated Learning (*i*Learning) Sales Specialist is a McGraw-Hill Ryerson representative who has the experience, product knowledge, training, and support to help you assess and integrate any of the above-noted products, technology, and services into your course for optimum teaching and learning performance. Whether it's how to use our test bank software, help your students improve their grades, or put your entire course online, your *i*Learning Sales Specialist is there to help. Contact your Specialist today to learn how to maximize all McGraw-Hill Ryerson resources!

*i*Services Program

McGraw-Hill Ryerson offers a unique *i*Services package designed for Canadian faculty. Our mission is to equip providers of higher education with superior tools and resources required for excellence in teaching. For additional information visit www.mcgrawhill.ca/highereducation/eservices.

Student Supplements

*i*Study for Human Resource Management (www.istudyhrm.ca)

NEW! This interactive study space was developed by Sandra Steen to help students master the concepts and achieve better grades. *i*Study HRM includes key study aids such as concept reviews, chapter summaries, self-testing modules in an interactive and fun format, what to watch for, flash cards, and much more. The site also contains links to relevant human resource management sites and resources and other supplemental information to help boost student success in HRM.

Student Online Learning Centre (www.mcgrawhill.ca/olc/steen)

The *Human Resource Management* Online Learning Centre (OLC) follows the text chapter by chapter, with additional experiential materials linked to the text, such as **"What's Your HR IQ?"** and quizzes to enhance the text and the classroom experience. Students can review concepts or prepare for exams by taking the self-grading quizzes that accompany each chapter or work through interactive exercises. The site also has links to relevant human resource management sites and resources and other supplemental information that complements the text material.

CCH Canada BusinessWorks©

Use the tools the professionals use! **CCH Canada BusinessWorks©**, available from the Online Learning Centre, provides a snapshot of the BusinessWorks information database. This online resource gives students and instructors access to laws, regulations, and developments in all major areas of human resource management, including health and safety, employment standards, and industrial relations.

CourseSmart

CourseSmart brings together thousands of textbooks across hundreds of courses in an eTextbook format providing unique benefits to students and faculty. By purchasing an eTextbook, students can save up to 50 percent off the cost of a print textbook; reduce their impact on the environment; and gain access to powerful Web tools for learning, including full text search, notes and highlighting, and e-mail tools for sharing notes between classmates. For faculty, CourseSmart provides instant access to review and compare textbooks and course materials in their discipline area without the time, cost, and environmental impact of mailing print examination copies. For further details contact your *i*Learning Sales Specialist or go to www.coursesmart.com.

Acknowledgments

The second edition of *Human Resource Management* represents the efforts of an extraordinary publishing team at McGraw-Hill Ryerson. Although work is increasingly performed in teams, it is a special accomplishment when your team members become your trusted advisors, coaches, and friends! This result was made possible by first and foremost an inspiring leader—Kim Brewster, Senior Sponsoring Editor, who provided the type of leadership that we hope everyone can experience at least once in their career. Tracey Haggert, Developmental Editor, who masterfully managed the entire writing and review process. Tracey was always just a BlackBerry message away and provided both the support and structure to complete the research and writing through a tight schedule. And Christine Lomas, Senior Editorial Associate, who handled every photo idea and permission request with unwavering enthusiasm and unparalleled organizational skills. For this edition, we also are very grateful for the skills and contributions of Cathy Biribauer, our Supervising Editor who guided the production process, and Rodney Rawlings, Copy Editor, for his keen copyediting skills.

Many instructors across Canada reviewed *Human Resource Management*. Their detailed feedback, timely comments, and suggestions improved the final product. The following people from Canadian colleges and universities are among those who provided their insights:

Carol Ann Samhaber, *Algonquin College*

Linda Eligh, *University of Western Ontario*

Maureen Nummelin, *Conestoga College*

R. Blake Jelley, *University of Prince Edward Island*

David Morrison, *Durham College*

Janice Foley, *University of Regina*

Suzanne Kavanagh, *George Brown College*

Coreen Hrabluik, *University of Toronto, Rotman School of Management*

Nelson Lacroix, *Niagara College*

Jim Hebert, *Red River College of Applied Arts, Science and Technology*

Jennifer Percival, *University of Ontario Institute of Technology*

Gary Gannon, *Durham College*

Ron Schlegelmilch, *University of Alberta*

Paul Nyhof, *University of Manitoba*

Celia Moore, *University of Toronto, Rotman School of Management*

Sue Deegan, *Georgian College*

Maria Galang, *University of Victoria*

Jana Raver, *Queens University*

Melanie Peacock, *Mount Royal College*

Rajeev Sachdev, *University of Ontario Institute of Technology*

Indira Somwaru, *Seneca College of Applied Arts and Technology*

Grace O'Farrell, *University of Winnipeg*

PEDAGOGICAL FEATURES

Each of these features has been designed to take human resource management out of the classroom and into the real world—with either a practical exercise, a trip to the Web, a headline news feature, or an example of a best practice or innovation in the workplace.

Chapter 3

Safe and Engaging Work Environments

What Do I Need to Know? After reading this chapter, you should be able to:

1. Explain the context for workplace health and safety.
2. Identify employers' duties and employees' rights and responsibilities related to workforce health and safety.
3. Discuss ways employers promote worker health and safety.
4. Describe how organizations contribute to employee job satisfaction and engagement and retain employees.

WHAT DO I NEED TO KNOW?

Student learning objectives open each chapter. They bring attention to the key topics in the chapter and are then referenced in the page margins of the chapter discussion so students can easily see where each topic is explored.

Real People in HR

...Joy Serne, Senior Director Culture, Farm Credit Canada

Joy Serne is the Senior Director Culture, Organizational Development and Workforce Planning, with Farm Credit Canada (FCC). Joy previously held positions throughout FCC in the areas of Operations, Re-engineering, and IT. She holds a bachelor of science in agriculture and agricultural economics from the University of Saskatchewan.

Name...
Joy Serne.

Job...
Senior Director Culture, Organizational Development and Workforce Planning—Farm Credit Canada (FCC).

Most challenging aspect of your job...
Finding the time to do everything that can be done.

Most rewarding aspect of your job...
Seeing new HR strategies come to life and hearing others in the business say we really add value to FCC.

REAL PEOPLE IN HR—*NEW!*

Each Part opens with a brief profile of a Canadian HR professional. These "in my own words" profiles offer students some insights into how HRM is practised by actual HR professionals and reinforce the text's commitment to "real world" application of the concepts and theories presented in the part.

THINKING ETHICALLY

Checking Out a Candidate's Facebook Profile

The Internet has become the first stop for many recruiters and hiring managers to determine if a potential candidate is a good fit. Many job seekers are not aware of these instant background checks. In a recent Adecco Workplace Insights survey, 66 percent of Generation Y respondents were unaware that seemingly private photos, comments, and statements were audited by potential employers.

"It's a lot more common than I think the prospective employees realize," says Lynne Perry-Reid, a Calgary recruiter and co-founder of Corporate Connections. "Especially now that a lot of recruiters tend

to be younger, maybe in their 30's, everyone is really involved in things like MySpace or Facebook," she says, "so you can easily just type in someone's name to find out about them because you're already hooked into that network."

In a formal job interview, employers are not legally permitted to ask questions about a candidate's age, marital status, sexual orientation, or ethnicity but the individual's profile can reveal all of these things to a prospective employer. Even individuals who are very careful about photos and information on their own profile, may not be

aware of being in a photo that appears on another person's profile. "All of a sudden there are pictures of you drunk and half-naked—do you want your prospective employer to see those pictures before they have actually met you?"

SOURCES: "Your Profile on Social Sites Can Make or Break Your Job Opportunities," Financial Post, September 19, 2007, www.canada .com/nationalpost/news/working/ story, retrieved September 21, 2007; Derek Sankey, "Facebook Background Checks," Calgary Herald, 2007, http:// working.canada.com/calgary/resources/ story, retrieved April 4, 2008; Kristin Gissaro, "The Invasion of Recruiters on Social Networking Sites," www.ere.net .blogs/generational_recruiting, retrieved April 4, 2008.

Questions
1. Are employers crossing the line when they look up job candidates on a social networking site such as Facebook?

THINKING ETHICALLY—*NEW!*

The "Thinking Ethically" feature at the end of each chapter confronts students with ethical issues regarding managing human resources and asks them to make and justify their decisions. Examples include: "Talent Poaching" and "Whose Business Is It When You Blog?"

Introduction

Wardrop Engineering Inc., based in Winnipeg Manitoba, is a multidisciplinary consulting engineering, environmental, and information technology firm that holds the distinction of being one of the Top 100 Employers in Canada for eight consecutive years. This award-winning firm makes use of a balanced scorecard as part of its approach to "ensure everyone is pushing in the same direction." "Balanced scorecard can get everyone working together," says CEO Shayne Smith. It also helps ensure that the work

CHAPTER OPENING VIGNETTES

Each chapter opens with a look at events and people in real organizations (see "Introduction") to encourage students to critically evaluate and apply each situation to the chapter content.

pay equity
Principle of nondiscrimination in wages that requires men and women doing work of equal value to be paid the same.

equal value, or pay equity. **Pay equity** is a principle of nondiscrimination in wages that requires men and women doing work of equal value to the employer to be paid the same. Most provinces and the Yukon, as well as Australia, Scandinavian countries, and many U.S. states, have laws to ensure women and men working in female-dominated jobs, for example, nursing, clerical, and retail sales, are paid fairly. The four criteria usually applied are *skill, effort, responsibility,* and *working conditions*.

Pay equity legislation is intended to address the wage gap—the difference between the earnings of women working full-time versus the earnings of men working full-time. "In Canada, today, women working full-time still make an average of

KEY TERMS

Key terms and definitions appear in the text margins, so terms are highlighted where they are discussed for easy review and in order to introduce the language of HRM.

BEST PRACTICES

Canadian Cancer Society Launches New Onboarding Program

People Remember Stories

New employees can become overwhelmed by having to absorb too much too soon. They don't yet have the organization-specific navigational skills to discern what's important in the mountain of binders, reports, intranet resources, and other information provided. The HR team's solution was to develop an approach that reinforces the society's brand and ensures a consistent and reliable method of providing information.

A typical volunteer, Ray, was selected to help guide the new employee through the organization's massive intranet and essential links. Through his story as both a

example, Ray talks about his community work and his family's participation in the Canadian Cancer Society Relay for Life, a national fundraising event. He then invites the new hire to click on appropriate links to drill deeper into fundraising information.

Experience: Managers Can't Do It All

Recognizing the importance of developing quality relationships early in a new employee's tenure, the society developed a series of discussion guides to help new employees, their managers, and their internal and external clients talk about mutual expectations. In one guide, a new hire and her

employee interview key clients to understand their priorities and expectations. This helps the employee take action and establish credibility early on.

Future Plans Include Measurement, Enhancements

While the onboarding program is still in its early days, there are already plans to measure the effectiveness.

And future program enhancements include the development of specific departmental orientation modules and a survey that solicits confidential feedback about program usage and impact from both new hires and hiring managers. This will provide quantitative and

BEST PRACTICES

The Best Practices boxes give specific examples of what is working well in HRM. Illustrating real-world examples of effective practices that have been put in place and have been successful helps students understand how to apply what they're learning in the text. Examples include: "Suncor Energy's Journey-to-Zero Safety Initiative Receives CAPP President Award" and "Deloitte Develops a Global Workforce."

E-HRM

Recruiting Real Talent in a Virtual World

At a recent recruitment session for the Vancouver police, Inspector Kevin McQuiggin was surrounded by job seekers with spiky hairdos, exotic wardrobes, and even wings. "Any one of those individuals may make an excellent police officer," McQuiggin says. After all, this was Second Life, so he was not at all alarmed by this unusual cast of characters. The Vancouver Police Department, like Hewlett-Packard, Manpower, Kelly, CareerBuilder, and Microsoft, are recruiting on

We have to recruit people that are going to understand that," he says. "The kind of people we attract through Second Life are people who have a predisposition to technology."

In Second Life, both job seekers and recruiters create avatars or online personas that interact in a virtual community, also sometimes referred to as a *virtual social world,* the 3-D *Internet,* or *participatory media.* The appearance, dress, and even species of the avatar can be customized to the user's preferences.

of interest as they meet with employers in virtual booths. If both the employer and job seeker are interested in further discussion, they go to a virtual conference room to chat, share files, and have further discussions that may result in a real-world interview. The main pitfall of virtual world recruiting is the amount of time, energy, and patience required to set up your avatar. As a result, the base of job seekers tends to be younger and more technologically savvy.

E-HRM

The e-HRM boxes appear in each chapter and emphasize the increasing use of technology in human resource management today and how it is changing how things are done. Examples include: "Paperless Performance Appraisal" and "Triple Creek Associates Puts Mentoring Online."

HR HOW-TO

Measuring Worker Engagement

To identify the elements of worker engagement, Gallup conducted hundreds of focus groups and many thousands of worker interviews in all kinds of organizations, and at all levels, in most industries, and in many countries. The result was 12 key employee expectations that, when satisfied, form the foundation of strong feelings of engagement.

These are Gallup's 12 questions:

• Do you know what is expected of you at work?
• Do you have the materials and equipment you need to do your work right?
• At work, do you have the opportunity to do what you do best every day?
• In the last seven days, have

you received recognition or praise for doing good work?
• Does your supervisor, or someone at work, seem to care about you as a person?
• Is there someone at work who encourages your development?
• At work, do your opinions seem to count?
• Does the mission/purpose of your company make you feel your job is important?
• Are your associates (fellow employees) committed to doing quality work?
• Do you have a best friend at work?
• In the last six months, has someone at work talked to you about your progress?
• In the last year, have you had opportunities at work to learn and grow?

The 12 engagement questions are answered by employees on a scale of one to five, according to their weak or strong agreement. The process also involves a feedback methodology for improving engagement by creating a factual base for discussion and debate of the causes behind the numbers. In this way, it yields actionable input from staff and managers for changes in behaviour, attitudes, policies, and processes. Follow-up surveys are conducted to track long-term progress—or backsliding—on the 12 questions.

SOURCE: John Thackray, "Feedback for Real," March 15, 2001, http://gmj.gallup.com/content/811/Feedback-Real.aspx, retrieved August 28, 2008.

HR HOW-TO

The HR How-To boxes discuss steps to creating HRM programs and include examples of how companies have tackled challenges. This feature helps students to understand the common functions of human resource professionals. Examples include: "Writing a Job Description" and "Maintaining Legal Compliance When Collecting and Using Employee Information—PIPEDA."

PEDAGOGICAL FEATURES

CHAPTER SUMMARIES recap the "What Do I Need to Know?" objectives from the beginning of each chapter with brief summary discussions.

CASES in each chapter look at organizations and how their practices illustrate or apply concepts from the chapter. They provide external examples to bring into a lecture, along with questions for assignments or classroom discussion.

VIDEO CASES at the end of each Part include summaries and challenging questions about current HRM issues. Teaching notes to the video cases are included in the Instructor's Manual. ●

VIDEO CASE

PCL Internal Orientation Video

This video puts you inside one of North America's largest construction companies—PCL, headquartered in Edmonton, Alberta. This video is used as part of PCL's orientation process for new employees. PCL's values and dedication to construction excellence and its talent are discussed in a series of personal vignettes from a diverse group of employees including the CEO.

For example, PCL's College of Construction, illustrated in the introduction to Chapter 7, is mentioned as one of the tangible ways that PCL supports the development of people.

Questions
1. What evidence does the video provide that PCL is committed to valuing and developing its talent (people)?

2. If you were watching this video as part of an orientation (onboarding) process at PCL, what expectations would you have about the kinds of training, development, and career opportunities you will have as a PCL employee?
3. Does PCL sound like a good place to build a career? Why or why not?

REVIEW AND DISCUSSION QUESTIONS at the end of each chapter help link the contents in the chapter to potential applications requiring critical thinking. ●

REVIEW AND DISCUSSION QUESTIONS

1. Some individuals evaluate prospective employers' job offers based only on direct pay considerations. What additional factors should be considered when evaluating job offers from employers?
2. Why might an organization choose to pay employees more than the market rate? Why might it choose to pay less? What are the consequences of paying more or less than the market rate?
3. What are the advantages of establishing pay ranges, rather than specific pay levels, for each job? What are the drawbacks of this approach?
4. Suppose a small startup business wants to establish a competency-based pay structure. What would be some advantages of this approach? List the issues the company should be prepared to address in setting up this system. Consider the kinds of information you will need and the ways employees may react to the new pay structure.
5. With some organizations and jobs, pay is primarily wages or salaries, and with others, incentive pay is more important. For each of the following jobs, state whether you think the pay should emphasize base pay (wages and salaries) or incentive pay (bonuses, profit sharing, and so on). Give a reason for each.
   a. An accountant at a manufacturing company
   b. A salesperson for a software company

c. A mechanic for a major airline
d. A marketing manager for a consumer packaged-goods firm
e. A recruitment specialist for the federal government
6. Why do some organizations link incentive pay to the organization's overall performance? Is it appropriate to use stock performance as an incentive for employees at all levels? Why or why not?
7. Why do employers provide employee benefits, rather than providing all compensation in the form of pay and letting employees buy the services they want?
8. Of the benefits discussed in this chapter, list the ones you consider essential—those benefits you would require in any job offer. Why are these benefits important to you?
9. Why is it important to communicate information about total rewards? Suppose you work in the HR department of a company that has decided to add new elements to its total rewards—onsite massage plus an increased budget to support learning and development opportunities for all employees. How would you recommend communicating this change? What information should your messages include?
10. Do you think executive total compensation is too high? Why or why not?

WHAT'S YOUR HR IQ? sections at the end of each chapter reference the assessment activities included on the Online Learning Centre, which are hands-on activities to reinforce the specific chapter content. ●

WHAT'S YOUR HR IQ?

Online Learning Centre
The Online Learning Centre offers more ways to check what you've learned so far. Find experiential exercises as well as Test Your Knowledge Quizzes, Videos, and many other resources at www.mcgrawhill.ca/olc/steen.

Excalibur Case:
Smith Rubber

EXCALIBUR
Excellence • calibre

EXCALIBUR CASES are featured in some chapters. These cases were used in Excalibur, the Canadian University Tournament in Human Resources. ●

Located in the Eastern Townships region of Quebec, Smith Rubber grew from a small family-owned business into a medium-sized company. The organization is now facing a great deal of competition within Quebec and across North America. Its success has always been tied to its ability to compete with Japanese and Mexican companies that also supply the automobile industry.

Steve Smith Jr. is now president of Smith Rubber. At the time of his promotion some years ago, the company was not unionized. During this period he wondered how to best recognize employees and reward their performance while encouraging them to increase productivity. He hesitated about increasing wages because he feared losing his competitive edge if his fixed costs rose.

Three years ago, Smith Rubber had a particularly good year in terms of sales and profits. As a result, Steve

thought that a Christmas bonus would be the best way to reward employees. In fact, he told David Sanders, his human resource manager, "There is nothing like cold hard cash to make employees work harder." He set out his bonus system as follows:

Compensation	Bonus
$30,000 and under	$2,500
$30,001–$35,000	$3,000
$35,001–$40,000	$3,500
$40,001–$45,000	$4,000
$45,001–$50,000	$4,500
$50,001 or higher	10% of salary

The bonuses were a hit. Many employees thanked the president personally. Moreover, in February, David Sanders

Part 1

The Human Resource Environment

Real People in HR

Merrill Brinton, President of the Canadian Council of Human Resources Associations, has over three decades of experience in HR and industrial relations. He is currently the Human Resource Practice Leader for Meyers Norris Penny's Saskatchewan region and sits on the board of the North American Human Resources Management Association (NAHRM).

Name...
Merrill Brinton.

Job...
President, CCHRA and Human Resource Practice Leader—Myers Norris Penny.

Adjective people would use to describe you...
I would hope "respected."

First job...
Bottle washer in a major dairy in Halifax.

First HR job...
Labour Relations Officer in the construction industry. They wanted someone with no experience but a lot of "moxie." I went back and asked my professor from Dalhousie who recommended me for the job what "moxie" was. He said it is the ability to have people quickly, almost instantly, like and trust you so that they will open up and let you know what is really going on. It actually took me a long time to realize that it was in fact the combination of leadership competencies that created moxie.

Top three issues facing HR professionals in the next five years...
The near future is all about talent, and the top three issues would be recruitment, retention, and creating an employer/manager of choice organization culture.

Most challenging HR-related problem encountered...
There have been many; however, I would suggest that the most recent ones involve recruiting the "right" people into the "right" fit for both them and the hiring organization. Another would be convincing employers that they should use external coaches to help coach employees who they have a significant investment in and are perceived to be struggling in their role rather than simply trying to replace them.

Most important deliverables of the HR function and how to measure them...
As an external consultant I am exposed to customer scrutiny and am accountable for the "scope" of the project I am working on. I always begin a project with a client by asking what "success" will look like from their perspective at the end—whether it is a recruitment, a career transition, or performance coaching situation.

Everyone has service delivery standards and they should be honed and continually improved as you gain experience. A simple, yet appropriate, example in my opinion is training. At the beginning of a session I always "flipchart" what each participant would like to leave with, and then return at the end and ask each one if they got what they wanted. That is also measurement.

Four essential attributes that make someone a great HR professional...

Integrity, excellent interpersonal skills, the ability to be flexible, and a willingness to be accountable.

If you had to pick an alternative career...

Probably marketing or acting.

Best career advice that you ever received...

I used to be the "devil's advocate" on an executive team, which created a perception that I was negative and not a team player. My president took me aside and asked me to focus on how we could make things happen instead of why they wouldn't. This would create a perception that I was on the team and looking for ways to improve and implement new ideas, processes, etc., with other team members. If there were barriers, we would find them together, and either find ways to remove them or not, but it would be done collaboratively—not me versus them.

Advice for someone beginning an HR career...

Do the best possible job you can, learn as much as you can, ask lots of questions, and be a team player. The most important thing you can possibly do is to do what you say you will.

Chapter 1

Strategies, Trends, and Challenges in Human Resource Management

What Do I Need to Know? After reading this chapter, you should be able to:

1. Define human resource management, identify the roles and responsibilities of human resource departments, and explain how human resource management contributes to an organization's performance.

2. Summarize areas in which human resource management can support organizational strategies.

3. Identify the Required Professional Capabilities and certification process for HR professionals.

4. Explain the role of supervisors and line managers in human resource management.

5. Describe typical careers in human resource management.

6. Describe trends in the labour force composition and how they affect human resource management.

7. Discuss the role of high-performance work systems and how technological developments are affecting human resource management.

8. Explain how the nature of the employment relationship is changing and how the need for flexibility affects human resource management.

Introduction

What do Research in Motion, the Royal Canadian Mint, Farm Credit Canada, the Halifax Herald, Ontario Public Service, and Google Inc. have in common? They have all been recently recognized as excellent employers with progressive human resource management practices. The list of employment awards is growing, raising the bar on what it takes to attract, retain, and engage top talent. As labour markets become increasingly competitive, human resource professionals are being called upon to provide people management practices that not only support the organization's priorities but also provide for competitive success in a global marketplace. Organizations also strive to create an employment brand that resonates with specific employees. In addition to Mediacorp Canada's "Top 100 Employers," there are several additional annual competitions, including "Canada's Top 10 Employers for Young People," "Canada's Most Earth-Friendly Employers," "Best Employers for New Canadians," and "Canada's Top 10 Family Friendly Employers." Organizations are also considered for regional recognition including "Greater Toronto's Top 50 Employers," "New Brunswick's Top Employers," and Manitoba's Top 10 Employers."

Perhaps no organization has received more attention or has a stronger brand than Google. Google is known for its people practices and employee-first culture that directly contribute to its success. The work environment provides "Googlers" unlimited amounts of free, chef-prepared food at all times of the day, lap pools, onsite massages, car washes, oil changes, drycleaning, laundry service, and haircuts. Google's "20-percent time" gives employees 20 percent of their day to "work on what they're really passionate about"—and tangible organizational outcomes often result. For example, Gmail came about from one Google employee's 20-percent time efforts. Perhaps it is no surprise that Google receives 1300 résumés every day and is able to attract and retain some of the world's top talent.[1]

Google has been ranked multiple times as #1 on Fortune Magazine's 100 Best Companies to Work For.

Organizations of all sizes and in all industries are increasingly recognizing the importance of people. "This is a time of rapid change in the market—a time when Canadian organizations are constantly trying to keep pace and remain competitive. In today's knowledge-based economy, we rely on people to generate, develop, and implement ideas."[2] and the "human resource function has an important role in ensuring that organizations have the people capacity to execute strategic objectives."[3]

Strategic HRM

FIGURE 1.1

Human Resource
Management Practices

Company
Performance

Human resource management (HRM), centres on the policies, practices, and systems that influence employees' behaviour, attitudes, and performance. Many companies refer to HRM as "people practices." Figure 1.1 emphasizes that there are several important HRM practices that contribute to an organization's ability to realize the full benefit of its talent: analyzing work and designing jobs, attracting potential employees (recruiting), choosing employees (selection), preparing employees to perform their jobs and for the future (training and development), supporting their performance (performance management), rewarding employees (compensation), creating a positive work environment (employee and labour relations), and supporting the organization's strategy (workforce planning and change management). In addition, HRM has responsibility for providing safe work environments and assuring compliance with legal requirements that will be discussed in Chapter 2. An organization performs best when all of these practices are managed systemically. At companies with effective HRM, employees and customers tend to be more satisfied, and the companies tend to be more innovative, have greater productivity, and develop a more favourable reputation in the community.[4]

In this chapter, we introduce the scope of human resource management, including the ways HRM facilitates and supports organizational strategy. We begin by discussing why human resource management is an essential element of an organization's success. We then turn to the elements of managing human resources: the roles and capabilities needed for effective human resource management. Next, the chapter describes how all managers, not just human resource professionals, participate in the functions and processes of human resource management. We then provide an overview of careers in human resource management and the highlights of practices covered in the remainder of the book. The chapter concludes by discussing a variety of trends and developments that impact HRM.

L01 - Define human resource management, identify the roles and responsibilities of human resource departments, and explain how human resource management contributes to an organization's performance.

1,2

human resource management (HRM)
The policies, practices, and systems that influence employees' behaviour, attitudes, and performance.

The Value of People

Managers and economists traditionally have seen human resource management as a necessary expense, rather than as a source of value to their organizations. Economic value is usually associated with *capital*—equipment, technology, and facilities. However, "in the changing corporate environment, more and more organizations are awakening to the importance of human capital as the next competitive advantage."[5]

A barrier to business expansion is not only availability of financial capital but also access to talent—that is, human capital. In summary, people are crucial to organizational success and the human and intellectual capital of an organization's workforce provides an opportunity for substantial competitive advantage. "As the 'resident people experts,' HR leaders are ideally suited to advise their organization on the best means for realizing their objectives."[6] Decisions such as whom to hire, what to pay, what training to offer, and how to evaluate employee performance directly affect employees' motivation, engagement, and ability to provide goods and services that customers value. Companies that attempt to increase their competitiveness by investing in new technology and promoting quality throughout the organization also invest in state-of-the-art staffing, training, and compensation practices.[7] These types of practices indicate that employees are viewed as valuable investments.[8]

human capital
An organization's employees, described in terms of their training, experience, judgment, intelligence, relationships, and insight.

The concept of "human resource management" implies that employees are *resources* of the employer. As a type of resource, **human capital** means the organization's employees, described in terms of their training, experience, judgment, intelligence, relationships, and insight—the employee characteristics that can add economic value to the organization. In other words, whether it manufactures bicycles or forecasts the weather, for an organization to succeed at what it does, it needs employees with certain qualities, such as particular kinds of skills and experience. This view means employees in today's organizations are not interchangeable, easily replaced parts of a system but the source of the company's success or failure. By influencing *who* works for the organization and *how* those people work, human resource management therefore contributes to such basic measures of an organization's success as quality, profitability, and customer satisfaction. Figure 1.2 shows this relationship.

Human resource management is critical to the success of organizations, because human capital has certain qualities that make it valuable. In terms of business strategy, an organization can succeed if it has a *sustainable competitive advantage* (is better than competitors at something, and can hold that advantage over a sustained period of time). Therefore, we can conclude that organizations need the kind of

FIGURE 1.2

Impact of Human Resource Management

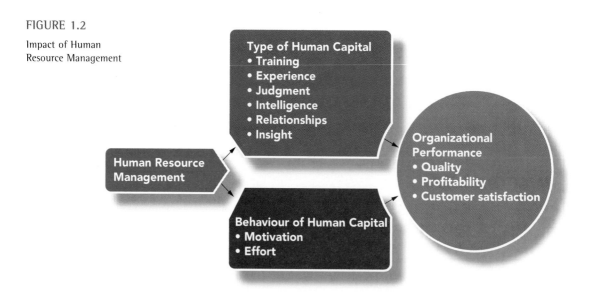

At WestJet, a key focus is on keeping employees motivated, trained, and compensated effectively. In turn, there is a low turnover rate and a high rate of customer satisfaction.

resources that will give them such an advantage. Human resources have these necessary qualities:

- Human resources are *valuable*. High-quality employees provide a needed service as they perform many critical functions.
- Human resources are *rare* in the sense that a person with high levels of the needed skills and knowledge is not common. An organization might spend months looking for a talented and experienced manager or technician.
- Human resources *cannot be imitated*. To imitate human resources at a high-performing competitor, you would have to figure out which employees are providing the advantage and how. Then you would have to recruit people who can do precisely the same thing and set up the systems that enable those people to imitate your competitor.
- Human resources have *no good substitutes*. When people are well trained and highly motivated, they learn, develop their abilities, and care about customers. It is difficult to imagine another resource that can match committed and talented employees.

These qualities imply that human resources have enormous potential. An organization realizes this potential through its approach to *human capital management*, that is, how it practises human resource management.

Effective management of human resources can form the foundation of a **high-performance work system**—an organization in which technology, organizational structure, people, and processes all work together to give an organization an advantage in the competitive environment. As technology changes how organizations manufacture, transport, communicate, and keep track of information, human resource management must ensure that the organization has the right kinds of people to meet the new challenges. Maintaining a high-performance work system might include development of training programs, recruitment of people with new skill sets, and establishment of rewards for such behaviours as teamwork, flexibility, and learning. Chapter 12 examines high-performance work systems in greater detail.

high-performance work system
An organization in which technology, organizational structure, people, and processes all work together to give an organization an advantage in the competitive environment.

Responsibilities of Human Resource Departments

In all but the smallest organizations, a human resource department is responsible for the functions of human resource management. On average, an organization has one HR staff person for every 100 employees served by the department; however, this ratio may vary widely across organizations. Another general guideline is that a specialized HR role is often created when an organization has reached the size of approximately 40 employees. Table 1.1 details the responsibilities of human resource departments. These responsibilities include the practices introduced in Figure 1.1 plus two areas of responsibility that support those practices: (1) establishing and administering human resource policies and (2) ensuring compliance with legal requirements.

Although the human resource department has responsibility for these areas, many of the requirements are performed by supervisors or others inside or outside the organization. No two human resource departments have precisely the same roles, because of differences in organization sizes and characteristics of the workforce, the industry, and management's values. In some companies, the HR department handles all the activities listed in Table 1.1. In others, it may share the roles and duties with managers and supervisors of other departments such as finance, operations, or information technology. When managers and supervisors actively perform a variety of HR activities, the HR department usually retains responsibility for consistency and compliance with all legal requirements. In some companies, the HR department actively advises top management. In others, the department responds to top-level management decisions and implements staffing, training, and compensation activities in light of company strategy and policies.

TABLE 1.1

Responsibilities of HR Departments

FUNCTION	RESPONSIBILITIES
Analysis and design of work	Work analysis; job design; job descriptions
Recruitment and selection	Identify needs; recruiting; interviewing and screening; deployment of staff; and outplacement
Training and development	Orientation; learning strategies; design, deliver, and evaluate programs; career development
Performance management	Integrate performance measures; performance appraisal systems; assist and coach supervisors
Compensation and rewards	Develop and administer compensation and incentive programs; benefit program design and implementation; pension plans; payroll
Employee and labour relations	Terms and conditions of employment, communication; employee involvement; labour relations
Strategy	Strategic partner in organizational effectiveness; change and development; workforce planning
Human resource policies	Guide and implement policy; create and manage systems to collect and safeguard HR information
Compliance with legislation	Implement policies to ensure compliance with all legal requirements; reporting requirements

SOURCE: Based on Canadian Council of Human Resources Associations National Standards for Human Resources Professionals, www.cchra-caarh.ca/en/phaseireport, retrieved March 22, 2004.

Let's take a look at an overview of the HR functions and some of the options available for carrying them out. Human resource management involves both the selection of which options to use and the activities related to implementation. Later chapters will explore each function in greater detail.

Analyzing and Designing Jobs

To produce their given product or service (or set of products or services), companies require that a number of tasks be performed. The tasks are grouped in various combinations to form jobs. Ideally, the tasks should be grouped in ways that help the organization to operate efficiently and to obtain people with the right qualifications to do the jobs well. This function involves the activities of job analysis and job design. **Job analysis** is the process of getting detailed information about jobs. **Job design** is the process of defining the way work will be performed and the tasks that a given job requires.

Recruiting and Hiring Employees

On the basis of job analysis and job design, an organization can determine the kinds of employees it needs. With this knowledge, it carries out the function of recruiting and hiring employees. **Recruitment** is the process through which the organization seeks applicants for potential employment. **Selection** refers to the process by which the organization attempts to identify applicants with the necessary knowledge, skills, abilities, and other characteristics that will help the organization achieve its goals. An organization makes selection decisions in order to add employees to its workforce, as well as to transfer existing employees to new positions.

At some organizations, the selection process may focus on specific skills, such as experience with a particular programming language or type of equipment. At others, selection may focus on general abilities, such as the ability to work as part of a team or find creative solutions. The focus an organization favours will affect many choices, from the way the organization measures ability, to the questions it asks in interviews, to the places it recruits. Table 1.2 lists employability skills, attitudes, and behaviours needed to participate and progress in today's dynamic world of work. HR professionals also provide guidance related to redeploying employees, termination, and outplacement.

job analysis
The process of getting detailed information about jobs.

job design
The process of defining the way work will be performed and the tasks that a given job requires.

recruitment
The process through which the organization seeks applicants for potential employment.

selection
The process by which the organization attempts to identify applicants with the necessary knowledge, skills, abilities, and other characteristics that will help the organization achieve its goals.

FUNDAMENTAL SKILLS	PERSONAL MANAGEMENT SKILLS	TEAMWORK SKILLS
• Communicate	• Demonstrate positive attitudes and behaviours	• Work with others
• Manage information	• Be responsible	• Participate in projects and tasks
• Use numbers	• Be adaptive	
• Think and solve problems	• Learn continuously	
	• Work safely	

TABLE 1.2

Employability Skills

SOURCE: "Employability Skills 2000+," *Brochure 2000 E/F* (Ottawa: The Conference Board of Canada, 2000), www.conferenceboard.ca/education/learning-tools/employability-skills.htm, retrieved February 28, 2004.

Training and Developing Employees

training
A planned effort to enable employees to learn job-related knowledge, skills, and behaviour.

Although organizations base hiring decisions on candidates' existing qualifications, most organizations provide ways for their employees to broaden or deepen their knowledge, skills, and abilities. To do this, organizations provide for employee training and development. **Training** is a planned effort to enable employees to learn job-related knowledge, skills, and behaviour. For example, many organizations offer safety training to teach employees safe work habits. **Development** involves acquiring knowledge, skills, and behaviour that improve employees' ability to meet the challenges of a variety of new or existing jobs, including the client and customer demands of those jobs. Development programs often focus on preparing employees for management responsibility.

development
The acquisition of knowledge, skills, and behaviours that improve an employee's ability to meet changes in job requirements and in customer demands.

Managing Performance

Managing human resources includes keeping track of how well employees are performing relative to objectives such as job descriptions and goals for a particular position. The process of ensuring that employees' activities and outputs match the organization's goals is called **performance management**. The activities of performance management include specifying the tasks and outcomes of a job that contribute to the organization's success. Then various measures are used to compare the employee's performance over some time period with the desired performance. Often, rewards—the topic of the next section—are developed to encourage good performance.

performance management
The process of ensuring that employees' activities and outputs match the organization's goals.

Compensation and Rewards

Planning pay and benefits involves many decisions, often complex and based on knowledge of a multitude of legal requirements. An important decision is how much to offer in salary or wages, as opposed to bonuses, commissions, and other performance-related pay. Other decisions involve which benefits to offer, from retirement plans to various kinds of insurance to other more intangible rewards such as opportunities for learning and personal growth. All such decisions have implications for the organization's bottom line, as well as for employee motivation.

Administering pay and benefits is another big responsibility. Organizations need systems for keeping track of each employee's earnings and benefits. Employees need information about their health plan, retirement plan, and other benefits. Keeping track of this involves extensive record keeping and reporting to management, employees, and others, while ensuring compliance with all applicable legislation.

Maintaining Positive Employee and Labour Relations

Organizations often depend on human resource professionals to help them identify and perform many of the tasks related to maintaining positive relations with employees. This function often includes providing for communications to employees.

In organizations where employees belong to a union, labour relations entails additional responsibilities. The organization periodically conducts collective bargaining to negotiate an employment contract with union members. The HR department also maintains communication with union representatives to ensure that issues are resolved as they arise.

Establishing and Administering Human Resource Policies

All the human resource activities described so far require fair and consistent decisions, and most require substantial record keeping. Organizations depend on their HR department to help establish policies related to hiring, discipline, promotions, benefits, and the other activities of human resource management.

All aspects of human resource management require HR professionals to collect and safeguard information. From the preparation of employee handbooks, to processing job applications, performance appraisals, benefits enrolment, and government-mandated reports, handling records about employees requires accuracy as well as sensitivity to employee privacy.

Ensuring Compliance with Federal and Provincial Legislation

As we will discuss in later chapters, especially in Chapters 2 and 3, the government has many laws and regulations concerning the treatment of employees. These laws govern such matters as human rights, employment equity, employee safety and health, employee compensation and benefits, and employee privacy. Most managers depend on human resource professionals to help them keep up to date and on track with these requirements. Ensuring compliance with laws requires that human resource professionals keep watch over a rapidly changing legal landscape.

Focus on Strategy

L02 - Summarize areas in which human resource management can support organizational strategies.

Traditional management thinking treated human resource management primarily as an administrative function, but managers are increasingly seeing a more central role for HRM. They are looking at HRM as a means to support a company's *strategy*—its plan for meeting broad goals such as profitability, quality, and market share.[9] This strategic role for HRM has evolved gradually. At many organizations, managers still treat HR professionals primarily as experts in designing and delivering HR systems. But at a growing number of organizations, HR professionals are strategic partners with other managers.[10] This means they use their knowledge of the business and of human resources to help the organization develop strategies and to align HRM policies and practices with those strategies.

In a recent study of almost 200 Canadian organizations surveyed by Deloitte Consulting and the University of Toronto's Centre of Industrial Relations, 41 percent of human resource leaders describe their departments as strategic partners while 31 percent still view themselves as administrative champions. Part of the problem for HR professionals is that employees are concerned about getting help with traditional human resource administrative responsibilities such as completing benefit forms while executives want senior HR leaders to be partners in strategic planning.[11]

The specific ways human resource professionals support the organization's strategy vary according to their level of involvement and the nature of the strategy. Strategic issues include emphasis on productivity improvement; attracting, engaging, and retaining talent; international expansion and outsourcing decisions.

Another important element of this responsibility is **workforce planning**, identifying the numbers and types of employees the organization will require in order to meet its objectives. Using these estimates, the human resource department helps

workforce planning
Identifying the numbers and types of employees the organization will require to meet its objectives.

the organization forecast its needs for hiring, training, and reassigning employees. Planning also may show that the organization will need fewer employees to meet anticipated needs. In that situation, human resource planning includes how to handle or avoid layoffs.

Often, an organization's strategy requires some type of change—for example, adding, moving or closing facilities, applying new technology, or entering markets in other regions or countries. Common reactions to change include fear, anger, and confusion. The organization may turn to its human resource department for help in managing the change process. Skilled human resource professionals can apply knowledge of human behaviour, along with performance management tools, to help the organization manage change constructively.

Productivity Improvement

productivity
The relationship between an organization's outputs (products, information or services) and its inputs (e.g., people, facilities, equipment, data, and materials).

To compete in today's global economy, companies need to enhance productivity. The relationship between an organization's outputs (products, information, or services) and its inputs (e.g., people, facilities, equipment, data, and materials) is referred to as **productivity**. Canada's labour force productivity growth is forecast to average 1.5 percent per year between 2003 and 2015 in contrast with 1.7 percent per year in the United States. This productivity gap between Canada and the United States threatens Canada's ability to compete globally. As illustrated in Figure 1.3, Canada is also a productivity laggard from a global perspective, significantly underperforming not only the United States but many other nations as well. In 2006, Canada placed 16th, while the U.S. placed sixth in actual productivity levels.[12]

Expanding into Global Markets

Companies are finding that to survive and prosper they must compete in international markets as well as fend off foreign competitors' attempts to gain ground in Canada. To meet these challenges, Canadian businesses must develop global markets, keep up

FIGURE 1.3

Average Labour
Productivity Growth (%)

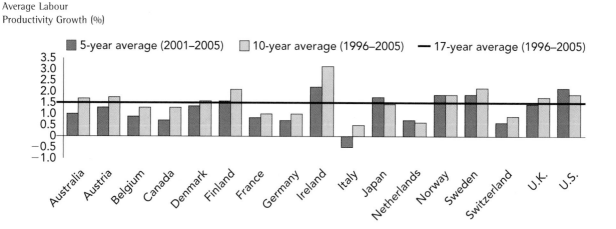

SOURCE: "How Canada Performs: A Report Card on Canada." © OECD, 2007.

with competition from overseas, hire from an international labour pool, and prepare employees for global assignments.

Study of companies that are successful and widely admired suggests that these companies not only operate on a multinational scale, but also have workforces and corporate cultures that reflect their global markets.[13] These companies, which include Research in Motion, Scotiabank, General Electric, Microsoft, RBC, and Intel, focus on customer satisfaction and innovation. In addition, they operate on the belief that people are the company's most important asset. Placing this value on employees requires the companies to emphasize human resource practices, including rewards for superior performance, measures of employee satisfaction, careful selection of employees, promotion from within, and investment in employee development.

The Global Workforce

For today's and tomorrow's employers, talent comes from a global workforce. Organizations with international operations hire at least some of their employees in the foreign countries where they operate. And even small businesses that stick close to home hire qualified candidates who are immigrants to Canada.

For an organization to operate in other countries, its HR practices must take into consideration differences in culture and business practices. Consider how Starbucks Coffee handled its expansion into Beijing, China.[14] Demand for qualified managers in Beijing exceeds the local supply, so Starbucks researched the motivation and needs of potential managers. The company learned that in traditional Chinese-owned companies, rules and regulations allowed little creativity and self-direction. Starbucks distinguished itself as an employer by emphasizing its casual culture and opportunities for career development. The company also spends considerable time training employees.

Even hiring at home may involve selection of employees from other countries. The 21st century, like the beginning of the last century, have been years of significant immigration. Foreign-born people account for virtually one in five of Canada's total population—the highest level in 75 years.[15] The impact of immigration is especially significant in some regions of Canada—more than one-fourth of the population of British Columbia and Ontario are foreign-born.[16]

Figure 1.4 illustrates the percentage of the population that is foreign-born for each province and territory. Canada's largest cities attract the largest number of immigrants. For example, 43.7 percent of Toronto's population and 37.5 percent of Vancouver's population are foreign-born.[17]

Because of declining population and labour shortages predicted for the future, employers will increasingly turn to immigrants to fill available job openings. In fact, Canada's current levels of immigration will need to increase by a multiple of 0.8 just to maintain replacement population levels.[18] Employers in tight labour markets—such as those seeking experts in computer science, engineering, and information systems—are especially likely to recruit international students.[19]

Starbucks Coffee President and CEO Howard Schultz, left, poses with Yuji Tsunoda, President of Starbucks Japan.

FIGURE 1.4

Percentage of the Population That Is Foreign-Born

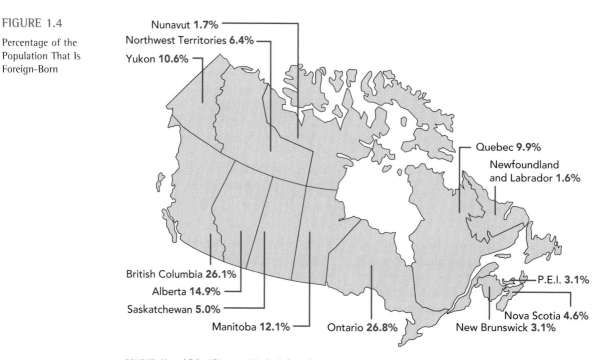

Nunavut **1.7%**
Northwest Territories **6.4%**
Yukon **10.6%**

Quebec **9.9%**
Newfoundland and Labrador **1.6%**

British Columbia **26.1%**
Alberta **14.9%**
Saskatchewan **5.0%**
Manitoba **12.1%**
Ontario **26.8%**
P.E.I. **3.1%**
Nova Scotia **4.6%**
New Brunswick **3.1%**

SOURCE: Karnal Dib, "Diversity Works," *Canadian Business*, March 29–April 11, 2004, p. 54.

International Assignments

Besides hiring an international workforce, organizations must be prepared to send employees to other countries. This requires HR expertise in selecting employees for international assignments and preparing them for those assignments. Employees who take assignments in other countries are called **expatriates**.

Canadian companies must prepare employees to work in other countries. Canadian companies must carefully select employees to work abroad on the basis of their ability to understand and respect the cultural and business norms of the host country. Qualified candidates also need language skills and technical ability. In Chapter 11, we discuss practices for training employees to understand other cultures.

expatriates
Employees who take assignments in other countries.

Outsourcing

Many organizations are increasingly outsourcing and offshoring business activities. **Outsourcing** refers to the practice of having another company (a vendor, third-party provider, or consultant) provide services. For instance, a manufacturing company might outsource its accounting and transportation functions to businesses that specialize in these activities. Outsourcing gives the company access to in-depth expertise and is often more economical as well. In addition to manufacturing, software development and call centre operations are other functions typically considered for outsourcing. **Offshoring**, on the other hand, refers to setting up a business enterprise in another country, for example, setting up a factory in China to manufacture products at less cost than in Canada. Increasingly, organizations are *offshore outsourcing*, that is, the company providing outsourced services is located in another country rather than the organization's home country. For example, The Portables, a trade-show display and exhibits maker based in Richmond, B.C., have increased annual sales dramatically since starting its use of offshore outsourcing. Hanif Mulijinai, president

outsourcing
The practice of having another company (a vendor, third-party provider, or consultant) provide services.

offshoring
Setting up a business enterprise in another country (e.g., building a factory in China).

of The Portables, says offshore outsourcing was never the plan for his company. "But we find with some of the newer products, it's a lot easier to get some of the products manufactured in China. It's a lot quicker and less expensive," he says. "Some of the quality of the work they do is very scary, it's so good."[20]

Overall there are two primary categories of outsourcing and offshoring implications to Canada:

- *Canadian companies are likely to increase their use of outsourcing and offshoring.* To cut costs and reduce capital investment, Canadian companies are likely to increase their use of outsourcing and offshoring to the ever-growing list of countries such as India, China, Russia, and Mexico that are actively seeking economic diversification and investment. For example, Bombardier Inc.'s train unit now outsources low-level engineering work such as transferring 2D drawings to 3D from peak-capacity plants to a variety of outside firms around the world.[21] Montreal-based CGI Group Inc., Canada's largest computer services firm, has expanded its development operations in Bangalore and Mumbai India to 650 from 500 in the past year.[22]

- *Canada is losing its attractiveness as an outsourcing destination.* Canada has slipped from second to eighth place as an attractive outsourcing destination behind India, China, Malaysia, Czech Republic, Singapore, Philippines, and Brazil in a study conducted by A. T. Kearney.[23] For example, Canadian industries such as the auto industry could come under continuing pressure if the United States turns inward or to other countries to put together automobiles.

Not only do HR departments help with a transition to outsourcing, but many HR functions are being outsourced. A survey by the Society for Human Resource Management found that almost three-quarters of companies outsource at least one HR function.[24] HR functions that are commonly outsourced to companies such as Ceridian and Hewitt Associates, Inc. include payroll administration, training, and recruitment and selection of employees. For example, BMO has a ten-year contract with Hewitt Associates to manage much of the bank's HR function. BMO's HR department was cut as payroll and benefits administration, HR call centre management, employee records, and other administrative functions were outsourced.[25] This arrangement frees HR managers at BMO to work on strategy and vision, focusing them on HRM responsibilities that add value to the business. Rogers Communication has also outsourced "business process" duties of its HR department including payroll and maintaining support employee database records. "Rogers, like the Bank of Montreal and Air Canada, has decided that in order to concentrate on their core competencies they will focus on just the strategic elements of HR and leave most of the administrative HR work to us," said Shauna Cooper, who heads up business process outsourcing for Hewitt in Canada.[26]

Mergers and Acquisitions

Increasingly, organizations are joining forces through mergers (two companies becoming one) and acquisitions (one company buying another). These deals do not always meet expectations, and often failures may be due to "people issues." Recognizing this, some companies now heavily weigh the other organization's culture before they embark on a merger or acquisition. HRM should have a significant role in carrying out a merger or acquisition. Differences between the businesses involved in the deal make conflict inevitable. Training efforts should therefore include development of skills in conflict resolution. Also, HR professionals have to sort out differences in the two

1,2

companies' practices with regard to rewards, performance appraisal, and other HR systems. Settling on a consistent structure to meet the combined organization's goals may help to bring employees together. HR's role in engaging top talent and keeping them on board with challenging opportunities following a merger or acquisition will be explored further in Chapter 12.

L03 - Identify the Required Professional Capabilities and certification process for HR professionals.

Required Professional Capabilities (RPCs™) and Certification of HR Professionals

The knowledge, skills, abilities, and other attributes required by an individual working in HR to demonstrate professional competence has been researched and defined by the Canadian Council of Human Resources Associations. The resulting Required Professional Capabilities (187 in total) are grouped into seven functional dimensions as shown in Figure 1.5.

With such varied responsibilities, human resource professionals need both academic knowledge and experiential knowledge. There are two national examinations, the National Knowledge Exam™ (tests academic knowledge) and the National Professional Practice Assessment™ (tests experiential knowledge) leading to the Certified Human Resources Professional (CHRP) designation. In summary, the RPCs encompass what an HR professional needs to know and be able to do while working in the profession.[27]

Currently more than 17,000 HR practitioners from across Canada have earned their CHRP designation.[28] To retain the CHRP designation, HR professionals must maintain membership with a provincial CHRP-granting HR association and recertify every three years either by re-writing the National Professional Practice Assessment™ or engaging in a variety of professional development activities. As of January 1, 2011, CHRP candidates (those who have passed the National Knowledge Exam™) will require a minimum of a bachelor's degree from an accredited college or university in order to register for the National Professional Practice Assessment™ and qualify for the CHRP designation.[29] The e-HRM box provides sample interactive questions from the CHRP examinations.

FIGURE 1.5

Required Professional Capabilities Grouped by Functional Dimensions

- Professional Practice in Human Resources — 22.4%
- Organizational Effectiveness
- Staffing
- Employee & Labour Relations
- Total Compensation
- Organizational Learning, Training & Development
- Occupational Health, Safety & Wellness

9.1% 13.9% 13.4% 13.4% 16.0% 11.8%

SOURCE: www.cchra.ca/Web/certification/content.aspx?f=29967, retrieved March 12, 2008. © Reproduced with permission by the Canadian Council of Human Resources Associations.

E- HRM

Certified Human Resources Professional (CHRP) National Examination Preparation

HR Practitioners apply their knowledge to contribute to organizational effectiveness. The Canadian Council of Human Resources Associations provides interactive online study resources. These questions and answers are a valuable resource not only to CHRP Exam registrants and CHRP candidates preparing for the examinations but also to current HR professionals who can access these questions and scenarios as a resource in implementing both strategic and day-to-day responsibilities.

National Knowledge Exam™ Sample Questions

1. What should be the relationship between human resources planning and corporate strategic planning?
   a. HR planning should drive strategic planning.
   b. HR planning should only follow and support the outcome of a strategic planning process.
   c. None, these are distinct and independent functions.
   d. Reciprocal and interdependent, each should contribute to the other.
2. The main advantage of having the organization design

and build a human resource information system (HRIS) itself rather than purchase a HRIS off-the-shelf from an external software supplier is the opportunity to
   a. Better reflect internal business processes
   b. Avoid making an outdated system
   c. Make updates easier
   d. Have better access to documentation and training resources

National Professional Practice Assessment™ Sample Question

3. You are an HR manager working in a community-based organization. HR policies are outdated and practices are inconsistent across the organization. You note that management always appears to be working in a mode that further reflects the lack of organization in the HR department. What should you do?

   a. Develop and administer a survey to cover all areas of human resources and use the data collected to establish new HR policies and practices.
   b. Develop a set of policies and procedures based on

your previous experience as an HR manager. Communicate to employees through a handbook.
   c. Identify another organization that carries out similar activities. Meet their HR manager to get their handbook and use it. Agree to share your experiences based on their handbook with them.
   d. With the members of the executive committee, develop an HR strategy based on the organization's objectives. Analyze HR policies and practices currently in effect. Identify HR policies to revise and develop. Educate all managers and communicate the new strategies and policies to employees.

SOURCE: Canadian Council of Human Resources Associations, www.cchra .ca/Web/exam/nke_answers.aspx; www.cchra.ca/Web/exam/nppa_ answers.aspx, retrieved March 12, 2008. © Reproduced with permission by the Canadian Council of Human Resources Associations.

ANSWERS: 1: d; 2: a;
3: a = 2 Points, b = 0 Points,
c = 2 Points, d = 5 Points. This last answer includes HR strategy and organizational objectives in developing HR policies.

Ethics in Human Resource Management

ethics
The fundamental principles of right and wrong.

Whenever people's actions affect one another, ethical issues arise, and business decisions are no exception. **Ethics** refers to the fundamental principles of right and wrong; ethical behaviour is behaviour that is consistent with those principles. Business decisions, including HRM decisions, should be ethical, but the evidence suggests that is not always what happens. Recent surveys indicate that the general public and managers do not have positive perceptions of the ethical conduct of businesses. For example, in a survey conducted by the *Wall Street Journal*, 4 out of 10 executives reported they had been asked to behave unethically.[30]

The HR How-To box here provides the Code of Ethics for the Canadian Council of Human Resources Associations (CCHRA) that identifies standards for professional and ethical conduct of HR practitioners. For human resource practices to be considered ethical, they must satisfy the three basic standards summarized in Figure 1.6.[31] First, HRM practices must result in the greatest good for the greatest number of people. Second, human resource practices must respect legal requirements including human rights and privacy. Third, managers must treat employees and customers equitably and fairly. To explore how ethical principles apply to a variety of decisions, throughout the book we will highlight ethical dilemmas in human resource management practices.

Closely related to the discussion of ethics and ethical practices is HR's role in organizational values and corporate social responsibility. For example, "there is increasing evidence that interest in environmental issues is motivating people's behaviour as consumers, employees and jobseekers."[32] In Chapter 3, we will explore this subject in more depth including a discussion of how eco-friendly firms may have an edge in their ability to attract, retain, and engage top talent.

FIGURE 1.6

Standards for Identifying Ethical Practices

HR HOW-TO

CCHRA's National Code of Ethics

1. *Preamble.* As HR practitioners in the following categories:

   Certified Human Resources Professionals

   CHRP Candidates, or

   CHRP Exam Registrants,

   We commit to abide by all requirements of the Code of Ethics of the Canadian Council of Human Resources Associations (CCHRA), as listed in this document. (Where provincial codes are legislated, those will prevail.)

2. *Competence.* Maintain competence in carrying out professional responsibilities and provide services in an honest and diligent manner. Ensure that activities engaged in are within the limits of one's knowledge, experience, and skill. When providing services outside one's level of competence, or the profession, the necessary assistance must be sought so as not to compromise professional responsibility.

3. *Legal requirements.* Adhere to any statutory acts, regulation, or by-laws which relate to the field of human resources management, as well as all civil and criminal laws, regulations, and statutes that apply in one's jurisdiction. Not knowingly or otherwise engage in or condone any activity or attempt to circumvent the clear intention of the law.

4. *Dignity in the workplace.* Support, promote and apply the principles of human rights, equity, dignity and respect in the workplace, within the profession, and in society as a whole.

5. *Balancing interests.* Strive to balance organizational and employee needs and interests in the practice of the profession.

6. *Confidentiality.* Hold in strict confidence all confidential information acquired in the course of the performance of one's duties, and not divulge

confidential information unless required by law and/or where serious harm is imminent.

7. *Conflict of interest.* Either avoid or disclose a potential conflict of interest that might influence or might be perceived to influence personal actions or judgments.

8. *Professional growth and support of other professionals.* Maintain personal and professional growth in human resources management by engaging in activities that enhance the credibility and value of the profession.

9. *Enforcement.* The Canadian Council of Human Resources Associations works collaboratively with its Member Associations to develop and enforce high standards of ethical practice among all its members.

SOURCE: © Reproduced with permission by the Canadian Council of Human Resources Associations. www. cchra.ca/Web/ethics/content.aspx?f = 2956, retrieved March 12, 2008.

HR Responsibilities of Supervisors and Line Managers

L04 - Explain the role of supervisors and line managers in human resource management.

Although many organizations have human resource departments, HR activities are by no means limited to the specialists who staff those departments. In large organizations, HR departments advise and support the activities of the other departments. In small organizations, there may be an HR specialist, but many HR activities are carried out by supervisors and other line managers. Either way, non-HR managers need to be familiar with the basics of HRM and their role with regard to managing human resources.

As we will see in later chapters, supervisors and non-HR managers typically have responsibilities related to all the HR functions. Figure 1.7 shows some HR responsibilities that supervisors and line managers are likely to be involved in. Organizations depend on supervisors to help them determine what kinds of work need to be done (job analysis and design) and in what quantities (workforce planning). Supervisors and line managers typically interview job candidates and participate in the decisions about which candidates to hire. Many organizations expect supervisors to train employees in some or all aspects of the employees' jobs. Supervisors conduct performance appraisals and may recommend pay increases. And, of course, supervisors and line managers play a key role in employee relations, because they are most often the voice of management for their employees, representing the company on a day-to-day basis. Throughout these activities, supervisors and line managers can participate in HRM by taking into consideration how decisions and policies will affect their employees. Understanding the principles of communication, motivation, and other elements of human behaviour can help supervisors and line managers engage and inspire the best from the organization's human resources.

L05 - Describe typical careers in human resource management.

Careers in Human Resource Management

There are many different types of jobs in the HRM profession. Figure 1.8 shows selected HRM positions and their salaries. The salaries vary according to education and experience, as well as the type of industry in which the person works.

The Government of Canada's National Occupational Classification (NOC) identifies one specific broad classification of human resources occupations: "Specialists in Human Resources." Figure 1.9 provides a summary of average hourly

FIGURE 1.7

Typical Areas of Involvement of Supervisors and Line Managers in HRM

Help define jobs

Provide motivational environment

Forecast HR needs

Communicate policies and comply with legal requirements

Train, coach, and develop employees

Interview (and select) candidates

Recommend pay increases and promotions

Appraise performance

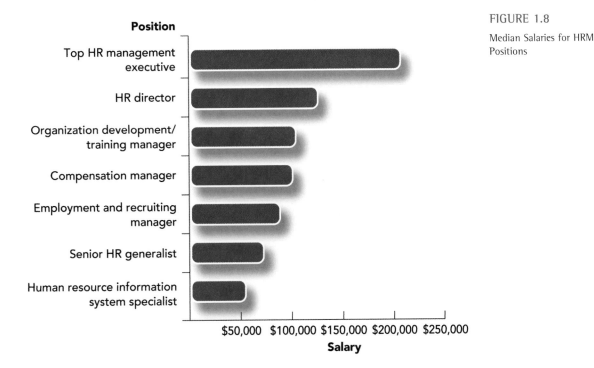

FIGURE 1.8

Median Salaries for HRM
Positions

SOURCE: Based on Society for Human Resource Management—Mercer Survey 2003, as reported in J. Vocino, "On the Rise," *HR Magazine*, November 2003, pp. 75–84; and F. Hansen, "2003 Data Bank Annual," *Workforce Management* 82, no. 13 (2003), p. 88. Based on Society for Human Resource Management—2003 as reported in J. Vocino, "On the Rise," *HR Magazine*, pp. 75–84; and F. Hansen, "2003 Data Bank Annual," *Workforce Management* 82, no. 13 (2003), p. 88.

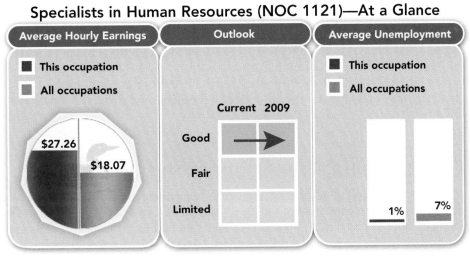

FIGURE 1.9

Average Hourly Earnings,
Outlook, and Average
Unemployment for
Specialists in Human
Resources

SOURCE: National Occupational Classification, Service Canada, www.jobfutures.ca/jobfutures/noc/1121.shtml, retrieved June 1, 2008.

HRPA (Human Resources Professionals Association) of Ontario provides education, information services, seminars, government and media representation, online services, and publications such as *HR Professional*.

earnings, employment outlook, and average levels of unemployment. This resource also provides similar information for thousands of other occupations in Canada.

Some positions in HRM involve work in specialized areas such as recruiting, training, or labour and industrial relations. Other positions call for generalists to perform a full range of HRM activities, including recruiting, training, compensation, and employee relations. Many recent entrants have a university degree or college diploma. As discussed earlier in the chapter, in 2011, CHRP candidates will require a degree to qualify for the CHRP designation, a change likely to advance the status of the CHRP among employers.

A well-rounded educational background will likely serve a person well. As one HR professional noted,

> One of the biggest misconceptions is that [HRM] is all warm and fuzzy communications with the workers. Or that it is creative and involved in making a more congenial atmosphere for people at work. Actually it is both of those some of the time, but most of the time it is a big mountain of paperwork which calls on a myriad of skills besides the "people" type. It is law, accounting, philosophy, and logic as well as psychology, spirituality, tolerance, and humility.[33]

In addition to the HRM professionals who hold the CHRP designation, many more are members of professional associations. The largest Canadian professional organization for HRM is the Canadian Council of Human Resources Associations (CCHRA), which represents the collaborative efforts of ten provincial and specialist Human Resource Associations and includes more than 25,000 professionals across Canada. Visit the CCHRA's website at www.cchra.ca to see their services and link to the associated provincial and specialist association websites.

Environmental Trends Impacting HRM

Major environmental trends that are impacting human resource management include changes related to composition of the workforce and how HRM can support a number of organizational strategies, from efforts to maintain high-performance work systems to changes in the organization's size and structure. Major changes in technology, especially the role of the Internet are changing organizations themselves, as well as providing new ways to carry out human resource management. Finally, we explore the changing nature of the employment relationship, in which careers and jobs are becoming more flexible.

Change in the Labour Force

The *labour force* is a general way to refer to all the people willing and able to work. For an organization, the **internal labour force** consists of the organization's workers—its employees and the people who work at the organization. This internal labour force is drawn from the organization's **external labour market**, that is, individuals who are actively seeking employment. The number and kinds of people in the external labour market determine the kinds of human resources available to an organization (and their cost). Human resource professionals need to be aware of trends in the composition of the external labour market, because these trends affect the organization's options for creating a well-skilled, motivated internal labour force. One significant trend relates to the impending shortage of workers as the labour force actually shrinks in some developed countries. See Figure 1.10.

An Aging Workforce

John Murphy has done the math, and it doesn't look good: over the next five years, his company will likely need to replace more than a quarter of its 11,000 employees. Murphy, executive vice-president of human resources at Ontario Power Generation, the Crown corporation that manages provincial electricity supply, says there isn't much he can do to avoid it. Average age of OPG's workforce is 45, its ranks filled with baby boomers who have their sights set on retirement. Many of those leaving the corporation in the next few years will be senior engineers and managers, who, after decades on the job, will give up their desk for good—taking valuable skills and experience with them.[34]

Canada's population and its labour force are aging. The fastest-growing age segment of the labour force will be workers aged 45+, as the baby-boom generation (born 1946–1964) continues to age. There will be sustained growth in the working-age population until 2010 as the "echo-boom" generation (the children of the baby boomers) reaches working age.[35] However, as illustrated in Figure 1.10, growth of the labour force in Canada and other developed countries will decline dramatically after 2010

L06 - Describe trends in the labour force composition and how they affect human resource management.

internal labour force
An organization's workers (its employees and the people who work at the organization).

external labour market
Individuals who are actively seeking employment.

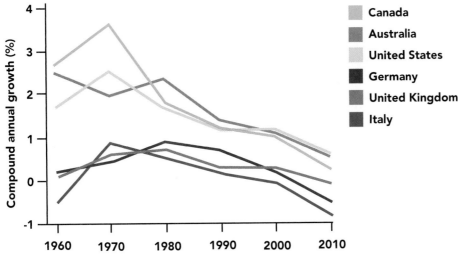

FIGURE 1.10

Decline of Labour Forces in Many Developed Countries by 2010

SOURCE: Andrew Wahl, "Leaders Wanted," *Canadian Business*, March 1–14, 2004, p. 32.

FIGURE 1.11

Age Distribution Projection of the Canadian Population, 2006 and 2016

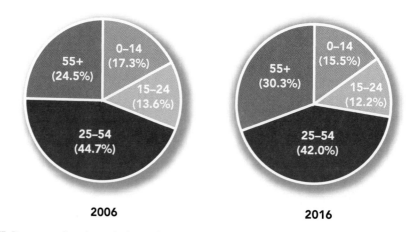

2006   **2016**

NOTE: Due to rounding, the totals do not always add up to the sum of the figure.

SOURCE: "Age Distribution Projection of the Canadian Population 2006 and 2016," adapted from Statistics Canada website, www40.statcan.ca/l01/cst01/demo23a.htm and www40.statcan.ca/l01/cst01/demo23b.htm, retrieved April 16, 2008.

because of decreased numbers of the population aged 15 years and younger. By 2010, the labour forces in many developed countries will be shrinking.[36]

Human resource professionals will therefore spend much of their time on concerns related to retirement planning, retraining older workers, and motivating workers whose careers have plateaued. Organizations will struggle with ways to control the rising costs of health-related and other benefits. At the same time, organizations will have to find ways to attract, retain, and prepare the newest entrants to the labour force and effectively deal with the increasing generational diversity of the workforce.

Generation X (born 1965–1980) grew up in the wake of the baby boomers. Dual-income families produced a generation of children with greater responsibility for taking care of themselves. Generation X employees are inclined to be cynical about the future because of their experience with recessions and downsizing and tend to be independent, technology-savvy, and results-driven. Generation Y (born 1981–2000) have been born and raised in a multicultural society resulting in tolerance to differences in race, religion, and culture.[37]

Employees view work as a means to self-fulfillment—that is, a means to more fully use their skills and abilities, meet their interests, and live a desirable lifestyle.[38] One report indicates that if employees receive opportunities to fully use and develop their skills, have greater job responsibilities, believe the promotion system is fair, and have a trustworthy manager who represents the employee's best interests, they are more committed to their companies.[39] Fostering these values requires organizations to develop HRM practices that provide more opportunity for individual contribution and entrepreneurship (in this context, taking responsibility for starting up something new).[40] Because many employees place more value on the quality of nonwork activities and family life than on pay and production, employees will demand more flexible work policies that allow them to choose work hours and the places where work is performed.

Employers will likely find that many talented older workers want to continue contributing through their work, though not necessarily in a traditional eight-to-five job. For organizations to attract and keep talented older workers, many will have to rethink how they design jobs. Phyllis Ostrowsky, in her mid-fifties, enjoyed her position as a store manager for 13 years, and she went out of her way to provide good customer service. But her job responsibilities and hours expanded to the point they

FIGURE 1.12

HRM Practices That
Support Diversity
Management

SOURCE: Based on M. Loden and J. B. Rosener, *Workforce America!* (Homewood, IL: Business One Irwin, 1991).

became excessive. She eventually was working 12-hour days and was too busy to give customers the personal touch she liked to deliver. Ostrowsky therefore left her store job for a position as an office manager with another company.[41]

A Diverse Workforce

Another change affecting the Canadian labour force is that it is growing more diverse. Over 200 ethnic groups were reported in Canada's most recent census. Employment equity is now recognized as an effective Canadian tool for efficient use of skilled human resources—and is increasingly borrowed by many industrialized countries. The four designated groups under the federal Employment Equity Act (women, Aboriginal peoples, persons with disabilities, and members of visible minorities) represent a strategic resource that numbers approximately 10 million individuals in Canada's labour force.[42] Employment equity considerations will be discussed in more detail in Chapter 2. Figure 1.12 summarizes some ways HRM can support the management of diversity for organizational success.

> A diversified workforce has paid off at Lea International Ltd., a Markham, Ontario, company that creates transport and urban planning systems. It recently won a contract to redesign seven railway stations in Mumbai, India, for a commuter network that carries 6.1 million people a day. "The fact that we have a workforce from around the world gives me competitive knowledge," says president John Farrow, who points out that 34 percent of his employees are visible minorities and 12 percent are immigrants whose first language was not English.[43]

The banks also have good business cases for diversity: they need to reflect the communities and clients to which they sell services. "There is a natural tendency to hire people who look like the people on the other side of the counter," says Amy Hanen, vice-president of human resource policy and governance at CIBC.[44] The Best Practices box discusses how one Canadian organization provides for effective integration of diverse cultures.

Participation rates of women in the labour force are increasing. In 2006, women represented 46.9 percent of Canada's paid workforce.[45] Even as recently as 1990,

BEST PRACTICES

OMNI's Success in Managing Diversity

OMNI, a multilingual TV station owned by Rogers Communications, Inc., is a leading provider of ethnocultural television programming. The station, which can be seen as a microcosm of the larger workplace community, is described as a virtual United Nations of nearly 400 employees who produce broadcasts in 44 languages, representing Cantonese, Portuguese, Italian, Hindi, Polish, and Ukrainian communities, to name a few. Where there is such a great mix of employees, "people are acculturated and more accepting of differences," vice-president and general manager Madeline Ziniak says. However, this success in managing diversity does not happen without the planful effort of OMNI.

To help integrate employees from different cultures and create a harmonious workplace, OMNI conducts orientation sessions with a twofold aim:

- For employees new to Canada, they help to clarify expectations and accepted practices.
- For employees born and raised in Canada, they help to promote greater understanding and tolerance.

"We really do become citizens of the world here," Ms. Ziniak says. "So [employees become] very well-versed in the kind of interaction that is acceptable and respectful between different ethno-cultural communities." In addition, Ms. Ziniak says many training sessions focus on issues of communication, since "culturally, there's different ways

of communicating. In some cultures, looking someone right in the eye is not respectful. In our courses, we say you have to look at the person directly." Specialized sessions like these run four or five times a year, and senior managers attend two annual conferences on diversity.

In addition, interoffice multicultural events help build understanding and tolerance while making minorities feel welcome. OMNI also hosts many international delegations, sent by the foreign affairs and international trade ministries, to learn about working in a diverse environment.

SOURCES: Sherry Noik-Bent, "By Being Visible: How to Manage Multiculti Maze," *The Globe and Mail*, November 24, 2004, pp. C1, C2; www.rogers.com.

women made up only 9 percent of executive positions at the Bank of Montreal; now, they make up 33 and 47 percent of middle and other managers.[46] The population of Aboriginal peoples surpassed 1 million in 2006. Almost one-third of the Aboriginal population is under age 15, in contrast with 17 percent of the non-Aboriginal population,[47] thus providing opportunities for a significant source of skilled workers in the future. Persons with disabilities comprise a productive but historically overlooked sector of the workforce. Some persons with disabilities require accommodation on the job to be effective; however, more often than not, this accommodation can be provided at little or no cost, for example, by providing large print software or arranging office furniture to promote ease of access.[48]

Throughout this book, we will show how diversity affects HRM practices. For example, from a staffing perspective, it is important to ensure that tests used to select employees are not unfairly biased. From the perspective of work design, employees need flexible schedules that allow them to meet nonwork needs. In terms of training, it is clear that employees must be made aware of the damage that stereotypes can do. With regard to compensation and rewards, organizations are providing benefits such as child and elder care as a way to accommodate the needs of a diverse workforce.

Skill Deficiencies of the Workforce

The increasing use of computers to do routine tasks has shifted the kinds of skills needed for employees. Such qualities as physical strength and mastery of a particular piece of machinery are no longer important for many jobs. More employers are looking for mathematical, verbal, and interpersonal skills, such as the ability to solve math problems or reach decisions as part of a team. Often, when organizations are looking for technical skills, they are looking for skills related to computers and using the Internet. When employees lack advanced literacy and thinking skills, they may be unable to perform their jobs competently and will experience difficulty adjusting to changes in the workplace.[49] Today's employees must be able to handle a variety of responsibilities, interact with customers, and think creatively.

To find such employees, most organizations are looking for educational achievements. A college diploma or university degree is a basic requirement for many jobs today. Competition for qualified college and university graduates in many fields is intense. At the other extreme, workers with less education often have to settle for low-paying jobs. Some companies are unable to find qualified employees and instead rely on training to correct skill deficiencies.[50] Other companies team up with universities, colleges, and high schools to design and teach courses ranging from basic reading to design blueprint reading.

High-Performance Work Systems

Human resource management is playing an important role in helping organizations gain and keep an advantage over competitors by becoming high-performance work systems. These are organizations that have the best possible fit between their social system (people and how they interact) and technical system (equipment and processes).[51] As the nature of the workforce and the technology available to organizations have changed, so have the requirements for creating a high-performance work system. Customers are demanding high quality and customized products, employees are seeking flexible work arrangements, and employers are looking for ways to tap people's creativity and interpersonal skills. Such demands require that organizations make full use of their people's knowledge and skill, and skilled human resource management can help organizations do this.

Among the trends that are occurring in today's high-performance work systems are reliance on knowledge workers, employee engagement, the use of teamwork, and the increasing levels of education of the workforce. The following sections describe these four trends, and Chapter 12 will explore the ways HRM can support the creation and maintenance of a high-performance work system. HR professionals who keep up with change are well positioned to help create high-performance work systems.

LO7 - Discuss the role of high-performance work systems and how technological developments are affecting human resource management.

Knowledge Workers

To meet their human capital needs, companies are increasingly trying to attract, develop, and retain knowledge workers. **Knowledge workers** are employees whose main contribution to the organization is specialized knowledge, such as knowledge of customers, a process, or a profession. Knowledge workers are especially needed for jobs in health services, business services, social services, engineering, and management.

Knowledge workers are in a position of power, because they own the knowledge that the company needs in order to produce its products and services, and they must share their knowledge and collaborate with others in order for their employer to succeed.

knowledge workers
Employees whose main contribution to the organization is specialized knowledge, such as knowledge of customers, a process, or a profession.

Knowledge workers are employees whose value to their employers stems primarily from what they know. Employees such as the ones pictured here have in-depth knowledge of their profession and are hard to replace because of their special knowledge.

An employer cannot simply order these employees to perform tasks. Managers depend on the employees' willingness to share information. Furthermore, skilled knowledge workers have many job opportunities, even in a slow economy. If they choose, they can leave a company and take their knowledge to another employer. Replacing them may be difficult and time-consuming.

As more organizations become knowledge-based, they must promote and capture learning at the level of employees, teams, and the overall organization.

The reliance on knowledge workers also affects organizations' decisions about the kinds of people they are recruiting and selecting.[52] They are shifting away from focusing on specific skills, such as how to operate a particular kind of machinery, and toward a greater emphasis on general cognitive skills (thinking and problem solving) and interpersonal skills. Employers are more interested in evidence that job candidates will excel at working in teams or interacting with customers. These skills also support an employee's ability to gather and share knowledge, helping the organization to innovate and meet customer needs. To the extent that technical skills are important, employers often are most interested in the ability to use information technology, including the Internet and statistical software.

The editors at *Canadian Business* spoke to academics, consultants, and industry representatives across Canada to find what the high-demand jobs for skilled labour will be in the coming years. Table 1.3 summarizes their picks.

TABLE 1.3

Some of Tomorrow's Hot Jobs

SECTOR	WANTED	CURRENT SALARY
Any	Managers of all types	Varies
Utilities	Engineers, load managers, line technicians	$44,000–$70,000
Oil and gas	Engineers, geologist, geophysicists, mechanics, equipment operators	$50,000–$150,000
Technology	Computer systems and software engineers	$47,000–$90,000
Health care	Surgeons, nurses, pharmacists	$32,000–$280,000
Financial services	Financial planners	$75,000–$500,000
Any	Accounting, insurance and finance professionals	$55,000–$235,000

SOURCE: Raizel Robin, "Tomorrow's Hot Jobs," *Canadian Business*, March 1–14, 2004, pp. 39, 40.

Employee Engagement

To completely benefit from employees' knowledge, organizations need a management style that focuses on developing and engaging employees. **Employee engagement** refers to the extent that employees are satisfied, committed to, and prepared to support what is important to the organization.

HRM practices such as performance management, training, career management, work design, and employee relations are important for creating employee engagement. Jobs must be designed to give employees the necessary latitude for making a variety of decisions. Employees must be properly trained to exert their wider authority and use information resources such as the Internet, as well as tools for communicating information. Employees also need feedback to help them evaluate their success. Pay and other rewards should reflect employees' authority and be related to successful handling of their responsibility. In addition, for engagement to occur, managers must be trained to link employees to resources within and outside the organization, such as customers, co-workers in other departments, and websites with needed information. Managers must also encourage employees to interact with staff throughout the organization, must ensure that employees receive the information they need, and must reward cooperation.

As with the need for knowledge workers, employee engagement shifts the recruiting focus away from technical skills and toward general cognitive and interpersonal skills. Employees who have responsibility for a final product or service must be able to listen to customers, adapt to changing needs, and creatively solve a variety of problems. Chapter 3 will explore employee engagement practices and outcomes in more detail.

employee engagement
The extent that employees are satisfied, committed to, and prepared to support what is important to the organization.

Teamwork

Modern technology places the information that employees need for improving quality and providing customer service right at the point of sale or production. As a result, the employees engaging in selling and producing must also be able to make decisions about how to do their work. Organizations need to set up work in a way that gives employees the authority and ability to make those decisions. One of the most popular ways to increase employee responsibility and control is to assign work to teams. **Teamwork** is the assignment of work to groups of employees with various skills who interact to assemble a product or provide a service.

teamwork
The assignment of work to groups of employees with various skills who interact to assemble a product or provide a service.

Increasing Levels of Education

The educational attainment of Canada's population is increasing. In 2006, 17.3 percent of Canada's population 15 years and older had a college certificate or diploma; 11.6 percent a bachelor's degree. These figures are up from 8.3 percent and 9.6 percent respectively, from 1986.[53]

In a recent survey conducted for a TD Bank Financial Group paper, economists Craig Alexander and Eric Lascalles examined the work of a dozen researchers to discover the rate of return of postsecondary education. The rate of return was calculated using the present value difference between the lifetime earnings of a postsecondary graduate and those of a high-school graduate, factoring in the cost of tuition, academic fees, and lost earnings while students were in school. Annual rates of return for a university degree ranged from 12 percent to 17 percent for men and 16 percent to 20 percent for women; for a college diploma, rates of return were between 15 percent and 28 percent for men, and 18 percent and 28 percent for women.[54]

Technological Change in HRM

Advances in computer-related technology have had a major impact on the use of information for managing human resources. Large quantities of employee data (including training records, skills, compensation rates, and benefits usage and cost) can easily be stored on personal computers and manipulated with user-friendly spreadsheets or statistical software. Often these features are combined in a **human resource information system (HRIS)**, a computer system used to acquire, store, manipulate, analyze, retrieve, and distribute information related to an organization's human resources.[55] An HRIS can support strategic decision making, help the organization avoid lawsuits, provide data for evaluating programs or policies, and support day-to-day HR decisions.

The support of an HRIS can help HR professionals navigate the challenges of today's complex business environment. For example, rapidly changing technology can cause employees' skills to become obsolete. Organizations must therefore carefully monitor their employees' skills and the organization's needed skills. Often the employees and needs are distributed among several locations, perhaps among several countries, requiring a global HRIS. Northern Telecom has facilities in 90 countries, including the United Kingdom, China, and the United States, and needed access to information about employees located worldwide. The company has created a central database built on a common set of core elements. Anyone with authorization can view employee records from around the globe. Data on the number of employees, salaries, and recruiting efforts are continually updated as changes are made around the world. The system is customized to specific country needs, but several common data fields and elements are used globally. Northern Telecom's system has enabled managers around the world to obtain up-to-date employee data to meet customer needs and address internal staffing issues.[56]

The Internet Economy

The way business is conducted has changed rapidly during the past few years and will continue to do so. Many companies are connecting to the Internet to gain an advantage over (or keep up with) competitors. Greater use of the Internet has prompted the spread of **electronic business (e-business)**—any process that a business conducts electronically, especially business involving use of the Internet. E-business includes several forms of buying and selling goods and business services:

- Business-to-consumer transactions, such as purchasing books and tickets and conducting services, including banking, online

- Business-to-business transactions, including sales among manufacturers, retailers, wholesalers, and construction firms

- Consumer-to-consumer transactions—in particular, individuals buying and selling through auctions

E-business relies on the Internet to enable buyers to obtain information online, directly order products and services, receive after-sale technical support, and view the status of orders and deliveries. Internet sites may also allow the customer and seller to communicate with each other through email, chat, and voice connections. Companies may set up customer service centres offering email and live telephone connections to provide help, advice, or product information not found on their websites.

E-business creates many HRM challenges.[57] The fast pace of change in information technology requires companies to continually update their skill requirements and then recruit and train people to meet those requirements. The competition for such employees may be stiff and, as described earlier, often involves recruiting on an international scale.

human resource information system (HRIS)
A computer system used to acquire, store, manipulate, analyze, retrieve, and distribute information related to an organization's human resources.

electronic business (e-business)
Any process that a business conducts electronically, especially business involving use of the Internet.

Motivation can also be a challenge. A decade ago, many e-business organizations were small startup companies founded by young, forward-looking people who saw the potential of a then-new technology. These companies sometimes made up for inexperienced management with a culture based on creativity, enthusiasm, and intense commitment. Policies and procedures sometimes took a back seat to team spirit and workplace fun. But as competition heated up and investors withdrew funding, the startup companies were acquired, went out of business, or had to radically cut back hiring and spending. In this changed environment, many employees are beginning to demand overtime pay for their 60-hour workweeks and refusing stock options as substitutes for pay raises. In an extreme case, current and former employees of videogame company Electronic Arts filed a lawsuit complaining that it had not paid them overtime wages to which they were entitled.[58] In this environment, HRM needs to help companies comply with labour laws, motivate employees, and craft human resource policies that seem fair to workers and meet employers' competitive demands.

electronic human resource management (e-HRM)
The processing and transmission of digitized HR information, especially using computer networking and the Internet.

e-HRM Applications

The development of e-business has included ways to move HRM activities onto the Internet. Electronic HRM applications let employees enrol in and participate in training programs online. Employees can go online to select from items in a benefits package and enrol in the benefits they choose. They can look up answers to HR-related questions and read company news. This processing and transmission of digitized HR information is called **electronic human resource management (e-HRM)**.

The Internet and e-HRM are helpful for employees who work outside the office because they can receive and share information online easily. The benefits of products such as PDAs and BlackBerrys are enormous, but is it possible to be too accessible?

e-HRM has the potential to change all traditional HRM functions. Table 1.4 shows some major implications of e-HRM. For example, employees in different geographic areas can work together. Use of the Internet lets companies search for talent without

HRM PRACTICES	IMPLICATIONS OF E-HRM
Analysis and design of work	Employees in geographically dispersed locations can work together in virtual teams using video, email, and the Internet.
Recruiting	Employers can post job openings online; candidates can apply for jobs online.
Selection	Online simulations, including tests, videos, and email, can measure job candidates' ability to deal with real-life business challenges.
Training	Online learning can bring training to employees anywhere, anytime.
Total rewards	Employees can review salary and incentives information and seek information about and enrol in benefit plans.

TABLE 1.4

Implications of e-HRM for HRM Practices

geographic limitations. Recruiting can include online job postings, applications, and candidate screening from the company's website or the websites of companies that specialize in online recruiting. Employees from different geographic locations can all receive the same training over the company's computer network.

Privacy is an important issue in e-HRM. A great deal of HR information is confidential and not suitable for posting on a website for everyone to see. Therefore, e-HRM typically is set up on an *intranet*, which is a network that uses Internet tools but limits access to authorized users in the organization.

employee self-service
System in which employees have online access to information about HR issues and go online to enrol themselves in programs and provide feedback through surveys.

Sharing of Human Resource Information

Information technology is changing the way HR departments handle record keeping and information sharing. Today, HR employees use technology to automate much of their work in managing employee records and giving employees access to information and enrolment forms for training, benefits, and other programs. As a result, HR employees play a smaller role in maintaining records, and employees now get information through **employee self-service**. This means employees have online access to information about HR issues such as training, benefits, compensation, and contracts; go online to enrol themselves in programs and services; and provide feedback through online surveys.

LO8 - Explain how the nature of the employment relationship is changing and how the need for flexibility affects human resource management.

Change in the Employment Relationship

Economic downturns resulting in layoffs and bankruptcies have played a major role in changing the basic relationship between employers and employees.

A New Psychological Contract

psychological contract
A description of what an employee expects to contribute in an employment relationship and what the employer will provide the employee in exchange for those contributions.

We can think of the relationship between employers and employees in terms of a **psychological contract**, a description of what an employee expects to contribute in an employment relationship and what the employer will provide the employee in exchange for those contributions.[59] Unlike a sales contract, the psychological contract is not formally put into writing. Instead, it describes unspoken expectations that are widely held by employers and employees. In the traditional version of this psychological contract, organizations expected their employees to contribute time, effort, skills, abilities, and loyalty. In return, the organizations would provide job security and opportunities for promotion.

However, this arrangement is being replaced with a new type of psychological contract.[60] To stay competitive, modern organizations must frequently change the quality, innovation, creativeness, and timeliness of employee contributions and the skills needed to make those contributions. This need has led to organizational restructuring, mergers and acquisitions, layoffs, and longer hours for many employees. Companies demand excellent customer service and high productivity levels. They expect employees to take more responsibility for their own careers, from seeking training to balancing work and family. These expectations result in less job security for employees, who can count on working for several companies over the course of a career. Today, the average length of time a person holds a job is seven years.[61]

In exchange for top performance and working longer hours without job security, employees want companies to provide flexible work schedules, effective work environments, more control over how they accomplish work, training and development opportunities, and financial incentives based on how the organization performs. (Figure 1.13 provides a humorous look at an employee who seems to have benefited from this modern psychological contract by obtaining a family-friendly work arrangement.) Employees realize that companies cannot provide employment security, so they want *employability*. This means they want their company to provide training and job experiences to help ensure that they can find other employment opportunities.

SPEED BUMP   **Dave Coverly**

FIGURE 1.13

A Family-Friendly Work Arrangement

Flexibility

The new psychological contract largely results from the HRM challenge of building a committed, productive workforce in turbulent economic conditions that offer opportunity for financial success but can also quickly turn sour, making every employee expendable. From the organization's perspective, the key to survival in a fast-changing environment is flexibility. Organizations want to be able to change as fast as customer needs and economic conditions change. Flexibility in human resource management includes flexible staffing levels and flexible work schedules.

Flexible Staffing Levels

A flexible workforce is one the organization can quickly reshape and resize to meet its changing needs. To be able to do this without massive hiring and firing campaigns, organizations are using more **flexible staffing arrangements**. Flexible staffing arrangements are methods of staffing other than the traditional hiring of full-time employees. There are a variety of methods, the following being most common:

- *Independent contractors* are self-employed individuals with multiple clients.
- *On-call workers* are persons who work for an organization only when they are needed.
- *Temporary workers* are employed by a temporary agency; client organizations pay the agency for the services of these workers.
- *Contract company workers* are employed directly by a company for a specific time specified in a written contract.

CBC News recently reported that an estimated one-third or greater of working Canadians are working in a non-standard work arrangement including part-time or casual status jobs, temporary or contract work, self-employment, holding multiple jobs, and those working from home.[62] More workers are choosing these arrangements, but preferences vary. Most independent contractors and contract workers have this type of arrangement by choice. In contrast, temporary agency workers and on-call workers are likely to prefer traditional full-time employment. With flexible staffing, organizations can more easily modify the number of their employees. Continually adjusting staffing levels is especially cost-effective for an organization

flexible staffing arrangements
Methods of staffing other than the traditional hiring of full-time employees (e.g., use of independent contractors, on-call workers, temporary workers, and contract company workers).

that has fluctuating demand for its products and services. And when an organization downsizes by laying off temporary and part-time employees, the damage to morale among permanent full-time workers is likely to be less severe. From the employee's perspective, alternative work arrangements provide some flexibility for balancing work and nonwork activities.

Organization of This Book

This chapter has provided an overview of human resource management as well as a summary of challenges and trends impacting Canadian organizations, employees, and HR professionals. In this book, the topics are organized according to the broad areas of human resource management shown in Table 1.5.

Each chapter includes principles and examples showing how the human resource management practices covered in that chapter helps a company maintain

TABLE 1.5

Topics Covered in This Book

PART 1 THE HUMAN RESOURCE ENVIRONMENT
• To be effective, human resource management must begin with an awareness of the trends and challenges shaping this field, including changes in the workforce, technology, and society as well as the profession of HR itself (Chapter 1).
• On a more detailed level, human resource management must also ensure that the organization's actions comply with legal requirements, the topic of Chapter 2. Chapter 3 addresses how organizations provide safe and engaging work environments.
PART 2 PREPARING FOR AND ACQUIRING HUMAN RESOURCES
• Explores the responsibilities involved in acquiring and selecting human resources.
• Chapter 4 covers the topics of analyzing work and designing jobs. Chapter 5 explains how to plan for human resource needs and recruit candidates to meet those needs. Chapter 6 discusses the selection of employees and their placement into jobs or teams.
PART 3 MANAGING TALENT
• The discussion turns to the development of human resources.
• Chapter 7 addresses various ways organizations train and develop their employees to perform their jobs, prepare for future jobs and help establish career paths that take into account work interests, goals, values, and other career issues. Chapter 8 describes the various activities involved in managing performance, including regular performance appraisals.
PART 4 REWARDING HUMAN RESOURCES
• An important element of attracting, retaining, and engaging human resources is the employee's belief that he or she is being fairly rewarded for the work performed.
• Chapter 9 explores decisions related to the organization's overall pay structure, discusses ways organizations can use pay to recognize individual and group contributions to the organization's performance, considers benefits (forms of total compensation other than pay), and looks at how to create a total rewards culture.

PART 5   MEETING OTHER HR GOALS

- Addresses a number of special topics that human resource managers face today.
- Chapter 10 discusses responsibilities of HRM in organizations where employees have or are seeking union representation. Chapter 11 explores issues that arise when the organizations has people working in more than one country. And Chapter 12, the last chapter, returns to the topic of high-performance organizations, taking a closer look at how human resource management can foster high performance.

high performance. Best Practices boxes highlight success stories related to these topics. HR How-To boxes provide a more detailed look at how to carry out a practice in each of these areas. e-HRM boxes identify the ways human resource professionals are applying information technology and the Internet to help their organizations excel in the fast-changing dynamic world. Finally, the Thinking Ethically box at the end of each chapter demonstrates ethical issues in managing human resources.

THINKING ETHICALLY

Whose Business Is It When You Blog?

Just as companies have become used to the idea of warning employees that their email messages are not private, along come blogs (Web logs), with their own set of issues. Although some companies have begun to use blogs as a new marketing tool, most blogs are written by individuals who enjoy posting their thoughts online. The dilemma involves the line between what people do as employees and what they do on their own time.

Consider the case of Mark Jen. After he obtained a job with Google, he began posting his observations about the company in a blog he named

Ninetyninezeros. (Coincidentally or not, this title has one less zero than the number of zeros in a googol, the number that inspired Google's name.) About a week after the entries began, they disappeared temporarily, and they reappeared after some editing. Jen noted that Google was "pretty cool about" his blog, but a few days later, word leaked that he was no longer working for Google.

Other bloggers weighed in. Jeremy Zawodny, who works for Yahoo! and said he spoke to Jen, wrote, "He doesn't believe he was doing anything wrong (neither do I based on what he told me)." Robert Scoble, a

Microsoft employee, cautioned, "It's not easy writing in public. All it takes is one paragraph to lose credibility, have people laugh at you, get you sued, create a PR firestorm, or get your boss mad at you."

Jen is not the first blogger to lose his job. Ellen Simonetti was fired after her Queen of the Sky blog posted pictures of herself posed humorously and a little provocatively in her flight attendant uniform. Bank employee Peter Whitney was fired after co-workers came across his Gravity Spike blog, which included complaints about work. Heather Armstrong's blog

THINKING ETHICALLY

at www.dooce.com included exaggerated stories about work. They were intended to amuse her family and friends, but her boss, alerted by an anonymous tip, was not amused.

SOURCE: Evan Hansen, "Google Blogger Has Left the Building," *ONetNews.com*, February 8, 2005, www.news.com; Neville Hobson, "Google Blogger Firing Highlights Why Guidelines Are Essential," *WebProNews.com*, February 10, 2005,

www.webpronews.com; and Todd Wallack, "Beware If Your Blog Is Related to Work," San Francisco Chronicle, January 24, 2005, www.sfgate.com.

Questions

1. Who might be affected by a blog written about a company? What kinds of work-related information are public? What information does a company have a right to keep private?
2. Imagine that you work in HR and you learn that an employee of your company has mentioned work-related topics in a blog. What would you do?

SUMMARY

L01

Define human resource management, identify the roles and responsibilities of human resource departments, and explain how human resource management contributes to an organization's performance.

- Human resource management consists of an organization's "people practices"—the policies, practices, and systems that influence employees' behaviour, attitudes, and performance.

- The HRM process begins with analyzing and designing jobs, then recruiting and selecting employees to fill those jobs. Training and development equip employees to carry out their present jobs and follow a career path in the organization. Performance management ensures employees' activities and outputs match the organization's goals.

- Human resource departments also plan and administer the organization's pay and benefits. They carry out activities in support of employee and labour relations, such as communication programs and collective bargaining. Conducting all these activities involves the establishment and administration of human resource policies.

- Management depends on human resource professionals for help in ensuring compliance with legislation, as well as for support for the organization's strategy—for example, workforce planning and change management.

- HRM contributes to organizational performance by influencing who works for the organization and how these people work. These human resources, if well managed, have the potential to be a source of sustainable competitive advantage, contributing to basic objectives such as productivity, profits, and customer satisfaction.

L02

Summarize areas in which human resource management can support organizational strategies.

- HR professionals should be familiar with the organization's strategy and may even play a role in developing the strategy.

- Specific HR practices vary according to the type of strategy. Productivity improvements require HR leadership including effective feedback and rewards. When organizations with international operations hire employees in foreign countries where they operate, they need to be mindful of the differences in culture and business practices. Even small businesses serving local markets discover that qualified candidates include skilled immigrants who account for a significant and growing share of the Canadian labour market. Therefore, HRM requires knowledge of different cultures.

- Organizations must be able to select and prepare employees for global assignments.
- Outsourcing requires effective job design, planning, recruitment and selection, and compensation practices to realize the potential benefits.

LO3

Identify the Required Professional Capabilities and certification process for HR professionals.

- HR professionals require both academic knowledge and experiential knowledge of the profession. The Required Professional Capabilities (RPCs) include varied areas of knowledge and professional application.
- Many human resource professionals have achieved the nationally standardized designation, Certified Human Resources Professional (CHRP).
- Human resource professionals are required to uphold high ethical standards. Some areas in which ethical issues arise include adherence to legislation, protecting confidentiality, and maintaining professional competence.

LO4

Explain the role of supervisors and line managers in human resource management.

- Although many organizations have human resource departments, supervisors and line managers must be familiar with the basics of HRM and their own role with regard to managing human resources.
- Supervisors and line managers typically have responsibilities related to all the HR functions. Supervisors help analyze work, interview job candidates, participate in selection decisions, provide training, conduct performance appraisals, and recommend pay increases. On a day-to-day basis, supervisors and line managers represent the company to their employees, so they also play an important role in employee relations.

LO5

Describe typical careers in human resource management.

- Careers in HRM may involve specialized work in fields such as recruiting, training, or labour relations.
- HR professionals may also be generalists, performing the full range of HR activities described in this chapter. People in these positions usually have a university degree or college diploma in business or the social sciences.

LO6

Describe trends in the labour force composition and how they affect human resource management.

- An organization's internal labour force comes from its external labour market—individuals who are actively seeking employment. In Canada, this labour market is aging and becoming more diverse. The share of women in the Canadian workforce has grown to nearly half of the total.
- To compete for talent, organizations must be flexible enough to meet the needs of older workers, possibly redesigning jobs. Organizations must recruit from a diverse population, establish bias-free HR systems, and help employees understand and appreciate cultural differences.
- Organizations also need employees with skills in decision making, customer service, and teamwork, as well as technical skills. The competition for such talent is intense. Organizations facing a skills shortage often hire employees who lack certain skills, then train them for their jobs.

LO7

Discuss the role of high-performance work systems and how technological developments are affecting human resource management.

- HRM can help organizations find and keep the best possible fit between their social system and technical system. Recruiting and selection decisions are especially important for organizations that rely on knowledge workers. Job design and appropriate systems for assessment and rewards have a central role in supporting employee engagement and teamwork.
- The widespread use of the Internet includes HRM applications. Organizations search for talent globally using online job postings and screening candidates online. Organizations' websites feature information

directed toward potential employees. Employees may receive training online. At many companies, online information sharing enables employee self-service for many HR needs, from application forms to training modules to information about the details of company policies and benefits.

L08 Explain how the nature of the employment relationship is changing and how the need for flexibility affects human resource management.

- The employment relationship takes the form of a "psychological contract" that describes what employees and employers expect from the employment relationship. Traditionally, organizations expected employees to contribute their skills and loyalty in exchange for job security and opportunities for promotion. Today, organizations are requiring top performance and longer work hours but often cannot provide job security.

- Organizations seek flexibility in staffing through non-standard work arrangements. They may use outsourcing as well as temporary and contract workers. The use of such workers can affect job design, as well as the motivation of the organization's permanent employees.

REVIEW AND DISCUSSION QUESTIONS

1. How can human resource management contribute to a company's success?
2. Why do organizations outsource HRM functions? How does outsourcing affect the role of human resource professionals? As an HR professional, would you rather work for the HR department of a large organization or for a firm that provides HR outsourcing services such as Hewitt Associates Inc.? Explain your answer.
3. What skills are important for success in human resource management? Which of these skills are already strengths of yours? Which would you like to develop further?
4. Traditionally, human resource management practices were developed and administered by the company's human resource department. Increasingly, supervisors and line managers are playing an active HRM role.

What are the potential benefits of supervisors and line managers taking a more active role in HRM? Potential problems?
5. Does a career in human resource management appeal to you? Why or why not?
6. How does each of the following labour force trends affect HRM?
   a. Aging of the workforce
   b. Diversity
   c. Skill deficiencies
   d. Higher levels of education
7. What HRM functions could an organization provide through self-service? What are some advantages and disadvantages of using self-service for these functions?
8. How does the employment relationship typical of today's organizations differ from that of a generation ago?

WHAT'S YOUR HR IQ?

Online Learning Centre The Online Learning Centre offers more ways to check what you've learned so far. Find experiential exercises as well as Test Your Knowledge Quizzes, Videos, and many other resources at www.mcgrawhill.ca/olc/steen.

Case:
Suncor Strives for a Representative Workforce

Suncor Energy Inc. is a world leader in mining and extracting crude oil from Alberta's oil sands. Suncor also explores for, develops, and markets natural gas, operates major refineries in Sarnia, Ontario and Denver, Colorado and is actively involved in renewable energy initiatives such as wind power projects. Suncor also operates a chain of Sunoco service stations across Ontario and Phillips

66 service stations in Colorado and Wyoming. Suncor employs approximately 4,000 employees.

Nineteen percent of Suncor's employees are women, 7 percent are visible minorities, and in the past eight years the Aboriginal workforce in its oil sands division has grown to more than 10 percent from 3 percent. Heather Kennedy, vice-president of human resources and community affairs, says 10 percent is good, but not good enough. To attract more Aboriginal employees to better reflect the local population, Suncor sponsors scholarships and literacy and mentorship programs, and every summer hires 130 students, up to a third of them Aboriginal.

One beneficiary is Florida Proulx, from the Athabasca Chipewyan First Nation. A summer accounting assistant, she has since been hired by Suncor and plans to become a certified general accountant. Before that, she worked for an employment centre in Wood Buffalo, where she helped find jobs for Aboriginal peoples, many of them at Suncor. "The company is proactive," Proulx says.

"They go out and meet people in smaller communities and let them know they're there. Consultation is part of operating in the oilpatch—companies must show regulators they have consulted with stakeholders. But it's also good business," says Heather Kennedy. "We're equals in this region. It's not a matter of meeting our obligations, but working with Aboriginals to determine what their needs and our needs are, and pulling them together."

Suncor recently sponsored an event held in conjunction with the National Aboriginal Achievement Foundation Awards to provide opportunities for high-school students from across Canada to meet Aboriginal role models and leaders such as Tina Keeper, television star of *North of 60*. The National Aboriginal Achievement Foundation Awards were developed to encourage and celebrate excellence in the Aboriginal community.

Questions

1. How might Suncor benefit from employing a diverse workforce and supporting Aboriginal initiatives?
2. What does Suncor's human resource department need to do to ensure these potential benefits are achieved? Refer to the human resource management functions and responsibilities identified in Table 1.1 in developing your answer.

SOURCES: www.suncor.com; Richard W. Yerema, *Canada's Top 100 Employers 2004* (Toronto: Mediacorp Canada Inc.), p. 325; "Aboriginal Voices," *Canadian Business*, March 29–April 11, 2004, p. 50; www.naaf.ca/naaaright.html, retrieved April 3, 2004.

Excalibur Case:
Le Cirque du Soleil: How to Manage Growth

EXCALIBUR
Excellence ∎ calibre

You are a team of consultants specializing in human resources and labour relations management. Your firm of consultants enjoys a good reputation for the quality of the services offered, especially to large-scale international companies. Having heard tell of the excellence of your services, Cirque du Soleil has approached you. After several meetings with representatives from their Human Resources Department, you have noted the following facts:

Cirque du Soleil
Founded in 1984 by a group of young street performers, Cirque du Soleil has been in constant evolution since its creation. The company enjoys excellent international recognition and is reputed to have reinvented circus arts. While Cirque du Soleil had sales of $1.7 million, 50 employees, and 23 performers in 1984, in 2000, sales reached $407 million and it employed 1,370 employees and 445 performers. It presented seven shows in 2000 on three continents: North America, Europe, and Asia. Also, to manage adequately all its personnel, it has four separate headquarters. As well as International Headquarters in Montreal, it has four other head offices: Headquarters—America, also in Montreal, Headquarters—Europe in Amsterdam, Headquarters—Las Vegas in Las Vegas, and lastly, Headquarters—Asia-Pacific in Singapore.

While Cirque du Soleil would like to find and exploit new niches related to presenting shows, most of its revenues come from ticket sales. Thus, the nucleus of the Cirque remains presenting shows. The Cirque has four fixed shows, two touring shows in Asia, one in North America, and another in Europe. A touring show comprises 150 to 200 people, including 50 to 70 performers, and it has to relocate, on average, every six weeks, which demands very skilled logistics and effective planning of the entry authorizations for the different countries on the tour. Relocating means moving personnel, their baggage, and the Cirque's equipment from town to town. It also means lodging all these people and ensuring they get the required visas and work permits to be able to practice their art in the countries the tour is visiting. To reach the level of excellence set by Cirque du Soleil, talent scouts and recruiters travel the globe in search of artists, creators, coaches, musicians, etc. Consequently, the Cirque's performers and personnel come from more than 30 countries and speak various languages. Also, while the average age of employees is relatively young at 32, the age of the performers and employees varies from 3 to 62.

Development Project
As well as continuing to create and produce new shows, Cirque du Soleil wants to diversify its commercial activities. Indeed, it would like to see itself develop the production of audiovisual works such as the soundtracks of the different shows, explore the field of publishing, and continue to promote some strategic agreements with partners in the hotel business. It has also set itself the objective of adding two or three tours within five years, which will bring the number of employees required to about 2,000.

Management

Cirque du Soleil has adopted a management style in its own image: dynamic, vibrant, and imaginative. The organic nature of how it operates puts each employee in a position that allows him or her to contribute to a common work. Cirque du Soleil firmly believes that by appealing to everyone's intelligence all objectives are achievable. Also, communications are open and the moral authority that certain hierarchical titles might impose is almost nonexistent. A core value of Cirque du Soleil's is respect for cultural diversity. Despite the continuous growth the company has experienced, it has always known how to ensure cohesion among employees and maintain a strong sense of belonging.

Challenges to Be Met

Given its growth plans, both by the number of shows presented and the establishment of new commercial activities, Cirque du Soleil must apply itself to adapting its structure, and above all to ensuring that its managers have the ability to support such development. Several managers who have grown up with Cirque du Soleil and who have thus acquired broad operating experience are having difficulty moving to a strategic management mode. Given their extensive knowledge of how the Cirque operates, they too often remain occupied or preoccupied with operating questions, rather than investing their energy more in strategic planning. Also, given the increased number of tours planned, another problem that already exists is likely to get bigger. Because of the difficult touring conditions, such as the frequent relocations, the increased number of shows per week, and working conditions in general, the turnover of employees is very high. On average, they work for the Cirque between 19 and 24 months, which creates a turnover rate of 18–22 percent. Despite the efforts made to reduce the inconveniences inherent in touring, problems remain. For example, the Cirque offers the services of a tutor to child performers and to the children of performers. However, because of the costs this would entail, this service cannot be offered to all the children of its personnel. Despite the advantageous salaries, Cirque du Soleil is having trouble retaining touring personnel.

Finally, it is important to note that, in the touring shows and in International Headquarters in Montreal, the presence of many people of different nationalities, speaking different languages, is a challenge. Indeed, while the presence of Quebec or Canadian performers at International Headquarters and on tours is often secondary, having several nationalities greatly influences the quality of communications. And, depending on the cultural baggage of each person, the perception of the message communicated can differ greatly. Since cultural references are very divergent, what are innocuous gestures to some have unexpected implications for others. Although Cirque du Soleil has always greatly valued cultural diversity and emphasized the richness it brings rather than the differences it creates, it has to constantly manage stereotypes and prejudices. This situation is even more palpable at International Headquarters in Montreal, since the performers who work there are passing through, either with the aim of learning a new number or to take up training again following an injury. Also, people of the same nationality often remain among themselves without mixing much with other performers of different nationalities.

Your Mandate

You have been given a mandate by Le Cirque du Soleil to propose solutions to the problems raised by the facts described. To do so, you must

1. State your understanding of the situation at Cirque du Soleil
2. Precisely determine the needs of Cirque du Soleil in the short and the medium term
3. Because of those needs, make provisions for the obstacles envisaged
4. Establish a plan of action by formulating possible solutions, taking into account the values transmitted by Cirque du Soleil

SOURCE: www.rhri.org/excalibur, retrieved March 2, 2004. Case is adapted from the online publication *Effectif*, September/October 2001, pp. 12–14.
Note: This case study was used in the 15th edition of Excalibur (the Canadian University Tournament of Human Resources).

Chapter

2

The Legal Context for Human Resource Management

What Do I Need to Know? After reading this chapter, you should be able to:

1. Describe the legal framework for human resource management in Canada.

2. Summarize the major federal and provincial laws impacting human resource management.

3. Identify the agencies that enforce employment equality and privacy legislation and describe their roles.

4. Describe ways employers can avoid illegal discrimination and meet the duty to accommodate.

5. Define harassment and sexual harassment and discuss how employers can eliminate or minimize them.

6. Discuss the importance of valuing diversity.

7. Describe and introduce the protection of employee health and safety in the workplace.

Introduction

He's breaking barriers. Steven Fletcher is Canada's first quadriplegic MP. In 1996, Steven, a two-time Manitoba kayaking champion, was paralyzed from the neck down in a car collision with a moose. Elected in 2004, 2006, and again in 2008, in a highly competitive constituency in Winnipeg, Steven continues to create change within Parliament.

Steven Fletcher, Canada's first quadriplegic MP, is creating a legacy of accomplishments, advocating a national cancer strategy, embryonic stem cell research, and the labelling of trans fats.

Fletcher ran his campaign on increased access to postsecondary education, greater government accountability, and improving health care. One of Fletcher's immediate impacts was directly on the House of Commons where aisles are too narrow and elevators too small for his motorized wheelchair. Many of the buildings are 75 to 140 years old and are not as accessible as one might expect. Because Fletcher needs help to perform the day-to-day aspects of his job—for example, turning the pages of a report—an aide is by his side. But Steven is focused on his ability to contribute, "I made the decision to use what I have. What's important is from the neck up."

A variety of necessary arrangements were needed for him do his job as a parliamentarian. These accommodations included not only building adaptations such as lifts and ramps, but also information technology needs such as wireless voice-activated dialling for his phone system and use of a head mouse for his computer. Although the initial focus was on accommodating Steven Fletcher's needs to allow him to do his job, his legacy will likely include creating awareness and improving the situation for many others. For example, Steven serves as the Parliamentary Secretary of Health and on the Legislative Committee for Bill C-20, a Criminal Code amendment to increase the protection of children from sexual exploitation. Steven adds, "let's lay the foundation so we'll see people in wheelchairs contributing . . . and it's natural."[1]

As we saw in Chapter 1, human resource management takes place in the context of the company's goals and society's expectations for how a company should operate. In Canada, the federal, provincial, and territorial governments have set some limits on how an organization can practise human resource management. Among these limits are requirements intended to prevent discrimination in hiring and employment practices and to protect the health and safety of workers while they are on the job. Questions about a company's compliance with these requirements can result in human rights complaints, lawsuits, and negative publicity that often cause serious problems for a company's success and survival. Conversely, a company that skillfully navigates the maze of regulations can gain an advantage over its competitors.

This chapter provides an overview of the ways government bodies regulate human resource management. It introduces you to major laws affecting employers in these areas, as well as the agencies charged with enforcing those laws. The chapter also discusses ways organizations can develop practices that ensure they are in compliance with the laws.

One point to make at the outset is that managers often want a list of dos and don'ts that will keep them out of legal trouble. Some managers rely on strict rules such as

"Don't ever ask a female applicant if she is married," rather than learning the reasons behind those rules. Clearly, certain practices are illegal or at least inadvisable, and this chapter will provide guidance on avoiding such practices. However, managers who merely focus on how to avoid breaking the law are not thinking about how to be ethical or how to acquire and use human resources in the best way to carry out the company's mission. This chapter introduces ways to think proactively about the legal requirements for HRM.

R₽C

1,2,3,4

The Legal Framework for Human Resource Management

LO1 - Describe the legal framework for human resource management in Canada.

Federal, provincial, and territorial governments in Canada all play an important role in creating the legal environment for human resource management. Approximately 90 percent of Canadian employers and their employees are covered by provincial and territorial legislation. The remaining 10 percent are covered by federal legislation. Table 2.1 summarizes the types of organizations that fall under federal versus provincial legislation.

Federal, provincial, and territorial employment-related laws tend to mirror one another; however, some differences exist. It is important for employers to ensure they are aware of and comply with all legal requirements. For organizations with workers in more than one province, territory, or industry it can be time-consuming and challenging to maintain compliance with this web of legal requirements. In addition, many proactive human resource departments and their organizations are moving beyond

FEDERALLY REGULATED ORGANIZATIONS	PROVINCIALLY REGULATED ORGANIZATIONS
• Federal departments, agencies, and Crown corporations	All other businesses not listed. Examples include
• Chartered banks	• Retail and hospitality businesses, such as a store, a restaurant, a hotel, etc.
• Airlines	• Hospitals or health care providers
• Television and radio stations	• Schools, colleges, or universities
• Interprovincial communication and telecommunication companies	• Most manufacturers
• Buses and railways that travel between provinces	
• First Nations	
• Other federally regulated industries, such as uranium, mining, grain elevators, flour and seed mills, and feed warehouses	

TABLE 2.1

Summary of Federally versus Provincially Regulated Organizations

SOURCES: "Canadian Human Rights Commission Overview," www.chrc-ccdp.ca/discrimination/federally_regulated-en.asp, retrieved April 13, 2008; *Anti-Discrimination Casebook*, p. 1, www.chrc-ccdp.ca/Legis&Poli, retrieved February 18, 2004; and Human Resource Management Laws and Regulations Government of Canada, http://hrmanagement.gc.ca, retrieved February 18, 2004.

compliance and are recognizing the strategic importance of valuing the various goals pursued through the legislation, for example, diversity, health and safety of employees, and privacy protection. Table 2.2 provides an overview of federal, provincial, and territorial human rights, employment standards, and health and safety laws in Canada.

TABLE 2.2

Human Rights, Employment Standards, and Health and Safety Laws in Canada

JURISDICTION	HUMAN RIGHTS	EMPLOYMENT STANDARDS	HEALTH & SAFETY
Federal	Canadian Human Rights Act www.chrc-ccdp.ca	Canada Labour Code www.hrsdc.gc.ca	Canada Labour Code www.hrsdc.gc.ca
British Columbia	Human Rights Code www.bchrt.gov.bc.ca	Employment Standards Act www.gov.bc.ca	Workers Compensation Act www.gov.bc.ca
Alberta	Human Rights Citizenship and Multiculturalism Act www.albertahumanrights.ab.ca	Employment Standards Code www.gov.ab.ca	Occupational Health and Safety Act www.gov.ab.ca
Saskatchewan	Human Rights Code www.shrc.gov.sk.ca	Labour Standards Act www.gov.sk.ca	Occupational Health and Safety Act www.gov.sk.ca
Manitoba	Human Rights Code www.gov.mb.ca/hrc	Employment Standards Code www.gov.mb.ca	Workplace Safety and Health Act www.gov.mb.ca
Ontario	Human Rights Code www.ohrc.on.ca	Employment Standards Act www.gov.on.ca	Occupational Health and Safety Act and Workplace Safety and Insurance Act www.gov.on.ca
Quebec	Charter of Human Rights and Freedoms www.cdpdj.qc.ca	Labour Standards Act www.cnt.gouv.qc.ca	Act Respecting Occupational Health and Safety www.gouv.qc.ca
New Brunswick	Human Rights Act www.gnb.ca/hrc-cdp	Employment Standards Act www.gnb.ca	Occupational Health and Safety Act www.gnb.ca
Nova Scotia	Human Rights Act www.gov.ns.ca/humanrights	Labour Standards Code www.gov.ns.ca	Occupational Health and Safety Act www.gov.ns.ca
Prince Edward Island	Human Rights Act www.gov.pe.ca/humanrights	Employment Standards Act www.gov.pe.ca	Occupational Health and Safety Act www.gov.pe.ca
Newfoundland and Labrador	Human Rights Code www.justice.gov.nl.ca/hrc	Labour Standards Act www.gov.nl.ca	Occupational Health and Safety Act www.gov.nl.ca
Yukon	Human Rights Act www.yhrc.yk.ca	Employment Standards Act www.gov.yk.ca	Occupational Health and Safety Act www.wcb.yk.ca
Northwest Territories	Human Rights Act www.assembly.gov.nt.ca	Labour Standards Act www.gov.nt.ca	Occupational Health and Safety Regulations www.gov.nt.ca
Nunavut	Fair Practices Act www.cbsc.org/nunavut	Labour Standards Act www.gov.nu.ca	Workers' Compensation Act www.gov.nu.ca

Equality in Employment

Among the most significant efforts to regulate human resource management are those aimed at achieving equality in employment and eliminating discrimination based on a protected ground such as race, age, colour, or sex. **Discrimination** means to "treat someone differently or unfairly because of a personal characteristic."[2] However, it may be helpful to note that it is acceptable, and in fact encouraged to *discriminate* on the basis of performance—for example, providing a bonus or other rewards only to individuals or teams that meet or exceed objective job-related performance standards.

All individuals have a right to an equal chance to be hired, keep a job, get a promotion, or receive other work benefit regardless of personal characteristics including race, colour, national or ethnic origin, religion, sexual orientation, age, marital status, sex, family status, physical or mental disability, or pardoned conviction.

Direct discrimination involves policies or practices that clearly make a distinction on the basis of a prohibited ground (see Figure 2.1). **Indirect discrimination** involves

discrimination
To treat someone differently or unfairly because of a personal characteristic.

direct discrimination
Policies or practices that clearly make a distinction on the basis of a prohibited ground.

FIGURE 2.1

Prohibited Grounds of Discrimination in Employment

PROHIBITED GROUND	FEDERAL	BC	AB	SK	MB	ON	QUE	NB	NS	PEI	NL	NWT	YK	NU
Race	*	*	*	*	*	*	*	*	*	*	*	*	*	*
National or ethnic origin	*	*	*	*	*	*	*	*	*	*	*	*	*	*
Colour	*	*	*	*	*	*	*	*	*	*	*	*	*	*
Religion or religious creed	*	*	*	*	*	*	*	*	*	*	*	*	*	*
Age	*	*	*	*	*	*	*	*	*	*	*	*	*	*
		19+	18+	18+		18+					19+			
Sex (including pregnancy & childbearing)	*	*	*	*	*	*	*	*	*	*	*	*	*	*
Sexual orientation	*	*	*	*	*	*	*	*	*	*	*	*	*	*
Marital status	*	*	*	*	*	*	*	*	*	*	*	*	*	*
Family status	*	*	*	*	*	*	*		*	*		*	*	*
Physical or mental disability (includes dependence on drugs or alcohol, with the exception of Quebec, NWT, and Yukon)	*	*	*	*	*	*	*	*	*	*	*	*	*	*
Pardoned conviction	*	*				*	*					*		
Ancestry or place of origin		*	*	*	*	*		*				*	*	*
Political belief		*			*		*		*	*	*	*	*	
Source of income (social condition)		*	*	*	*		*		*	*		*		

SOURCE: From Canadian Human Rights Commission, "Prohibited Grounds of Discrimination in Canada," pp. 1–3, 1998. Reproduced with the permission of the Minister of Public Works and Government Services Canada, 2004, www.chrc-ccdp.ca/discrimination/grounds-en.asp, retrieved December 6, 2004. *Updates*: From www.chrc-ccdp.ca/publications/prohibited_grounds.en.asp, retrieved April 19, 2008; "Mandatory Retirement in Canada," www.hrsdc.gc.ca/en/lp/spila/clli/eslc/19mandatory_retirement.shtml, retrieved April 13, 2008; "Retiring Mandatory Retirement," February 21, 2008, www.cbc.ca/newsbackground/retirement/mandatory/retirement.html, retrieved April 19, 2008. *Note*: This chart is for quick reference only; for interpretation or further details, contact the appropriate Human Rights Commission.

FIGURE 2.2

Examples of
Inappropriate
Discriminatory Behaviour
in Employment

INAPPROPRIATE DISCRIMINATORY BEHAVIOUR IN EMPLOYMENT

- Denying someone a job because of a disability that can be accommodated or doesn't affect job performance
- Internet or recorded telephone hate messages
- Firing an employee for filing a human rights complaint
- Including employment requirements not related to the job, e.g., asking for previous Canadian work experience

SOURCE: Adapted from the *Canadian Human Rights Act: A Guide*, pp. 2, 3, www.chrc-ccdp.ca/publications/chra_guide/ledp.asp, retrieved February 18, 2004.

indirect discrimination
Policies or practices that appear to be neutral but have an adverse effect on the basis of a prohibited ground.

policies or practices that appear to be neutral but have an *adverse effect* on the basis of a prohibited ground. For example, requiring a job applicant to have a driver's licence appears to be applied equally to all applicants. However, the effect of this requirement is not neutral—someone who does not have a driver's licence because of suffering from epilepsy would not be able to apply for the job.[3] See Figure 2.2 for examples of discriminatory behaviour in employment.

L02 - Summarize the major federal and provincial laws impacting human resource management.

Legislation in Canada

Canadian law recognizes the equality of people and prohibits discrimination in employment practices. Canadian law also requires employers to identify and remove barriers in employment.

1,2,3,4

Canadian Human Rights Act
Federal legislation that protects individuals from discrimination on the basis of 11 prohibited (protected) grounds.

The Canadian Human Rights Act (1977)

The **Canadian Human Rights Act** is federal legislation that protects individuals from discrimination based on 11 prohibited (protected) grounds:

- Race
- National or ethnic origin
- Colour
- Religion
- Age
- Sex (including pregnancy and childbirth)
- Sexual orientation (1996)
- Marital status
- Family status
- Physical or mental disability (including dependence on alcohol or drugs)
- Pardoned criminal conviction[4]

See Figure 2.4 later in the chapter for a discussion of each of the prohibited (protected) grounds along with some real examples of disputes and settlements.

The Charter of Rights and Freedoms (1982)

The Charter of Rights and Freedoms was the first constitutional recognition of the right to equality. It identifies fundamental rights and freedoms including the right to equality (including the equality of men and women), Aboriginal peoples' rights, the right to seek employment anywhere in Canada, and the right to use either of Canada's official languages.[5]

The Employment Equity Act (1986)

The Employment Equity Act requires federally regulated employers as well as private-sector contractors with more than 100 employees in Canada and with contracts valued at more than $200,000 to eliminate employment barriers to the four designated groups:

- Women
- Members of visible minorities ("persons other than Aboriginal peoples, who are non-Caucasian in race or non-white in colour")[6]
- Aboriginal peoples ("persons who are Indians, Inuit, or Metis")[7]
- Persons with disabilities ("persons who have a long-term or recurring physical mental, sensory, psychiatric or learning impairment")[8]

See Table 2.3 for the representation of these four designated workforce groups.

By June 1 every year, over 400 federally regulated employers (employers with 1001+ employees) must submit a report outlining what they have done to improve the situation for the designated groups within their workforce. Employers also need to submit statistics including the representation of the designated groups in their workforce relative to the composition of the Canadian labour force. Employers receive ratings based on their results. Top ratings earned are "A's" and "B's" indicating superior to good performance. Less-than-average-to-poor performance is indicated with "C's" and "D's." A rating of "Z" indicates that an organization does not have any members of one or more of the designated group in its workforce. In addition, more organizations are integrating their employment equity plans into their business planning as a tool to achieve equality in their workforce and capitalize on the benefits of a diverse workforce.

Best practices of exemplary organizations are recognized in the *Employment Equity Act Annual Reports*. Recent examples include the Royal Canadian Mint, which accommodates employees with disabilities at its Ottawa and Winnipeg plants by providing portable wireless communications devices to employees with hearing impairments."[9]

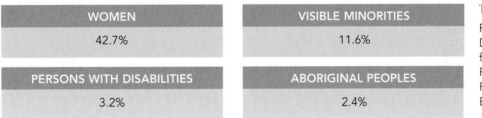

WOMEN	VISIBLE MINORITIES
42.7%	11.6%
PERSONS WITH DISABILITIES	ABORIGINAL PEOPLES
3.2%	2.4%

TABLE 2.3

Representation of Designated Groups for All Employees Reporting Under the Federal Employment Equity Act

SOURCE: *Annual Report Employment Equity Act*, 2006, p. 13, www.hrsdc.gc.ca/en, retrieved April 13, 2008.

Operating similarly to a cellular phone, this accommodation helps employees with hearing impairments feel safe and comfortable in their workplace. Spectra Energy was also recently recognized for the partnerships it has developed to increase recruitment of Aboriginal peoples. Northern Opportunities is a partnership of schools and colleges in northeastern British Columbia, Aboriginal communities, and businesses that "attempts to provide a seamless learning pathway from secondary school to post-secondary trades/technology training and careers." Spectra Energy has invested $1.88 million into the program which will bring returns in the ability to attract potential employees that are already trained to the organization's needs.[10]

The Official Languages Act (1988)

The Official Languages Act provides English and French-speaking Canadians equal opportunities in employment in federally regulated organizations.

Personal Information Protection and Electronic Documents Act (PIPEDA) (2004)

Personal Information Protection and Electronic Documents Act (PIPEDA)

Provides rules for how organizations can collect, use, or disclose information about you in the course of commercial activities.

The **Personal Information Protection and Electronic Documents Act (PIPEDA)** came into effect in three stages over a three-year period from 2001–2004 and provides rules for how organizations can "collect, use, or disclose information about you in the course of commercial activities."[11]

The Act's ten principles establish national standards for privacy practices and have implications for human resource departments and their responsibilities to safeguard employee privacy. Recent complaints to the federal Privacy Commissioner indicate that although employers can collect information on employees about performance, attendance, and potential for advancement there is little an employer can keep from an employee.

In a recent case, an employee of Human Resources and Social Development Canada demanded to see all the information obtained about her during an assessment review. The employee wanted to see the notes made by the contractor hired to conduct the assessment. These notes contained feedback and comments from other employees. The federal Privacy Commissioner ruled the employee was entitled to this information and that employees cannot be promised confidentiality when they make statements about another person.[12] The HR How-To box discusses some of the implications of PIPEDA.

Employment Standards Legislation

Federal, provincial, and territorial laws are in place to provide the minimum standards employees receive. Some of the areas covered include

- Minimum wage
- Hours of work
- General holidays
- Annual vacations
- Unjust dismissals
- Layoff procedures
- Severance pay

HR HOW-TO

Maintaining Legal Compliance When Collecting and Using Employee Information—PIPEDA

The implications to HRM of this relatively new federal legislation and similar laws passed in Alberta (PIPA Alberta) and British Columbia (PIPA BC) are still being tested. However, the Act's ten principles serve as a guide to organizations and HR professionals as to how to maintain legal compliance when collecting and using employee information needed for administration and decision making. HR professionals need to consider the following principles when collecting and using employee personal information in the course of all HR activities to avoid employee complaints:

1. *Accountability*. The organization is responsible for personal information it controls. Start by appointing a privacy officer(s).

2. *Identifying purpose*. Before collecting information, the organization needs to identify why they are collecting the information and how it will be used. Conduct a "privacy audit" to determine what information is collected and why it is collected.

3. *Consent*. The organization is responsible for ensuring that consent is given. Consider what type of consent is needed for each type of information on the basis of criteria such as the sensitivity of the information.

4. *Limiting collection*. Care must be taken to make sure that the collection of personal information is limited to what is needed for the stated purpose. Use a "reasonable person" test to determine what is considered appropriate.

5. *Limiting use, disclosure, and retention*. Personal information cannot be used or disclosed to others without consent and information can only be retained to meet the stated purposes. Additional care must be taken when HR functions are outsourced. Create minimum and maximum retention times for information collected.

6. *Accuracy*. Information of employees must be current and correct. Keep information accurate and introduce a process to correct errors in a timely way.

7. *Safeguards*. Security protection needs to be put in place. Implement both technical and physical security measures to safeguard employee information.

8. *Openness*. Communicate privacy policies and practices. Consider developing training materials, brochures, or other means of communication about the organization's approach to privacy protection.

9. *Individual access*. Be responsive to employees when they request access to information the organization holds about them. Have a method in place to deal with employee concerns about the accuracy and completeness of information.

10. *Compliance challenges*. Individuals have the power to challenge what the organization does to comply with the principles just described. Be open to employee concerns and be willing to adapt policies and practices to ensure compliance with all aspects.

SOURCES: www.privcom.gc.ca/information, retrieved March 21, 2004; Dianne Rinehart, "The ABC's of the New Privacy Legislation," *Small Business Canada Magazine* 6, no. 2 (Spring 2004), p. 7; "The 10 Principles of the Federal Privacy Law," *Canadian HR Reporter*, March 6, 2004, p. G7.

Each jurisdiction has relevant laws to provide minimum employment standards. Refer to Table 2.2 and its summary of the relevant employment standards legislation for each jurisdiction along with the addresses of searchable weblinks where detailed, specific information can be accessed.

A variety of important changes to employment standards laws have recently been made in several jurisdictions. In British Columbia, the Employment Standards Act was amended in order to introduce compassionate care benefits and the federal Employment Insurance Act has expanded the list of persons of whom an employee can claim compassionate care benefits. Minimum wages have increased in several provinces, federal legislation was enacted to provide workers quick payment of unpaid wages in cases of bankruptcy or receivership, and Nova Scotia made several amendments related to retail workers. It was also recently announced that Ontario is considering amending its Employment Standards Act to provide living organ donors with job-protected leave to help offset financial hardships.[13]

5

pay equity
Principle of nondiscrimination in wages that requires men and women doing work of equal value to be paid the same.

Pay Equity

Federally regulated employers are responsible for providing equal pay for work of equal value, or pay equity. **Pay equity** is a principle of nondiscrimination in wages that requires men and women doing work of equal value to the employer to be paid the same. Most provinces and the Yukon, as well as Australia, Scandinavian countries, and many U.S. states, have laws to ensure women and men working in female-dominated jobs, for example, nursing, clerical, and retail sales, are paid fairly. The four criteria usually applied are *skill*, *effort*, *responsibility*, and *working conditions*.

Pay equity legislation is intended to address the wage gap—the difference between the earnings of women working full-time versus the earnings of men working full-time. "In Canada, today, women working full-time still make an average of only 72 cents for every dollar earned by men, and this wage gap has narrowed by just 8 percent since the late 1960s."[14] The irony is that men and women tend to begin their career on an approximately equal footing; however, women fall behind later—often after time away from paid employment to have children. As a result men end up with more experience. Also, men tend to work longer hours, have more education, and are less likely than women to work part-time.[15] Cumulatively, however, these factors do not explain the entire wage gap or earnings gap between men and women. Statistics Canada reported the results of a study of 29 universities related to the salaries of male and female professors. The study revealed that "male university professors earned on average up to $17,300 more than female colleagues."[16] According to the Canadian Association of University Teachers (CAUT), one reason for the wage gap is that women are underrepresented in the highest-paying position of full professor.[17] "Despite comprising about one-third of faculty in 2004–2005, women made up just 19 per cent of the country's full professors, the top academic rank—up from 8 per cent in 1990–91, Statistics Canada data show."[18]

The pay equity system has been criticized for the overall lack of progress, and the federal government has recently completed an extensive pay equity review process expected to result in a more proactive model.[19]

The Government's Role in Providing for Equality and Privacy Protection

At minimum, employers must comply with the legal requirements of their jurisdictions. To enforce these laws, the federal government, for example, has the Canadian Human Rights Commission and the Privacy Commissioner of Canada.

In addition, the provinces and territories have Human Rights Commissions (or a similar structure) to enforce the human rights legislation for their jurisdiction. For example, the **Canadian Human Rights Commission (CHRC)** provides individuals under federal jurisdiction a means to resolve complaints of discrimination (see Figure 2.3). The CHRC has the power to receive and address allegations of discrimination or harassment complaints based on the 11 prohibited grounds of outlined in the Canadian Human Rights Act. The CHRC tries to resolve complaints using mediation and conciliation; however, some complaints only get resolved by using a tribunal. Cases may also be ultimately appealed all the way to the Supreme Court of Canada for final resolution. Recent efforts have also been directed toward early dispute resolution in order to save time, money, and stress associated with the complaint process. In 2007, the average age of the active caseload was 9.1 months, down from 9.5 months in 2006, indicating progress is being made to resolve disputes faster, sometimes before a formal complaint is filed.[20] Figure 2.4 discusses each of the prohibited grounds and provides an example of an actual allegation of discrimination or harassment made in a work-related situation along with the settlement that the complainant received.

L03 - Identify the agencies that enforce employment equality and privacy legislation and describe their roles.

Canadian Human Rights Commission (CHRC)
Provides individuals under federal jurisdiction a means to resolve complaints of discrimination.

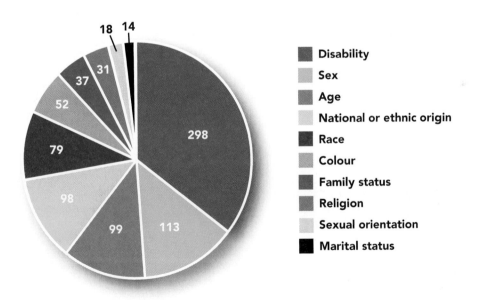

FIGURE 2.3

Types of Signed Complaints Filed with the Canadian Human Rights Commission in 2007

- Disability
- Sex
- Age
- National or ethnic origin
- Race
- Colour
- Family status
- Religion
- Sexual orientation
- Marital status

NOTE: One "pardoned conviction" signed complaint was received in 2007.

SOURCE: "Resolving Disputes Report," www.chrc-ccdp.ca/publications/ar_2007_ra/page6-en.asp#41, Canadian Human Rights Commission. Reproduced with permission of the Ministry of Public Works and Government Services, 2008; Canadian Human Rights Commission, "Overview-Resolving Disputes: Settlement Examples," www.chrc-ccdp.ca/DisputeResolutions. Author/Organization: Canadian Human Rights Commission. Reproduced with the permission of the Ministry of Public Works and Government Services, 2008.

FIGURE 2.4

Federal Prohibited Grounds, Allegations, and Settlements

PROHIBITED GROUND	DESCRIPTION	ALLEGATION	SETTLEMENT
Race, colour, and national or ethnic origin	These three grounds are related, and it is often difficult to draw clear distinctions between them. They are intended to get at the societal problem referred to as "racism."	The complainant alleged that a disgruntled customer used a distasteful tone and made racial slurs. She alleged that the respondent (employer) asked her to deal with the situation by hiding whenever the customer entered her area. Her employment was subsequently terminated for poor performance.	• Letter of reference • Financial compensation for general damages • Financial compensation for pain and suffering • Reimbursement of legal fees • Assistance with job search
Religion or religious creed	Discrimination has occurred because of knowledge of one's religion or a perception of that religion. *Note:* When an individual alleges adverse effect discrimination from some policy or decision the following three questions must be answered "yes": • Is the belief sincerely held? • Is it religious? • Is it the cause of the objection being made?	The complainant cannot work on Sundays because of her religious beliefs. She alleged that, because of this, her supervisor required her to work every Saturday. Eventually, her employment was terminated.	• Financial compensation for general damages • Letter of regret
Age	The ground can refer to: • An individual's actual age • Membership in a specific age-group, e.g., over 55 • A generalized characterization of his or her age, e.g., too old, or too young	The complainant, who is 47 years old, alleged that he was denied education assistance normally provided to younger employees. The complainant also alleged that remarks about his age were made and written comments included in his personnel file.	• Removal from the complainant's file of all reference to his age or to the number of years he could remain as an employee • Assurance that having filed a complaint will not negatively affect his employment • Financial compensation for future tuition and books • Reimbursement for tuition and books for past courses

PROHIBITED GROUND	DESCRIPTION	ALLEGATION	SETTLEMENT
Sex (including pregnancy and childbearing)	Refers to the condition of being: • Male or female	The complainant handed in her resignation at one point because of an excessive workload, but her employer refused to accept it and she continued working. After she announced that she was pregnant two months later, she alleges that her employer suddenly decided to accept her resignation.	• Financial compensation for lost wages and general damages • Letter of recommendation
Sexual orientation	Refers to: • Heterosexuality • Homosexuality • Bisexuality	The complainant alleged that, during a job interview, he was asked inappropriate questions about his sexual orientation. In the end, the complainant got the job.	• Letter of regret • Training for all interviewers on the Canadian Human Rights Act
Marital status	Condition of being: • Single • Legally married • Common-law spouses (opposite-sex or same-sex) • Widowed • Divorced	The complainant and his partner filed separate complaints alleging that the respondent did not take action against a co-worker who made defamatory and harassing remarks about their personal relationship. They allege that the respondent did not provide a harassment-free work environment. *Note:* This allegation included two grounds: marital status and sex.	• Development of protocol for future instances of sexual harassment • Joint management and union anti-harassment and human rights training • Posting of the respondent's human rights and employment equity policy, and relevant provisions of the collective agreement • Financial compensation for pain and suffering
Family status	Refers to the interrelationship that arises as a result of marriage, legal adoption, ancestral relationship, as well as the relationships between spouses, siblings, uncles or aunts, cousins, etc.	The complainant alleged that her employer denied her several career-enhancing opportunities when she returned to work from maternity leave, and that it ultimately terminated her employment on the pretext that it was downsizing and that her job no longer existed. *Note:* This allegation included two grounds: family status and sex.	• Expression of regret to the complainant • Financial compensation for general damages

(continued)

FIGURE 2.4 (concluded)

PROHIBITED GROUND	DESCRIPTION	ALLEGATION	SETTLEMENT
Physical or mental disability (including dependence on alcohol or drugs)	Disability is defined as being either: • Physical or mental • Previous or existing • Including dependence on alcohol or a drug *Note:* A disability can be either permanent or temporary (e.g., a temporary impairment as a result of an accident, or a treatable illness).	The complainant, who has multiple sclerosis, alleged that her employer, by refusing her a work schedule recommended by her doctor, failed to accommodate her disability.	• Adjustment of the complainant's work schedule to reflect the doctor's recommendations • Briefing session for employees on multiple sclerosis and non-visible disabilities • Occupational training, with half of the training program to be determined by one of the two parties • Reinstatement of leave • Letter of regret • Withdrawal of related grievances
Pardoned criminal conviction	A conviction for which a pardon has been granted by any authority under law.	The complainant is a truck driver who was required to travel to the U.S. Although he had been granted a pardon for a conviction in Canada, he was nevertheless denied entry in the U.S. Consequently, his employer laid him off on the ground that he could not fulfill all the requirements of the job.	• Financial compensation

SOURCES: Canadian Human Rights Commission, "Overview—Resolving Disputes: Discrimination and Harassment," www.chrc-ccdp.ca/discrimination, retrieved April 14, 2008; and Canadian Human Rights Commission, "Overview—Resolving Disputes: Settlement Examples," www.chrc-ccdp.ca/DisputeResolutions, retrieved April 14, 2008.

The Canadian Human Rights Commission is also responsible for auditing federally regulated employers to ensure compliance with the Employment Equity Act. Figure 2.5 provides a portion of a sample survey questionnaire used in the federal audit process. In addition, the CHRC enforces pay equity requirements. Approximately 70,000 employees have obtained equal pay increases due to cases involving the CHRC. Some of the jobs where equal pay has been achieved are nurses and paramedics, librarians and historical researchers, and kitchen workers and janitors.[21]

FIGURE 2.5

Employment Equity Audit: Excerpt from Survey Questionnaire

---

1. WORKFORCE SURVEY & DATA SYSTEMS

1.1 Has your organization conducted a self-identification survey of the entire workforce? .... ❒ Yes   ❒ No   ❒ In part

If so, in what year? _____ What was the return rate?* (___%) (*If no, go to section 2.*)

*The return rate is calculated by dividing the number of identifiable questionnaires which have been returned (completed or not) by the full population of the organization.

1.2 Do you have a process to invite new employees to self-identify? .... ❒ Yes   ❒ No

If so, **please provide a copy of the self-identification package for new employees.**

1.3 If your survey took place more than one year ago, have the results been updated? .... ❒ Yes   ❒ No

If so, **please include a description of the update process and its frequency.**

1.4 Please provide a copy of the self-identification package including the questionnaire, any accompanying material or campaign communications, used at the time of the full survey. **Please include a description of the process, including any lead-up or follow-up strategy used.**

1.5 How do you store the information collected?   ❒ Manually   ❒ Electronically

Does this data system allow you to generate up-to-date representation data:

a) on the whole work force? .... ❒ Yes   ❒ No   ❒ In part

b) for each designated group? .... ❒ Yes   ❒ No   ❒ In part

c) by occupational group or category? .... ❒ Yes   ❒ No   ❒ In part

1.6 Please indicate the percentage of current employees for which a record of a self-identification questionnaire exists. _____

1.7 Do you collect data for designated groups on the following:

(*Please check all appropriate boxes*)

Hiring ❒   Applications ❒   Screening/selection ❒

Promotions ❒   Terminations ❒   Salary ❒

---

2. WORKFORCE ANALYSIS

2.1 Has your organization conducted a workforce analysis? .... ❒ Yes   ❒ No

(*If no, please go to section 3.*)

(*continued*)

FIGURE 2.5 (concluded)

2.2 **Please provide a copy of the report on your workforce analysis** and, if not included in the report, a copy or description of the following:

a) the availability estimates and a description of how they were developed and calculated; .... Incl. ❑ Not avail. ❑

b) how appropriate geographic areas and occupational qualifications were considered in this process; .... Incl. ❑ Not avail. ❑

c) a copy of any background calculations and data (4-digit NOC group and regional) which were used to prepare the available estimates; .... Incl. ❑ Not avail. ❑

d) summary table(s) listing total workforce, representation and availability, and the gap, in actual numbers as well as percentages, by occupational group/category for all designated groups; Incl. ❑ Not avail. ❑

e) summary tables listing the results of the analysis of hires, promotions and terminations if applicable; .... Incl. ❑ Not avail. ❑

f) a description of the results of your analysis and its conclusions including identification of gaps. .... Incl. ❑ Not avail. ❑

2.3 Did your analysis include the following:

a) calculation of the **internal representation** of all designated groups in each occupational group/category .... ❑ Yes ❑ No

b) development of **external representation/availability estimates** for all designated groups in each occupational group/category .... ❑ Yes ❑ No

c) a **comparison of internal representation with external availability** to determine degree of underrepresentation (gap), if any, for each designated group in each occupational group/category .... ❑ Yes ❑ No

2.4 In those occupational groups/categories where underrepresentation was found, have you done a comparative analysis of the affected designated groups in terms of:

a) shares* of hiring/recruitment with external representation? .... ❑ Yes ❑ No

b) shares of promotions with internal representation? .... ❑ Yes ❑ No

c) shares* of terminations/separations with internal representation or termination/ separation rates* with those of non-designated group members? .... ❑ Yes ❑ No

d) clustering in the lower levels? .... ❑ Yes ❑ No

*"Share" means the % of total hiring or promotions received by members of a particular designated group. "Rate" means the % of employees from a particular group who have been terminated over a defined period of time.

SOURCE: Canadian Human Rights Commission, "Framework for Compliance Audits Under the Employment Equity Act: Audit Process," *Assessment Factors and Survey Questionnaire*, January 2000, pp. 50–51. Reproduced with the permission of the Minister of Public Works and Government Services Canada, 2004.

The Privacy Commissioner of Canada

The Privacy Commissioner of Canada is responsible for ensuring compliance with the Personal Information Protection and Electronic Documents Act. The Privacy Commissioner has the power to investigate complaints and recommend solutions to employers. To ensure compliance, the Commissioner can publicly identify organizations violating individuals' privacy rights and take the complaint to the Federal Court of Canada. If unable to resolve the complaint, the Court can order the organization to take specific actions and can also award damages.[22]

Employers' Role in Meeting Legal Requirements

Rare is the business owner or manager who wants to wait for the government to identify that his or her organization has failed to meet its legal requirements to treat employees fairly. Instead, out of motives ranging from concern for employee well-being to the desire to avoid costly lawsuits and negative publicity, most companies recognize the importance of complying with these laws. Often, management depends on the expertise of human resource professionals to help in identifying how to comply. These professionals can help organizations take steps to avoid discrimination and provide reasonable accommodation.

L04 - Describe ways employers can avoid illegal discrimination and meet the duty to accommodate.

1,3,4

Avoiding Discrimination

How would you know if you had been discriminated against? Decisions about human resources are so complex that discrimination is often difficult to identify and prove. However, legal scholars and court rulings have arrived at some ways to show evidence of discrimination.

Differential Treatment

One sign of discrimination is **differential treatment**—differing treatment of individuals, where the differences are based on a prohibited ground of discrimination such as the individuals' race, colour, religion, sex, national origin, age, or disability status. For example, differential treatment would include hiring or promoting one person over an equally qualified person because of the individual's race. Suppose a company fails to hire women with school-age children (claiming the women will be frequently absent) but hires men with school-age children. In that situation, the women are victims of differential treatment, because they are being treated differently on the basis of their sex.

> **differential treatment**
> Differing treatment of individuals where the differences are based on a prohibited ground.

To avoid complaints of differential treatment, companies can evaluate the questions and investigations they use in making employment decisions. These should be applied consistently. For example, if the company investigates conviction records of job applicants, it should investigate them for all applicants, not just for applicants from certain racial groups. Companies may want to avoid some types of questions altogether. For example, questions about marital status can cause problems, because interviewers may unfairly make different assumptions about men and women. (Common stereotypes about women have been that a married woman is less flexible or more likely to get pregnant than a single woman, in contrast to the assumption that a married man is more stable and committed to his work.)

bona fide occupational requirement (BFOR)
A necessary (not merely preferred) requirement for performing a job.

Is differential treatment ever legal? The courts have held that in some situations, a factor such as sex or race may be a **bona fide occupational requirement (BFOR)**, that is, a necessary (not merely preferred) qualification for performing a job. A typical example is a job that includes handing out towels in a locker room. Requiring that employees who perform this job in the women's locker room be female is a BFOR. However, it is very difficult to think of many jobs where criteria such as sex and race are BFORs. In some cases, a core function of the job may be related to a protected ground. For example, a job may require a specified level of visual capability to be performed effectively and safely, thereby eliminating someone who does not meet this requirement. Employers should seek ways to perform the job so that these restrictions are not needed.

It is the employer's responsibility to prove the existence of a BFOR if any complaint of discrimination should arise. In the widely publicized *Meiorin* case from 1999, Tawny Meiorin, a female forest firefighter, lost her job when she failed to meet a required aerobic fitness standard that had been established by the British Columbia Public Service Employee Relations Commission. This standard had been put in place as a minimum requirement for all firefighters. She lost her job after failing *one* aspect of a minimum fitness standard—taking 49.4 seconds too long to complete a 2.5 kilometre run.[22] She filed a complaint stating that the fitness standard discriminated against women because women usually have less aerobic capability than men. Although the employer argued the standard was a bona fide occupational requirement of the job, the Supreme Court of Canada ultimately ruled the standard was not a BFOR—not reasonably necessary to fulfill a legitimate work-related purpose.[23] Ms. Meiorin was reinstated to her job and received compensation for lost wages and benefits.

Mandatory Retirement

The practice of forcing an employee to retire for the reason of age is a human rights issue and falls under the regulation of human rights legislations. As of July 2009, all jurisdictions in Canada have enacted legislation that makes mandatory retirement discriminatory unless there is a bona fide occupational requirement due to a specific employment requirement.[24]

1,3,4

duty to accommodate
An employer's duty to consider how an employee's characteristic such as disability, religion, or sex can be accommodated and to take action so the employee can perform the job.

The Duty to Accommodate

An employer has a duty to consider how an employee's characteristic such as disability, religion, or sex can be accommodated and to take action so that the employee can perform the job. This duty is referred to as the **duty to accommodate**.

The employer's duty to accommodate has been evolving since it became a part of human rights law in the 1980s. Accommodation frequently involves an employee with a disability. Employer awareness of the duty to accommodate has increased since the *Meiorin* decision by the Supreme Court of Canada in 1999. The duty to accommodate is the employer's responsibility. Accommodation may even require that the employee perform another job within their capabilities. Employers' duty to accommodate extends to the point of *undue hardship*—"undue" meaning only if it is so high that the very survival of the organization or business would be threatened or essentially changed.[25]

In the context of religion, this principle recognizes that for some individuals, religious observations and practices may present a conflict with work duties, dress codes, or company practices. For example, some religions require head coverings, or to be able to pray at a particular time, or individuals might need time off to observe the Sabbath or other holy days, when the company might have them scheduled to work. When the employee has a legitimate religious belief requiring accommodation, the employee should demonstrate this need to the employer. Assuming that it would not present an undue hardship, employers are required to accommodate such religious practices. They may have to adjust schedules so that employees do not have to work on days when their religion forbids it, or they may have to alter dress or grooming requirements.

Equipment like this can help employers make reasonable accommodation for an employee with a physical disability.

For employees with disabilities, accommodations also vary according to the individuals' needs. As shown in Figure 2.6, employers may restructure jobs, make facilities in the workplace more accessible, modify equipment, or reassign an employee to a job that the person can perform. In some situations, an individual with a disability may provide his or her own accommodation, which the employer allows, as in the case of a blind worker who brings a guide dog to work for assistance.

FIGURE 2.6

Examples of Accommodations

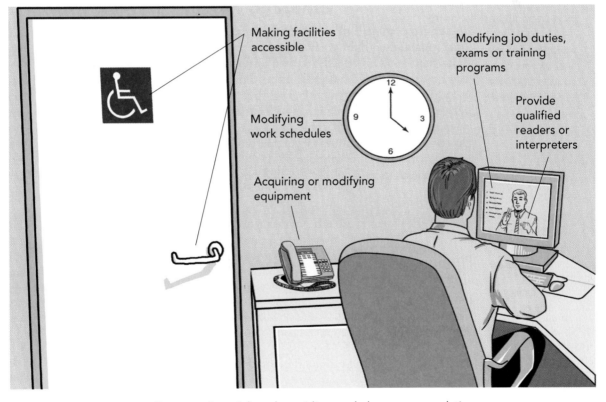

Restructuring a job and providing workplace accommodation

SOURCE: Equal Employment Opportunity Commission, "The ADA: Questions and Answers," www.eeoc.gov/facts/adaqa1.html, retrieved August 28, 2008. Types of signed complaints filed with the Canadian Human Rights Commission. *Note:* Reasonable accommodations do not include hiring an unqualified person, lowering quality standards, or compromising coworkers' safety.

E- HRM

Access to Workplace Accommodation Tools and Resources

Ensuring appropriate accommodations for employees and job applicants are key responsibilities of supervisors, managers, and HR professionals. Although the employee or applicant has a responsibility to request accommodation including the possible types of accommodation that may be needed, it may be a challenge even for the most experienced managers and HR professionals to anticipate how best to remove workplace barriers that might negatively affect an individual and his or her desire to fully contribute in the workplace. Extensive resources and expert guidance are just a couple of clicks away through the Job Accommodation Network website (www.jan.wvu .edu/media/fact.html) as well as through online resources offered by Industry Canada (www.apt.gc.ca/wat/wb11100E .asp?pId = 260).

The Accommodation Fact Sheet Series provides a centralized source of background advice and resources, and accommodations for an extensive list of employment settings:

- Job Accommodations for People with Brain Injuries (e.g., increase natural lighting)
- Job Accommodations for People with Cancer (e.g., allow work from home)
- Job Accommodations for People with HIV/AIDS (e.g., provide access to a refrigerator to store food supplements or medications)
- Job Accommodations for People with Diabetes (e.g., provide appropriate containers for disposal of syringes)
- Job Accommodations Related to Service Animals (e.g., allow periodic breaks so employee can care for the

service animal's basic daily needs)

Industry Canada's online Workplace Accommodation Toolkit (WAT) is organized by:

- Product Type (e.g. Assistive Technology)
- Disability
- Keywords

In addition, a tutorial, demos, and resources such as frequently asked questions and downloadable proactive disclosure documents are all available online.

SOURCES: "Workplace Accommodation in Human Resources Development Canada," www1.servicecanada.gc.ca/ en/mb/accomodation, retrieved April 14, 2008; "Industry Canada: Workplace Accommodation Toolkit (WAT)," www.apt.gc.ca/wat/wb11100E .asp?pId = 260, retrieved April 18, 2008; "Job Accommodation Network: Accommodation Fact Sheet Series," www.jan.wvu.edu/media/fact.html, retrieved April 14, 2008.

L05 - Define harassment and sexual harassment and discuss how employers can eliminate or minimize them.

harassment
Any behaviour that demeans, humiliates, or embarrasses a person, and that a reasonable person should have known would be unwelcome.

Preventing Harassment

Human rights legislation prohibits **harassment** related to any of the protected grounds in their jurisdiction, for example, race, colour, religion, sex, etc. Human rights legislation also prohibits all forms of harassment. Harassment is "any behaviour that demeans, humiliates, or embarrasses a person, and that a reasonable person should have known would be unwelcome."[26]

Seneca Colleges' Discrimination and Harassment Policy states:

It is the policy of Seneca College that all employees and students have a right to study in an environment that asserts the personal worth and dignity of each individual. In order to achieve this objective, Seneca College will not tolerate any form of discrimination and/or harassment in its employment, education, accommodation, or business. Every member of the College community has the right to file a compliant of discrimination/harassment.[27]

Sexual harassment refers to unwelcome behaviour that is of a sexual nature or is related to a person's sex. Examples are

- Question or discussion about a person's sexual life
- Comments about someone's sexual attractiveness (or unattractiveness)
- Continuing to ask for a date after being refused
- Writing sexually suggestive notes
- Telling a woman she should not be performing a particular job[28]

In general, the most obvious examples of sexual harassment involve *quid pro quo harassment*, meaning that a person makes a benefit (or punishment) contingent on an employee's submitting to (or rejecting) sexual advances. For example, a manager who promises a raise to an employee who will participate in sexual activities is engaging in quid pro quo harassment. Likewise, it would be sexual harassment to threaten to reassign someone to a less desirable job if that person refuses sexual favours.

A more subtle, and possibly more pervasive, form of sexual harassment is to create or permit a *hostile work environment*. This occurs when someone's behaviour in the workplace creates an environment in which it is difficult for someone of a particular sex to work. Common complaints in sexual harassment lawsuits include claims that harassers ran their fingers through the plaintiffs' hair, made suggestive remarks, touched intimate body parts, posted pictures with sexual content in the workplace, and used sexually explicit language or told sex-related jokes. In Europe, employers can be liable for creating a hostile work environment if they fail to protect workers from receiving sexually explicit emails such as racy spam messages.[29]

Although a large majority of sexual harassment complaints received involve women being harassed by men, sexual harassment can affect anyone. Men have filed complaints that they were harassed by women, and in at least one case a male employee won a lawsuit claiming sexual harassment by his male boss.[30]

To ensure a workplace free from harassment, organizations can follow some important steps. Federally regulated employees are required to develop an anti-harassment policy making it very clear that harassment will not be tolerated in the workplace. Second, all employees need to be made aware of the policy and receive training related to anti-harassment. In addition, the organization can develop a mechanism for reporting harassment in a way that encourages people to speak out. Finally, management can prepare to act promptly to discipline those who engage in harassment, as well as to protect the victims of harassment.

The case of a former British Columbia RCMP officer serves to illustrate the significant consequences of harassment. Ex-Mountie Nancy Sulz was awarded $950,000 by the B.C. Supreme Court for "damages, lost wages, and loss of future earnings" after finding her Staff Sgt. and two subordinate officers caused Sulz "serious psychological harm" related to incidents arising after the birth of a child.[31]

Recently, the definition of harassment has been expanded to include "psychological harassment"—which includes behaviours such as *workplace bullying*. Researchers have recently found that bullying may is more destructive than sexual harassment to workers and workplaces. "Bullying is where sexual harassment was 30 years ago," said Janice Rubin, an employment lawyer with Rubin Thomlinson LLP. "Employers are trying to wrap their heads around how to deal with it." Presently only Quebec and Saskatchewan have anti-bullying laws that prohibit workplace behaviours such as yelling, rudeness, gossip, or other torments that are forms of psychological harassment.[32] Some new respect-at-work guidelines cite behaviours such as "excessive nitpicking" and "phoning

sexual harassment
Unwelcome behaviour that is of a sexual nature or is related to a person's sex.

BEST PRACTICES

Quebec's New Labour Law

Quebec's Labour Standards Division recently introduced a new law against workplace psychological harassment. This legislation, the first of its kind in North America, was based on a similar law introduced in France in 2002. The law is intended to improve workplace morale and result in improved productivity. The law defines psychological harassment as "any vexatious behaviour in the form of repeated and hostile or unwanted conduct, verbal comments, actions, or gestures that affect an employee's dignity, psychological, or physical integrity and that results in a harmful work environment for the employee."

Quebec employers are assessing their current policies and practices to ensure compliance with the new legislation that expands protection of workers from bullying bosses and co-workers. Under the new law, employers need to undertake the following proactive measures:

- Provide a work environment that promotes respectful interpersonal communications
- Manage conflict quickly and effectively
- Consider providing specialized counselling services

Quebec's new law will raise awareness about an employee's right to an effective work environment where hostile or intimidating behaviour and abuse of power are not only unacceptable, but also illegal. Although critics of the new law say that too much responsibility is placed on employers to manage behaviour in organizations, others say this new law will help change workplaces for the better.

SOURCE: Wallace Immen, "Quebec Squares Off Against Bullies," *The Globe and Mail*, May 26, 2004, pp. C1, C6. Reprinted with permission from The Globe and Mail.

---

negligent hiring
Legal concept where an employer may be found liable for harm that an employee causes to others when references and background checks were not performed adequately at the time of hiring.

off-duty colleagues at home with work demands" as forms of mistreatment.[33] The Best Practices box discusses Quebec's law that makes it illegal to engage in psychological harassment.

Employers are also have a duty to protect workers and the public from harassment or violence arising from placing an unfit or dangerous person in the workplace. **Negligent hiring** is a legal concept whereby an employer may be found liable for harm an employee causes to others because references and background checks were not performed adequately at the time of hiring. Employer liability for negligent hiring usually occurs when the "employer knows or should have known" that a employee might cause harm to others in the workplace and proper background and reference checks were not conducted.

Employers are recognized for providing Canada's most inclusive workplaces.

LO6 - Discuss the importance of valuing diversity.

1,2,3,4

Valuing Diversity

As we mentioned in Chapter 1, Canada is a diverse nation, and becoming more so. In addition, many Canadian companies have customers and operations in more than one country. Managers differ in how they approach the challenges related to this diversity. Some define a diverse workforce as a competitive advantage that brings them a wider pool of talent and greater insight into the needs and behaviours of their diverse customers. These organizations say they have a policy of *valuing diversity*. Canada's Top 100 Employers recently added a new category to recognize employers that provide the most inclusive workplaces, "Canada's Best Diversity Employers." Recent winners included Boeing Canada Technology Ltd. (Winnipeg), University of British Columbia (Vancouver), Saskatchewan Government Insurance (Regina), University of Toronto (Toronto), and Enbridge Inc. (Calgary).[34]

Employers are recognized for providing Canada's most inclusive workplaces.

The practice of valuing diversity has no single form; it is not written into law or business theory. One of the concerns about diversity is that "the majority of Canadian organizations rank diversity as a priority, but 42 per cent of them have no strategic plan to foster it" according to a recent report from the Conference Board of Canada.[35] Another hurdle to fostering diversity in the workplace relates to subtle forms of discrimination referred to as "microinequities." A **microinequity** is defined as "a subtle message, sometimes subconscious, that devalues, discourages and ultimately impairs performance in the workplace." According to Mary P. Rowe, special assistant to the president and adjunct professor at the Massachusetts Institute of Technology, "microinequities occur whenever people are perceived to be different. That can be Caucasians in a Japanese-owned company, women in a traditionally male environment, Jews and Muslims in a traditionally Protestant environment." Because companies' diversity efforts tend to focus on obvious differences among individuals, these subtle forms of discrimination may affect an organization's ability to create inclusivity unless commitment from the top and open discussion is fostered in the organization.[36] The Thinking Ethically box describes how IBM is fostering discussion with a community of employees who may experience both direct and subtle discrimination in the workplace.

microinequity
Subtle message, sometimes subconscious, that devalues, discourages and ultimately impairs performance in the workplace

Organizations that value diversity may also actively work to meet employment equity goals, discussed earlier. Bell Canada speaks to the benefits of diversity: business objectives, and our objectives for diversity and employment equity go hand in hand. And as we apply our considerable strengths to achieving our business goals with a strong diversity focus, we see no limits to what we are able to accomplish as individuals, as a company, and even as a nation."[37] They may have policies stating their value of understanding and respecting differences. Wal-Mart's website includes a statement that reinforces the company's folksy image along with its policy with regard to diversity: "All kinds of people work and shop at Wal-Mart—and we like it that way."[38] Organizations may try to hire, reward, and promote employees who demonstrate respect for others. They may sponsor training programs designed to teach employees about differences among groups. Whatever their form, these efforts are intended to make every individual feel respected. Also, these actions can support diversity by cultivating an environment in which individuals feel valued and able to perform to their potential.

Occupational Health and Safety

The protection of employee health and safety is regulated by the government. As outlined in Table 2.2, occupational health and safety legislation is in place for all jurisdictions. However, the effective management of health and safety in the workplace includes more than legal compliance. Increasingly, organizations are taking a strategic approach to occupational health and safety by adopting a values-based commitment to safe operations as a way to protect people. Additional benefits to business include cost savings by reducing worker injuries, fatalities, occupational disease, and property damage as well as improved employee relations and reliability and productivity improvement.[39] Employers and employees share responsibility for creating and maintaining safe and healthy work environments. Employer–employee partnerships are put in place to ensure compliance and create a climate and culture of safety in the organization.[40] Chapter 3 will explore this topic in more detail.

L07 - Describe and introduce the protection of employee health and safety in the workplace.

7

THINKING ETHICALLY

Simple Questions and Awkward Situations: The Impact of the Closet at Work

"What did you do on the weekend?" It sounds like a simple question that managers might ask their employees to build a team atmosphere and show interest in their lives outside work. But for gay, lesbian, bisexual, or transgender (GLBT) employees who may not be "out" to their bosses, it can be one of the hardest questions to answer. Companies that promote diversity emphasize hiring, training, and retention of people protected by human rights and employment equity legislation. Some companies take diversity efforts further. For example, IBM Canada has four diversity network groups: East Asian, South Asian, Black, and GLBT. These network groups share information, provide coaching and mentoring, participate in community outreach activities, and plan and implement social, cultural, and educational events. An example of how these groups contribute to building an inclusive work environment is found in the recent activity of IBM's GLBT Network Group.

The group has been active in Canada since the early 1990s.

At first, its work involved advising the human resource department in establishing benefit rights for partners and creating a forum for sharing with fellow GLBT members. As the group evolved, it has taken on a larger mandate of community involvement. One of the most successful examples of this is the executive breakfast series hosted by members of the GLBT group.

The program is designed to educate IBM executives on the sensitivities of working with a member of the GLBT constituency who may not be "out" in the workplace. Since GLBT employees are less identifiable, the group felt it was important to be more visible and provide names and faces that can help drive home issues. The sessions are designed so participants can "walk in the shoes" of a GLBT member. In the latest session, 22 senior executives had breakfast with members of IBM's GLBT constituency to discuss ways to improve workplace climate. Members of the GLBT group shared personal

stories that highlighted how an inclusive work environment can have a positive impact on the productivity of talented employees. One member of the Global GLBT Executive Task Force shared a story illustrating the lost productivity, reduced team cohesion, and decreased employee morale resulting from GLBT employees hiding their personal lives because they may not be comfortable being "out" in the workplace.

Executives were surprised when one member discussed how difficult it is for him to attend the breakfast without saying where he was going. By not being "out" to his own manager, the person had to be creative about the morning absence. This example helped drive home the importance for managers to develop an inclusive environment within their departments.

SOURCE: Susan Turner, "Simple Questions and Awkward Situations: The Impact of the Closet at Work," *Canadian HR Reporter*, December 20, 2004, p. 10.

Questions

1. How does including GLBT employees in IBM's diversity efforts affect IBM's workforce? Its managers? Its work environment? Its customers and investors?
2. Is IBM's policy toward GLBT employees good business? Is it good ethics? Should a company pursue a diversity policy that goes beyond legal requirements?

SUMMARY

LO1 **Describe the legal framework for human resource management in Canada.**

- Approximately 90 percent of Canadian employees are covered by provincial and territorial legislation. The remaining 10 percent are covered by federal legislation.
- Although jurisdictional differences exist, laws tend to mirror one another.

LO2 **Summarize the major federal and provincial laws impacting human resource management.**

- Several Canadian laws create the foundation for equality in employment—for example, Charter of Rights and Freedoms, Official Languages Act, Employment Equity Act (1986), and Human Rights Acts.
- The Personal Information Protection and Electronic Documents Act (PIPEDA) provides rules about how organizations can collect, use, and disclose information about you.
- Employment standards legislation deals with the minimum standards an employee will receive.
- Pay equity provisions help assure equal pay for work of equal value.

LO3 **Identify the agencies that enforce employment equality and privacy legislation and describe their roles.**

- Human Rights Commissions are responsible for enforcing human rights legislation in their respective jurisdictions. The Canadian Human Rights Commission is responsible for enforcing the Canadian Human Rights Act, the Employment Equity Act, and the Pay Equity Act.
- The Privacy Commissioner of Canada is responsible for enforcing the Personal Information Protection and Electronic Documents Act (PIPEDA).

LO4 **Describe ways employers can avoid illegal discrimination and meet the duty to accommodate.**

- Employers can avoid discrimination by avoiding differential treatment of job applicants and employees. Organizations can develop and enforce practices and policies that demonstrate a high value placed on diversity.
- Employment equity initiatives may remove employment barriers to the designated groups.
- To provide accommodation, companies should recognize individuals' needs. Employers may need to make such accommodations as adjusting schedules or dress codes, making the workplace more accessible, or restructuring jobs.

LO5 **Define harassment and sexual harassment and discuss how employers can eliminate or minimize them.**

- Harassment is any behaviour that demeans, humiliates, or embarrasses a person, and that a reasonable person should have known would be unwelcome.
- Sexual harassment is unwelcome behaviour of a sexual nature or related to a person's sex.
- Organizations can prevent harassment by developing a policy that defines and forbids it, training employees to recognize and avoid this behaviour, and providing a means for employees to complain and be protected.

LO6 **Discuss the importance of valuing diversity.**

- Although the practice of valuing diversity has no single form, organizations that value diversity are likely to be mindful of the benefits of diversity and work actively to create a work environment in which individuals feel valued and able to perform to their potential.

LO7 **Describe and introduce the protection of employee health and safety in the workplace.**

- All jurisdictions in Canada have occupational health and safety legislation. Canada's approach to safety in the workplace is based on the internal responsibility system in which both employers and employees are responsible for safety.

REVIEW AND DISCUSSION QUESTIONS

1. What are the major laws that impact human resource management in your province or territory? Compare and contrast this legislation to the corresponding federal legislation.
2. How does the Personal Information Protection and Electronic Documents Act (PIPEDA) impact HRM?
3. Research minimum wages across various jurisdictions in Canada, for example, Alberta, Saskatchewan, and Ontario. Also, conduct online research regarding advertised salaries at traditionally "minimum wage" service-sector jobs such as retail sales and fast-food restaurants in Alberta, Saskatchewan, and Ontario. What are your observations and conclusions?
4. What is the ground of discrimination most frequently cited in complaints to the Canadian Human Rights Commission? Why do you think this ground of discrimination is so frequently cited in discrimination complaints?
5. Have you ever experienced illegal discrimination in an employment situation? What might have the organization done to prevent this discrimination from occurring?
6. On the basis of your knowledge of diverse religious practices, what types of accommodations might an employer be expected to provide?
7. An employer says, "I pay the same wages to men and women doing the same job." Would this meet an employer's pay equity obligations where legally required?
8. What is sexual harassment? What are some types of behaviour likely considered to be sexual harassment in a workplace?
9. Should organizations have a policy on psychological harassment even if it is not a legal requirement in their jurisdiction? Why or why not? What would an effective policy include?
10. "Organizations that value diversity are more likely to meet their employment equity goals." Do you agree or disagree with this statement? Why or why not?

WHAT'S YOUR HR IQ?

Online LearningCentre The Online Learning Centre offers more ways to check what you've learned so far. Find experiential exercises as well as Test Your Knowledge Quizzes, Videos, and many other resources at www.mcgrawhill.ca/olc/steen.

Case:
Airport Screener Suspended for Altering Uniform to Comply with Her Religious Beliefs

Halima Muse, 33, a practising Muslim, immigrated to Canada from Somalia and had been employed for six years with Garda, a company contracted by the Canadian Air Transport Security Authority (CATSA) to screen passengers and their luggage at Toronto's Pearson International Airport. At the airport, security employees are provided a standard uniform. Female employees had a choice of wearing either a knee-length skirt or slacks. Muse had been wearing slacks, because knee-length skirts violate the modesty standards of her religion. However, due to her Islamic beliefs she also felt uncomfortable exposing the shape of her body by wearing slacks and always wore a blazer to cover her hips. Finally, she asked her employer if she could wear a non-standard loose-fitting skirt that she had made of similar colour and fabric. She received approval to wear the ankle-length skirt; however, several months later, the Canadian Air Transport Security Authority insisted that she wear one of the two standard uniforms, that is, slacks or knee-length skirt. When she refused to give up the ankle-length skirt she was suspended. Although she filed a grievance with her union, Teamsters 847, her employer advised her that CATSA, not Garda, controlled the policy related to uniforms.

CATSA defended its strict policy regarding uniforms on the grounds that maintaining a professional image in airport security was very important.

SOURCES: Jeffrey R. Smith, "Airport Screener Suspended for Wearing Long Skirt," *Canadian HR Reporter*, December 17, 2007, pp. 1, 11; "Suspended Muslim Airport Screener Offered New Job," *The Globe and Mail*, November 22, 2007, p. A17; John Goddard, "Guard to Get Back Pay Pending Uniform Review; Airport Screener Will Do Alternative Work During Uniform Assessment," *Toronto Star*, November 21, 2007, p. A14.

Questions

1. By offering Muse a choice of slacks or a knee-length skirt do you feel CATSA provided a reasonable accommodation to this employee? Justify your answer.
2. Because Muse agreed to wear slacks for several years before telling her employer about her concerns should there be any reduced duty on her employer or CATSA to accommodate? Explain.
3. If you had been Muse's supervisor, how would you have handled her request? Is there anything you would have done differently?

Case:
Class-Action Lawsuits over Unpaid Overtime

CIBC, Scotiabank, KPMG, and CN are all facing class-action lawsuits on behalf of employees over allegations of unpaid overtime, and the stakes are high. Canadian Imperial Bank of Commerce faces a $600 million lawsuit that could involve more than 10,000 current and former CIBC employees from across Canada. The suit alleges that front-line employees such as tellers, account executives, and commercial and personal bankers are given workloads too heavy to be handled in regular working hours. The lead plaintiff in the CIBC case, Dara Fresco, claims to have been denied approximately $50,000 in unpaid overtime over ten years of employment. "What is unfair is that my colleagues and I are rarely being paid for the overtime that we are working, and that's just not right," said Fresco. The CIBC suit claims that CIBC has failed to pay for overtime work that was required or at least permitted, which is in contravention to the Canada Labour Code. However, CIBC maintains it has a "clearly defined" overtime policy that "exceeds legislative requirements."

KPMG LLP in Ontario faces litigation seeking $20 million on behalf of employees including non-chartered accountant staff, lawyers, and other employees who worked more than 44 hours in a week without extra pay. The lead plaintiff, Alison Corless, who worked as a "technician" responsible for compiling tax returns, claims she is owed $87,000 in overtime for the 4½ years she worked at KPMG. Shilpa Kotecha, a spokesperson for KPMG, states that the firm "provides a competitive compensation and benefits package in keeping with its goal of being an employer of choice."

At Canadian National, Michael McCracken is leading the lawsuit of more than 1,000 present and former CN first-line supervisors across Canada. The suit alleges that CN "misclassified first line supervisors as management employees in order to escape its obligations to pay overtime under the Canada Labour Code."

SOURCES: "CN faces $250M class action lawsuit," www.cbc.ca/money/story/2008/03/25/en.html, retrieved April 14, 2008; "CN Hit with Class-Action Lawsuit on Unpaid Overtime," *Canadian HR Reporter*, website posting, www.hrreporter.com, March 25, 2008; Gary Norris, "KPMG Faces Employee Class Action Lawsuit in Ontario for Overtime Pay," www.cbc.ca/cp/business/070904/b0904111A.html, retrieved October 4, 2007; Virginia Galt and Janet McFarland, "CIBC Faces Massive Overtime Lawsuit," *The Globe and Mail*, June 5, 2007, www.theglobeandmail.com, retrieved March 18, 2008; "CIBC Faces $600-Million Suit over Unpaid Overtime," *CanWest News Service*, June 5, 2007, www.canada.com/components, retrieved March 18, 2008.

Questions

1. Review the relevant labour standards legislation. On the basis of your assessment, do you agree or disagree with the employees' position they were entitled to receive overtime pay?
2. What should an employer do to reduce the likelihood of overtime misunderstandings or allegations of the type raised in this case?
3. Do the employees' allegations and lawsuits affect your perception of these organizations as "employers of choice"? Explain your response.

3

Safe and Engaging Work Environments

What Do I Need to Know? After reading this chapter, you should be able to:

1. Explain the context for workplace health and safety.

2. Identify employers' duties and employees' rights and responsibilities related to workforce health and safety.

3. Discuss ways employers promote worker health and safety.

4. Describe how organizations contribute to employee job satisfaction and engagement and retain employees.

5. Distinguish between voluntary and involuntary turnover, and describe their effects on an organization.

6. Summarize ways in which organizations can fairly discipline employees.

7. Identify how corporate social responsibility contributes to employee engagement and retention.

Introduction

About three years ago, an employee at NB Power walked into an off-limits area and was electrocuted. His burns were so bad that he still hasn't returned to work and might never be able to, says Paul Theriault, vice-president of human resources. The employee's team did everything right that day. They had the required daily "tailboard" conference—a meeting to discuss the day's jobs and the safety implications of each job. All of the workers had received extensive safety training and everyone, including the injured worker, knew not to enter the off-limits area. However, there was no physical barrier cordoning off the area. This incident is also an example of how a person's state of mind can affect his safety on the job. Even without the physical barrier, the worker knew not to enter the area, he knew it wasn't safe, but he did so anyway, says Theriault. "To this day, he would not be able to tell you what happened to his state of mind that day," he says.

That's why NB Power takes a holistic approach to health and safety and makes it one of the eight integrated HR functions. The other seven functions are recruitment, compensation, diversity, leadership, relationship management, well-being, and labour relations. Too often, HR issues have been dealt with in isolation, not taking into consideration the impact, one event or issue can have on the others, says Theriault. For example, if an employee has an issue around compensation and that issue isn't addressed to his satisfaction, he will probably be distracted while doing his other work and in a high-risk organization such as NB Power, that distraction can result in a serious injury. It is only by ensuring employees are in the best possible state of mind that the company has a chance of mitigating, or possibly eliminating, workplace accidents, says Theriault. "You certainly would not think of putting the mental well-being of an operation under anything but HR and I certainly would see the physical part being in the same category."[1]

Paul Theriault, vice-president of human resources at NB Power. The Fredericton-based utility company integrates health and safety with other HR functions.

This chapter explores the challenges of providing work environments that are at once both safe and engaging. Although the protection of employee safety and health is regulated by the government, some organizations are going well beyond the legal requirements to create a culture of safety. Similarly, many organizations are committed to creating work environments that connect with employees in the effort to encourage them to stay and contribute to their full potential. In today's highly competitive job markets, organizations are also reflecting on their reputation for corporate social responsibility and supporting green initiatives, volunteerism, and high ethical standards as part of their commitment to attracting and retaining similarly-minded top talent. These topics provide a transition between Parts 1 and 2. The previous chapters in Part 1 considered the strategic aspects of HRM and the legal requirements that influence HR practices. Part 2 then moves into some of the more technical aspects of the practice of HRM such as analyzing work and workforce planning, as well as building on the discussion started in this chapter about employer reputation and branding that will be explored more thoroughly in the context of recruiting and selecting employees in Part 2.

2,7

Workplace Health and Safety

In Chapter 2, we briefly outlined occupational health and safety legislation and introduced the importance of taking a strategic approach to health and safety. The protection of employee health and safety is regulated by the government. As outlined in Chapter 2, occupational health and safety legislation is in place for all jurisdictions; however, the effective management of health and safety in the workplace includes more than legal compliance. Increasingly, organizations including NB Power are taking a strategic approach to occupational health and safety by adopting a values-based commitment to safe operations as a way to protect people. Additional benefits to business include cost savings by reducing worker injuries, fatalities, occupational disease, and property damage, as well as improved employee relations, reliability, and productivity.[2]

LO1 - Explain the context for workplace health and safety.

7

internal responsibility system
Philosophy of occupational health and safety whereby employers and employees share responsibility for creating and maintaining safe and healthy work environments.

workplace health and safety committee
A committee jointly appointed by the employer and employees at large (or union) to address health and safety issues in a workplace.

LO2 - Identify employers' duties and employees' rights and responsibilities related to workforce health and safety.

Internal Responsibility System

In Canada, safety in the workplace is based on the foundation of an **internal responsibility system**. The internal responsibility system is a philosophy of occupational health and safety whereby employers and employees share responsibility for creating and maintaining safe and healthy work environments. Employer–employee partnerships are put in place to ensure compliance and create a culture of safety in the organization.[3]

Workplace Health and Safety Committees

Workplace health and safety committees, a key feature of the internal responsibility system, are jointly appointed by the employer and employees at large (or union) to address health and safety issues in a workplace (see Figure 3.1). Under federal law, a workplace health and safety committee is required for every workplace that has 20 or more employees. The committee must consist of at least two persons and is required to meet at least nine times a year, at regular intervals, during normal working hours. The premise is that it is the people employed in a particular workplace who know the most about hazards and unhealthy conditions.[4]

General and Specific Duties

Employers and supervisors have a duty to provide a safe workplace. At minimum, supervisors must

- Ensure that appropriate occupational health and safety policies and practices are in place
- Understand and follow policies and practices related to working safely
- Identify the need for training for employees and themselves
- Determine hazards that may exist and ensure employees are aware of these hazards
- Eliminate or at least reduce hazards
- Ensure employees comply with safety policies and practices[5]

FIGURE 3.1

Power and Duties of a Workplace Health and Safety Committee

POWER AND DUTIES OF A WORKPLACE HEALTH AND SAFETY COMMITTEE

- Consider and deal with health and safety complaints in a timely manner.
- Participate in the development, implementation, and monitoring of programs to prevent workplace hazards and provide protective equipment, devices, and clothing.
- Participate in safety inquiries and safety assessments, and ensure that effective records are kept.
- Perform workplace inspections.
- Be provided full access to all reports, studies, and tests related to the health and safety of workers.

SOURCE: Government of Canada, "Information on Occupational Health and Safety: 6B Workplace Health and Safety Committees," http://info.load-otea.hrdc-drhc.gc.ca/publications/ohs/committees.pdf, retrieved February 25, 2004.

Employers need to assess and be alert to workplace hazards and safety issues. For example, "a study published in the *British Medical Journal* found drivers talking on a cellphone are four times more likely to be involved in a serious crash."[6] In another study, psychologists concluded that "using a hands-free cellphone while driving could impair drivers as much as having a blood-alcohol level of 0.08 per cent,"[7] the maximum legal limit in Canada. Imperial Oil and ExxonMobil Canada introduced a safety initiative that forbids the use of cellphones while driving on company business. Imperial Oil's director of Safety, Health, and Environment, Jim Levins says, "since driving is one of the more hazardous tasks we do during a normal work day, this new initiative will help us all achieve our goal of zero injuries."[8]

Employers must keep records of work-related deaths, injuries, and hazardous occurrences and provide an annual summary of these records. Figure 3.2 provides a sample of the form federally regulated employers must complete annually.

Enforcement of Occupational Health and Safety Regulations

Enforcement responsibilities exist within the federal, provincial, and territorial governments. Occupational health and safety officers/inspectors have the authority to inspect workplaces and issue orders to employers and workers. Ontario recently hired 200 new health and safety inspectors, which almost doubled its enforcement staff. The Ontario government is planning to target 6,000 workplaces with poor safety records.[9] In some jurisdictions such as Nova Scotia and Ontario, safety officers/inspectors can issue tickets to people and organizations when these orders are not followed. In Nova Scotia, occupational health and safety officers can write tickets for up to $800 as a tool to ensure compliance.[10]

In addition, the Criminal Code was amended in 2004 to create additional legal duties on employers to ensure the safety of workers and the public. This amendment, **Bill C-45 (Westray Bill)**, named after the Nova Scotia mining disaster in 1992 that killed 26 workers, makes organizations and anyone who directs the work of others criminally liable for safety offences. Maximum fines were increased to $100,000 from $25,000 for less serious offences and provides an unlimited fine for more serious offences. Anyone who directs the work of others can also face serious charges—criminal conviction, a criminal record, and even life imprisonment for failing to provide for health and safety in the workplace.[11] One of the chapter-ending cases discusses the first criminal conviction handed down since the amendments came into force.

Bill C-45 (Westray Bill) Amendment to the Criminal Code making organizations and anyone who directs the work of others criminally liable for safety offences.

Employee Rights and Responsibilities

Although employers are responsible for protecting workers from health and safety hazards, employees have responsibilities as well. They have to follow safety rules and regulations governing employee behaviour. Employees also have a duty to report hazardous conditions.

Along with those responsibilities go certain rights. All Canadian workers have three fundamental rights that are protected by occupational health and safety legislation:

- *The right to know* about known or foreseeable hazards in the workplace
- *The right to participate* in identifying and resolving job-related safety and health problems
- *The right to refuse* dangerous work[12]

FIGURE 3.2

Federal Employer's Annual Hazardous Occurrence Report

Human Resources Development Canada — Développement des ressources humaines Canada

Year - Année

SCHEDULE - ANNEXE

CANADA OCCUPATIONAL SAFETY AND HEALTH REGULATIONS (Section 15.10)

RÉGLEMENT CANADIEN SUR LA SÉCURITÉ ET LA SANTÉ AU TRAVAIL (Article 15.10)

Page of - de

EMPLOYER'S ANNUAL HAZARDOUS OCCURRENCE REPORT - RAPPORT ANNUEL DE L'EMPLOYEUR CONCERNANT LES SITUATIONS COMPORTANT DES RISQUES

Employer identification number		Address of work place	Number of disabling injuries	Number of deaths	Number of minor injuries	Number of other hazardous occurrences	Total number of employees	Number of office employees	Total number of hours worked
Numéro d'identification de l'employeur		Adresse du lieu de travail	Nombre de blessures invalidantes	Nombre de décès	Nombre de blessures légères	Nbre d'autres situations comportant des risques	Nombre total d'employés	Nombre d'employés de bureau	Total des heures travaillées

GUIDE TO COMPLETION ON REVERSE SIDE

EXPLICATIONS AU VERSO

Submitting officer's name and title - Nom et titre de l'auteur du rapport	Signature	Date of submission - Date de présentation / Telephone - Téléphone ( ) ___-___

NHQ/LAB 1009 (10-03) B

If this address is incorrect, please correct.

Si cette adresse est inexacte veuillez la corriger

Canada

SOURCE: "Human Resources and Skills Development Canada," Canada Occupational Safety and Health Regulations (Section 15.10), Employer's Annual Hazardous Occurrence Report. Reproduced with the permission of Her Majesty the Queen in Right of Canada 2005, www100.hrdc.gc.ca/indlab1009e.shtml.

Occupational Health & Safety Inspectors
Industrial

Apply your experience/knowledge gained in industrial processes/health-and-safety hazards/controls in one of these critical positions (11 bilingual). You will: enforce *Occupational Health and Safety Act*, regulations; conduct site inspections/investigations; write orders/reports; engage in enforcement activities, including prosecutions; promote safe work practices/working conditions with workers, unions, management (Internal Responsibility System). **Locations: Toronto East/Scarborough (11 positions) – File LBCR-21; Toronto West/Downsview (4) – File LBCR-25; Toronto North/Downsview (3) – File LBCR-28; Peel North/Mississauga (6) – File LBCR-32; York/Newmarket (3) – File LBCR-35; Durham/Oshawa (1) – File LBCR-39; Kingston (2) – File LBER-03; Peterborough (1) – File LBER-05; Ottawa East (1) – File LBER-07; Ottawa West (2) – File LBER-11; North Bay (1) – File LBNR-30; Sault Ste. Marie (1) – File LBNR-31; Sudbury East (1) – File LBNR-33; Thunder Bay/Dryden (1) – File LBNR-32; Timmins/South Porcupine (1) – File LBNR-27; Brant/Hamilton (2) – File LBWR-03; Hamilton (5) – File LBWR-06; Halton/Hamilton (2) – File LBWR-08; Kitchener-Waterloo/Waterloo (5) – File LBWR-10; London North (3) – File LBWR-12; London South (4) – File LBWR-14; Niagara/St. Catharines (4) – File LBWR-17; Windsor (2) – File LBWR-19. BILINGUAL POSITIONS: Toronto East/Scarborough (1) – File LBCR-22; Toronto West/Downsview (1) – File LBCR-26; Peel South/Mississauga (1) – File LBCR-30; Peel North/ Mississauga (1) – File LBCR-33; Ottawa East (2) – File LBER-08; Ottawa West (1) – File LBER-12; North Bay (1) – File LBNR-18; Timmins/South Porcupine (1) – File LBNR-23; Brant/Hamilton (1) – File LBWR-04; London South (1) – File LBWR-15.**

Qualifications: working knowledge of/practical experience in broad range of industrial processes, to identify, evaluate, control hazards associated with chemical/biological/physical agents; working knowledge of *Occupational Health and Safety Act*, regulations, standards, legislation re industrial/institutional workplaces; demonstrated ability to conduct investigations, enforce legislation, participate in court procedures, handle labour/management issues, resolve conflicts, use notebook technology in Windows environment; sound planning, organization, communication skills; experience writing clear, concise reports; ability to travel extensively and respond to after-hours calls; valid driver's licence. Candidates are required to be available for 7.25-hour work periods during days, evenings and some weekends. Bilingual positions also require proficiency in English and French.

Applicants who do not have the full range of practical experience in industrial processes, but have working knowledge typically acquired through a combination of practical experience and completion of relevant educational/training programs, may be considered on an underfill basis.

Salary range: $1,134 - $1,352 per week

Ontario has turned up its ability to monitor and enforce workplace health and safety, hiring 200 new enforcement positions in the Ministry of Labour.

In federally regulated organizations, employees' right to refuse dangerous work has been expanded to include refusing work on the *potential for* risk versus existing danger. This expanded definition was put into practice in the precedent-setting *Verville v. Canada* (*Correctional Services*) case where maximum security prison guards at the Kent Penitentiary in British Columbia performed a work refusal when guards were prohibited from carrying handcuffs. Although Correctional Services Canada said availability of handcuffs at control posts was adequate, the judge ruled that employees can refuse work if there is a reasonable possibility of danger.[13]

Employees may file a complaint and request an inspection of the workplace, and their employers cannot retaliate against them for complaining. Employees also have a right to receive information about any hazardous products they handle in the course of their jobs.

material safety data sheets (MSDSs)
Detailed hazard information concerning a controlled (hazardous) product.

The Workplace Hazardous Materials Information System or WHMIS is related to the worker's "right to know." "WHMIS is Canada's national hazard communication program consisting of symbols and warning labels for consumers and material-specific safety data sheets that guide the handling of dangerous substances in the workplace, as well as related worker education and training."[14] WHMIS is implemented through coordinated federal, provincial, and territorial legislation to ensure that hazardous products are properly labelled, used, stored, handled, and disposed of safely. The circled skull-and-crossbones is one sample of a familiar warning label indicating materials causing immediate and serious toxic effects.

WHMIS Classes and Hazard Symbols

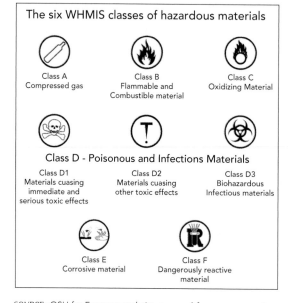

The six WHMIS classes of hazardous materials

Class A
Compressed gas

Class B
Flammable and Combustible material

Class C
Oxidizing Material

Class D - Poisonous and Infections Materials

Class D1
Materials cuasing immediate and serious toxic effects

Class D2
Materials cuasing other toxic effects

Class D3
Biohazardous Infectious materials

Class E
Corrosive material

Class F
Dangerously reactive material

SOURCE: OSH for Everyone website, www.oshforeveryone.org/wsib/files/ont_whsc/swapwhms.htm, retrieved August 28, 2008. Courtesy of WHMIS.

Organizations must have **material safety data sheets (MSDSs)** for hazardous products that employees are exposed to. An MSDS form details the hazards associated with a chemical; the chemical's producer or importer is responsible for identifying these hazards and detailing them on the form. Employers must also ensure that all containers of hazardous chemicals are labelled with information about the hazards, and they must train employees in safe handling of the chemicals. Canada is currently working with other countries to harmonize the existing hazard communication systems on chemicals. "It made sense that as international trade in chemical products grows that we should have a standardized system. Canada, the United States, Japan, the European Union (EU), and some other countries had all developed their own systems. But they pretty much agree there should be one,"[15] says Gordon Lloyd, the vice-president of technical affairs at Ottawa-based Canadian Chemical Producer's Association (CCPA), a contributing organization to WHMIS. The Globally Harmonized System of Classification and Labelling of Chemicals System (GHS) is now ready for worldwide implementation. Technical and implementation consultations were performed in 2007, and next steps include economic analysis, development of final recommendations, draft regulations and processes, and phasing in implementation.[16]

7

Impact of Occupational Health and Safety Legislation

Legislation has unquestionably succeeded in raising the level of awareness of occupational safety. However, as depicted in Figure 3.3, the number of Canadians killed on the job has increased in recent years despite a significant reduction in time-loss injuries (Figure 3.4). For example, in Ontario, the number of fatalities has increased from 238 in 1996 to 373 in 2006—an increase of 57 percent.[17]

FIGURE 3.3

Workplace Fatalities in
Canada, 1996–2006

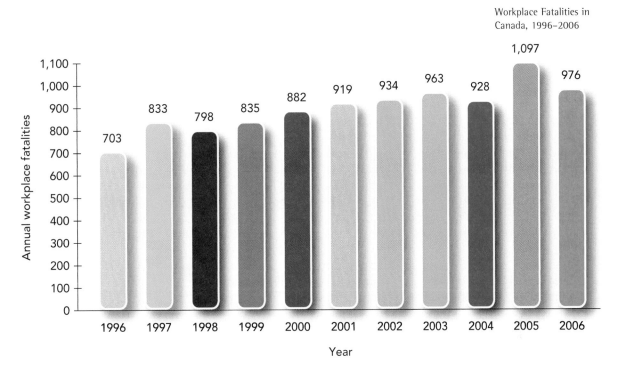

SOURCE: Association of Workers' Compensation Boards of Canada, "Table 14: Number of Fatalities, by Jurisdiction, 1993–2006," www.awcbc.org, retrieved May 29, 2008.

FIGURE 3.4

Time-Loss Injuries in
Canada, 1996–2006

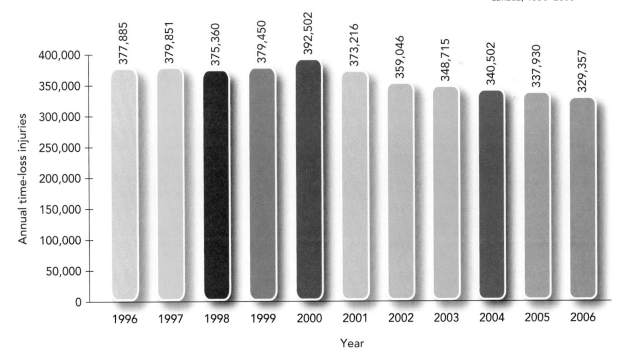

SOURCE: Association of Workers' Compensation Boards of Canada, "Table 1: Number of Accepted Time-Loss Injuries, by Jurisdiction, 1993–2006," www.awcbc.org, retrieved May 29, 2008.

E- HRM

Technology Enhancing Workplace Health and Safety

Access to information and resources is a key part of creating a safe and healthy workplace. Technology can provide new tools to employees to provide access to services and knowledge. Technology can come into play by providing links to reliable Internet sites for online information, briefing materials, best practices, statistics, safety assessments, presentations, and compliance information with national standards such as Workplace Hazardous Materials Information System (WHMIS). The official Canadian WHMIS website is a comprehensive resource and source of information (www.whmis.net).

Technology also provides employers the ability to maintain accurate information about employees to ensure all legal requirements are met including analysis of hazards and accurate reporting of workplace accidents and injuries.

Online instruction can provide employees with information about preventative measures to reduce workplace accidents and injuries.

Technology also provides access to resources for employers and workers. For example, the Association of Workers' Compensation Boards of Canada's website (www. awcbc.org) is a comprehensive resource that provides links to

relevant legislation, statistics, and research findings, a well as resources designed specifically to support the needs of young workers, healthcare and other safety-sensitive industries. WorkSafeBC's web site (www. worksafebc.com) provides injured workers, employers, and health care providers the ability to view the current status of claims. Workers can even view their most recent wage-loss payments.

SOURCE: Jeff Koven, "Technology for a Healthy Workplace," *Canadian HR Reporter*, April 19, 2004, pp. 17, 21. © *Canadian HR Reporter*, April 19, 2004, by permission of Carswell, Toronto, Ontario, 1-800-387-5164, www.hrreporter.com; www.awcbc.org; www.worksafebc.com/ claims/managing_claims/claim_status/ default.asp, retrieved June 3, 2008.

Many workplace accidents are a product of unsafe behaviours, not unsafe working conditions. Because legislation does not directly regulate employee behaviour, little behaviour change can be expected unless employees are convinced of the standards' importance.[18] This principle has been recognized by labour leaders. For example, Lynn Williams, president of the United Steelworkers, has noted, "We can't count on government. We can't count on employers. We must rely on ourselves to bring about the safety and health of our workers."[19]

Because conforming to the law alone does not necessarily guarantee their employees will be safe, many employers go beyond the letter of the law. In the next section we examine various kinds of employer-initiated safety awareness programs that comply with, and in some cases exceed, legal requirements.

LO3 - Discuss ways employers promote worker health and safety.

Employer-Sponsored Health and Safety Programs

Many employers establish safety awareness programs to go beyond mere compliance with occupational health and safety regulations and attempt to instil an emphasis on safety. A safety awareness program has three primary components: identifying and communicating hazards, reinforcing safe practices, and promoting safety internationally.

BEST PRACTICES

Suncor Energy's Journey-to-Zero Safety Initiative Receives CAPP President Award

Suncor is one of Canada's most diversified energy companies, producing more than 280,000 barrels of oil per day from its oil sands operations; developing and producing natural gas; and operating an ethanol plant and refinery in Ontario, a refinery in Colorado, Sunoco retail service stations in Ontario, and wind power projects in Saskatchewan, Alberta, and Ontario.

Suncor's "Journey to Zero" initiative is intended to embed a safety culture into every aspect of the business. The aim is to achieve a level of safety excellence that results in an injury-free work site. Suncor wants all work processes and systems to be safe, and the company demands employees and contractors take individual responsibility for safety. Since launching Journey to Zero back in 2002, Suncor has made significant progress in two key measures of safety performance: the frequency of lost-time injuries among Suncor employees and contractors has fallen by two-thirds, and the frequency of recordable injuries has been reduced by nearly one-half.

Journey to Zero recently received the President's Award in the Stewards of Excellence Awards of the Canadian Association of Petroleum Producers. "Thanks to tremendous effort by our employees and contractors, safety is becoming integrated into the way we do business," says Steve Williams, Suncor's chief operating officer. "This unwavering commitment to safety is essential for a busy, growing company like Suncor and we remain focused on achieving our vision of a workplace free of occupational injuries and illnesses."

SOURCE: "CAPP Stewardship Awards," *BNET*, http://findarticles.com/p/articles/mi_qa5406/is_200705/ai_n21290245, retrieved May 28, 2008; "Journey to Zero" and "Suncor Energy Safety Initiative Receives CAPP President's Award," www.suncor.com/default.aspx?ID = 2569, retrieved May 28, 2008.

Identifying and Communicating Job Hazards

Employees, supervisors, and other knowledgeable sources need to sit down and discuss potential problems related to safety. One method for doing this is the **job hazard analysis technique**.[20] With this technique, each job is broken down into basic elements, and each of these is rated for its potential for harm or injury. If there is agreement that some job element has high hazard potential, the group isolates the element and considers possible technological or behaviour changes to reduce or eliminate the hazard.

Another means of isolating unsafe job elements is to study past accidents. The **technic of operations review (TOR)** is an analysis method for determining which specific element of a job led to a past accident.[21] The first step in a TOR analysis is to establish the facts surrounding the incident. To accomplish this, all members of the work group involved in the accident give their initial impressions of what happened. The group must then, through discussion, come to an agreement on the single, systematic failure that most likely contributed to the incident, as well as two or three major secondary factors that contributed to it.

An analysis of jobs at Burger King, for example, revealed that certain jobs required employees to walk across wet or slippery surfaces, which led to many falls. Specific corrective action was taken on the basis of analysis of where people were falling and

job hazard analysis technique
Safety promotion technique that involves breaking down a job into basic elements, then rating each element for its potential for harm or injury.

technic of operations review (TOR)
Method of promoting safety by determining which specific element of a job led to a past accident.

WorkSafeBC produces a variety of posters and other resources to communicate job hazards and promote working safely.

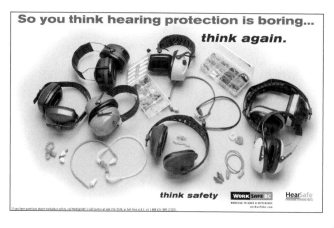

what conditions led to those falls. Now Burger King provides mats at critical locations and has generally upgraded its floor maintenance. The company also makes slip-resistant shoes available to employees in certain job categories.[22]

To communicate with employees about job hazards, managers should talk directly with their employees about safety. Written communications also are important, because the written communication helps establish a "paper trail" that can later document due diligence and a history of the employer's concern regarding the job hazard. Posters, especially if placed near the hazard, serve as a constant reminder, reinforcing other messages.

In communicating risk, managers should recognize that different groups of individuals may constitute different audiences. Research reported by Human Resources and Social Development Canada indicates that younger workers (15–24 years) have a higher incidence of time-loss injuries than any other age group. In Ontario alone, "almost two young workers are injured every hour of every day and night, seven days a week, and it's often because of what they didn't know."[23] The employer's primary concern with respect to younger workers is to inform them. Training should include specific information about safe procedures, first aid, and any protective equipment related to the job.

Experienced employees need retraining to jar them from complacency about the real dangers associated with their work.[24] This is especially the case if the hazard in question poses a greater threat to older employees. For example, accidents that involve falling off a ladder are a greater threat to older workers than to younger ones. Over 20 percent of such falls lead to a fatality for workers in the 55-to-65 age group, as against 10 percent for all other workers.[25]

Reinforcing Safe Practices

To ensure safe behaviours, employers should not only define how to work safely but also reinforce the desired behaviour. One common technique for reinforcing safe practices is implementing a safety incentive program to reward workers for their support of and commitment to safety goals. Such programs start by focusing on monthly or quarterly goals or by encouraging suggestions for improving safety. Goals might include good housekeeping practices, adherence to safety rules, and proper use of protective equipment. Later, the program expands to include more wide-ranging, long-term goals. Typically, the employer distributes prizes in highly public forums, such as company or department meetings. Using merchandise for prizes, instead of cash, provides a lasting symbol of achievement. At Regina-based USF Water Group, the company is using a health and safety bingo. Bingo numbers are given out every day and employees can win a variety of prizes. If a lost-time accident occurs, the game board is erased and employees have to start over. Prizes include gift certificates, free lunches, and even a trip to Edmonton for an NHL game.[26] A good deal of evidence suggests that such incentive programs are effective in reducing the number and cost of injuries.[27]

Besides focusing on specific jobs, organizations can target particular types of injuries or disabilities, especially those for which employees may be at risk. For example, the National Society to Prevent Blindness estimates that 1,000 eye injuries occur every day in occupational settings.[28] Organizations can prevent such injuries through a combination of job analysis, written policies, safety training, protective eyewear, rewards and sanctions for safe and unsafe behaviour, and management support for the safety effort. Industries and occupational groups also provide overall organizational safety awards. DRG Resources Corporation, a national resource company, was the recipient of the BC and Yukon Chamber of Mines' Exploration and Safety Award. In a one-year time period DRG had no lost-day accidents in 24,800 hours of copper and gold exploration work.[29]

Promoting Safety Internationally

Given the increasing focus on international management, organizations also need to consider how to ensure the safety of their employees regardless of the nation in which they operate. Cultural differences may make this more difficult than it seems. For example, a study examined the impact of one standardized corporation-wide safety policy on employees in three different countries: the United States, France, and Argentina. The results of this study indicate that employees in the three countries interpreted the policy differently because of cultural differences. The individualistic, control-oriented culture of the United States stressed the role of top management in ensuring safety in a top-down fashion. However, this policy failed to work in Argentina, where the culture is more "collectivist" (emphasizing the group). Argentine employees tend to feel that safety is everyone's joint concern, so the safety programs needed to be defined from the bottom of the organization up.[30]

Another challenge in promoting safety internationally is that laws, enforcement practices, and political climates vary from country to country. With the increasing use of offshoring, described in Chapter 1, more companies have operations in countries where safety requirements are far less strict than Canadian standards. Managers and employees in these countries may not think the company is serious about protecting workers' health and safety. In that case, strong communication and consistent actions will be necessary if the company intends to adhere to the ethical principle of valuing its foreign workers' safety as much as that of its Canadian workers.

Satisfying and Engaging Work Environments

As the opening vignette of this chapter shows, an employee's state of mind impacts work-related behaviours and outcomes on the job. Organizations need to promote **job satisfaction**, a pleasant feeling resulting from the perception that one's job fulfills or allows for the fulfillment of one's important job values.[31] A condition underpinning any high-performance organization is that employees experience job satisfaction. Research supports the idea that employees' job satisfaction and job performance are related.[32] Higher performance at the individual level should contribute to higher performance for the organization as a whole.

L04 - Describe how organizations contribute to employee job satisfaction and engagement and retain employees.

2,4

job satisfaction
A pleasant feeling resulting from the perception that one's job fulfills or allows for the fulfillment of one's important job values.

One study looked at job satisfaction in teachers and the overall performance of their schools.[33] It found a significant link between teachers' satisfaction and their schools' performance according to a variety of measures, including students' behaviour and academic achievement. More recently, a study by Watson Wyatt Worldwide found that companies with high employee commitment (which includes employees' satisfaction with their jobs and the company) enjoyed higher total returns to shareholders, a basic measure of a company's financial performance.[34] An extensive study by Sears also demonstrated a link between employee satisfaction and profits. The Sears study showed that when "employees felt good about their jobs and the company, their behaviour with customers was more positive. Sears found that if a store increased its employee satisfaction score by five measuring units in a quarter, the following quarter its customer satisfaction score would go up by 2 percent. This in turn would lead to a revenue growth of half a percent above the national average." Satisfied employees produce more revenue—that's something that gets the attention of executives.[35]

Organizations can promote job satisfaction in a number of ways: making jobs more interesting, setting clear and challenging goals, and providing valued rewards linked to performance in a performance management system that employees consider fair.

Research has found that teachers' job satisfaction is associated with high performance of the schools where they teach. In what other ways can organizations promote and foster employee satisfaction and engagement?

As discussed in Chapter 1, some organizations are moving beyond concern with job satisfaction and trying to foster employee engagement—the extent that employees are satisfied, committed to, and prepared to support what is important to the organization. "An organization's capacity to manage employee engagement is closely related to its ability to achieve superior results."[36] That's the conclusion of a compilation of data from Hewitt Associates that makes the strongest link yet between engaged employees and business success. An analysis of the Hewitt Associates Employee Engagement and Best Employer Database of 1,500 companies over a four-year period showed that companies with high engagement levels had markedly higher total shareholder return (TSR) than those with low employee engagement. Specifically, companies with 60–100 percent employee engagement achieved an average TSR of 24.2 percent. With engagement scores of 49–60 percent, TSR dropped off to 9.1 percent. Companies with engagement below 25 percent suffered negative TSR.[37]

Measuring Employee Satisfaction and Engagement

The usual way to measure satisfaction or engagement is with a survey. A systematic, ongoing program of employee surveys should be part of the organization's human resource strategy. This allows the organization to monitor trends and prevent *voluntary turnover*. For example, if satisfaction with promotion opportunities has been falling over several years, the trend may signal a need for better career management (a topic of Chapter 7). An organizational change, such as a merger, also might have important consequences. In addition, ongoing surveys give the organization a way to measure whether new policies improve job satisfaction and employee engagement. Organizations can also compare results from different departments to identify groups with successful practices that may apply elsewhere in the organization. Another benefit

Job Satisfaction from the Faces Scale

Consider all aspects of your job. Circle the face that best describes your feelings about your job in general.

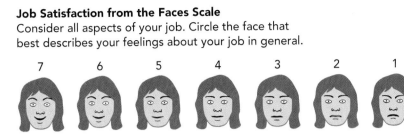

SOURCE: R. B. Dunham and J. B. Herman and published in the *Journal of Applied Psychology* (1975), pp. 629–31. © 1975 by the American Psychological Association. Adapted with permission.

FIGURE 3.5

Job Satisfaction from the Faces Scale

is that some scales provide data that organizations can use to compare themselves to others in the same industry. This information will be valuable for creating and reviewing human resource policies that enable organizations to attract and retain employees in a competitive job market. Finally, conducting surveys gives employees a chance to be heard, so the practice itself can contribute to employee satisfaction.

To obtain a survey instrument, an excellent place to begin is with one of the many established scales. The validity and reliability of many satisfaction scales have been tested, so it is possible to compare the instruments. The main reason for an organization to create its own scale would be that it wants to measure satisfaction with aspects of work specific to the organization (such as satisfaction with a specific training initiative).

Some satisfaction scales measure general satisfaction, using broad questions such as "All in all, how satisfied are you with your job?"[38] Some scales avoid language altogether, relying on pictures. The faces scale in Figure 3.5 is an example of this type of measure. Other scales exist for measuring more specific aspects of satisfaction. For example, the Pay Satisfaction Questionnaire (PSQ) measures satisfaction with specific aspects of pay, such as pay levels, structure, and raises.[39]

Conducting surveys is not something an organization should take lightly. Especially when the program is new, they often raise employees' expectations. The organization should therefore be ready to act on the results. At the Canadian division of the Swiss pharmaceutical company, Hoffman-La Roche Ltd., comments from employee surveys are quickly acted on. For example, on the basis of the surveys, a holiday-hours program was recently set up, giving full-time employees an extra day off on long weekends. This attention to employees recently earned Hoffman-La Roche one of the top spots on Hewitt Associates' list of the 50 Best Employers in Canada.[40]

However, critics describe the traditional employee satisfaction feedback process as: "The individual has his or her moment of self-expression, a fleeting participation in the great collective search for truth, then silence, nada, frustration as the status quo prevails."[41] With this in mind, the Gallup Organization set about to create a better employee feedback process that linked the elements of employee engagement to improved business outcomes, for example, sales growth, productivity, customer loyalty, and the generation of value.[42] The HR How-To box identifies Gallup's questions for measuring employee engagement.

The global HR consulting firm Towers Perrin recently surveyed nearly 90,000 workers from 18 countries and found that just 21 percent of employees reported "being engaged in their work and willing to go the extra mile to help their companies succeed."[43] This study also found that engaged employees are more likely to see a direct connection between what they do and company results. More than 80 percent of engaged employees believe they can and do contribute to the quality of products

HR HOW-TO

Measuring Worker Engagement

To identify the elements of worker engagement, Gallup conducted hundreds of focus groups and many thousands of worker interviews in all kinds of organizations, and at all levels, in most industries, and in many countries. The result was 12 key employee expectations that, when satisfied, form the foundation of strong feelings of engagement.

These are Gallup's 12 questions:

- Do you know what is expected of you at work?
- Do you have the materials and equipment you need to do your work right?
- At work, do you have the opportunity to do what you do best every day?
- In the last seven days, have you received recognition or praise for doing good work?
- Does your supervisor, or someone at work, seem to care about you as a person?
- Is there someone at work who encourages your development?
- At work, do your opinions seem to count?
- Does the mission/purpose of your company make you feel your job is important?
- Are your associates (fellow employees) committed to doing quality work?
- Do you have a best friend at work?
- In the last six months, has someone at work talked to you about your progress?
- In the last year, have you had opportunities at work to learn and grow?

The 12 engagement questions are answered by employees on a scale of one to five, according to their weak or strong agree-ment. The process also involves a feedback methodo-logy for improving engagement by creating a factual base for discussion and debate of the causes behind the numbers. In this way, it yields actionable input from staff and managers for changes in behaviour, atti-tudes, poli-cies, and processes. Follow-up surveys are conduc-ted to track long-term progress—or backsliding—on the 12 questions.

SOURCE: John Thackray, "Feedback for Real," March 15, 2001, http://gmj.gallup.com/content/811/Feedback-Real.aspx, retrieved August 28, 2008.

---

and services and to customer satisfaction, whereas only half as many of the disengaged share that view. In addition, engagement was found to have a direct impact on retaining employees. "Half of the engaged employees had no plans to leave their companies, compared with just 15 per cent of the disengaged. Less than 5 per cent of the engaged employees said they were actively looking for other jobs, compared with more than one-quarter of the disengaged employees."[44]

exit interview
A meeting of a departing employee with the employee's supervisor and/or human resource specialist to discuss the employee's reasons for leaving.

In spite of surveys and other efforts to retain employees, some employees inevitably will leave the organization. This presents another opportunity to gather information for retaining employees: the **exit interview**—a meeting of the departing employee with the employee's supervisor and/or a human resource specialist to discuss the employee's reasons for leaving. A well-conducted exit interview can uncover reasons why employees leave and perhaps set the stage for some of them to return.[45] HR professionals can help make exit interviews more successful by arranging for the employee to talk to someone from the HR department (rather than the departing employee's supervisor) in a neutral location.[46] Questions should start out open-ended and general, to give the employee a chance to name the source of the dissatisfaction.

FIGURE 3.6

Top Five Reasons Why
Employees Will Stay

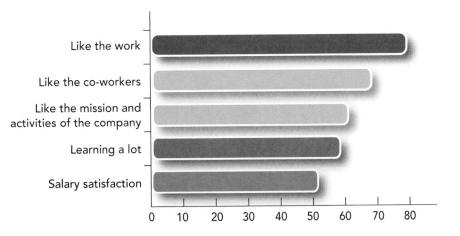

SOURCE: Ipsos-Reid for Workopolis (2001), appearing in "On the Charts," *Canadian HR Reporter*, May 17, 2004, p. G3.

A recruiter armed with information about what caused a specific person to leave may be able to negotiate a return when the situation changes. And when several exiting employees give similar reasons for leaving, management should consider whether this indicates a need for change. Most white-collar workers feel their job responsibilities are what ultimately cause them to decide to stay with an organization. Figure 3.6 illustrates the results of an Ipsos-Reid study of 1,000 full-time white-collar workers in Canada and what matters the most when it comes to retention. Ultimately in the war for talent, the best way to manage retention is to engage in a battle for every valued employee, even when it looks as if the battle has been lost. A recent twist on the exit interview is a **stay interview**—a meeting with an employee to explore his or her thoughts and feelings about the job and to uncover issues in the effort to prevent that employee from becoming disgruntled.[47] The competitive job market, impending retirement of the baby boomers, and the multigenerational workforce are all placing more importance on engagement in the workplace. These factors are pressing organizations to find ways to retain their top talent, and that is also necessitating the need for engaged workers.[48]

Managing Voluntary and Involuntary Turnover

To maintain an environment that supports employee satisfaction and engagement, organizations must try to ensure that good performers want to stay with the organization and that employees whose performance is chronically low are encouraged—or forced—to leave. Both of these challenges involve *employee turnover*, that is, employees leaving the organization. When the organization initiates the turnover (often with employees who would prefer to stay), the result is **involuntary turnover**. Examples include terminating an employee for theft or laying off employees during a downturn. Most organizations use the word *termination* to refer only to a discharge related to a discipline problem, but some organizations call any involuntary turnover a termination. When the employees initiate the turnover (often when the organization would prefer to keep them), it is **voluntary turnover**. Employees may leave to retire or to take a job with a different organization, particularly in competitive labour markets when employees have many options should they become unhappy with their current job or employer.

stay interview
A meeting with an employee to explore his or her thoughts and feelings about the job and to uncover issues in the effort to prevent that employee from becoming disgruntled.

3,4

L05 - Distinguish between voluntary and involuntary turnover, and describe their effects on an organization.

involuntary turnover
Turnover initiated by an employer (often with employees who would prefer to stay).

voluntary turnover
Turnover initiated by employees (often when the organization would prefer to keep them).

FIGURE 3.7

Voluntary Turnover Rates
(%, average)

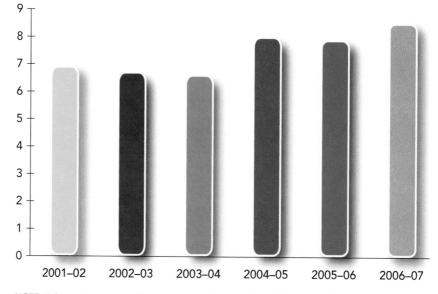

NOTE: Voluntary turnover applies to regular employees only, and does not include early retirements or severances.

SOURCE: Stephen Clarke, "Compensation Planning Outlook 2008," *The Conference Board of Canada,* October 2007, p. 16.

In general, organizations try to avoid the need for involuntary turnover and to minimize voluntary turnover, especially among top performers. Figure 3.7 shows how voluntary turnover has increased in Canada in recent years. Both kinds of turnover are costly, as summarized in Table 3.1. Replacing workers is expensive, and new employees need time to learn their jobs. Although estimates of the cost of turnover fluctuate widely, Hay Group's vice-president of HR consulting, David Sissons, cites the cost of turnover as 1.5 times the annual salary for a manager or professional, 0.5 times the annual salary for an hourly worker, and as much as 2.0 times annual salary for a top sales or senior-level person.[49] In addition, people today are more likely to take legal action against a former employer if they feel they were unfairly dismissed. The prospect of workplace violence also raises the risk associated with discharging employees. Effective human resource management can help the organization minimize both kinds of turnover, as well as carry it out effectively when necessary. Despite a company's best efforts at selection, training, and compensation, some employees will fail to meet expectations or will violate company policies. When this

TABLE 3.1

Costs Associated
with Turnover

INVOLUNTARY TURNOVER	VOLUNTARY TURNOVER
Recruiting, selecting, and training replacements	Recruiting, selecting, and training replacements
Lost productivity	Lost productivity
Lawsuits	Loss of talented employees
Workplace violence	

happens, organizations need to apply a discipline program that might ultimately lead to discharging the individual.

For a number of reasons, discharging employees can be a very difficult but potentially important way to maintain a high-performance and engaging work culture. The decision also has legal aspects that can affect the organization. Historically, if the organization and employee do not have a specific employment contract, the employer or employee may end the employment relationship at any time. This is the *employment-at-will doctrine*. This doctrine has eroded significantly, however. Employees who have been terminated sometimes sue their employers for wrongful dismissal, and in such cases the courts may award employees significant financial settlements. Publicity associated with the proceedings may also be embarrassing or harmful to the employer's reputation.

Employment/labour standards laws in each of the federal, provincial, and territorial jurisdictions set out the legal minimum requirements employers must follow when terminating or laying off employees. No notice or compensation is needed if the employee quit or retired, the employee had been employed for less than the required minimum (usually three months), the employee was employed on an "on-call" basis, or the employee was terminated for "just cause." Examples of "just cause" or dismissal that are considered serious violations of the employment relationship are dishonesty; willful disobedience to a supervisor; and failure to comply with known policies or procedures or meet performance requirements.[50]

Employers have a right to terminate workers for reasons other than for "just cause"; however, they must provide notice, termination pay, or severance pay as prescribed in the relevant employment/labour standards legislation. **Termination pay** is a lump-sum payment equal to the regular wages for a regular workweek that an employee would have earned during the notice period. **Severance pay** is compensation that recognizes the employee's years of service and compensates the employee for loss of job-related earnings.[51] Employers cannot avoid paying termination or severance pay by attempting to force an employee to resign. **Constructive dismissal** occurs when the employer makes a significant change to a worker's condition of employment. Examples may include changing the employee's hours of work, authority, travel requirements, or other elements that may cause the employee to feel they have no choice but to resign.

Sometimes terminations may occur because the organization determines that for economic reasons it must close a facility. An organization that plans such a broad-scale layoff must consult with their employment/labour standards office to ensure that all the requirements for their jurisdiction are handled appropriately. An organization should also seek legal advice before implementing a mass termination.

Along with the financial risks of dismissing an employee, there are issues related to personal safety. Distressing as it is that some former employees go to the courts, even more problematic are the employees who react to a termination decision with violence. Violence in the workplace has become a major organizational problem. Workplace homicide is the fastest-growing form of murder.[52] Although any number of organizational actions or decisions may incite violence among employees, the "nothing to lose" aspect of an employee's dismissal makes the situation dangerous.

Because of the critical financial and personal risks associated with employee dismissal, it is easy to see why organizations must develop a standardized, systematic approach to discipline and discharge. These decisions should not be left solely to the discretion of individual managers or supervisors. Policies that can lead to employee

5

termination pay
A lump-sum payment equal to the regular wages for a regular workweek that an employee would have earned during the notice period.

severance pay
Compensation that recognizes the employee's years of service and compensates the employee for loss of job-related earnings.

constructive dismissal
Occurs when the employer makes a significant change to a worker's condition of employment.

4

separation should be based on principles of justice and law, and they should allow for various ways to intervene.

Ultimately, employees' satisfaction, engagement, and intent to stay with an organization are impacted by their conclusions about the system's fairness on the basis of the system's outcomes and procedures and how managers treat employees when carrying out those procedures. Figure 3.8 summarizes these principles as outcome fairness, procedural justice, and interactional justice. Outcome fairness involves the ends of a discipline process, while procedural and interactional justice focus on the means to those ends.

outcome fairness
A judgment that the consequences given to employees are just.

People's perception of **outcome fairness** depends on their judgment that the consequences of a decision to employees are just. As shown in Figure 3.8, one employee's consequences should be consistent with other employees' consequences. Organizations promote outcome fairness when they clearly communicate policies regarding the consequences of inappropriate behaviour. Finally, the outcome should be proportionate to the behaviour. Terminating an employee for being late to work, especially if this is the first time the employee has been late, would seem out of proportion to the offence in most situations. Employees' sense of outcome fairness would usually reserve loss of a job for the most serious offences.

procedural justice
A judgment that fair methods were used to determine the consequences an employee receives.

People's perception of **procedural justice** is their judgment that fair methods were used to determine the consequences an employee receives. Figure 3.8 shows six principles that determine whether people perceive procedures as fair. The procedures should be consistent from one person to another, and the manager using them should suppress any personal biases. The procedures should be based on accurate information, not rumours or falsehoods. The procedures should also be correctable, meaning the system includes safeguards, such as channels for appealing a decision or correcting errors. The procedures should take into account the concerns of all the groups affected—for example, by gathering information from employees, customers, and managers. Finally, the procedures should be consistent with prevailing ethical standards, such as concerns for privacy and honesty.

FIGURE 3.8

Principles of Justice

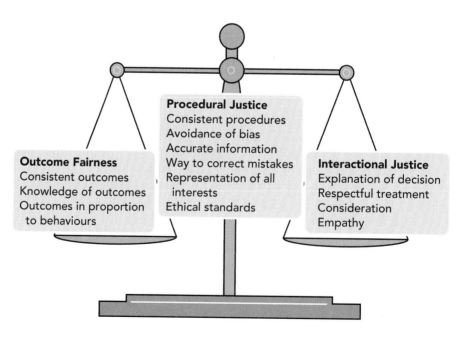

A perception of **interactional justice** is a judgment that the organization carried out its actions in a way that took the employee's feelings into account. It is a judgment about the ways that managers interact with their employees. A disciplinary action meets the standards of interactional justice if the manager explains to the employee how the action is procedurally just. The manager should listen to the employee. The manager should also treat the employee with dignity and respect and should empathize with the employee's feelings. The precedent-setting Supreme Court case of *Wallace v. United Grain Growers* (1997) sent a clear message that employers must act fairly and respectfully when handling an employee termination. The *Wallace* case gave judges a legal precedent to award employees additional notice or damages if the employer treats an employee callously or unfairly during termination.

The issue of off-the-job behaviour is also of concern to employers. Employers are frequently concerned if a worker's off-the-job behaviour might affect the organization's business or reputation in some way. Violet Legere, a YMCA-YWCA employee, ran into her colleague and neighbour at a grocery store. They had been on opposing sides of a bitter environmental dispute in the community. The colleague, who was with her four-year old daughter, approached Legere and said "Hi." Legere lost it and told the colleague, "You f*** right off." Shortly after this incident, she was dismissed from her job at the YMCA-YWCA where she was responsible for running an after-school program. The employer said she had cursed in front of children and this violated the Y's code of conduct. However, a New Brunswick Court of Queen's Bench judge ruled in Legere's favour and concluded that Legere had exercised her right to free speech and the phrase she used was just an intense way of saying, "Go away."[53]

An employee who has been discharged is likely to feel angry and confused about what to do next. If the person feels there is nothing to lose and nowhere else to turn, the potential for violence, a lawsuit, or other negative impacts on remaining employees and the general work environment is greater than most organizations are willing to tolerate. This concern is one reason many organizations provide **outplacement counselling**, which tries to help dismissed employees manage the transition from one job to another.

Some organizations have their own staff for conducting outplacement counselling. Other organizations have contracts with outside providers to help with individual cases. Either way, the goals for outplacement programs are to help the former employee address the psychological issues associated with losing a job—grief, depression, and fear—while at the same time helping the person find a new job.

Employee Discipline

In order to maintain a positive and motivating work environment for all employees, organizations look for methods of handling problem behaviour that are fair, legal, and effective. A popular principle for responding effectively is the **hot-stove rule**. According to this principle, discipline should be like a hot stove: the glowing or burning stove gives warning not to touch. Anyone who ignores the warning will be burned. The stove has no feelings to influence which people it burns, and it delivers the same burn to any touch. Finally, the burn is immediate. Like the hot stove, an organization's discipline should give warning and have consequences that are consistent, objective, and immediate.

interactional justice
A judgment that the organization carried out its actions in a way that took the employee's feelings into account.

outplacement counselling
A service in which professionals try to help dismissed employees manage the transition from one job to another.

L06 - Summarize ways in which organizations can fairly discipline employees.

hot-stove rule
Principle of discipline that says discipline should be like a hot stove, giving clear warning and following up with consistent, objective, immediate consequences.

FIGURE 3.9

Progressive Discipline
Responses

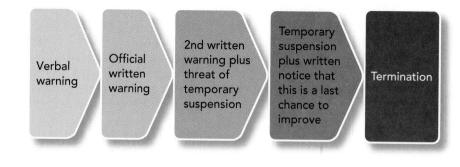

progressive discipline

A formal discipline process in which the consequences become more serious if the employee repeats the offence.

The principles of justice suggest that the organization prepare for problems by establishing a formal discipline process in which the consequences become more serious if the employee repeats the offence. Such a system is called **progressive discipline**. A typical progressive discipline system identifies and communicates inappropriate behaviours and responds to a series of offences with the actions shown in Figure 3.9—verbal and then written warnings, temporary suspension, and finally, termination. This process fulfills the purpose of discipline by teaching employees what is expected of them and creating a situation in which employees must try to do what is expected. It seeks to prevent inappropriate behaviour (by publishing rules) and to correct, rather than merely punish, inappropriate behaviour.

Such procedures may seem exasperatingly slow, especially when the employee's misdeeds hurt the team's performance. In the end, however, if an employee must be discharged, careful use of the procedure increases other employees' belief that the organization is fair and reduces the likelihood that the employee will take legal action (or at least that the employee will win in court). For situations in which inappropriate behaviour is dangerous, the organization may establish a stricter policy, even terminating an employee for the first offence. In that case, it is especially important to communicate the procedure—not only to ensure fairness, but also to prevent the dangerous inappropriate behaviour.

Creating a formal discipline process is a primary responsibility of the human resource department. The HR professional should consult with supervisors and managers to identify inappropriate behaviours and establish rules and consequences for violating the rules. The rules should cover disciplinary problems such as the ones identified in Table 3.2. For each infraction, the HR professional would identify a series of responses, such as those in Figure 3.9. In addition, the organization must communicate these rules and consequences in writing to every employee. Ways of publishing rules include presenting them in an employee handbook, posting them on the company's intranet, and displaying them on a bulletin board. Supervisors should be familiar with the rules, so that they can discuss them with employees and apply them consistently.

Along with rules and a progression of consequences for violating the rules, a progressive discipline system should have requirements for documenting the rules, offences, and responses.

As we noted in the earlier discussion of procedural justice, the discipline system should provide an opportunity to hear every point of view and to correct errors. Before discussing and filing records of inappropriate behaviour, it is important for the supervisor to investigate the incident. The employee should be made aware of what he or she is said to have done wrong and should have an opportunity to present his or her version of events.

Tardiness
Absenteeism
Unsafe work practices
Poor quantity or quality of work
Sexual harassment of coworkers
Theft of company property
Cyberslacking (surfing the Internet at work)

TABLE 3.2

Common Problems Requiring Discipline

Alternative Dispute Resolution

Sometimes workplace issues are easier to solve when an impartial person helps to create the solution. Therefore, at various points in the discipline process, the employee or organization might want to bring in someone to help with problem solving. Rather than turning to the courts every time an outsider is desired, more and more organizations are using **alternative dispute resolution (ADR)**. A variety of ADR techniques show promise for resolving disputes in a timely, constructive, cost-effective manner.

In general, a system for alternative dispute resolution proceeds through the four stages shown in Figure 3.10:

1. *Open-door policy.* On the expectation that two people in conflict should first try to arrive at a settlement together, the organization has a policy of making managers available to hear complaints. Typically, the first "open door" is that of the employee's immediate supervisor, and if the employee does not get a resolution from that person, the employee may appeal to managers at higher levels. This policy works only to the degree that managers who hear complaints listen and are able to act.
2. **Peer review**. If the people in conflict cannot reach an agreement, they take their conflict to a panel composed of representatives from the organization at the same levels as the people in the dispute. The panel hears the case and tries to help the parties arrive at a settlement.
3. **Mediation**. If the peer review does not lead to a settlement, a neutral party from outside the organization hears the case and tries to help the people in conflict arrive at a settlement. The process is not binding, meaning the mediator cannot force a solution.

alternative dispute resolution (ADR)
Methods of solving a problem by bringing in an impartial outsider but not using the court system.

peer review
Process for resolving disputes by taking them to a panel composed of representatives from the organization at the same levels as the people in the dispute.

mediation
Nonbinding process in which a neutral party from outside the organization hears the case and tries to help the people in conflict arrive at a settlement.

FIGURE 3.10

Typical Stages of Alternative Dispute Resolution

arbitration
Binding process in which a professional arbitrator from outside the organization (usually a lawyer or judge) hears the case and resolves it by making a decision.

4. **Arbitration.** If mediation fails, a professional arbitrator from outside the organization hears the case and resolves it by making a decision. Most arbitrators are experienced employment lawyers or retired judges. The employee and employer both have to accept the person's decision.

Each stage reflects a somewhat broader involvement of people outside the dispute. The hope is that the conflict will be resolved at earlier stages, at which the costs, time, and impact of employees and other organizational stakeholders are lowest.

Employee Assistance Programs

employee assistance program (EAP)
A referral service employees can use to seek professional treatment for emotional problems or substance abuse

While ADR is effective in dealing with problems related to performance and disputes between people at work, many of the problems that lead an organization to want to terminate an employee involve drug or alcohol abuse or personal issues. In these cases, the organization's discipline program should also incorporate an **employee assistance program (EAP)**—a referral service employees can use to seek professional and confidential treatment for emotional problems or substance abuse.

EAPs vary widely, but most share some basic elements. First, the programs are usually identified in official documents published by the employer, such as employee handbooks. Supervisors (and line managers) are trained to use the referral service for employees whom they suspect of having health-related problems. The organization also trains employees to use the system to refer themselves when necessary, and the services are usually made available to the employee's partner and family members.

2,4

L07 - Identify how corporate social responsibility contributes to employee engagement and retention.

Corporate Social Responsibility

corporate social responsibility (CSR)
An evolving concept integrating social, environmental, and economic concerns into an organization's values, culture, decision making, strategy, and operations in a way that creates wealth and improves society.

In the long run, a high-performance organization fosters the kind of work culture that encourages high levels of motivation, satisfaction, commitment, and engagement. The newer generations in the workforce are much more likely to speak up, saying: "I'm not a happy camper and you need to do more to keep me here, or I am going to pick up my skill set and go somewhere else."[54] **Corporate social responsibility (CSR)** is an evolving concept integrating social, environmental, and economic concerns into an organization's values, culture, decision making, strategy and operations in a way that creates wealth and improves society.[55] CSR may also be referred to as *corporate responsibility*, *corporate citizenship*, *responsible business*, or *triple bottom line* (social, environmental, and economic performance) just to name a few frequently used alternative terms. Canada is recognized as a leader in social responsibility and "CSR remains a concept that is openly embraced by a strong majority of Canadians."[56] For example, research firm GlobeScan found that 92 percent of Canadians said that "the more socially and environmentally responsible a company is, the more likely they are to purchase its products or services." Additionally, "91 per cent of Canadians surveyed prefer to work for a company that is socially and environmentally responsible." The more socially and environmentally responsible a company is, the more attractive it becomes as an employer.[57]

Demonstrating corporate social responsibility such as sustainability, promoting volunteerism, providing meaningful work, and having high ethical standards are important factors to retain and engage employees. These factors may be particularly important among young employees.

Sustainability—Going Green

There is a growing trend among young, intelligent employees leaving lucrative private sector jobs to integrate their personal values with their professional goals. Monica Da Ponte, manager of marketing alliances for World Wildlife Fund (WWF)—Canada, spent seven years with a leading consumer packaged-goods company after finishing her undergraduate degree. "After some travelling and a better understanding of what was happening globally, I realized I was doing all this great work for something I did not believe in. That's when I started volunteering at WWF-Canada and pursuing my MBA with a focus on sustainability and nonprofit management," say Da Ponte. Now Da Ponte has struck a balance where to gets to 'walk her talk' with respect to her values, while fully utilizing her business knowledge and skills.[58] According to Ron Dembo, CEO of Zerofootprint, a Toronto-based consultancy focusing on sustainable commerce: "Two years ago, if you went to a company's corporate responsibility person, you would have found that environmental issues did not rank high." The cultural change has been so sudden that a lot of corporations haven't caught up to the fact that this issue can have an impact on employee morale, loyalty, and engagement, he said.[59] For example, a recent poll on green employment by MonsterTRAK.com, a job website for students and entry-level hires, found that "92 percent would be more inclined to work for an environmentally friendly company and 80 percent of young professionals are interested in securing a job that has a positive impact on the environment."[60]

In 2006, Vancouver-based credit union Vancity, set a goal to become carbon-neutral by 2010—meaning the amount of carbon dioxide the company emits will be equal to the amount of carbon dioxide reduced through the company's investment in green projects that are saving emissions. Vancity met this goal two years ahead of schedule with the help of experts including the University of British Columbia, Ecotrust Canada, and the David Suzuki Foundation.[61] Vancity has been committed to the environment since the early 1990s. The company makes it easier for employees to commute to work. For example, in 1995 Vancity built its corporate head office on the SkyTrain line, encourages carpooling, and provides a cash incentive of about $2000 to employees who purchase a car with low carbon dioxide emissions. Vancity invests 30 percent of its annual profits into programs that support their three corporate social responsibility initiatives—acting on climate change, facing poverty, and growing the social economy.[62]

Climate change is one of the ways Vancity rates its success as a business. Vancity set a goal to be carbon-neutral by 2010, and they reached this goal two years ahead of schedule.

Volunteerism

Charitable initiatives—whether ongoing fundraisers or annual events—foster a sense of community within an organization, thereby increasing employees' satisfaction, engagement, and retention. For example, one of Deloitte's company values is "commitment to each other." Deloitte "believes that supporting the communities in which we do business makes good business sense and is an important part of our corporate responsibility." Last year, Deloitte staff raised $2 million for United Way across Canada, and it sponsors a nationwide Impact Day on which employees are encouraged to spend one paid workday together involved in local community projects. Beth Tyndall, senior manager of human resources at Deloitte, says, "By supporting people through their community activities, Deloitte generates employee engagement and commitment. Local charities benefit as well."[63]

QLT Inc., a Vancouver-based global biopharmaceutical company, also commits to volunteering as a team. For example, QLT's more than 300 employees recently spent a half-day working together to clean up the beach in downtown Vancouver. "We filled literally thousands of garbage bags," said senior vice-president of human resources Linda Lupini.[64] A similar sense of volunteerism is fostered at TD Bank Financial Group, where employees are provided time off to work as volunteers for a charitable organization of their choice. If they put in more than 40 hours of volunteering, they can even apply for a $500 grant that goes directly to their charity. So far, $550,000 in grant money has been provided; that's in addition to the money that TD directly gives to charities—more than $33 million annually. Says Teri Currie, executive vice-president of human resources, "Pride in an organization is best described as what employees are doing when no one is looking: Are they engaged with customers? With fellow employees? With the larger community?"[65]

Meaningful Work

Another way organizations foster engagement is to match employees with on-the-job roles and projects that are connected to their values and create a sense of meaning and purpose for the employee. For example, when John Hancock joined Microsoft Canada in Toronto as a consultant, he went to work on an 18-month project with law enforcement agencies to develop a Child Exploitation Tracking System (CETS) to battle online sexual abuse. Now five years later he is still using his software development skills at Microsoft and is in charge of helping police forces around the world get CETS up and running. He says he's proud that the resources of Microsoft could be put toward developing such an important social tool. "Knowing that Microsoft Canada was the driving force behind the initiative is part of the attraction of coming into work every day."[66] Fostering pride and engagement through the opportunity to make a difference is also being promoted by governments across the country. For example the Nova Scotia government promotes pride in the public sector through the slogan "Make a Difference" as part of its strategy to attract, engage, and retain employees.[67]

Ethics

Ethics, defined in Chapter 1, establishes fundamental principles for behaviour, such as honesty and fairness. Organizations and their employees must meet these standards if they are to maintain positive long-term relationships with their employees, customers, and community. For example, Gerline Herrmann, president of The Herrmann Group, an HR management consulting firm in Ontario, cautions employers not to make empty promises about being an eco-friendly organization to attract candidates—a practice experts call *greenwashing*. Herrmann, who serves on SHRM's Corporate Social Responsibility and Sustainability Special Expertise Panel, notes that potential employees check organizations' backgrounds and talk with employees to find out whether organizations deliver.[68]

Ethical behaviour is most likely to result from values held by the organization's leaders combined with systems that promote ethical behaviour. Charles O. Holliday Jr., the chairman and chief executive officer of DuPont Company, is an example of an executive who cares about ethics. For Holliday, ethics is a matter of behaving in ways that promote trust: "Just saying you're ethical isn't very useful. You have to earn trust by what you do every day."[69] Holliday experienced this kind of leadership himself when he first joined DuPont. The CEO at that time, Dick Heckert, told him, "This company lives by the letter of its contracts and the intent of those contracts," speaking with such conviction that he imprinted the lesson on Holliday's mind.

A number of organizational systems can promote ethical behaviour.[70] These include a written code of ethics that the organization distributes to employees and expects them to use in decision making. Publishing a list of ethical standards is not enough, however. The organization should reinforce ethical behaviour. For example, performance measures should include ethical standards. The organization should provide channels employees can use to ask questions about ethical behaviour or to seek help if they are expected to do something they believe is wrong. Organizations also can provide training in ethical decision making.

As these examples suggest, ethical behaviour is a human resource management concern. The systems that promote ethical behaviour include such HRM functions as training, performance management, and discipline policies. In today's business climate, ethical behaviour also can affect recruiting. Recent high-profile scandals involving fraudulent accounting practices and executive fraud have hastened the collapse of some companies and put thousands of employees out of work. Job candidates want to avoid employers whose misdeeds might cost them their jobs and their reputations. Many job candidates have asked recruiters how well their organizations promote ethical behaviour.[71]

Many organizations are developing and clarifying expectations for ethical behaviour. For example, CIBC clearly defines its requirements for employee behaviour in its "Code of Conduct"[72] and director behaviour in a "Code of Ethics."[73] The most common ethics initiatives undertaken by Canadian businesses are providing a secure forum for employees to report unethical behaviour and implementing ethics training, according to a recent CEO/Business Leader Poll by COMPAS in the *Financial Post*.[74]

THINKING ETHICALLY

Green or Greenwashing?

Michael Adams, president of The Environics Group of research and communications consulting companies in Toronto, said he sees people increasingly concerned about whether they work for environmentally responsible companies. "They don't want to go home and have to apologize to their children about where they work and what they do. They want to feel proud of what they do," said Adams. The surge of environmental awareness in North America is unmistakable. It has been documented by researchers and widely reported in the popular press. Environmental concerns have emerged as an issue not only for consumers but also for employees. As a result, organizations are developing sophisticated strategies to secure their reputation as sustainable and eco-friendly in order to attract, retain, and engage both customers and employees. Less studied

(continued)

THINKING ETHICALLY

is the apparent increase in "greenwashing"—false or misleading green marketing claims in the hope of making a quick buck on consumer and/or employee goodwill.

"We live in an era of both idealism and cynicism. Our kids are brought up watching Homer Simpson, *The Family Guy*, and *South Park*. They are much more aware that authority figures can be wrong, whether it's the church, the state, or Dad." So when companies ostentatiously display idealism, they are going to be watching for whether or not they carry through—the danger is that the talk may outpace the walk, and claims of CSR may be just that—claims.

SOURCE: Uyen Vu, "Climate Change Sparks Attitude Shift," *Canadian HR Reporter*, March 26, 2007, p. 11; Adine Mees and Jamie Bonham, "Corporate Social Responsibility Belongs with HR," *Canadian HR Reporter*, April 4, 2004, p. 11; "The Six Sins of Greenwashing TM," *terrachoice environmental marketing*, 2007, www.terrachoice.com, retrieved June 4, 2008.

Questions

1. Do organizations have an ethical obligation to improve social and environmental conditions? Why or why not?
2. Can or should HR push the CSR agenda? Why or why not?
3. What steps would you take to protect yourself from being "greenwashed" by a potential employer?

SUMMARY

L01 Explain the context for workplace health and safety.

- All jurisdictions in Canada have occupational health and safety legislation. Canada's approach to safety in the workplace is based on the internal responsibility system whereby both employers and employees are responsible for safety.

L02 Identify employers' duties and employees' rights and responsibilities related to workforce health and safety.

- Employers and supervisors have a duty to provide a safe workplace.
- Canada workers have three fundamental rights that are protected by occupational health and safety legislation.
- A recent amendment to the Criminal Code (Bill C-45) has created an additional legal duty on employers to ensure the safety of workers. Employees also have responsibilities including following safety rules and reporting hazardous conditions.

L03 Discuss ways employers promote worker health and safety.

- Besides complying with occupational health and safety regulations, employers often establish safety awareness programs designed to instil an emphasis on safety.
- They may identify and communicate hazards through the job hazard analysis technique or the technic of operations review. They may adapt communications and training to the needs of different employees, such as differences in experience levels or cultural differences from one country to another. Employers may also establish incentive programs to reward safe behaviour.

L04   **Describe how organizations contribute to employee job satisfaction and engagement and retain employees.**

- Job satisfaction and engagement are factors that contribute directly to the achievement of organizational results and high levels of performance. The usual way to measure employee satisfaction and engagement is with a survey, and systematic approaches should be part of the organization's human resource strategy.

- Exit interviews and stay interviews are effective methods to uncover employee issues in the effort to retain employees over the long-term.

L05   **Distinguish between voluntary and involuntary turnover, and describe their effects on an organization.**

- Voluntary turnover occurs when employees initiate the turnover, often when the organization would prefer to keep them. Involuntary turnover occurs when the organization requires employees to leave, often when they would prefer to stay. Both are costly because of the need to recruit, hire, and train replacements.

- Employees draw conclusions about fairness on the outcomes of decision regarding them, the procedures applied, and the way managers treat employees when carrying out those procedures.

L06   **Summarize ways in which organizations can fairly discipline employees.**

- Discipline should follow the principles of the hot-stove rule, meaning discipline should give warning and have consequences that are consistent, objective, and immediate. A system that can meet these requirements is referred to as progressive discipline.

- Organizations may also resolve problems through alternative dispute resolution, including an open-door policy, peer review, mediation, and arbitration.

L07   **Identify how corporate social responsibility contributes to employee engagement and retention.**

- High-performance organizations foster a work culture that encourages engagement and retention. Corporate social responsibility involves integrating social, environmental, and economic concerns.

- Issues such sustainability, volunteerism, meaningful work, and high ethical standards are factors that are increasingly important to an organization's ability to attract, retain, and engage employees—particularly younger ones.

REVIEW AND DISCUSSION QUESTIONS

1. What is the role of a workplace health and safety committee in reducing workplace accidents and injuries?
2. What effect will Bill C-45 (Westray Bill) likely have on supervisors' behaviours and attitudes related to workplace safety?
3. How can organizations motivate employees to promote safety and health in the workplace?
4. Why do you think younger workers are more likely to be injured on the job?
5. For each of the following occupations, identify at least one possible hazard and at least one action employees could take to minimize the risk of an injury or illness related to that hazard.
   a. Worker in a fast-food restaurant
   b. Computer programmer
   c. Worker in a special care home for seniors
   d. House painter
6. Why are exit interviews and stay interviews important? Should an organization care about the opinions of people who are leaving or are at risk of leaving?
7. What are the direct and indirect costs associated with employee turnover?
8. What should HR's role be in corporate social responsibility?
9. How important is your organization's reputation? Would you be prepared to earn less to work for an organization with an outstanding corporate social responsibility track record?
10. Do you see issues such as concern for the environment and ethics as short-term fads or long-term factors important to organizational success? Explain your perspective.

WHAT'S YOUR HR IQ?

The Online Learning Centre offers more ways to check what you've learned so far. Find experiential exercises as well as Test Your Knowledge Quizzes, Videos, and many other resources at www.mcgrawhill.ca/olc/steen.

Case:
Quebec Company Fined $110,000 in Worker's Death

In a historic sentencing, a Quebec court has ordered a company convicted of criminal negligence in the death of a worker to pay $110,000. In December 2007, Transpavé, a paving-stone manufacturer in Saint-Eustache, Quebec, pleaded guilty to criminal negligence in the 2005 death of 23-year-old Steve L'Écuyer.

Quebec court Judge Paul Chevalier handed down the $110,000 fine on March 17, 2008. Andrée Beaulieu, L'Écuyer's mother, told reporters she was disappointed with the fine and that she had expected a penalty in the millions. In October 2005, L'Écuyer was crushed by a machine that stacks concrete blocks after pallets with concrete had backed up on the conveyer belt. Inspectors found the machine's safety guard had been disabled for nearly two years.

Transpavé was charged with, and pleaded guilty to, criminal negligence causing death under the amendments to the Criminal Code brought in by Bill C-45, known as the "corporate killing law." This was the first criminal conviction since the amendments came into force in 2004.

In his ruling, the judge said the company, managers and employees weren't aware that the safety guard wasn't working and that there was no intent on the company's part for the system to be down. He also stated the fine reflected the company's willingness to take responsibility for the incident and the $500,000 in safety upgrades the company has made since 2006 to bring the plant in line with European standards, which are more stringent than North American standards.

In a statement after the sentencing, the company reiterated its "most sincere regrets to L'Écuyer's family."

In its own written statement, the Quebec Federation of Labour stated company managers should have been held accountable for the incident, not just the company as a corporate entity. Only a significant fine, for which they would be personally responsible for paying, will make managers truly value employee health and safety, said Michel Arsenault, president of the federation. Arsenault also said the Crown botched the case by describing the company as exemplary in its health and safety record while there were numerous health and safety complaints lodged against the company.

However, Transpavé's lawyer Claude Mageau said a safety commission employee testified that while there were complaints, there were no convictions or fines.

SOURCE: "Quebec Company Fined $110,000 in Worker's Death," *Canadian HR Reporter*, March 18, 2008, www.hrreporter.com, retrieved March 18, 2008.

Questions
1. How would you rate Transpavé's commitment to safety? Explain your answer.
2. Do you think company managers should also have been held accountable for this workplace fatality? Why or why not?
3. If you were a manager at Transpavé, what would you do differently in the future to protect the health and safety of employees?

Case:
Fairmont Finds It's Easy Being Green

While the health of the world's ecosystem is a hot topic, it has been a priority at Fairmont Hotels and Resorts since 1990. With the debut of its Green Partnership, the Toronto-based company initated a chain-wide environmental program. Since then, the program has expanded to 40 locations around the world, garnered several international awards, and been an inspiration for others in the hospitality industry and beyond. The move to greener pastures was prompted by the company's locations (then known as Canadian Pacific Hotels) in sensitive environments, such as national parks, biosphere reserves, and

coastal zones or wetlands. "We realized we had to mitigate our operation impacts on the environment, because if you take care of the environment, you take care of the very resource that brings your guests to explore in the first place," said Michelle White, director of environmental affairs at Fairmont.

Looking to have a gentler environmental footprint, the company first focused on waste management (recycling, organics diversion, and food and goods redistribution), energy conservation (lighting retrofits, HVAC upgrades, alternative technology, and sustainability), and water conservation (tap aerators, low-flow shower heads, low-flush toilets, and wastewater recycling).

The rise of responsible tourism has also meant Fairmont is sharing the benefits of business with the community, particularly in emerging markets where economic development is a challenge. A Fairmont property in Mexico is selling local tours, and giving part of the proceeds back to the community and the rest to a conservation fund for the biosphere. "Over time, we realized you couldn't be a really green hotel and good corporate citizen unless you also look at your community involvement," said White.

Beyond helping the environment, Fairmont has seen gains in areas such as guest loyalty, brand identity, and media interest, while developing a reputation as an environmental leader and demonstrating corporate social responsibility. There have also been cost efficiencies, such as lighting or retrofits that reduce utilities consumption, though White admits costs can vary, depending on the supporting infrastructure.

Fairmont has garnered award-praise for its efforts. In 2006, it received the global tourism business award for the best corporate social responsibility program at MKG's Worldwide Hospitality Awards and the global tourism business award from the World Travel and Tourism Council. But behind it all is the commitment and enthusiasm of its 26,000 employees around the world, including 10,500 in Canada. "Before implementing a program of this scale, you want to make sure you have a lot of employee buy-in," she said. "If they care about those things at home, they like to see that brought over to their workplace as well."

"The biggest challenge in any environmental program is making sure your employees are engaged, and that often comes with making sure employees are informed," White adds. For every new hotel or new market, the green program has been heartily embraced, said Mike Taylor, manager of media relations for Fairmont. "It's definitely something new employees latch on to and feel passionate about and are very connected to from day one," said Taylor. "At every single hotel, that's the predominant program that really resonates with new employees."

While the program is administered corporately, volunteer "green teams" at each property meet monthly to discuss and review ways to improve the operational performance in various departments. Fairmont also runs an environmental incentive program that recognizes the green team that has performed the best on a quarterly basis, and rewards two hotels that have had the best overall environmental performance each year. The green focus is definitely used as a retention tool and makes employees feel empowered. "They have an ownership or a management group that supports that approach to sustainable tourism," said Taylor. "And at the end of the day, it's right thing to do and it's the right thing for the planet."

SOURCE: Sarah Dobson, "Fairmont Finds It's Easy Being Green," *Canadian HR Reporter*, March 26, 2007, p. 14.

Questions

1. On the basis of the information provided in the case, what costs and benefits has Fairmont experienced by implementing its Green Partnership program?
2. Would you be more likely to be satisfied, engaged, and/or loyal, and/or remain with a company that shows evidence of corporate social responsibility such as being committed to the environment? Explain your response.

VIDEO CASE

Made in Canada

A strong dollar and cheap labour overseas are killing the country's manufacturing sector. Since 2004, 200,000 Canadian manufacturing sector jobs have been lost—most due to offshoring manufacturing to lower labour cost countries such as China.

Canada's own Mountain Equipment Co-op (MEC) maintains a vigorous social agenda including commitment to the environment, fair trade, and making a deliberate decision to sell a significant portion of Canadian goods even if it means making less profit. Although most of the hard goods such as tents and sleeping bags that MEC sells are manufactured overseas, CEO Peter Robinson describes how they are striving to support Canadian clothing factories. As of 2007, half of MEC's brand-name clothing was Canadian-made, a drop from 70 percent in 2002.

Questions

1. Would you be willing to pay more for a product to protect jobs in Canada? Why or why not?
2. Would you be more likely to buy products from MEC because of their demonstration of corporate social responsibility including commitment to the environment and to keeping Canadian clothing manufacturers in business?

SOURCE: Based on CBC, "Made in Canada," *The National*, May 30, 2007.

Preparing for and Acquiring Human Resources

Real People in HR

...Lyne Levasseur, Senior Market Manager, Randstad Canada

Lyne Levasseur is the Senior Market Manager with Randstad Canada, one of the largest staffing agencies in Canada. Lyne has over 20 years of management experience in the field of human resources, eight of which she gained at Randstad.

Name...
Lyne Levasseur.

Job...
Senior Market Manager—Randstad Canada.

Adjective people would use to describe you...
Determined.

First job...
Real estate sales.

First HR job...
As a manager for the past 20 years, I have been actively involved with many areas of human resources including recruitment, labour relations, and benefits.

What companies can do to prepare for talent shortages...
I think more and more companies are realizing that retirement does not always mean a complete loss of this individual's contribution. A lot of organizations have programs that allow older employees to stay on in some capacity—consultants, working part-time, or through mentorship programs with up-and-coming talent.

Organizations also need to consider the talent they currently have. It is of the utmost importance that employers understand Generation Y. Their views are different than preceding generations, no doubt. However, as the saying goes, we need to "get with the times." This generation is talented, they have much to offer, and it's our job as human resource professionals to ensure organizations have tactics in place to effectively attract, coach and develop, and retain this generation. Essentially, without a successful plan covering both aspects—retiring boomers and understanding the mindset of Generation Y—our future may hold in store poor performance, untapped potential, and higher-than-necessary attrition.

Most rewarding aspect of your job...
Helping people with their careers. Finding the right job opportunity for an individual helps them not only with income and security, but the right job, in the right environment, can positively impact so many areas of a person's life. The same can be said for the rewarding aspects of helping organizations build their team. We help with productivity, morale, retention, client satisfaction and so on. The environment is very fast-paced and can be demanding. The biggest challenge is managing priorities and remaining focused.

Four essential attributes that make someone a great HR professional...

Speaking specifically about recruitment, I would say that number one, in order to properly assess candidates and recognize talent, you need to have a genuine interest in others. Talent is not always obvious, so be engaged, learn their story! The second thing you need is to develop good questioning techniques that put people at ease. People are more likely to respond in a straightforward manner when the interviewer is on their side. Don't interrogate! Give candidates the opportunity to think and express themselves. You will be much more likely to extract valid, accurate, and pertinent data about the interviewee. The third essential attribute is you have to be kind and empathetic. Searching for a job is often not a pleasurable experience. Job seekers deal with the inevitable rejection and worries associated with their future and financial security, and often question their self-worth. Whether or not they are successful in obtaining a position through you, they should remember speaking with you and dealing with your company as a positive experience. Finally, act with urgency. Talented people are not unemployed or actively searching for long, and you need to appreciate that they are in demand. Respond quickly, move the process along as fast as possible to ensure both parties have the opportunity to consider each other before they accept someone else's job offer.

If you had to pick an alternative career...

It would definitely involve direct and frequent contact with people, where I could have impact on their careers or bring value in some way.

Best career advice that you ever received...

In retrospect, Career Advice 101 ... just plain good common sense: understand your talents and make sure that the environment you are in highly values those talents. Those qualities should be precisely what will drive your career and success in that position or environment.

Advice for hiring managers and potential employees...

Find a partnership with an organization that understands you. Work closely with your staffing consultant; take the time to teach them about your requirements. And then trust them to find solutions for you. Their recommendations and advice are based on specialized expertise in your field of interest. Fit goes beyond a job description or résumé. A successful placement involves assessment of boss fit, job fit, and cultural fit.

Advice for someone beginning an HR career...

Do your homework on any potential employer's values prior to accepting an employment offer. These should closely match your own. On a daily basis, you will be executing and making decisions in line with the organization's values—if these do not closely match your own, you may find yourself in conflict with your own beliefs of right and wrong. Ask for their values and look for past examples of actions that have supported those. Ask them what their position would be in hypothetical situations you may face.

4

Analyzing Work and Designing Jobs

What Do I Need to Know? After reading this chapter, you should be able to:

1. Summarize the elements of work flow analysis.

2. Describe how work flow is related to an organization's structure.

3. Define the elements of a job analysis, and discuss their significance for human resource management.

4. Tell how to obtain job analysis information.

5. Summarize recent trends in job analysis.

6. Describe methods for designing a job so that it can be done efficiently.

7. Identify approaches to designing a job to make it motivating.

8. Explain how organizations apply ergonomics to design safe jobs.

9. Discuss how organizations can plan for the mental demands of a job.

Introduction

The Information and Communications Technology Council (ICTC) works to address skills and human resource issues that impact companies in the information and communications technology (ICT) sector. The ICTC regularly receives calls from HR professionals complaining they are unable to find qualified candidates to fill vacant

ICT positions, says Paul Swinwood, president of the council. The problem is that too many different definitions are being used to describe job requirements and qualifications, resulting in rejections of applicants actually having the needed skills. The extent of the problem was demonstrated in a new survey of the Canadian ICT labour market, the *National Survey of Information Technology Occupations*, that involved more than 25,000 employers and 35,000 employees in both the private and public sectors.

"The study confirms that there is a lack of common understanding and definitions of what the ICT jobs are," says Swinwood. The Online Skills Profile Model (OSPM) is a human resource reference for ICT occupations that allows jobs to be compared across industries. In addition, an online self-assessment tool to assess knowledge and skills against industry standards for more than 35 jobs—for example, System Programming, Help Desk, Technical Writing, and Design Engineering—is available on ICTC's website (www.ictc-ctic.ca).

The council is striving to ensure that all ICT employees, and the organizations that employ them, share a clear picture of employer expectations for ICT occupations. The ICTC works closely with its sponsors, Human Resources and Social Development Canada, and Industry Canada, as well as its members from industry, educational institutions, and government. A sampling of member organizations includes McMaster University, Intuit Canada, Cisco Systems, NAIT, Algonquin College, Alberta Research Council, and the Canadian Council of Professional Engineers (CCPE).[1]

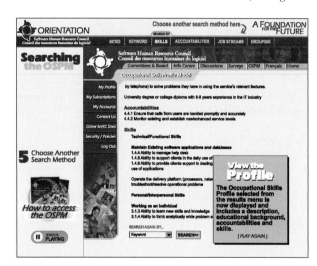

The ability to define jobs provides for the identification of the competencies required for success, and they in turn help to narrow the field of people who will succeed in an ICT career. Consideration of such elements is at the heart of analyzing work, whether in a small-to-medium-sized business, a multinational corporation, or the public sector.

This chapter discusses the analysis and design of work and, in doing so, lays out some considerations that go into making informed decisions about how to create and link jobs. The chapter begins with a look at the big-picture issues related to analyzing work flow and organizational structure. The discussion then turns to the more specific issues of analyzing and designing jobs. Traditionally, job analysis has emphasized the study of existing jobs in order to make decisions such as employee selection, training, and compensation. In contrast, job design has emphasized making jobs more efficient or more motivating. However, as this chapter shows, the two activities are interrelated.

Work Flow in Organizations

work flow design
The process of analyzing the tasks necessary for the production of a product or service.

job
A set of related duties.

position
The set of duties (job) performed by a particular person.

Informed decisions about jobs take place in the context of the organization's overall work flow. Through the process of **work flow design**, managers analyze the tasks needed to produce a product or service. With this information, they assign these tasks to specific jobs and positions. (A **job** is a set of related duties. A **position** is the set of duties performed by one person. A school has many teaching *positions*; the person filling each of those positions is performing the *job* of teacher.) Basing these decisions on work flow design can lead to better results than the more traditional practice of looking at jobs individually.

Work Flow Analysis

Before designing its work flow, the organization's planners need to analyze what work needs to be done. Figure 4.1 shows the elements of a work flow analysis. For each type of work, such as producing a product line or providing a support service (accounting, legal support, and so on), the analysis identifies the output of the process, the activities involved, and three categories of inputs: raw inputs (materials and information), equipment, and human resources.

Outputs are the products of any work unit, whether a department, team, or individual. An output can be as readily identifiable as a completed purchase order, an employment test, or a hot, juicy hamburger. An output can also be a service, such as transportation, cleaning, or answering questions about employee benefits. Even at an organization that produces tangible goods, such as computers, many employees produce other outputs, such as components of the computers, marketing plans, and building security. Work flow analysis identifies the outputs of particular work units. The analysis considers not only the amount of output but also quality standards. This attention to outputs has only recently gained attention among HR professionals. However, it gives a clearer view of how to increase the effectiveness of each work unit.

For the outputs identified, work flow analysis then examines the work processes used to generate those outputs. Work processes are the activities that members of a work unit engage in to produce a given output. Every process consists of operating procedures that specify how things should be done at each stage of developing the output. These procedures include all the tasks that must be performed in producing the output. Usually, the analysis breaks down the tasks into those performed by each person in the work unit. This analysis helps with design of efficient work systems by clarifying which tasks are necessary. Typically, when a unit's work load increases, the unit adds people, and when the work load decreases, some members of the unit may busy themselves with unrelated tasks in an effort to appear busy. Without knowledge of work processes, it is more difficult to identify whether the work unit is properly staffed. Knowledge of work processes also can guide staffing changes when work is automated or outsourced. At Unifi, a textile producer, high-speed data lines send shop floor data in real time to analysts at the company's headquarters. Unifi no longer requires supervisors to carry out the tasks of monitoring and reporting on production.[2] The final stage in work flow analysis is to identify the inputs used in the development of the work unit's product. As shown in Figure 4.1, these inputs can be broken down into the raw inputs (materials and knowledge), equipment, and human skills needed to perform the tasks. Makers of athletic shoes need nylon and leather, shoemaking machinery, and workers to operate the machinery, among other inputs. Nike and Reebok minimize the cost of inputs by subcontracting manufacturing to factories in countries where wages are low. In contrast, New Balance Athletic Shoes operates a factory in the United States, where modern

LO1 - Summarize the elements of work flow analysis.

Firefighters work as a team. They and their equipment are the "inputs" (they do the work), and the "output" is an extinguished fire and the rescue of people and pets. In any organization or team, workers need to be cross-trained in several skills to create an effective team. If these firefighters are trained to do any part of the job, the chief can deploy them rapidly as needed.

FIGURE 4.1

Developing a Work-Unit Activity Analysis

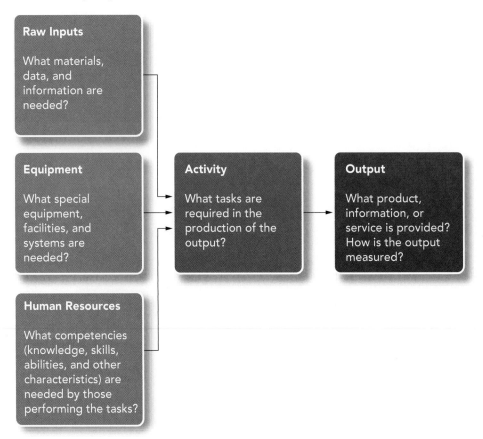

technology and worker training enable the company to afford North American workers. Teams of employees use automated equipment that operates over 20 sewing machines simultaneously. The employees are cross-trained in all tasks. The highly efficient factory produces shoes much faster than a typical shoe factory in China.[3]

LO2 - Describe how work flow is related to an organization's structure.

Work Flow Design and Organization's Structure

Besides looking at the work flow of each process, it is important to see how the work fits within the context of the organization's structure. Within an organization, units and individuals must cooperate to create outputs. Ideally, the organization's structure brings together the people who must collaborate in order to efficiently produce the desired outputs. The structure may do this in a way that is highly centralized (i.e., with authority concentrated in a few people at the top of the organization) or decentralized (with authority spread among many people). The organization may group jobs according to functions (e.g., welding, painting, packaging), or it may set up divisions to focus on products or customer groups.

Although there are an infinite number of ways to combine the elements of an organization's structure, we can make some general observations about structure and work design. If the structure is strongly based on function, workers tend to have low authority and to work alone at highly specialized jobs. Jobs that involve teamwork or broad responsibility tend to require a structure based on divisions other than functions. When the goal is to engage employees, companies therefore need to set up structures and jobs that enable broad responsibility, such as jobs that involve employees in serving a particular group of customers or producing a particular product, rather than performing a narrowly defined function. An extreme example would be W. L. Gore, described in the Best Practices box toward the end of this chapter. The organization's structure also affects managers' jobs. Managing a division responsible for a product or customer group tends to require more experience and cognitive (thinking) ability than managing a department that handles a specific function.[4]

Work design often emphasizes the analysis and design of jobs, as described in the remainder of this chapter. Although all of these approaches can succeed, each focuses on one isolated job at a time. These approaches do not necessarily consider how that single job fits into the overall work flow or structure of the organization. To use these techniques effectively, human resource professionals should also understand their organization as a whole. Without this big-picture appreciation, they might redesign a job in a way that makes sense for the job but is out of line with the organization's work flow, structure, or strategy.

Job Analysis

To achieve high-quality performance, organizations have to understand and match job requirements and people. This understanding requires **job analysis**, the process of getting detailed information about jobs. Analyzing jobs and understanding what is required to carry out a job provide essential knowledge for staffing, training, performance appraisal, and many other HR activities. For instance, a supervisor's evaluation of an employee's work should be based on performance relative to job requirements. In very small organizations, line managers may perform a job analysis, but usually the work is done by a human resource professional. A large company may have a compensation management or total rewards function that includes job analysts. Organizations may also contract with firms that provide this service.

Job Descriptions

A key outcome of job analysis is the creation of job descriptions. A **job description** is a list of the tasks, duties, and responsibilities (TDRs) that a job entails. TDRs are observable actions. For example, a news photographer's job requires the jobholder to use a camera to take photographs. If you were to observe someone in that position for a day, you would almost certainly see some pictures being taken. When a manager attempts to evaluate job performance, it is most important to have detailed information about the work performed in the job (i.e., the TDRs). This information makes it possible to determine how well an individual is meeting each job requirement.

A job description typically has the format shown in Figure 4.2. It includes the job title, a brief description of the TDRs, and a list of the essential duties with detailed specifications of the tasks involved in carrying out each duty. Although organizations may modify this format according to their needs, all job descriptions within an organization should follow the same format. This helps the organization make consistent decisions about such matters as pay and promotions. It also helps the organization show that it makes human resource decisions fairly.

LO3 - Define the elements of a job analysis, and discuss their significance for human resource management.

3

job analysis
The process of getting detailed information about jobs.

job description
A list of the tasks, duties, and responsibilities (TDRs) that a particular job entails.

FIGURE 4.2

Sample Job Description

PART-TIME SALES ASSOCIATE

Customer service and interaction with customers are key responsibilities of this position. A sales associate must work effectively with customers and other store associates and provide information about products and/or projects. This position also involves stocking merchandise, using tools and equipment, and maintenance duties (e.g., sweeping aisles, down-stocking shelves, etc.).

Position Responsibilities

- Provide outstanding customer service from initial greeting to the final sale
- Assess customer needs and provide expert advice about available products
- Create customer agreements for special order merchandise
- Demonstrate features and benefits of any product, which may complement the sale
- Merchandise and maintain the assigned area to its best image, i.e. displays, presentations, labels, signage, and ordering needs
- Participate in ensuring maintenance of department facing, stocking, and signing
- Complete paperwork on price changes
- Fill stock outs, end caps, and clip strips

SOURCE: Home Depot Canada website, http://jobsearch.homedepotcareers.ca, retrieved March 21, 2008.

HR HOW-TO

Writing a Job Description

Preparing a job description begins with gathering information from sources who can identify the details of performing a task. These sources may include persons already performing the job and, the supervisor, team leader, or, if the job is new, managers who are creating the new position. Asking the purpose of the new position can provide insight into what the company expects this person to accomplish. Besides people, sources of information may include the company's human resource files, such as past job advertisements and job descriptions, as well as

general sources of information about similar jobs, such as Human Resources and Social Development Canada's National Occupational Classification (NOC) system.

There are several ways to gather information about the duties of a job:

- Employees can fill out a questionnaire that asks about what they do or complete a diary that details their activities over several days.
- A job analyst can visit the workplace and watch or videotape an employee performing the job. This

method is most appropriate for jobs that are repetitive and involve physical activity.

- A job analyst can visit the workplace and ask an employee to show what the job entails. This method is most appropriate for clerical and technical jobs.
- A manager or supervisor can describe what a person holding the job must do to be successful. What would the jobholder's outputs be? Would customers have clear answers to their questions? Would decision makers in the organization have accurate and timely data from this

(continued)

HR HOW-TO

Writing a Job Description

person? The analyst can identify the activities necessary to create these outputs.

- A supervisor or job analyst can review company records related to performing the job—for example, work orders or summaries of customer calls. These records can show the kinds of problems a person solves in the course of doing a job.

After gathering information, the next thing to do is list all the activities and evaluate which are essential duties. One way to do this is to rate all the duties on a scale of 1 to 5, where 1 is most important. A rating scale could also rank the tasks according to how much time the person spends on them. Perhaps the ratings will show that some tasks are desirable but not essential.

Gathering information from many sources helps to verify which tasks are essential. Perhaps the jobholder is aware of some activities that others do not notice. In other cases, he or she might perform activities that are merely habits or holdovers from a time when they were essential. When different people analyzing a job come to different conclusions about which activities are essential, the person writing the job description should compare the listed activities with the company's goals and work flow

to see which are essential. A group discussion also may help categorize tasks as essential, ideal, and unnecessary.

From these sources, the writer of the job description obtains the important elements of the description:

- *Title of the job.* The title should be descriptive and, if appropriate, indicate the job's level in the organization by using terms such as junior, senior, assistant, and executive.
- *Administrative information about the job.* Depending on the company's size and requirements, the job description may identify a division, department, supervisor's title, date of the analysis, name of the analyst, and other information for administering the company's human resource activities.
- *Summary of the job, focusing on its purpose and duties.* This summary should be brief and as specific as possible, including types of responsibilities, tools and equipment used, and level of authority (e.g., the degree of authority and responsibility of the jobholder—how closely the person is supervised and how closely the person supervises others or participates in teamwork).

- *Essential duties of the job.* These should be listed in order of importance to successful performance of the job and should include details such as physical requirements (e.g., the amount of weight to be lifted), the persons with whom an employee in this job interacts, and the results to be accomplished. This section should include only duties that the job analysis identified as essential.
- *Additional responsibilities.* The job description may have a section stating that the position requires additional responsibilities as requested by the supervisor.
- *Job specifications.* The specifications cover the knowledge, skills, abilities, and other characteristics required for a person to be qualified to perform the job successfully. These may appear at the end of the job description or as a separate document.

SOURCE: D. B. Bordeaux, "Writing Job Descriptions," *Motor Age*, November 2001, retrieved from Findarticles .com; "Job Descriptions and the ADA," *HRNext*, www.hrnext.com, retrieved March 7, 2002; "Simple Job Analysis," *HRNext*, www.hrnext.com, retrieved March 7, 2002; C. Joinson, "Refocusing Job Descriptions," *HR Magazine*, January 2001, retrieved from Findarticles.com; and Lou Adler, "Know What You're Looking For," *Inc.com*, March 2005, www.inc.com.

Whenever the organization creates a new job, it needs to prepare a job description, using a process such as the one detailed in the HR How-To box. Job descriptions should then be reviewed periodically (say once a year) and updated if necessary. Performance appraisals can provide a good opportunity for updating job descriptions, as the employee and supervisor compare what the employee has been doing against the details of the job description.

When organizations prepare many job descriptions, the process can become repetitive and time-consuming. To address this challenge, a number of companies have developed software that provides forms into which the job analyst can insert details about the specific job. Typically, the job analyst would use a library of basic descriptions, selecting one that is for a similar type of job and then modifying it to fit the organization's needs.

Organizations should provide each newly hired employee a copy of his or her job description. This helps the employee to understand what is expected, but it shouldn't be presented as limiting the employee's commitment to quality and customer satisfaction. Ideally, employees will want to go above and beyond the listed duties when the situation and their abilities call for that. Many job descriptions include the phrase *and other duties as required* as a way to remind employees not to tell their supervisor, "But that's not part of my job."

Job Specifications

job specification
A list of the competencies an individual must have to perform a particular job.

Whereas the job description focuses on the activities involved in carrying out a job, a **job specification** looks at the qualities of the person performing the job. It is a list of the **competencies**, that is, knowledge, skills, abilities, and other characteristics associated with effective job performance. *Knowledge* refers to factual or procedural information necessary for successfully performing a task. For example, this course is providing you with knowledge in how to manage human resources. A *skill* is an individual's level of proficiency at performing a particular task—the capability to perform it well. With knowledge and experience, you could acquire skill in the task of preparing job specifications. *Ability*, in contrast to skill, refers to a more general enduring capability that an individual possesses. A person might have the ability to cooperate with others or to write clearly and precisely. Finally, *other characteristics* might be personality traits such as someone's persistence or motivation to achieve. Some jobs also have legal requirements, such as licensing or certification. Figure 4.3 gives a set of sample job specifications for the job description in Figure 4.2.

competencies
Knowledge, skills, abilities, and other characteristics associated with effective job performance.

In developing job specifications, it is important to consider all of the elements of the competencies. As with writing a job description, the information can come from a combination of people performing the job, people supervising or planning for the job, and trained job analysts. At Acxiom Corporation, job specifications are based on an analysis of employees' roles and competencies (what they must be able to do), stated in terms of behaviours. To reach these definitions, groups studied what the company's good performers were doing and looked for the underlying abilities. For example, according to Jeff Standridge, Acxiom's organizational development leader, they might ask a panel about a high-performing software developer, and panel members might identify the employee's knowledge of the Java and C++ programming languages. Then, Standridge says, the job analysts would probe for the abilities behind this knowledge: "When we asked, 'If Java becomes obsolete in five years, will this person no longer be successful?' the panel responded, 'Oh no, he'll update his skills and be great in the new language.' . . . The employee's strength was not just in his specific skills but in his ability to learn."[5] On a less serious level, the cartoon in

FIGURE 4.3

Sample Job
Specifications

PART-TIME SALES ASSOCIATE

Experience/Knowledge Required

- Excellent communication skills with a strong sense of customer service

- Knowledge and adherence to Home Depot policies and procedures

- Self-motivated and able to work independently

- High level of enthusiasm

- Excellent team player and able to work with people at all levels

- Mature attitude and a strong work ethic are essentials

- Good decision-making abilities and problem-solving skills

SOURCE: Home Depot Canada website, http://jobsearch.homedepotcareers.ca, retrieved March 21, 2008.

Figure 4.4 shows a young team member who seems to have an abundance of basketball skills but a limited supply of other desirable characteristics, such as orientation toward teamwork.

In contrast to tasks, duties, and responsibilities, competencies are characteristics of people and are observable only when individuals are carrying out the TDRs of the job—and afterward, if they can show the product of their labour. Thus, if someone applied for a job as a news photographer, you could not simply look at the individual to determine whether he or she can spot and take effective photographs. However, you would be able to draw conclusions later about the person's skills by looking at examples of his or her photographs.

Accurate information about competencies is especially important for making decisions about who will fill a job. A manager attempting to fill a position needs information about the characteristics required, and about the characteristics of each applicant. Interviews and selection decisions should therefore focus on competencies. In the earlier example of computer programming at Acxiom, the company would look for

FIGURE 4.4

Does This Player Have the Right Competencies to Succeed?

SOURCE: CLEATS © Bill Hinds. Reprinted with permission of Universal Press Syndicate. All rights reserved.

someone who knows the computer languages currently used, but also has a track record of taking the initiative to learn new computer languages as they are developed.

The identification of competencies is also being implemented widely in the public sector. The federal government has developed a Corporate Competency Profile for Middle Managers that identifies 14 leadership competencies. These competencies include detailed descriptions, such as the behaviours as well as the knowledge, skills, and abilities associated with each competency. Competencies identified for middle managers in the federal public sector include intellectual competencies (e.g., cognitive capacity); management competencies (e.g., teamwork); relationship competencies (e.g., communication); and personal competencies (e.g., stamina or stress resistance).[6]

Operations that need to run 24 hours a day have special job requirements. For example, shutting down certain equipment at night may be inefficient or cause production problems; and some industries, such as security and health care, may have customers who demand services around the clock. Globalization often means that operations take place across many time zones, requiring management at all hours. When a job entails working night shifts, job specifications should reflect this requirement. For most people, working at night disrupts their normal functioning and may cause disorders such as fatigue, depression, and obesity. However, people show wide variability in how well they respond to working at night. Research has found that people who work well at night tend to prefer sleeping late in the morning and staying up late. They also tend to sleep easily at different times of day, like to take naps, and exercise regularly. When job specifications call for nighttime work, a person's ability to handle a nocturnal work life may be the most critical competency.[7]

Sources of Job Information

L04 - Tell how to obtain job analysis information.

Information for analyzing an existing job often comes from incumbents, that is, people who currently hold that position in the organization. They are a logical source of information, because they are most acquainted with the details of the job. Incumbents should be able to provide very accurate information.

A drawback of relying solely on incumbents' information is that they may have an incentive to exaggerate what they do, to appear more valuable to the organization. Information from incumbents should therefore be supplemented with information from observers, such as supervisors. Supervisors should review the information provided by incumbents, looking for a match between what incumbents are doing and what they are supposed to do. Research suggests that incumbents may provide the most *accurate* estimates of the actual time spent performing job tasks, while supervisors may be more accurate in reporting information about the *importance* of job duties.[8]

National Occupational Classification (NOC)

Tool created by the federal government to provide a standardized source of information about jobs in Canada's labour market.

The federal government also provides background information for analyzing jobs. Human Resources and Social Development Canada working with Statistics Canada created the **National Occupational Classification (NOC)** to provide standardized sources of information about jobs in Canada's labour market. The NOC is a tool that uses a four-digit code to classify occupations based on the types and levels of skills required. The NOC classification system (www.hrsdc.gc.ca) supports the needs of employers, individual job seekers, as well as career counsellors, statisticians, and labour market analysts, by providing a consistent way to identify and interpret the nature of work. A recent addition to the site is a publication titled "Job Descriptions: An Employers' Handbook" that may be particularly helpful to managers and human resource professionals.

Other significant sources of information about jobs in Canada are organized according to the NOC classifications. For example, Job Futures (www.jobfutures.ca) provides information about occupational outlooks. Figure 4.5 shows job duties and requirements for the job of a Specialist in Human Resources as identified by the NOC.

FIGURE 4.5

Job Description and Job Specifications for Specialists in Human Resources (NOC 1121)

SPECIALISTS IN HUMAN RESOURCES (NOC 1121)

What They Do (Job Description)

Specialists in human resources perform some or all of the following duties:

- Advise managers and employees on the interpretation of personnel policies, compensation and benefit programs and collective agreements.

- Research employee benefit and health and safety practices and recommend changes or modifications to existing policies.

- Plan, develop, implement and evaluate personnel and labour relations strategies including policies, programs and procedures to address an organization's human resource requirements.

- Negotiate collective agreements on behalf of employers or workers, mediate labour disputes and grievances and provide advice on employee and labour relations.

- Research and prepare occupational classifications, job descriptions, salary scales and competency appraisal measures and systems.

- Plan and administer staffing, total compensation, training and career development, employee assistance, employment equity and affirmative action programs.

- Manage programs and maintain human resources information and related records systems.

- Hire and oversee training of staff.

- Coordinate employee performance and appraisal programs.

What You Need (Job Specifications)

- You must complete either a university degree or a professional development program or college diploma in personnel administration or a related field (business administration, industrial relations, commerce, psychology) and five years of experience.

- You may be required to gain experience in a clerical or administrative position related to personnel administration.

- With experience, you may move up the ranks to become a manager.

- One of the factors creating additional complexity in the skills required is the growing and changing body of law applied to human resources. You will be required to interpret and apply these laws and to keep pace with changes.

- Most recent entrants have an undergraduate university degree or a college diploma.

SOURCE: Service Canada website, www.jobfutures.ca/noc/1121.shtml, retrieved March 21, 2008. Reproduced with the permission of the Minister of Public Works and Government Services, 2008.

Position Analysis Questionnaire

After gathering information, the job analyst uses the information to analyze the job. One of the broadest and best-researched instruments for analyzing jobs is the **Position Analysis Questionnaire (PAQ)**, a standardized tool containing 194 items that represent work behaviours, work conditions, and job characteristics that apply to a wide variety of jobs, and are organized into six sections concerning different aspects of the job:

Position Analysis Questionnaire (PAQ)
A standardized job analysis questionnaire containing 194 questions about work behaviours, work conditions, and job characteristics that apply to a wide variety of jobs.

1. *Information input.* Where and how a worker gets information needed to perform the job.
2. *Mental processes.* The reasoning, decision making, planning, and information processing activities involved in performing the job.
3. *Work output.* The physical activities, tools, and devices used by the worker to perform the job.
4. *Relationships with other persons.* The relationships with other people required in performing the job.
5. *Job context.* The physical and social contexts where the work is performed.
6. *Other characteristics.* The activities, conditions, and characteristics other than those previously described that are relevant to the job.

The person analyzing a job determines whether each item on the questionnaire applies to the job being analyzed. The analyst rates each item on six scales: extent of use, amount of time, importance to the job, possibility of occurrence, applicability, and special code (special rating scales used with a particular item). The PAQ headquarters uses a computer to score the questionnaire and generate a report that describes the scores on the job dimensions.

Using the PAQ provides an organization with information that helps in comparing jobs, even when they are dissimilar. The PAQ also has the advantage that it considers the whole work process, from inputs through outputs. However, the person who fills out the questionnaire must have postsecondary-level reading skills, and the PAQ is meant to be completed only by job analysts trained in this method.[9] Also, the descriptions in the PAQ reports are rather abstract, so the reports may not be useful for writing job descriptions or redesigning jobs.

Task Analysis Inventory

task analysis inventory
Job analysis method that involves listing the tasks performed in a job and rating each task according to a defined set of criteria.

Another type of job analysis method, the **task analysis inventory**, focuses on the tasks performed in a job. This method has several variations. In one, the task inventory–CODAP method, subject-matter experts such as job incumbents generate a list of the tasks performed in a job. Then they rate each task in terms of time spent on the task, frequency of task performance, relative importance, relative difficulty, and length of time required to learn the job. The CODAP computer program organizes the responses into dimensions of similar tasks.[10]

Task analysis inventories can be very detailed, including 100 or more tasks. This level of detail can be helpful for developing employment tests and criteria for performance appraisal. However, they do not directly identify competencies needed for success in a job.

Fleishman Job Analysis System

To gather information about worker requirements, the **Fleishman Job Analysis System** asks subject-matter experts (typically job incumbents) to evaluate a job in terms of the abilities required to perform the job.[11] The survey is based on 52 categories of abilities, ranging from written comprehension to deductive reasoning, manual dexterity, stamina, and originality. As in the example in Figure 4.6, the survey items are arranged into a scale for each ability. Each begins with a description of the ability and a comparison to related abilities. Below this is a seven-point scale with phrases describing extremely high and low levels of the ability. The person completing the survey indicates which point on the scale represents the level of the ability required for performing the job being analyzed.

Fleishman Job Analysis System
Job analysis technique that asks subject-matter experts to evaluate a job in terms of the abilities required to perform the job.

Written Comprehension

This is the ability to understand written sentences and paragraphs.
How written comprehension is different from other abilities:

This Ability   **Other Abilities**

Understand written English words, sentences, and paragraphs.   vs. *Oral comprehension* (1): *Listen and understand spoken* English words and sentences.

vs. *Oral expression* (3): and *written expression* (4): *Speak or write* English words and sentences so others will understand.

Requires understanding of complex or detailed information in **writing** containing unusual words and phrases and involving fine distinctions in meaning among words.

7 ← Understand an instruction book on repairing a missile guidance system.
6
5
4 ← Understand an apartment lease.
3
2
1 ← Read a road map.

Requires understanding short, simple **written** information containing common words and phrases.

FIGURE 4.6

Example of an Ability from the Fleishman Job Analysis System

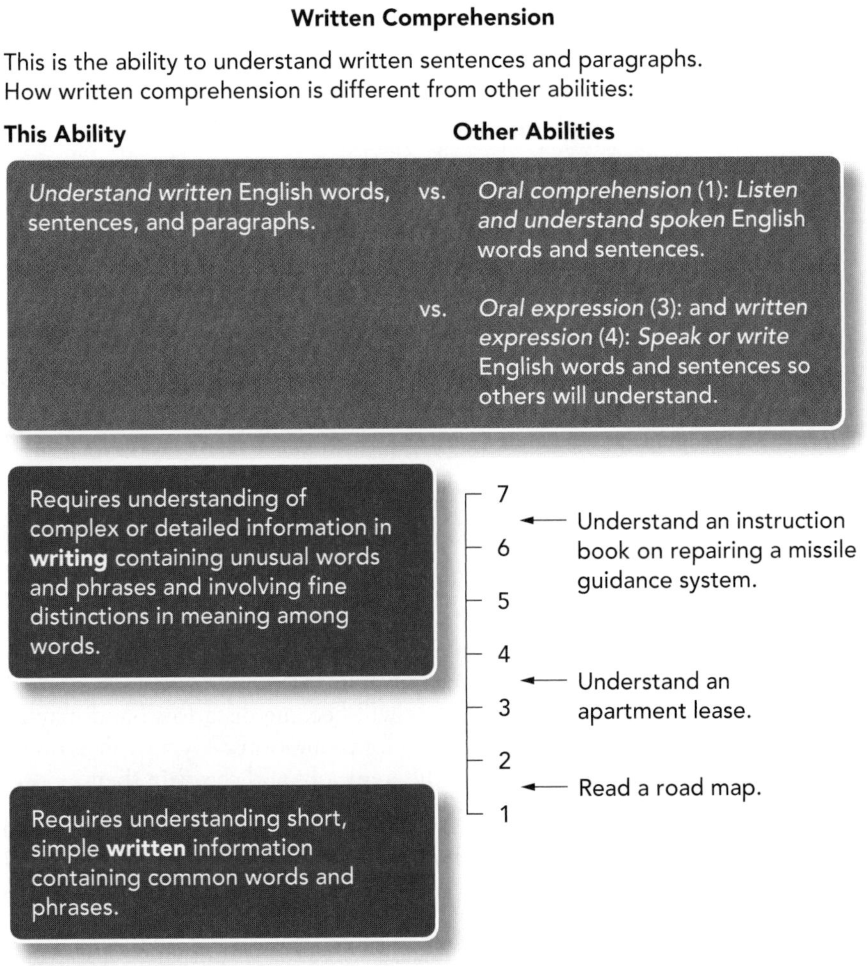

SOURCE: A. Fleishman and M. D. Mumford, "Evaluating Classifications of Job Behavior: A Construct Validation of the Ability Requirements Scales," *Personnel Psychology* 44 (1991), pp. 523–76. The complete set of ability requirement scales, along with instructions for their use, may be found in E. A. Fleishman, *Fleishman Job Analysis Survey (F-JAS)* (Palo Alto, CA: Consulting Psychologists Press, 1992). Used with permission.

When the survey has been completed in all 52 categories, the results provide a picture of the ability requirements of a job. Such information is especially useful for employee selection, training, and career development.

Importance of Job Analysis

Job analysis is so important to HR managers that it has been called the building block of everything that HR does.[12] The fact is that almost every human resource management program requires some type of information gleaned from job analysis:[13]

- *Work redesign.* Often an organization seeks to redesign work to make it more efficient or to improve quality. The redesign requires detailed information about the existing job(s). In addition, preparing the redesign is similar to analyzing a job that does not yet exist.

- *Workforce planning.* As planners analyze human resource needs and how to meet those needs, they must have accurate information about the levels of skill required in various jobs, so that they can tell what kinds of human resources will be needed.

- *Selection.* To identify the most qualified applicants for various positions, decision makers need to know what tasks the individuals must perform, as well as the necessary knowledge, skills, and abilities.

- *Training.* Almost every employee hired by an organization will require training. Any training program requires knowledge of the tasks performed in a job, so that the training is related to the necessary knowledge and skills.

- *Performance appraisal.* An accurate performance appraisal requires information about how well each employee is performing in order to reward employees who perform well and to improve their performance if it is below expectations. Job analysis helps in identifying the behaviours and the results associated with effective performance.

- *Career planning.* Matching an individual's skills and aspirations with career opportunities requires that those responsible for developing career planning processes know the skill requirements of the various jobs. This facilitates matching of individuals to jobs in which they will succeed and be satisfied.

- *Job evaluation.* The process of job evaluation involves assessing the relative value of each job to the organization in order to set up fair pay structures. If employees do not believe pay structures are fair, they will become dissatisfied and may quit, or they will not see much benefit in striving for promotions. To put values on jobs, it is necessary to get information about different jobs and compare them.

Job analysis supports several of these activities when it comes to automating major job duties, as described in the e-HRM box. The Royal Canadian Mounted Police (RCMP) has an automated resource, a database that identifies the functions and competency requirements of specific RCMP jobs; it integrates information about jobs to various HR functions. For example, the database links "Job Profiles," materials to help understand what the job is all about, with "Development Activities," which provide information about formal learning opportunities including workshops, online courses, and offline resources such as articles and videos. The link "Problem-Based Learning" leads to scenarios that test one's skills, and "Performance Management" allows employees and their supervisors to get assistance in determining competencies for further development.[14]

E- HRM

Self-Service Kiosks Make Work Different at Airport Terminals

Airport ticket agents once had jobs that were largely repetitive. One by one, passengers approached them, tickets in hand, to check in, receive seat assignments and boarding passes, and check their baggage. Today, however, airline passengers are more likely to bypass the ticket agent.

The technology behind the change is the Internet coupled with the airport self-service kiosk. Travellers today go online to make reservations. Instead of a printed ticket, they are likely to receive an e-ticket, or confirmation of their online reservation. Then, when travellers arrive at the airport, hundreds of thousands of them head for self-service kiosks, such as those used by Air Canada. These travellers would rather do much of the check-in work themselves instead of waiting in line for an agent. By swiping a credit card and touching a screen, they can obtain their boarding passes and find out which gate to go to. Air Canada self-service kiosks also provide travellers expanded capabilities

such as requesting an earlier departure, entering frequent-flyer information, entering passport information, and even checking in groups.

More and more airline passengers are checking themselves in. In 2007, the proportion of travellers buying tickets online for flights was 49 percent, confirming that booking via the Internet is becoming the norm. There is a sharp jump in the number of travellers using self-check-in—up overall from 23 percent in 2006 to 30 percent in 2007, with business travellers most likely to opt for self-service.

The main attraction is time-saving. Besides being able to quickly and easily check in at the airport, passengers also like the direct access to information. Instead of discussing seat assignments with an agent, hoping to be clear about what they want, they can look at a seating chart and choose an available seat that suits them best. Airport kiosks also offer information in several languages, an option few agents can match.

When airlines began using airport kiosks, some worried that ticket agents' jobs would be phased out. In fact, airlines have been making cuts in recent years but not primarily among ticket agents. The main impact on agents is that their jobs have changed rather than been eliminated. Instead of processing a steady stream of routine check-ins, the agents now handle special problems and requests. Airlines need agents who can respond to unusual concerns and develop solutions aimed at satisfying travellers. This change must affect the recruiting, selection, training, and performance evaluation of ticket agents.

SOURCE: Based on: Charles Fishman, "The Tool of a New Machine," *Fast Company*, May 2004, pp. 90–95; "Passenger Self-Service: Beyond the Hype: Complex Challenges and SITA Solutions" and "Power to the People—the Dominance of Self-Service," www.sita.aero, retrieved March 20, 2008; www.aircanada.com/en/travelinfo/airport/expresscheckin; "Case-Study—Air Canada Passengers & IBM Self-Service Kiosk," http://whitepapers.silicon.com, retrieved March 20, 2008.

Job analysis is also important from a legal standpoint. As we saw in Chapter 2, governments impose requirements related to human rights and pay equity. Detailed, accurate, objective job specifications help decision makers comply with these requirements by keeping the focus on tasks and abilities. Employers have a legal obligation to eliminate discrimination against employees and prospective employees with disabilities. Job redesign may be required to consider the needs of the job applicant to ensure that accommodation is provided. When accommodation is discussed with the employee or job applicant, it is important to use language that focuses on the person's abilities, rather than the person's disability. For example, ask all employees regardless of whether they have a disability, "Will you require accommodation to perform this task?" rather than, "Can you perform this task?"[15]

Besides helping human resource professionals, job analysis helps supervisors and other managers carry out their duties. Data from job analysis can help managers identify the types of work in their units, as well as provide information about the work flow process, so that managers can evaluate whether work is done in the most efficient way. Job analysis information also supports managers as they make hiring decisions, review performance, and recommend rewards.

Trends in Job Analysis

L05 - Summarize recent trends in job analysis.

2,3

As we noted in the earlier discussion of work flow analysis, organizations are beginning to appreciate the need to analyze jobs in the context of the organization's structure and strategy. In addition, organizations are recognizing that today's workplace is constantly subject to change and must be adaptable. Thus, although we tend to think of "jobs" as something stable, they actually evolve. Those who occupy or manage jobs often make minor adjustments to match personal preferences or changing conditions.[16] Indeed, although errors in job analysis can have many sources, most of the inaccuracy is likely to result from job descriptions being outdated. For this reason, job analysis must not only define jobs when they are created, but also detect changes in jobs as time passes. Competency requirements of a job may be more stable and long-lasting than the tasks, duties, and responsibilities associated with that job. In addition, an organization also requires specific competencies to be successful in a dynamic environment. Many organizations have developed a **competency framework** that identifies the competencies the entire organization requires to be successful. This framework is then used to assist in determining the competencies required by specific departments, teams, and jobs within the organization.

competency framework
Competencies the entire organization requires to be successful.

In today's world of rapidly changing products and markets, some observers have even begun to suggest that the concept of a "job" is obsolete. Some researchers and businesspeople have observed a trend they call *dejobbing*—viewing organizations as a field of work needing to be done, rather than as a set or series of jobs held by individuals. For example, at Amazon.com, HR director Scott Pitasky notes, "Here, a person might be in the same 'job,' but three months later be doing completely different work."[17] This means Amazon.com puts more emphasis on broad worker competencies ("entrepreneurial and customer-focused") than on detailed job descriptions ("HTML programming"), which may not be descriptive one year down the road.

Amazon.com practises "dejobbing," or designing work by project rather than by jobs. What would appeal to you about working for a company organized like this?

These changes in the nature of work and the expanded use of "project-based" organizational structures require the type of broader understanding that comes from an analysis of work flows. Because the work can change rapidly and it is impossible to rewrite job descriptions every week, job descriptions and specifications need to be flexible. At the same time, legal requirements (as discussed in Chapter 2) may discourage organizations from writing flexible job descriptions, so organizations must balance the need for flexibility with the need for legal documentation. This presents one of the major challenges to be faced by HRM departments in the next decade. Many professionals are meeting this challenge with a greater emphasis on careful job design.

Job Design

Although job analysis, as just described, is important for an understanding of existing jobs, organizations also must plan for new jobs and periodically consider whether they should revise existing jobs. When an organization is expanding, supervisors and human resource professionals must help plan for new or growing work units. When an organization is trying to improve quality or efficiency, a review of work units and processes may require a fresh look at how jobs are designed.

These situations call for **job design**, the process of defining the way work will be performed and the tasks that a given job requires, or *job redesign*, a similar process that involves changing an existing job design. To design jobs effectively, a person must thoroughly understand the job itself (through job analysis) and its place in the larger work unit's work flow process (through work flow analysis). Having a detailed knowledge of the tasks performed in the work unit and in the job, a manager then has many alternative ways to design a job. As shown in Figure 4.7, the available approaches emphasize different aspects of the job: the mechanics of doing a job efficiently, the job's impact on motivation, the use of safe work practices, and the mental demands of the job.

job design
The process of defining the way work will be performed and the tasks that a given job requires.

Designing Efficient Jobs

If workers perform tasks as efficiently as possible, not only does the organization benefit from lower costs and greater output per worker, but workers should be less fatigued. This point of view has for years formed the basis of classical **industrial engineering**, which looks for the simplest way to structure work in order to maximize

LO6 - Describe methods for designing a job so that it can be done efficiently.

industrial engineering
The study of jobs to find the simplest way to structure work in order to maximize efficiency.

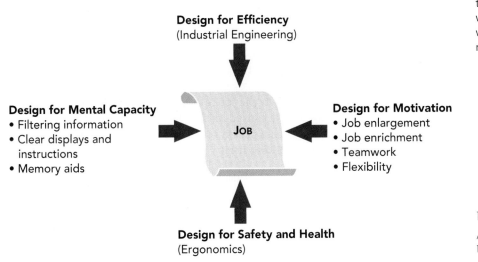

FIGURE 4.7

Approaches to Job Design

efficiency. Typically, applying industrial engineering to a job reduces the complexity of the work, making it so simple that almost anyone can be trained quickly and easily to perform the job. Such jobs tend to be highly specialized and repetitive.

In practice, the scientific method traditionally seeks the "one best way" to perform a job by performing time-and-motion studies to identify the most efficient movements for workers to make. Once the engineers have identified the most efficient sequence of motions, the organization should select workers based on their ability to do the job, then train them in the details of the "one best way" to perform that job. The company also should offer pay structured to motivate workers to do their best. (Chapter 9 discusses pay and pay structures.)

Despite the logical benefits of industrial engineering, a focus on efficiency alone can create jobs that are so simple and repetitive that workers get bored. Workers performing these jobs may feel their work is meaningless. Hence, most organizations combine industrial engineering with other approaches to job design.

Designing Jobs That Motivate

L07 - Identify approaches to designing a job to make it motivating.

Especially when organizations have to compete for employees, depend on skilled knowledge workers, or need a workforce that cares about customer satisfaction, a pure focus on efficiency will not achieve human resource objectives. These organizations need jobs that employees find interesting and satisfying, and job design should take into account factors that make jobs motivating to employees.

The quest for meaningful work draws people to such career paths as teaching and public service. For example, when Patrick Bernhardt was laid off from his job as a marketing executive, he seized on the chance to switch fields. Bernhardt became a computer science teacher and enrolled in evening classes. When he switched to this job, Bernhardt took a 50 percent pay cut, but he doesn't mind: "This is the hardest thing I've ever done, but the sense of satisfaction makes it worth it."[18]

A model that shows how to make jobs more motivating is the Job Characteristics Model, developed by Richard Hackman and Greg Oldham. This model describes jobs in terms of five characteristics:[19]

1. *Skill variety.* The extent to which a job requires a variety of skills to carry out the tasks involved.
2. *Task identity.* The degree to which a job requires completing a "whole" piece of work from beginning to end (e.g., building an entire component or resolving a customer's complaint).
3. *Task significance.* The extent to which the job has an important impact on the lives of other people.
4. *Autonomy.* The degree to which the job allows an individual to make decisions about the way the work will be carried out.
5. *Feedback.* The extent to which a person receives clear information about performance effectiveness from the work itself.

As shown in Figure 4.8, the more of each of these characteristics a job has, the more motivating the job will be, according to the Job Characteristics Model. The model predicts that a person with such a job will be more satisfied and will produce more and better work. This approach to designing jobs includes such techniques as job enlargement, job enrichment, self-managing work teams, flexible work schedules, and telework.

FIGURE 4.8

Characteristics of a Motivating Job

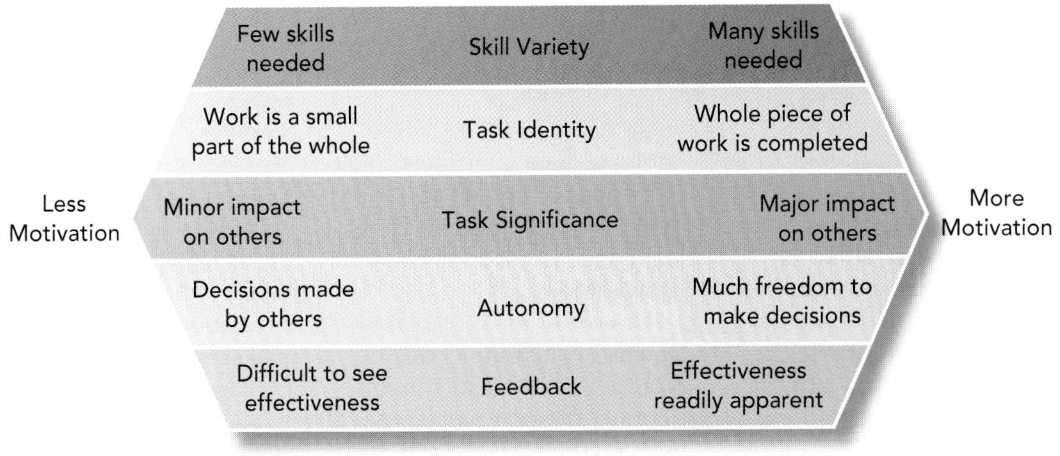

Few skills needed	Skill Variety	Many skills needed
Work is a small part of the whole	Task Identity	Whole piece of work is completed
Minor impact on others	Task Significance	Major impact on others
Decisions made by others	Autonomy	Much freedom to make decisions
Difficult to see effectiveness	Feedback	Effectiveness readily apparent

Less Motivation   More Motivation

Job Enlargement

In a job design, **job enlargement** refers to broadening the types of tasks performed. The objective of job enlargement is to make jobs less repetitive and more interesting. Methods of job enlargement include job extension and job rotation.

Job extension is enlarging jobs by combining several relatively simple jobs to form a job with a wider range of tasks. An example might be combining the jobs of receptionist, data entry clerk, and file clerk into jobs containing all three kinds of work. This approach to job enlargement is relatively simple, but if all the tasks are dull, workers will not necessarily be more motivated by the redesigned job.

Job rotation does not actually redesign the jobs themselves, but moves employees among several different jobs. This approach to job enlargement is common among production teams. During the course of a week, a team member may carry out each of the jobs handled by the team. Team members might assemble components one day and pack products into cases another day. As with job extension, the enlarged jobs may still consist of repetitious activities, but with greater variation among those activities.

Job Enrichment

The idea of **job enrichment**, or engaging workers by adding more decision-making authority to their jobs, comes from the work of Frederick Herzberg. According to Herzberg's two-factor theory, individuals are motivated more by the intrinsic aspects of work (e.g., the meaningfulness of a job) than by extrinsic rewards such as pay. Herzberg identified five factors he associated with motivating jobs: achievement, recognition, growth, responsibility, and performance of the entire job. Thus, ways to enrich a manufacturing job might include giving employees authority to stop production when quality standards are not being met and having each employee perform several tasks to complete a particular stage of the process, rather than dividing up the tasks among the employees. For a salesperson in a store, job enrichment might involve the authority to resolve customer problems, including the authority to decide whether to issue refunds or replace merchandise.

job enlargement
Broadening the types of tasks performed in a job.

job extension
Enlarging jobs by combining several relatively simple jobs to form a job with a wider range of tasks.

job rotation
Enlarging jobs by moving employees among several different jobs.

job enrichment
Engaging workers by adding more decision-making authority to jobs.

BEST PRACTICES

Jobs Without Titles Promote Innovation at W. L. Gore

When *Fast Company* magazine set out to find an innovative company, they eliminated some of the biggest contenders and settled on W. L. Gore & Associates, best known for creating Gore-Tex fabrics. Besides Gore-Tex, the company makes fabrics for such tough applications as clothing for soldiers and astronauts. It also makes medical products, air pollution filters, and hundreds of other items as diverse as dental floss and guitar strings. In fact, the company thrives on innovation: Gore employees are urged to look everywhere for opportunities to make something better than what is currently on the market.

How do you structure work when the commitment is to creativity? Structure might seem to stifle creativity, but Gore's work design is actually extremely flexible. The organizational structure is remarkably flat, with communication rather than formal authority as the basis for getting work done. Gore is organized into four broad product divisions, each with a division leader, but most employees don't have job titles. The only way to know who is doing what is to learn what everyone does. The company keeps facilities small (factories contain up to 200 people) so that people can learn each other's skills and knowledge.

The experience of Diana Davidson illustrates how the type of work design affects people. The company hired her for its Citywear project, applying Gore-Tex fabrics to clothing designs suitable for office or party wear. From her experience in the hierarchical men's shoe business, Davidson found the freedom of Gore confusing at first. She was assigned to a mentor, who discouraged her repeated questions about who her boss was. Eventually, Davidson concluded, "Your team is your boss, because you don't want to let them down." She figured out that people didn't need strict titles and job descriptions because their work was guided by whatever commitment they had made to their team— commitments that might bring together several functions, such as sales and product design.

Davidson and others find that this work design requires patience to learn team members' skills and roles. John Mongan, who has participated in several Gore teams, says the first job on a new team is to spend a few months getting to know the team. He adds, "It takes 18 months to build credibility. Early on, it's really frustrating. In hindsight, it makes sense."

This flat structure with limited formal job design might stop a routine company in its tracks, but Gore is far from routine. It hires talented people and then enables them to draw on the best of each other's skills to produce one high-value product after another. As they gain skills, employees are expected to find new roles in which they can apply their additional skills. Because Gore is a privately held company (not traded on the stock market), it doesn't publish the financial statements used to compare businesses' success. But its growing product line, increasing payroll, and satisfied customers and employees testify to the company's success.

SOURCE: Alan Deutschman, "The Fabric of Creativity," *Fast Company,* December 2004, pp. 54–55, 58–62, www.fastcompany.com/magazine/89/open_gore.html, retrieved August 28, 2008.

Self-Managing Work Teams

Instead of merely enriching individual jobs, some organizations engage employees by designing work to be done by self-managing work teams. As described in Chapter 1, these teams have authority for an entire work process or segment. Team members typically have authority to schedule work, hire team members, resolve problems related to the team's performance, and perform other duties traditionally handled by management. Teamwork can give a job such motivating characteristics as autonomy, skill variety, and task identity.

Because team members' responsibilities are great, their jobs usually are defined broadly and include sharing of work assignments. Team members may, at one time or another, perform every duty of the team. The challenge for the organization is to provide enough training so that the team members can learn the necessary skills. Another approach, when teams are responsible for particular work processes or customers, is to assign the team responsibility for the process or customer, then let the team decide which members will carry out which tasks.

Teamwork can certainly make jobs more interesting, but teamwork's effectiveness is not guaranteed. Self-managing teams are most likely to accomplish their goals if they involve 6 to 18 employees who share the same technology (tools or ideas), location, and work hours. Such teams can be especially beneficial when a group's skills are relatively easy to learn (so that employees can readily learn one another's jobs) and demand for particular activities shifts from day to day (requiring flexibility). In addition, the job specifications should help the organization identify employees who will be willing and able to cooperate for the team's success. Such employees likely will have good problem-solving skills and be able to communicate well.

A study of work teams at a large financial services company found that the right job design was associated with effective teamwork.[20] In particular, when teams are self-managed and team members are highly involved in decision making, teams are more productive, employees more satisfied, and managers more pleased with performance. Teams also tend to do better when each team member performs a variety of tasks and when team members view their effort as significant.

Employees who have enriched jobs and/or work in self-managed teams can be engaged and motivated when they have decision-making authority.

3

Flexible Work Schedules

One way an organization can give employees some say in how their work is structured is to offer flexible work schedules. Depending on the requirements of the organization and the individual jobs, organizations may be able to be flexible in terms of when employees work. As introduced in Chapter 1, types of flexibility include flextime and job sharing. Figure 4.9 illustrates alternatives to the traditional 40-hour workweek.

Flextime is a scheduling policy in which full-time employees may choose starting and ending times within guidelines specified by the organization. The flextime policy may require that employees be at work between certain hours, say, 10:00 a.m. and 3:00 p.m. Employees work additional hours before or after this period in order to work the full day. One employee might arrive early in the morning in order to leave at 3:00 p.m. to pick up children after school. Another employee might be a night-owl who prefers to arrive at 10:00 a.m. and work until 6:00, 7:00, or even later in the evening. A flextime policy may also enable workers to adjust a specific day's hours in order to make time for doctor's appointments, children's activities, hobbies, or volunteer work. A work schedule that allows time for community and family interests can be extremely motivating for some employees.

Job sharing is a work option in which two part-time employees carry out the tasks associated with a single job. Such arrangements can enable an organization to attract or retain valued employees who want more time to attend school or to care for family members. The job requirements in such an arrangement include the ability to work cooperatively and coordinate the details of one's job with another person.

flextime
A scheduling policy in which full-time employees may choose starting and ending times within guidelines specified by the organization.

job sharing
A work option in which two part-time employees carry out the tasks associated with a single job.

FIGURE 4.9

Alternatives to the 8-to-5 Job

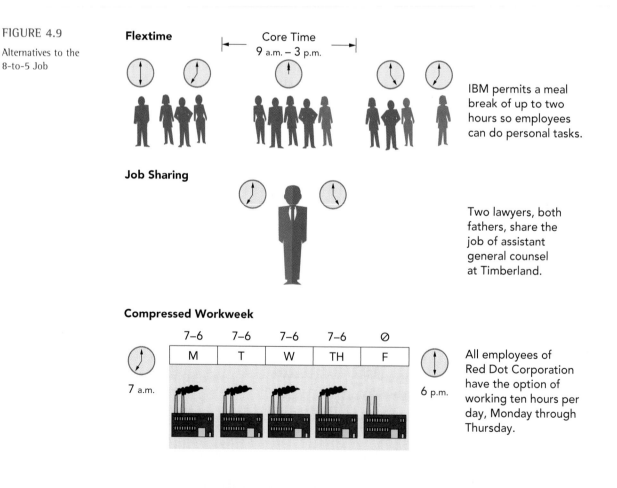

Flextime

Core Time
9 a.m. – 3 p.m.

IBM permits a meal break of up to two hours so employees can do personal tasks.

Job Sharing

Two lawyers, both fathers, share the job of assistant general counsel at Timberland.

Compressed Workweek

7–6	7–6	7–6	7–6	∅
M	T	W	TH	F

7 a.m.   6 p.m.

All employees of Red Dot Corporation have the option of working ten hours per day, Monday through Thursday.

Although not strictly a form of flexibility on the level of individual employees, another scheduling alternative is the *compressed workweek*. A compressed workweek is a schedule in which full-time workers complete their weekly hours in fewer than five days. For example, instead of working eight hours a day for five days, the employees might complete 40 hours of work in four 10-hour days. This alternative is most common, but some companies use other alternatives, such as scheduling 80 hours over nine days (with a three-day weekend every other week) or reducing the workweek from 40 to 38 or 36 hours. Employees may appreciate the extra days available for leisure, family, or volunteer activities. An organization might even use this schedule to offer a kind of flexibility—for example, letting workers vote on whether they want a compressed workweek during the summer months. This type of schedule has a couple of drawbacks, however. One is that employees may become exhausted on the longer workdays. Another is that if the arrangement involves working more than a specific number of hours during a week, employment (labour) standards legislation may require the payment of overtime wages to nonsupervisory employees.

Remote Work Arrangements

Flexibility can extend to work locations as well as work schedules. Before the Industrial Revolution, most people worked either close to or inside their own homes. Mass production technologies changed all this, separating work life from home life, as people began to travel to centrally located factories and offices. Today, however, prices for gasoline, office space, combined with drastically reduced prices for computers and communication technologies and easy access to the Internet—for example wireless access and hot spots—seem poised to reverse this trend. The broad term for doing one's work away from a centrally located office is *remote work*, *telework*, or *telecommuting*. Recently, the concept known as *distributed work* has been increasingly made available to employees in companies including Bell Canada ("flexSpace"), IBM ("eMobility"), Sun Microsystems ("iWork"), Boeing ("Virtual Office"), and T4G, the company featured along with Bell Canada in the chapter-ending case study. **Distributed work** is "a combination of work options, including work from the

distributed work
A combination of work options, including work from the corporate office, work from home, work from a satellite office, or work from another remote location.

FIGURE 4.10

Distributed Work—Working Where You Are

"YOU KNOW YOUR PROBLEM, HARLAN? YOU NEED TO GET IN TOUCH WITH YOUR 'INNER BEACH BUM.'"

corporate office, work from home, work from a satellite office or work from another remote location.[21] Distributed work programs might require employees to give up a dedicated office space.

For employers, advantages of distributed work include less need for office space and the ability to offer greater flexibility to employees. "The demographic skills crunch is coming. More employees, particularly the baby boomers, are interested in flexible work arrangements but, ironically, so are Generations X and Y. So you have three generations right now, for different reasons, looking for flexible work arrangements," says George Horhota, co-founder and executive vice-president of SuiteWorks, a Barrie, Ontario–based provider of satellite office space. "Employees love distributed work. It empowers them to have a choice as to where they work best today."[22] Approximately 10 percent of the workforce are classified as teleworkers, but there has been a recent stall in telework numbers as reported by Statistics Canada.[23] However, the overall trend to distributed work is becoming the norm for knowledge workers, for example, people in managerial, professional, or sales jobs. As is illustrated in Figure 4.11, *where* work is being performed is being transformed from the traditional office setting to a variety of remote locations including clients' offices, airplanes, airport lounges, hotels, cottages and vacation properties, coffee shops, homes, and satellite offices located close to employees' homes.[24]

Central British Columbia's Interior Health Authority delivers services to a region with difficult winter driving conditions, where in recent years a doctor and a nurse have been killed in motor vehicle accidents. Dr. David Stewart, urologist and chief of the department of surgery at the Royal Inland Hospital in Kamloops, is one of this growing number of Canadians accessing their workplace technologies from remote locations. Dr. Stewart uses a remote access system to examine X-ray images over the Internet while consulting with a local physician who can view the same image simultaneously. He can view patients' lab results and charts from his home computer before making his hospital rounds. As a result, Dr. Stewart has more time with his family, while the health authority, through accurate offsite diagnoses, reduces costs associated with unnecessary ambulance trips and hospital stays.[25]

FIGURE 4.11

Evolution of the Workplace

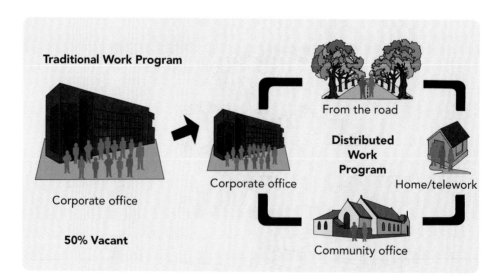

Designing Ergonomic Jobs

How people use their bodies when they work—whether toting heavy furniture onto a moving van or sitting quietly before a computer screen—affects their physical well-being and may affect how well and how long they can work. The study of the interface between individuals' physiology and the characteristics of the physical work environment is called **ergonomics.** The goal of ergonomics is to minimize physical strain on the worker by structuring the physical work environment around the way the human body works. Ergonomics therefore focuses on outcomes such as reducing physical fatigue, aches and pains, and health complaints.

L08 - Explain how organizations apply ergonomics to design safe jobs.

3,7

ergonomics
The study of the interface between individuals' physiology and the characteristics of the physical work environment.

Ergonomic job design has been applied in redesigning equipment used in jobs that are physically demanding. Such redesign is often aimed at reducing the physical demands of certain jobs so that anyone can perform them. In addition, many interventions focus on redesigning machines and technology—for instance, adjusting the height of a computer keyboard to minimize occupational illnesses, such as carpal tunnel syndrome. The design of chairs and desks to fit posture requirements is very important in many office jobs. One study found that having employees participate in an ergonomic redesign effort significantly reduced the number and severity of repetitive strain injuries (injuries that result from performing the same movement over and over), lost production time, and restricted-duty days.[26]

Often, redesigning work to make it more worker-friendly also leads to increased efficiencies. For example, at International Truck and Engine Corporation, one of the most difficult aspects of truck production was pinning the axles to the truck frame. Traditionally, the frame was lowered onto the axle, and a crew of six people, armed with oversized hammers and crowbars, forced the frame onto the axle. Because the workers could not see the bolts they had to tighten under the frame, the bolts were often fastened improperly, and many workers injured themselves in the process. After a brainstorming session, the workers and engineers concluded it would be better to flip the frame upside down and attach the axles from above. The result was a job that could be done twice as fast by half as many workers, who were much less likely to make mistakes or get injured.[27]

Ergonomically designed workstations have adjustable components, enabling the employee to modify the workstation to accommodate various job and physical requirements.

Similarly, at a 3M plant, the company spent $60,000 on new ramps and forklifts specifically to help its aging workers lift crates filled with the company's product. The crates weighed over 125 pounds and were the source of numerous employee complaints. The result of this change in work processes was that productivity went up (expressed in terms of time to load trucks) and workers' compensation claims in the factory went to zero in the next year—down from an average of 20 over the past five years. These positive outcomes far outstripped the cost of the changes, again illustrating how a change aimed at improving the work from an ergonomic point of view often leads to cost savings as well.[28]

The Canadian Centre for Occupational Health and Safety identifies several workplace conditions that pose ergonomic hazards:[29]

- Repetitive and forceful movements
- Vibration
- Temperature extremes
- Awkward postures that arise from improper work methods
- Improperly designed workstations, tools, and equipment

When jobs have these conditions, employers should be vigilant about opportunities to improve work design, for the benefit of both workers and the organization.

LO9 - Discuss how organizations can plan for the mental demands of a job.

Designing Jobs That Meet Mental Capabilities and Limitations

Just as the human body has capabilities and limitations, addressed by ergonomics, the mind, too, has capabilities and limitations. As more and more work activities become information processing activities, the need to consider *cognitive ergonomics* is likely to be an emerging trend.[30] Besides hiring people with certain mental skills, organizations can design jobs so that they can be accurately and safely performed given the way the brain processes information. Generally, this means reducing the information processing requirements of a job. In these simpler jobs, workers may be less likely to make mistakes or have accidents. Of course, the simpler jobs may also be less motivating.

There are several ways to simplify a job's mental demands. One is to limit the amount of information and memorization the job requires. Organizations can also provide adequate lighting, easy-to-understand gauges and displays, simple-to-operate equipment, and clear instructions. Often, employees try to simplify some of the mental demands of their own jobs by creating checklists, charts, or other aids. Finally, every job requires some degree of thinking, remembering, and paying attention, so for every job, organizations need to evaluate whether their employees can handle the job's mental demands.

Applying the perceptual approach to the job of cashier, electronic cash registers have simplified some aspects of this job. In the past, a cashier read the total price displayed by a cash register, received payment, then calculated any change due the customer. Today, most stores have cash registers that compute the change due and display that amount. The cash register display makes the job easier. However, some cashiers may have been proud of their ability to calculate change due, and for these people, the introduction of electronic cash registers may have reduced their job satisfaction. In this way, simplifying the mental demands of a job can also make it less interesting.

Because of this drawback to simplifying jobs, it can be most beneficial to simplify jobs where employees will most appreciate having the mental demands reduced (as in a job that is extremely challenging) or where the costs of errors are severe (as in the job of a surgeon or air-traffic controller). A relatively recent source of complexity in many jobs is the need to process a daily flood of messages beyond just email, including instant messaging and mobile messaging. Canadian Internet users, on average, receive more than 200 emails every week. A recent study released by Ipsos Reid has found that although 66 percent of Canadian prefer communicating via email over other methods, 44 percent say that can hardly keep up with their email.[31]

Organizations take various steps to manage this challenge. Many have established policies—for example, limiting personal use of company email and restricting the number of Internet discussion groups to which employees may subscribe. Some companies delete email messages once a month. Another alternative is to install software that filters spam (electronic "junk mail") by looking for and blocking messages that match spam databases or have characteristics of spam. Of course, generators of spam continuously look for ways to evade these filters, so individual employees have to develop ways of managing email, just as they have simplified other aspects of their jobs in the past.[32] For highly mobile knowledge workers, the ability to be "always reachable" makes additional mental demands. For example, 92 percent of knowledge workers read, send, make or take work-related messages in nonwork situations.[33]

THINKING ETHICALLY

Who's Responsible When Workers Get Hurt?

One of the considerations of job design is ergonomics, but which measures are effective is still being debated. Without universal standards and with little history from which to learn, many employers worry that failing to fully address ergonomic job design may have very big implications: worker plain and suffering; compromised attendance, morale and productivity; and potentially crippling costs.

A "bed war" is being waged among luxury hotel chains—guests enjoy more luxurious mattresses, bed linens, and pillows. However, the impact on room attendants includes heavier workloads, and a higher risk of developing repetitive strain injuries (RSIs). Consider the recent dispute between Fairmont Royal York and its room attendants, represented by Local 75 of UNITE HERE.

The Fairmont Royal York brought in an ergonomics expert to evaluate staff techniques and provided training on how to perform tasks and minimize injury risk when its new mattresses were introduced, says Tammy Lynn Phillips, director of public relations for Fairmont Royal York. To reduce risk of RSIs for room attendants "we introduced fitted sheets to eliminate the need to lift the mattress" and "we have stopped all mattress flipping and now rotate the mattress using the handles."

However, according to Union spokesperson Andrea Calver, "23 of the hotel's 150 attendants are on modified work duties because of RSIs." She places the blame for the injuries on a 16-room shift quota combined with the increased workload. "Anything that requires a room attendant to do the same thing over and over and over again has the potential to lead to a repetitive strain injury," Calver says.

SOURCE: Based on Vanessa Mariga, "RSIs the Cost of Luxury, Union Contends," *OH & S Canada*, January/February 2006, p. 20.

Questions

1. What obligations, if any, do employers have to reduce the physical demands of jobs when workers experience fatigue, soreness, or injury from their work?
2. If you worked in a human resources department and workers complained to you about pain associated with repetitive motions, what would you recommend that the company do?

SUMMARY

LO1 **Summarize the elements of work flow analysis.**

- The analysis identifies the amount and quality of a work unit's outputs, which may be products, parts of products, or services.
- Next, the analyst determines the work processes required to produce these outputs, breaking down tasks into those performed by each person in the work unit.
- Finally, the work flow analysis identifies the inputs used to carry out the processes and produce the outputs.

LO2 **Describe how work flow is related to an organization's structure.**

- Within an organization, units and individuals must cooperate to create outputs, and the organization's structure brings people together for this purpose. The structure may be centralized or decentralized, and people may be grouped according to function or into divisions focusing on particular products or customer groups.
- A functional structure is most appropriate for people who perform highly specialized jobs and hold relatively little authority. Employee engagement and teamwork succeed best in a divisional structure. Because of these links between structure and types of jobs, considering such issues improves the success of job design.

LO3 **Define the elements of a job analysis, and discuss their significance for human resource management.**

- Job analysis is the process of getting detailed information about jobs. It includes preparation of job descriptions and job specifications.
- A job description lists the tasks, duties, and responsibilities of a job. Job specifications look at the qualities needed in a person performing the job. They list the competencies, that is, knowledge, skills, abilities, and other characteristics, that are required for successful performance of a job.
- Job analysis provides a foundation for carrying out many HRM responsibilities, including work redesign, workforce planning, employee selection and training, performance appraisal, career planning, and job evaluation to determine pay scales.

LO4 **Tell how to obtain job analysis information.**

- Information for analyzing an existing job often comes from incumbents and their supervisors. The federal government provides background information about jobs in the National Occupational Classification (NOC).
- Job analysts, employees, and managers may complete a Position Analysis Questionnaire or task analysis inventory, or fill out a survey for the Fleishman Job Analysis System.

LO5 **Summarize recent trends in job analysis.**

- Some organizations are *dejobbing*, or viewing organizations in terms of a field of work needing to be done, rather than as a set or series of jobs. These organizations look for employees who can take on different responsibilities as the field of work changes.
- Organizations are also adopting project-based structures and teamwork, which also require flexibility and the ability to handle broad responsibilities.

LO6 **Describe methods for designing a job so that it can be done efficiently.**

- The basic technique for designing efficient jobs is industrial engineering, which looks for the simplest way to structure work in order to maximize efficiency. Through methods such as time-and-motion studies, the industrial engineer creates jobs that are relatively simple and typically repetitive. These jobs may bore workers because they are so simple.

L07 Identify approaches to designing a job to make it motivating.

- According to the Job Characteristics Model, jobs are more motivating if they have greater skill variety, task identity, task significance, autonomy, and feedback about performance effectiveness. Ways to create such jobs include job enlargement (through job extension or job rotation) and job enrichment.

- Self-managing work teams offer greater skill variety and task identity. Flexible work schedules and telework offer greater autonomy.

L08 Explain how organizations apply ergonomics to design safe jobs.

- The goal of ergonomics is to minimize physical strain on the worker by structuring the physical work environment around the way the human body works.

- Ergonomic design may involve modifying equipment to reduce the physical demands of performing certain jobs or redesigning the jobs themselves to reduce strain. Ergonomic design may target working conditions associated with ergonomic hazards including repetitive and forceful movements, vibration, temperature extremes, and awkward postures that arise from improper work methods and improperly designed workstations, tools, and equipment.

L09 Discuss how organizations can plan for the mental demands of a job.

- Employers may seek to reduce mental as well as physical strain. The job design may limit the amount of information and memorization involved. Adequate lighting, easy-to-read gauges and displays, simple-to-operate equipment, and clear instructions can also minimize mental strain.

- Computer software can simplify jobs—for example, by performing calculations or filtering out spam from relevant email. Finally, organizations can select employees with the necessary abilities to handle a job's mental demands.

REVIEW AND DISCUSSION QUESTIONS

1. Assume you are the manager of a fast-food restaurant. What are the outputs of your work unit? What are the activities required to produce those outputs? What are the inputs?

2. With question 1 in mind, consider the cashier's job in the restaurant. What are the outputs, activities, and inputs for that job?

3. Consider the "job" of university or college student. Perform a job analysis on this job. What tasks are required in the job? What competencies are necessary to perform those tasks? Prepare a job description based on your analysis.

4. Discuss how the following trends are changing the skill requirements for managerial jobs in Canada:
   a. Increasing use of teamwork
   b. Increasing global competition
   c. Increasing cognitive job demands including the need to be reachable at all times

5. How can a job analysis of each job in the work unit help a supervisor to do his or her job?

6. Consider the job of a customer service representative who fields telephone calls from customers of a retailer that sells online and through catalogues. What measures can an employer take to design this job to make it efficient? What might be some drawbacks or challenges of designing this job for efficiency?

7. How might the job in question 6 be designed to make it more motivating? Would these considerations apply to the manager's job in question 1?

8. What ergonomic considerations might apply to each of the following jobs? For each job, what kinds of costs would result from addressing ergonomics? What costs might result from failing to address ergonomics?
   a. A computer programmer
   b. A UPS delivery person
   c. A child care worker

9. The chapter said that modern electronics have eliminated the need for a store's cashiers to calculate change due on a purchase. How does this development modify the job description for a cashier? If you were a store manager, how would it affect the skills and qualities of job candidates you would want to hire? Does this change in mental processing requirements affect what you would expect from a cashier? How?

10. Consider a job you hold now or have held recently. Would you want this job to be redesigned to place more emphasis on efficiency, motivation, ergonomics, or mental processing? What changes would you want, and why? (Or why do you not want the job to be redesigned?)

WHAT'S YOUR HR IQ?

The Online Learning Centre offers more ways to check what you've learned so far. Find experiential exercises as well as Test Your Knowledge Quizzes, Videos, and many other resources at www.mcgrawhill.ca/olc/steen.

BusinessWeek Case:
Why the "Laptop-on-a-Stick" Is a Hard-Pressed RN's Best Friend　BusinessWeek

When Melanie Weigeshoff joined Hackensack University Medical Center in 1998 as a nursing assistant, the hospital was still in the Dark Ages. Most medication orders, lab test results, and doctors' instructions for patient care were recorded on paper, in giant three-ring binders. Weigeshoff was constantly on the phone clarifying doctors' quickly scribbled notes, and she spent hours chronicling her patients' progress by hand. "We were always flipping, flipping, flipping through pages," she recalls, reenacting the frustration with frantic waves of her arms.

Today that primitive hospital is just a memory for Weigeshoff, now a staff nurse. Although she still uses paper on occasion, her primary tool is now a laptop-on-a-stick, a PC that rolls around on what looks like an IV stand. As she greets patients at the start of each shift, she logs in to their electronic records through a wireless connection. She reviews vital signs—temperature, heart rate—which had been entered into the computer by a nurse's aid earlier. Then she clicks over to the medication orders, making note of each dose on the computer after she delivers it. "Charting is more accurate now," she says, "because we're right there, doing everything in real time." Best of all she has shaved an hour of overtime off her day.

As the health care industry grapples with an unrelenting nursing shortage, technology has taken a leading role in keeping employees like Weigeshoff happy. Many of the demands of health care have been heaped onto nurses, burdening them with more patients to care for in less time and an endless flood of paperwork. The pressures have driven so many out of the profession that the supply of nurses is expected to fall 20 percent below the demand by 2010. Surveys reveal that one out of every three nurses under 30 plans to leave the job within a year. Technology that makes nurses' jobs easier won't be a panacea, but "it's an important consideration in making the hospital a better work environment, "says Carol J. Bickford, senior policy fellow.

Technology is lightening Weigeshoff's administrative load in all kinds of ways. As she prepares to visit patient Alvest Williams, she grabs the laptop and wheels it into his room. Earlier that day, a roboticized sorting machine in the pharmacy downstairs had read Alvest's prescriptions on his electronic chart and sent them to Weigeshoff's unit. As she checks each prescription on the screen, Williams calls out the names of the drugs in her basket to make sure Weigeshoff has everything, gesturing toward the laptop as if it were another person there to help him feel better. "Protonix?" asks the 60-year-old, who is recovering from pneumonia. "Yep," says Weigeshoff. In the past, she would have had to collect handwritten prescriptions, enter them into paper charts, and fax them to the pharmacy.

For Weigeshoff, the laptop-on-a-stick frees her to be the nurse she dreamed about being when she was growing up. As a teen, she relished the job of big sister, coddling her toddler brother and sister when they needed a Band-Aid on a scraped knee or a kiss on a bumped head. "I love taking care of people," says the ebullient nurse.

But when she first starting in nursing, she often struggled to find time for the caregiving part of her job. She was always on the phone with the pharmacy, pressing them for medication refills, or with doctors, trying to decipher handwriting. Now the system ensures that the pharmacy gets drugs to nurses on schedule and that almost every piece of information she needs is at her fingertips.

Weaning the nurses off traditional paper charts isn't always easy, though. "On the first day we go live [with the computer system] on a unit, everyone wants to kill me," says Teresa C. Moore, the hospital's manager of clinical informatics. "It's a drastic change." Unlike most of the doctors at Hackensack, the nurses are employees and are required to use technology in their jobs. Moore runs weekly user groups to gather feedback.

Weigeshoff welcomes any technology that will make her job easier. Paper charts won't go away anytime soon—the hospital still requires printed copies of everything entered in the computer, and some notes can't be made digitally yet. "I would love to never have to write again," she says. A dream? Maybe. But at Hackensack, it's getting closer to reality.

SOURCE: "The Nurse: Melanie Weigeshoff," *BusinessWeek*, March 28, 2005, www.businessweek.com/magazine/content/05_13/b3926007_mz001.htm, retrieved August 17, 2008.

Questions

1. Keeping in mind the information given, identify as many tasks, duties, and responsibilities of Weigeshoff's original job as you can. Then identify tasks, duties, and responsibilities of her job after the new technology was introduced.

2. Keeping in mind the information given, identify competencies—knowledge, skills, abilities, and other characteristics—required for successfully performing Weigeshoff's original job. Then do the same for her job with the new technology.

3. To complete a job description and job specifications for Weigeshoff's new job, what additional information would you need? How might you gather that information if you worked in the human resource department at the hospital where Weigeshoff works?

Case:
T4G and Bell Canada Offer Employees Distributed Work Programs

T4G

Real estate savings may be pegged as the chief reason distributed work is an appealing strategy to employers; but at T4G, a Toronto-based information technology firm specializing in Web and software development, there has been no attempt to cut down on office space. Every one of the 200 or so employees at T4G has a designated desk at one of the company's offices in Toronto, Saint John, Halifax, or Vancouver. That said, according to the company's vice-president of strategy, Paul Barter, employees spend less than half of their time in the office—they're either working from home or at a client site.

People are used to working on virtual teams at T4G, so it makes little difference where they are. The company's Microsoft Outlook is programmed to integrate voicemail and email. Whenever someone leaves a phone message, an alert appears in Outlook and the employee can retrieve the message via email. Conversely, the employee can use the telephone to have email read to him. In place of office chatter, employees use instant messaging to bounce ideas off each other. The company pays for everyone's laptop and high-speed Internet connection at home.

"We believe that work is an activity and not a location. As long as they get a job done, we don't care where they are," said Barter. The same mindset applies to the company's flexible-hour policy. "As long as they can keep the customer happy, we really don't care whether they start at 7 a.m. or 10 a.m. or whether they're in our office or at the customer office or at their home," said Barter.

The key to ensuring productivity does not fall off is to manage people by very specific metrics, such as expectations on deliverables and time frames relative to deliverables, he said. Financial results are reported every week so the executive team can find out quickly if any customer issues come up. Barter said the prime benefit of such a program has been the retention of people.

"From an HR perspective, we're in a market that was very tight in 1999–2000. And then there was too much capacity and the market slackened. And now it's tight again. The type of people we hire really do have a lot of options. And they're mature, self-managed individuals, working on individual projects," he said. That makes it easy to manage them remotely. On top of low employee turnover, Barter said the company has doubled in size in the last two years.

"The market certainly hasn't grown at that level," he said. "We're outgrowing the market and one reason for that is we can attract and retain employees when our major competitors have a more difficult time in attracting and retaining employees."

Bell Canada

Whether on contract or working full-time, all employees at Bell are eligible to take part in the company's distributed work program. All that's required is for the manager and the employee to agree the work allows for it and to sign an agreement. The program, which has been around more than 15 years, has three elements. The full-time telework element allows employees to work 100 percent of the time from home, with the company paying for the entire cost of home equipment. For those signed up for partial telework, the company pays for the computer and VPN access but not high-speed Internet.

The third option was introduced only last year, and that's to work a few days a week at one of Bell's six satellite offices in Quebec and Ontario. This option, branded *flexSpace*, allows people to cut down on commuting time or to take advantage of telework benefits even if they don't have the right setup at home, said Jean-Marc Ciot, senior consultant of information systems and information technology at Bell.

So far, out of an employee population of 45,000, 2,000 have signed up for full-time telework and 18,000 to 19,000 people are doing partial telework. The number of flexSpace participants is not yet available, but there are 40 spaces at each of the six sites and they're almost fully used.

The objective is to give flexibility to employees and offer them a different way to work, Ciot said, particularly mothers with young children who might want to spend more time at home for a couple of years. To make sure participants stay productive, the company offers training to both the full-time teleworker and to the employee's manager. The latter might cover such issues as the need for constant communication or the need to ensure the full-time teleworker does not feel excluded. Ciot said he rarely hears of communication or management issues from people working remotely.

"A person doing telework needs to be reachable every time, even more so than if they're in the office. If you work in the office these days, you'll find people not talking to their bosses every day. Often at Bell, a person might be working in Quebec and reporting to a boss in Toronto. It's not very different."

SOURCE: Uyen Vu, "A Variety of Options Gives Boost to Remote Work," *Canadian HR Reporter,* August 14, 2006, p. 15.

Questions

1. What are the benefits of distributed work to T4G and Bell Canada? What are the benefits of distributed work to employees at T4G and Bell Canada?
2. How does distributed work impact the tasks, duties, and responsibilities of jobs at T4G and Bell Canada?
3. How does distributed work impact the competency requirements of jobs at T4G and Bell Canada?
4. Is distributed work appealing to you? Why or why not?

Chapter 5

Planning for and Recruiting Human Resources

What Do I Need to Know? After reading this chapter, you should be able to:

1. Discuss how to plan for the human resources needed to carry out the organization's strategy.

2. Determine the demand for and supply of workers in various job categories.

3. Summarize the advantages and disadvantages of ways to eliminate a labour surplus and avoid a labour shortage.

4. Discuss the use of employment branding and recruitment policies organizations use to make job vacancies more attractive.

5. List and compare sources of job applicants.

6. Describe the recruiter's role in the recruitment process, including limits and opportunities.

Introduction

Would you meet the eligibility requirements to immigrate to Canada as a skilled worker or professional? The Citizenship and Immigration Canada website (www.cic .gc.ca) provides a test to help potential immigrants assess whether they would meet the requirements to immigrate to Canada as a skilled worker or professional.

Weiling Qian, a systems engineer from China, left, and Agnes van Haeren, the human resource manager for Motorola Canada, who hired Ms. Qian as an intern under the Career Bridge program: "I began to look for a job but employment agents who saw my résumé said I needed Canadian experience," Ms. Qian says.

The passing grade is 67 points out of a possible 100 points. Maximum points for education—25 points—requires applicants to have at least 17 years of full-time or full-time equivalent study and to hold a master's degree or a Ph.D. (two bachelor's degrees earns 22 points; a college diploma, trade certificate, or apprenticeship and at least 14 years of full-time equivalent study earns 20 points). Other criteria include ability in English and/or French, age (10 points if you are 21 to 49 years old), arranged employment in Canada and adaptability.[1]

Although Canada will require immigrants to fill various jobs and meet demand for skilled workers, internationally trained professionals face recruitment barriers. Ontario recently announced a $4 million program to assist internationally trained professionals in teaching, engineering, and health care gain access to jobs without duplicating education and training received outside Canada. One specific initiative, Career Bridge, provides employers in cities across Ontario and in Vancouver with access to internationally qualified professionals in areas such as business, information technology, and engineering. More than 130 participating organizations, including Motorola Canada, Bell Canada, Manulife Financial, the City of Toronto, FedEx, the Humber Institute of Technology, York University, and Hudson's Bay Company, have provided internships and paid positions lasting 4, 6, 9, or 12 months to job-ready immigrants legally able to work in Canada.[2]

Trends and events that affect the economy create opportunities and problems in obtaining human resources. When customer demand rises (or falls), organizations may need more (or fewer) employees. When the labour market changes—as when more people pursue postsecondary education or when a sizable share of the population retires—the supply of qualified workers may grow, shrink, or change in nature. Organizations recently have had difficulty filling information technology jobs, because the demand for people with these skills outstrips the supply. To prepare for and respond to these challenges, organizations engage in *workforce planning*—defined in Chapter 1 as identifying the numbers and types of employees the organization will require to meet its objectives.

This chapter describes how organizations carry out workforce planning. In the first part of the chapter, we lay out the steps that go into developing and implementing a human resource plan. Throughout each section, we focus especially on recent trends and practices, including downsizing, employing temporary workers, and outsourcing. The remainder of the chapter explores the process of recruiting. We discuss the importance of employment branding in attracting potential employees, the process by which organizations look for people to fill job openings, and the sources of job candidates. Finally, we discuss the role of recruiters.

1,2,3

The Process of Workforce Planning

Organizations should carry out workforce planning so as to meet business objectives and gain an advantage over competitors. To do this, organizations need a clear idea of the strengths and weaknesses of their existing internal labour force. They also must know what they want to be doing in the future—what size they want the organization to be, what products and services it should be producing, and so on. This knowledge helps them define the number and kinds of employees they will need. Workforce planning compares the present state of the organization with its goals for the future, then identifies what changes it must make in its human resources to meet those goals. The changes may include downsizing, training existing employees in new skills, or hiring new employees. The overall goal of workforce planning is to ensure the organization has the right people with the right skills in the right places at the right time.

These activities give a general view of workforce planning. They take place in the workforce planning process shown in Figure 5.1. The process consists of three stages: forecasting, goal setting and strategic planning, and program implementation and evaluation.

L01 - Discuss how to plan for the human resources needed to carry out the organization's strategy.

FIGURE 5.1

Overview of the Workforce Planning Process

Forecasting

The first step in workforce planning is **forecasting**, as shown in the top portion of Figure 5.1. In forecasting, the HR professional tries to determine the *supply* of and *demand* for various types of human resources. The primary goal is to predict which areas of the organization will experience labour shortages or surpluses.

Forecasting supply and demand can use statistical methods or judgment. Statistical methods capture historic trends in a company's demand for labour. Under the right conditions, these methods predict demand and supply more precisely than a human forecaster can using subjective judgment. But many important events in the labour market have no precedent. When such events occur, statistical methods are of little use. To prepare for these situations, the organization must rely on the subjective judgments of experts. Pooling their "best guesses" is an important source of ideas about the future.

Forecasting the Demand for Labour

Usually, an organization forecasts demand for specific job categories or skill areas. After identifying the relevant job categories or skills, the planner investigates the likely demand for each. The planner must forecast whether the need for people with the necessary skills and experience will increase or decrease. There are several ways of making such forecasts.

At the most sophisticated level, an organization might use **trend analysis**, constructing and applying statistical models that predict labour demand for the next year, given relatively objective statistics from the previous year. These statistics are called **leading indicators**—objective measures that accurately predict future labour demand. They might include measures of the economy (such as sales or inventory levels), actions of competitors, changes in technology, and trends in the composition of the workforce. For example, a manufacturer of automobile parts that sells its product to automakers would use statistics on the auto industry, using the numbers from recent time periods to predict the demand for the company's product in a later time period.

Statistical planning models are useful when there is a long, stable history that can be used to reliably detect relationships among variables. However, these models almost always have to be complemented with subjective judgments of experts. There are simply too many "once in a lifetime" changes to consider, and statistical models cannot capture them.

Determining Labour Supply

Once a company has forecast the demand for labour, it needs an indication of the firm's labour supply. Determining the internal labour supply calls for a detailed analysis of how many people are currently in various job categories or have specific skills within the organization. The planner then modifies this analysis to reflect changes expected in the near future as a result of retirements, promotions, transfers, voluntary turnover, and terminations.

One type of statistical procedure that can be used for this purpose is the analysis of a **transitional matrix**, which is a chart that lists job categories held in one period and shows the proportion of employees in each of those job categories in a future period. It answers two questions: "Where did people who were in each job category go?" and "Where did people now in each job category come from?" This process of tracking

TABLE 5.1

Transitional Matrix: Example for an Aerospace Parts Manufacturer

2006	2008							
	(1) Sales Manager	(2) Sales Rep	(3) Sales Apprentice	(4) Assistant Plant Manager	(5) Production Manager	(6) Production Assembler	(7) Clerical	(8) Not in Organization
1. Sales Manager	0.95							0.05
2. Sales Rep	0.05	0.60						0.35
3. Sales Apprentice		0.20	0.50					0.30
4. Assistant Plant Manager				0.90	0.05			0.05
5. Production Manager				0.10	0.75			0.15
6. Production Assembler					0.10	0.80		0.10
7. Clerical							0.70	0.30
8. Not in Organization	0.00	0.20	0.50	0.00	0.10	0.20	0.30	

and analyzing employee movement through jobs is also referred to as *Markov analysis*. Table 5.1 is an example of a transitional matrix.

This example lists job categories for an auto parts manufacturer. The jobs listed at the left were held in 2006; the numbers across show what happened to the people in 2008. The numbers represent proportions. For example, 0.95 means 95 percent of the people represented by a row in the matrix. The column headings under 2008 refer to the row numbers. The first row is "Sales Manager," so the numbers under column 1 represent people who were sales managers in 2008. Reading across the first row, we see that 95 percent of the people who were sales managers in 2006 were still sales managers in 2008. The other 5 percent correspond to column 8, "Not in Organization," meaning that 5 percent of people who were sales managers in 2006 left the organization. The second row is "Sales Reps." Of those who were sales reps in 2006, 5 percent were promoted to sales manager, 60 percent were still sales reps, and 35 percent left the organization. In row 3, half (50 percent) of "Sales Apprentices" were still in that job in 2008, but 20 percent are now sales reps, and 30 percent left the organization. This pattern shows a career path from sales apprentice to sales representative to sales manager. Of course, not everyone is promoted, and some people leave instead.

Reading down the columns provides another kind of information: the sources of employees holding the positions in 2008. In the first column, we see that most sales managers (95 percent) held that same job two years earlier. The other 5 percent were promoted from sales rep positions. Skipping to column 3, half the sales apprentices on the payroll in 2008 held the same job two years before, and the other half were hired from outside the organization. This suggests that the organization fills sales manager positions primarily through promotions, so planning for this job would focus on preparing sales representatives. In contrast, planning to meet the organization's needs for sales apprentices would emphasize recruitment and selection of new employees.

Matrices like this are extremely useful for charting historical trends in the company's supply of labour. More importantly, if conditions remain somewhat constant, they can also be used to plan for the future. For example, if we think we are going to have a surplus of labour in the production assembler job category in the next two years, we can plan to avoid layoffs. Still, historical data may not always reliably indicate future trends. Planners need to combine statistical forecasts of labour supply with expert judgments. For example, managers in the organization may see that a new training program will likely increase the number of employees qualified for new openings. Forecasts of labour supply also should take into account the organization's pool of skills. Many organizations include inventories of employees' skills in an HR database. When the organization forecasts that it will need new skills in the future, planners can consult the database to see how many existing employees have those skills.

Besides looking at the labour supply within the organization, the planner should examine trends in the external labour market. The planner should keep abreast of labour market forecasts, including the size of the labour market, the unemployment rate, and the kinds of people who will be in the labour market. For example, we saw in Chapter 1 that the labour market is aging and that immigration is an important source of new workers. Important sources of data on the external labour market are available from Statistics Canada. Details and news (releases from *The Daily*) are available at the Statistics Canada website (www.statcan.ca).

Determining Labour Surplus or Shortage

On the basis of the forecasts for labour demand and supply, the planner can compare the figures to determine whether there will be a shortage or surplus of labour for each job category. Determining expected shortages and surpluses allows the organization to plan how to address these challenges.

Issues related to a labour surplus or shortage can pose serious challenges for the organization. General Motors Corporation has addressed a labour surplus by instituting several hiring freezes over the last few years. One consequence is that the average age of its labour force is relatively old (estimated at age 48) with fully half of GM workers eligible to retire within the next few years. At the same time, GM has estimated that it needs to reduce its workforce by close to 20 percent, so its aging workforce offers an advantage. GM can wait and let retirement and natural attrition (people choosing to leave) take care of the needed downsizing. In terms of numbers, this solves the labour surplus problem, but it does not give the company control over which workers leave. The company has to make sure that the remaining employees have the necessary skills and are prepared to handle work that had been performed by the retiring employees. Also, GM spends more than most companies to pay pension and health care benefits for retirees. This substantial expense requires management as well.[3]

2,3

LO3 - Summarize the advantages and disadvantages of ways to eliminate a labour surplus and avoid a labour shortage.

Goal Setting and Strategic Planning

The second step in workforce planning is goal setting and strategic planning, as shown in the middle of Figure 5.1. The purpose of setting specific numerical goals is to focus attention on the problem and provide a basis for measuring the organization's success in addressing labour shortages and surpluses. The goals should come directly from the analysis of labour supply and demand. They should include a specific figure indicating what should happen with the job category or skill area and a specific timetable for when the results should be achieved.

TABLE 5.2

HR Strategies for
Addressing a Labour
Shortage or Surplus

OPTIONS FOR REDUCING A SURPLUS		
OPTION	SPEED OF RESULTS	AMOUNT OF SUFFERING CAUSED
Downsizing	Fast	High
Pay reductions	Fast	High
Demotions	Fast	High
Transfers	Fast	Moderate
Work sharing	Fast	Moderate
Hiring freeze	Slow	Low
Natural attrition	Slow	Low
Early retirement	Slow	Low
Retraining	Slow	Low

OPTIONS FOR AVOIDING A SHORTAGE		
OPTION LATER	SPEED OF RESULTS	ABILITY TO CHANGE
Overtime	Fast	High
Temporary employees	Fast	High
Outsourcing	Fast	High
Retrained transfers	Slow	High
Turnover reductions	Slow	Moderate
New external hires	Slow	Low
Technological innovation	Slow	Low

For each goal, the organization must choose one or more human resource strategies. A variety of strategies are available for handling expected shortages and surpluses of labour. The top of Table 5.2 shows major options for reducing an expected labour surplus, and the bottom of the table lists options for avoiding an expected labour shortage.

This planning stage is critical. The options differ widely in their expense, speed, and effectiveness. Options for reducing a labour surplus cause differing amounts of human suffering. The options for avoiding a labour shortage differ in terms of how easily the organization can undo the change if it no longer faces a labour shortage. For example, an organization probably would not want to handle every expected labour shortage by hiring new employees. The process is relatively slow and involves expenses to find and train new employees. Also, if the shortage becomes a surplus, the organization will have to consider laying off some of the employees. Layoffs involve another set of expenses, such as severance pay, and they are costly in terms of human suffering.

Another consideration in choosing an HR strategy is whether the employees needed will contribute directly to the organization's success. Organizations are most likely to benefit from hiring and retaining employees who provide an organizational **core competency**—that is, a set of knowledge and skills that provide the organization with a competitive advantage and create value for customers.. These core competencies taken together form a competency framework as discussed in Chapter 4. At a store,

core competency
A set of knowledge
and skills that
provide the
organization with
a competitive
advantage and
create value for
customers.

for example, core competencies include choosing merchandise that shoppers want and providing shoppers with excellent service. For other work not associated with a core competency—say cleaning the store and providing security—the organization may benefit from using HR strategies other than hiring full-time employees.

Organizations try to anticipate labour surpluses far enough ahead that they can freeze hiring and let natural attrition (people leaving on their own) reduce the labour force. Unfortunately for many workers, in the past decade, the typical way organizations have responded to a surplus of labour has been downsizing, which delivers fast results. Beyond the obvious economic impact, downsizing has a psychological impact that spills over and affects families, increasing the rates of divorce, child abuse, and drug and alcohol addiction.[4] To handle a labour shortage, organizations typically hire temporary employees or use outsourcing. Because downsizing, using temporary employees, and outsourcing are most common, we will look at each of these in greater detail in the following sections.

Downsizing

downsizing
The planned elimination of large numbers of personnel with the goal of enhancing the organization's competitiveness.

As we discussed in Chapter 1, **downsizing** is the planned elimination of large numbers of employees with the goal of enhancing the organization's competitiveness. Nortel Networks has gone through major downsizing worldwide. Nortel has cut approximately 60,000 jobs and is now only about one-third of its former size.[5] Over 85 percent of the Fortune 1000 firms downsized since 1987, resulting in more than 8 million permanent layoffs. The jobs eliminated were not temporary losses due to downturns in the business cycle, but permanent losses resulting from changes in the competitive pressures faced by businesses today. In fact, eight out of every ten companies that underwent downsizing were earning a profit at the same time.[6]

The primary reason organizations engage in downsizing is to promote future competitiveness. According to surveys, they do this by meeting four objectives:

1. *Reducing costs.* Labour is a large part of a company's total costs, so downsizing is an attractive place to start cutting costs.
2. *Replacing labour with technology.* Closing outdated factories, automating, or introducing other technological changes reduces the need for labour. Often, the labour savings outweighs the cost of the new technology.
3. *Mergers and acquisitions.* When organizations combine, they often need less bureaucratic overhead, so they lay off managers and some professional staff members. After software maker Oracle Corporation acquired PeopleSoft, it laid off about 5,000 employees, almost one out of ten. It kept most of PeopleSoft's technical employees so that the company could continue meeting plans for product development and support, meaning the vulnerable positions were those involving administrative functions.[7]
4. *Moving to more economical locations.* In recent years, British Columbia has been attractive to U.S. film and television production companies. Other moves, however, have shifted Canadian jobs to other countries. Celestica Inc. announced that it would close an electronics factory employing 700 people in the Montreal area. Celestica has been shifting operations from North America and Western Europe to low-cost Asian countries.[8]

Although the jury is still out on whether these downsizing efforts have enhanced performance, some indications are that the results have *not* lived up to expectations. According to a study of 52 Fortune 100 firms, most firms that announced a downsizing campaign showed worse, rather than better, financial performance in the years that followed.[9]

Why do so many downsizing efforts fail to meet expectations? There seem to be several reasons. First, although the initial cost savings give a temporary boost to profits, the long-term effects of an improperly managed downsizing effort can be negative. Downsizing leads to a loss of talent, and it often disrupts the social networks through which people are creative and flexible.[10] When Roche Holding acquired Syntex Corporation, half the Syntex jobs were eliminated. Most of the employees left voluntarily, taking advantage of a lucrative severance package that included two to three years of full compensation. Many felt that this downsizing strategy encouraged turnover among the best, most marketable scientists and managers.[11]

Also, many companies wind up rehiring. Downsizing campaigns often eliminate people who turn out to be irreplaceable. In one survey, 80 percent of the firms that had downsized wound up replacing some of the very people they had laid off. One senior manager of a Fortune 100 firm described a situation in which a bookkeeper making $9 an hour was let go. Later, the company realized she knew many things

The Team Tim Hortons Scholarship program is one of the ways Tim Hortons attracts talent in tight labour markets.

about the company that no one else knew, so she was hired back as a consultant—for $42 an hour.[12] Hiring back formerly laid-off workers has become so routine that many organizations track their laid-off employees, using software formerly used for tracking job applicants. If the organization ever faces a labour shortage, it can quickly contact these persons and restore them to the payroll.[13]

Finally, downsizing efforts often fail, because employees who survive the purge become self-absorbed and afraid to take risks. Motivation drops, because any hope of future promotions—or any future—with the company dies. Many employees start looking for other employment opportunities. The negative publicity associated with a downsizing campaign can also hurt the company's image in the labour market, so it is harder to recruit employees later. The key to avoiding this kind of damage is to ensure that the need for the layoff is well explained and that procedures for carrying out the layoff are fair.[14] Although this advice may sound like common sense, organizations are often reluctant to provide complete information, especially when a layoff results from top-level mismanagement.[15]

Many problems with downsizing can be reduced with better planning. Still, downsizing hardly guarantees an increase in an organization's competitiveness. Organizations should more carefully consider using all the other avenues for eliminating a labour surplus (shown in Table 5.2). Many of these take effect slowly, so organizations must improve their forecasting or be stuck with downsizing as their only viable option.

Early-Retirement Programs

Another popular way to reduce a labour surplus is with an early-retirement program. As we discussed in Chapter 1, the average age of the Canadian workforce is increasing. But even though many baby boomers are approaching traditional retirement age, early indications are that this group has no intention of retiring soon.[16] Several forces fuel the drawing out of older workers' careers. First, the improved health of older people in general, combined with the decreased physical labour required by many jobs, has made working longer a viable option. Also, many workers fear their retirement savings and pension plans supplemented by the Canada Pension Plan will still not be enough to cover their expenses. Finally, protection from discrimination and eliminating mandatory retirement have limited organizations' ability to induce older workers to retire. Under the pressures associated with an aging labour force, many employers try to encourage older workers to leave voluntarily by offering a variety of early-retirement incentives. The more lucrative of these programs succeed by some measures. Research suggests that these programs encourage lower-performing older workers to retire.[17] Sometimes they work so well that too many workers retire.

Many organizations are moving from early-retirement programs to *phased-retirement programs*. In a phased-retirement program, the organization can continue to enjoy the experience of older workers while reducing the number of hours these employees work, as well as the cost of those employees. This option also can give older employees the psychological benefit of easing into retirement, rather than being thrust entirely into a new way of life.[18]

Employing Temporary and Contract Workers

While downsizing has been a popular way to reduce a labour surplus, the most widespread methods for eliminating a labour shortage are hiring temporary and contract workers and outsourcing work. Employers may arrange to hire a temporary worker through an agency that specializes in linking employers with people who have the necessary skills. The employer pays the agency, whom in turn pays the temporary worker. Temporary employment is popular with employers, because it gives them flexibility they need to operate efficiently when demand for their products changes rapidly. Adecco Group, one of the world's largest staffing services companies, estimates that temporary staffing accounts for $140 billion of revenues worldwide.[19] Adecco has nearly 650,000 associates on payroll on an average day serving 100,000 clients from 5,800 offices worldwide. During the year, Adecco employs close to 4 million people.[20] Employers also may contract directly with individuals, often professionals, to provide a particular service.

Temporary Workers

In addition to flexibility, temporary employment often offers lower costs. Using temporary workers frees the employer from many administrative tasks and financial burdens associated with being the "employer of record." The cost of employee benefits, including vacations, pension, life insurance, workers' compensation, and employment insurance, may account for 40 percent of payroll expenses for permanent employees. Assuming the agency pays for these benefits, a company using temporary workers may save money even if it pays the agency a higher rate for that worker than the usual wage paid to a permanent employee.

Agencies that provide temporary employees also may handle some of the tasks associated with hiring. Small companies that cannot afford their own testing programs often get employees who have been tested by a temporary agency.

Many staffing companies train employees before sending them to employers. This reduces employers' training costs and eases the transition for the temporary worker

Companies such as Adecco offer organizations flexible staffing solutions to meet changing operational and business requirements.

and employer. When United Parcel Service (UPS) signed on with a temporary agency to supply data-entry personnel, the agency designed a computer screen that simulates those used at UPS. A temporary worker assigned to UPS is required to be able to enter data at a minimum speed on the simulated screens.[21]

Finally, temporary workers may offer benefits not available from permanent employees. Because the temporary worker has little experience at the employer's organization, this person brings an objective point of view to the organization's problems and procedures. Also, a temporary worker may have a great deal of experience in other organizations.

Employee or Contractor?

Besides using a temporary-employment agency, a company can obtain workers for limited assignments by entering into contracts with them. If the person providing the services in an independent contractor, rather than an employee, the company does not pay employee benefits, such as health insurance and vacations. As with using temporary employees, the savings can be significant, even if the contractor works at a higher rate of pay.

FedEx Ground recently built up an efficient delivery system by signing on drivers to work as independent contractors. These drivers lease delivery vehicles and buy uniforms from FedEx and take responsibility for the deliveries along a particular route. They are also responsible for their business expenses, including fuel and maintenance of their vehicles. FedEx pays them according to the number of packages they deliver plus a bonus based on its own information about customer satisfaction. The payment method provides an incentive for the contractors to work hard and drum up new business. Some successful drivers have hired their own employees and leased additional vehicles.[22]

This strategy carries risks, however. If the person providing the service is a contractor and not an employee, the company is not supposed to directly supervise the worker. The company can tell the contractor what criteria the finished assignment should meet, but not, for example, where or what hours to work. This distinction is significant, because if the company treats the contractor as an employee, the company has certain legal obligations, related to overtime pay and withholding income taxes.

With regard to FedEx Ground, some drivers have become dissatisfied with their working arrangement and complained that they are actually employees. For FedEx, the challenge is to figure out whether it can continue an arrangement it says many drivers prefer, exert enough influence to ensure contractors meet its standards, and also meet the legal requirements for these drivers to have independent contractor status.[23]

When an organization wants to consider using independent contractors as a way to expand its labour force temporarily, human resource professionals can help by alerting the company to the need to verify that the arrangement will meet legal requirements. A good place to start is with the advice provided at the Canada Revenue Agency website (www.cra.gc.ca). In addition, the organization may need to obtain legal or financial services advice.

Guidelines for Using Temporary Employees and Contractors

To benefit from using contract or temporary workers, organizations must overcome the disadvantages associated with this type of labour force. One drawback is that tension often exists between temporary and permanent employees. According to surveys, one-third of full-time employees perceive temporary workers as a threat to their own job security. Such an attitude can interfere with cooperation and, in some cases, lead to outright sabotage if the situation is not well managed.

One way organizations should manage this situation is to complete any downsizing efforts before bringing in temporary or contract workers. Surviving a downsizing is almost like experiencing a death in the family. In this context, a reasonable time interval needs to occur before new temporary workers are introduced. Without the delay, the surviving employees will associate the downsizing effort (which was a threat) with the new temporary employees (who could be perceived as outsiders brought in to replace old friends). If an upswing in demand follows a downsizing effort, the organization should probably begin meeting its expanded demand for labour by granting overtime to core employees. If the demand persists, the organization will be more certain that the upswing will last and future layoffs will be unnecessary. The extended stretches of overtime will eventually tax the full-time employees, so they will accept using temporary workers to help lessen their load.

Organizations that use temporary workers must avoid treating them as second-class citizens. One way to do this is to ensure that the temporary agency provides temporaries with benefits comparable to those enjoyed by the organization's permanent workers. For example, one temporary agency, MacTemps, gives its workers long-term health coverage, full disability insurance, and complete dental coverage. This not only reduces the benefit gap between the temporary and permanent workers but also helps attract the best temporary workers in the first place. Similarly, employers must ensure temporary employees are treated no differently than permanent employees when it comes to human rights protections and internal complaint procedures.[24]

Outsourcing

Instead of using a temporary employee to fill a single job, an organization might want a broader set of services. As discussed in Chapter 1, contracting with another organization to perform a broad set of services is called *outsourcing*. Organizations use outsourcing as a way to operate more efficiently and save money. They choose outsourcing firms that promise to deliver the same or better quality at a lower cost. One reason they can do this is that the outside company specializes in the services and can benefit from economies of scale (the economic principle that producing something in large volume tends to cost less for each additional unit than producing in small volume). This efficiency is often the attraction for outsourcing human resource functions such as payroll. Costs also are lower when the outsourcing firm is located in a part of the world where wages are relatively low.

The first uses of outsourcing emphasized manufacturing and routine tasks. However, technological advances in computer networks and transmission have speeded up the outsourcing process and have helped it spread beyond manufacturing areas and low-skilled jobs. For example, Xpitax provides for the outsourcing of income tax preparation. Accounting firms send the company electronic files of clients' data, and Xpitax puts the data on a secure Internet server. In India, Xpitax accountants retrieve the data and prepare the tax returns.[25]

In the case of manufacturing, outsourcing may make good sense in the short term but may hurt Canadian firms' competitiveness. Outsourcing reduces manufacturing costs, but companies eventually will have more and more difficulty designing products that apply innovations in technology. According to this argument, unrestrained outsourcing starts a downward spiral of more and more outsourcing until the organization no longer produces anything of value. Companies that manufacture goods develop their own design teams and compete directly, and with a substantial competitive advantage.

Organizations interested in outsourcing should plan how they will avoid problems. Outsourcing an operation means giving up direct control, particularly when outsourcing to another company. Some companies that have tried outsourcing have been disappointed by the results. Sometimes cost savings have been lost to quality-control problems, security violations, and poor customer service. Figure 5.2 provides a comparison of international salaries and Canadian salaries for programmers.

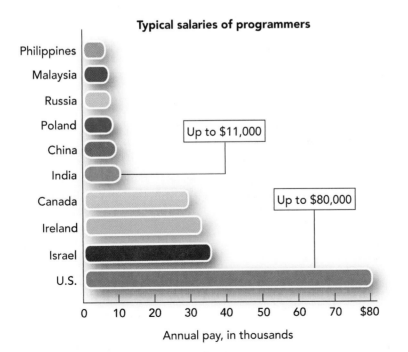

FIGURE 5.2

International Salaries and Canadian Salaries for Programmers

SOURCE: Jyoti Thottam, "The Great Jobs Debate," *Time* (Canadian Edition), March 1, 2004, p. 18.

Overtime and Expanded Hours

Organizations facing a labour shortage may be reluctant to hire employees, even temporary workers, or to commit to an outsourcing arrangement. Especially if the organization expects the shortage to be temporary, it may prefer an arrangement that is simpler and less costly. Under some conditions, these organizations may try to garner more hours from the existing labour force. Many employers opted for this strategy during the 1990s. As a result, 6 percent of the automobiles assembled in North America resulted from overtime production—equivalent to the output of an additional four auto plants running on straight time (no overtime).[26]

A major downside of overtime is that the employer must pay nonmanagement employees additional pay above and beyond their normal wages for work done overtime. Even so, employers see overtime pay as preferable to the costs of hiring and training new employees. The preference is especially strong if the organization doubts that the current higher level of demand for its products will last long.

For a short time at least, many workers appreciate the added compensation for working overtime. Over extended periods, however, employees feel stress and frustration from working long hours. Overtime therefore is best suited for short-term labour shortages.

Implementing and Evaluating the HR Plan

For whatever HR strategies are selected, the final stage of workforce planning involves implementing the strategies and evaluating the outcomes. This stage is represented by the bottom part of Figure 5.1. When implementing the HR strategy, the organization must hold some individual accountable for achieving the goals. That person also must have the authority and resources needed to accomplish those goals. It is also important that this person issue regular progress reports, so the organization can be sure that all activities occur on schedule and that the early results are as expected.

In evaluating the results, the most obvious step is checking whether the organization has succeeded in avoiding labour shortages or surpluses. Along with measuring these numbers, the evaluation should identify which parts of the planning process contributed to success or failure.

Applying Workforce Planning to Employment Equity

As we discussed in Chapter 2, many organizations have a human resource strategy that includes employment equity to manage diversity or meet government requirements. Meeting employment equity goals requires that employers carry out an additional level of workforce planning aimed at those goals. In other words, besides looking at its overall workforce and needs, the organization looks at the representation of subgroups in its labour force—for example, the proportion of women and visible minorities.

workforce utilization review
A comparison of the proportion of employees in protected groups with the proportion that each group represents in the relevant labour market.

Employment equity plans forecast and monitor the proportion of employees who are members of various protected groups (women, Aboriginal peoples, people with disabilities, and visible minorities). The planning looks at the representation of these employees in the organization's job categories and career tracks. The planner can compare the proportion of employees who are in each group with the proportion each group represents in the labour market. For example, the organization might note that in a labour market that consists of 20 percent visible minorities, 60 percent of its customer service employees are members of a visible minority. This type of comparison is called a **workforce utilization review**. The organization can use this process to determine whether there is any subgroup whose proportion in the relevant labour market differs substantially from the proportion in the job category.

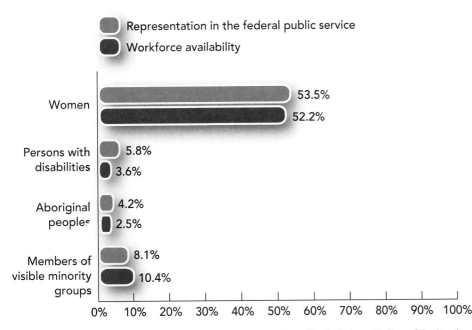

FIGURE 5.3

Employment Equity in the Federal Public Service Compared to Workforce Availability

SOURCE: "Employment Equity in the Federal Public Service—Not There Yet: Preliminary Findings of the Standing Senate Committee on Human Rights," February 2007, pp. 11–12, www.parl.gc.ca/39/1/parlbus/commbus/senate/com-e/huma-e/rep-e/rep07feb07-e.pdf, retrieved May 23, 2008.

If the workforce utilization review indicates that some group—for example, Aboriginal peoples—makes up 10 percent of the relevant labour market for a job category but that this same group constitutes only 5 percent of the employees actually in the job category at the organization, this is evidence of *underutilization*. That situation could result from problems in selection or from problems in internal movement (promotions or other movement along a career path). One way to diagnose the situation would be to use transitional matrices, such as that shown in Table 5.1 earlier in this chapter. The federal public service is the largest employer in Canada with more than 176,000 employees.[27] Figure 5.3 compares participation of its employment equity groups with workforce availability.

The steps in a workforce utilization review are identical to the steps in the workforce planning process shown in Figure 5.1. The organization must assess current utilization patterns, then forecast how these are likely to change in the near future. If these analyses suggest the organization is underutilizing certain groups and if forecasts suggest this pattern is likely to continue, the organization may need to set goals and timetables for changing. The planning process may identify new strategies for recruitment or selection. The organization carries out these HR strategies and evaluates their success.

Recruiting Human Resources

As the first part of this chapter shows, it is difficult to always predict exactly how many (if any) new employees the organization will have to hire in a given year in a given job category. The role of human resource recruitment is to build a supply of potential new hires that the organization can draw on as the need arises. In some regions and industries in Canada, labour shortages have become the norm, and employers are

2,3

passive job seekers
Individuals who are not actively seeking a job.

recruiting
Any activity carried on by the organization with the primary purpose of identifying and attracting potential employees.

becoming increasingly creative in their efforts to identify and attract both active and passive job seekers. **Passive job seekers** are not actively seeking a job, and are often the target of an organization's recruitment efforts because they represent a significant source of top talent. In human resource management, **recruiting** consists of in any practice or activity carried on by the organization with the primary purpose of identifying and attracting potential employees.[28] It thus creates a connection between planning and the actual selection of new employees (the topic of the next chapter).

Because of differences in companies' strategies, they may assign different degrees of importance to recruiting.[29] According to a survey of more than 400 human resource professionals conducted by Workopolis, 55 percent of respondents said, "recruiting/ staff retention is as important to their business as profitability."[30] In general, however, all companies have to make decisions in three areas of recruiting: human resource policies, recruitment sources, and the characteristics and behaviour of the recruiter. As shown in Figure 5.4, these aspects of recruiting have different effects on whom the organization ultimately hires. Human resource policies influence the characteristics of the positions to be filled. Recruitment sources influence the kinds of job applicants an organization reaches. And the nature and behaviour of the recruiter affect the characteristics of both the vacancies and the applicants. Ultimately, an applicant's decision to accept a job offer—and the organization's decision to make the offer—depend on the *fit* between vacancy characteristics and applicant characteristics.

Kelsey August has experienced the impact of this principle as she has struggled to find entry-level employees, including packers, shippers, and production workers, for her direct-marketing company, Lone Star Direct. Unskilled workers were just as happy to work for McDonald's and Wendy's, which were paying wages of $10 to $12 per hour. After such desperate efforts as hiring away the cashiers in stores where she shopped, August tried running a newspaper ad for part-time jobs. To August's surprise, a flood of applications poured in, mostly from women with children. Lone Star revised its human resource policies to suit this new group of employees, with benefits

FIGURE 5.4

Three Aspects of Recruiting

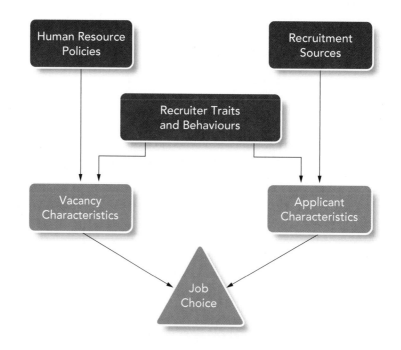

emphasizing flexible work hours and perks that appeal to young mothers. Many of these employees have not completed high school, so Lone Star brings in instructors to help them prepare for their high school equivalency diplomas. The company also started paying a $200 bonus to employees who refer candidates—which enabled the company to cut its budget for job advertising.[31]

The remainder of this chapter explores these three aspects of recruiting: human resource policies, recruitment sources, and recruiter traits and behaviours.

Human Resource Policies

An organization's *human resource policies* are its decisions about how it will carry out human resource management, including how it will fill job openings. These policies influence the nature of the positions that are vacant. (The Best Practices box describes how firms actively cultivate a continuing connection to former employees.) According to the research on recruitment, it is clear that characteristics of the vacancy are more important than recruiters or recruiting sources for predicting job choice.[32] Several policies are especially relevant to recruitment:

LO4 - Discuss the use of employment branding and recruitment policies organizations use to make job vacancies more attractive.

- Recruiting existing employees to fill vacancies or hiring from outside the organization
- Meeting or exceeding the market rate of pay
- Images of the organization conveyed in its employer branding activities

Let's explore the impact of each of these policy areas.

BEST PRACTICES

"Boomerang Employees" Bring Back Benefits for Employers

An employee who leaves a company to pursue other ventures and is later rehired is what has become known as a "boomerang employee." Many career experts say, that as competition for top talent intensifies, companies will open the door even wider to former top employees. "It'll be a growing trend because there's such a skills shortage, one that's only going to get worse," predicts Larry Gibbons,

vice-president of human resources at Kinectrics Inc., an engineering and technical services company in Toronto that has rehired former employees.

Few companies go as far as Ernst and Young LLP to stay on good terms with former employees. Through its alumni relations program, the Toronto-based accounting firm actively cultivates a continuing connection with those who have moved on.

"We want to have a life-long relationship with our people, no matter where they are," says Colleen Albiston, E&Y's director of national marketing. About five years ago, the company decided to substantially beef up the alumni program. Ms. Albiston travelled the country, asking former employees what they would like provided by the company. Continuing education was a top request. Now former

(continued)

BEST PRACTICES

"Boomerang Employees" Bring Back Benefits for Employers

staffers have access to webcasts sponsored by E&Y that discuss developments in the accounting profession, such as regulatory changes. A newsletter is sent out a couple of times a year and several social events are held for former staff. When people leave the firm, they're given a password to the alumni website, which includes a directory of current and former employees, updates on what former E&Y staff are doing, a place to post résumés, and a list of job vacancies at the company.

Encouraging former employees to consider E&Y again is definitely one of the aims of the program, Ms. Albiston says. "We wouldn't go aggressively recruiting someone but if there was a high performer showing an interest, we would look for the next

opportunity for them to rejoin us." At E&Y, 13 percent of new hires last year were boomerangs, the previous year the figure was 15 percent. "It's something we'd like to see continue to grow," Albiston adds. "They always bring back a lot of assets and understand clients on a level they wouldn't if they'd spent their whole career focused on this side of the business."

One of the benefits of rehiring former staff is the positive message it sends about the firm to those starting out. Luana Comin-Sartor, senior manager of audit and assurance business services in Toronto, rejoined Ernst & Young after a lengthy sojourn at Nortel Networks. Many of her younger colleagues seek out her advice about their own career prospects. "People see me as having a more objective

view, because I did leave." She also gets calls from former employees thinking about returning.

The chance to recapture some of its talent isn't the only reason E&Y puts so much effort into staying in touch. There are obvious business benefits for the consulting firm in maintaining a strong relationship with those who move on to other companies, which might need its services. "These are people we've trained, worked with, invested in," say Albiston. "Wherever they go, we'd like them to be an ambassador for the firm."

SOURCE: Ann Kerr, "Many Happy Returns" and "Accounting Firm Makes Sure to Stay in Touch with Past Staff," *The Globe and Mail*, June 30, 2004, p. C1.

Internal versus External Recruiting

Opportunities for advancement make a job more attractive to applicants and employees. Organizations with policies to "promote from within" try to fill upper-level vacancies by recruiting candidates internally—that is, finding candidates who already work for the organization. In a survey of students pursuing a master's degree in business administration (MBA), a policy of promotion from within was the students' top consideration when they were evaluating jobs at a company.[33]

As human resource policies, decisions about internal versus external recruiting affect the nature of jobs. As we will discuss later in the chapter, they also influence recruitment sources and the nature of applicants. For now, we will focus on the impact of these decisions as human resource policies. Promote-from-within policies signal to job applicants that the company provides opportunities for advancement, both for the present vacancy and for later vacancies created when people are promoted to fill higher-level vacancies. Besides providing a career path, internal recruiting can help prevent layoffs during a labour surplus, signalling a policy of retaining valued employees whenever possible.

McDonald's restaurants provide a good example of the virtues of promoting from within. McDonald's has a program with the goal of enabling low-income managers to buy franchises. Phil Hagans was once a cook at a McDonald's restaurant, who worked his way up, and thanks to his hard work and the McDonald's program for low-income employees, now owns two franchises. Hagans's restaurants not only turn a profit but also perform a valuable social function by providing needed employment and work experience.[34]

2,3,5

Lead-the-Market Pay Strategies

Pay is an important job characteristic for almost all applicants. Organizations have a recruiting advantage if their policy is to take a "lead the market" approach to pay—that is, pay more than the current market wages for a job. Higher pay can also make up for a job's less desirable features. For example, many organizations pay employees more for working midnight shifts than daytime shifts. (This practice is called paying a *shift differential*; we will take a closer look at these and other decisions about pay in Chapter 9.)

Organizations that compete for applicants on the basis of pay do so using forms other than wages or salary. For example, a survey found that nearly four out of ten employers used signing bonuses rather than higher wages to attract new hires. Almost two out of ten were using lucrative stock option plans (the right to buy company stock at a set price at a specified time).[35]

The Canadian Forces offers various recruitment allowances for applicants who have specific qualifications. For example, signing bonuses are offered to qualified technicians, tradespeople, and engineers in amounts ranging from $10,000 to $40,000. Trained doctors are eligible for signing bonuses of $225,000.[36] Due to competition for talent in Canada's pharmaceutical industry, Luc St-Pierre, vice-president of human resources for Pfizer Canada, states that signing bonuses for some candidates can "reach 10 to 25 percent of the salary."[37] Many employers prefer bonuses and stock options, because, unlike wages and salary, they tend not to grow over time (as with a percent raise every year) and can be administered more flexibly.

2,3

employer branding
A strategic approach of attaching a visual, emotional, or cultural brand to an organization.

Employer Branding

When labour markets tighten and unemployment levels fall, companies need to put their best foot forward to attract potential hires.[38] **Employer branding**, or *employment branding, or recruitment branding* is a strategic approach of attaching a visual, emotional, or cultural brand to an organization. Employer branding uses marketing techniques to attract, engage, and retain employees in the effort to become an *employer of choice*. For example, when an organization is recognized as one of "Canada's 50 Best Managed Companies" (www.canadas50best .com), the organization acquires the ability to use this well-known designation in various mediums—for example, print or a company website—to support and enhance their recruitment efforts. This logo identifies to current and prospective employees that the organization is part of a prestigious group of Canadian employers who exemplify sound business practices in areas such as human resource management. An employment brand is the impression the company makes on employees and job seekers. Marketing it successfully is the same as marketing any other brand.[39] "The secret to an effective employment brand is differentiating an organization from the competition, targeting key benefits of the job to the right labour segments, and using multiple platforms to reach the right audiences."[40]

When an organization is recognized as one of "Canada's 50 Best Managed Companies," they are likely to experience a dramatic increase in the number of résumés they receive.

The image an employer projects for potential hires, its *employment brand*, should be honest and paint a realistic picture of the company.[41] Just as marketers talk about the unique features of their products, employers need to first understand their own strengths and weaknesses and what they can offer top talent that their rivals cannot.[42]

Edmonton-based EBA Engineering Consultants developed an employment brand so compelling it convinced recruits in the United Kingdom to relocate to Western Canada. The company created a promotional tool that differentiated EBA in a powerful way. "A leather-bound album featured stunning photographs of Western Canada, testimonials from EBA employees who had been recruited from overseas and a USB key that linked candidates to a comprehensive informational website. At the back of the album, a leather luggage tag was mounted as a call-to-action, inviting candidates to pack their bags and join the EBA family in Canada."[43] As this example illustrates, an employment brand that resonates with job seekers, combined with effective recruiting processes and tools, can make the difference of whether a company can attract the talent it needs to be successful. Employer branding is not the exclusive domain of the private sector. "Savvy governments across the country are beginning to build and market a solid employment brand, creating catchy tag lines to grab the attention of jobseekers. The tag line for B.C.'s public service is 'Where Ideas Work' while in Nova Scotia it is 'Make a Difference.'"[44]

Image Advertising

Advertising designed to create a generally favourable impression of the organization is called *image advertising*. Image advertising is particularly important for organizations in highly competitive labour markets that perceive themselves as having a bad image.[45]

The Canadian Forces includes three partners: the Army, the Navy, and the Air Force. The Canadian Forces actively promotes in the labour market to raise awareness of the types of career opportunities available as well as to portray a positive image of employment with the Canadian Forces. The Canadian Forces website promotes the career advantages offered, such as subsidized training plans and recruitment allowances as well as targets specific groups within the overall labour market. For example, video testimonials are available at the Canadian Forces website (www.recruiting.forces .gc.ca) from women presently serving in the Army, the Air Force, and the Navy, and a video produced in collaboration with the APN Aboriginal Peoples Network shows what life in the military is like from the perspective of Aboriginal young people.[46]

Whether the goal is to influence the perception of the public in general or specific segments of the labour market, job seekers form beliefs about the nature of the organizations well before they have any direct interviewing experience with these companies. Thus, organizations must assess their reputation in the labour market and correct any shortcomings they detect in people's actual image of them.[47]

LO5 - List and compare sources of job applicants.

Recruitment Sources

Another critical element of an organization's recruitment strategy is its decisions about where to look for applicants. The total labour market is enormous and spread over the entire globe. As a practical matter, an organization will draw from a small fraction of that total market. The methods the organization chooses for communicating its labour needs and the audiences it targets will determine the size and nature of the labour market the organization taps to fill its vacant positions.[48] A person who responds to

FIGURE 5.5

Recruitment Sources

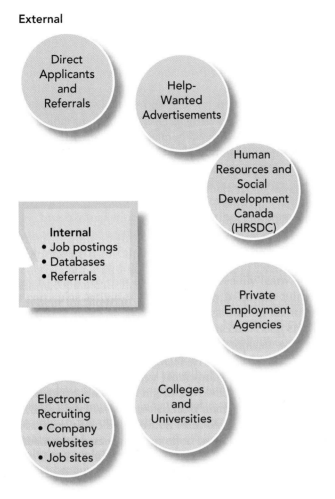

a job advertisement on the Internet is likely to be different from a person responding to a sign hanging outside a factory. Figure 5.5 summarizes major sources from which organizations draw recruits. Each source has advantages and disadvantages.

Internal Sources

As we discussed with regard to human resource policies, an organization may emphasize internal or external sources of job applicants. Internal sources are employees who currently hold other positions in the organization. Organizations recruit existing employees through **job posting**, or communicating information about the vacancy on company bulletin boards, in employee publications, on corporate intranets, and anywhere else the organization communicates with employees. Managers also may identify candidates to recommend for vacancies. Policies that emphasize promotions and even lateral moves to achieve broader career experience can give applicants a favourable impression of the organization's jobs. The use of internal sources also affects what kinds of people the organization recruits.

job posting
The process of communicating information about a job vacancy on company bulletin boards, in employee publications, on corporate intranets, and anywhere else the organization communicates with employees.

For the employer, relying on internal sources offers several advantages.[49] First, it generates applicants who are well known to the organization. In addition, these applicants are relatively knowledgeable about the organization's vacancies, which minimizes the possibility they will have unrealistic expectations about the job. Finally, filling vacancies through internal recruiting is generally cheaper and faster than looking outside the organization.

CCL Industries, a Toronto manufacturing company, has provided leadership training to about 1,000 employees since the 1990s to grow talent within the organization. This "leadership pool" is used to staff projects and assignments as well as prepare employees for additional responsibilities and challenges. In addition, CCL attributes this initiative to enhanced employee morale—employees feel valued because of the investment the company is making in them.[50]

External Sources

Despite the advantages of internal recruitment, organizations often have good reasons to recruit externally.[51] For entry-level positions and perhaps for specialized upper-level positions, the organization has no internal recruits from which to draw. Also, bringing in outsiders may expose the organization to new ideas or new ways of doing business. An organization that uses only internal recruitment can wind up with a workforce whose members all think alike and therefore may be poorly suited to innovation.[52] In order to attract a more diverse workforce, organizations often recruit through direct applicants and referrals, advertisements, employment agencies, schools, and websites. For example, due to language requirements, the province of Quebec targets health care workers in France and Switzerland in addressing the shortage of doctors and nursing specialists.[53]

Direct Applicants and Referrals

direct applicants
People who apply for a vacancy without prompting from the organization.

referrals
People who apply for a vacancy because someone in the organization prompted them to do so.

Even without a formal effort to reach job applicants, an organization may hear from candidates through direct applicants and referrals. **Direct applicants** are people who apply for a vacancy without prompting from the organization. **Referrals** are people who apply because someone in the organization prompted them to do so. According to a recent survey of large companies, the largest share of new employees hired (about one-third) came from referrals, and the next-largest share (30 percent) came from online applications, about half of which were direct applications made at the employer's website.[54] These two sources of recruits share characteristics that make them excellent pools from which to draw.

One advantage is that many direct applicants are to some extent already "sold" on the organization. Most have done some research and concluded there is enough fit between themselves and the vacant position to warrant submitting an application, a process called *self-selection*, which, when it works, eases the pressure on the organization's recruiting and selection systems. A form of aided self-selection occurs with referrals. Many job seekers look to friends, relatives, and acquaintances to help find employment. Using these social networks not only helps the job seeker, but also simplifies recruitment for employers. Current employees (who are familiar with the vacancy as well as the person they are referring) decide that there is a fit between the person and the vacancy, so they convince the person to apply for the job.

An additional benefit of using such sources is that it costs much less than formal recruiting efforts. Considering these combined benefits, referrals and direct applications are among the best sources of new hires. Some employers offer current employees financial incentives for referring applicants who are hired and perform acceptably on the job (e.g., if they stay 180 days).[55] Other companies play off their good reputations in the labour market to generate direct applications.

The major downside of referrals is that they limit the likelihood of exposing the organization to fresh viewpoints. People tend to refer others who are like themselves. Furthermore, sometimes referrals contribute to hiring practices that are or that appear unfair, an example being **nepotism**, or the hiring of relatives. Employees may resent the hiring and rapid promotion of "the boss's son" or "the boss's daughter," or even the boss's friend.

nepotism
The practice of hiring relatives.

Advertisements in Newspapers and Magazines

Open almost any newspaper or magazine and you can find advertisements of job openings. These ads typically generate a less desirable group of applicants than direct applications or referrals, and do so at greater expense. However, few employers can fill all their vacancies purely through direct applications and referrals, so they usually need to advertise. Also, an employer can take many steps to increase the effectiveness of recruitment through advertising.

The person designing a job advertisement needs to answer two questions:

- What do we need to say?
- To whom do we need to say it?

With respect to the first question, an ad should give readers enough information to evaluate the job and its requirements, so they can make a well-informed judgment about their qualifications. Providing enough information may require long advertisements, which cost more. The employer should evaluate the additional costs against the costs of providing too little information: vague ads generate a huge number of applicants, including many who are not reasonably qualified or would not accept the job if they learned more about it. Reviewing all these applications to eliminate unsuitable applicants is expensive.

Specifying whom to reach with the message helps the advertiser decide where to place the ad. The most common medium for advertising jobs is the classified section of local newspapers. These ads are relatively inexpensive, yet they reach many people in a specific geographic area who are currently looking for work (or at least interested enough to be reading the classifieds). On the downside, this medium offers little ability to target skill levels. Typically, many of the people reading classified ads are either over- or underqualified for the position. Also, people not looking for work rarely read the classifieds; these people may include candidates the organization might lure from their current employers. For reaching a specific part of the labour market, including certain skill levels and more people who are employed, the organization may get better results from advertising in professional or industry journals. Some employers also advertise on television—particularly cable television.[56]

Human Resources and Social Development Canada (HRSDC)

Human Resources and Social Development Canada clients include both people looking for jobs and potential employers. Clients can access services without charge by mail, telephone, in person, and via the Internet. Specific program responsibilities of the HRSDC (www.hrsdc.gc.ca) include job creation partnerships designed to provide participants the opportunity to enhance job skills and acquire work experience. Employers post job advertisements in the Job Bank (www.jobbank.gc.ca), an electronic listing of jobs, and receive financial assistance for hiring eligible participants.

Various links provide career information and resources to help job seekers prepare for their job search and to assist employers with their human resource management needs. Additional program responsibilities of the HRSDC include the Youth Employment Strategy, Aboriginal Human Resources Development Agreements, and administering the Canada Student Loan Program and the Employment Insurance Commission.

Staffing Services Companies

In addition to providing temporary employees, staffing services companies, such as Randstad, provide assistance to employers in attracting permanent applicants. Job seekers apply to the private employment agency and are usually screened for suitability. Private employment agencies differ significantly in the types of services provided. It is important for both job seekers and employers to research and thoroughly assess private agencies so as to work with the agency that will best meet their needs and expectations.

Staffing companies provide their services for a fee. Usually these fees are paid by the employer for the service of receiving employee referrals. The staffing services business in Canada has grown into a $4 billion industry that places thousands of job seekers in full-time, temporary, and contract assignments.[57]

For managers or professionals, an employer may use the services of a type of private agency called an *executive search firm* (ESF). People often call these agencies "headhunters" because, unlike other employment agencies, they find new jobs for people almost exclusively already employed. For job candidates, dealing with executive search firms can be sensitive. Typically, executives do not want to advertise their availability, because it might trigger a negative reaction from their current employer. ESFs serve as a buffer, providing confidentiality between the employer and the recruit. That benefit may give an employer access to candidates it cannot recruit in other, more direct ways. EmploymentAgencies.ca is a free Internet directory of employment agencies and executive search firms. Alternatively, the *Directory of Canadian Recruiters* and the *Canadian Directory of Search Firms* are sources of information about private employment agencies. Neither publication is free, but most libraries carry copies.[58]

Employing an executive search firm may be expensive because of direct and indirect costs. ESFs often charge one-third to one-half the salary of the executive who is eventually placed with the client.[59] Also, convincing a person to consider changing jobs requires that the employer offer something more attractive. A company in a growing industry may have to offer as much as 50 percent more than the executive's current pay.[60]

Universities and Colleges

Most universities and colleges have placement services that seek to help their graduates obtain employment. On-campus interviewing is the most important source of recruits for entry-level professional and managerial vacancies.[61] Organizations tend to focus especially on universities and colleges that have strong reputations in areas for which they have critical needs—say petroleum engineering or cost accounting.[62] The recruiting strategy at 3M includes concentrating on 25 to 30 selected

Vancouver Police Department recruiters recently created online personas on Second Life. The e-HRM box discusses how organizations are using virtual world recruiting to attract real-life employees.

universities. The company has a commitment to those selected universities and returns to them every year with new job openings. HR professionals make sure that the same person works with the same university year in and year out, to achieve "continuity of contact."[63]

Many employers have found that successfully competing for the best students requires more than just signing up prospective graduates for interview slots. One of the best ways to establish a stronger presence on a campus is with a cooperative education or internship program. For example, Research in Motion (RIM) provides a variety of employment opportunities for students, including four-month cooperative education placements. In addition to the opportunity to work for a leader in the mobile communications market, student employees are provided with a BlackBerry.[64] These programs give an organization early access to potential applicants and let the organization assess their capabilities directly.

Another way of increasing the employer's presence on campus is to participate in university and college job fairs. In general, a job fair is an event where many employers gather for a short time to meet large numbers of potential job applicants. Although job fairs can be held anywhere (such as at a hotel or convention centre), campuses are ideal because of the many well-educated, not-yet-employed individuals there. Job fairs are an inexpensive means of generating an on-campus presence. They can even provide one-on-one dialogue with potential recruits—dialogue that would be impossible through less interactive media such as newspaper ads. To support its student programs, Research in Motion employs a full-time "Campus Recruitment Specialist."[65] The popularity of social networking sites such as Facebook has also not gone unnoticed by university and college recruiters as discussed in the following section on "electronic recruiting."

Electronic Recruiting

The Internet has opened up new vistas for organizations trying to recruit talent, including talent from anywhere in the world. There are many ways to employ the Internet for recruiting. Increasingly, organizations are refining their use of this medium. The Internet has such a significant impact on recruitment that about 50 percent of all résumés are submitted electronically.[66] As shown in Figure 5.6, over one-third of HR executives responding to a survey indicated that electronic job boards were the most effective source of recruits for their organization.[67] As the e-HRM box describes, online recruiting has also diversified to include the use of participatory media, for example, virtual social worlds or what is also referred to as the *3D Internet*.

FIGURE 5.6

Sources of Recruits

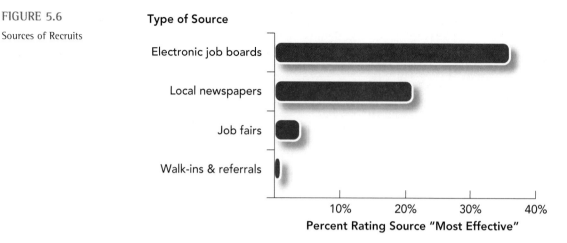

Type of Source

Electronic job boards

Local newspapers

Job fairs

Walk-ins & referrals

10%   20%   30%   40%

Percent Rating Source "Most Effective"

E- HRM

Recruiting Real Talent in a Virtual World

At a recent recruitment session for the Vancouver police, Inspector Kevin McQuiggin was surrounded by job seekers with spiky hairdos, exotic wardrobes, and even wings. "Any one of those individuals may make an excellent police officer," McQuiggin says. After all, this was Second Life, so he was not at all alarmed by this unusual cast of characters. The Vancouver Police Department, like Hewlett-Packard, Manpower, Kelly, CareerBuilder, and Microsoft, are recruiting on Second Life, joining a growing list of organizations turning to virtual online communities to find employees for real-life positions. Inspector McQuiggin was using Second Life as a way to attract tech-savvy individuals to apply for jobs investigating technology-related crimes. "We have to look at how technology is pervasive in society, and how it's going to become more so.

We have to recruit people that are going to understand that," he says. "The kind of people we attract through Second Life are people who have a predisposition to technology."

In Second Life, both job seekers and recruiters create *avatars* or online personas that interact in a virtual community, also sometimes referred to as a *virtual social world, the 3-D Internet,* or *participatory media.* The appearance, dress, and even species of the avatar can be customized to the user's preferences.

Even job fairs are going virtual. TMP Worldwide, a recruitment-advertising firm, recently hosted an online job fair. Recruiters walk around inside a large wide building and meet with prospective employees—or at least the avatars of prospective employees. In some virtual job fairs, job seekers carry a virtual briefcase and add jobs

of interest as they meet with employers in virtual booths. If both the employer and job seeker are interested in further discussion, they go to a virtual conference room to chat, share files, and have further discussions that may result in a real-world interview. The main pitfall of virtual world recruiting is the amount of time, energy, and patience required to set up your avatar. As a result, the base of job seekers tends to be younger and more technologically savvy.

SOURCE: Wency Leung, "Recruiting Real Talent in a Virtual World," Special to *The Globe and Mail,* July 16, 2007, www.theglobeandmail.com, retrieved March 30, 2008; Kathleen Schalch, "Virtual Recruiting for Real-World Jobs," *NPR,* August 22, 2007, www.npr.org, retrieved March 30, 2008; Kimberly Hill, "Virtual World Workforce Part 2: Real-Life Pitfalls," *LinuxInsider,* January 17, 2008, www.linuxinsider.com, retrieved March 30, 2008; "Technology: The Virtual Job Fair, *HR Professional,* December 2007/January 2008, p. 15.

One of the easiest ways to get into "e-cruiting" is simply to use the organization's own website to solicit applications. Less than a quarter of the websites of the world's largest firms were using this approach ten years ago; however, today it is becoming increasingly rare for any large organization *not* to be using this approach.

Although most large corporations have this capability, not all have learned to use it effectively. Some provide only generalities about careers at the company, but today's job seekers expect to find descriptions of open positions and an easy way to submit a résumé. A user-friendly career site is not complicated. Basics include a prominent link to career information from the company's home page and additional links to career information for categories of candidates, such as college or university graduates, or people in a particular profession. The user also should be able to link to information about the company, to evaluate whether it will be a good fit with the candidates' interests and strengths. There should also be a means to confirm receipt of the applicant's application.

Providing a way to submit applications at the company website is not so successful for smaller and less well-known organizations, because fewer people are likely to visit the site. These organizations might get better results by going to the national job board websites, such as Monster.ca, Workopolis.com, or www.working.canada.com, which attract a vast array of applicants. At these sites, job seekers submit standardized résumés. Employers can search the site's database for résumés that include specified key terms, and they can also submit information about their job opportunities, so that job seekers can search that information by key term. With both employers and job seekers submitting information to and conducting searches on them, these sites offer an efficient way to find matches between job seekers and job vacancies. However, a drawback is that the big job websites can provide too many leads of inferior quality, because they are so huge and serve all job seekers and employers, not a select segment.

Because of this limitation of the large websites, smaller, more tailored websites called "niche boards" focus on certain industries, occupations, or geographic areas. For example, Atlantic Canada's Career Beacon is a regional-based job board popular with applicants who live in Atlantic Canada and have no intention of relocating. The best evidence in favour of these boards is that the major websites are scrambling to create more focused subsections of their own.[68]

In addition, some *blogs* cover jobs in particular industries. Written informally, blogs attract job seekers who want to read firsthand comments and news about jobs in their specialty. Several recruiters at Microsoft write blogs about careers at that company. Other blogs are related to industries, rather than particular companies. From the company's perspective, blogs can reach people who are serious about researching a job. Companies are also using social network sites to keep in touch with prospective employees. For example, Ernst & Young's sponsored Facebook page contains information and discussion boards aimed at students.[69] The downside of both blogs and social networks as recruitment tools is that the company may have little control about the information itself or in the sources to which the information is linked.[70]

Riding the popularity of websites such as YouTube, some employers and recruitment websites have started offering video workplace "tours" to give potential employees a new way to get a glimpse of the organization's employer brand.[71]

A popular e-cruiting myth is that experienced candidates do not seek jobs online. However, employers are increasingly recognizing that potential employees of all types regard the Internet as the job search tool of choice. As a result, some of Canada's leading employers are already taking advantage of the power of their corporate career websites. For example, in a snapshot view, TELUS had 17 senior-level, management,

Ernst & Young keeps in touch with former employees through its Alumni Network.

and director-level career opportunities posted online, while Canadian Tire had seven. These websites also provide options to search career opportunities by level of experience, making things easier for senior- and executive-level candidates.[72]

Evaluating the Quality of a Source

In general, there are few rules that say what recruitment source is best for a given job vacancy. Therefore, it is wise for employers to monitor the quality of all their recruitment sources. One way to do this is to develop and compare **yield ratios** for each source.[73] A yield ratio expresses the percentage of applicants who successfully move from one stage of the recruitment and selection process to the next. For example, the organization might find the number of candidates interviewed as a percentage of the total number of résumés generated by a given source (i.e., number of interviews divided by number of résumés). A high yield ratio (large percentage) means the source is an effective way to find candidates to interview. By comparing the yield ratios of different recruitment sources, HR professionals can determine which is the best or most efficient for the type of vacancy.

Another measure of recruitment success is the *cost per hire*. To compute this amount, find the cost of using a particular recruitment source for a particular type of vacancy. Then divide that cost by the number of people hired to fill that type of vacancy. A low cost per hire means that the recruitment source is efficient; it delivers qualified candidates at minimal cost.

To see how HR professionals use these measures, look at the examples in Table 5.3. This table shows the results for a hypothetical organization that used six kinds of recruitment sources to fill a number of vacancies. For each recruitment source, the table shows four yield ratios and the cost per hire. To fill these jobs, the best two sources of recruits were local universities and employee referral programs. Company websites generated the largest number of recruits (1,000 résumés). However, only 20 were judged acceptable, of which only half accepted employment offers, for a cumulative yield ratio of 20/1,000, or 2 percent. Recruiting at renowned universities generated highly qualified applicants, but relatively few of them ultimately accepted positions with the organization. Executive search firms produced the highest cumulative yield ratio. These generated only 20 applicants, but all of them accepted interview offers,

yield ratio
A ratio that expresses the percentage of applicants who successfully move from one stage of the recruitment and selection process to the next.

TABLE 5.3

Results of a Hypothetical Recruiting Effort

	RECRUITING SOURCE					
	LOCAL COLLEGE/ UNIVERSITY	RENOWNED COLLEGE/ UNIVERSITY	EMPLOYEE REFERRALS	NEWSPAPER AD	EXECUTIVE SEARCH FIRMS	COMPANY WEBSITE
Résumés generated	200	400	50	500	20	1,000
Interview offers accepted	175	100	45	400	20	80
Yield ratio	**87%**	**25%**	**90%**	**80%**	**100%**	**8%**
Applicants judged acceptable	100	95	40	50	19	40
Yield ratio	**57%**	**95%**	**89%**	**12%**	**95%**	**50%**
Accept employment offers	90	10	35	25	15	20
Yield ratio	**90%**	**11%**	**88%**	**50%**	**79%**	**50%**
Cumulative yield ratio	90/200 **45%**	10/400 **3%**	35/50 **70%**	25/500 **5%**	15/20 **75%**	20/1,000 **2%**
Cost	$30,000	$50,000	$15,000	$20,000	$90,000	$500
Cost per hire	**$333**	**$5,000**	**$428**	**$800**	**$6,000**	**$25**

most were judged acceptable, and 79 percent of these acceptable candidates took jobs with the organization. However, notice the cost per hire. The executive search firms charged $90,000 for finding these 15 employees, resulting in the largest cost per hire. In contrast, local colleges and universities and company websites provided modest yield ratios at one of the lowest costs per hire. Employee referrals provided excellent yield ratios at a slightly higher cost.

Recruiter Traits and Behaviours

As we showed in Figure 5.4, the third influence on recruitment outcomes is the recruiter, including this person's characteristics and the way he or she behaves. The ideal recruiter is a "talent magnet," that is, top recruiters are able to attract talent. The recruiter affects the nature of both the job vacancy and the applicants generated. However, the recruiter often gets involved late in the recruitment process. In many cases, by the time a recruiter meets some applicants, they have already made up their minds about what they desire in a job, what the vacant job has to offer, and their likelihood of receiving a job offer.[74]

Many applicants approach the recruiter with some skepticism. Knowing it is the recruiter's job to sell them on a vacancy, some applicants discount what the recruiter says, in light of what they have heard from other sources, such as friends, magazine articles, and professors. For these and other reasons, recruiters' characteristics and behaviours seem to have limited impact on applicants' job choices. The HR How-To box discusses effective recruiting with an emphasis on the role of recruiters.

L06 - Describe the recruiter's role in the recruitment process, including limits and opportunities.

1,3

HR HOW-TO

10 Steps to Successful Corporate Recruiting

The best and brightest are highly coveted and, in turn have an abundance of options. The best recruiters understand that in the people business, you have to earn the opportunity to hire the very best candidates.

1. *Be likable.* People prefer to do business with, and work around and for people they like and trust. Often, before they come to work for you, they need to like you.

2. *Respect and serve.* Helping people determine fit, providing feedback, guidance, insights, and support through the recruiting process demonstrates sincere interest and respect for candidates who are making a critical life decision.

3. *Follow-up and -through.* Treating candidates like customers creates a sense of urgency. A-level talent is on the marketplace for a short period of time, so immediate follow-up is critical. Coveted candidates have lessening patience for long delays and limited feedback and communication.

4. *You are the company.* Every touch point is an opportunity to enhance the candidate experience and extend the relationship. Recruiters become the ultimate extension of the employment brand. Having a clearly defined, authentic employment value proposition extended through an employer branding strategy is essential to attracting A-level talent. In the eyes of the candidate, you are the company.

5. *Do your homework.* Make sure hiring managers are thoroughly prepared with all the background notes, detail, and relevant nuances to ensure a successful follow-up meeting. Preparation helps demonstrate keen interest in the candidate.

6. *Earn the talent.* Customer relationships are often cultivated through years of development and interface before finally being solidified. A recruiting culture that approaches engaging talent competitively has an advantage every time. You have to earn the opportunity to employ A-players.

7. *Be number one.* When recruiting passive candidates, strive to become the organization candidates think of first when they begin contemplating a career change. Work to stay relevant and top of mind to the talent you desire and aspire to be the first person they call when the timing is right.

8. *Keep it simple.* Make it easy for candidates to connect with your organization, understand career opportunities, and apply for a job. Review your career site. How compelling is the first impression you make? Is it simple and painless to search and apply for a job? Can a candidate leave his or her email address to get communication on the status of their application and updates on careers?

9. *After the yes.* The company should do everything it can to fulfil expectations extended during the recruitment process.

10. *Live and learn.* Enhance recruiting effectiveness by understanding lost opportunities and implement process improvements. Develop a mechanism for obtaining feedback from candidates who turn down job offers. Make a plan to shore up any gaps and remove barriers to acquiring valued prospective employees.

SOURCE: Ryan Estis, "Sales Effectiveness: 10 Steps to Successful Corporate Recruiting," *HR Professional*, December 2007/January 2008, pp. 42–43.

Characteristics of the Recruiter

Most organizations have to choose whether their recruiters are specialists in human resources or experts at particular jobs (i.e., those who currently hold the same kinds of jobs or supervise people who hold the jobs). According to some studies, applicants perceive HR specialists as less credible and are less attracted to jobs when recruiters are HR specialists.[75] The evidence does not completely discount a positive role for HR specialists in recruiting. It does indicate, however, that these specialists need to take extra steps to ensure that applicants perceive them as knowledgeable and credible.

In general, applicants respond positively to recruiters whom they perceive as warm and informative. "Warm" means the recruiter seems to care about the applicant and to be enthusiastic about the applicant's potential to contribute to the organization. "Informative" means the recruiter provides the kind of information the applicant is seeking. The evidence of impact of other characteristics of recruiters—including their age, sex, and race—is complex and inconsistent.[76]

Behaviour of the Recruiter

Recruiters affect results not only by providing plenty of information, but by providing the right kind of information. Perhaps the most researched aspect of recruiting is the level of realism in the recruiter's message. Because the recruiter's job is to attract candidates, recruiters may feel pressure to exaggerate the positive qualities of the vacancy and to downplay its negative qualities. Applicants are highly sensitive to negative information. The highest-quality applicants may be less willing to pursue jobs when this type of information comes out.[77] But if the recruiter goes too far in a positive direction, the candidate can be misled and lured into taking a job that has been misrepresented. Then unmet expectations can contribute to a high turnover rate. When recruiters describe jobs unrealistically, people who take those jobs may come to believe that the employer is deceitful.[78]

Many studies have looked at how well **realistic job previews**—background information about jobs' positive and negative qualities—can get around this problem and help organizations minimize turnover among new employees. On the whole, the research suggests that realistic job previews have a weak and inconsistent effect on turnover.[79] Although recruiters can go overboard in selling applicants on the desirability of a job vacancy, there is little support for the belief that informing people about the negative characteristics of a job will "inoculate" them so that the negative features don't cause them to quit.[80]

Finally, for affecting whether people choose to take a job, but even more so, whether they stick with a job, the recruiter seems less important than an organization's human resource policies that directly affect the job's features (pay, security, advancement opportunities, and so on).

realistic job preview
Background information about a job's positive and negative qualities.

Enhancing the Recruiter's Impact

Nevertheless, although recruiters are probably not the most important influence on people's job choices, this does not mean recruiters cannot have an impact. Most recruiters receive little training.[81] If we were to determine what does matter to job candidates, perhaps recruiters could be trained in those areas.

Researchers have tried to find the conditions in which recruiters do make a difference. Such research suggests that an organization can take several steps to increase the positive impact that recruiters have on job candidates:

- *Recruiters should provide timely feedback.* Applicants dislike delays in feedback. They may draw negative conclusions about the organization (for starters, that the organization doesn't care about their application).

- *Recruiters should avoid offensive behaviour.* They should avoid behaving in ways that might convey the wrong impression about the organization.[82] Figure 5.7 quotes applicants who felt they had extremely bad experiences with recruiters. Their statements provide examples of behaviours to avoid.

FIGURE 5.7

Recruits Who Were
Offended by Recruiters

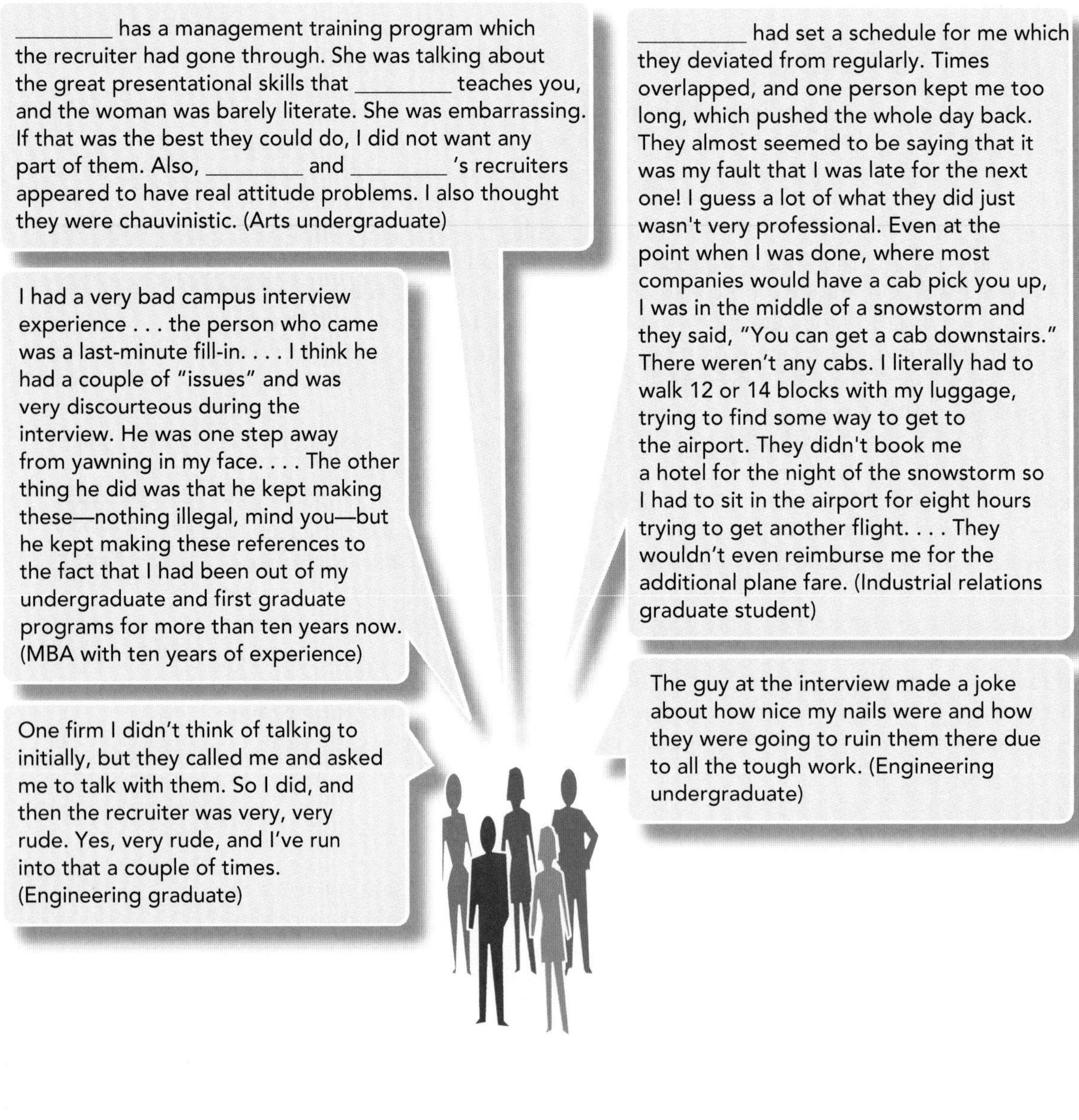

_____ has a management training program which the recruiter had gone through. She was talking about the great presentational skills that _____ teaches you, and the woman was barely literate. She was embarrassing. If that was the best they could do, I did not want any part of them. Also, _____ and _____ 's recruiters appeared to have real attitude problems. I also thought they were chauvinistic. (Arts undergraduate)

I had a very bad campus interview experience . . . the person who came was a last-minute fill-in. . . . I think he had a couple of "issues" and was very discourteous during the interview. He was one step away from yawning in my face. . . . The other thing he did was that he kept making these—nothing illegal, mind you—but he kept making these references to the fact that I had been out of my undergraduate and first graduate programs for more than ten years now. (MBA with ten years of experience)

One firm I didn't think of talking to initially, but they called me and asked me to talk with them. So I did, and then the recruiter was very, very rude. Yes, very rude, and I've run into that a couple of times. (Engineering graduate)

_____ had set a schedule for me which they deviated from regularly. Times overlapped, and one person kept me too long, which pushed the whole day back. They almost seemed to be saying that it was my fault that I was late for the next one! I guess a lot of what they did just wasn't very professional. Even at the point when I was done, where most companies would have a cab pick you up, I was in the middle of a snowstorm and they said, "You can get a cab downstairs." There weren't any cabs. I literally had to walk 12 or 14 blocks with my luggage, trying to find some way to get to the airport. They didn't book me a hotel for the night of the snowstorm so I had to sit in the airport for eight hours trying to get another flight. . . . They wouldn't even reimburse me for the additional plane fare. (Industrial relations graduate student)

The guy at the interview made a joke about how nice my nails were and how they were going to ruin them there due to all the tough work. (Engineering undergraduate)

- *The organization can recruit with teams rather than individual recruiters.* Applicants view job experts as more credible than HR specialists, and a team can include both kinds of recruiters. HR specialists on the team provide knowledge about company policies and procedures and ensure the integrity of the process, consistency, and compliance with human rights legislation.

Through such positive behaviour, recruiters can give organizations a better chance of competing for talented human resources. In the next chapter, we will describe how an organization selects the candidates that best meet its needs.

THINKING ETHICALLY

Talent Poachers

In the escalating war for top talent, the fine line between aggressive recruiting and the unethical solicitation of former colleagues is getting fuzzy. The object of "talent poachers" is to provide their clients with top talent. But not unlike an endangered species, this top talent is in scarce supply. As a result, talent poachers pursue employees who have not even expressed any interest in leaving their current organizations.

Accounting firm Mintz & Partners LLP creates "cones of silence" around their staff by installing spam filters on all of its computers to block incoming emails from all known recruiters. Receptionists flag incoming calls from potential recruiters and screen callers indicating "the person they seek is unavailable,"

says Lyle Strachan, Mintz's chief operating officer in Toronto. "Recruiting is rampant. We know our people are constantly getting tempting offers laid at their feet," Mr. Strachan says. "We're making it known that we value their contributions, and that we will do everything we possibly can to listen to their concerns, and meet their needs."

Talent poachers are well aware of these types of employer tactics and use some strategies of their own. Poachers will call potential "poachees" at home or create new email accounts to get around spam filters that block their names. Executives and professionals also respond favourably to poachers who remind them they are known to be well-respected, top performers in their field. It

is expected that the war for talent is just starting to heat up and recruiting will continue to get more aggressive for professional and executive talent. "In some industries, there used to be kind of a club, an unwritten agreement that they wouldn't try to go into each other's organizations," says Tom Long, a Toronto-based partner with Egon Zehnder International, a global executive recruiting firm with offices worldwide. "Frankly, I think that's a thing of the past."

SOURCES: Lisa Orndorff, Regan Halvorsen, and Anne St. Martin, "Taxing Expats, Poaching Talent, E-Newsletters," *HR Magazine,* May 2007, p. 33; Wallace Immen, "Warning: Poachers Will Be Fought on Site," *The Globe and Mail*, October 18, 2006, p. C1; Erin Pooley, "The Perils of Poaching," *Canadian Business,* January 31–February 13, 2005, p. 63.

Questions
1. Where is the line between aggressive recruiting and unethical solicitation of talent?
2. What obligations, if any, does an employee have to its current employer?
3. Is there any way for an organization to protect itself from talent poachers?

SUMMARY

LO1 **Discuss how to plan for the human resources needed to carry out the organization's strategy.**

- The first step in workforce planning is forecasting. Through trend analysis and good judgment, the planner tries to determine the supply of and demand for various human resources.

- On the basis of whether a surplus or a shortage is expected, the planner sets goals and creates a strategy for achieving those goals. The organization then implements its HR strategy and evaluates the results.

LO2 **Determine the demand for and supply of workers in various job categories.**

- The planner can look at leading indicators, assuming historical patterns will continue in the future. Trend analysis can convert several leading indicators into a single prediction of labour needs and supply.

- Analysis of a transitional matrix can help the planner identify which job categories can be filled internally and where high turnover is likely.

LO3 **Summarize the advantages and disadvantages of ways to eliminate a labour surplus and avoid a labour shortage.**

- To reduce a surplus, downsizing, pay reductions, and demotions deliver fast results but at a high cost in human suffering that may hurt surviving employees' motivation and future recruiting. Transferring employees, requiring them to share work, a hiring freeze, early-retirement packages, and retraining also have various advantages and disadvantages.

- To avoid a labour shortage, requiring overtime is the easiest and fastest strategy, which can easily be changed if conditions change. However, overtime may exhaust workers and can hurt morale. Similarly, using temporary employees, outsourcing, transferring, retraining, hiring new employees, and using technology offer advantages and disadvantages requiring careful consideration.

LO4 **Discuss the use of employment branding and recruitment policies organizations use to make job vacancies more attractive.**

- Internal recruiting (hiring from within) generally makes job vacancies more attractive, because candidates see opportunities for growth and advancement. Lead-the-market pay strategies make jobs economically desirable.

- Employer branding projects an image of the organization, including its culture and key benefits. Image advertising can give candidates the impression that the organization is a good place to work.

LO5 **List and compare sources of job applicants.**

- Internal sources, promoted through job postings, generate applicants who are familiar to the organization and motivate other employees by demonstrating opportunities for advancement. However, internal sources are usually insufficient for all of an organization's labour needs. Direct applicants and referrals, newspaper and magazine advertising, staffing agencies, and universities and colleges offer advantages and issues to be assessed.

- Electronic recruiting gives organizations access to a global labour market, tends to be inexpensive, and allows convenient searching of databases; however, organizations may receive many applications from unqualified applicants. E-cruiting has become increasingly targeted and sophisticated and has expanded to applications such as social networking and virtual world recruiting.

LO6 **Describe the recruiter's role in the recruitment process, including limits and opportunities.**

- Through their behaviour and other characteristics, recruiters influence the nature of the job vacancy and the kinds of applicants generated. Applicants tend to perceive job experts as more credible than recruiters who are HR specialists.

- Recruiters can improve their impact by providing timely feedback, avoiding behaviour that contributes to a negative impression of the organization, and teaming up with job experts.

REVIEW AND DISCUSSION QUESTIONS

1. Suppose an organization expects a labour shortage to develop in key job areas over the next few years. Recommend general responses the organization could make in each of the following areas:
   a. Recruitment
   b. Training
   c. Rewards (pay, employee benefits, and work environment)

2. Review the sample transitional matrix shown in Table 5.1. What jobs experience the greatest turnover (employees leaving the organization)? How might an organization with this combination of jobs reduce the turnover?

3. In the same transitional matrix, which jobs seem to rely the most on internal recruitment? Which seem to rely most on external recruitment? Why?

4. Why do organizations combine statistical and judgmental forecasts of labour demand, rather than relying on statistics or judgment alone? Give an example of a situation in which each type of forecast could be inaccurate.

5. Some organizations have detailed employment equity plans, complete with goals and timetables, for women, Aboriginal employees, people with disabilities, and visible minorities, yet have no formal human resource plan for the organization as a whole. Why might this be the case? What does this practice suggest about the role of human resource management in these organizations?

6. Give an example of a human resource policy that would help attract a larger pool of job candidates. Give an example of a human resource policy that would likely reduce the pool of candidates. Would you expect these policies to influence the quality as well as the number of applicants? Why or why not?

7. Discuss the relative merits of internal versus external recruitment. Give an example of a situation in which each of these approaches might be particularly effective.

8. List the jobs you have held. How were you recruited for each of these? From the organization's perspective, what were some pros and cons of recruiting you through these methods?

9. Recruiting people for jobs that require international assignments is increasingly important for many organizations. Where might an organization go to recruit people interested in such assignments?

10. A large share of HR professionals have rated electronic recruiting as their best source of new talent. What qualities of electronic recruiting do you think contribute to this opinion? What is your reaction to the use of social networks and virtual worlds for recruiting purposes?

11. How can organizations improve the effectiveness of their recruiters?

WHAT'S YOUR HR IQ?

The Online Learning Centre offers more ways to check what you've learned so far. Find experiential exercises as well as Test Your Knowledge Quizzes, Videos, and many other resources at www.mcgrawhill.ca/olc/steen.

Case:
The Downside of Boom

Ray English, CEO of Raydan Manufacturing Inc., no longer talks about milk and honey in Alberta. In March, he decided he couldn't afford to grow his 14-year-old, $14-million truck suspension business in the dangerously overheated economy of his native province. So the Edmonton-born English purchased two small firms in Ontario for $2.3 million—and is planning an expanded chassis-modification business in Breslau, just outside Kitchener-Waterloo. Central Canada offered two advantages Alberta currently lacks: affordable space and a supply of reliable workers. "We just got tired of fighting for labour with Syncrude and the other megaprojects," English explains. "It's overwhelming. Everything is so far out of whack it doesn't make sense."

Two years ago, English hired new staff, including mechanics and welders, only to later lose them to hungry oil and gas firms cannibalizing the marketplace. "Everyone is so transient," he complains. "You train them and then they are gone." After spending $52,000 on help-wanted ads in 24 different newspapers and magazines over a six-week period to little or no effect, English did the once-unthinkable: he hired a recruiting agency last fall. Even then, he couldn't find the workers necessary for an expansion. Alberta's real estate market didn't help matters, either. After prospective engineers from out-of-province took one look at local housing prices, ($250,000-plus), "they were gone," English says.

English wasn't the only local businessman experiencing labour difficulties in Nisku, a bustling industrial park just outside Edmonton. A brand new Burger King shut down last fall for lack of staff, as did a 20-year-old Dairy Queen franchise. English also started to see more and more teenagers dropping out of high school to take $20-an-hour wages as general labourers. "People from outside the province don't see our provincial economy eroding from the bottom up," he says.

While English has decided to expand in Ontario, others offer another bold and equally dramatic solution to Alberta's labour crunch: get control on megaprojects and limit them. Even John Lau, the president and CEO of Husky Energy Inc., seemed to support that cause when in April he said his company had all but ruled out building another megaproject in the oil sands due to chronic labour shortages and "cost overruns and delays."

Alberta's labour crisis, the product of an energy boom and a demonstrable deficit of government leadership, has now reached a tipping point. While many Calgary firms actively talk about importing temporary workers from China and Mexico, Todd Hirsch, chief economist at the Calgary-based Canada West Foundation, calls the situation "almost absurd." Just two years ago, he thought Alberta's labour shortage was confined to skilled professionals. Today, almost every business sector in the Edmonton-Calgary corridor, along with key oil-and-gas towns, including Grand Prairie and Fort McMurray, can't even find people to peel carrots for $14 an hour. The squeeze has not only driven up wages by 6.8 percent (more than twice the national average); it is also burning out employees, curtailing business expansion, driving up prices and encouraging rampant worker poaching. "Do we really want 8 percent to 9 percent GDP growth at the expense of infrastructure and the environment?" asks Hirsch. "We have to get real and say faster growth isn't better."

The dynamics driving the shortage of workers have been repeatedly foretold—and they're accelerating. Statistics Canada predicted skilled-labour shortages in the West years ago based solely on the country's biggest demographic trend: the aging of the baby boomers. But that well-publicized labour decline, which affects North America's entire workforce, has collided head-on in Alberta with an unprecedented global demand for oil that has now reached 1,000 barrels a second. And that has unleashed a chaotic building frenzy in Fort McMurray.

The oilpatch's insatiable hunger for labour also coincides with the rising economic fortunes of British Columbia, where huge capital projects have an immovable deadline in the 2010 Winter Olympics. Manitoba and Saskatchewan are also enjoying good times, leaving few idle fish in the nation's shrinking labour pools.

In fact, megaproject fever is now overfishing both provincial and national labour pools. With more than $120 billion worth of capital works projects on the books for the next decade in the public and private sector in Alberta, employers will need to fill 400,000 new jobs by 2010. But even with special programs to employ seniors, Aboriginal youth, and foreign workers, the provincial government predicts a staggering human-capital deficit of 100,000 people over ten years. As a result, most industries face worker shortages, inflationary wages or chronic poaching. A January survey by the Canadian Federation of Independent Business found that more than 80 percent of small-business owners in Alberta have had difficulty finding workers—and that more than half were coping by hiring underqualified individuals. A third had simply accepted reduced staff as a fact of life. "We not only have a skill shortage," says Sam Shaw, president of Northern Alberta Institute of Technology in Edmonton. "We have a people shortage in Alberta."

The oil sands have become a vortex sucking up workers. With nearly 50 megaprojects on the books, worth an estimated $75 billion, the population of Fort McMurray, Canada's fastest-growing frontier city, could swell from 56,000 to 80,000 people in the next five years. Yet the municipality is already struggling with a growing infrastructure deficit of $1.2 billion, overcrowded hospitals and schools, and a housing shortfall of 1,200 units. It also has the highest monthly rents in the nation, averaging $1,478 a month for a two-bedroom apartment. A 2006 consultant's report on 21 key indicators of the region's sustainability gloomily describes the affordability and availability of housing as "worsening."

As a consequence, many oil sands developers have gone to extreme measures to acquire workers. To kickstart its multibillion-dollar Horizon mining project, Canadian Natural Resources Ltd. built its own private airstrip to fly in tradesmen. Given that the average price of a house in Fort McMurray has quadrupled from a modest $105,000 in 1995 to about $415,000 today, Canadian Natural Resources also briefly considered housing staff 1,127 kilometres away in Kimberley, B.C., and flying in workers for four-day shifts. And in a highly controversial move, the company, which might employ 3,000 construction workers for several years, is looking into importing temporary workers from the depleted oilfields of northeastern China.

Gil McGowan, president of the Alberta Federation of Labour, doesn't think the mass migration of foreign workers is a smart solution, however. He admits that a tight labour market has produced shortages in some key trades, but adds "the sky is not falling." McGowan, like an increasing number of business leaders, believes the provincial government should exercise some discipline in the oil sands. "With a staggered approval system," he argues, "we wouldn't have this tight labour market, which is the direct result of an irrational approach to megaproject approvals."

McGowan calculates that staggered approvals could keep the construction trades well-employed for 20 steady years, instead of 10 chaotic ones. It would also ease inflationary costs, and make it easier for the public sector to tackle critical infrastructure projects, instead of competing with the private sector.

The hyperinflationary pressures of Alberta's energy boom are already undermining many sectors of the economy. The province's $3.7-billion forestry industry, which closed four mills in the past two years, has been particularly hard hit by a rising dollar and persistent labour shortages, according to Neil Shelly, executive director of the Alberta Forest Products Association. "The labour situation is increasing our operating costs, decreasing our operating flexibility, and putting us at a unique disadvantage nationally," he says. Even mills with a $20-an-hour starting wage can't find free hands. Shelly also fears that the province's new energy boom is now actively diminishing economic diversity in the province.

Other sectors are bleeding, too. Although the Alberta Hotel Association recently recorded its highest occupancy rates, it lost nearly 16,000 workers, including housekeepers and managers, to higher-paying jobs in the energy business last year. Even Michael Mazepa, the owner of five Edmonton-based hotels with 30 years' experience, is forced to clean hotel rooms on the weekends. "That's how desperate the labour shortage is," says Dave Kaiser, president and CEO of the association. The sector is importing 350 temporary workers from the Philippines as well as another 600 Sri Lankans for the food-service industry. "That won't even close the gap, but we really need to retain workers and stem the drain," says Kaiser.

The solutions to the province's labour woes are complex, expensive, and multifaceted. A novel Edmonton program (Women Building Futures) that prepares low-income women for skilled trades recently graduated 15 candidates, but had scores of employers lined up for the workers. The province proposes to boost immigration from 16,000 to 24,000 a year, but it hasn't invested in the social or educational services for successful integration. In the end, many Albertans are now hoping the labour shortage may help cool the overheated engine down. "It just might keep the economy from bubbling over and act as a natural break mechanism," proposes Hirsch. But for the province's non-energy-business crowd, that break may already be too little, too late.

SOURCE: Andrew Nikiforuk, "The Downside of Boom," *Canadian Business*, May 22–June 4, 2006, pp. 25–26.

Questions

1. On the basis of the information given in this case, why is Alberta facing a labour shortage?
2. What have the companies done to meet their human resource needs under these conditions?
3. What else could the companies do to align their human resources with the expected needs?

Excalibur Case:
Golden Thread Company

EXCALIBUR
Excellence ▪ calibre

You have just accepted the position of head of human resources at Golden Thread, an up-and-coming import-export company. The company was launched about ten years ago, and since then it has received many awards for achievement in the textile sector. Golden Thread enjoys an excellent financial position. It has been selling to the United States since the company's early days, and over the past 18 months has struck many agreements in Europe and Asia.

Golden Thread's main shareholder is also general manager of the company, an overworked individual with a strong entrepreneurial approach. There is often a need to conduct last-minute negotiations over the phone, but despite the pressure, the GM remains upbeat and pleased that business is doing so well.

The GM has asked you to give priority to settling the problem of recruiting an administrative assistant for him. He has had three since the beginning of the year, and they all left of their own accord. He is trying to understand what happened.

He adds that his previous assistant spent nearly eight years with the company, but left because of health

problems. Since then, new assistants have come and gone through the revolving door. His former assistant had been entrusted with many responsibilities and challenges, including client relations and the authority to solve any problems that arose.

As you speak to the GM, he asserts his proficiency at selling a position to a skeptical candidate. You also find out that hefty payments were made to three different employment agencies over the past year.

SOURCE: Richard Matte, CHRP, "Matte groupe conseil," www.rhri .org/excalibur/en/case_study, retrieved May 16, 2004. *Note:* This case study was used in the 17th edition (2003) of *Excalibur* (the Canadian University Tournament of Human Resources).

Questions

1. Summarize your understanding of the problem. Take no more than five lines to do so.
2. In light of the information provided, what steps should be taken (at least four) to ensure the success of the recruitment process?

Chapter 6

Selecting Employees

What Do I Need to Know? After reading this chapter, you should be able to:

1. Identify the elements of the selection process.

2. Define ways to measure the success of a selection method.

3. Summarize the legal requirements for employee selection.

4. Compare the common methods used for selecting human resources.

5. Describe major types of employment tests.

6. Discuss how to conduct effective interviews.

7. Explain how employers carry out the process of making a selection decision.

Introduction

Hiring the right person is perhaps the most important decision a manager can make. The inherent risks and potential costs of a bad hire are causing organizations of all sizes to spend a bit of money up front hiring a third party to conduct thorough background checks of potential employees.

Companies such as BackCheck™ specialize in pre-employment background checks such as criminal record checks, credit inquiries, education verifications, employment history verifications, driving records, and verification of information provided by references. Angus Stewart, vice-president of forensics and leader of corporate intelligence at KPMG LLP in Toronto, says that knowing what to look for is key to a successful search. "Education fraud is the most common," he says, adding that people lie about the degree they received or the institutions they attend. There is also the "diploma mill issue": people state degrees they ordered online from phoney institutions. "There's quite a bit of that."[1]

Hiring decisions are about finding the people who will be a good fit with the job and the organization. Any organization that appreciates the competitive edge provided by good people must take the utmost care in choosing its members. The organization's decisions about selecting people are central to its ability to survive, adapt, and grow. Selection decisions become especially critical when organizations face tight labour markets or must compete for talent with other organizations in the same industry. If a competitor keeps getting the best applicants, the remaining companies have to make do with who is left.

Checking out employees is a growth industry as more organizations such as BackCheck™ conduct background checks on potential employees. Advanced technology has helped reduce costs and streamline the process.

This chapter will familiarize you with ways to increase the effectiveness of employee selection. The chapter starts by describing the selection process and how to evaluate possible methods for carrying out that process. It then takes an in-depth look at the most widely used methods: applications and résumés, employment tests, and interviews. The chapter ends by describing the process by which organizations arrive at a final selection decision.

1,2,3

Selection Process

Through the process of **selection**, organizations make decisions about who will be chosen to fill job openings. Selection begins with the candidates identified through recruitment and attempts to reduce their number to the individuals best qualified to perform the available jobs and fit with the culture of the organization. At the end of the process, the selected individuals are placed in jobs with the organization.

The process of selecting employees varies considerably from organization to organization and from job to job. At most organizations, however, selection includes the steps illustrated in Figure 6.1. First, a human resource professional reviews the applications received to see which meet the requirements of the job. For candidates who meet the requirements, the organization administers tests and reviews work samples to assess the candidates' competencies. Those with the best capabilities

LO1 - Identify the elements of the selection process.

selection
The process through which organizations make decisions about who will be chosen to fill job openings.

FIGURE 6.1

Steps in the Selection Process

Screening Applications and Résumés → Testing and Reviewing Work Samples → Interviewing Candidates → Checking References and Background → Making a Selection

are invited to the organization for one or more interviews. Often, supervisors and team members are involved in this stage of the process. By this point, the decision makers are beginning to form opinions about which candidates are most desirable. For the top few candidates, the organization should check references and conduct background checks to verify that the organization's information is correct. Then supervisors, teams, and other decision makers select a person to receive a job offer. In some cases, the candidate may negotiate with the organization regarding salary, benefits, and the like. If the candidate accepts the job, the organization places him or her in that job.

How does an organization decide which of these elements to use, and in what order? Some organizations simply repeat a selection process that is familiar. If members of the organization underwent job interviews, they conduct job interviews, asking familiar questions. However, what organizations *should* do is to create a selection process in support of its job descriptions and specifications. In Chapter 4, we explained that a job specification identifies the competencies required for successfully performing a job. The selection process should be set up in such a way that it lets the organization identify people who have the necessary competencies. When the Canadian Security and Intelligence Service (CSIS) hires Intelligence Officers, it looks for people who have specific experience, characteristics, and personal attributes. For example, CSIS wants people who are highly motivated and interested in the Service. The selection process for Intelligence Officers assesses these attributes during the suitability interview, an in-depth panel interview, and a psychological assessment. Candidates who survive the entire range of interviews and tests, not to mention the intensive security screening process, also spend time in an interview with CSIS executives.[2]

This kind of strategic approach to selection requires ways to measure the effectiveness of selection tools. From science, we have basic standards for this. The best selection methods will provide information that is reliable and valid and can be generalized to apply to the organization's group of candidates. In addition, selection should measure characteristics that have practical benefits for the organization. Finally, selection criteria must meet the legal requirements in effect where the organization operates. Figure 6.2 summarizes these criteria.

FIGURE 6.2

Criteria for Evaluating Selection Methods

Reliability

The **reliability** of a type of measurement indicates how free that measurement is from random error.[3] A reliable measurement therefore generates consistent results. Assuming that a person's intelligence is fairly stable over time, a reliable test of intelligence should generate consistent results if the same person takes the test several times. Organizations that construct intelligence tests therefore should be able to provide (and explain) information about the reliability of their tests.

Usually, this information involves statistics such as *correlation coefficients*. These statistics meaxsure the degree to which two sets of numbers are related. A higher correlation coefficient signifies a stronger relationship. At one extreme, a correlation coefficient of 1.0 means a perfect positive relationship—as one set of numbers goes up, so does the other. If you took the same vision test three days in a row, those scores would probably have nearly a perfect correlation. At the other extreme, a correlation of –1.0 means a perfect negative correlation—when one set of numbers goes up, the other goes down. In the middle, a correlation of 0 means there is no correlation at all. For example, the correlation between weather and intelligence would be at or near 0. A reliable test would be one for which scores by the same person (or people with similar attributes) have a correlation close to 1.0.

Validity

For a selection measure, **validity** describes the extent to which performance on the measure (such as a test score) is related to what the measure is designed to assess (such as job performance). Although we can reliably measure such characteristics as weight and height, these measurements do not provide much information about how a person will perform most kinds of jobs. Thus, for most jobs height and weight provide little validity as selection criteria. One way to determine whether a measure is valid is to compare many people's scores on that measure with their job performance. For example, suppose people who score above 60 words per minute on a keyboarding test consistently get high marks for their performance in data-entry jobs. This observation suggests the keyboarding test is valid for predicting success in that job.

As with reliability, information about the validity of selection methods often uses correlation coefficients. A strong positive (or negative) correlation between a measure and job performance means the measure should be a valid basis for selecting (or rejecting) a candidate. This information is important, not only because it helps organizations identify the best employees, but also because organizations can ensure that their selection process is valid. Three ways of measuring validity are criterion-related, content, and construct validity.

Criterion-Related Validity

The first category, **criterion-related validity**, is a measure of validity based on showing a substantial correlation between test scores and job performance scores. In the example in Figure 6.3, a company compares two measures—an intelligence test and a university or college grade point average—with performance as sales representative. In the left graph, which shows the relationship between the intelligence test scores and job performance, the points for the 20 sales representatives fall near the 45-degree line. The correlation coefficient is near 0.90 (for a perfect 1.0, all the points would be on the 45-degree line). In the graph at the right, the points are scattered more

LO2 - Define ways to measure the success of a selection method.

3

reliability
The extent to which a measurement generates consistent results.

validity
The extent to which performance on a measure (such as a test score) is related to what the measure is designed to assess (such as job performance).

criterion-related validity
A measure of validity based on showing a substantial correlation between test scores and job performance scores.

FIGURE 6.3

Criterion-Related Measurements of a Student's Aptitude

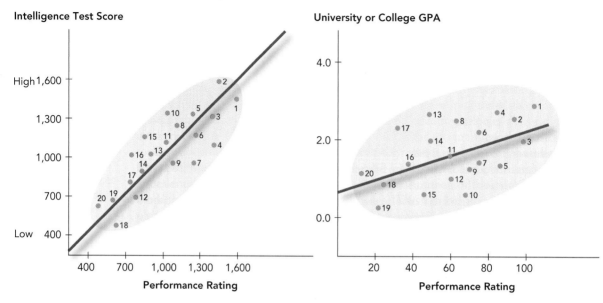

predictive validation
Research that uses the test scores of all applicants and looks for a relationship between the scores and future performance of the applicants who were hired.

widely. The correlation between university or college GPA and sales representatives' performance is much lower. In this hypothetical example, the intelligence test is more valid than GPA for predicting success at this job.

Two kinds of research are possible for arriving at criterion-related validity:

1. **Predictive validation.** This research uses the test scores of all applicants and looks for a relationship between the scores and future performance. The researcher administers the tests, waits a set period of time, and then measures the performance of the applicants who were hired.

2. **Concurrent validation.** This type of research administers a test to people who currently hold a job, then compares their scores to existing measures of job performance. If the people who score highest on the test also do better on the job, the test is assumed to be valid.

concurrent validation
Research that consists of administering a test to people who currently hold a job, then comparing their scores to existing measures of job performance.

Predictive validation is more time-consuming and difficult, but it is the best measure of validity. Job applicants tend to be more motivated to do well on the tests, and their performance on the tests is not influenced by their firsthand experience with the job. Also, the group studied is more likely to include people who perform poorly on the test—a necessary ingredient to accurately validate a test.[4]

Content and Construct Validity

Another way to show validity is to establish **content validity**—that is, consistency between the test items or problems and the kinds of situations or problems that occur on the job.[5] A test that is "content-valid" exposes the job applicant to situations likely to occur on the job. It tests whether the applicant has the knowledge, skills, or ability, that is, competencies to handle such situations.

content validity
Consistency between the test items or problems and the kinds of situations or problems that occur on the job.

For example, a general residential contracting firm needed to hire a construction superintendent.[6] This job involved organizing, supervising, and inspecting the work of many subcontractors. The tests developed for this position attempted to mirror the job. One test was a scrambled subcontractor test. The applicant had to take a random list of subcontractors (roofing, plumbing, electrical, and so on) and put them in the order in which each firm should appear on the construction site. A second test measured recognition of construction errors. In this test, the applicant went into a shed that was specially constructed to have 25 common and expensive errors, including faulty wiring and upside-down windows. The applicant was supposed to record all the problems he or she could detect. The content of these tests so closely parallels the content of the job that it was safe to use test performance as the basis for predicting job performance.

The usual basis for deciding that a test has content validity is through expert judgment. Experts can rate the test items according to whether they mirror essential functions of the job. Because establishing validity is based on the experts' subjective judgments, content validity is most suitable for measuring behaviour that is concrete and observable.

For tests that measure abstract qualities such as intelligence or leadership ability, establishment of validity may have to rely on **construct validity**. This involves establishing that tests really do measure intelligence, leadership ability, or other such "constructs," as well as showing that mastery of this construct is associated with successful performance of the job. For example, if you could show that a test measures something called "mechanical ability," and that people with superior mechanical ability perform well as assemblers, then the test has construct validity for the assembler job. Tests that measure a construct usually measure a combination of behaviours thought to be associated with the construct.

	construct validity Capability of a test to measure a construct such as intelligence and the relationship of this construct to successful job performance.

Ability to Generalize

Along with validity in general, we need to know whether a selection method is valid in the context in which the organization wants to use it. A **generalizable** method not only applies to the conditions in which the method was originally developed—such as job, organization, people, and time period—it also applies to other organizations, jobs, applicants, and so on. In other words, is a selection method that was valid in one context also valid in other contexts?

Researchers have studied whether tests of intelligence and thinking skills (called *cognitive ability*) can be generalized. The research has supported the idea that these tests are generalizable across many jobs. However, as jobs become more complex, the validity of many of these tests increases. In other words, they are most valid for complex jobs.[7]

generalizable Valid in other contexts beyond the context in which the selection method was developed.

Practical Value

Not only should selection methods such as tests and interview responses accurately predict how well individuals will perform, they should produce information that actually benefits the organization. Being valid, reliable, and generalizable adds value to a method. Another consideration is the cost of using the selection method. Selection procedures such as testing and interviewing cost money. They should cost significantly less than the benefits of hiring the new employees. Methods that provide economic value greater than the cost of using them are said to have **utility**.

The choice of a selection method may differ according to the job being filled. If the job involves providing a product or service of high value to the organization, it is worthwhile to spend more to find a top performer. At a company where salespeople are responsible for closing million-dollar deals, the company will be willing to invest

utility The extent to which something provides economic value greater than its cost.

more in selection decisions. At a fast-food restaurant, such an investment will not be worthwhile; the employer will prefer faster, simpler ways to select workers who enter orders, prepare food, and keep the facility clean.

LO3 - Summarize the legal requirements for employee selection.

1,3

Legal Standards for Selection

Whether selecting a new employee or promoting an employee from within the organization, the selection process needs to be conducted in a way that avoids human rights complaints. Human rights legislation and privacy legislation described in Chapter 2 has implications for the selection process.

- The interview needs to be conducted in a way that candidates can be assessed without drawing out information that is not relevant to the job being filled. As summarized in Table 6.1, the organization may not ask questions on an application form or in an interview that gathers information about a person's protected status, even indirectly. For example, asking candidates for the dates they attended high school might indirectly gather information about applicants' age.

- Interview notes are made by interviewers to help distinguish among candidates. Even if these notes are only used by the interviewers, they cannot include references to any prohibited ground of discrimination (e.g., "Asian man, 40-ish" would be an inappropriate comment to include in interview notes).[8]

- Candidates must provide their consent before a background check can be conducted. Because background checks may unearth information about protected grounds such as age or religious affiliation, it is recommended that employers "issue a conditional job offer to a candidate and then make it subject to the completion of successful background and reference checks."[9]

TABLE 6.1

Guidelines for Applications and Interviews

SUBJECT	AVOID ASKING	PREFERRED
Name	• About name change: whether it was changed by court order, marriage, or other reason • For maiden name	
Address	• For addresses outside Canada	• Ask place and duration of current or recent address.
Age	• For birth certificates, baptismal records, or about age in general	• Ask applicants whether they are eligible to work under Canadian laws regarding age restrictions.
Sex	• About pregnancy, childbearing plans, or child care arrangements	• Ask applicant if the attendance requirements can be met.
Marital status	• Whether the applicant is single, married, divorced, engaged, separated, widowed, or living common-law	• If transfer or travel is part of the job, the applicant can be asked whether he or she can meet these requirements.
	• About the spouse's employment	• Ask whether there are any circumstances that might prevent completion of a minimum service commitment.

(continued)

(continued)

Family status	• For number of children or dependants	• Ask if the applicant would be able to work the required hours and, where applicable, overtime.
National or ethic origin	• About birthplace, nationality of ancestors, spouse, or other relatives • Whether born in Canada • For proof of citizenship	• Ask if the applicant is legally entitled to work in Canada.
Photographs	• For photo to be attached to applications or sent to interviewer before interview	
Religion	• About religious affiliation • For references from clergy	• Explain the required work shift, and ask whether such a schedule poses problems for the applicant. NOTE: Accommodation of an employee's religious beliefs is the employer's duty.
Disability	• For a list of all disabilities, limitations, or health problems	• Ask whether the applicant has any condition that might affect ability to do the job. NOTE: Accommodation of an employee's disability is the employer's duty to the point of undue hardship.
Pardoned conviction	• Whether an applicant has ever been convicted • Whether the applicant has a criminal record	• If bonding is a job requirement, ask whether the applicant is eligible.
Sexual orientation	• About the applicant's sexual orientation	

NOTE: This table provides examples and is not intended as a complete listing of all guidelines. The examples are based on federal human rights legislation; some provincial laws vary and may affect these examples.

SOURCE: Canadian Human Rights Commission, "A Guide to Screening and Selection in Employment," February 2001, pp. 3–5, www.chrc-ccdp.ca/publications/employment_equity-en.asp, retrieved April 3, 2004. Reproduced with the permission of the Minister of Public Works and Government Services Canada, 2004.

An important principle of selection is to combine several sources of information about candidates, rather than relying solely on interviews or a single type of testing. The sources should be chosen carefully to relate to the characteristics identified in the job description. When organizations do this, they are increasing the validity of the decision criteria. They are more likely to make hiring decisions that are fair and unbiased. They also are more likely to choose the best candidates.

Job Applications and Résumés

LO4 - Compare the common methods used for selecting human resources.

Nearly all employers gather background information on applicants at the beginning of the selection process. The usual ways of gathering background information are by asking applicants to fill out application forms and provide résumés. Organizations also verify the information by checking references and conducting background checks.

3

Asking job candidates to provide background information is inexpensive. The organization can get reasonably accurate information by combining applications and résumés with background checks and well-designed interviews.[10] A major challenge with applications and résumés is the sheer volume of work they generate for the organization. Especially considering how easy it is for candidates to submit applications or résumés online, human resource departments need to take steps to ensure they are not swamped with more than they can carefully review. Solutions to this dilemma usually involve a software application that will be discussed in more detail later in this section.

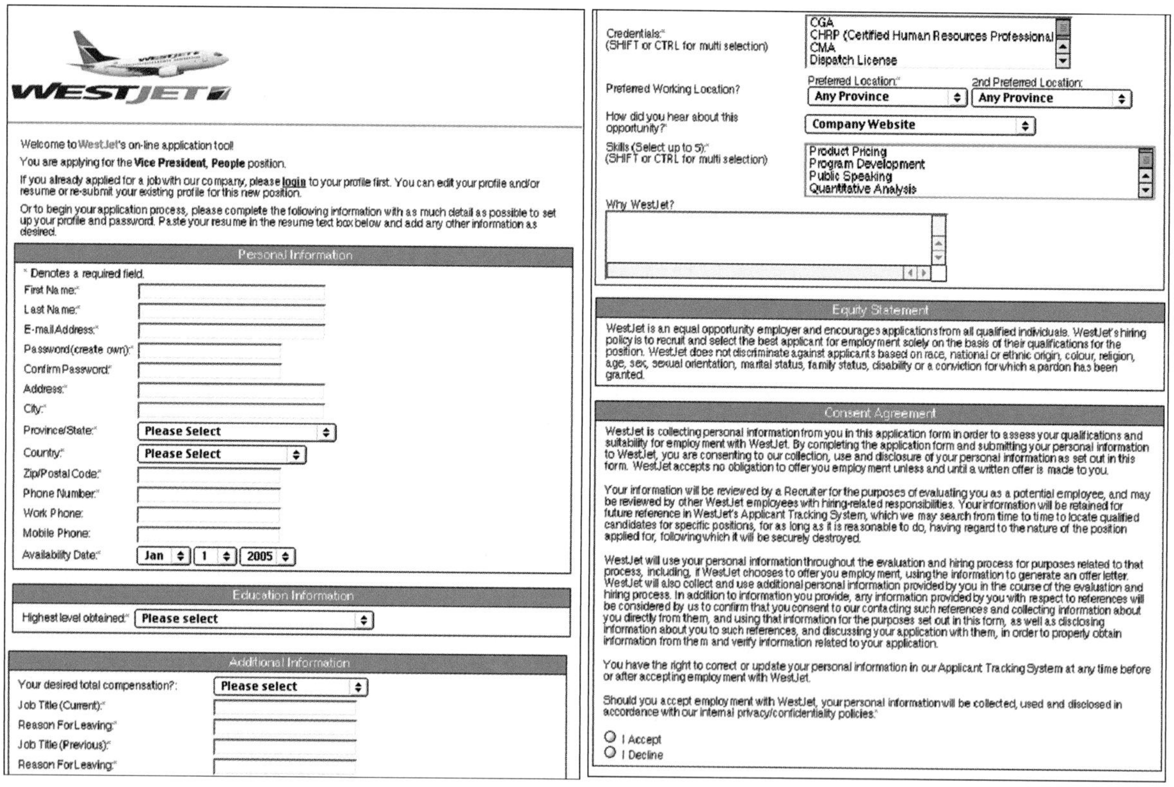

Application Forms

Asking each applicant to fill out an employment application is a low-cost way to gather basic data from many applicants. It also ensures that the organization has certain standard categories of information, such as mailing address and employment history, from each. Figure 6.4 is an example of an online application form for the "Vice President, People" job at WestJet.

Employment applications include areas for applicants to provide several types of information:

- *Contact information.* The employee's name, address, phone number, and email address.

FIGURE 6.4

WestJet's Online Application Form

SOURCE: www.westjet.com, retrieved March 31, 2005.

- *Work experience.* Companies the applicant worked for, job titles, and dates of employment.
- *Educational background.* High school, college, or universities attended and diploma(s) or degree(s) awarded.
- *Applicant's signature.* Signature or verification following a statement that the applicant has provided true and complete information.

The application form may include other areas for the applicant to provide additional information, such as specific work experiences, technical skills, certifications, or memberships in professional or trade associations. Also, including the date on an application is useful for keeping up-to-date records of job applicants. The application form should not request information that might violate human rights legislation. For example, questions about an applicant's birthplace, marital status, or number of children would be inappropriate.

By reviewing application forms, HR staff can identify which candidates meet minimum requirements for education and experience. They may be able to rank applicants—for example, giving applicants with five years' experience a higher ranking than applicants with two years' experience. In this way, the applications enable the organization to narrow the pool of candidates to a number it can afford to test and interview.

Résumés

The usual way applicants introduce themselves to a potential employer is by submitting a résumé. An obvious drawback of this information source is that applicants control the content of the information, as well as the way it is presented. This type of information is therefore biased in favour of the applicant and (although this is unethical) may not even be accurate. However, this inexpensive way to gather information does provide employers with a starting point. Organizations typically use résumés as a basis for deciding which candidates to investigate further.

As with employment applications, an HR staff member reviews the résumés to identify candidates meeting such requirements including competencies, educational background, related work performed, and types of equipment the person has used. Because résumés are created by the job applicants (or the applicants have at least approved résumés created by someone they hire), they also may provide some insight into how candidates communicate and present themselves. Employers tend to decide against applicants whose résumés are unclear, messy, or contain mistakes. On the positive side, résumés may enable applicants to highlight accomplishments that might not show up in the format of an employment application. Review of résumés is most valid when the content of the résumés is assessed in terms of the criteria associated with successful job performance.

1,3

Organizations are increasingly turning to Web-based applicant tracking systems to centralize the handling of résumés and job applications from both internal and external applicants. An **applicant tracking system (ATS)** is a software application that streamlines the flow of information between job seekers, HR staff, and hiring managers. As organizations expand their corporate websites into interactive career centres, applicant tracking systems provide capabilities including multilingual support for global locations, generating applicant confirmation letters, pre-screening applications and résumés for education, specific competencies, and experience. Applicant tracking systems also support various data handling and report generation

Applicant tracking system (ATS)
A software application that streamlines the flow of information between job seekers, HR staff, and hiring managers.

requirements associated with hiring employees, for example, storing résumés, tracking candidate sources, and connecting applications to specific hiring managers or job openings. By automating the process to match available talent with current job opportunities, the efficiency and speed of the overall hiring process is improved. Organizations can streamline the process, build relationships with candidates, cut hiring cycle-time, and increase the probability of hiring an available and interested candidate.[11]

References

Application forms often ask that applicants provide the names of several references. Applicants provide the names and contact information of former employers or others who can vouch for their abilities and past job performance. In some situations, the applicant may provide letters of reference written by those people. It is then up to the organization to have someone contact the references to gather information or verify the accuracy of the information provided by the applicant.

As you might expect, references are not an unbiased source of information. Most applicants are careful to choose references who will say something positive. In addition, former employers and others may be afraid that if they express negative opinions, they will be sued. Their fear is understandable. In the many thousands of lawsuits that have been filed over such matters, damage awards can run over $500,000.[12] Intuit Corporation, producer of Quicken software, gets around this problem by requiring as many as 12 letters of reference. Typically, the first two or three people listed provide glowing references, but people further down the list provide a fuller picture of the candidate.[13]

Usually the organization checks references after it has determined that the applicant is a finalist for the job. Contacting references for all applicants would be time-consuming, and it does put a burden on the people contacted. Part of that burden is the risk of giving information seen as too negative or too positive. If the person who is a reference gives negative information, there is a chance the candidate will claim *defamation*, meaning the person damaged the applicant's reputation by making statements that cannot be proved truthful.[14] At the other extreme, if the person gives a glowing statement about a candidate, and the new employer later learns of misdeeds such as sexual misconduct or workplace violence, the new employer might sue the former employer for *misrepresentation*.[15]

Because such situations occasionally arise, often with much publicity, people who give references tend to give as little information as possible. Most organizations have policies that the human resource department will handle all requests for references and that they will only verify employment dates and sometimes the employee's final salary. In organizations without such a policy, HR professionals should be careful— and train managers to be careful—to stick to observable, job-related behaviours and to avoid broad opinions that may be misinterpreted. In spite of these drawbacks of references, the risks of not learning about significant problems in a candidate's past outweigh the possibility of getting only a little information. "An HR manager may be in the interesting position of declining to give an elaborate reference for any employee who intends to leave her organization, yet demand one for a person she wishes to hire. And applicants may find themselves to be essentially unemployable, as they discover they can't be hired without a satisfactory reference from their former employer."[16]

Background Checks

A background check is a way to verify that applicants are as they represent themselves to be. Unfortunately, as is humorously illustrated in Figure 6.5, not all candidates are open and honest. About eight out of ten large companies and over two-thirds of smaller organizations say they conduct criminal record background checks.[17] The primary database is the Canadian Police Information Centre, operated by the RCMP. ADP Screening and Selection Services is another company that provides background checks on prospective employees. ADP found that more than half of candidates submitted false information—up from 40 percent in the previous year. These kinds of findings are prompting companies to increase their use of thorough background checks.[18] Also fuelling this growing use of background checks are applicants using complex and high-tech means to fraudulently impress employers. For example, a counterfeiting ring operating out of a house in Markham, Ontario may have supplied thousands of people with forged university degrees, and transcripts as well as forged immigration documents, according to York Regional Police. The police confiscated forged degrees from the University of Toronto, the University of Western Ontario, Cape Breton University, and many others. Even university officials were hard pressed to detect the fakes. "These were of such high quality that our university people had to do a double take," said Detective Fred Kerr. "From an employer point of view, you're not going to catch what's wrong with them."[19]

Besides verifying résumés and employment history, education, and references, businesses are also checking for criminal records, personal credit histories, and driving abstracts. However, employers must keep in mind that before performing a background check they have to get consent from the candidate. As discussed earlier in the chapter, conducting a background check after extending a contingent job offer can help to protect the potential employer from a discrimination claim if the

MISTER BOFFO

FIGURE 6.5

Job Candidate Who Inspires a Background Check

SOURCE: © 2005, Tribune Media Services. Reprinted with permission.

applicant is not hired. Consent is also needed to comply with Canada's Personal Information Protection and Electronic Documents Act (PIPEDA)[20] or similar provincial legislation.

L05 - Describe major types of employment tests.

Employment Tests and Work Samples

When the organization has identified candidates whose applications or résumés indicate they meet basic requirements, the organization continues the selection process with this narrower pool of candidates. Often, the next step is to gather objective data through one or more employment tests. These tests fall into two broad categories:

aptitude tests
Tests that assess how well a person can learn or acquire skills and abilities.

1. **Aptitude tests** assess how well a person can learn or acquire skills and abilities. In the realm of employment testing, the best-known aptitude test is the General Aptitude Test Battery (GATB). The Public Service Commission of Canada also provides other employment-related tests such as the Administrative Support: The Office Skills Test (OST) which assesses the individual's aptitude for following directions, filing, arithmetic, checking, and vocabulary.[21]

achievement tests
Tests that measure a person's existing knowledge and skills.

2. **Achievement tests** measure a person's existing knowledge and skills. For example, some organizations use interactive tests to assess applicants' skills using software such as Outlook, Excel, and PowerPoint.

Employment tests may assess general abilities, such as physical strength, or specific skills, such as keyboarding speed. Some organizations also use personality tests to find applicants who have personality traits associated with successful job performance and fit with the organization's culture, as well as integrity tests to weed out dishonest candidates. Before using any test, organizations should investigate the test's validity and reliability. Use of drug testing and medical examinations try to ensure that candidates meet physical job requirements and will not be impaired on the job. Besides asking the testing service to provide this information, it is wise to consult more impartial sources of information, such as the ones identified in Table 6.2. The HR How-To box discusses various types of employment tests used to screen job applicants.

The RCMP Police Aptitude Battery (RPAB) consists of the RCMP Police Aptitude Test (RPAT) and the Six Factor Personality Questionnaire (SFPQ). The RPAT

TABLE 6.2

Sources of Information About Employment Tests

Mental Measurements Yearbook	Descriptions and reviews of tests that are commercially available
Principles for the Validation and Use of Personnel Selection Procedures (Society for Industrial and Organizational Psychology)	Guide to help organizations evaluate tests
Standards for Educational and Psychological Tests (American Psychological Association)	Description of standards for testing programs
Tests: A Comprehensive Reference for Assessments in Psychology, Education, and Business	Descriptions of thousands of tests
Test Critiques	Reviews of tests, written by professionals in the field

HR HOW-TO

Testing 101

Intelligence Quotient

In use for about a century, we've all taken IQ tests in school. These are most often multiple-choice tests that determine how well you acquire verbal and mathematical knowledge, and how accurately you apply what you know.

Sample question: Which number does not belong: 4, 17, 18, 32? The answer is 17, the only odd number.

What it demonstrates: IQ score is based on an average. Scoring 100 means the person is technically higher than 50 percent of all people taking the test. An IQ of 130 is higher than 95 percent of the people taking the test.

Emotional Intelligence

Based on research by psychologist Dr. Daniel Goleman, who claims a combination of self-awareness, empathy, and social skills is as important as factual knowledge in achieving success.

Sample question: Rate on a five-point scale from strongly agree to disagree: "Even when I do my best, I feel guilty about the things that didn't get done." Strongly agreeing indicates the person is a perfectionist, which an employer might prize, but it could also be seen as obsessive, which could affect ability to work with others.

What it shows: Proponents claim the combination of self-awareness, empathy, and social skills these tests measure are vital to leadership.

Personality Test

More than 100 tests are on the market that ask questions about anger, anxiety, pain, honesty, and integrity to rate a person's approach to life and relationships.

Sample question: Rate yourself on a five-point scale from strongly agree to disagree: "I am a reliable worker; I can be careless at times; I tend to be disorganized."

What it measures: Traits—for instance, extroverted or introverted; agreeable or inflexible; creative or conservative.

SOURCE: Wallace Immen, "Testing 101," *The Globe and Mail,* January 26, 2005, p. C2. Reprinted with permission from The Globe and Mail.

is a multiple-choice test used to evaluate an individual's aptitude for police work by measuring seven skills deemed essential to performing the job: composition (spelling, grammar, and vocabulary), comprehension, memory, judgement, observation, logic, and computation. The SFPQ is used to assess the candidate's honesty, integrity, and commitment, and results in a conscientiousness score. Candidates with the best scores on the RPAB advance to the next step, where they take the Physical Abilities Requirement Evaluation (PARE). The PARE is a job-related physical ability test developed as a result of extensive research and simulates a critical incident in which a police officer chases, controls, and apprehends a suspect.[22]

Physical Ability Tests

Physical strength and endurance play less of a role in the modern workplace than in the past, thanks to the use of automation and current technology. Even so, many jobs still require certain physical abilities or psychomotor abilities (those connecting brain and body, as in the case of eye–hand coordination). When these abilities are essential to job performance or avoidance of injury, the organization may use physical ability tests. These evaluate one or more of the following areas of physical ability: muscular tension, muscular power, muscular endurance, cardiovascular endurance, flexibility, balance, and coordination.[23]

Although these tests can accurately predict success at certain kinds of jobs, they also tend to exclude women and people with disabilities. As a result, use of physical ability tests can make the organization vulnerable to human rights complaints. It is therefore important to be certain that the abilities tested for really are essential to job performance or that the absence of these abilities really does create a safety hazard.

3

cognitive ability tests
Tests designed to measure such mental abilities as verbal skills, quantitative skills, and reasoning ability.

Cognitive Ability Tests

Although fewer jobs require muscle power today, brainpower is essential for most jobs. Organizations therefore benefit from people who have strong mental abilities. **Cognitive ability tests**—sometimes called "intelligence tests"—are designed to measure such mental abilities as verbal skills (skill in using written and spoken language), quantitative skills (skill in working with numbers), and reasoning ability (skill in thinking through the answer to a problem). Many jobs require all of these cognitive skills, so employers often get valid information from general tests. The Public Service Commission of Canada uses the General Competency Test Level 1 (GCT1) to measure thinking skills (understanding written material, solving numerical problems, and drawing logical conclusions) for administrative support position selection decisions. See Figure 6.6 for a sample question and answer from the General Competency Test Level 1 (GCT1). The GCT2 is used to assess general cognitive abilities required for officer-level positions.[24] Many reliable tests are commercially available. The tests are especially valid for complex jobs and for those requiring adaptability in changing circumstances.[25]

FIGURE 6.6

Sample Question from the Public Service Commission of Canada's General Competency Test: Level 1 (GCT1)

Government   Gouvernement
of Canada   du Canada
MEMORANDUM   NOTE DE SERVICE

TO: All employees
FROM: Manager

We are pleased to announce that our Ministry's budget has been increased and consequently we will experience an increase in staff size. Because new positions will become available, we will be holding interviews within the next few weeks.

The main focus of this memo is to indicate a change concerning:

1. better ministerial policy.
2. better budget publicity.
3. more human resources.
4. more office space.

SOURCE: General Competency Test Level—GCT 1 Practice Test, www.psc-cfp.gc.ca/ppc/gct1_practice_test_info_e.htm. Reproduced with the permission of the Public Service Commission of Canada, April 2008.

Job Performance Tests and Work Samples

Many kinds of jobs require candidates that excel at performing specialized tasks, such as operating a certain machine, handling calls from customers, or designing advertising materials. To evaluate candidates for such jobs, the organization may administer tests of the necessary skills. Sometimes the candidates take tests that involve a sample of work, or they may show existing samples of their work. Examples of job performance tests include tests of keyboarding speed and *in-basket tests*, which measure the ability to juggle a variety of demands, as in a manager's job. The candidate is presented with simulated emails and messages describing the kinds of problems that confront a person in the job. The candidate has to decide how to respond to these messages, and in what order. Examples of jobs for which candidates provide work samples include graphic designers and writers. The e-HRM box describes how job simulation can be used as a selection tool in the real estate industry.

Pilots require high cognitive ability. Cognitive ability tests may be used to select individuals for such jobs. What other jobs might require measures of an individual's ability to handle their complexities?

E- HRM

Simulation Turns Selection into a Two-Way Street

Ken Church, the owner of Prudential Grand Valley Realty, a real estate firm in Kitchener, Ontario, is constantly on the lookout for new agents and competition for talent can be intense. Given its ambitious growth goals, recruitment and selection of new staff who would be top performers was one of his toughest challenges.

He started using job simulation as a selection tool. It's an online, video-based assessment that simulates the job of a real estate agent and gives candidates a realistic preview of what day-to-day life as a sales agent will be. It also evaluates the key skills required to succeed as an agent and compiles that information for review to help make a better hiring decision.

"Since we've implemented this tool, we are getting way more recruiting leads and are seeing a higher quality of applicants," said Church. "It's no secret that attracting people into the real estate industry is tough, because they have no real way of knowing if they have what it takes to be successful. The simulation helps them make a more informed decision."

In the simulation, the recruit plays the role of an agent and gets to interact with virtual clients who are interested in buying or selling property. The recruit is taken through the entire sales cycle from building rapport all the way to closing and must demonstrate the ability to handle objections, negotiate price, understand client needs, deal with personality clashes, and handle periodic rejection.

SOURCE: Igor Kotylar and Ravit Abelman, "Simulation Turns Recruitment into a Two-Way Street," *Canadian HR Reporter*, December 1, 2003, www.hrreporter.com, retrieved February 19, 2004. © *Canadian HR Reporter*, December 1, 2003, by permission of Carswell, Toronto, Ontario, 1-800-387-5164.

assessment centre
A wide variety of specific selection programs that use multiple selection methods to rate applicants or job incumbents on their management potential.

Tests for selecting managers may take the form of an **assessment centre**—a wide variety of specific selection programs that use multiple selection methods to rate applicants or job incumbents on their management potential. An assessment centre typically includes in-basket tests, tests of more general abilities, and personality tests. Combining several assessment methods increases the validity of this approach.

Job performance tests have the advantage of being job-specific—that is, tailored to the kind of work done in a specific job. These tests therefore have a high level of validity, especially when combined with cognitive ability tests and a highly structured interview.[26] This can become a disadvantage, however, if the organization wants to generalize the results of a test for one job to candidates for other jobs. The tests are more appropriate for identifying candidates generally able to solve the problems associated with a job, rather than for identifying which specific skills or traits the individual possesses.[27] Developing different tests for different jobs can become expensive. One way to save money is to prepare computerized tests that can be delivered online to various locations.

Personality Inventories

In some situations, employers may also want to know about candidates' personalities. For example, one way psychologists think of personality is in terms of the "Big Five" traits: extroversion, adjustment, agreeableness, conscientiousness, and inquisitiveness (explained in Table 6.3). There is evidence that people who score high on conscientiousness tend to excel at work, especially when they also have high cognitive ability.[28] For people-related jobs like sales and management, extroversion and agreeableness also seem to be associated with success.[29]

A recent Spherion Workplace Snapshot survey conducted by Harris Interactive suggests that workers are also interested in personality tests. Nearly one-third of workers (32 percent) agree personality tests can help determine if a prospective employee will fit in.[30] The usual way to identify a candidate's personality traits is to administer one of the personality tests that are commercially available. The employer pays for the use of the test, and the organization that owns the test then scores the responses and provides a report about the test taker's personality. An organization that provides such tests should be able to discuss the test's validity and reliability. Assuming the tests are valid for the organization's jobs, they have advantages. However, Shawn Bakker, a chartered psychologist at Psychometrics Canada (an Alberta firm that specializes in selection) cautions that personality tests were not designed for selection and work better for staff development purposes.[31]

TABLE 6.3

Five Major Personality Dimensions Measured by Personality Inventories

1. Extroversion	Sociable, gregarious, assertive, talkative, expressive
2. Adjustment	Emotionally stable, non-depressed, secure, content
3. Agreeableness	Courteous, trusting, good-natured, tolerant, cooperative, forgiving
4. Conscientiousness	Dependable, organized, persevering, thorough, achievement-oriented
5. Inquisitiveness	Curious, imaginative, artistically sensitive, broadminded, playful

Google is experimenting with an approach to hiring that uses an algorithm created by company mathematicians to predict how well a person will fit into its chaotic and competitive culture. Google receives more than 100,000 job applications each month and uses an elaborate online survey to explore job applicant's attitudes, behaviour and personality. Applicants' answers are fed into a series of formulas that calculates a score from zero to 100.[32]

Honesty, Alcohol, and Drug Tests

No matter what employees' personalities may be like, organizations want employees to be honest and to behave safely. Some organizations are satisfied to assess these qualities on the basis of judgments from reference checks and interviews. Others investigate these characteristics more directly through the use of tests.

1,3

The most famous kind of honesty test is the polygraph, the so-called "lie detector" test. As a result of controversies associated with the use of polygraph tests, testing services have developed paper-and-pencil honesty (or integrity) tests. Generally these tests ask applicants directly about their attitudes toward honesty and integrity and their own experiences in situations inside and outside work. Table 6.4 shows a sample of the items on such a test. Most of the research into the validity of these tests has been conducted by the testing companies, but evidence suggests they do have some ability to predict such behaviour as theft of the employer's property.[33]

As concerns about substance abuse and the harmful impacts of alcohol and drugs on employee safety and performance have grown, so has the use of alcohol and drug testing. As a measure of a person's past exposure to drugs, chemical testing is highly accurate. However, these tests are controversial for several reasons. Although breathalyzer tests can measure how much alcohol has been consumed and the person's level of impairment, current drug tests cannot measure impairment or assess if an employee is capable of performing the job.[34]

The use of pre-employment drug testing was recently dealt a blow by the Alberta Court of Queen's Bench decision regarding a case involving the use of a drug screen as part of the hiring process for Kellogg Brown & Root (KBR), a subsidiary of Houston-based oil-and-gas giant Haliburton. Although the court commended KBR's goal of workplace safety, Justice Martin "ordered KBR to cease its contravention of human rights legislation and refrain from breaching it again," that is, use of pre-employment drug testing.[35] Employers considering the use of drug or alcohol tests should ensure that their testing programs conform to the Canadian Human Rights Commission's drug and alcohol testing policy and all other relevant legal

TABLE 6.4

Sample Items from a Typical Honesty Test

1. It's OK to take something from a company that is making too much profit.
2. Stealing is just a way of getting your fair share.
3. When a store overcharges its customers, it's OK to change price tags on merchandise.
4. If you could get into a movie without paying and not get caught, would you do it?
5. Is it OK to go around the law if you don't actually break it?

SOURCE: "T or F? Honesty Tests," p. 104. Reprinted with permission, *Inc.* magazine, February 1992. © 1992 by Goldhirsh Group, Inc., 38 Commercial Wharf, Boston, MA 02110.

requirements. As discussed in Chapter 2, the Canadian Human Rights Act prohibits discrimination related to a disability, and dependence on drugs or alcohol is considered a disability that must be accommodated to the point of undue hardship.

At least partially in response to cases brought before the Supreme Court of Canada and the Ontario Court of Appeals, the Canadian Human Rights Commission has updated its policy on drug testing and created a framework for alcohol testing. As a result, the following kinds of testing became unacceptable:

- Pre-employment drug tests
- Random drug tests
- Random alcohol tests for employees in jobs not considered "safety-sensitive"

Note: At the time of writing, the Canadian Human Rights Commission's Policy on Alcohol and Drug Testing (2002) is being reviewed.[36]

Employers considering the use of alcohol or drug testing should get legal advice to make sure they can justify testing on the basis of a bona fide occupational requirement.

Medical Examinations

Especially for physically demanding jobs, organizations may wish to conduct medical examinations to see that the applicant can meet the job's requirements. Employers may also wish to establish an employee's physical condition at the beginning of employment, so that there is a basis for measuring whether the employee has suffered a work-related disability later on. At the same time, as described in Chapter 2, organizations may not discriminate against individuals with disabilities who could perform a job with reasonable accommodations. Likewise, they may not use a measure of physical ability that discriminates against women, older workers, etc., unless those requirements are valid in predicting the ability to perform a job. Medical exams must be related to job requirements and may not be given until the candidate has received a conditional job offer. Therefore, organizations must be careful in how they use medical examinations. Many organizations make selection decisions first, then conduct the exams to confirm that the employee can handle the job, with any reasonable accommodations required. Limiting the use of medical exams in this way also holds down the cost of what tends to be an expensive process.

L06 - Discuss how to conduct effective interviews.

Interviews

Supervisors and team members most often get involved in the selection process at the stage of employment interviews. These interviews bring together job applicants and representatives of the employer to obtain information and evaluate the applicant's qualifications and organizational fit. While the applicant is providing information, he or she is also forming opinions about what it is like to work for the organization. Most organizations use interviewing as part of the selection process. In fact, this method is used more than any other.

nondirective interview
A selection interview in which the interviewer has great discretion in choosing questions to ask each candidate.

Interviewing Techniques

An interview may be nondirective or structured. In a **nondirective interview**, the interviewer has great discretion in choosing questions to ask each candidate. For example, the interviewer might ask, "What is your greatest accomplishment in your current position?" The candidate's reply might suggest to the interviewer what other questions to ask. Often, these interviews include open-ended questions about the candidate's strengths, weaknesses, career goals, and work experience. Because nondirective interviews give the interviewer wide latitude, their reliability is not great. Also, interviewers do not necessarily ask valid questions. For example, asking a candidate, "If you were a tree, what kind of tree would you be?" is likely to lack both reliability and validity. Inexperienced or poorly informed interviewers may ask questions that are irrelevant or even illegal.

To manage the risks of a nondirective interview, many organizations substitute the use of a **structured interview**, which establishes a set of questions for the interviewer to ask. Ideally, these questions are related to the requirements set out in the job description. They should cover the candidate's knowledge required to perform this type of job, his or her experience in handling job-related situations, and other job-related personal requirements such as willingness to travel, work overtime, or learn new skills. The interviewer asks questions from the list and is supposed to avoid asking questions that are not on the list. Some interviewers object to being limited in this way, but a list of well-written questions can provide more valid and reliable results.

Some of the best results of interviewing come from the use of situational interviews. In this type of structured interview, the interviewer describes a situation likely to arise on the job, then asks the candidate what he or she would do in that situation. **Situational interviews** have been shown to have high validity in predicting job performance.[37] A variation is the **behavioural interview**, in which the interviewer asks the candidate to describe how he or she handled a type of situation in the past. Questions about the candidates' actual experiences tend to have the highest validity.[38] This extensively used method may also be referred to as a *behaviour description interview*, or as *behaviourally-based* or *competency-based interviewing*.

When Andrew Kindler was a hiring manager, he used open-ended behavioural questions to good effect. When interviewing candidates for management positions, he would ask them to describe the most difficult ethical dilemma they had to solve at work. Kindler's objective was to learn about each candidate's ethics and problem-solving style. In one instance, a candidate for a position as the corporation's general counsel (an important legal position) said he had never encountered an ethical

structured interview
A selection interview that consists of a predetermined set of questions for the interviewer to ask.

situational interviews
A structured interview in which the interviewer describes a situation likely to arise on the job, then asks the candidate what he or she would do in that situation.

behavioural interview
A structured interview in which the interviewer asks the candidate to describe how he or she handled a type of situation in the past.

When interviewing candidates, it's valid to ask about willingness to travel if that is part of the job. Interviewers might ask questions about previous business travel experiences and/or how interviewees handled situations requiring flexibility and self-motivation (qualities that would be an asset in someone who is travelling alone and solving business problems on the road).

BEST PRACTICES

Interview Questions That Can Get Boffo Results

Behavioural interviewing is based on the premise that past behaviour is the best predictor of future behaviour. Behavioural interviewing offers at least a couple of key advantages relative to traditional methods:

- By focusing on the critical competencies or attributes most important to successful job performance, the interview has a valid basis for person-to-job matching.
- Because candidates are asked similar questions, the interviewer can make objective comparisons between candidates.

Here are five behavioural interview questions that are somewhat unexpected and are likely to produce revealing results:

1. "Tell us about a best-in-class standard or practice that you've introduced."

- This question can uncover results-orientation and may be adapted for less senior positions, for example, "Tell us about a recent example of something you have done to improve your efficiency at work."

2. "Describe a situation when a subordinate was able to change your mind on a particular course of action."

- This question is useful to uncover team leadership capabilities.

3. "Tell us about the most unpopular decision you have made."

- This question can tell you a lot about a candidate's leadership and negotiation skills.

4. "Describe a time when you were faced with a challenging situation that involved balancing competing interests in your personal life with issues in the workplace."

- This question can uncover how employees effectively balance their work–life by using creative and innovative solutions.

5. "Describe a crisis situation and how you handled it."

- This question can provide key insights into the candidate's ability to assess and respond quickly.

Behavioural description interviews are flexible and can be applied and adapted to any situation or organization.

SOURCE: Sarah B. Hood, "Hire Echelon," *Canadian Business*, June 7–20, 2004, pp. 71–73.

---

dilemma. Kindler quickly eliminated that candidate from consideration, on the grounds that "a lawyer who has never encountered an ethical dilemma doesn't have ethics."[39]

The Best Practices box examines some specific questions that may be part of an effective behavioural interview. BMO Financial Group has been using behavioural interviews since the early 1990s for almost every position it fills. BMO Financial Group views behavioural interviews as most effective for external candidates because internal candidates have existing performance reviews and have been through the process at some point.[40]

The common setup for either a nondirective or structured interview is for an individual (an HR professional or the supervisor for the vacant position) to interview each candidate face to face. However, variations on this approach are possible. In a **panel interview**, several members of the organization meet to interview each

panel interview
Selection interview in which several members of the organization meet to interview each candidate.

candidate. A panel interview gives the candidate a chance to meet more people and see how people interact in that organization. It provides the organization with the judgments of more than one person, to reduce the effect of personal biases in selection decisions. Panel interviews can be especially appropriate in organizations that use teamwork. At the other extreme, some organizations conduct interviews without any interviewers; they use a computerized interviewing process. The candidate enters replies to the questions interactively and results are submitted electronically. Such a format eliminates a lot of personal bias—along with the opportunity to see how people interact. Therefore, electronic interviews are useful for gathering objective data, rather than assessing people skills.

Advantages and Disadvantages of Interviewing

The wide use of interviewing is not surprising. People naturally want to see prospective employees firsthand. As we noted in Chapter 1, the top qualities that employers seek in new hires include communication skills and interpersonal skills. Talking face to face can provide evidence of these skills. Interviews can give insights into candidates' personalities and interpersonal styles. They are more valid, however, when they focus on job knowledge and skill. Interviews also provide a means to check the accuracy of information on the applicant's résumé or job application. Asking applicants to elaborate about their experiences and offer details reduces the likelihood of a candidate being able to invent a work history.[41]

Despite these benefits, interviewing is not necessarily the most accurate basis for making a selection decision. Research has shown that interviews can be unreliable, low in validity,[42] and biased against a number of different groups.[43] Interviews are also costly. They require that at least one person devote time to interviewing each candidate, and the applicants typically have to be brought to one geographic location. Interviews are also subjective, so they place the organization at greater risk of discrimination complaints by applicants who were not hired, especially if those individuals were asked questions not entirely related to the job.

Organizations can avoid some of these pitfalls.[44] Human resource staff should keep the interviews focused, structured, and standardized. The interview should focus on accomplishing a few goals, so that at the end of the interview, the organization has ratings on several observable measures, such as ability to express ideas. The interview should not try to measure abilities and skills—for example, intelligence—that tests can measure better. As noted earlier, situational and behavioural interviews are especially effective for doing this. Organizations can prevent problems related to subjectivity by training interviewers and using more than one person to conduct interviews. Training typically includes focusing on the recording of observable facts, rather than on making subjective judgments, as well as developing interviewers' awareness of their biases.[45] Using a structured system for taking notes is helpful for limiting subjectivity and helping the interviewer remember and justify an evaluation later.[46] Finally, to address costs of interviewing, some organizations videotape interviews or use videoconferencing technologies.

Preparing to Interview

Organizations can reap the greatest benefits from interviewing if they prepare carefully. A well-planned interview should be standardized, comfortable for the participants, and focused on the job and the organization. The interviewer should have a quiet place in which to conduct interviews without interruption. This person should be trained in how to ask objective questions, what subject matter to avoid, and how to detect and handle his or her own personal biases or other distractions in order to fairly evaluate candidates.

The interviewer should have enough documents to conduct a complete interview. These should include a list of the questions to be asked, with plenty of space for recording the responses. When the questions are prepared, it is also helpful to determine how the answers will be assessed. For example, if questions are asked about how interviewees have handled certain situations, consider what responses are best in terms of meeting job requirements. If the job requires someone who develops new and creative solutions to problems, then a response that shows innovative behaviour would receive a higher score. The interviewer also should have a copy of the interviewee's employment application and résumé, to review before the interview and refer to during the interview. If possible, the interviewer should also have printed information about the organization and the job. Near the beginning of the interview, it is a good idea to go over the job specifications, organizational policies, and so on, so that the interviewee has a clearer understanding of the organization's needs and expectations.

The interviewer should schedule enough time to review the job requirements, discuss the interview questions, and give the interviewee a chance to ask questions. To close, the interviewer should thank the candidate for coming and provide information about what to expect—for example, that the organization will contact a few finalists within the next two weeks or that a decision will be made by the end of the week.

LO7 - Explain how employers carry out the process of making a selection decision.

1,3

Selection Decisions

After reviewing applications, scoring tests, conducting interviews, and checking references, the organization needs to make decisions about which candidates to place in which jobs. In practice, most organizations find more than one qualified candidate to fill an open position. The selection decision typically combines ranking based on objective criteria along with subjective judgments about which candidate will make the greatest contribution.

How Organizations Select Employees

The selection decision should not be a simple matter of whom the supervisor likes best or which candidate will take the lowest offer. Rather, the people making the selection should look for the best fit between candidate and position and candidate and organization. In general, the person's performance will result from a combination of ability and motivation. Often, the selection is a choice among a few people who possess the basic qualifications. The decision makers therefore have to decide which of those people have the best combination of ability and motivation to fit in the position and in the organization as a whole.

The usual process for arriving at a selection decision is to gradually narrow the pool of candidates for each job. This approach, called the **multiple-hurdle model**, is based on a process such as the one shown earlier in Figure 6.1. Each stage of the process is a hurdle, and candidates who overcome a hurdle continue to the next stage

multiple-hurdle model
Process of arriving at a selection decision by eliminating some candidates at each stage of the selection process.

of the process. For example, the organization reviews applications and/or résumés of all candidates, conducts some tests on those who meet minimum requirements, conducts initial interviews with those who had the highest test scores, follows up with additional interviews or testing, and then selects a candidate from the few who survived this process. Another, more expensive alternative is to take most applicants through all steps of the process and then to review all the scores to find the most desirable candidates. With this alternative, decision makers may use a **compensatory model**, in which a very high score on one type of assessment can make up for a low score on another.

Whether the organization uses a multiple-hurdle model or conducts the same assessments on all candidates, the decision maker(s) needs criteria for choosing among qualified candidates. An obvious strategy is to select the candidates who score highest on tests and interviews. However, employee performance depends on motivation as well as ability. It is possible that a candidate who scores very high on an ability test might be "overqualified," that is, the employee might be bored by the job the organization needs to fill, and a less-able employee might actually be a better fit. Similarly, a highly motivated person might learn some kinds of jobs very quickly, potentially outperforming someone who has the necessary skills. Furthermore, some organizations have policies of developing employees for career paths in the organization. Such organizations might put less emphasis on the skills needed for a particular job and more emphasis on hiring candidates who share the organization's values, show that they have the people skills to work with others in the organization, and are able to learn the skills needed for advancement.

Finally, organizations have choices about who will make the decision. Sometimes a supervisor makes the final decision, often alone. This person may couple knowledge of the job with a judgment about who will fit in best with others in the department. The decision could also be made by a human resource professional using standardized, objective criteria. Especially in organizations that value teamwork, selection decisions may be made by a work team or other panel of decision makers.

Communicating the Decision

The human resource department is often responsible for notifying applicants about the results of the selection process. When a candidate has been selected, the organization should communicate the offer to the candidate. The offer should include the job responsibilities, work schedule, rate of pay, starting date, and other relevant details. If placement in a job requires that the applicant complete a medical examination or drug test, the offer should state that contingency. The person communicating the offer should also indicate a date by which the candidate should reply with an acceptance or rejection of the offer. For some jobs, such as management and professional positions, the candidate and organization may negotiate pay, benefits, and work arrangements before they arrive at a final employment agreement.

The person who communicates this decision should keep accurate records of who was contacted, when, and for which position, as well as of the candidate's reply. The HR department and the supervisor also should be in close communication about the job offer. When an applicant accepts a job offer, the HR department must notify the supervisor, so that he or she can be prepared for the new employee's arrival.

compensatory model
Process of arriving at a selection decision in which a very high score on one type of assessment can make up for a low score on another.

THINKING ETHICALLY

Checking Out a Candidate's Facebook Profile

The Internet has become the first stop for many recruiters and hiring managers to determine if a potential candidate is a good fit. Many job seekers are not aware of these instant background checks. In a recent Adecco Workplace Insights survey, 66 percent of Generation Y respondents were unaware that seemingly private photos, comments, and statements were audited by potential employers.

"It's a lot more common than I think the prospective employees realize," says Lynne Perry-Reid, a Calgary recruiter and co-founder of Corporate Connections. "Especially now that a lot of recruiters tend to be younger, maybe in their 30's, everyone is really involved in things like MySpace or Facebook," she says, "so you can easily just type in someone's name to find out about them because you're already hooked into that network."

In a formal job interview, employers are not legally permitted to ask questions about a candidate's age, marital status, sexual orientation, or ethnicity but the individual's profile can reveal all of these things to a prospective employer. Even individuals who are very careful about photos and information on their own profile, may not be aware of being in a photo that appears on another person's profile. "All of a sudden there are pictures of you drunk and half-naked—do you want your prospective employer to see those pictures before they have actually met you?"

SOURCES: "Your Profile on Social Sites Can Make or Break Your Job Opportunities," *Financial Post,* September 19, 2007, www.canada .com/nationalpost/news/working/ story, retrieved September 21, 2007; Derek Sankey, "Facebook Background Checks," *Calgary Herald,* 2007, http:// working.canada.com/calgary/resources/ story, retrieved April 4, 2008; Kristin Gissaro, "The Invasion of Recruiters on Social Networking Sites," www.ere.net .blogs/generational_recruiting, retrieved April 4, 2008.

Questions

1. Are employers crossing the line when they look up job candidates on a social networking site such as Facebook?
2. Suppose you are a recruiter and have identified an applicant who possesses excellent knowledge, skills, ability, and other characteristics required for a position in your organization. Then you discover an awkward image of the prospective employee posted on their profile. What would you do? Would you need further information, and if so, what information?
3. Would your answer to question 2 be different if you identified two qualified candidates, and only one candidate's "Facebook background check" turned up a concern?

SUMMARY

L01 Identify the elements of the selection process.

- Selection typically begins with a review of candidates' employment applications and résumés. The organization administers tests to candidates who meet requirements, and qualified candidates undergo one or more interviews.

- Organizations check references and conduct background checks to verify the accuracy of information provided by candidates. A candidate is selected to fill each vacant position. Candidates who accept offers are placed in the positions for which they were selected.

L02   Define ways to measure the success of a selection method.

- One criterion is reliability, which indicates the method is free from random error, so that measurements are consistent. A selection method should also be valid, meaning that performance on the measure (such as a test score) is related to what the measure is designed to assess (such as job performance).

- A selection method also should be generalizable, so that it applies to more than one specific situation. Each selection method should have utility, meaning it provides economic value greater than its cost. Finally, selection methods should meet the legal requirements for employment decisions.

L03   Summarize the legal requirements for employee selection.

- The selection process must comply with human rights and privacy legislation and be conducted in a fair and consistent manner. Selection methods must be valid for job performance. Questions may not gather information about prohibited grounds.

L04   Compare the common methods used for selecting human resources.

- Nearly all organizations gather information through employment applications and résumés. These methods are inexpensive, and an application form standardizes basic information received from all applicants. The information is not necessarily reliable, because each applicant provides the information.

- References and background checks help to verify the accuracy of the information. Employment tests and work samples are more objective. To be legal, any test must measure abilities that actually are associated with successful job performance. Tests should be selected to be related to successful job performance and avoid human rights violations.

- Interviews are widely used to obtain information about a candidate's interpersonal and communication skills and to gather more detailed information about a candidate's background. Structured interviews are more valid than unstructured ones. Situational and behavioural interviews provide greater validity than general questions. Interviews are costly and may introduce bias into the selection process. Organizations can minimize the drawbacks through preparation and training.

L05   Describe major types of employment tests.

- Physical ability tests measure strength, endurance, psychomotor abilities, and other physical abilities. They can be accurate but can discriminate and are not always job-related.

- Cognitive ability tests, or intelligence tests, tend to be valid, especially for complex jobs and those requiring adaptability. Job performance tests tend to be valid but are not always generalizable.

- Personality tests measure personality traits such as extroversion and adjustment. Organizations may use honesty tests as well as alcohol and/or drug tests (if a bona fide occupational requirement such as safety justifies it). Passing a medical examination may be a condition of employment, but to avoid discrimination against persons with disabilities, organizations usually administer a medical exam only after making a conditional job offer.

L06   Discuss how to conduct effective interviews.

- Interviews should be focused, structured, and standardized. Interviewers should identify job requirements and create a list of questions related to the requirements. Interviewers should be trained to recognize their own personal biases and conduct objective interviews. Panel interviews can reduce problems related to interviewer bias. Interviewers also should be prepared to provide information about the job and the organization.

L07   Explain how employers carry out the process of making a selection decision.

- The organization should focus on the objective of finding the person who will be the best fit with the job and organization.

- Decision makers may use a multiple-hurdle model, in which each stage of the selection process eliminates some of the candidates from consideration at the following stages. An alternative is a compensatory model, in which all candidates are evaluated with all methods. A candidate who scores poorly with one method may be selected if he or she scores very high on another measure.

REVIEW AND DISCUSSION QUESTIONS

1. What activities are involved in the selection process? Think of the last time you were hired for a job. Which of those activities were used in selecting you? Should the organization that hired you have used other methods as well?

2. Why should the selection process be adapted to fit the organization's job specifications?

3. Choose two of the selection methods identified in this chapter. Describe how you can compare them in terms of reliability, validity, ability to generalize, utility, and compliance with human rights legislation.

4. Why does predictive validation provide better information than concurrent validation? Why is this type of validation more difficult?

5. How does human rights legislation affect organizations' use of interviews?

6. Suppose your organization needs to hire several computer programmers, and you are reviewing résumés you obtained from an online service. What kinds of information will you want to gather from the "work experience" portion of these résumés? What kinds of information will you want to gather from the "education" portion of these résumés? What methods would you use for verifying or exploring this information? Why would you use those methods?

7. For each of the following jobs, select two kinds of tests you think would be most important to include in the selection process. Explain why you chose those tests.
   a. City bus driver
   b. Pharmaceutical sales representative
   c. Member of a team that sells complex high-tech equipment to manufacturers
   d. Member of a team that makes a component of the equipment in (c)

8. Suppose you are a human resource professional at a large retail chain. You want to improve the company's hiring process by standardizing interviews, so that every time someone is interviewed for a particular job category, that person answers the same questions. You also want to make sure the questions asked are relevant to the job and comply with human rights legislation. Think of three questions to include in interviews for each of the following jobs. For each question, state why you think it should be included.
   a. Cashier at one of the company's stores
   b. Buyer of the teen clothing line
   c. Accounts payable clerk at company headquarters

9. How can organizations improve the quality of their interviewing so that interviews provide valid information?

10. The following questions are favourites of three seasoned hiring managers. For each of the following questions provide your opinion of:
    i. What you think the interviewer is after
    ii. The best answer
    iii. The worst answer
    a. Del Rollo, Director of Hospitality, Jackson-Triggs Niagara Estate, Niagara-on-the-Lake asks: "*What is the greatest service experience you've had?*"
    b. Gary Hellard, Manager of Recruiting, WestJet Airlines, Calgary asks: "*Tell us what began as your most frustrating or tough day, and what you did so that is ended up being your most productive day.*"
    c. Nancy Blair, Office Leader, Egon Zehnder International Inc., Calgary asks: "*What do you hope this job is not?*"

    SOURCE: Tony Martin, "Why Are They Asking Me This?" Report on Business, *The Globe and Mail,* September 26, 2007, www.theglobeandmail.com, retrieved September 27, 2007.

11. Some organizations set up a selection process that is long and complex. In some people's opinion, this kind of selection process not only is more valid but also has symbolic value. What can the use of a long, complex selection process symbolize to job seekers? How do you think this would affect the organization's ability to attract the best employees?

WHAT'S YOUR HR IQ?

Online **Learning Centre**

The Online Learning Centre offers more ways to check what you've learned so far. Find experiential exercises as well as Test Your Knowledge Quizzes, Videos, and many other resources at www.mcgrawhill.ca/olc/steen.

BusinessWeek Case:
How Google Searches for Talent

BusinessWeek

It is the first day of spring in India, a day celebrated with riotous colour and revelry. But in one corner of Bangalore, India's info tech hub, the sunny Saturday is heavy with tension. At an Internet café, a group of engineers and math majors, all in their twenties, hunch over terminals, ready to write some killer code—and with luck, launch careers with one of the world's premier tech companies, Google Inc.

It's the Google India Code Jam, a contest to find the most brilliant coder in South and Southeast Asia. The fastest will win $6,900—and more importantly, the offer of a coveted job at one of Google's research and development centres. At the stroke of 10:30 a.m., the contestants begin, emerging exhausted three hours later. "It's been incredibly difficult and awesome," says Nirin Gupta, a computer science undergrad at the Indian Institute of Technology at Bombay.

Google has staged Code Jams in the United States, but this is its first such bakeoff in Asia, and the response is huge. Some 14,000 aspirants registered from all over South and Southeast Asia for the first round in February. The top 50 were selected for the finals in Bangalore: 39 from India, 8 from Singapore, and 3 from Indonesia. "It's a dog-eat-dog world," says Robert Hughes, president of Top-Coder Inc., the testing company that runs the Code Jams. "Wherever the best talent is, Google wants them."

And the winner is ... one of these clever IIT grads from India, right? Surprisingly, no. Ardian Poernomo, a third-year undergrad computer engineering student at Singapore's Nanyang Technological University, lands in first place. The number two finisher, Pascal Alfadian, a second-year student at the Universitas Katolik Parahyangan in West Java, is Indonesian, too. Poernomo didn't commit to taking a job with Google, however. He may go for a doctorate degree in computer science in the United States.

Still, Google now has a new pool of Asian talent to choose from. According to Krishna Bharat, head of Google's India research and development centre, all the finalists will be offered jobs. And Google needs them. The search company has been frustrated by its inability to find top-notch engineers for its year-old Indian centre, according to industry insiders.

Google's frustrations in India stem from two factors. One is the red-hot job market in Indian tech. Engineering students are assured of a job a year before they graduate. But Google makes things hard for itself by having some of the most exacting hiring standards going. The contest is an example. Participants are tested on aptitude in problem solving, on designing and writing code, and on testing peer-written work. Finalists are asked to create and test software for unique Web searches and to get from point A to B in a city with a minimum number of turns. The final challenge is programming a war-based board game, a task so complex that only winner Poernomo completed it.

For Google, the Code Jam will serve as a shortcut through its hiring regime. Candidates normally go through a seven-stage process that can last months—and at the end of it, they're more likely to be rejected than hired. Much of that screening can be set aside for Code Jam winners.

For Wunderkinder like Poernomo, Google can be patient. Stanford grad Jon McAlister was the 2001 winner of TopCoder's U.S. Collegiate Code Jam, but didn't sign up with Google until 2004. He eventually rejected competing offers from other prominent companies, including Microsoft. "Google is the genuine engineering company," says McAlister. Google hopes its India finalists think so, too.

SOURCE: Josey Puliyenthuruthel, "How Google Searches—for Talent," *BusinessWeek*, April 11, 2005, http://web6.infotrac.galegroup.com.

Questions

1. Google's product is the Internet search engine of the same name. Why do you think the company uses a contest (the Code Jam) as one of its selection methods? What are some benefits of this method?
2. What knowledge, skills, abilities, or other characteristics of computer programmers would the Code Jam *not* evaluate?
3. Would you predict that the Code Jam is a valid and reliable selection method for Google programmers? Would you advise Google to use similar methods for other positions in the company? Explain.

Case:
A Dozen First Impressions

McMaster University in Hamilton, Ontario, is Canada's third-largest medical school. McMaster uses a screening method that requires medical school candidates to answer

questions and dash from one room to the next when a bell rings. This interviewing method was designed to enhance the quality of the selection process by getting an insight into the candidates' qualities related to the requirements of a medical career.

Traditional interviews for medical school involve interviews with a panel of professors. However, Chairman of Admissions, Dr. Harold Reiter explains, "It's hoped that by being able to differentiate which candidates are stronger in the desired personal qualities, we will be producing better physicians."

Applicants rotate through 12 mini-interviews that are exactly eight minutes long. They are given the chance to discuss one scenario or answer one question before having to move quickly to the next interview when a bell sounds. The mini-interviews focus on both ethical issues and realistic medical scenarios. For example, one mini-interview scenario requires applicants to answer a question about a patient who requests a faith healer after refusing traditional medical treatment. Another mini-interview requires applicants to confront a situation in which a law requires the physician to notify the police of treatment for a gunshot wound.

The use of these mini-interviews in the McMaster medical school's selection process takes the form of an assessment centre approach. This approach was put into place following three years of research into how to enhance the selection process. The medical school recently conducted these mini-interviews with 384 candidates in a two-week period to fill 138 available spots.

SOURCE: Anne Marie Owens, "Medical School's Novel Entrance Test—12 Eight Minute Interviews," *National Post*, April 5, 2004, pp. A1, A5. Reprinted with express permission of The National Post Company, a CanWest Partnership.

Questions

1. In your opinion, does this selection method increase the validity of the selection process at McMaster's medical school? Why or why not?
2. What additional selection methods might be appropriate for the initial screening of medical school applicants (i.e., prior to the intensive mini-interview process)?
3. Would you prefer this interview process to a traditional panel interview? Why or why not?

VIDEO CASE

Canada on Points

Canada has set the bar high for skilled workers to qualify to immigrate here. If today's standards had been in place in the past two centuries, the ancestors of many famous Canadians would have been unable to immigrate to Canada. Notable examples mentioned in the video include Sir John A. Macdonald, Tommy Douglas, and Wayne Gretzky. Canada's immigration system for skilled immigrants is based on a point system as outlined in the introduction to Chapter 5. Many the feel the bar is set too high—individuals might be lacking a college or university education but yet be able to contribute to Canada's economic growth; for example, skilled trades are often unable to meet the present requirements.

Questions

1. How does Canada's immigration policy impact workforce planning?
2. What advice would you offer Canada's prime minister about immigration policy given labour shortages threatening many Canadian organizations?
3. In your opinion what requirements and competencies are most critical to skilled immigrants' ability to make a meaningful contribution to Canada's economic well-being? How is your list the same or different from the current points system?

SOURCE: Based on CBC, "Canada on Points," *The National*, April 21, 2008.

Part 3

Managing Talent

Real People in HR

...Joy Serne, Senior Director Culture, Farm Credit Canada

Joy Serne is the Senior Director Culture, Organizational Development and Workforce Planning, with Farm Credit Canada (FCC). Joy previously held positions throughout FCC in the areas of Operations, Re-engineering, and IT. She holds a bachelor of science in agriculture and agricultural economics from the University of Saskatchewan.

Name...

Joy Serne.

Job...

Senior Director Culture, Organizational Development and Workforce Planning—Farm Credit Canada (FCC).

Adjective people would use to describe you...

Focused.

First job...

Working at Kentucky Fried Chicken as a cashier.

First HR job...

Compensation and Classification Advisor.

Biggest challenges or issues facing FCC from a talent management perspective...

We're currently in a great position as an employer of choice in Canada. We know the competition is going to get a lot tougher as the talent pool shrinks. Our big challenge is to keep striving to improve our employee experience so we can attract and keep the best of the best.

Most challenging aspect of your job...

Finding the time to do everything that can be done.

Most rewarding aspect of your job...

Seeing new HR strategies come to life and hearing others in the business say we really add value to FCC.

How FCC decides what training methods to use...

FCC bases its methods on *The Six Disciplines of Breakthrough Learning: How to Turn Training and Development into Business Results*. This is the essential guidebook for developing training that helps employees transfer what they learn into day-to-day actions that drive business results.

FCC's approach to management and leadership development...

We believe that the primary job of leaders is to inspire others to achieve outstanding results. We are currently building a new leadership strategy to ensure we support our leaders and equip them to effectively communicate, coach, and model our culture.

Four essential attributes that make someone a great HR professional...

1. Integrity displayed through both words and actions

2. Passion for people and the business

3. Vision for how HR can help move the business forward

4. Willingness to continually listen and learn

If you had to pick an alternative career...
Finance.

Best career advice that you ever received...
Find work you are passionate about and you will always be happy.

Advice for someone beginning an HR career...
Work hard and don't be scared to take on new challenges and ask questions. If you want to be respected by others in your organization, apply yourself to understanding the business and its environment so you can speak the language and connect with others.

Chapter 7

Training and Developing Employees

What Do I Need to Know? After reading this chapter, you should be able to:

1. Discuss how to link training and development to organizational needs and strategy.

2. Explain how to assess training needs and determine employees' readiness.

3. Describe how to plan and design an effective training program and compare training methods.

4. Summarize how to implement and evaluate a successful training program.

5. Describe training methods for employee orientation and diversity management.

6. Discuss the approaches organizations use for employee development.

7. Explain how managers and peers develop employees through mentoring and coaching.

8. Identify the steps in the career management process.

9. Discuss how organizations are meeting the challenges of the "glass ceiling" and succession planning.

Introduction

The PCL family of companies, established in 1906, is the largest general contracting organization in Canada, and among the largest in the United States. The PCL College of Construction, unique to the construction industry, has a campus or private learning space in each operating centre. The goal is to communicate today's technology to employees and help prepare them for tomorrow's challenges, whether through self-directed learning activities, instructor-directed learning, or some other teaching or mentoring activity. PCL describes its strategy to be the employer of choice in the North American Construction industry as "They invest in us; we invest in them." PCL expanded its commitment to the College of Construction by building the $13 million Centennial Learning Centre to commemorate PCL's 100th anniversary. The 29,000-square-foot addition to PCL's existing ten-acre business park in south Edmonton, serves as the training and development hub for the construction group.

The College of Construction offers courses and learning materials that develop skills in five main areas:

Personal: To enrich our personal abilities to learn, to communicate, and to organize ourselves.
Interpersonal: To build on our skills to interact effectively with one another.
Leadership and management: To demonstrate and practise new methods for the management of our key resources: our people, our time, our materials/equipment, and our finances.
Technical: To ensure that PCL employees have the appropriate opportunities to become and remain technically competent in key construction techniques, computer skills, and safety.
QUEST (skills for continuous improvement): To help develop innovative ways for working that will help prepare PCL employees for the variety of challenges facing the organization now and in a more competitive, complex, and rapidly changing future.[1]

In today's demanding and rapidly changing business environment, more and more companies are viewing employees as the talent upon which the organization's success is dependent. Organizations and their employees must constantly expand their competencies to meet customer needs and operate globally. More companies organize work in terms of projects or customers, rather than specialized functions, so employees need to acquire a broad range of technical and interpersonal skills. Many companies expect employees at all levels to perform roles once reserved for management. Organizations are required to provide training and development opportunities to employees without regard to prohibited grounds of discrimination discussed in Chapter 2, including characteristics such as sex, race, ethnic origin, and age. In this climate, organizations are placing greater emphasis on training and development.

PCL's Centennial Learning Centre is the focal point of the contracting organization's headquarters in Edmonton, Alberta.

	TRAINING	DEVELOPMENT
Focus	Current	Future
Use of work experiences	Low	High
Goal	Preparation for current job	Preparation for changes
Participation	Required	Voluntary

TABLE 7.1

Training versus Development

Training consists of an organization's planned efforts to help employees acquire job-related competencies with the goal of applying these on the job. A training program may range from formal classes to one-on-one coaching, and it may take place on the job or at remote locations. No matter what its form, training can benefit the organization when it is linked to organizational needs and when it motivates employees.

As we noted in Chapter 1, employees' commitment to their organization depends on how their managers treat them. To "win the war for talent" managers must be able to identify high-potential employees, make sure the organization uses the talents of these people, and reassure them of their value, so that they do not become dissatisfied and leave the organization. Managers also must be able to listen. Although new employees need direction, they expect to be able to think independently and be treated with respect. In all these ways, managers provide for **employee development**—the combination of formal education, job experiences, relationships, and assessment of personality and competencies to help employees prepare for the future of their careers. Human resource management establishes a process for employee development that prepares employees to help the organization meet its goals. Table 7.1 summarizes the traditional differences between training and development.

This chapter describes how to plan and carry out an effective training program and explores the purpose and activities of employee development. We begin by discussing how to develop effective training in the context of the organization's strategy. Next, we discuss how organizations assess employees' training needs. We then review training methods and the process of evaluating a training program, and discuss some special applications of training: orientation of new employees and the management of diversity. We also examine the relationships among development, training, and career management and look at development approaches, including formal education, assessment, job experiences, and interpersonal relationships. The chapter emphasizes the types of competencies that are strengthened by each development method, so employees and their managers can choose appropriate methods when planning for development. The steps of the career management process, emphasizing the responsibilities of employee and employer at each step of the process are discussed. The chapter concludes with a discussion of special challenges related to employee development—succession planning, and the so-called glass ceiling.

training
An organization's planned efforts to help employees acquire job-related competencies with the goal of applying these on the job.

employee development
The combination of formal education, job experiences, relationships, and assessment of personality and competencies to help employees prepare for the future of their careers.

2,6

Training and Development Linked to Organizational Needs and Strategy

Workplace training and employee development are key ingredients in the competitiveness of firms and ultimately of national competitiveness.[2] Rapid change, especially in the area of technology, requires that employees continually learn new

L01 - Discuss how to link training and development to organizational needs and strategy.

skills and upgrade their current skills. The new psychological contract, described in Chapter 1, has created the expectation that employees invest in their own career development. Employees with this expectation will value employment at an organization that provides learning opportunities. Growing reliance on teamwork creates a demand for the ability to solve problems in teams, an ability that often requires formal training. Finally, the diversity of the Canadian population, coupled with the globalization of business, requires that employees be able to work well with people who are different from them. Successful organizations often take the lead in developing this ability.

Some organizations are developing their employer brand and reputation as a talent developer. These organizations emphasize training, career, and developmental opportunities as a means of gaining competitive advantage in the war for talent.[3] How are Canadian firms investing in and supporting learning? How does Canada compare with other countries? The Conference Board of Canada explores these and other questions in its *Training and Development Outlook Report*. The study reveals that Canadian firms continue to under-invest in learning and that Canada lags the United States and other countries in employee training, This could have serious adverse effects on long-term productivity as well as have serious ramifications for competitiveness—for both workers and markets—on the world stage.[4]

This survey of employers found that training remained relatively flat compared with previous years. Average training dollars represented 1.8 percent of payroll (the average per capita direct expenditure on training and development across all industries in Canada was $852 in 2006) down by 17 percent since 1996 in real terms (factoring inflation into the calculation). The average Canadian employee received 25 hours—or more than three workdays—of training in 2006. This is down 10 percent from 2004, when the average employee received 28 hours.[5] Organizations indicated that approximately one-third of employees did not receive any formal training at all.[6] Overall, Canada does *not* compare favourably with other

TABLE 7.2

International Rankings of Employee Training, 2002–06

	2002	2004	2006
Denmark	3	2	1
Finland	1	1	1
Japan	9	7	4
Norway	15	10	8
United States	10	23	9
Germany	7	16	10
Australia	18	15	16
Canada	**12**	**20**	**21**
Hong Kong	32	37	24
China	39	34	25
France	24	28	28
United Kingdom	35	44	42

SOURCE: P. Derek Hughes and Michael Grant, "Learning and Development Outlook 2007" (Ottawa: The Conference Board of Canada, April 23, 2007), p. 14. Based on data from International Institute for Management Development, *World Competitiveness Yearbook, 2006* (Lausanne, Switzerland: 2007).

competitor countries. The International Institute for Management Development (IMD) suggests that Canada has slipped by various measures of employee training investment. The IMD ranked Canada as 12th place in 2002 and 21st place in 2006.[7] Table 7.2 illustrates how Canada's participation in job-related continuing education and training compares with that of other countries.

With training so essential in modern organizations, it is important to provide training that is effective. An effective training program actually teaches what it is designed to teach, and it teaches skills and behaviours that will help the organization achieve its goals. Training programs may prepare employees for future positions in the organization, enable the organization to respond to change, reduce turnover, enhance worker safety, improve customer service and product design, and meet many other goals. To achieve those goals, HR professionals approach training through **instructional design**—a process of systematically developing training to meet specified needs.

A complete instructional design process includes the steps shown in Figure 7.1. It begins with an assessment of the needs for training—what the organization requires that its people know and be able to do. Next, the organization ensures that employees are ready for training in terms of their attitudes, motivation, basic skills, and work environment. The third step is to plan the training program, including the program's objectives, instructors, and methods. The organization then implements the program. Finally, evaluating the results of the training provides feedback for planning future training programs.

instructional design
A process of systematically developing training to meet specified needs.

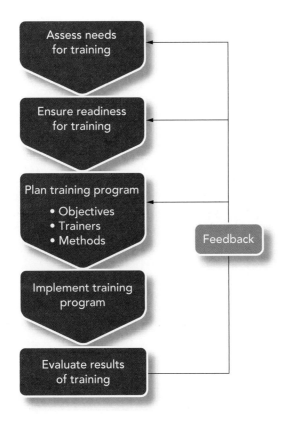

FIGURE 7.1

Stages of Instructional Design

FIGURE 7.2

Needs Assessment

L02 - Explain how to assess training needs and determine employees' readiness.

Needs Assessment and Assessing Readiness for Training

Instructional design logically should begin with a **needs assessment**, the process of evaluating the organization, individual employees, and employees' tasks to determine what kinds of training, if any, are necessary. As this definition indicates, the needs assessment answers questions in the three broad areas shown in Figure 7.2.[8]

1. *Organization.* What is the context in which training will occur?
2. *Person.* Who needs training?
3. *Task.* What topics should the training cover?

The answers to these questions provide the basis for planning an effective training program.

A variety of conditions may prompt an organization to conduct a needs assessment. Management may observe that some employees lack basic skills or are performing poorly. Decisions to produce new products, apply new technology, or design new jobs should prompt a needs assessment, because these changes tend to require new skills. The decision to conduct a needs assessment also may be prompted by outside forces, such as customer requests or legal requirements.

The outcome of the needs assessment is a set of decisions about how to address the issues that prompted the needs assessment. These decisions do not necessarily include a training program, because some issues should be resolved through methods other than training—for example, plans for better rewards to improve motivation, better hiring decisions, and better safety precautions.

Organization Analysis

needs assessment
The process of evaluating the organization, individual employees, and employees' tasks to determine what kinds of training, if any, are necessary.

organization analysis
A process for determining the appropriateness of training by evaluating the characteristics of the organization.

Usually, the needs assessment begins with the **organization analysis**. This is a process for determining the appropriateness of training by evaluating the characteristics of the organization. The organization analysis looks at training needs in light of the organization's strategy, resources available for training, and management's support for training activities.

Training needs will vary depending on whether the organization's strategy is based on growing or shrinking its workforce, whether it is seeking to serve a broad customer base or focusing on the specific needs of a narrow market segment, and various other strategic scenarios. A company cutting costs with a downsizing strategy may need to train employees in job search skills. The employees who will remain following a downsizing may need cross-training so they can handle a wider variety of responsibilities. An organization that concentrates on serving a niche market may need to continually update its employees on a specialized skills set.

Anyone planning a training program must consider whether the organization has the budget, time, and expertise for training. For example, if the company is installing computer-based manufacturing equipment in one of its plants, it can ensure it has the necessary computer-literate employees in one of three ways: (1) if it has the technical experts on its staff, it can train the employees affected by the change; (2) it can use testing to determine which of its employees are already computer-literate and then replace or reassign employees who lack the necessary skills; or (3) it can purchase training from an outside individual or organization. Even if training fits the organization's strategy, it can be viable only if the organization is willing to invest in this type of activity. Managers play a key role by supporting employees' needs and ensuring employees have opportunities to apply their competencies on the job.[9] Conversely, the managers will be most likely to support training if the people planning it can show that it will solve a significant problem or result in a significant improvement, relative to its cost. Managers appreciate training proposals with specific goals, timetables, budgets, and methods for measuring success.

Person Analysis

Following the organizational assessment, needs assessment turns to the remaining areas of analysis: person and task. The **person analysis** is a process for determining individuals' needs and readiness for training. It involves answering several questions:

person analysis
A process for determining individuals' needs and readiness for training.

- Do performance deficiencies result from a competency gap—that is, a lack of knowledge, skill, or ability? (If so, training is appropriate; if not, other solutions are more relevant.)
- Who needs training?
- Are these employees ready for training?

The answers to these questions help the manager identify whether training is appropriate and which employees need training. In certain situations, such as the introduction of a new technology or service, all employees may need training. However, when needs assessment is conducted in response to a performance problem, training is not always the best solution.

The person analysis is therefore critical when training is considered in response to a performance problem. In assessing the need for training, the manager should identify all the variables that can influence performance. The primary variables are the person's ability and skills, his or her attitudes and motivation, the organization's input (including clear directions, necessary resources, and freedom from interference and distractions), performance feedback (including praise and performance standards), and positive consequences to motivate good performance. Of these variables, only ability and skills can be affected by training. Therefore, before planning a training program, it is important to be sure that any performance problem results from a deficiency in knowledge and skills. Otherwise, training dollars will be wasted, because the training is unlikely to have much effect on performance.

The person analysis also should determine whether employees are ready to undergo training. In other words, the employees to receive training not only should require additional knowledge and skill, but must be willing and able to learn. We will explore this aspect a little later in this chapter.

Task Analysis

The third area of needs assessment is **task analysis**, the process of identifying the tasks and competencies (knowledge, skills, and behaviour) that training should emphasize. Usually, task analysis is conducted along with person analysis. Understanding shortcomings in performance usually requires knowledge about the tasks and work environment as well as the employee.

To carry out the task analysis, the HR professional looks at the conditions in which tasks are performed. These conditions include the equipment and environment of the job, time constraints (e.g., deadlines), safety considerations, and performance standards. These observations form the basis for a description of work activities, or the tasks required by the person's job. For a selected job, the analyst interviews employees and their supervisors to prepare a list of tasks performed in that job. Then the analyst validates the list by showing it to employees, supervisors, and other subject-matter experts and asking them to complete a questionnaire about the importance, frequency, and difficulty of the tasks. The information from these questionnaires is the basis for determining which tasks will be the focus of the training.

Readiness for Training

Effective training requires not only a program that addresses real needs, but also a condition of employee readiness. **Readiness for training** is a combination of employee characteristics and positive work environment that permit training. The necessary employee characteristics include ability to learn the subject matter, favourable attitudes toward the training, and motivation to learn. A positive work environment is one that encourages learning and avoids interfering with the training program.

Employee Readiness Characteristics

Employees learn more from training programs when they are highly motivated to learn—that is, when they really want to learn the content of the training program.[10] Employees tend to feel this way if they believe they are able to learn, see potential benefits from the training program, are aware of their need to learn, see a fit between the training and their career goals, and have the basic skills needed for participating in the program. Managers can influence a ready attitude in a variety of ways. For example, they can provide feedback that encourages employees, establish rewards for learning, and communicate with employees about the organization's career paths and future needs.

Work Environment

Readiness for training also depends on two broad characteristics of the work environment: situational constraints and social support.[11] *Situational constraints* are the limits on training's effectiveness that arise from the situation or the conditions within the organization. Constraints can include a lack of money for training, lack of time for training or practising, and failure to provide proper tools and materials for learning or applying the lessons of training.

Social support refers to the ways the organization's people encourage training, including giving trainees praise and encouraging words, sharing information about participating in training programs, and expressing positive attitudes toward the organization's training programs. Support can come from employees' peers as well as from supervisors and managers. The organization can formally provide peer support by

Extreme Hockey and Sport, located in Regina, Saskatchewan, has developed a reputation for satisfied customers served by knowledgeable and dedicated employees. Management of this retail sports speciality store supports employee training through intensive product knowledge sessions that provide an environment that encourages employees to stay with the company.

establishing groups of employees who meet regularly to discuss their progress. Another way to encourage peer support is for the human resource department or others in the organization to publish a newsletter with articles relevant to training. The newsletter might include interviews with employees who successfully applied new skills. Finally, the organization can assign experienced employees as coaches to trainees, providing advice and support related to the training.

Planning and Designing the Training Program

When the needs assessment indicates a need for training and employees are ready to learn, the person responsible for training should plan a training program that directly relates to the needs identified. Planning begins with establishing objectives for the training program. On the basis of those objectives, the planner decides who will provide the training, what topics the training will cover, what training methods to use, and how to evaluate the training.

L03 - Describe how to plan and design an effective training program and compare training methods.

Objectives of the Program

Formally establishing objectives for the training program has several benefits. First, a training program based on clear objectives will be more focused and more likely to succeed. In addition, when trainers know the objectives, they can communicate them to the employees participating in the program. Employees learn best when they know what the training is supposed to accomplish. Finally, down the road, establishing objectives provides a basis for measuring whether the program succeeded, as we will discuss later in this chapter.

Effective training objectives have three components:

1. A statement of what the employee is expected to do (performance or outcome)
2. A statement of the quality or level of performance that is acceptable
3. A statement of the conditions under which the trainee is expected to apply what he or she learned (for instance, physical conditions, mental stresses, or equipment failure)[12]

If possible, the objectives should include measurable performance standards.

Finally, training objectives should identify any resources required to carry out the desired performance or outcome. This helps the organization ensure that employees will be able to apply what they have learned.

A related issue at the outset is who will participate in the training program. Some training programs are developed for all employees of the organization or all members of a team. Other training programs identify individuals who lack desirable skills or have potential to be promoted, then provide training in the areas of need that are identified for the particular employees. When deciding whom to include in training, the organization has to avoid illegal discrimination. The organization should not—intentionally or unintentionally—exclude anyone due to a prohibited ground of discrimination, for example, sex, race, colour, ethnic background, sexual orientation, or age. During the training, all participants should receive equal treatment, such as equal opportunities for practice. In addition, the training program should provide accommodation for trainees with disabilities.

In-House or Contracted Out?

An organization can provide an effective training program, even if it lacks expertise in training. Many companies and consultants provide training services to organizations. Colleges and technical institutes often work with employers to train employees in a variety of skills. When ESSO Resources needed power engineering certificate upgrading for employees at their Devon and Bonnie Glen plants, they called NAIT (Northern Alberta Institute of Technology), located in Edmonton, Alberta. NAIT staff has delivered customized training to a diverse group of companies, including TELUS and the Department of National Defence.[13]

To select a training service, an organization can mail several vendors a *request for proposal (RFP)*, a document outlining the type of service needed, the type and number of references needed, the number of employees to be trained, the date by which the training is to be completed, and the date by which proposals should be received. A complete RFP also indicates funding for the project and the process by which the organization will determine its level of satisfaction. Putting together a request for proposal is time-consuming, but worthwhile because it helps the organization clarify its objectives, compare vendors, and measure results.

Vendors that believe they are able to provide the services outlined in the RFP submit proposals that provide the types of information requested. The organization reviews the proposals to eliminate any vendors that do not meet requirements and to compare the vendors that do qualify. They check references and select a candidate, based on the proposal and the vendor's answers to questions such as those listed in Table 7.3.

TABLE 7.3

Questions to Ask Vendors and Consultants

- How much and what type of experience does your company have in designing and delivering training?
- What are the qualifications and experiences of your staff?
- Can you provide demonstrations or examples of training programs you have developed?
- Would you provide references of clients for whom you worked?
- What evidence do you have that your programs work?

SOURCE: Based on R. Zemke and J. Armstrong, "Evaluating Multimedia Developers," *Training*, November 1996, pp. 33–38. Adapted with permission. Lakewood Publications, Minneapolis, MN.

The cost of purchasing training from a contractor can vary substantially. In general, it is much costlier to purchase specialized training tailored to the organization's requirements than to participate in a seminar or training course that teaches general skills or knowledge. Even in organizations that send employees to outside training programs, someone in the organization may be responsible for coordinating the overall training program. This responsibility, called *training administration*, is typically given to a human resources professional. It includes activities before, during, and after training sessions such as communicating with and enrolling employees, preparing and processing pretests, arranging the training facility, distributing training materials, and maintaining records.

Choice of Training Methods

Whether the organization prepares its own training programs or buys training from other organizations, it is important to verify that the content of the training relates directly to the training objectives. Such relevance to the organization's needs and objectives ensures that training money is well spent. Tying training content closely to objectives also improves trainees' learning, because it increases the likelihood that the training will be meaningful and helpful. After deciding on the goals and content of the training program, planners must decide how the training will be conducted. A wide variety of methods are available for conducting training. Figure 7.3 shows

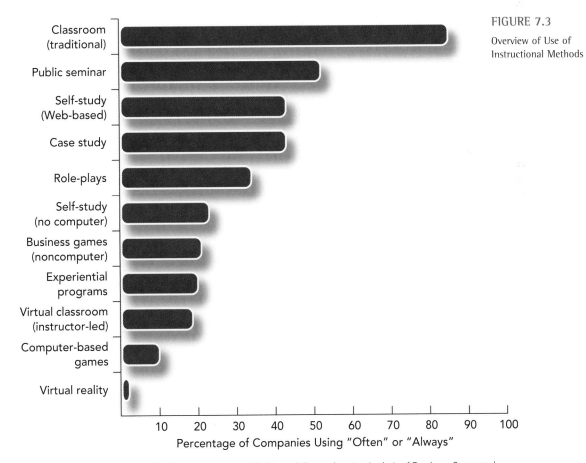

FIGURE 7.3

Overview of Use of Instructional Methods

SOURCE: Based on Holly Dolezalek, "*Training* Magazine's 23rd Annual Comprehensive Analysis of Employer-Sponsored Training in the United States," *Training*, October 2004, http://web5.infotrac.galegroup.com.

the percentages of companies using various training methods: classroom instruction, seminars (face-to-face and remote), self-study, role-plays, case studies, learning games, experiential programs. Of these methods, the most widely used are traditional classroom training, public seminars, self-study online, and case studies.

Classroom Instruction

At school, we tend to associate learning with classroom instruction, and that type of training is most widely used in the workplace, too. Classroom instruction typically involves an instructor leading a group. Instructors often use slides, discussions, case studies, question-and-answer sessions, and role playing. Actively involving trainees enhances learning.

When the course objectives call for presenting information on a specific topic to many trainees, classroom instruction is one of the least expensive and least time-consuming ways to accomplish that goal. Learning will be more effective if trainers enhance lectures with job-related examples and opportunities for hands-on learning.

Technology has expanded the notion of the classroom to classes of trainees scattered in various locations. With *distance learning*, trainees at different locations attend programs over phone and computer lines. Through audio- and videoconferencing, they can hear and see lectures and participate in discussions.

Audiovisual Training

Training need not require that trainees attend a class. Trainees can also work independently, using course material prepared in podcasts, videos, or workbooks. These methods can also supplement classroom instruction. Users of audiovisual training often have some control over the presentation. They can review material and may be able to slow down or speed up the lesson. Videos can show situations and equipment that cannot be easily demonstrated in a classroom. Another advantage of audiovisual presentations is that they give trainees a consistent presentation, not affected by an individual trainer's goals and skills. The problems associated with these methods may include their trying to present too much material, poorly written dialogue, overuse of features such as humour or music, and drama that distracts from the key points. A well-written and carefully produced video can overcome these problems.

Computer-Based Training

Although almost all organizations use classroom training, new technologies are gaining in popularity as technology improves and becomes less expensive. With computer-based training, participants receive course materials and instruction distributed over the Internet or on CD-ROM. Often, these materials are interactive, so participants can answer questions and try out techniques, with course materials adjusted according to participants' responses. Online training programs may allow trainees to submit questions via email and to participate in online discussions. Multimedia capabilities enable computers to provide sounds, images, and video presentations, along with text.

Computer-based training is generally less expensive than putting an instructor in a classroom of trainees. The low cost to deliver information gives the company flexibility in scheduling training, so that it can fit around work requirements. Training can be delivered in smaller doses, so material is easier to remember.[14] Finally, it is easier to customize computer-based training for individual learners.

Electronic Performance Support Systems

Computers can support trainees in applying training content to their jobs. *Electronic performance support systems (EPSSs)* are computer applications that provide access to skills training, information, and expert advice when a problem occurs on the job.[15] An EPSS gives trainees an electronic information source that they can refer to as they try applying new skills on the job.

E-Learning

Receiving training via the Internet or the organization's intranet is called **e-learning** or online learning. E-learning may bring together Web-based training, distance learning, virtual classrooms, and the use of CD-ROMs. Course content is presented with a combination of text, video, graphics, and sound. E-learning has three important characteristics. First, it involves electronic networks that enable the delivery, sharing, and updating of information and instruction. Second, e-learning is delivered to the trainee via computers with Internet access. Finally, it goes beyond traditional training objectives to offer tools and information that will help trainees improve performance. The system also may handle course enrolment, testing and evaluation of participants, and monitoring of progress. For example, Vancouver City Savings Credit Union (Vancity) has created DiscoverU, an e-learning tool that allows employees to map their career path and to create links between performance management, individual career development plans, and the corporate talent pool.[16]

With e-learning, trainees have a great deal of control. They determine what they learn, how fast they progress through the program, how much time they practise, and when they learn. E-learners also may choose to collaborate or interact with other trainees and experts. They may use the training system's links to other learning resources such as reference materials, company websites, and other training programs.

To enable organizations to bring together diverse computer-based training tools or authoring systems, a course management system (CMS) may be used. For example, WebCT and Moodle is utilized in thousands of colleges and universities around the world to provide a flexible blend of e-learning and classroom-based teaching.

Like other forms of computer-based learning, e-learning can reduce training costs and time. Trainees often appreciate the multimedia capabilities, which appeal to several senses, and the opportunity to actively participate in learning and apply it to situations on the job. The best e-learning combines the advantages of the Internet with the principles of a good learning environment. It takes advantage of the Web's dynamic nature and ability to use many positive learning features, including hyperlinks to other training sites and content, control by the trainee, and ability for trainees to collaborate.

On-the-Job Training

Although people often associate training with classrooms, much learning occurs while employees are performing their jobs. **On-the-job training (OJT)** refers to training methods in which a person with job experience and skill guides trainees in practising job skills at the workplace. This type of training takes various forms, including apprenticeships and internships.

An **apprenticeship** is a work-study training method that teaches job skills through a combination of on-the-job training and technical training.[17] The OJT component

e-learning
Receiving training via the Internet or the organization's intranet.

on-the-job training (OJT)
Training methods in which a person with job experience and skill guides trainees in practising job skills at the workplace.

apprenticeship
A work-study training method that teaches job skills through a combination of on-the-job training and technical training.

of an apprenticeship involves the apprentice assisting a certified journeyperson in the work place. Typically, the technical training is provided by local trade schools, high schools, community colleges, and technical institutes. On average, 85 percent of the apprentice's two-to-five-year training is spent in the workplace, the rest is spent at a training institution.[18] Some apprenticeship programs are sponsored by individual companies, others by employee unions. Apprenticeship programs are usually administered by provincial and territorial government departments with support from advisory bodies such as apprenticeship and certification boards. To provide greater mobility across Canada for skilled workers, apprentices who have completed their training and certified journeypersons are able to obtain a "Red Seal" endorsement after completing an interprovincial standards exam that allows them to practise their trade anywhere in Canada.[19] For trainees, a major advantage of apprenticeship is the ability to earn an income while learning a trade, that is, "earning while learning." In addition, training through an apprenticeship is usually effective because it involves hands-on learning and extensive practice.

An **internship** is on-the-job learning sponsored by an educational institution as a component of an academic program. The sponsoring school works with local employers to place students in positions where they can gain experience related to their area of study. For example, summer internships have become an integral component of UBC's 15-month MBA program and a requirement of graduation.[20]

Cooperative education is a plan of higher education that incorporates paid work experience as an integral part of academic studies. Cooperative education is being readily accepted by government, business, and industry in Canada and throughout the world. Universities, colleges, technical schools, and high schools are offering co-op programs to thousands of students in a growing number of disciplines.[21]

To be effective, OJT programs should include several characteristics:

- The organization should issue a policy statement describing the purpose of OJT and emphasizing the organization's support for it.

- The organization should specify who is accountable for conducting OJT. This accountability should be included in the relevant job descriptions.

- The organization should review OJT practices at companies in similar industries.

- Managers and peers should be trained in OJT principles.

- Employees who conduct OJT should have access to lesson plans, checklists, procedure manuals, training manuals, learning contracts, and progress report forms.

- Before conducting OJT with an employee, the organization should assess the employees' level of basic skills.[22]

The OJT program at Canadian Air Transport Security Authority (CATSA) has many of these characteristics. After completing extensive classroom training including role-plays, and hands-on practice in a training lab, screening officers participate in "live-line-on-the-job training." Point leaders pay careful attention to the screening officers while they conduct various searches and investigations of passengers and their belongings. One class of trainees intercepted an item that looked like a rocket propelled grenade on the X-ray machine. After the police responded and searched the bag, it turned out to be cologne. Ten minutes later, on the same screening line, the search of a passenger's carry-on bag yielded over $30,000 in U.S. currency. Local police and Canadian Border Services Agency officers attended the checkpoint and

internship
On-the-job learning sponsored by an educational institution as a component of an academic program.

cooperative education
A plan of higher education that incorporates paid work experience as an integral part of academic studies.

conducted their investigations. Through this live-line OJT trainees received invaluable first-hand experience of how to deal with the discovery of contraband at the screening checkpoint and work with stakeholders such as police, airport security, air carriers, and airport authorities.[23]

Simulations

A **simulation** is a training method that represents a real-life situation, with trainees making decisions resulting in outcomes that mirror what would happen on the job. Simulations enable trainees to see the impact of their decisions in an artificial, risk-free environment. They are used to teach production and process skills as well as management and interpersonal skills.

Simulators must have elements identical to those found in the work environment. The simulator needs to respond exactly as equipment would under the conditions and response given by the trainee. For this reason, simulators are expensive to develop and need constant updating as new information about the work environment becomes available. Still, they are an excellent training method when the risks of a mistake on the job are great. Trainees do not have to be afraid of the impact of wrong decisions when using the simulator, as they would be with on-the-job training.

A recent development in simulations is the use of virtual reality technology. **Virtual reality** is a computer-based technology that provides an interactive, three-dimensional learning experience. Using specialized equipment or viewing the virtual model on a computer screen, trainees move through the simulated environment and interact with its components.[24] Devices relay information from the environment to the trainees' senses. For example, audio interfaces, gloves that provide a sense of touch, treadmills, or motion platforms create a realistic but artificial environment. Devices also communicate information about the trainee's movements to a computer. Virtual worlds, and participatory media such as Second Life discussed in Chapter 5, are also transforming training in many organizations through collaborative and experiential learning. One example is British Petroleum's use of Second Life to train new gas station employees in the safety features of gasoline storage tanks and piping systems. In Second Life, BP built three-dimensional renderings of the tank and pipe systems at a typical gas station. Trainees could "see" underground and observe the effect of using safety devices to control the flow of gasoline in a way they could never have done in real life.[25]

simulation
A training method that represents a real-life situation, with trainees making decisions resulting in outcomes that mirror what would happen on the job.

virtual reality
A computer-based technology that provides an interactive, three-dimensional learning experience.

Business Games and Case Studies

Training programs use business games and case studies to develop employees' management skills. A case study is a detailed description of a situation that trainees study and discuss. Cases are designed to develop higher-order thinking skills, such as the ability to analyze and evaluate information. They also can be a safe way to encourage trainees to take appropriate risks, by giving them practice in weighing and acting on uncertain outcomes. There are many sources of case studies, including the Richard Ivey School of Business, Wilfrid Laurier University, Harvard Business School, and McGraw-Hill Education.

With business games, trainees gather information, analyze it, and make decisions that influence the outcome of the game. For instance, Markstrat integrated into a marketing course, requires participants to use strategic thinking (such as analyzing competitors) to increase their share of the market.[26] Games stimulate learning because they actively involve participants and mirror the competitive nature of business. A realistic game may be more meaningful to trainees than techniques such as classroom instruction.

Training with case studies and games requires that participants come together to discuss the cases or the progress of the game. This requires face-to-face or electronic meetings. Also, participants must be willing to be actively involved in analyzing the situation and defending their decisions.

Behaviour Modelling

Research suggests that one of the most effective ways to teach interpersonal skills is through behaviour modelling.[27] This involves training sessions in which participants observe other people demonstrating the desired behaviour, then have opportunities to practise the behaviour themselves. For example, a training program could involve four-hour sessions, each focusing on one interpersonal skill, such as communicating or coaching. At the beginning of each session, participants hear the reasons for using the key behaviours, then they watch a video of an expert performing the key behaviours. They practise through role-playing and receive feedback about their performance. In addition, they evaluate the performance of the model in the videotape and discuss how they can apply the behaviour on the job.

Team Training and Learning

An important consideration in implementing training in organizations is understanding group process. A great deal of the work in organizations gets done by bringing together individuals with different knowledge, expertise, and backgrounds to discuss issues and collaborate on decisions in the effort to achieve a common goal. Team learning has been defined in several way including being viewed as an aggregate of individual learning, a process for creating change as individual team members create, acquire, and share knowledge, and as a dynamic system in which the individuals in the team and the team itself changes behaviours as the team learns.[28]

experiential programs
Training programs in which participants learn concepts and apply them by simulating behaviours involved and analyzing the activity, connecting it with real-life situations

An organization may benefit from providing training to groups when group members must share information and team performance depends on the performance of the individual members. Success depends on individuals coordinating their activities to make decisions, perhaps in dangerous situations.

To develop teamwork and leadership skills, some organizations enrol their employees in a form of training called **experiential programs**. In experiential programs, participants learn concepts and then apply them by simulating the behaviours involved and analyzing the activity, connecting it with real-life situations.[29] In France, some businesses are signing up their managers to attend cooking schools, where they whip up a gourmet meal together. Jacques Bally, who works for a school run by one of France's top chefs, says cooking is a great way to learn teamwork: "It's like in any squad, everyone is responsible for playing their part, they have their own tasks but a common objective—and if they want to eat in the end, then they have to get the meal ready."[30]

adventure learning
A teamwork and leadership training program based on the use of challenging, structured outdoor activities.

Experiential training programs should follow several guidelines. A program should be related to a specific business problem. Participants should feel challenged and move outside their comfort zones but within limits that keep their motivation strong and help them understand the purpose of the program. One form of experiential program, called **adventure learning**, uses challenging, structured outdoor activities, which may include difficult sports such as dogsledding or mountain-climbing. Other activities may be structured tasks like climbing walls or completing rope courses.

Before requiring employees to participate in experiential programs, the organization should consider the possible drawbacks. Because these programs are usually physically demanding and often require participants to touch each other, companies face certain risks. Some employees may be injured or may feel that they were sexually harassed or that their privacy was invaded. Also, human rights and employment equity legislation (discussed in Chapter 2) raises questions about requiring employees with disabilities to participate in physically demanding training experiences.

Ways to conduct team training also include cross-training and coordination training.[31] In **cross-training**, team members understand and practise each other's skills so that they are prepared to step in and take another member's place. For example, Toronto Hydro cross-trains supervisors so they can work across specializations. Jodi Engle, manager of organizational development and performance at Toronto Hydro says, "This enhances their skills. It's a great retention strategy, it gives them more variety and makes their job more meaningful."[32]

Coordination training trains the team in how to share information and decisions to obtain the best team performance. Both of these kinds of teams must monitor different aspects of equipment and the environment at the same time sharing information to make the most effective decisions.

Another form of group building is **action learning**. In this type of training, teams or work groups get an actual problem, work on solving it, commit to an action plan, and are accountable for carrying out the plan.[33] Typically, 6 to 30 employees participate in action learning; sometimes the participants include customers and vendors. For instance, a group might include a customer that buys the product involved in the problem to be solved. Another arrangement is to bring together employees from various functions affected by the problem.

The effectiveness of action learning has not been formally evaluated. This type of training seems to result in a great deal of learning, however; and employees are able to apply what they learn, because it involves actual problems the organization is facing. The group approach also helps teams identify behaviours that interfere with problem solving.

cross-training
Team training in which team members understand and practise each other's skills so that they are prepared to step in and take another member's place.

coordination training
Team training that teaches the team how to share information and make decisions to obtain the best team performance.

action learning
Training in which teams get an actual problem, work on solving it and commit to an action plan, and are accountable for carrying it out.

One of the most important features of organizations today is teamwork. Experiential programs include team-building exercises like wall-climbing and rafting help build trust and cooperation among employees.

1,6

L04 - Summarize how to implement and evaluate a successful training program.

Implementing and Evaluating the Training Program

Implementing and evaluating the training program are the remaining stages of instructional design.

Principles of Learning

Learning permanently changes behaviour. For employees to acquire knowledge and skills in the training program and apply what they have learned in their jobs, the training program must be implemented in a way that applies what we know about how people learn. Researchers have identified a number of ways employees learn best.[34] Table 7.4 summarizes ways training can best encourage learning. In general, effective training communicates learning objectives clearly, presents information in distinctive and memorable ways, and helps trainees link the subject matter to their jobs.

TABLE 7.4

Ways That Training Helps Employees Learn

TRAINING ACTIVITY	WAYS TO PROVIDE TRAINING ACTIVITY
Communicate the learning objective.	• Demonstrate the performance to be expected. • Give examples of questions to be answered.
Use distinctive, attention-getting messages.	• Emphasize key points. • Use pictures, not just words.
Limit the content of training.	• Group lengthy material into chunks. • Provide a visual image of the course material. • Provide opportunities to repeat and practise material.
Guide trainees as they learn.	• Use words as reminders about sequence of activities. • Use words and pictures to relate concepts to one another and to their context.
Elaborate on the subject.	• Present the material in different contexts and settings. • Relate new ideas to previously learned concepts. • Practise in a variety of contexts and settings.
Provide memory cues.	• Suggest memory aids. • Use familiar sounds or rhymes as memory cues.
Transfer course content to the workplace.	• Design the learning environment so that it has elements in common with the workplace. • Require learners to develop action plans that apply training content to their jobs. • Use words that link the course to the workplace.
Provide feedback about performance.	• Tell trainees how accurately and quickly they are performing their new skill. • Show how trainees have met the objectives of the training.

SOURCE: Adapted from R. M. Gagne, "Learning Processes and Instruction," *Training Research Journal* 1 (1995/96), pp. 17–28.

Employees are most likely to learn when training is linked to their current job experiences and tasks.[35] There are a number of ways trainers can make this link. Training sessions should present material using familiar concepts, terms, and examples. As far as possible, the training context—such as the physical setting or the images presented on a computer—should mirror the work environment. Along with physical elements, the context should include emotional elements. For example, in training store employees to handle upset customers, the physical context is more relevant if it includes trainees acting out scenarios of employees dealing with unhappy customers. The role-play interaction between trainees adds emotional realism and further enhances learning.

To fully understand and remember the content of the training, employees need a chance to demonstrate and practise what they have learned. Trainers should provide ways to actively involve the trainees, have them practise repeatedly, and have them complete tasks within a time that is appropriate in light of the learning objectives. Practice requires physically carrying out the desired behaviours, not just describing them. Practice sessions might include role-playing interactions, filling out relevant forms, or operating machinery or equipment to be used on the job. The more the trainee practises these activities, the more comfortable he or she will be in applying the skills on the job. People tend to benefit most from practice that occurs over several sessions, rather than one long practice session.[36] For complex tasks, it may be most effective to practise a few skills or behaviours at a time, then combine them in later practice sessions.

Trainees need to understand whether they are succeeding. Therefore, training sessions should offer feedback. Effective feedback focuses on specific behaviours and is delivered as soon as possible after the trainees practise or demonstrate what they have learned.[37]

Well-designed training helps people remember the content. Training programs need to break information into chunks that people can remember. Research suggests that people can attend to no more than four to five items at a time. If a concept or procedure involves more than five items, the training program should deliver information in shorter sessions or chunks.[38] Other ways to make information more memorable include presenting it with visual images and practising some tasks enough that they become automatic.

Workplace literacy is a relative rather than an absolute concept, involving prose, document, and quantitative capabilities in the languages in which business is conducted. Increasingly, organizations are recognizing the literacy skills that enabled employees to do their jobs effectively are no longer adequate in today's competitive marketplace.[39] A recent survey sponsored by the National Literacy Secretariat and Human Resources and Social Development Canada found that "42 percent of Canadian workers have literacy skills below the level they need to succeed and perform well in most jobs."[40]

Palliser Furniture Ltd. employs an ethnically and linguistically diverse workforce and regards employees' basic skills as fundamental to business success. This Winnipeg-based manufacturer recently received an Award for Excellence in Workplace Literacy from the Conference Board of Canada in recognition of its workplace literacy contributions. Palliser provides employees with courses including English as a second language, reading and writing for lead hands, and various math modules to enhance employees' literacy skills, as they progress in employment and take on additional responsibilities that require advanced skills.[41]

workplace literacy
Prose, document, and quantitative capabilities in the languages in which business is conducted.

HR HOW-TO

8 Steps to Effective Training Feedback

Imagine spending one-half of a year's salary on a new car and just leaving it parked in front of the house forever. The car never roars down the highway, so there's no way to gauge performance. It's never taken grocery shopping, so it's impossible to assess the trunk space. And the sound system is never cranked up. So nobody has any idea how good it is. Few people would do that with a new car. But a remarkable number of organizations do the equivalent with employee training. They invest a substantial amount of money without ever doing preparatory work beforehand or seeking an accurate picture afterward on what they gained for their money.

There are eight key steps to getting the most value from training budgets and obtaining the best information about training outcomes:

1. *Identify training needs.* Before training even starts, identify the kind of training the organization needs and wants to do, whether for new regulations, new technology or differentiation in the market. Regardless of whether it is offered in-house or by an outside supplier, run pilot projects and learn from them before deploying programs more widely throughout the organization.

2. *Create employee competency profiles.* Before training actually starts, prepare a core competency profile for all employees. This helps determine which employees need what training and, as an added bonus, provides the organization with a system-wide inventory of the skills that already exist in-house.

3. *Ask the basics.* As soon as an individual has completed training, it is a good idea to ask the basic question: "Did you find the training satisfactory?" This helps send a signal to the employee that the organization cares about training quality.

4. *Find out what was learned.* Organizations need to go beyond the basics and ask the employee: "Have you learned anything?" Follow up by asking for elaboration. Not enough organizations take this step, even though it is useful to gauge relevance and determine where training programs need tweaking.

5. *Gauge the mid-term impact on the job.* Few companies actually get to the heart of the impact of training on an individual's job. But new tools can make this step easy. Web-based tools, including 360-degree feedback, can help a trainer prepare detailed questionnaires for the employee and his/her peers, subordinates, clients, suppliers and supervisor, asking for observations about changed or improved behaviour. This

should be done about three months after the training.

6. *Determine the effect on business.* To gain a precise measurement of the impact training has had on business results, ask: "Did the trainee's division log improved sales or operating efficiencies since the training?" "Has there been a dollars-and-cents improvement to the bottom-line that can be traced back to the training?" "Has customer satisfaction improved against specific objectives?"

7. *Measure the return on investment.* Measuring the return on investment of training and reporting back to executives helps mould the shape of future training programs. Ask: "How much did sales or earnings rise for every dollar spent on training?"

8. *Gauge the long-term job impact.* Prepare detailed questionnaires for the employee and those around him/her about six to 12 months after training completion. The questions should be tied to what the employee does and is supposed to do. This kind of long-term follow-up is rarely done but can provide invaluable data about the long-term value of different kinds of training.

SOURCE: Jacques Gaumond, "8 Steps to Effective Training Feedback," *Canadian HR Reporter*, November 5, 2007, pp. 24–25.

Measuring Results of Training

After a training program ends, or at intervals during an ongoing training program, organizations should ensure that the training is meeting objectives. The HR How-To box discusses steps to increase the value obtained form training. The stage to prepare for evaluating a training program is when the program is being developed. Along with designing course objectives and content, the planner should identify how to measure achievement of objectives. Depending on the objectives, the evaluation can use one or more of the measures shown in Figure 7.4:[42]

1,2,6

- *Reaction.* Satisfaction with the program.
- *Learning.* Knowledge and skills gained.
- *Behaviour.* Behaviour changes.
- *Results.* Improvements in individual and organizational performance.

The Conference Board of Canada reports that over 89 percent of organizations administer reaction-level training evaluations, and that an increasing number of organizations are conducting learning, behaviour, and results-level training evaluations.[43]

The usual way to measure whether participants have acquired information is to administer tests on paper or electronically. Trainers or supervisors can observe whether participants demonstrate the desired competencies. Changes in company performance have a variety of measures, many of which organizations keep track of for preparing performance appraisals, annual reports, and other routine documents, in order to demonstrate the final measure of success shown in Figure 7.4 results, including return on investment (ROI).

Evaluation Methods

Evaluation of training should look for **transfer of training**, or on-the-job use of competencies enhanced in training. Transfer of training requires that employees actually learn the content of the training program and that the necessary conditions are in place for employees to apply what they learned. Thus, the assessment can look at

transfer of training
On-the-job use of competencies enhanced in training.

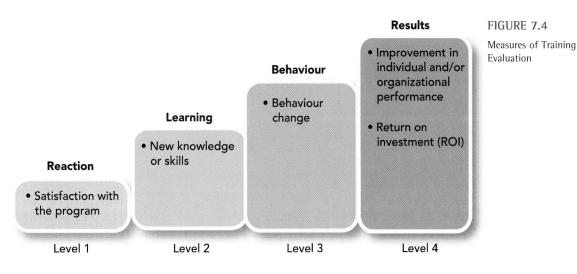

FIGURE 7.4

Measures of Training Evaluation

Results
- Improvement in individual and/or organizational performance
- Return on investment (ROI)

Behaviour
- Behaviour change

Learning
- New knowledge or skills

Reaction
- Satisfaction with the program

Level 1   Level 2   Level 3   Level 4

whether employees have an opportunity to perform the skills related to the training. The organization can measure this by asking employees three questions about specific training-related tasks:

1. Do you perform the task?
2. How many times do you perform the task?
3. To what extent do you perform difficult and challenging learned tasks?

Assessment of training also should evaluate training *outcomes*, that is, what (if anything) has changed as a result of the training. The relevant training outcomes are the ones related to the organization's goals for the training and its overall performance. Possible outcomes include the following:

- Trainee and supervisor satisfaction with the training program (reaction)

- Information such as facts, techniques, and procedures that trainees can recall after the training (learning)

- Skills that trainees can demonstrate in tests or on the job (behaviour)

- Changes in behaviour related to the content of the training, for example, concern for safety or support of diversity (behaviour)

- Improvements in individual, group, or company performance, for example, greater customer satisfaction, more sales, fewer defects (results)

Training is a significant part of many organizations' budgets. Therefore, economic measures are an important way to evaluate the success of a training program. Businesses that invest in training want to achieve a high return on investment—the monetary benefits of the investment compared to the amount invested, expressed as a percentage. For example, IBM's e-learning program for new managers, Basic Blue, costs $8,708 per manager.[44] The company has measured an improvement in each new manager's performance worth $415,000. That gives IBM a benefit of $415,000 − $8,708 = $406,292 for each manager. This is an extremely large return on investment: $406,292/$8,708 = 46.65, or 4,665 percent! In other words, for every $1 that IBM invests in Basic Blue, it receives almost $47.

For any of these methods, the most accurate but most costly way to evaluate the training program is to assess performance, knowledge, or behaviours among all employees before the training, then to train only some of the employees. After the training is complete, the performance, knowledge, or behaviour are again assessed, and the trained group is compared to the untrained group. A simpler but less accurate way to assess the training is to conduct a *pre-test* and *post-test* on all trainees, comparing their performance, knowledge, or behaviours before and after the training. This form of measurement does not rule out the possibility that change resulted from something other than training (e.g., a change in the compensation system). The simplest approach is to use only a post-test. Of course, this type of measurement does not enable accurate comparisons, but it may be sufficient, depending on the cost and purpose of the training.

Applying the Evaluation

The purpose of evaluating training is to help with future decisions about the organization's training programs. Using the evaluation, the organization may identify a need to modify the training and gain information about the kinds of changes needed. The organization may decide to expand on successful areas of training and cut back on training that has not delivered significant benefits.

TD Bank Financial Group evaluates the effectiveness of training using both quantitative and qualitative measures. TD uses a comprehensive process that includes assessment of knowledge increase, on-the-job confidence, effectiveness of materials and methods, as well as the business impact of their training programs.[45]

Applications of Training

1,2,3,6

Two categories of training that have become widespread among North American companies are orientation of new employees and training in how to manage workforce diversity.

L05 - Describe training methods for employee orientation and diversity management.

Orientation of New Employees—Onboarding

Many employees receive their first training during their first days on the job. This training is the organization's **orientation** program—its training designed to prepare employees to perform their job effectively, learn about the organization, and establish work relationships. Organizations provide for orientation because, no matter how realistic the information provided during employment interviews and site visits, people feel shock and surprise when they start a new job.[46] Also, employees need to become familiar with job tasks and learn the details of the organization's practices, policies, and procedures. Many HR professionals are rethinking traditional approaches to orientation due to pressures to maximize early productivity and engagement by creating a positive first impression. According to the Human Capital Institute, 90 percent of newly hired employees decide whether they'll remain with the company during the first six months.[47] Increasingly, employee orientation is referred to as *onboarding*, reflecting the critical role these programs play. The Best Practices box describes the Canadian Cancer Society's new onboarding program.

orientation
Training designed to prepare employees to perform their jobs effectively, learn about their organization, and establish work relationships.

The objectives of orientation programs include making new employees familiar with the organization's rules, policies, and procedures. Such a program provides information about the overall company and about the department in which the new employee will be working. The topics include social as well as technical aspects of the job.

Orientation processes may combine various training methods such as printed and audiovisual materials, classroom instruction, on-the-job training, and e-learning. Decisions about how to conduct the orientation depend on the type of material to be covered and the number of new employees, among other factors. At Toronto-based I Love Rewards, the first five days on the job are spent in the "I Love Rewards University," where new recruits "sit in a room together and learn everything from dress code to how to make the organization's drink of choice, the RedPoint (part Sour Puss raspberry liqueur, part Crown Royal, and part Red Bull)."[48] At Bayer Inc. new employee orientation starts with making the new hires feel like they're already part of the company well before they show up for work. Bayer Inc.'s Toronto office uses an approach to onboarding new employees called "Hello Bayer," in which new hires enter an extranet website and take a virtual tour of the facility—"great for locating their cubicle's nearest washroom—or read up on workplace minutiae like parking spaces, security passes, and even company acronyms." Philip Blake, president and CEO of Bayer says, "It's all about feeling comfortable, fitting in and feeling wanted and welcome. This onboarding gives people the opportunity to see everything that they're coming to."[49]

BEST PRACTICES

Canadian Cancer Society Launches New Onboarding Program

The Canadian Cancer Society, Ontario Division, decided to take a more strategic approach to onboarding. The division has hundreds of employees and thousands of volunteers across Ontario who carry out the society's mission to eradicate cancer and enhance the quality of life of those living with the disease.

One objective was to reduce voluntary turnover by equipping new hires with a greater understanding of, and connection to, the work of the society as a whole. In an organization that is geographically diverse (46 locations across the province), multifaceted (portfolios include prevention, advocacy, research, and education) and has many external alliances, it is important to get people up to speed quickly so they can make a strong, sustainable start.

Foundation Knowledge

The onboarding plan contained many elements. One part focused on "foundation knowledge." The objective was to give every new hire, regardless of his/her position or level, a consistent macro understanding of the society—including things such as key people, portfolios, and programs. Thought was given to the timing of different onboarding activities so the process would unfold in a logical and integrated way throughout the first year of employment. These activities are incorporated into detailed checklists to promote a consistent experience and ensure all elements are covered.

People Remember Stories

New employees can become overwhelmed by having to absorb too much too soon. They don't yet have the organization-specific navigational skills to discern what's important in the mountain of binders, reports, intranet resources, and other information provided. The HR team's solution was to develop an approach that reinforces the society's brand and ensures a consistent and reliable method of providing information.

A typical volunteer, Ray, was selected to help guide the new employee through the organization's massive intranet and essential links. Through his story as both a volunteer and cancer survivor, Ray helps the new hire absorb static information—mission, cancer research, and statistics, organization structure, and fundraising activities—in a more logical, dynamic, and memorable way. For example, Ray talks about his community work and his family's participation in the Canadian Cancer Society Relay for Life, a national fundraising event. He then invites the new hire to click on appropriate links to drill deeper into fundraising information.

Experience: Managers Can't Do It All

Recognizing the importance of developing quality relationships early in a new employee's tenure, the society developed a series of discussion guides to help new employees, their managers, and their internal and external clients talk about mutual expectations. In one guide, a new hire and her manager ask each other a set of questions to help define the "soft" side of the working relationship. For example: "What type of recognition is important to you?" and "How do you prefer to collaborate?" Another guide helps a new employee interview key clients to understand their priorities and expectations. This helps the employee take action and establish credibility early on.

Future Plans Include Measurement, Enhancements

While the onboarding program is still in its early days, there are already plans to measure the effectiveness.

BEST PRACTICES

And future program enhancements include the development of specific departmental orientation modules and a survey that solicits confidential feedback about program usage and

impact from both new hires and hiring managers. This will provide quantitative and qualitative information that can be translated into design enhancements.

SOURCE: Adapted from Deborah Kyrzakos and Sue Nador, "Canadian Cancer Society Launches New Onboarding Program," *Canadian HR Reporter*, March 10, 2008, p. 12.

Diversity Training

In response to human rights and employment equity legislation and market forces, many organizations today are concerned about managing diversity—creating an inclusive environment that allows all employees to contribute to organizational goals and experience personal growth. This environment includes access to jobs as well as fair and positive treatment of all employees. Chapter 2 described how organizations manage diversity by complying with legal requirements. Besides these efforts, many organizations provide training designed to teach employees attitudes and behaviours that support the management of diversity. Training designed to change employee attitudes about diversity and/or develop skills needed to work with a diverse workforce is called **diversity training**. These programs generally emphasize either attitude awareness and change or behaviour change.

diversity training
Training designed to change employee attitudes about diversity and/or develop skills needed to work with a diverse workforce.

Programs that focus on attitudes have objectives to increase participants' awareness of cultural and ethnic differences, as well as differences in personal characteristics and physical characteristics (such as disabilities). For example, at Air Canada, employees receive training about the nuances of different cultures. "Cultures are very different and little gestures that you may experience from a customer, you may experience them differently than they're meant to be," says Louise McEvoy, general manager of languages and diversity for Air Canada.[50]

Programs that focus on behaviour aim at changing the organizational policies and individual behaviours that inhibit employees' personal growth and productivity. Sometimes these programs identify incidents that discourage employees from achieving their potential. The existing evidence regarding diversity training suggests that some characteristics make diversity training more effective.[51] Most importantly, the training should be tied to business objectives, such as understanding customers. The support and involvement of top management, and the involvement of stakeholders at all levels, also are important. For example, Gayle Johnson, human resources head of Regina-based Conexus Credit Union went to the nearby Piapot Reserve to meet with its chief, band councillors, and community members to learn the best way to hire and retain Aboriginal employees. She decided to hire groups of ten Aboriginal employees at a time to reduce their sense of isolation in the workplace and tailored a ten-week training program for these new hires. She also prepared her staff for the arrival of the new employees by discussing cultural differences and why the diversity initiative was key to the business.[52] Diversity training should emphasize learning behaviours and skills, not blaming employees. Finally, the program should be well structured, connected to the organization's rewards for performance, and include a way to measure the success of the training.

Approaches to Employee Development

The definition of employee development provided near the beginning of this chapter indicates that it is future-oriented. Development implies learning that is not necessarily related to the employee's current job.[53] Instead, it prepares employees for other positions in the organization and increases their ability to move into jobs that may not yet exist.[54] Development also may help employees prepare for changes in their current jobs, such as changes resulting from new technology, work designs, or customers. So development is about preparing for change and achieving one's full potential in the form of new jobs, new responsibilities, or new requirements.

In contrast, training traditionally focuses on helping employees improve performance in their current jobs. Many organizations have focused on linking training programs to business goals. In these organizations, the distinction between training and development is more blurred.

Development for Careers

The concept of a career has changed in recent years. In the traditional view, a career consists of a sequence of positions within an occupation or organization.[55] For example, an engineer might start as a staff engineer, then with greater experience earn promotions to the positions of advisory engineer, senior engineer, and vice-president of engineering. In these examples, the career resembles a set of stairs from the entry to a profession or organization to the senior levels.

Changes such as downsizing, restructuring, bankruptcy, and growth have become the norm in the modern business environment. As this has happened, the concept of career has become more fluid. The new concept of a career is often referred to as

Irving Managers, from left, Kevin Scott, Tanya Chapman, Daniel Goodwin, and Greg Bambury: "We wanted to be explicit about our people strategy and talk about it in the same way that we often talk about our marketing strategy and our financial strategy," Greg Bambury says. Irving Oil recently received a Human Resources Innovation Award from Atlantic Canada Human Resources Awards (ACHRA) for its Mutual Value Promise (MVP) program that includes a wide range of learning and development opportunities for employees and managers.

a **protean career**—that is, a career that frequently changes based on changes in the person's interests, abilities, and values and in the work environment. For example, an engineer might decide to take a sabbatical from her position to work in a management role with the United Way for a year. The purpose of this change could be to develop her managerial skills and evaluate whether she likes managerial work more than engineering. As in this example, the concept of a protean career assumes that employees will take major responsibility for managing their careers. This concept is consistent with the modern *psychological contract* we described in Chapter 1. In place of the traditional expectation of job security and advancement within a company, today's employees need to take control over their careers and personal responsibility for managing their careers. They look for organizations that will support them by providing development opportunities and flexible work arrangements so they can pursue their goals.

In this environment, employees need to develop new skills, rather than rely on an unchanging base of knowledge. This need results from employers' efforts to respond to customer demands.

The many approaches to employee development fall into four broad categories: formal education, assessment, job experiences, and interpersonal relationships.[56] Figure 7.5 summarizes these four methods. Many organizations combine these approaches.

protean career
A career that frequently changes based on changes in the person's interests, abilities, and values and in the work environment.

Formal Education

Organizations may support employee development through a variety of formal educational programs, either at the workplace or offsite. These may include workshops designed specifically for the organization's employees, short courses offered by consultants, colleges, or universities, and MBA and executive MBA programs. These programs may involve lectures by business experts, business games and simulations, experiential programs, and meetings with customers.

FIGURE 7.5

The Four Approaches to Employee Development

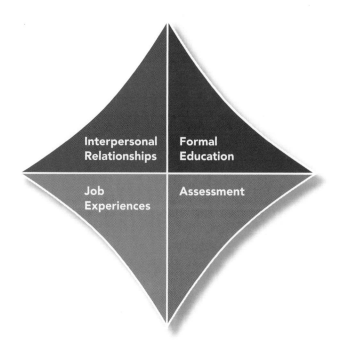

Many companies, including SaskTel, IBM, BMO, and KPMG LLP, operate training and development centres that offer in-house training. Universities including Queen's, the University of Western Ontario, the University of Alberta, and UBC as well as colleges including Humber, Conestoga, Durham, Seneca, and Grant MacEwan offer management and professional development programs to organizations. A growing number of companies and educational institutions are also using distance learning and other e-learning options to reach their audiences.

Another trend in formal education is for employers and the education provider to create short courses with content designed specifically for the audience. An example of this type of customized learning is Toronto's University Health Network's leadership development program that was developed with the help of the Rotman School of Management.[57] For over a decade, BMO has offered an MBA program on company time. Participants meet for week-long sessions at the bank's learning centre on the outskirts of Toronto with professors from Dalhousie who fly in to deliver each of the 16 modules that make up the program.[58]

Assessment

assessment
Collecting information and providing feedback to employees about their behaviour, communication style, or skills.

Another way to provide for employee development is **assessment**—collecting information and providing feedback to employees about their behaviour, communication style, or skills.[59] Information for assessment may come from the employees, their peers, managers, and customers. The most frequent uses of assessment are to identify employees with managerial potential to measure current managers' strengths and weaknesses. Organizations also use assessment to identify managers with potential to move into higher-level executive positions. Organizations that assign work to teams may use assessment to identify the strengths and weaknesses of individual team members and the effects of the team members' decision-making and communication styles on the team's productivity.

For assessment to support development, the information must be shared with the employee being assessed. Along with that assessment information, the employee needs suggestions for correcting skill weaknesses and for using skills already learned. The suggestions might be to participate in training courses or develop skills through new job experiences. On the basis of the assessment information and available development opportunities, employees should develop action plans to guide their efforts at self-improvement.

It is increasingly recognized that excellent technical skills are not enough for individuals or organizations to be successful. "Strong people skills are equally important to attracting clients, building lasting relationships with both clients and colleagues, and expanding business."[60] As a result, organizations vary in the methods and sources of information they use in developmental assessment. Many organizations appraise performance. Organizations with sophisticated development systems may use psychological tests to measure employees' skills, personality types, and communication styles. They may collect self, peer, and manager ratings of employees' behaviour and style of working with others. Assessment of emotional intelligence (EQ) increases an employee's self-awareness and facilitates their development with respect to intrapersonal and interpersonal skills, adaptability, and handling of stress.[61] Applying this kind of information about employees' preferences or tendencies helps organizations understand the communication, motivation, teamwork, work styles, and leadership of the people in their groups.

TABLE 7.5

Skills Related
to Success as a
Manager

Resourcefulness	Can think strategically, engage in flexible problem solving, and work effectively with higher management.
Doing whatever it takes	Has perseverance and focus in the face of obstacles.
Being a quick study	Quickly masters new technical and business knowledge.
Building and mending relationships	Knows how to build and maintain working relationships with co-workers and external parties.
Leading subordinates	Delegates to employees effectively, broadens their opportunities, and acts with fairness toward them.
Compassion and sensitivity	Shows genuine interest in others and sensitivity to employees' needs.
Straightforwardness and composure	Is honourable and steadfast.
Setting a developmental climate	Provides a challenging climate to encourage employees' development.
Confronting difficult employee situations	Acts decisively and fairly when dealing with difficult employee situations.
Team orientation	Accomplishes tasks through managing others.
Balance between personal life and work	Balances work priorities with personal life so that neither is neglected.
Decisiveness	Prefers quick and approximate actions to slow and precise ones in many management situations.
Self-awareness	Has an accurate picture of strengths and weaknesses and is willing to improve.
Hiring talented staff	Hires talented people for the team.
Putting people at ease	Displays warmth and a good sense of humour.
Acting with flexibility	Can behave in ways that are often seen as opposites.

SOURCE: Adapted with permission from C. D. McCauley, M. M. Lombardo, and C. J. Usher, "Diagnosing Management Development Needs: An Instrument Based on How Managers Develop," *Journal of Management* 15 (1989), pp. 389–403.

360-Degree Feedback

As we will discuss in more detail in Chapter 8, a recent trend in performance appraisals, is *360-degree feedback*—performance measurement by the employee's supervisor, peers, direct reports, and customers. Often the feedback involves rating the individual in terms of skills, competencies, and work-related behaviours. Table 7.5 provides a summary of management skills. Research has found that managers who have these skills are more likely to receive positive performance evaluations, be considered promotable, and be promoted.[62] For development purposes, the rater would identify an area of behaviour as a strength of that employee or an area requiring further development. The results presented to the employee show how he or she was rated on each item and how self-evaluations differ from other

FIGURE 7.6

Steps in the TELUS
Development System

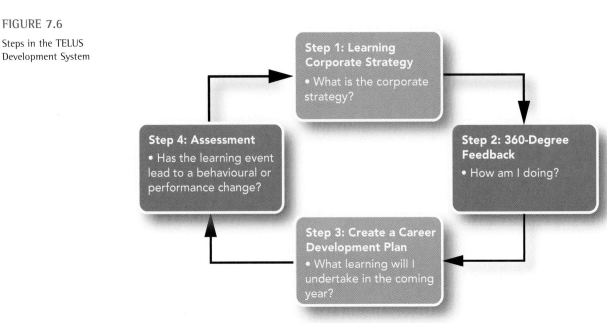

SOURCE: "TELUS Awarded for Development System," *Canadian HR Reporter,* March 8, 2004, p. 16.

raters' evaluations. The individual reviews the results, seeks clarification from the raters, and sets specific development goals based on the strengths and weaknesses identified.[63]

However, the 360-degree feedback is often viewed as more successful when used for development purposes rather than for performance appraisal. Consider how TELUS uses development planning with 360-degree feedback. As illustrated in Figure 7.6, TELUS uses a four-step process that encourages all employees to create a development plan with objectives for learning and performance. This process relies on 360-degree feedback as a critical step.

Job Experiences

job experiences
The combination of relationships, problems, demands, tasks, and other features of an employee's jobs.

Most employee development occurs through **job experiences**[64] the combination of relationships, problems, demands, tasks, and other features of an employee's jobs. Using job experiences for employee development assumes that development is most likely to occur when the employee's skills and experiences do not entirely match the skills required for the employee's current job. To succeed, employees must stretch their skills. In other words, they must learn new skills, apply their skills and knowledge in new ways, and master new experiences.[65] For example, companies that want to prepare employees to expand overseas markets are assigning them to a variety of international jobs.

Most of what we know about development through job experiences comes from a series of studies conducted by the Center for Creative Leadership.[66] These studies asked executives to identify key career events that made a difference in their managerial styles and the lessons they learned from these experiences. The key events included job assignments (such as fixing a failed operation), interpersonal relationships (getting along with supervisors), and types of transitions (situations in which the manager at first lacked the necessary background). Through job experiences like these, managers learn how to handle common challenges, prove themselves, lead change, handle pressure, and influence others.

The usefulness of job experiences for employee development varies depending on whether the employee views the experiences as positive or negative sources of stress. When employees view job experiences as positive stressors, the experiences challenge them and stimulate learning. When they view job experiences as negative stressors, employees may suffer from high levels of harmful stress. Of the job demands studied, managers were most likely to experience negative stress from creating change and overcoming obstacles (adverse business conditions, lack of management support, lack of personal support, or a difficult boss). Research suggests that all of the job demands except obstacles are related to learning.[67] Organizations should offer job experiences that are most likely to increase learning, and they should consider the consequences of situations that involve negative stress.

Although the research on development through job experiences has focused on managers, line employees also can learn through job experiences. Organizations may, for example, use job experiences to develop skills needed for teamwork, including conflict resolution, data analysis, and customer service. These experiences may occur when forming a team and when employees switch roles within a team. Effem Inc., the organization that makes consumer products including Mars chocolate bars employs about 500 people in Canada. Effem's approach to career development starts "at recruitment when associates are not hired for 'The Job' but assessed for their potential to transfer into different roles."[68]

Various job assignments can provide for employee development. The organization may enlarge the employee's current job or move the employee to different jobs. Lateral moves include job rotation, transfer, or temporary assignment to another or organization. The organization may also use downward moves or promotions as a source of job experience. Figure 7.7 summarizes these alternatives.

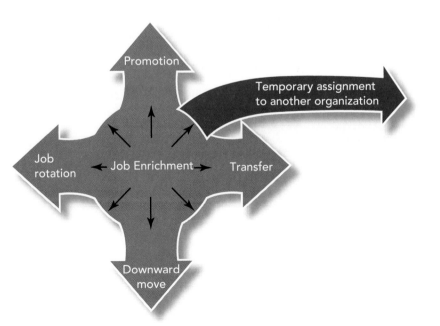

FIGURE 7.7

How Job Experiences Are Used for Employee Development

Job Enrichment

Job enrichment involves adding challenges or new responsibilities to employees' current jobs. Examples include completing a special project, switching roles within a work team, or researching new ways to serve customers. An accountant might join a task force developing new career paths for technical employees. The work on the project could give the accountant a leadership role through which the engineer learns about the company's career development system while also practising leadership skills to help the task force reach its goals. In this way, job enrichment not only makes a job more interesting, but also creates an opportunity for employees to develop new competencies.

Job Rotation

Another job design technique that can be applied to employee development is *job rotation*, moving employees through a series of job assignments in one or more functional areas. At Purdy's Chocolates in British Columbia, employees are provided development opportunities. Plant workers are given the chance to run a shift to see if they have the potential to replace a lead hand or become a warehouse manager in the future.[69]

Job rotation helps employees gain an appreciation for the company's goals, increases their understanding of different company functions, develops a network of contacts, and improves problem-solving and decision-making competencies.[70] Job rotation also helps employees increase their salary and earn promotions faster. At RBC Financial Group, 12,000 of the bank's 70,000 employees move to new positions through internal job postings every year.[71] Zabeen Hirji, RBC's senior vice-president of human resources, says, "job hopping helps employees provide better customer service because they learn about different areas of the company."[72] However, the rotation of employees through a department may hurt productivity and increase the workload of those who remain after employees are rotated out. Job rotation is most likely to succeed when it meets certain conditions:[73]

- Job rotation is used for developing competencies as well as gaining experience for management careers.
- Employees understand specifically what competencies rotation is to develop.
- The organization uses job rotation for all levels and types of employees.
- Job rotation is linked with the career management process so employees know what development needs each assignment addresses.
- The organization manages the timing of rotations to maximize their benefits and minimize their costs.
- All employees have equal opportunities for job rotation, without facing discrimination due to their ethnic origin, sexual orientation, age, or other prohibited grounds of discrimination.

transfer
Assignment of an employee to a position in a different area of the company, usually in a lateral move.

Transfers, Promotions, and Downward Moves

Most companies use upward, downward, and lateral moves as an option for employee development. In a **transfer**, the organization assigns an employee to a position in a different area of the company. Transfers do not necessarily increase job responsibilities or compensation. They are usually lateral moves, that is, moves to a job with a similar level of responsibility. They may involve relocation to another part of the country or even to another country.

Because transfers can provoke anxiety, many companies have difficulty getting employees to accept them. Employees most willing to accept transfers tend to be those with high career ambitions, a belief that the organization offers a promising future, and a belief that accepting the transfer will help the company succeed.[74]

A **downward move** occurs when an employee is given less responsibility and authority. The organization may demote an employee because of poor performance or move the employee to a lower-level position in another function so that the employee can develop different skills. The temporary cross-functional move is the most common way to use downward moves for employee development. For example, engineers who want to move into management often take lower-level positions, such as shift supervisor, to develop their management skills.

Many employees have difficulty associating transfers and downward moves with development; these changes may feel more like forms of punishment. Employees will be more likely to accept transfers and downward moves as development opportunities if the organization provides information about the change and its possible benefits and involves the employee in planning the change. Employees are also more likely to be positive about such a recommendation if the organization provides clear performance objectives and frequent feedback.

A **promotion** involves moving an employee into a position with greater challenges, more responsibility, and more authority than in the previous job. Usually promotions include pay increases. Because promotions improve the person's pay, status, and feelings of accomplishment, employees are more willing to accept promotions than lateral or downward moves. Even so, employers can increase the likelihood that employees will accept promotions by providing the same kind of information and assistance that are used to support transfers and downward moves. Organizations can more easily offer promotions if they are profitable and growing. In other conditions, opportunities for promoting employees may be limited.

Temporary Assignments with Other Organizations

In some cases, an employer may benefit from the skills an employee can learn at another organization. The employer may encourage the employee to participate in an **externship**—a full-time temporary position at another organization. Mercer Management, a consulting firm, uses externships to develop employees who want experience in a specific industry.[75] Mercer Management promises to employ the externs after their assignments end. One employee with several years' experience as a Mercer consultant became vice-president of Internet services for Binney and Smith, the maker of Crayola crayons. He had been consulting on an Internet project for Binney and Smith and wanted to implement his recommendations, rather than just give them to the client and move on to another project. He started working at Binney and Smith while remaining employed by Mercer Management, though his pay comes from the former. Mercer believes that employees who participate in its externship program will remain committed to the consulting firm, because they have a chance to learn and grow professionally without the demands of a job search.

Temporary assignments can include a **sabbatical**—a leave of absence from an organization to renew or develop skills. Employees on sabbatical often receive full pay and benefits. Sabbaticals let employees get away from the day-to-day stresses of their

downward move
Assignment of an employee to a position with less responsibility and authority.

promotion
Assignment of an employee to a position with greater challenges, more responsibility, and more authority than in the previous job, usually accompanied by a pay increase.

externship
Employee development through a full-time temporary position at another organization.

sabbatical
A leave of absence from an organization to renew or develop skills.

jobs and acquire new skills and perspectives. Sabbaticals also allow employees more time for personal pursuits such as writing a book or spending more time with family members. Morningstar, which tracks and reports the performance of mutual funds, provides a six-week paid sabbatical every four years for all employees.[76]

L07 - Explain how managers and peers develop employees through mentoring and coaching.

Interpersonal Relationships

Employees can also develop skills and increase their knowledge about the organization and its customers by interacting with a more experienced organization member. Two types of relationships used for employee development are *mentoring* and *coaching*.

Mentors

mentor

An experienced, productive senior employee who helps develop a less experienced employee (a protégé or mentee).

A **mentor** is an experienced, productive senior employee who helps develop a less experienced employee, called the *protégé* or *mentee*. Most mentoring relationships develop informally as a result of interests or values shared by the mentor and protégé. According to research, the employees most likely to seek and attract a mentor have certain personality characteristics: emotional stability, ability to adapt their behaviour to the situation, and high needs for power and achievement.[77] Mentoring relationships also can develop as part of the organization's planned effort to bring together successful senior employees with less experienced employees.

One major advantage of formal mentoring programs is that they ensure access to mentors for all employees. An advantage is that participants in a company-sponsored mentoring program know what is expected of them.[78] However, in an artificially created relationship, mentors may have difficulty providing counselling and coaching.[79] Mentoring programs tend to be most successful when they are *voluntary* and participants understand the details of the program. Rewarding managers for employee development is also important, because it signals that mentoring and other development activities are worthwhile. In addition, the organization should carefully select mentors on the basis of their interpersonal and technical competencies, train them for the role, and evaluate whether the program has met its objectives. Information technology can help organizations meet some of these guidelines. The e-HRM box describes how computer software by Triple Creek Associates helps employees find and select their mentors and stay on track to meeting their development goals.

Bell Canada's mentoring program, "Mentor Match," has been recognized as one of the best. Mentor Match is open to employees at all levels and uses an online cross-functional mentoring program. Protégés/mentees browse a pool of possible mentors using a search tool. A list of suitable mentors is generated according to the profile of the protégé/mentee. From a strategic perspective, Mentor Match is expected to improve employee retention, enhance performance and productivity, and accelerate the development of employees. Because it is fully automated, Mentor Match can track data and generate results such as signup statistics. All the necessary mentoring tools such as mentoring agreements, suggestions, and templates are available online.[80]

Mentors and protégés can both benefit from a mentoring relationship. Table 7.6 summarizes the advantages of mentoring programs to both protégés and mentors. Protégés receive career support, including coaching, protection, sponsorship, challenging assignments, and visibility among the organization's managers. They also receive benefits of a positive relationship—a friend and role model who accepts them, has a

E- HRM

Triple Creek Associates Puts Mentoring Online

One of the big challenges of mentoring is finding the right matches between employees with development needs and people with experience in the areas requiring development. If finding a match sounds a lot like a dating service, then the service offered by Triple Creek Associates is not surprising; an electronic matchmaking service for mentoring. In a typical arrangement, a Triple Creek client recruits people willing to serve as mentors, builds up a database in which these people provide information about their skills and work experience, and then begins offering the mentoring program to its employees. Triple Creek hosts the software for the process and usually tailors it to the company's human resource requirements.

To use the system, an employee completes a self-profile that indicates that employee's areas of development need. The system then searches the database, looking for potential mentors and rating them according to how well their strengths match

the person's development needs. The employee can see which of these potential mentors rank as the closest matches and can select one or more to interview in person, over the phone, or online. When the employee has found a good match, the mentoring relationship begins, proceeding along the terms of a formal mentoring agreement established by the pair. During the process, the Triple Creek system provides meeting reminders and evaluation forms so that the participants can track their progress.

One of the companies that uses the Triple Creek system is Dow Chemical, which has 1,500 mentoring pairs enrolled in the system. With offices in 167 countries, the company's management knew it couldn't rely on employees to physically find the mentors with the necessary background—the best match for an employee in Sarnia, Ontario, might be a manager in Germany.

When Dow employee Michael Witt wanted to deepen his management ability and

knowledge of the corporation, he found a mentor through this system. Witt, whose title was Products Stewardship Specialist, was surprised to find that the closest match was the company's Chief Information Officer, David Kepler. Though Witt, in his words, "hadn't even been to the executive offices," he contacted Kepler, and they began meeting periodically to discuss Witt's career and the company's products. The mentoring relationship helped Witt serve on a team that oversees product development, and Witt is optimistic about his career prospects at Dow. Kepler, too, is pleased with the mentoring system. He praises the requirement that protégés do the work of establishing goals, choosing a mentor, and evaluating progress. Says Kepler, "That forces them to think about what they want out of the relationship."

SOURCE: Based on Eve Tahmincioglu, "Looking for a Mentor? Technology Can Help Make the Right Match," *Workforce Management*, December 2004, pp. 63–65; and Triple Creek Associates, "Tour," www.3creek.com, retrieved May 12, 2005.

positive opinion toward them, and gives them a chance to talk about their concerns. Employees with mentors are also more likely to be promoted, earn higher salaries, and have more influence within their organization.[81] Acting as a mentor gives managers a chance to develop their interpersonal skills and increase their feeling they are contributing something important. Working with the protégé on technical matters such as new research in the field may also increase the mentor's technical knowledge.

TABLE 7.6

Advantages of
Mentoring Programs

FOR PROTÉGÉS/MENTEES	FOR MENTORS
• Breaks down "silos" throughout the organization	• Maintains a pulse on the organization by keeping regular contact and communication with employees
• Increases communication	• Enhances interpersonal and leadership competencies
• Supports continuous learning throughout all levels of the organization	
• Enhances career development and growth	
• Improves employee satisfaction and engagement	
• Fosters a culture where employees support and help one another	

SOURCE: Adapted from Conference Board of Canada, "Mentoring—Low Cost, Big Benefits," www.conferenceboard.ca/humanresource/mentoring-inside.htm, retrieved February 24, 2005.

So that more employees can benefit from mentoring, some organizations use *group mentoring programs*, which assign four to six protégés to a successful senior employee. A potential advantage of group mentoring is that protégés can learn from each other as well as from the mentor. The leader helps protégés/mentees understand the organization, guides them in analyzing their experiences, and helps them clarify career directions. Each member of the group may complete specific assignments, or the group may work together on a problem or issue.

Coaching

coach

A peer or manager who works with an employee to provide a source of motivation, help him or her develop skills, and provide reinforcement and feedback.

A **coach** is a peer or manager who works with an employee to provide a source of motivation, help him or her develop skills, and provide reinforcement and feedback. Coaches may play one or more of three roles:[82]

1. Working one-on-one with an employee, as when giving feedback
2. Helping employees learn for themselves—for example, helping them find experts and teaching them to obtain feedback from others
3. Providing resources such as mentors, courses, or job experiences

William Gray, president of Corporate Mentoring Solutions Inc. and former UBC professor, draws a distinction between mentoring and coaching. Gray describes mentoring as developing the "whole person" and coaching involves developing a specific skill set.[83]

Best Buy, a consumer-electronics retailer, has invested nearly $10 million on coaches for all top managers.[84] Once a month, top executives spend a few hours with an industrial psychologist who helps them work through leadership issues. One manager discussed with his coach how to balance the needs of some of the managers who worked for him with the company's business needs. His managers were more comfortable focusing on traditional store retailing at a time when the company needed a focus on competition on the Internet. The manager being coached needed to learn how to lead his team and push new ideas without squelching team members.

FIGURE 7.8

Steps and Responsibilities in the Career Management Process

	Self-assessment	Reality check	Goal setting	Action planning
Employee responsibility	Identify opportunities and development needs.	Identify what needs are realistic to develop.	Identify goals and method to determine goal progress.	Identify steps and timetable to reach goals.
Company responsibility	Provide assessment information to identify strengths, weaknesses, interests, and values.	Communicate performance evaluation, where employee fits in long-range plans of the company.	Ensure that goals are specific, challenging, and attainable; commit to help employee reach the goals.	Identify resources employee needs to reach goals, including education, work experiences, relationships.

Career Management Systems

Employee development is most likely to meet the organization's needs if it is part of a human resource system of career management. In practice, organizations' career management systems vary. Some rely heavily on informal relationships, while others are sophisticated programs. As shown in Figure 7.8, a basic career management system involves four steps: self-assessment, reality check, goal setting, and action planning. At each step, both the employee and the organization have responsibilities. The system is most likely to be beneficial if it is linked to the organization's objectives and needs, has support from top management, and is created with employee participation.[85] Human resource professionals can also contribute to the system's success by ensuring it is linked to other HR practices such as performance management, training, and recruiting.

A recent Conference Board of Canada survey noted that 78 percent of participating organizations have a formal career development planning process. Almost half of these organizations say that both the employee and the organization share responsibility for an employee's career development plan.[86]

LO8 - Identify the steps in the career management process.

R P C
6

Self-Assessment

In discussing the methods of employee development, we highlighted several assessment tools. Such tools may be applied to the first stage of career development, **self-assessment**. This is the use of information by employees to determine their career interests, values, aptitudes, and behavioural tendencies. The employee's responsibility is to identify opportunities and development needs. The organization's responsibility is to provide assessment information for identifying strengths, weaknesses, interests, and values.

Self-assessment tools often include psychological tests such as the Myers-Briggs Type Inventory, the Strong-Campbell Interest Inventory, and the Self-Directed Search. The Strong-Campbell Inventory helps employees identify their occupational and job interests. The Self-Directed Search identifies employees' preferences for working in different kinds of environments—sales, counselling, and so on. Tests may

self-assessment
The use of information by employees to determine their career interests, values, aptitudes, and behavioural tendencies.

also help employees identify the relative value they place on work and leisure activities. Self-assessment tools can help an employee consider his or her current career status, future plans, and the fit between the career and current situation and resources. Some organizations provide counsellors to help employees in the self-assessment process and to interpret the results of psychological tests.

Completing a self-assessment can help employees identify a development need. This need can result from gaps between current skills or interests and the type of work or position the employee has or wants.

Reality Check

reality check
Information employers give employees about their competencies and where these assets fit into the organization's plans.

career path
The identified pattern or progression of jobs or roles within an organization.

In the next step of career management, the **reality check**, employees receive information about their competencies and where these assets fit into the organization's plans. The employee's responsibility is to identify what skills she or he could realistically develop in light of the opportunities available. The organization's responsibility is to communicate the performance evaluation and the opportunities available to the employee, given the organization's long-range plans. Opportunities might include promotions and transfers. Some organizations develop and communicate **career paths** —the identified pattern or progression of jobs or roles within an organization to provide clarity about how an employee may progress into more senior positions. Career paths may include a wide variety of jobs or may provide specific information related to cumulative responsibilities for a managerial, technical, or professional career. Career-path information can also enhance the discussion of opportunities between employees and their managers by providing consistent language related to how jobs and roles are defined in the organization.[87] Figure 7.9 provides information about career paths in Building Operations at PCL.

Usually the employer conducts the reality check as part of a performance appraisal or as the feedback stage of performance management. In well-developed career

FIGURE 7.9

Career Paths—Building Operations at PCL

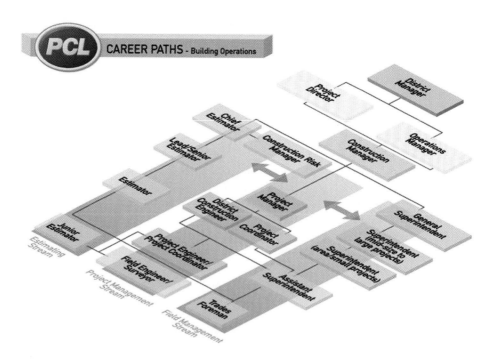

SOURCE: PCL Family of Companies website, www.pcl.com/html/homesection/careers/career_path.html.

management systems, the manager may hold separate discussions for performance feedback and career development. Another form of reality check encouraged by career coaches involves "checking your Google score" to see how many pages on the Web have your name on them. This awareness will help detect misconceptions about your "personal brand." Whether you took part in a 10 kilometre run and your time made it to the sponsor's site, your bio appears on your company's website, or your Facebook profile has been indexed, you have an online identity that can be viewed by anyone with access to a search engine.[88] That fact is well known to technology-savvy employers and could help or hinder your career.

Goal Setting

On the basis of the information from the self-assessment and reality check, the employee sets short- and long-term career objectives. These goals usually involve one or more of the following categories:

- Desired roles, such as becoming a team leader within three years
- Level of competency—for example, to apply one's budgeting skills to improve the unit's cash flow problems
- Work setting—for example, to move to corporate marketing within two years
- Skill acquisition, such as learning how to use the company's human resource information system

As in these examples, the goals should be specific, and they should include a date by which the goal is to be achieved. It is the employee's responsibility to identify the goal and the method of determining her or his progress toward each goal. Usually the employee discusses the goals with his or her manager. The organization's responsibilities are to ensure that the goal is specific, challenging, and achievable, and to help the employee reach the goal.

Action Planning

In the final step, employees prepare an action plan for *how* they will achieve their short- and long-term development goals. The employee is responsible for identifying the steps and timetable to reach the goals. The employer should identify resources needed, including courses, work experiences, and relationships.

Action plans may involve any one or a combination of the development methods discussed earlier in the chapter—training, assessment, job experiences, or the help of a mentor or coach. The approach used depends on the particular developmental needs and career objectives. For example, suppose the program manager in an information systems department uses feedback from performance appraisals to determine that greater knowledge of project management software is needed. The manager plans to increase that knowledge by reading articles (formal education), meeting with software vendors, and contacting the vendors' customers to ask them about the software they have used (job experiences). The manager and his supervisor agree that six months will be the target date for achieving the higher level of knowledge through these activities.

The outcome of action planning often takes the form of a development plan. Figure 7.10 is an example of a development plan for a product manager. Development plans usually include descriptions of strengths and weaknesses, career goals, and development activities for reaching each goal.

FIGURE 7.10

Development Plan

| **Name:** | **Title:** Project Manager | **Immediate Manager:** |

Competencies

Please identify your three greatest strengths and areas for improvement.

Strengths

- Strategic thinking and execution (confidence, command skills, action orientation)
- Results orientation (creating a motivating work environment, perseverance)
- Spirit for winning (building team spirit, customer focus, respect colleagues)

Areas for Improvement

- Patience (tolerance of people or processes and sensitivity to pacing)
- Written communications (ability to write clearly and succinctly)
- Overly ambitious (too much focus on successful completion of projects rather than developing relationships with individuals involved in the projects)

Career Goals

Please describe your overall career goals.

- *Long-term.* Accept positions of increased responsibility to a level of general manager (or beyond). The areas of specific interest include but are not limited to product and brand management, technology and development, strategic planning, and marketing.
- *Short-term.* Continue to improve my skills in marketing and brand management while utilizing my skills in product management, strategic planning, and global relations.

Next Assignments

Identify potential next assignments (including timing) that would help you develop toward your career goals.

- Manager or director level in planning, development, product, or brand management. Timing estimated to be Spring 2010.

Training and Development Needs

List both training and development activities that will either help you develop in your current assignment or provide overall career development.

- Master's degree classes will allow me to practise and improve my written communications skills. The dynamics of my current position, teamwork, and reliance on other individuals allow me to practise patience and to focus on individual team members' needs along with the success of the project.

Employee _____ **Date** _____

Immediate Manager _____ **Date** _____

Mentor _____ **Date** _____

L09 - Discuss how organizations are meeting the challenges of the "glass ceiling" and succession planning.

Development-Related Challenges

A well-designed system for employee development can help organizations face three widespread challenges: the glass ceiling, succession planning, and dysfunctional behaviour by managers.

The Glass Ceiling

As we mentioned in Chapter 1, women and other members of the employment equity target groups are rare in the top level of Canadian corporations. According to the most recent data from Catalyst, only 15.1 percent of corporate officer jobs and 13 percent of board seats in Canada's FP 500 companies are held by women.[89] Observers of this situation have noted that it looks as if an invisible barrier is keeping these individuals from reaching the top jobs, a barrier that has come to be known as the **glass ceiling**. However, the glass ceiling metaphor has been criticized because it describes an absolute barrier at a specific high level in organizations and fails to incorporate the complex and varied challenges women and other members of the employment equity target groups face in their careers. A better metaphor may be a *labyrinth*, connoting a complex journey with many twists and turns and puzzles to solve along the way to the top jobs.[90] According to research, women and men have equal access to job experiences involving transitions or creating change.[91] But male managers receive significantly more assignments involving great responsibility (high stakes, managing business diversity, handling external pressure) than female managers of similar ability and managerial level. Also, female managers report experiencing more challenge due to lack of personal support. With regard to developmental relationships, women and visible minorities often have trouble finding mentors. They may not participate in the organization's, profession's, or community's "old boys' network." Also, managers in the organization may prefer to interact with people who have similar status, or may avoid interacting with certain people because of discomfort or negative stereotypes.[92]

Organizations can use development systems to help break through the glass ceiling or "navigate the labyrinth." Managers making developmental assignments need to carefully consider whether stereotypes are influencing the types of assignments men and women receive. A formal process for regularly identifying development needs and creating action plans can make these decisions more objective. An organization actively working to eliminate the glass ceiling is Deloitte & Touche, an accounting, tax, and consulting firm with offices throughout North America. Deloitte & Touche had been experiencing high turnover of talented women, so it set up a task force chaired by the company's chief executive officer to analyze the problem and develop recommendations. The task force gathered data by having every management professional in the company attend a workshop designed to explore how attitudes about gender affected the work environment. The workshops included discussions, videos, and case studies, such as one case in which two promising candidates, one male and one female, with identical skills were evaluated. The workshops also focused on how work assignments were allocated. The workshops found differences in the ways men and women were evaluated and in the kinds of assignments they were given, based on managers' assumptions about men and women. As a result, Deloitte & Touche began to rethink how assignments were given, to make sure women had opportunities for highly visible assignments. The company started a formal process for career planning for all employees, and began offering networking events at which women could meet successful female partners and high-level managers. Deloitte & Touche began measuring turnover and promotion rates and linking rewards to meeting career development objectives. Through these changes, the company improved its retention of women, and reducing turnover has saved $250 million in hiring and training costs.[93]

2,6

glass ceiling
Circumstances resembling an invisible barrier that keep most women and other members of the employment equity target groups from attaining the top jobs in organizations.

2,3,6

Succession Planning

Organizations have always had to prepare for the retirement of their leaders, but the need is more intense than ever. The aging of the workforce means that a greater share of employees are reaching retirement age. Many organizations are fuelling the trend by downsizing through early-retirement programs. As positions at the top of organizations become vacant, many organizations have determined that their middle managers are fewer and often unprepared for top-level responsibility. This situation has raised awareness of the need for **succession planning**—the process of identifying and tracking high-potential employees who will be able to fill top management positions when they become vacant. Forty-five percent of Purdy's Chocolates employees will be eligible to retire in a decade. Because Purdy's prefers to promote from within they are developing a succession plan to deal with future retirements of store managers from their 48 retail-store chains in Alberta and British Columbia.[94]

Succession planning offers several benefits.[95] It forces senior management to regularly and thoughtfully review the company's leadership talent. It assures that top-level management talent is available. It provides a set of development experiences that managers must complete to be considered for top management positions, so the organization does not promote managers before they are ready. Succession planning systems also help attract and retain ambitious managerial employees by providing development opportunities.

Succession planning focuses on *high-potential employees*, that is, employees the organization believes can succeed in higher-level business positions such as general manager of a business unit, director of a function (such as marketing or finance), or chief executive officer.[96] A typical approach to development of high-potential employees is to have them complete an individual development program including education, executive mentoring and coaching, and rotation through job assignments. Job assignments are based on the successful career paths of the managers whom the high-potential employees are preparing to replace. High-potential employees may also receive special assignments, such as making presentations and serving on committees and task forces. Research shows that an effective program for developing high-potential employees has three stages:[97]

1. *Selection of high-potential employees.* Organizations may select outstanding performers and employees who have completed academic programs, such as earning a master's degree in business administration. They may also use the results of psychological tests and assessment centres.

2. *Developmental experiences.* As employees participate in developmental experiences, the organization identifies those who succeed in the experiences. The organization looks for employees who continue to show qualities associated with success in top jobs, such as communication skills, leadership talent, and willingness to make sacrifices for the organization. Employees who display these qualities continue to be considered high-potential employees.

3. *Active involvement with the CEO.* High-potential employees seen by top management as fitting into the organization's culture and having personality characteristics necessary for representing the company become actively involved with the chief executive officer. The CEO exposes these employees to the organization's key people and gives them a greater understanding of the organization's culture. The development of high-potential employees is a slow process. Reaching stage 3 may take many years.

succession planning
The process of identifying and tracking high-potential employees who will be able to fill top management positions when they become vacant.

Figure 7.11 breaks this process into seven steps. It begins with identifying the positions to be planned for and the employees to be included in the plan. Planning should also include establishing position requirements and deciding how to measure employees' potential for being able to fill those requirements. The organization needs to develop a process for reviewing the existing talent. The next step is to link succession planning with other human resource systems. Finally, the organization needs a way to provide employees with feedback about career paths available to them and how they are progressing toward their goals.

At some organizations, succession planning systems identify a few potential managers for each position. This limited approach allows the organization to target development activities to the most talented managers, but it may not prepare enough managers to fill vacant positions. High-potential employees who are not on the short list for managerial jobs may leave. Some organizations avoid this problem by identifying many qualified leaders, which builds commitment to the company.

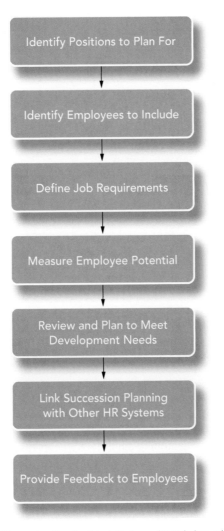

FIGURE 7.11

Process for Developing a Succession Plan

SOURCE: Based on B. Dowell, "Succession Planning," in J. Hedge and E. Pulaskos, eds., *Implementing Organizational Interventions* (San Francisco: Jossey-Bass, 2002), pp. 78–109.

THINKING | ETHICALLY

Can You Teach People to Be Ethical?

This chapter looked at training and development as a way to ensure that employees have a variety of skills and abilities, such as knowing how to perform the tasks involved in a particular job and being able to work constructively with a diverse group of people. Some organizations also provide training to help their employees make decisions.

The Molson Coors Brewing Company offers employees several resources related to ethics, including interactive e-learning, ethics leadership training, and a visual "map" to guide ethical decision making. These training resources support detailed ethics policies and supplement a company help line to call for guidance in specific situations. According to Warren Malmquist, who developed the ethics training for Adolph Coors Company before its merger with Molson, "The goal of the program is to step beyond rules and guidelines and teach employees how to think, clarify, and analyze situations." The e-learning program presents scenarios and provides feedback to help employees see the ethical principles related to their decisions. The program includes a series of modules presented as an "expedition" from a base camp to the top of the mountain. As the employee ascends through the modules, the topics become more complex and the choices less obvious. All new hires must complete this course within 90 days, and existing employees must take refresher courses.

SOURCE: Based on Samuel Greengard, "Golden Values," *Workforce Management,* March 2005, pp. 52–53.

Questions

1. To make ethical decisions, what skills and abilities do you need? What else you need besides skills and abilities?
2. Do you think the ethics training described here will help make Molson Coors' employees more ethical? Explain.
3. Suppose you became responsible for providing ethics training at Molson Coors. What additional ideas from the chapter or your own experience would you want to apply to the program described here?

SUMMARY

L01 | **Discuss how to link training and development to organizational needs and strategy.**

- Organizations need to establish training programs that are effective.
- Organizations create such programs through instructional design. This process begins with a needs assessment, then ensures readiness for training, plans a training program, implements the program, and evaluates the results.

L02 | **Explain how to assess training needs and determine employees' readiness.**

- Needs assessment consists of an organization analysis, person analysis, and task analysis.
- The organization analysis determines the appropriateness of training by evaluating the characteristics of the organization, including its strategy, resources, and management support. The person analysis determines individuals' needs and readiness for training. The task analysis identifies the tasks, knowledge, skills, and behaviours that training should emphasize.
- Readiness for training is a combination of employee characteristics and positive work environment that permit training.

LO3 **Describe how to plan and design an effective training program and compare training methods.**

- Planning begins with establishing objectives for the training program. These should define an expected performance or outcome, the desired level of performance, and the conditions under which the performance should occur.
- On the basis of the objectives, the planner decides who will provide the training, what topics the training will cover, what training methods to use, and how to evaluate the training.
- Even when organizations purchase outside training, someone in the organization, usually a member of the HR department, is responsible for training administration.
- The training methods selected should be related to the objectives and content of the training program. Methods include classroom instruction; audiovisual instruction; computer-based training; on-the-job training methods such as apprenticeships, internships, and cooperative education; business games and cases; experiential programs; and team training.

LO4 **Summarize how to implement and evaluate a successful training program.**

- Implementation should apply principles of learning. In general, effective training communicates learning objectives, presents information in distinctive and memorable ways, and helps trainees link the subject matter to their jobs. Consideration should also be given to ensuring employees have the required workplace literacy skills to succeed and perform well in their jobs.
- Training can be evaluated at four levels—reaction, learning, behaviour, and results. Evaluation of training should look for transfer of training by measuring whether employees are performing the tasks taught in the training program. Assessment of training also should evaluate training outcomes.

LO5 **Describe training methods for employee orientation and diversity management.**

- Employee orientation is training designed to prepare new employees to perform their job effectively, learn about the organization, and establish work relationships. A typical orientation program includes information about the overall company and the department in which the new employee will be working, covering social as well as technical aspects of the job.
- Orientation programs may combine several training methods, from printed materials to on-the-job training to e-learning.
- Diversity training is designed to change employee attitudes about diversity and/or develop skills needed to work with a diverse workforce.

LO6 **Discuss the approaches organizations use for employee development.**

- Organizations may use formal educational programs at the workplace or offsite such as in workshops, college and university programs, company-sponsored training, or programs offered by independent institutions.
- Organizations may use the assessment process to help employees identify strengths and areas requiring further development.
- Job experiences help employees develop by stretching competencies as they meet new challenges.
- Interpersonal relationships with a more experienced member of the organization—often in the role of mentor or coach can help employees develop their understanding of the organization and its customers.

LO7 **Explain how managers and peers develop employees through mentoring and coaching.**

- A mentor is an experienced, productive senior employee who helps develop a less experienced employee. Although most mentoring relationships develop informally, organizations can link mentoring to development goals by establishing a formal mentoring program.
- A coach is a peer or manager who works with an employee to motivate the employee, help him or her develop skills, and provide reinforcement and feedback.

LO8 **Identify the steps in the career management process.**

- First, during self-assessment, employees determine their career interests, values, aptitudes, and behavioural tendencies, looking for opportunities and areas needing development.
- The second step is the reality check, during which the organization communicates information about the employee's skills and knowledge and how these fit into the organization's plan.

- The employee then sets goals and discusses them with his or her manager, who ensures that the goals are specific, challenging, and attainable.
- Finally, the employee works with his or her manager to create an action plan for development activities that will help the employee achieve the goals.

L09 Discuss how organizations are meeting the challenges of the "glass ceiling" and succession planning.

- The "glass ceiling" is a barrier that has been observed preventing women and other members of the employment equity target groups from achieving top jobs in an organization. Development programs can ensure that these employees receive access to development resources.
- Succession planning ensures that the organization prepares qualified employees to fill critical organizational roles by focusing on applying employee development to high-potential employees.

REVIEW AND DISCUSSION QUESTIONS

1. "Melinda!," bellowed Toran to the company's HR specialist, "I've got a problem, and you've got to solve it. I can't get people in this plant to work together as a team. As if I don't have enough trouble with our competitors and our past-due accounts, now I have to put up with running a zoo. You're responsible for seeing that the staff gets along. I want a training proposal on my desk by Monday." Assume you are Melinda.
   a. Is training the solution to this problem? How can you determine the need for training?
   b. Summarize how you would conduct a needs assessment.
   c. How do Toran's comments suggest readiness (or lack of readiness) for learning?

2. Assume you are the human resource manager of a small seafood company. The general manager has told you that customers have begun complaining about the quality of your company's fresh fish. Currently, training consists of senior fish cleaners showing new employees how to perform the job. Assuming your needs assessment indicates a need for training, how would you plan a training program? What steps should you take in planning the program?

3. Many organizations turn to e-learning as a less expensive alternative to classroom training. What are some other advantages of substituting e-learning for classroom training? What are some disadvantages?

4. A manufacturing company employs several maintenance employees. When a problem occurs with the equipment, a maintenance employee receives a description of the symptoms and is supposed to locate and fix the source of the problem. The company recently installed a new, complex electronics system. To prepare its maintenance workers, the company provided classroom training. The trainer displayed electrical drawings of system components and posed problems about the system. The trainer would point to a component in a drawing and ask, "What would happen if this component were faulty?" Trainees would study the diagrams, describe the likely symptoms, and discuss how to repair the problem. If you were responsible for this company's training, how would

you evaluate the success of this training program?

5. Consider your current job, or one you have held recently.
   a. How was orientation handled?
   b. What types of training did you receive for the job?
   c. How did orientation and training affect your performance on the job? Your commitment to the organization?
   d. Is there anything the organization could have done to make the orientation and/or training processes more effective?

6. Why do organizations provide diversity training? What kinds of goals are most suitable for such training?

7. What are the four broad categories of development methods? Why might it be beneficial to combine all of these methods into a formal development program?

8. Recommend a development method for each of the following situations, and explain why you chose that method.
   a. An employee recently promoted to the job of plant supervisor is having difficulty motivating employees to meet quality standards.
   b. A sales manager annoys salespeople by directing every detail of their work.
   c. An employee has excellent leadership skills but lacks knowledge of the financial side of business.
   d. An organization is planning to organize its production workers into teams for the first time.

9. Many employees are unwilling to relocate because they like their current community and family members prefer not to move. Yet preparation for management requires that employees develop new skills, strengthen areas of weakness, and be exposed to new aspects of the organization's business. How can an organization change an employee's current job to develop management skills?

10. Many people feel that mentoring relationships should occur naturally, in situations where senior managers feel inclined to play that role. What are some advantages of setting up a formal mentoring program, rather than letting senior managers decide how and whom to help?

11. What are the manager's roles in a career management system? Which role do you think is most difficult for the typical manager? Which is the easiest role? List reasons why managers might resist becoming involved in career management.

12. What metaphors were used to describe the barriers that women and other employment equity group members still face to advancement into senior executive positions? Can you think of any other relevant metaphors? Which metaphor do you feel is most relevant? Why? Can employee development or succession planning help with this problem? Explain.

WHAT'S YOUR HR IQ?

The Online Learning Centre offers more ways to check what you've learned so far. Find experiential exercises as well as Test Your Knowledge Quizzes, Videos, and many other resources at www.mcgrawhill.ca/olc/steen.

Case:
Learning Technologies in the Workplace—SaskTel

SaskTel is Saskatchewan's leading full-service telecommunications company. The company employs over 4,000 people, who work in more than 50 communities throughout the province. SaskTel conducts business through the Internet and develops e-business solutions for its customers. SaskTel's transition to an electronic environment put pressure on its employees to develop their computer literacy and e-business skills. Recognizing the opportunities the Internet affords for online training, the company aggressively uses technology to enhance learning in the workplace. SaskTel was recently the recipient of the Conference Board of Canada's Learning Technologies in the Workplace Award for demonstrating an innovative approach to its transition to an e-learning strategy.

SaskTel makes e-learning opportunities available to all of its employees, regardless of where they live. Employees can currently access over 450 online courses from work or home.

The employee barriers encountered during the transition included the difficulty for employees to make the connection between participating in e-learning and supporting SaskTel's e-business strategy and the need for call centre service representatives to develop a sales focus as well as a service focus. From a company perspective, SaskTel needed to measure the effectiveness of online learning including measuring performance gains made based on e-learning and developing line managers' project management skills, including their ability to give timely and constructive feedback to employees regarding learning needs and performance. In addition, SaskTel wanted to ensure opportunities were provided to employees who had made use of online learning to apply, challenge, enhance, and reinforce their recently learned or honed skills.

Four keys to success for the company have been:

1. *Building strategic awareness.* Communicating the impact of technology-based changes on employees.
2. *Soft-launching the e-learning strategy.* Offering online courses for four years before the launch of online learning provided SaskTel time to build up a repertoire of courses. In addition, line managers are encouraged to promote the benefits of e-learning.
3. *Building a culture of engagement in e-learning.* Making online learning fun, recognizing employee accomplishments and completion of online learning modules, and linking online learning back to employees' development plans.
4. *Taking a broad approach to e-learning.* Blending traditional and electronic approaches to teaching and learning according to what works best (e.g., online learning, classroom-led learning, team meetings).

Some of the outcomes achieved include:

- Approximately 50 percent of training at SaskTel is currently done online.
- Relevant portions of SaskTel's call centre curriculum are now being converted into online modules complete with pre- and post-assessment and opportunities for employee learners to collaborate.
- SaskTel employees completed 5,480 online courses—on average, more than one course per employee.

SaskTel's approach to implementing an e-learning training strategy may be used as a model by other organizations that are prepared to support a long-term cultural shift. SaskTel immersed its employees in online learning when its business was being transformed by the imperatives of e-business. SaskTel also integrated modular and course-based online learning with content conceived in a much more targeted way. For example, while their customers are on the telephone, call centre representatives can use quick links to obtain product and service information. In addition, self-directed online learning is also connected with help desk functions within the company.

SOURCE: Adapted from Kurtis Kitagawa, "Learning Technologies in the Workplace Award Winner 2002: SaskTel" (Ottawa: Conference Board of Canada, 2002), www.conferenceboard.ca, retrieved February 28, 2004.

Questions

1. What considerations are needed for e-learning to be effective? Explain.
2. Because many organizations expect trainees to complete e-learning during breaks or outside work hours, online learning blurs the boundaries between training and work. Is this expectation realistic? Why or why not?
3. What measures can an organization take to improve employees' motivation to participate in e-learning?

Case:
Learning Is Business at Nokia

Nokia Corporation, the world leader in mobile communications, has over 50,000 employees and net sales of $30 billion. Nokia consists of two business groups: Nokia Networks and Nokia Mobile Phones. The company also includes the separate Nokia Ventures Organization and a corporate research unit, Nokia Research Centre. Nokia's goal is to strengthen the company's position as the leading communication technology and systems provider by offering personalized communication technology and entering new business segments that the company predicts will experience fast growth. As the demand for wireless access to services increases, Nokia plans to lead the development and commercialization of networks and systems required to make wireless content more accessible and rewarding for customers.

The management approach at Nokia, known as the "Nokia way," consists of the Nokia values, its organizational competencies, and its operations and processes used to maintain efficiency. The company has built its current and future strength on the Nokia way. The company has a flat, decentralized structure, and it emphasizes networking, speed, and flexibility in decision making. Nokia's values include customer satisfaction, respect for the individual, achievement, and continuous learning.

Continuous learning provides employees with the opportunity to develop themselves and to stay technologically current. Employees are encouraged to share experiences, take risks, and learn together. Continuous learning goes beyond formal training classes. At Nokia, continuous learning means employees support each other's growth, developing and improving relationships by exchanging and developing ideas. The company uses e-learning to give employees the freedom to choose the best possible time and place for personal development.

Nokia's top management is committed to continuous learning. the business group presidents are "owners" of all global management and leadership programs for senior managers. They provide input into the development of these programs and appoint "godfathers" from their management teams to participate throughout each program and design the program's content. Together with the training and development staff, the godfathers help the learning processes. Most of the programs involve active learning in the form of strategic projects the participants must complete. Top managers review the projects and have authority to take action based on recommendations from the project team.

The value Nokia places on continuous learning translates into opportunities for personal and professional growth. Employees are encouraged to create their own development plan and use available learning methods. Highly skilled employees serve as coaches to help other employees develop and share ideas with one another. Nokia employees have access to a wide variety of training and development opportunities including learning centres and the Learning Marketplace Internet, which has information on all the available learning opportunities such as e-learning and classroom courses. These programs bring together employees from all of Nokia's business groups. Nokia believes that this creates knowledge as employees share their different traditions and experiences.

In addition to formal programs, Nokia emphasizes on-the-job learning through job rotation and challenging work assignments. Managers also have a wide range of opportunities to improve their management and leadership skills. Some of these result from the performance management process, during which employees and their managers set goals and review performance.

Nokia emphasizes that learning should result in improved operations and better business results, so the company uses a combination of measures to evaluate the results of training. After employees have completed a program, Nokia asks them for their immediate reactions. Other measures include whether the employees have attained the expected level of competence. Nokia's top managers believe that the main benefits of its learning programs are the sharing of knowledge, the reinforcement of continuous learning, and the commitment of employees to the company.

SOURCE: Based on the Nokia Corporation website, www.nokia.com, retrieved August 22, 2003; and L. Masalin, "Nokia Leads Change Through Continuous Learning," *Academy of Management Learning and Education* 2 (2003), pp. 68–72.

Questions

1. Nokia's commitment to continuous learning emphasizes a belief that the organization benefits when employees share their knowledge with each other. Which of the methods and ideas in this chapter would contribute to this kind of knowledge sharing?
2. How might the company's training department promote the sharing of knowledge?
3. Is there a difference between support for learning (which Nokia expresses) and support for training and development? Explain.

Chapter 8

Managing Employees' Performance

What Do I Need to Know? After reading this chapter, you should be able to:

1. Identify the activities involved in performance management.

2. Discuss the purposes of performance management systems.

3. Define five criteria for measuring the effectiveness of a performance management system.

4. Compare the major methods for measuring performance.

5. Describe major sources of performance information in terms of their advantages and disadvantages.

6. Define types of rating errors and explain how to minimize them.

7. Explain how to effectively provide performance feedback.

8. Summarize ways to achieve performance improvement.

9. Discuss legal and ethical issues that affect performance management.

Introduction

Wardrop Engineering Inc., based in Winnipeg Manitoba, is a multidisciplinary consulting engineering, environmental, and information technology firm that holds the distinction of being one of the Top 100 Employers in Canada for eight consecutive years. This award-winning firm makes use of a balanced scorecard as part of its approach to "ensure everyone is pushing in the same direction." "Balanced scorecard can get everyone working together," says CEO Shayne Smith. It also helps ensure that the work

performance management
The process of ensuring that employees' activities and outputs match the organization's goals.

Wardrop Engineering has earned a global reputation for high performance. CanadaArm2 is one of Wardrop's many high-profile projects.

of key corporate functions is aligned with those of operations, reinforcing the collaborative environment that Smith feels is critical to competing successfully against larger firms. Wardrop employees receive individual performance reviews every six months. As part of the performance management process, feedback is solicited from co-workers and other managers familiar with the employee's work and employees can provide confidential feedback on their manager's performance. Wardrop Engineering's ideals and culture are expressed by the phrase "People, Passion, Performance—Trusted Globally." Wardrop has worked on many high-profile projects, including the CanadaArm, the partial decommissioning of the Chernobyl nuclear reactor in the Ukraine, and rebuilding New York's subway line under the former World Trade Centre.[1]

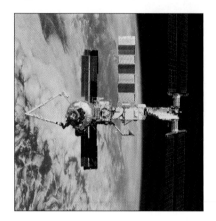

Performance management is the process of ensuring that employees' activities and outputs match the organization's goals. This process requires knowing what activities and outputs are desired, observing whether they occur, and providing feedback to help employees meet expectations. In the course of providing feedback, managers and employees may identify performance issues and establish ways to resolve those issues.

In this chapter we examine a variety of approaches to performance management. We begin by describing the activities involved in managing performance, then discuss the purpose of carrying out this process. Next, we discuss specific approaches to performance appraisal, including the strengths and weaknesses of each approach. We also look at various sources of performance information. The next section explores the kinds of errors that commonly occur during the assessment of performance, as well as ways to reduce those errors. Then we describe ways of giving performance feedback effectively and intervening when performance needs to improve. Finally, we summarize legal and ethical issues affecting performance management.

LO1 - Identify the activities involved in performance management.

performance appraisal
The measurement of specified areas of an employee's performance.

The Process of Performance Management

Traditional approaches to management have viewed **performance appraisal**, or the measurement of specified areas of an employee's performance, as the primary means of performance management. In the traditional approaches, the human resource department is responsible for setting up and managing a performance appraisal system. Managers conduct performance appraisals as one of their administrative duties. They tend to view the appraisals as a yearly ritual in which they quickly fill out forms and present the information to their employees, one by one. Appraisals include negative information (areas needing improvement), so the meetings for discussing performance appraisals tend to be uncomfortable for managers and employees alike. Often, managers feel they do not know how to evaluate performance effectively, and employees feel they are excluded from the process and that their contributions are not recognized.[2] The left side of Table 8.1 lists some of the criticisms that have been levelled against this style of performance management.

As is indicated on the right side of Table 8.1, these problems can be solved through a more effective approach to performance management. Appraising performance need not cause the problems listed in the table. If done correctly, the process can provide

PROBLEM	SOLUTION
Discourages teamwork.	Make collaboration a criterion on which employees will be evaluated.
Evaluators are inconsistent or use different criterion and standards.	Provide training for managers; have the HR department look for patterns on appraisals that suggest bias or over- or underevaluation; ensure employees' goals clearly align with team, departmental, and organizational goals.
Only valuable for very good or very poor employees.	Evaluate specific behaviours or results to show specifically what employees need to improve.
Encourages employees to achieve short-term goals.	Include both long-term and short-term goals in the appraisal process.
Manager has complete power over the employee.	Managers should be appraised for how they appraise their employees.
Too subjective.	Evaluate specific behaviour or results.
Produces emotional anguish.	Focus on behaviour; do not criticize employees; conduct appraisal on time; ensure appraisal is linked to ongoing development of the employee.

TABLE 8.1

Performance Appraisal Problems and Performance Management Solutions

SOURCE: Based on J. A. Siegel, "86 Your Appraisal Process?" *HR Magazine,* October 2000, pp. 199–202.

valuable benefits to employees and the organization alike. For example, a performance management system can tell top performers that they are valued, encourage communication between managers and their employees, establish uniform standards for evaluating employees, and help the organization identify its strongest and weakest performers. Over the past few years, there has been an overall increase in the "perceived effectiveness of performance management systems."[3] As illustrated in Figure 8.1, a recent study by the Conference Board of Canada found that 40 percent of organizations view their

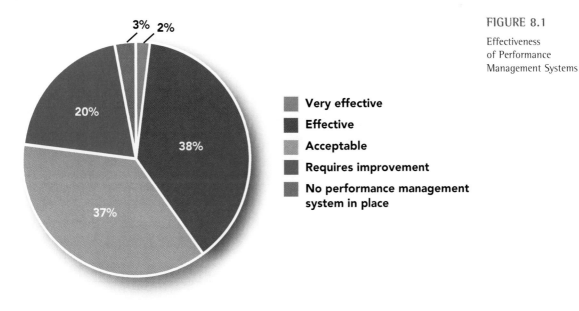

FIGURE 8.1

Effectiveness of Performance Management Systems

- Very effective
- Effective
- Acceptable
- Requires improvement
- No performance management system in place

SOURCE: "Compensation Planning Outlook 2008" (Ottawa: Conference Board of Canada), p. 16.

systems as either "very effective" or "effective." However, almost one-quarter of organizations said their performance management systems required improvement or that they are lacking a performance management system altogether.[4]

According to the Hay Group, companies on its Global Most Admired list, which it prepares for *Fortune* magazine, have chief executive officers who understand that performance measurement helps the organization motivate people and link performance to rewards.[5] Many of these executives report that performance measurement encourages employees to cooperate and helps the company focus on smooth operations, customer loyalty, and employee development. And in a recent survey of 164 chief financial officers (CFOs), performance management emerged as a top priority—73 percent said that, within their first one hundred days on the job, "they were expected to come up with a new plan for performance management."[6]

To meet these objectives, performance management extends beyond mere appraisals to include several activities. As is shown in Figure 8.2, these are defining performance, measuring performance, and feeding back performance information. First, the organization specifies which aspects of performance are relevant to the organization. These decisions are based on the organization's environment and overall objectives, as well as job analysis, described in Chapter 4. Next, the organization measures the relevant aspects of performance by conducting performance appraisals. Finally, through performance feedback sessions, managers give employees information about their performance so they can adjust their behaviour to meet the organization's goals. When there are performance gaps, the feedback session should include efforts to identify and resolve the underlying problems. In addition, performance feedback can come through the organization's rewards, as described in Chapter 9.

Using this performance management process in place of the traditional performance appraisal routine helps managers and employees focus on the organization's goals.

Computer software is available to help managers at various stages of performance management.[7] Software can help managers customize performance measurement forms. The manager uses the software to establish a set of performance standards for each job. The manager rates each employee according to the predetermined standards, and the software provides a report that compares the employee's performance to the standards and identifies the employee's strengths and weaknesses. Other software offers help with diagnosing performance gaps. This type of software

FIGURE 8.2

Stages of the
Performance
Management Process

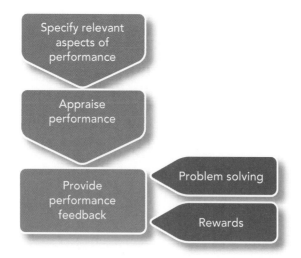

asks questions—for example, "Does the employee work under time pressure?" The answers suggest reasons for performance problems and ways the manager can help the employee improve. These technological tools can also provide strategic analysis of an organization's or department's key performance indicators. A competency gap analysis report can then be generated to determine which of these skills the organization has and which ones it still needs.[8] In addition, services such as PerformanceReview .com offer managers online help with writing performance reviews. This service is offered as either a single-use or an unlimited-use subscription.[9]

Purposes of Performance Management

LO2 - Discuss the purposes of performance management systems.

Organizations establish performance management systems to meet three broad purposes: strategic, administrative, and developmental. *Strategic purpose* means effective performance management helps the organization achieve its business objectives. It does this by helping to link employees' behaviour with the organization's goals. Performance management starts with defining what the organization expects from each employee. It measures each employee's performance to identify where those expectations are and are not being met. This enables the organization to take corrective action, such as training, incentives, or discipline. Performance management can achieve its strategic purpose only when measurements are truly aligned with the organization's goals and when the goals and feedback about performance are communicated to employees.

2,3,5,6

The *administrative purpose* of a performance management system refers to how organizations use the system to provide information for day-to-day decisions about salary, benefits, and recognition programs. Performance management can also support decision making related to employee retention, termination, and hiring or layoffs. Because performance management supports these administrative decisions, the information in a performance appraisal can have a great impact on the future of individual employees. Managers recognize this, which is the reason they may feel uncomfortable conducting performance appraisals when the appraisal information is negative and, therefore, likely to lead to a layoff, disappointing pay increase, or other negative outcome.

Finally, performance management has a *developmental purpose*, meaning that it serves as a basis for developing employees' competencies. Even employees who are meeting expectations can become more valuable when they hear and discuss performance feedback. Effective performance feedback makes employees aware of their strengths and of the areas in which they can improve. Discussing areas in which employees fall short can help the employees and their manager uncover the source of problems and identify steps for improvement. Although discussing shortcomings may feel uncomfortable, it is necessary when performance management has a developmental purpose. TELUS, the British Columbia-based communication company, was recently recognized by the American Society for Training and Development for its "Growing for High Performance" initiative that integrates performance management and the organization's learning systems. TELUS has restructured its corporate learning function "so that it is more of a performance consulting organization. That basically means working together with the line groups to identify their performance gaps and then identify training or learning solutions to directly work toward closing those performance gaps," or taking performance that meets expectations and taking it to the next level.[10] The HR How-To box recommends ways to develop a performance management system that can meet its strategic, administrative, and developmental purposes.

HR | HOW-TO

Setting Up a Performance Management System to Meet Goals

No single performance management system is ideal for all organizations. But the system is most likely to fulfill its purposes if it follows several guidelines:

- *The system should support the organization's values and beliefs.* For example, if employee involvement is an important value, then performance measurement should include self- or peer appraisals.
- *The organization's top management must show that it supports the system.* In most companies, senior management is involved in designing and implementing the performance management system. Their positive involvement encourages others in the organization to take responsibility for ensuring that evaluations are completed on time and that the system is used consistently.
- *Those planning the system should identify the most*

important measures of company performance. These should measure how well the company is doing relative to its business goals and strategy. Goals for individual employees should support the overall company goals.

- *Job descriptions should be linked to the performance management system.* This helps employees see that the activities they are supposed to do, the goals for which they are rewarded, and the goals of the organization are all related.
- *Verify that the performance management system assesses employees fairly and objectively according to clearly understood standards of performance or in terms of their contribution relative to that of other employees.* Employees should understand what constitutes poor, good, and excellent performance.
- *Managers must be trained how to use the performance measurement system and*

how to give performance feedback daily, not just in annual reviews. For employees, training programs should be related to the skills and behaviours necessary for meeting performance goals.

- *The performance management system should be linked to financial rewards.* For this connection to work as intended, the organization must communicate with employees about how the program works.
- *The performance management system needs to be evaluated.* The organization should verify that it meets company goals. On the basis of the evaluation, the organization should adjust the system.

SOURCE: Based on L. Weatherly, *Performance Management: Getting It Right from the Start* (Alexandria, VA: Society for Human Resource Management, 2004); and E. Lawler and M. McDermott, "Current Performance Management Practices," *World at Work Journal* 12, no. 2 (2003), pp. 49–60.

LO3 - Define five criteria for measuring the effectiveness of a performance management system.

Criteria for Effective Performance Management

In Chapter 6, we saw that there are many ways to predict performance of a job candidate. Similarly, there are many ways to measure the performance of an employee. For performance management to achieve its goals, its methods for measuring performance must be effective. Selecting these measures is a critical part of planning

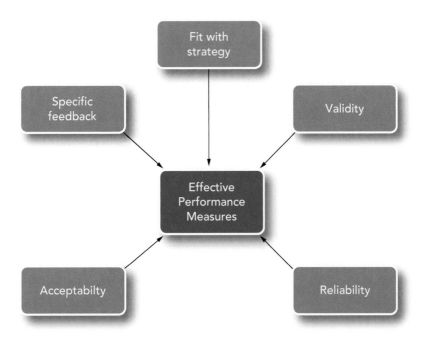

FIGURE 8.3

Criteria for Effective
Performance Measures

a performance management system. Criteria that determine the effectiveness of performance measures include each measure's fit with the organization's strategy, its validity, its reliability, the degree to which it is acceptable to the organization, and the extent to which it gives employees specific feedback. These criteria are summarized in Figure 8.3.

A performance management system should ensure the organization's strategic goals are translated into specific unit, function, and individual goals and objectives.

> By starting with the broadest organizational objectives and then drilling down through the functions that affect their achievement, employees can be reminded that all goals are interdependent across organizational units and levels. For example, an organizational objective to expand market penetration of a given product can be translated into specific goals for employees in sales, marketing, research and development, customer service, information technology, and training.[11]

A performance management system should aim at achieving employee behaviour and attitudes that support the organization's strategy, goals, and culture. If a company emphasizes customer service, then its performance management system should define the kinds of behaviour that contribute to good customer service. Performance appraisals should measure whether employees are engaging in those behaviours. Feedback should help employees improve in those areas. When an organization's strategy changes, human resource professionals should help managers assess how the performance management system should change to serve the new strategy.

As we discussed in Chapter 6, *validity* is the extent to which a measurement tool actually measures what it is intended to measure. In the case of performance

FIGURE 8.4

Contamination and
Deficiency of a Job
Performance Measure

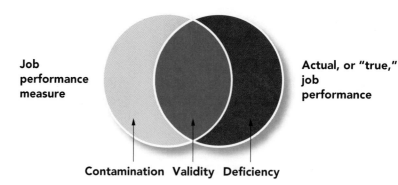

Job performance measure

Actual, or "true," job performance

Contamination Validity Deficiency

appraisal, validity refers to whether the appraisal measures all the relevant aspects of performance and omits irrelevant aspects of performance. Figure 8.4 shows two sets of information. The circle on the left represents all the information in a performance appraisal; the circle on the right represents all relevant measures of job performance. The overlap of the circles contains the valid information. Information that is gathered but irrelevant is "contamination." Comparing salespeople on the basis of how many calls they make to customers could be a contaminated measure. Making a lot of calls does not necessarily improve sales or customer satisfaction, unless every salesperson makes only well-planned calls. Information that is not gathered but is relevant represents a deficiency of the performance measure. For example, suppose a company measures whether employees have good attendance records but not whether they work efficiently. This limited performance appraisal is unlikely to provide a full picture of employees' contribution to the company. Performance measures should minimize both contamination and deficiency.

With regard to a performance measure, reliability describes the consistency of the results that the performance measure will deliver. *Interrater reliability* is consistency of results when more than one person measures performance. Simply asking a supervisor to rate an employee's performance on a scale of 1 to 5 would likely have low interrater reliability; the rating will differ depending on who is scoring the employees. *Test-retest reliability* refers to consistency of results over time. If a performance measure lacks test-retest reliability, determining whether an employee's performance has truly changed over time will be impossible.

Whether or not a measure is valid and reliable, it must meet the practical standard of being acceptable to the people who use it. For example, the people who use a performance measure must believe that it is not too time-consuming. Likewise, if employees believe the measure is unfair, they will not use the feedback as a basis for improving their performance.

Finally, a performance measure should communicate to employees what is expected of them and how they can meet those expectations. Being specific helps performance management meet the goals of supporting strategy and developing employees. Being specific also means the performance measures can usually be defined in quantitative terms. If a measure does not specify what an employee must do to help the organization achieve its goals, it does not support the strategy. If the measure fails to point out employees' performance gaps, they will not know how to improve.

Methods for Measuring Performance

LO4 - Compare the major methods for measuring performance.

Organizations have developed a wide variety of methods for measuring performance. A Conference Board of Canada study concluded that about 87 percent of all Canadian employers use some form of performance appraisal rating system.[12] Some methods rank each employee to compare employees' performance. Other methods break down the evaluation into ratings of individual competencies, behaviours, or results. Many organizations use a measurement system that includes a variety of these measures. Table 8.2 compares these methods in terms of our criteria for effective performance management.

Making Comparisons

The performance appraisal method may require the rater to compare one individual's performance with that of others. This method involves some form of ranking, in which some employees are the highest performers, some are average, and others are not meeting expectations. The usual techniques for making comparisons are simple ranking, forced distribution, and paired comparison.

TABLE 8.2

Basic Approaches to Performance Management

| APPROACH | CRITERIA | | | | |
	FIT WITH STRATEGY	VALIDITY	RELIABILITY	ACCEPTABILITY	SPECIFICITY
Comparative	Poor, unless manager takes time to make link	Can be high if ratings are done carefully	Depends on rater, but usually no measure of agreement used	Moderate; easy to develop and use but resistant to normative standard	Very low
Competency	Usually low; requires manager to make link	Usually low; can be fine if developed carefully	Usually low; can be improved by specific definitions of attributes	High; easy to develop and use	Very low
Behavioural	Can be quite high	Usually high; minimizes contamination and deficiency	Usually high	Moderate; difficult to develop, but accepted well for use	Very high
Results	Very high	Usually high; can be both contaminated and deficient	High; main problem can be test-retest—depends on timing of measure	High; usually developed with input from those to be evaluated	High regarding results, but low regarding behaviours necessary to achieve them

simple ranking
Method of performance measurement that requires managers to rank employees in their group from the highest to the lowest performer.

Simple ranking requires managers to rank employees in their group from the highest performer to the lowest performer. In a variation on this approach, *alternation ranking*, the manager works from a list of employees. First, the manager decides which employee is the highest performer and crosses that person's name off the list. From the remaining names, the manager selects the lowest performing employee and crosses off that name. The process continues with the manager selecting the second-highest, second-lowest, third-highest, and so on until all the employees have been ranked. The major downside of ranking involves validity. To state a performance measure as broadly as "highest" or "lowest" doesn't define what exactly is effective or ineffective about the person's contribution to the organization. Ranking therefore raises questions about fairness.

forced-distribution method
Method of performance measurement that assigns a certain percentage of employees to each category in a set of categories.

Another way to compare employees' performance is with the **forced-distribution method**. This type of performance measurement assigns a certain percentage of employees to each category in a set of categories. For example, the organization might establish the following percentages and categories:

- Exceptional—5 percent
- Exceeds expectations—25 percent
- Meets expectations—55 percent
- Room for improvement—10 percent
- Not acceptable—5 percent

The manager completing the performance appraisal would rate 5 percent of his or her employees as exceptional, 25 percent as exceeding standards, and so on. A forced-distribution approach works best if the members of a group really do vary this much in terms of their performance. It overcomes the temptation to rate everyone high in order to avoid conflict. However, a manager who does very well at selecting, motivating, and training employees will have a group of high performers. This manager would have difficulty assigning employees to the bottom categories. In that situation, saying that some employees require improvement or are "not acceptable" not only will be inaccurate, but will hurt morale.

The Conference Board of Canada reports that although only 13 percent of organizations use a forced-distribution performance management system, an additional 3 percent of organizations are considering its use in the coming year and a further 42 percent of organizations have guidelines or recommendations to ensure a normal distribution of performance ratings.[13] Figure 8.5 provides an illustration of these findings. Maple Leaf Foods, a Toronto-based food processing company, uses the forced-distribution method for assessing its 5,000 salaried employees. Wayne Johnson, vice-president of human resources, explains, "A's make up the top 20 percent, B's the middle 70 percent, and C's the bottom 10 percent."[14]

paired-comparison method
Method of performance measurement that compares each employee with every other one to establish rankings.

Another variation on rankings is the **paired-comparison method**. This approach involves comparing each employee with each other employee to establish rankings. Suppose a manager has five employees, Allen, Barbara, Caitlin, David, and Edgar. The manager compares Allen's performance to Barbara's and assigns one point to whichever employer is the higher performer. Then the manager compares Allen's performance to Caitlin's, then to David's, and finally to Edgar's. The manager repeats this process with Barbara, comparing her performance to Caitlin's, David's, and Edgar's. When the manager has compared every pair of employees, the manager

FIGURE 8.5

Forced-Distribution Performance and Guidelines

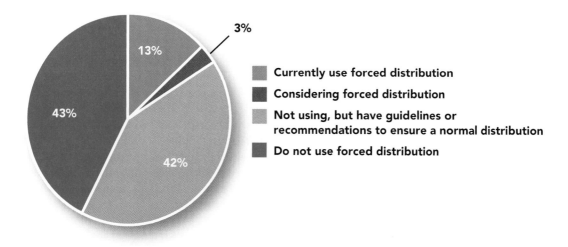

■	**Currently use forced distribution**
■	**Considering forced distribution**
■	**Not using, but have guidelines or recommendations to ensure a normal distribution**
■	**Do not use forced distribution**

NOTE: Total does not add up to 100 due to rounding.

SOURCE: "Compensation Planning Outlook 2008" (Ottawa: Conference Board of Canada), p. 17.

counts the number of points for each employee. The employee with the most points is considered the top-ranked employee. Clearly, this method is time-consuming if a group has more than a handful of employees. For a group of 15, the manager must make 105 comparisons.

In spite of the drawbacks, ranking employees offers some benefits. It counteracts the tendency to avoid controversy by rating everyone favourably or near the centre of the scale. Also, if some managers tend to evaluate behaviour more strictly (or more leniently) than others, a ranking system can erase that tendency from performance scores. Therefore, ranking systems can be useful for supporting decisions about how to distribute pay raises or layoffs. Some ranking systems are easy to use, which makes them acceptable to the managers who use them. A major drawback of rankings is that often they are not linked to the organization's goals. Also, a simple ranking system leaves the basis for ranking open to interpretation. Such rankings are not helpful for employee development and may hurt morale or result in legal challenges.

Rating Individuals

Instead of focusing on arranging a group of employees from best to worst, performance measurement can look at each employee's performance relative to a uniform set of standards. The measurement may evaluate employees in terms of competencies believed necessary for success in the job or in the organization. These measurements may identify whether employees have *behaved* in desirable ways, such as closing sales or completing assignments. The performance management system must identify the desired competencies or behaviours, then provide a form on which the manager can

graphic rating scale
Method of performance measurement that lists competencies and provides a rating scale for each competency; the employer uses the scale to indicate the extent to which an employee displays each competency.

mixed-standard scales
Method of performance measurement that uses several statements describing each competency to produce a final score for that competency.

rate the employee in terms of those competencies or behaviours. Typically, the form includes a rating scale, such as a scale from 1 to 5, where 1 is the worst performance and 5 is the best.

Rating Competencies

The most widely used method for rating competencies is the **graphic rating scale**. This method lists competencies and provides a rating scale for each. The employer uses the scale to indicate the extent to which the employee being rated displays the competencies. The rating scale may provide points to circle (as on a scale going from 1 for poor to 5 for distinguished), or it may provide a line representing a range of scores, with the manager marking a place along the line. Figure 8.6 shows an example of a graphic rating scale that uses a set of ratings from 1 to 5. A drawback of this approach is that it leaves to the particular manager the decisions about what is "excellent initiative" or "commendable teamwork" or "poor interpersonal skills." The result is low reliability, because managers are likely to arrive at different judgments.

To avoid this problem, some organizations use **mixed-standard scales**, which use several statements describing each competency to produce a final score for that competency. The manager scores the employee in terms of how the employee compares to each statement. Consider the sample mixed-standard scale in Figure 8.7. To create this scale, the organization determined that the relevant competencies are initiative, client orientation, and relations with others. For each competency, sentences were written to describe a person having a high level of that competency, a medium level, and a low level. The sentences for the traits were rearranged so that the nine statements about the three traits are mixed together. The manager who uses this scale

FIGURE 8.6

Example of a Graphic Rating Scale

The following areas of performance are significant to most positions. Indicate your assessment of performance on each dimension by circling the appropriate rating.

COMPETENCY	RATING				
	DISTINGUISHED	EXCEPTIONAL	COMMENDABLE	BARELY ADEQUATE	POOR
Client service	5	4	3	2	1
Communication	5	4	3	2	1
Leadership	5	4	3	2	1
Professionalism	5	4	3	2	1
Teamwork	5	4	3	2	1
Interpersonal skills	5	4	3	2	1
Initiative	5	4	3	2	1
Creativity	5	4	3	2	1
Problem solving	5	4	3	2	1

FIGURE 8.7

Example of a Mixed-Standard Scale

Three competencies being assessed:	Levels of performance in statements:
Initiative (INTV)	High (H)
Client orientation (CLO)	Medium (M)
Relations with others (RWO)	Low (L)

Instructions. Please indicate next to each statement whether the employee's performance is above (+), equal to (0), or below (–) the statement.

INTV	H	1.	This employee is a real self-starter. The employee always takes the initiative and his/her supervisor never has to prod this individual.	+
CLO	M	2.	Although this employee has some difficulty anticipating client needs, s/he is usually friendly and approachable.	+
RWO	L	3.	This employee has a tendency to get into unnecessary conflicts with other people.	0
INTV	M	4.	While generally this employee shows initiative, occasionally his/her supervisor must prod him/her to complete work.	+
CLO	L	5.	This employee frequently needs assistance in handling customer requests.	+
RWO	H	6.	This employee is on good terms with everyone. S/he can get along with people even when s/he does not agree with them.	–
INTV	L	7.	This employee has a bit of a tendency to sit around and wait for directions.	+
CLO	H	8.	This employee creates and maintains long-term client relationships.	–
RWO	M	9.	This employee gets along with most people. Only very occasionally does s/he have conflicts with others on the job, and these are likely to be minor.	–

Scoring Key:

STATEMENTS			SCORE
HIGH	MEDIUM	LOW	
+	+	+	7
0	+	+	6
–	+	+	5
–	0	+	4
–	–	+	3
–	–	0	2
–	–	–	1

Example score from preceding ratings:

	STATEMENTS			SCORE
	HIGH	MEDIUM	LOW	
Initiative	+	+	+	7
Client orientation	–	+	+	5
Relations with others	–	–	0	2

reads each sentence, then indicates whether the employee performs above (+), at (0), or below (−) the level described. The key in the middle section of Figure 8.7 tells how to use the pluses, zeros, and minuses to score performance. Someone who excels at every level of performance (pluses for high, medium, and low performance) receives a score of 7 for that competency. Someone who fails to live up to every description of performance (minuses for high, medium, and low) receives a score of 1 for that competency. The bottom of Figure 8.7 calculates the scores for the ratings used in this example.

An employee's performance measurement differs from job to job. For example, a car dealer's performance is measured by the dollar amount of sales, the number of new customers, and customer satisfaction surveys. How would the performance measurement of a car dealer differ from those of a company CEO?

Assessing competencies is the most popular way to measure performance in organizations. In general, competency-based performance methods are easy to develop and can be applied to a wide variety of jobs and organizations. If the organization is careful to identify which competencies are associated with high performance, and to define them carefully on the appraisal form, these methods can be reliable and valid. However, appraisal forms often fail to meet this standard. In addition, measurement of competencies may not be clearly linked to the organization's strategy. Furthermore, employees tend perhaps rightly to be defensive about receiving a mere numerical rating on some competency. How would you feel if you were told you scored 2 on a 5-point scale of initiative or communication skill? The number might seem arbitrary, and it doesn't tell you how to improve.

Rating Behaviours

A key way to enhance a competency-based approach to performance is to assess employees' behaviour. To rate behaviours, the organization begins by defining which behaviours are associated with success on the job. Which kinds of employee behaviour help the organization achieve its goals? The appraisal form asks the manager to rate an employee in terms of each of the identified behaviours.

critical-incident method
Method of performance measurement based on managers' records of specific examples of the employee behaving in ways that are either effective or ineffective.

One way to rate behaviours is with the **critical-incident method**. This approach requires managers to keep a record of specific examples of the employee behaving in ways that are either effective or ineffective. Here's an example of a critical incident in the performance evaluation of an appliance repairperson:

> A customer called in about a refrigerator that was not cooling and was making a clicking noise every few minutes. The technician prediagnosed the cause of the problem and checked his truck for the necessary parts. When he found he did not have them, he checked the parts out from inventory so that the customer's refrigerator would be repaired on his first visit and the customer would be satisfied promptly.

This incident provides evidence of the employee's knowledge of refrigerator repair and concern for efficiency and customer satisfaction. Evaluating performance in this specific way gives employees feedback about what they do well and what requires improvement. The manager can also relate the incidents to how the employee is helping the company achieve its goals. Keeping a daily or weekly log of critical incidents requires significant effort, however, and managers may resist this requirement. Also, critical incidents may be unique, so they may not support comparisons among employees.

A **behaviourally anchored rating scale (BARS)** builds on the critical incident approach. The BARS method is intended to define competency dimensions specifically, using statements of behaviour that describe different levels of the competency.[15] (The statements are "anchors" of the competency levels.) The scale in Figure 8.8 shows various competency levels for "listening, understanding, and responding." The statement at the top (rating 4) describes the highest level of listening, understanding, and responding. The statement at the bottom describes behaviour associated with ineffective or counterproductive performance. These statements are based on data about past performance. The organization gathers many critical incidents representing effective and ineffective performance, then classifies them from most to least effective. When experts about the job agree the statements clearly represent

behaviourally anchored rating scale (BARS)
Method of performance measurement that rates behaviour in terms of a scale showing specific statements of behaviour that describe different levels of performance.

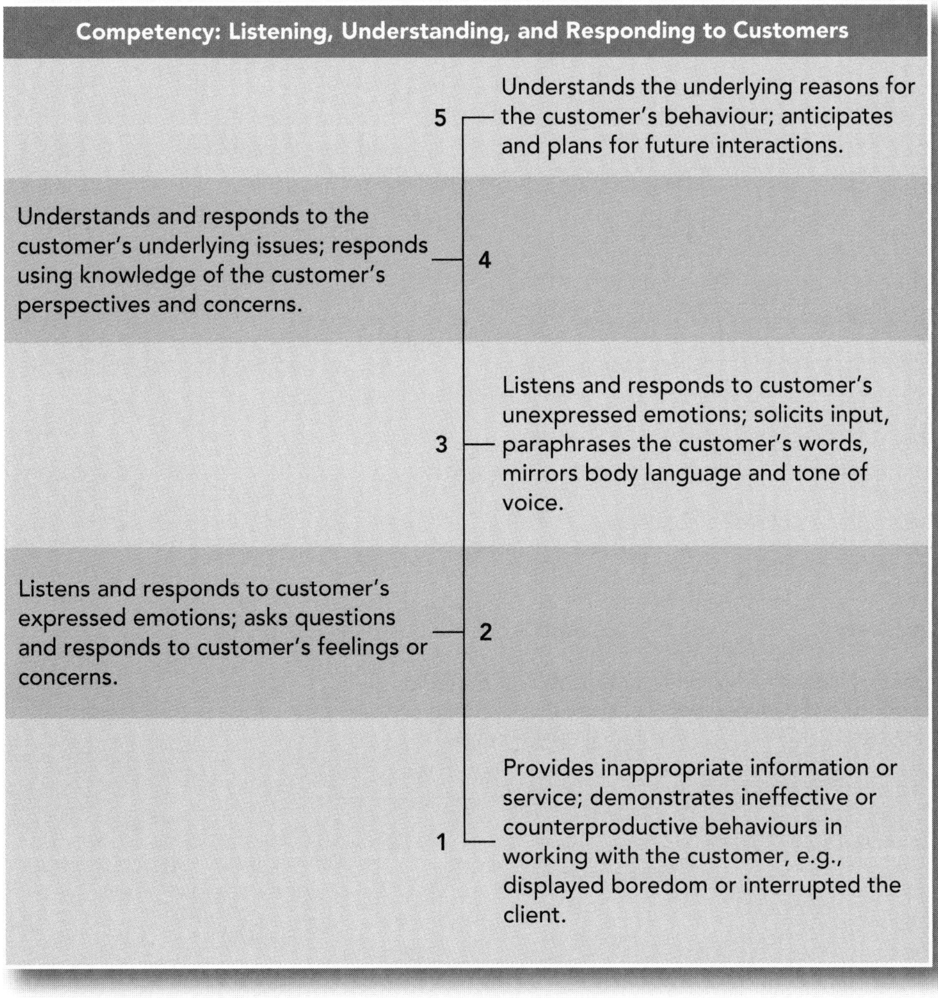

Competency: Listening, Understanding, and Responding to Customers

5 — Understands the underlying reasons for the customer's behaviour; anticipates and plans for future interactions.

Understands and responds to the customer's underlying issues; responds using knowledge of the customer's perspectives and concerns. — 4

3 — Listens and responds to customer's unexpressed emotions; solicits input, paraphrases the customer's words, mirrors body language and tone of voice.

Listens and responds to customer's expressed emotions; asks questions and responds to customer's feelings or concerns. — 2

1 — Provides inappropriate information or service; demonstrates ineffective or counterproductive behaviours in working with the customer, e.g., displayed boredom or interrupted the client.

FIGURE 8.8

BARS Rating Dimension: Customer Service Representative

SOURCE: Adapted from BC Public Service Agency, "Manager's HR Toolkit," www.hrtoolkit.gov.bc.ca/staffing, retrieved February 16, 2005.

levels of a competency, they are used as anchors to guide the rater. Although BARS can improve interrater reliability, this method can bias the manager's memory. The statements used as anchors can help managers remember similar behaviours, but at the expense of other critical incidents.[16]

behavioural observation scale (BOS)
A variation of BARS which uses all behaviours necessary for effective performance to rate performance at a task.

A **behavioural observation scale (BOS)** is a variation on a BARS. Like a BARS, a BOS is developed from critical incidents.[17] However, while a BARS discards many examples in creating the rating scale, a BOS uses many of them to define all behaviours necessary for effective performance (or behaviours that signal ineffective performance). As a result, a BOS may use 15 behaviours to define levels of performance. Also, a BOS asks the manager to rate the frequency with which the employee has exhibited the behaviour during the rating period. Figure 8.9 provides a simplified example of a BOS for measuring the behaviour "overcoming resistance to change."

A major drawback of this method is the amount of information required. A BOS can have 80 or more behaviours, and the manager must remember how often the

FIGURE 8.9

Example of a Behavioural Observation Scale

Overcoming Resistance to Change

Directions. Rate the frequency of each behaviour from 1 (Almost Never) to 5 (Almost Always).

1. Describes the details of the change to employees.
   Almost Never 1   2   3   4   5   Almost Always

2. Explains why the change is necessary.
   Almost Never 1   2   3   4   5   Almost Always

3. Discusses how the change will affect the employee.
   Almost Never 1   2   3   4   5   Almost Always

4. Listens to the employee's concerns.
   Almost Never 1   2   3   4   5   Almost Always

5. Asks the employee for help in making the change work.
   Almost Never 1   2   3   4   5   Almost Always

6. If necessary, specifies the date for a follow-up meeting
   to respond to the employee's concerns.
   Almost Never 1   2   3   4   5   Almost Always

Score. Total number of points = _____

Performance

Points	Performance Rating
6–10	Below adequate
11–15	Adequate
16–20	Full
21–25	Excellent
26–30	Superior

Scores are set by management.

employee exhibited each behaviour in a 6-to-12-month rating period. This is taxing enough for one employee, but managers often must rate ten or more employees. Even so, compared to BARS and graphic rating scales, managers and employees have said they prefer BOS for ease of use, providing feedback, maintaining objectivity, and suggesting training needs.[18]

Another approach to assessment builds directly on a branch of psychology called *behaviourism*, which holds that individuals' future behaviour is determined by their past experiences—specifically, the ways in which past behaviours have been reinforced. People tend to repeat behaviours that have been rewarded in the past. Providing feedback and reinforcement can therefore modify individuals' future behaviour. Applied to behaviour in organizations, **organizational behaviour modification (OBM)** is a plan for managing the behaviour of employees through a formal system of feedback and reinforcement. Specific OBM techniques vary, but most have four components:[19]

organizational behaviour modification (OBM) A plan for managing the behaviour of employees through a formal system of feedback and reinforcement.

1. Define a set of key behaviours necessary for job performance.
2. Use a measurement system to assess whether the employee exhibits the key behaviours.
3. Inform employees of the key behaviours, perhaps in terms of goals for how often to exhibit the behaviours.
4. Provide feedback and reinforcement based on employees' behaviour.

OBM techniques have been used in a variety of settings. For example, a community health agency used OBM to increase the rates and timeliness of critical job behaviours by showing employees the connection between job behaviours and the agency's accomplishments.[20] This process identified job behaviours related to administration, record keeping, and service provided to clients. Feedback and reinforcement improved staff performance. OBM also increased the frequency of safety behaviours in a processing plant.[21]

Behavioural approaches such as organizational behaviour modification and rating scales can be very effective. These methods can link the company's goals to the specific behaviour required to achieve those goals. Behavioural methods also can generate specific feedback, along with guidance in areas requiring improvements. As a result, these methods tend to be valid. The people to be measured often help in developing the measures, so acceptance tends to be high as well. When raters are well trained, reliability also tends to be high. However, behavioural methods do not work as well for complex jobs in which it is difficult to see a link between behaviour and results or there is more than one good way to achieve success.[22]

Measuring Results

Performance measurement can focus on managing the objective, measurable results of a job or work group. Results might include sales, costs, or productivity (output per worker or per dollar spent on production), among many possible measures. Two of the most popular methods for measuring results are measurement of productivity and management by objectives.

Productivity is an important measure of success, because getting more done with a smaller amount of resources (money or people) increases the company's profits. Productivity usually refers to the output of production workers, but it can be used more generally as a performance measure. To do this, the organization identifies the products—set of activities or objectives—it expects a group or individual to accomplish. At a repair shop, for instance, a product might be something like "quality of repair." The next step is to define how to measure production of these products. For quality of repair, the repair shop could track the percentage of items returned because they still do not work after a repair and the percentage of quality-control inspections passed. For each measure, the organization decides what level of performance is desired. Finally, the organization sets up a system for tracking these measures and giving employees feedback about their performance in terms of these measures. This type of performance measurement can be time-consuming to set up, but research suggests it can improve productivity.[23]

Management by Objectives

management by objectives (MBO)
A system in which people at each level of the organization set goals in a process that flows from top to bottom, so employees at all levels are contributing to the organization's overall goals; these goals become the standards for evaluating each employee's performance.

Management by objectives (MBO) is a system in which people at each level of the organization set goals in a process that flows from top to bottom, so employees at all levels are contributing to the organization's overall goals. These goals become the standards for evaluating each employee's performance. An MBO system has three components:[24]

1. Goals and objectives should be "SMART":

   - **S**pecific. Precise behaviour or outcome is identified
   - **M**easurable. Stated in quantifiable terms
   - **A**chievable. Challenging but achievable
   - **R**elevant. Within the employee's control and is important to the organization
   - **T**imed. A defined completion date

   The goals listed in the second column of Table 8.3 provide two examples for a Vice-President Human Resources.

2. Managers and their employees work together to set the goals.

TABLE 8.3

Management by Objectives: Two Goals for a Vice-President of Human Resources

KEY RESULT AREA	OBJECTIVE	COMPLETE	ACTUAL PERFORMANCE
Human resource strategy linked to business goals	92% employee retention for the period January 1–December 31, 2008	103%	95% employee retention in 2008.
Motivated and productive HR team	100% of HR employees have a documented development plan by December 31, 2008	100%	100% of HR employees have a documented development plan that was completed by December 31, 2008.

SOURCE: Adapted from "Vice-President Human Resources Example Performance Plan," Zigon Performance Group website, www.zigonperf.com/resources/examples/hrvp.asp, retrieved July 15, 2004.

BEST PRACTICES

Calibrating Talent

Effective performance management systems rate performance consistently. This foundation is the basis for reliability of performance management systems, and it is critical to creating fairness in how employees' performance is assessed. By definition, performance management systems assess how well an employee meets the expectations associated with the job and the organization's goals; but according to a study of 5,970 employees who each report to two managers, the majority of the employees received inconsistent performance ratings. "The study found that employees rated outstanding by one manager were rated lower by

their other manager 62 percent of the time."

Many companies use a calibration process to make sure that performance appraisals are consistent across managers. This process is ideally led by an experienced facilitator such as a senior human resource professional, who brings together supervisors and managers to discuss each employee's rating and its rationale. Some organizations are taking this a step further, using these meetings not only to calibrate performance but also to have meaningful discussions about the organization's talent. These types of discussions reinforce succession planning.

A Toronto-based utility, Direct Energy, also enhances

the calibration process with technology that provides real-time access to performance ratings as they happen. Terry Fox, director of HR operations, describes how calibration works at Direct Energy: "The focus is on the high-value discussion about who the high-performers are and why, and finding ways to share the pool of high-performing employees with peers to help those people develop."

SOURCE: Joanne Sammer, "Calibrating Consistency," *HR Magazine*, January 2008, pp. 73–75; Christee Gabour Atwood, "Implementing Your Succession Plan," *T + D*, November 2007, p. 54; David Brown, "Performance Management Systems Need Fixing," *Canadian HR Reporter*, April 11, 2005, p. 1.

3. The manager gives objective feedback through the rating period to monitor progress toward the goals. The two right-hand columns in Table 8.3 are examples of feedback given after one year.

MBO can have a very positive effect on an organization's performance. In 70 studies of MBO's performance, 68 showed that productivity improved.[25] The productivity gains tended to be greatest when top management was highly committed to MBO. Also, because staff members are involved in setting goals, it is likely that MBO systems effectively link individual employees' performance with the organization's overall goals. The Best Practices box discusses methods to ensure employees' performance ratings are assessed consistently.

In general, evaluation of results can be less subjective than other kinds of performance measurement. This makes

A coach provides feedback to team members or students, just as managers give feedback to their employees. Feedback provides information about what you're doing well and how you can change to improve. Feedback can contribute to a feeling of achievement.

measuring results highly acceptable to employees and managers alike. Results-oriented performance measurement is also relatively easy to link to the organization's goals. However, measuring results has problems with validity, because results may be affected by circumstances beyond each employee's performance. Also, if the organization measures only final results, it may fail to measure significant aspects of performance that are not directly related to those results. If individuals focus only on aspects of performance that are measured, they may neglect significant skills or behaviours. For example, if the organization measures only productivity, employees may not be concerned enough with customer service. The outcome may be high efficiency (costs are low) but low effectiveness (sales are low, too).[26] Finally, focusing strictly on results does not provide guidance on how to improve. If baseball players are in a hitting slump, simply telling them that their batting average is .190 may not improve their hitting. The coach would help more by providing feedback about how or what to change (e.g., taking one's eye off the ball or dropping one's shoulder).[27]

balanced scorecard
An organizational approach to performance management that integrates strategic perspectives including financial, customer, internal business processes, and learning and growth.

Balanced Scorecard

The **balanced scorecard** is an organizational approach to performance management that integrates strategic perspectives including financial, customer, internal business processes, and learning and growth. Robert S. Kaplan and David P. Norton developed this widely adopted approach, illustrated in Figure 8.10. The basic idea is that managers are encouraged to go beyond meeting just traditional financial targets, and recognize

FIGURE 8.10

The Balanced Scorecard

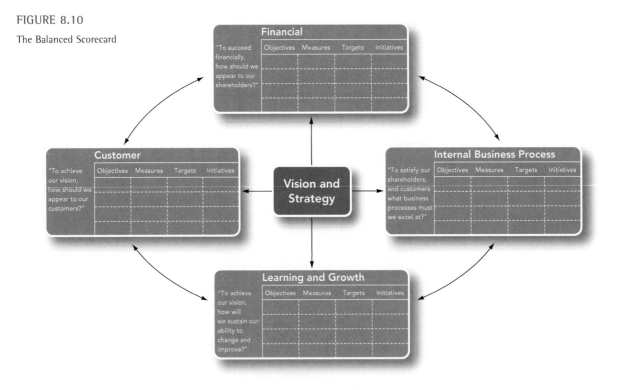

and simultaneously monitor the progress of other important goals such as customer and employee satisfaction.[28] Use of a balanced scorecard provides the means to align strategy at all levels of the organization and serves as "an excellent guide to measure and manage the performance of all employees."[29] Balanced scorecards are widely used in both the public and private sector. A sampling of the organizations that use balanced scorecards as part of their strategic management and performance management systems include: J. D. Irving Ltd., Canadian Cancer Society, Canadian Federal Government, Bell Aliant, McCain Foods, the Cooperators, Great-West Life Assurance Company, and Wardrop Engineering (featured at the beginning of the chapter).

Sources of Performance Information

L05 - Describe major sources of performance information in terms of their advantages and disadvantages.

All the methods of performance measurement require decisions about who will collect and analyze the performance information. To qualify for this task, a person should have an understanding of the job requirements and the opportunity to see the employee doing the job. The traditional approach is for managers to gather information about their employees' performance and arrive at performance ratings. However, many sources are possible. As is illustrated in Figure 8.11, possibilities of information sources include managers, peers, direct reports, self, and customers.

Using just one person as a source of information poses certain problems. People tend to like some people more than others, and those feelings can bias how an employee's efforts are perceived. Also, one person is likely to see an employee in a limited number of situations. A supervisor, for example, cannot see how an employee behaves when the supervisor is not there—for example, when a service technician is at the customer's facility. To get as complete an assessment as possible, some organizations combine information from most or all of the possible sources, in what is called a multi-rater or **360-degree performance appraisal**. The e-HRM box describes how online 360-degree performance appraisal has improved performance management at Sandy Hill Community Health Centre in Ottawa.

The John Molson School of Business at Montreal's Concordia University conducted a recent study to learn about the experiences of 101 large Canadian organizations with 360-degree programs. The study found that 43 percent of the organizations surveyed used 360-degree, that is, multi-rater approaches. Companies are using 360-degree performance appraisal because of advantages including

360-degree performance appraisal
Performance measurement that combines information from the employee's managers, peers, direct reports, self, and customers.

FIGURE 8.11

Sources of Performance Information

E- HRM

Paperless Performance Appraisal

Sandy Hill Community Health Centre (SHCHC) in downtown Ottawa decided its approach to performance appraisals was "time consuming, labour intensive, and lethal to forests everywhere." Although the 360-degree approach was valued by both management and staff, managers were overwhelmed with the administrative burden.

Initially, a performance appraisal reference group was assembled with leadership from the centre's HR officer. This group created a new competency-based performance evaluation tool, however the paper format still created confidentiality concerns when distributed through internal mail. In addition, the appraisal process created a large volume of paper that was described as a "literal stumbling block."

Matthew Garrison, the HR director at SHCHC researched and sampled approximately two dozen different Web-based performance appraisal tools in the effort to find an online tool that would meet SHCHC's needs. He ultimately found a U.K.-based application called Quask that allowed their organization to design a form that could be completed online

using a secure website. The software also provided SHCHC the flexibility it required to choose not only the content of the performance appraisal but also customize the rating scale that would be used to assess employees.

The new software application compiles performance assessments for each employee and provides the employee's manager with a summary of results for each question. The reporting format is flexible enough to allow results to be easily imported into a database, spreadsheet, or HTML application. A pilot of the new online performance evaluation tool was completed and additional enhancements such as drop-down menus were added to make the tool more user-friendly. With approval from SHCHC's management team, the technology was incorporated into their intranet and the system became fully functional.

According to Matthew Garrison, "The ability to conduct performance reviews online provides us with information that we would not have been able to gather through traditional paper means." Garrison also hopes

to take the next step to add the performance appraisal data to their Human Resources Information System (HRIS). The executive director of the SHCHC, David Gibson, also describes the ability of the new performance appraisal system to assess not only people but also to assess the effectiveness and efficiency of the centre's programs and processes. The goal is to measure "progress in meeting strategic goals and objectives, gather and analyze performance data, and then use this data to drive improvements in our organization and successfully translate strategy into action."

By implementing the new online performance evaluation software, the SHCHC has already met several key objectives including improving the efficiency of the performance process, saving management and staff time, and maintaining a 360-degree approach.

SOURCE: Dave Silverstone, "Paperless Performance Reviews," *HR Professional*, February 2005, www. hrpao.org/HRPAO/Knowledge Centre/ HRProfessional/newscluster/Paperless + Performance + Reviews.htm, retrieved February 19, 2005.

increased measurement accuracy and perceived fairness. Respondents also identified challenges such as resistance from individuals because of concerns about the process being time-, cost-, and energy-consuming, trust issues including anonymity of feedback, and the need to ensure a clear purpose and link to organizational strategy are in place before implementing 360-degree appraisal.[30]

Managers

The most-used source of performance information is the employee's manager. It is usually safe for organizations to assume that supervisors have extensive knowledge of the job requirements and that they have enough opportunity to observe their employees. In other words, managers possess the basic qualifications for this responsibility. Another advantage of using managers to evaluate performance is that they have an incentive to provide accurate and helpful feedback, because their own success depends so much on their employees' performance.[31] Finally, when managers try to observe employee behaviour or discuss performance issues in the feedback session, their feedback can improve performance, and employees tend to perceive the appraisal as accurate.[32]

Still, in some situations, problems can occur with using supervisors as the source of performance information. For employees in some jobs, the supervisor does not have enough opportunity to observe the employee performing job duties. A sales manager with many outside salespeople cannot be with the salespeople on many visits to customers. Even if the sales manager does make a point of travelling with salespeople for a few days, they are likely to be on their best behaviour while the manager is there. The manager cannot observe how they perform at other times.

Peers

Another source of performance information is the employee's peers or coworkers. Peers are an excellent source of information about performance in a job where the supervisor does not often observe the employee. Examples include law enforcement and sales. For these and other jobs, peers may have the most opportunity to observe the employee in day-to-day activities. Peers have expert knowledge of job requirements. They also bring a different perspective to the evaluation and can provide extremely valid assessments of performance.[33]

Peer evaluations obviously have some potential disadvantages. Friendships (or rivalries) have the potential to bias ratings. Research, however, has provided little evidence that this is a problem.[34] Another disadvantage is that when the evaluations are done to support administrative decisions, peers are uncomfortable with rating employees for decisions that may affect themselves. Generally, peers are more willing to participate in reviews to be used for employee development.[35]

Direct Reports

For evaluating the performance of managers, direct reports are an especially valuable source of information. Direct reports—the people reporting to the manager—often have the best chance to see how well a manager treats employees.

Direct report evaluations have some potential problems because of the power relationships involved. Direct reports are reluctant to say negative things about the person to whom they report; they prefer to provide feedback anonymously. Managers, however, have a more positive reaction to this type of feedback when the employees are identified. When feedback requires that the direct reports identify themselves, they tend to give the manager higher ratings.[36] Another problem is that when managers receive ratings from direct reports, the employees have more power, so managers tend to emphasize employee satisfaction, even at the expense of productivity. This issue arises primarily when the evaluations are used for administrative decisions. Therefore, as with peer evaluations, direct report evaluations are most appropriate for developmental purposes. To protect employees, the process should be anonymous and use at least three employees to rate each manager.

Self

No one has a greater chance to observe the employee's behaviour on the job than does the employee himself or herself. Self-ratings are rarely used alone, but they can contribute valuable information. A common approach is to have employees evaluate their own performance before the feedback session. This activity gets employees thinking about their performance. Areas of disagreement between the self-appraisal and other evaluations can be fruitful topics for the feedback session. Employee self-assessment offers a way to balance power in a process that tends to be manager-dominated. Areas of disagreement between the self-rating and the manager's rating should be used to create dialogue and reach mutual agreement during the feedback session.[37]

The obvious problem with self-ratings is that individuals have a tendency to inflate assessments of their performance. Especially if the ratings will be used for administrative decisions, exaggerating one's contributions has practical benefits. Also, social psychologists have found that, in general, people tend to blame outside circumstances for their failures while taking a large part of the credit for their successes. Supervisors can soften this tendency by providing frequent feedback, but, because people tend to perceive situations this way, self-appraisals are not appropriate as the basis for administrative decisions.[38]

Customers

Service industries continue to account for significant job growth. Services are often produced and consumed on the spot—so the customer is often the only person who directly observes the service performance, and therefore the customer may be the best source of performance information.

Many companies in service industries have introduced customer evaluations of employee performance. Marriott Corporation provides a customer satisfaction card in every room and mails surveys to a random sample of its hotel customers. Whirlpool's Consumer Services Division conducts both mail and telephone surveys of customers after factory technicians have serviced their appliances. These surveys allow the company to evaluate an individual technician's customer-service behaviours while in the customer's home. Many organizations also use mystery-shopper services. Tell Us About Us, a Winnipeg-based company, was recently contracted for a seven-figure, multiyear deal to provide customer evaluations at 5,500 Dunkin Donuts, Baskin-Robbins, and Togo's in Canada and the United States.[39]

Using customer evaluations of employee performance is appropriate in two situations.[40] The first is when an employee's job requires direct service to the customer or linking the customer to other services within the organization. Second, customer evaluations are appropriate when the organization is interested in gathering information to determine what products and services the customer wants. That is, customer evaluations contribute to the organization's goals by enabling HRM to support the organization's marketing activities. In this regard, customer evaluations are useful both for evaluating an employee's performance and for helping to determine whether the organization can improve customer service by making changes in HRM activities such as training or compensation.

The weakness of using customer feedback for performance measurement is the expense. Many organizations therefore limit the information gathering to short periods once a year.

Errors in Performance Measurement

LO6 - Define types of rating errors and explain how to minimize them.

As we noted in the previous section, one reason for gathering information from several sources is that performance measurements are not completely objective, and errors can occur. People observe behaviour, and they have no practical way of knowing all the circumstances, intentions, and outcomes related to that behaviour, so they interpret what they see. In doing so, observers make a number of judgment calls, and in some situations may even distort information on purpose. Therefore, fairness in rating performance and interpreting performance appraisals requires that managers understand the kinds of distortions that commonly occur.

Types of Rating Errors

Several kinds of errors and biases commonly influence performance measurements. Usually people make these errors unintentionally, especially when the criteria for measuring performance are not very specific.

Similar to Me

A common human tendency is to give a higher evaluation to people we consider similar to ourselves. Most of us tend to think of ourselves as effective. If others seem to be like us in some way—physical characteristics, family or economic background, attitudes, or beliefs—we expect them to be effective as well. Research has demonstrated that this effect, called the **similar-to-me error**, is strong. One unfortunate result (besides inaccuracy) is that when similarity is based on characteristics such as race or sex, the decisions may be discriminatory.[41]

similar-to-me error Rating error of giving a higher evaluation to people who seem similar to oneself.

Contrast

Sometimes, instead of comparing an individual's performance against an objective standard, the rater compares that individual with other employees. Suppose an employee is completely competent and does exactly what the job requires. But that employee has several co-workers who are outstanding; they keep breaking sales records or thinking up clever ways to shave time off production processes. If the person rating the employee is contrasting the employee's performance with the exceptional co-workers and gives lower performance ratings than the employee deserves, this is **contrast error**. The lowered rating does not accurately reflect what the employee is doing.

contrast error Rating error caused by comparing employee's performance to co-workers rather than to an objective standard.

Errors in Distribution

Raters often tend to use only one part of a rating scale—the low scores, the high scores, or the middle of the range. Sometimes a group of employees really do perform equally well (or poorly). In many cases, however, similar ratings for all members of a group are not an accurate description of performance, but an error in distribution. When a rater inaccurately assigns high ratings to all employees, this error is called **leniency**.

leniency error Rating error of assigning inaccurately high ratings to all employees.

strictness error
Rating error of giving low ratings to all employees, holding them to unreasonably high standards.

central tendency
Incorrectly rating all employees at or near the middle of a rating scale.

recency emphasis
Rating error that occurs when an annual rating is based only on most recent work performed.

focus on activities
Rating error when employees are assessed on how busy they appear rather than how effective they are in achieving results.

halo error
Rating error that occurs when the rater reacts to one positive performance aspect by rating the employee positively in all areas of performance.

horns error
Rating error that occurs when the rater responds to one negative aspect by rating an employee low in other aspects.

When a rater incorrectly gives low ratings to all employees, holding them to unreasonably high standards, the resulting error is called **strictness**. Rating all employees as somehow "average" or in the middle of the scale is called the **central tendency**. These errors pose two problems. First, they make it difficult to distinguish among employees rated by the same person. Decisions about promotions, job assignments, and so on are more difficult if employees all seem to be performing at the same level. Second, these errors create problems in comparing the performance of individuals rated by different raters. If one rater is lenient and the other is strict, employees of the strict rater will receive significantly fewer rewards than employees of the lenient rater. The rewards are not tied to actual performance but are to some degree erroneous.

Recency Emphasis

Raters sometimes base an annual rating only on the employee's most recent work. Raters may have difficulty remembering things that happened several months to a year ago versus work from a few weeks before the performance review. This **recency emphasis** error can also occur when the supervisor is rushing the evaluation process because of heavy workload or lack of time.[42]

Focus on Activities

Rushing due to insufficient time or heavy workload may also contribute to a **focus on activities**, which happens when employees are assessed on how busy they appear rather than how effective they are in achieving results.[43]

Halo and Horns

Another common problem is that raters often fail to distinguish among different aspects of performance. Consider a research lab that hires chemists. A chemist who expresses herself very well may appear to have greater knowledge of chemistry than a chemist with poor communication skills. In this example, a rater could easily fail to distinguish between communication skills and scientific skills.

This type of error can make a person look better, or worse, overall. When the rater reacts to one positive performance aspect by rating the employee positively in all areas of performance, the bias is called the **halo error**. As in the example of the chemist who communicates well, giving the impression of overall intelligence. In contrast, when the rater responds to one negative aspect by rating an employee low in other aspects, the bias is called the **horns error**. Suppose an employee sometimes arrives to work late. The rater takes this as a sign of lack of motivation, lack of ambition, and inability to follow through with responsibility—an example of the horns error.

When raters make halo and horns errors, the performance measurements cannot provide the specific information needed for useful feedback. Halo error signals that no aspects of an employee's performance need improvement, possibly missing opportunities for employee development. Horns error tells the employee that the rater has a low opinion of the employee. The employee is likely to feel defensive and frustrated, rather than motivated to improve.

Ways to Reduce Errors

Training can reduce rating errors.[44] Raters can be trained how to avoid rating errors.[45] Prospective raters watch video segments with story lines designed to lead them to make specific rating errors. After rating the fictional employees in the video segments, raters discuss their rating decisions and how such errors affected their rating decisions. Training programs offer tips for avoiding the errors in the future.

Another training method for raters focuses not on errors in rating, but on the complex nature of employee performance.[46] Raters learn to look at many aspects of performance that deserve their attention. Actual examples of performance are studied to bring out various performance dimensions and the standards for those dimensions. The objective of this training is to help raters evaluate employees' performance more thoroughly and accurately.

Political Behaviour in Performance Appraisals

Unintentional errors are not the only cause of inaccurate performance measurement. Sometimes the people rating performance distort an evaluation on purpose, to advance their personal goals. This kind of appraisal politics is unhealthy, especially because the resulting feedback does not focus on helping employees contribute to the organization's goals. High-performing employees who are rated unfairly will become frustrated, and low-performing employees who are overrated will be rewarded rather than encouraged to improve. Therefore, organizations try to identify and discourage appraisal politics.

Several characteristics of appraisal systems and company culture tend to encourage appraisal politics. Appraisal politics are most likely to occur when raters are accountable to the employee being rated, the goals of rating are not compatible with one another, performance appraisal is directly linked to highly desirable rewards, top executives tolerate or ignore distorted ratings, and senior employees tell newcomers company "folklore" that includes stories about distorted ratings.

Political behaviour occurs in every organization. Organizations can minimize appraisal politics by establishing an appraisal system that is fair. Some ways to promote fairness are to involve managers and employees in developing the system, use consistent standards for evaluating different employees, require that feedback be timely and complete, allow employees to challenge their evaluation, and communicate expectations about performance standards, evaluations, and rewards.[47] The organization can also help managers give accurate and fair appraisals by training them to use the appraisal process, encouraging them to recognize accomplishments that the employees themselves have not identified, and fostering a climate of openness in which employees feel they can be honest about their weaknesses.[48]

Giving Performance Feedback

Once the manager and others have measured an employee's performance, this information must be given to the employee. Only after the employee has received feedback can he or she begin to plan how to improve performance. Although the feedback stage of performance management is essential, it may be uncomfortable to managers and employees. Delivering feedback feels to the manager as if he or she is standing in judgment of others—a role few people enjoy. Receiving criticism feels even worse. Fortunately, managers can do much to smooth the feedback process and make it effective.

LO7 - Explain how to effectively provide performance feedback.

1,2,3

Scheduling Performance Feedback

Performance feedback should be a regular, expected management activity. The practice or policy at many organizations is to give formal performance feedback once a year. But annual feedback is not enough. One reason is that managers are responsible for dealing with performance gaps as soon as they occur. If the manager notices a problem with an employee's behaviour in June, but the annual appraisal is scheduled for November, the employee will miss months of opportunities for improvement. Generational differences in the workplace also contribute to different perspectives about what is timely feedback. Gen-Y employees may expect immediate feedback because their reference points are often built around short-time frames and accomplishments.[49]

Another reason for frequent performance feedback is that feedback is most effective when the information does not surprise the employee. If an employee has to wait for up to a year to learn what the manager thinks of his work, the employee will wonder whether he is meeting expectations. Employees should instead receive feedback so often that they know what the manager will say during their annual performance review.

Preparing for a Feedback Session

Managers should be well prepared for each formal feedback session. The manager should create the right context for the meeting. The location should be neutral. If the manager's office is the site of unpleasant conversations, a conference room may be more appropriate. In announcing the meeting to an employee, the manager should describe it as a chance to discuss the role of the employee, the role of the manager, and relationship between them. Managers should also say (and believe) that they would like the meeting to be an open dialogue.

When giving performance feedback, do it in an appropriate meeting place. Meet in a setting that is neutral and free of distractions. What other factors are important for a feedback session?

Managers should also enable the employee to be well prepared. The manager should ask the employee to complete a self-assessment ahead of time. The self-assessment requires employees to think about their performance over the past rating period and to be aware of their strengths and weaknesses, so they can participate more fully in the discussion. Even though employees may tend to overstate their accomplishments, the self-assessment can help the manager and employee identify areas for discussion. When the purpose of the assessment is to define areas for development, employees may actually understate their performance. Also, differences between the manager's and the employee's rating may be fruitful areas for discussion.

Conducting the Feedback Session

During the feedback session, managers can take any of three approaches. In the "tell-and-sell" approach, managers tell the employees their ratings and then justify those ratings. In the "tell-and-listen" approach, managers tell employees their ratings and then let the employees explain their side of the story. In the "problem-solving" approach, managers and employees work together to solve performance problems in an atmosphere of respect and encouragement. Not surprisingly, research demonstrates that the problem-solving approach is superior. Perhaps surprisingly, most managers rely on the tell-and-sell approach.[50] Managers can improve employee satisfaction with the feedback process and improve performance by creating two-way communication, by letting employees voice their opinions and discuss performance goals.[51]

Applying some additional principles will also make performance feedback more effective. Feedback should include a balanced and accurate assessment of how the employee is doing. The discussion should include a specific discussion of areas in which the employee's performance met, exceeded, and fell short of expectations. Any areas of required improvement should lead to problem solving. The content of the feedback should emphasize behaviour, not personalities. For example, "You did not meet the deadline" can open a conversation about what needs to change, but "You're not motivated" may make the employee feel defensive and angry. The feedback session should end with goal setting and a decision about when to follow up.

Performance Improvement

When performance evaluation indicates that an employee's performance is below expectations, the feedback process should launch an effort to address the performance gap. Even when the employee is meeting current standards, the feedback session may identify areas in which the employee can improve in order to contribute more to the organization in a current or future job. In sum, the final feedback stage of performance management involves identifying areas for improvement and ways to improve performance in those areas.

As is shown in Figure 8.12, the most effective way to improve performance varies according to the employee's ability and motivation. In general, when employees have high levels of ability and motivation, they perform at or above expectations. But when they lack ability, motivation, or both, corrective action is needed. The type of action called for depends on what the employee lacks.

To determine an employee's ability level, the manager should consider whether the employee has the competencies needed to perform the job effectively. Sometimes lack of ability is an issue when an employee is new or the job has changed. When a motivated employee lacks knowledge, skills, or abilities in some area, there are a number of ways to help the employee improve. The manager may offer coaching, training, and more detailed feedback. Sometimes it is appropriate to restructure the job so that its demands no longer exceed the employee's abilities.

To determine an employee's level of motivation, managers need to consider whether the employee is holding a job he or she wants. A belief that pay and other rewards are too small can also hurt motivation. Sometimes personal problems are such a distraction that they interfere with motivation. Managers with an unmotivated employee can explore ways to demonstrate that the employee is being treated

LO8 - Summarize ways to achieve performance improvement.

2,4

FIGURE 8.12

Improving Performance

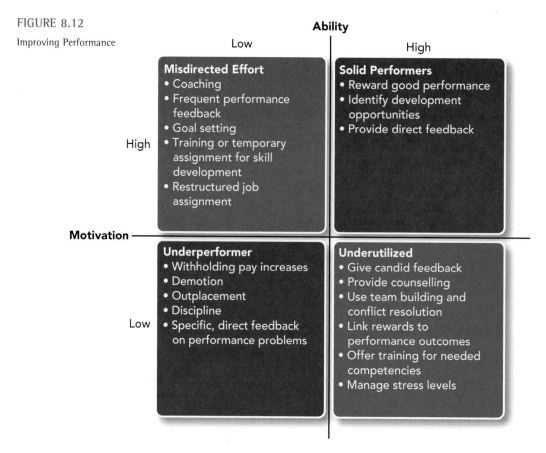

SOURCE: Based on M. London, *Job Feedback* (Mahwah, NJ: Lawrence Erlbaum Associates, 1997), pp. 96, 97. Used by permission.

fairly and rewarded adequately. The solution may be as simple as delivering more positive feedback. Employees may also benefit from a referral for counselling or help with stress management.

Employees whose performance is below expectations because they have neither the motivation nor the ability to perform the job may not be a good fit for the position. Performance may improve if the manager directs their attention to the significance of the problem by withholding rewards or by providing specific feedback. A documented performance improvement plan may be introduced by the supervisor as a means to discuss and reach agreement on next steps. A **performance improvement plan** is a summary of performance gaps and includes an action plan mutually agreed to by the employee and supervisor with specific dates to review progress. If employees do not respond by improving their performance, the organization may have to discipline or terminate these underperformers. Chapter 3 included a discussion of involuntary turnover.

As a rule, employees who combine high ability with high motivation are solid performers. As Figure 8.12 indicates, managers should by no means ignore these employees on the grounds of leaving well enough alone. Rather, such employees are likely to appreciate opportunities for further development. Rewards and direct feedback help to maintain these employees' high motivation levels.

performance improvement plan
Summary of performance gaps and includes an action plan mutually agreed to by the employee and supervisor with specific dates to review progress.

Legal and Ethical Issues in Performance Management

LO9 - Discuss legal and ethical issues that affect performance management.

2,3,4

In developing and using performance management systems, human resource professionals need to ensure that these systems meet legal requirements, such as the avoidance of discrimination related to any of the prohibited grounds, avoiding psychological harassment, and protecting employees' privacy.

Legal Requirements for Performance Management

Because performance measures play a central role in decisions about pay, promotions, and discipline, employment-related legal challenges may be directed at an organization's performance management system. Legal challenges related to performance management usually involve charges of illegal discrimination or unjust dismissal.

Claims often allege that the performance management system discriminated against employees on the basis of one of the protected grounds identified in human rights legislation such as age or sex. Many performance measures are subjective, and measurement errors, such as those described earlier in the chapter, can easily occur.

With regard to lawsuits filed on the grounds of unjust dismissal, the usual claim is that the person was dismissed for reasons besides the ones that the employer states. Health Canada recently fired three veterinary scientists who have attracted international attention for their public criticism of Canada's drug approval process and the use of drugs such as growth hormones in cattle. The scientists disclosed they were terminated for "insubordination"; however, the scientists' union, the Professional Institute of Public Servants, is likely to argue that the firings were a way to punish the employees for blowing the whistle.[52] In this type of situation, courts generally focus on the employer's performance management system, looking to see whether the dismissal could have been based on poor performance. To defend itself, the

You bring **flavor** to the **world.** Why not bring it **to work?**

The individuality you bring to the world is important to us at Pepsi-Cola North America. The distinctive flavor found in each of our beverages is proudly reflected in our people.

We offer a wide variety of job opportunities designed to challenge the right side of your brain or the left, with positions available across the country or just across town. Most important, they reflect the cultural and professional scope of the world you enhance and live in. Working for Pepsi-Cola North America now, doesn't that sound refreshing?

For more information visit our Web site: www.pepsijobs.com

PEPSI-COLA COMPANY

PepsiCo is dedicated to the policy of equal employment opportunity for all applicants without regard to their race, color, religion, gender, age, disability, national origin, sexual orientation or any other category protected by law.

Getting ratings from a diverse group of employees and thus getting a variety of viewpoints could be a check on one person's rating errors. Other ways to avoid bias in performance management are to have a valid rating system, to train raters in how to use the system, and to provide a way for employees to appeal an evaluation they think is inaccurate.

employer would need a performance management system that provides evidence to support its employment decisions.

To protect against both kinds of legal challenges, it is important to have a performance management system based on valid job analyses, as described in Chapter 4, with the requirements for job success clearly communicated to employees. Performance measurement should evaluate behaviours or results, on the basis of objective criteria. The organization should use multiple raters (including self-appraisals) and train raters in how to use the system. The organization should provide for a review of all performance ratings by upper-level managers and set up a system for employees to appeal when they believe they were evaluated unfairly. Along with feedback, the system should include a process for coaching or training employees to help them improve, rather than simply dismissing poor performers. Supervisors must also be careful to ensure performance feedback does not go beyond "reasonable criticism." As discussed in Chapter 2, Saskatchewan and Quebec have passed legislation which expands the definition of harassment, but employees in other provinces also have protection from employers who go too far in their criticism of employees.[53] One of the chapter-ending cases explores a recent example.

Employee Monitoring and Employee Privacy

Computer technology and other types of employee monitoring now support many performance management systems. Organizations often store records of employees' performance ratings, disciplinary actions, and work-rule violations in electronic databases. Many companies use personal computers to monitor productivity and other performance measures electronically.[54] The Society for Human Resource Management (SHRM) recently reported that more than one-third of organizations are stepping up their efforts to keep tabs on workers.[55] Figure 8.13 explains what employers monitor in the workplace.

Organizations need to consider how employees react to this type of performance measurement. Monitoring provides detailed, accurate information, but employees may find it demoralizing, degrading, and stressful. They are more likely to accept employee monitoring if the organization explains its purpose and links it to help in improving performance. For example, companies use global positioning systems (GPS) to create what is called a geofence—an invisible boundary based on GPS coordinates. If an employee strays outside his or her designated work area (geofence), GPS tracking software can alert the boss by email or instant messaging.[56] Although companies tend to argue that GPS is used to improve the efficiency of locating, dispatching, and routing employees to job sites, Canada's Privacy Commissioner Jennifer Stoddart

FIGURE 8.13

What Is Monitored in the Workplace

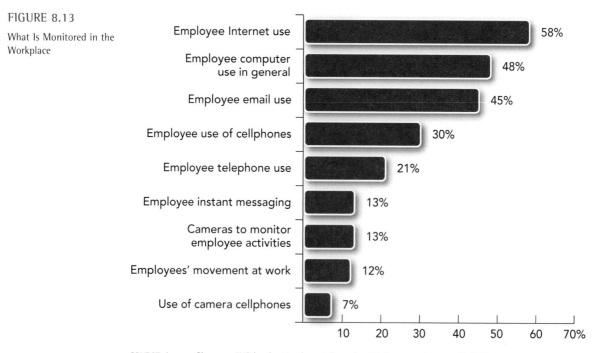

SOURCE: Lauren Chesney, "HR by the Numbers," *Canadian HR Reporter*, January 15, 2007, p. 4.

cautions employers to consider the privacy rights of workers before installing GPS in their vehicle fleets and to clearly explain to employees how GPS will be used.[57] As discussed in Chapter 2, the federal Personal Information Protection and Electronic Documents Act (PIPEDA) has additional implications for performance management. For example, organizations are required to ensure that personal information including an employee's performance review is securely protected, retained only for a specified time, and accessible to the employee.

THINKING ETHICALLY

Do Financial Goals Get Managers in Trouble?

The owners of a corporation naturally expect the company's managers and employees to work to increase the company's value (often expressed in terms of its stock price). Other basic financial goals for a business are to increase profits through greater sales or lower costs. But can a company's people focus on those goals too much?

Susan Annunzio of the Hudson Highland Center for High Performance conducted a study in which she concluded that the main cause of employees' difficulties in improving profits and innovating was an excessive focus on short-term financial results. When she talked to employees about their group's performance, 10 percent said they worked in high-performing groups, and 38 percent said they working in "nonperforming" groups.

Of those in the nonperforming groups, one-third said their groups used to be high-performing, but they began to fail when managers started raising their standards at the same time they were reducing budgets and staff.

Why does that happen? One opinion is that managers feel pressured to keep cutting costs to deliver greater profits in each quarterly financial statement. They can eliminate valuable employees, and the remainder feel their jobs are becoming impossible. Organizational psychologist Richard Hagberg worked with a sales vice-president who was urged to meet daily sales targets yet at the same time to cut staff to meet profit goals. The vice-president wanted to plan improvements to the product line and develop a

new competitive strategy, but his time was spent figuring out how to squeeze more work from a shrinking staff.

Other employees fear that the only way to meet targets is through unethical practices such as faking their performance data. Annunzio interviewed a factory manager who was given the goal of reducing operating costs. The manager thought of ways to meet the target within a month, but he spread the improvements over a year so that his boss wouldn't immediately come back with a stiffer goal for him to meet.

SOURCE: Based on Carol Hymowitz, "When Meeting Targets Becomes the Strategy, CEO Is on Wrong Path," *The Wall Street Journal*, March 8, 2005, http://online.wsj.com.

Questions

1. Who benefits when a company's employees are focused on making the company more profitable?
2. Do goals related to short-term profits—for this month or this quarter ever conflict with longer-term goals? Explain. Do these goals conflict with ethical standards? Explain.
3. Imagine that you are one of the managers described in this story or another manager who believes you cannot meet financial targets without deception or harm to the company. What should you do?

SUMMARY

LO1

Identify the activities involved in performance management.

- Performance management is the process through which managers ensure that employees' activities and outputs contribute to the organization's goals.

- The organization begins by specifying which aspects of performance are relevant; the relevant aspects of performance are measured through performance appraisal; and finally, in performance feedback sessions, managers provide employees with information about their performance so they can modify their behaviour to meet the organization's goals.

LO2

Discuss the purposes of performance management systems.

- Organizations establish performance management systems to meet three broad purposes:

- *Strategic purposes*. Meeting business objectives by helping to link employees' behaviour with the organization's goals.

- *Administrative purpose*. Providing information for day-to-day decisions about salary, benefits, recognition, and retention or termination.

- *Developmental purpose*. Using the system as a basis for developing employees' competencies.

LO3

Define five criteria for measuring the effectiveness of a performance management system.

- Performance measures should fit with the organization's strategy by supporting its goals and culture.

- Performance measures should be valid, that is, measure all the relevant aspects of performance and not measure irrelevant aspects of performance.

- Measures should provide interrater and test-retest reliability, that is, appraisals are consistent among raters and over time.

- Measures should be acceptable to the people who use them or receive feedback from them.

- Finally, a performance measure should specifically tell employees what is expected of them and how they can meet those expectations.

LO4

Compare the major methods for measuring performance.

- Performance measurement may use ranking systems such as simple ranking, forced distribution, or paired comparisons to compare one individual's performance with that of other employees.

- Although time-consuming, and may be seen as unfair under some circumstances, ranking counteracts some forms of rater bias and helps distinguish employees for administrative decisions.

- Other approaches involve rating employees' competencies, behaviours, or outcomes. Rating competencies is relatively simple but not always valid and requires a great deal of information, but these methods can be very effective.

- Rating results, such as productivity or achievement of objectives, tends to be less subjective than other kinds of rating; however, validity may be a problem because of factors outside the employee's control.

- A balanced scorecard is a widely used strategic approach.

LO5

Describe major sources of performance information in terms of their advantages and disadvantages.

- Performance information may come from an employee's self-appraisal and from appraisals by the employee's manager, employees, peers, and customers.

- Organizations may combine many sources into a 360-degree performance appraisal.

- Employees' supervisors may produce accurate information, and peers are an excellent source of information about performance in a job where the supervisor does not often observe the employee. Disadvantages are that friendships (or rivalries) may bias ratings and peers may be uncomfortable with the role of rating a friend. Direct reports often have the best chance to see how a manager treats employees; however, employees may be reluctant to contribute candid opinions about a supervisor unless they can provide information anonymously.

- Self-appraisals may be biased, but they do come from the person with the most knowledge of the employee's behaviour on the job, and they provide a basis for discussion in feedback sessions, opening up fruitful comparisons and areas of disagreement between the self-appraisal and other appraisals.

- Customers may be an excellent source of performance information, although obtaining customer feedback tends to be expensive.

LO6 Define types of rating errors and explain how to minimize them.

- A common tendency is to give higher evaluations to people we consider similar to ourselves.

- Other errors involve using only part of the rating scale or contrasting an employee unfavourably with very high performers.

- Giving all employees ratings at the high end of the scale is called leniency error. Rating everyone at the low end of the scale is called strictness error. Rating at or near the middle is called central tendency.

- Basing an employee's rating only on the most recent work performed is called recency emphasis; and focusing on activities—for example, how busy the employee looks, rather than results—is also problematic. Halo/horns error refers to rating employees positively/negatively in all areas because of strong/weak performance observed in one area.

- Ways to reduce rater error are training raters to be aware of their tendencies to make rating errors and training them to be sensitive to the complex nature of employee performance so they will consider many aspects of performance in greater depth.

- Politics also may influence ratings. Organizations can minimize appraisal politics by establishing a fair appraisal system, involving managers and employees in developing the system, allowing employees to challenge evaluations, communicating expectations, and fostering a climate of open discussion.

LO7 Explain how to effectively provide performance feedback.

- Performance feedback should be a regular, scheduled management activity, so that employees can correct problems as soon as they occur.

- Managers should prepare by establishing a neutral location, emphasizing that the feedback session will be a chance for discussion and asking the employee to prepare a self-assessment.

- During the feedback session, managers should strive for a problem-solving approach and encourage employees to voice their opinions and discuss performance goals. The manager should look for opportunities to reinforce desired behaviour and should limit criticism. The discussion should focus on behaviour and results rather than on personalities.

LO8 Summarize ways to achieve performance improvement.

- If an employee is motivated but lacks ability, provide coaching and training, give detailed feedback about performance, and consider restructuring the job.

- For an employee with ability but lacking motivation, investigate whether outside problems are a distraction, and if so refer the employee for help.

- If the problem has to do with the employee not feeling appreciated or rewarded, try to meet the employee's needs and evaluate whether additional rewards are appropriate.

- For an employee lacking both ability and motivation, consider whether the employee is a good fit for the position. Specific feedback or withholding rewards may spur improvement, or the employee may have to be demoted or terminated.

- Solid employees who are high in ability and motivation will continue so and may be able to contribute even more if the manager provides appropriate direct feedback, rewards, and opportunities for development.

L09 | Discuss legal and ethical issues that affect performance management.

- Lawsuits related to performance management usually involve charges of discrimination, psychological harassment, or unjust dismissal.

- Managers must make sure that performance management systems and decisions treat employees equally, without regard to their age, sex, or other protected grounds.

- A system is more likely to be legally defensible if it is based on behaviours and results, and if multiple raters evaluate each person's performance.

- An ethical issue of performance management is the use of employee monitoring. This type of performance measurement provides detailed, accurate information, but employees may find it demoralizing, degrading, and stressful.

REVIEW AND DISCUSSION QUESTIONS

1. How does a complete performance management system differ from the use of annual performance appraisals?

2. Give two examples of an administrative decision that would be based on performance management information. Give two examples of developmental decisions based on this type of information.

3. How can involving employees in the creation of performance standards improve the effectiveness of a performance management system? (Consider the criteria for effectiveness shown in Figure 8.3.)

4. Consider how you might rate the performance of three instructors from whom you are currently taking a course. (If you are currently taking only one or two courses, consider this course and two you recently completed.)

    a. Would it be harder to *rate* the instructors' performance or to *rank* their performance? Why?

    b. Write three items to use in rating the instructors—one each to rate them in terms of a competency, a behaviour, and an outcome.

    c. Which of the three items do you think is most valid? Most reliable? Why?

    d. Many educational institutions use questionnaires to gather data from students about their instructors' performance. Would it be appropriate to use the data for administrative decisions? Developmental decisions? Other decisions? Why or why not?

5. Imagine that a pet supply store is establishing a new performance management system to help employees provide better customer service. Management needs to decide who should participate in measuring the performance of each of the store's salespeople. From what sources should the store gather information? Why?

6. Would the same sources be appropriate if the store in question 5 will use the performance appraisals to support decisions about which employees to promote? Explain.

7. Suppose you were recently promoted to a supervisory job in a company where you have worked for two years. You genuinely like almost all your co-workers, who now report to you. The only exception is one employee, who dresses more formally than the others and frequently tells jokes that embarrass you and the other workers. Given your preexisting feelings for the employees, how can you measure their performance fairly and effectively?

8. Continuing the example in question 7, imagine that you are preparing for your first performance feedback session. You want the feedback to be effective—that is, you want the feedback to result in improved performance. List five or six steps you can take to achieve your goal.

9. Besides giving employees feedback, what steps can a manager take to improve employees' performance?

10. Suppose you are a human resource professional helping to improve the performance management system of a company that sells and services office equipment. The company operates a call centre that takes calls from customers having problems with their equipment. Call centre employees are supposed to verify that the problem is not one the customer can easily handle (e.g., equipment that will not operate because it has come unplugged). Then, if the problem is not resolved over the phone, the employees arrange for service technicians to visit the customer. The company can charge the customer only if a service technician visits, so performance management of the call centre employees focuses on productivity—how quickly they can complete a call and move on to the next caller. To measure this performance efficiently and accurately, the company uses employee monitoring.

    a. How would you expect the employees to react to the monitoring? How might the organization address the employees' concerns?

b. Besides productivity in terms of number of calls, what other performance measures should the performance management system include?

c. How should the organization gather information about the other performance measures?

WHAT'S YOUR HR IQ?

The Online Learning Centre offers more ways to check what you've learned so far. Find experiential exercises as well as Test Your Knowledge Quizzes, Videos, and many other resources at www.mcgrawhill.ca/olc/steen.

Case:
Forced Rankings Popular at Big Corporations

Many big companies, including Ford Motor Company, General Electric, Microsoft, and Hewlett-Packard, use forced-ranking systems and forced-distribution systems. Their use of the systems has sometimes generated lawsuits and negative publicity and triggered poor employee morale.

At General Electric, forced distribution was advocated by the company's former chief executive, Jack Welch. Welch insisted that GE annually identify and remove the bottom-performing 10 percent of the workforce. Such performance ranking takes several forms. Most commonly, employees are grouped into three, four, or five categories—usually of unequal size—indicating the best workers, the worst workers, and one to three categories in between. At General Electric, managers were required to place employees into the top 20 percent, middle 70 percent, and bottom 10 percent. The bottom 10 percent received no bonuses and could be terminated.

Why are forced-distribution systems popular? Top-level managers at many companies have observed that despite corporate performance being flat or decreasing, compensation costs have continued to spiral upward, and performance ratings remain high. They question how there can be so little connection between corporate performance and employees' evaluations and compensation. Forced-distribution systems are a way to help match company and employee performance with compensation. Poor performers receive no salary increase, and average performers receive smaller increases than are given to top performers.

A forced-distribution system also helps managers tailor development activities to employees based on their performance. For example, poor performers are given specific feedback about what they need to improve and what the timetable is for making the changes. If they do not improve, they are dismissed. Top performers are encouraged to participate in development activities such as challenging job experiences and leadership programs to prepare them for top management positions. So the use of a forced-distribution system is a way for companies to increase performance, motivate employees, and open the door for new talent to join the company in place of poor performers.

Still, the practice has problems. Forced distribution asks managers to differentiate between good, average, and poor performers, a distinction many managers find difficult to make. The systems have been difficult to implement, and some companies have gotten into trouble.

In 2002, Ford settled two class-action lawsuits for $10.5 million. Ford said it needed its forced-ranking system because its culture discouraged frankness in performance evaluations. The Ford Motors Performance Management System involved grading 1,800 middle managers as A, B, or C, with 10 percent receiving a C. Managers who received a C for one year received no bonus; two years at the C level meant possible demotion and termination. Some employees claimed the system harmed older, white workers because they received a larger proportion of C grades.

Dow Chemical Global had a forced-ranking system until the mid-1990s. The system caused a lot of problems. A study showed that the system took too much time and energy, and managers were focused on the appraisal instead of improving employee performance. The same employees were consistently evaluated in the top 15 percent, so other employees wondered how they could ever achieve a higher ranking. The company also found that the system was used to deny employees raises. In addition, it did not fit with Dow's philosophy of recruiting the best employees: If the company hired the best, how then could some be rated as poor performers? Dow replaced the system with one in which managers define performance expectations and then communicate them along with the company's values and the employee's role in maintaining those values. Employees are compared against performance standards, rather than against one another.

Goodyear Tire and Rubber used a system in which 10 percent of its staff would be rated as A performers and singled out for promotion. Another 10 percent would be rated as C performers and targeted for improvement or dismissal. After getting a second C rating in two years, a chemist at Goodyear was fired. He was fired a few days before he received a patent for a new kind of aircraft tire. The chemist and seven other Goodyear employees sued the company, claiming the forced-ranking system targeted older employees and not poor performers. Although Goodyear contested the lawsuit, it also abandoned the labelling of employees as A, B, or C. Its new categories are "exceeds expectations," "meets expectations," and "unsatisfactory." Employees in the bottom category are still expected to improve or to face reassignment or firing.

SOURCE: S. Bates, "Forced Ranking," *HR Magazine*, June 2003, pp. 63–68; A. Meisler, "Deadman's Curve," *Workforce Management*, July 2003, pp. 44–49; M. Lowery, "Forcing the Issue," *Human Resource Executive*, October 16, 2003, pp. 26–29; and M. Boyle, "Performance Reviews: Perilous Curves Ahead," *Fortune*, May 28, 2001, pp. 187–188.

Questions

1. What are the pros and cons of forced-distribution and forced-ranking systems?
2. Suppose Ford, Goodyear, or Dow Chemical contracted with you to modify its performance management system to avoid some of the problems it has experienced. What would you suggest the company do?
3. What advantages will your ideas have over the company's current system? How will you measure the success of your ideas?

Case:
When Does Performance Feedback Become Psychological Harassment?

Psychological harassment has become a hot topic among managers and HR professionals in Canada. Perhaps the best known common-law claim for psychological harassment is *Shah v. Xerox Canada Ltd.* Viren Shah was a 12-year employee at Xerox who consistently received good performance reviews throughout his career. When he took on a new position he started to experience difficulty getting along with his manager. Shah alleged that his manager gave him critical performance reviews that were not based on any substantiated concerns and that his boss's general attitude was "authoritarian, impatient, and intolerant." As a result of these difficult working conditions, Shah became ill, requested a leave of absence (which was denied) and was placed on probation for poor performance.

The case was ultimately decided by the Ontario Court of Appeal, which provided the following guidance with respect to the definition of what a supervisor can and cannot do in the context of performance appraisal and performance improvement. "An employer is entitled to be critical of the unsatisfactory work of its employees and, in general, to take such measures as it believes to be appropriate to remedy the situation," the court said. However, in this case the court determined that Shah's manager passed beyond the "bounds of reasonableness."

Although this case provides an extreme example of performance appraisal gone wrong, there are lessons for all supervisors and HR professionals that arise from discussion of this case.

SOURCE: James Heeney, "Personal Harassment Liability Always a Danger for Employers," *Canadian HR Reporter*, October 22, 2007, p. B15; Stuart Rudner, "Psychological Harassment Hurts Employees' Productivity," *Canadian HR Reporter*, October 22, 2007, p. 31; Christopher M. Andree Crawford, "Poor Treatment Is Constructive Dismissal," *Canadian Bar Association*, www.cba.org/CBA/newsletters/lab-2003/18.aspx, retrieved April 27, 2008; "Bullying at Work: Another Form of Workplace Violence," www.emond-harnden.com/publications/feb03/bullies.shtml, retrieved April 27, 2008.

Questions

1. What supervisory behaviours may be viewed as humiliating or intimidating to an employee receiving performance feedback?
2. What should supervisors do to reduce the likelihood they will be accused of personal or psychological harassment while conducting a performance review?
3. What steps should HR take to reduce the organization's liability and support supervisors responsible for conducting performance reviews?
4. Does this threat of personal harassment liability affect whether you would accept a supervisory or managerial job in the future? Why or why not?

VIDEO CASE

PCL Internal Orientation Video

This video puts you inside one of North America's largest construction companies—PCL, headquartered in Edmonton, Alberta. This video is used as part of PCL's orientation process for new employees. PCL's values and dedication to construction excellence and its talent are discussed in a series of personal vignettes from a diverse group of employees including the CEO.

For example, PCL's College of Construction, illustrated in the introduction to Chapter 7, is mentioned as one of the tangible ways that PCL supports the development of people.

Questions

1. What evidence does the video provide that PCL is committed to valuing and developing its talent (people)?

2. If you were watching this video as part of an orientation (onboarding) process at PCL, what expectations would you have about the kinds of training, development, and career opportunities you will have as a PCL employee?

3. Does PCL sound like a good place to build a career? Why or why not?

Part **4**

Compensating and Rewarding Human Resources

Chapter 9
  Total Rewards

Real People in HR

Lori Pavely, Human Resources Business Partner at Hallmark Canada. Lori has been with Hallmark Canada, in various roles, for over 20 years. Since 1995 she has worked in Human Resources, where she specializes in Compensation and Benefits Administration.

Name...
Lori Pavely.

Job...
Human Resources Business Partner at Hallmark Canada.

Adjective people would use to describe you...
Positive attitude.

First job...
Compositor at a newspaper.

First HR job...
Receptionist.

Most challenging aspect of your job...
Finding the time to be proactive instead of just reactive.

Most rewarding aspect of your job...
Working with a client to effect a change that employees embrace and that supports business success. Working with so many different people, both union and management and government.

Hallmark's total rewards approach to compensation...
The total rewards approach reflected the company's commitment to valuing the whole person, and that was the driving force behind the implementation. Thus far, feedback has been favourable, although this approach is still very new to employees. We offer a number of rewards designed to appeal to younger employees. These include a subsidized cafeteria and vending, flexible work arrangements, educational assistance, personal and floater days, a fitness subsidy, company-sponsored social events, and, of course, a solid core-benefits package.

Four essential attributes that make someone a great HR professional...
HR is about people, so be empathetic. I think that honesty is also an essential attribute. Being innovative and able to adapt to change are the other two attributes that I think contribute to one's success as an HR professional.

If you had to pick an alternative career...
Librarian.

Best career advice that you ever received...
Be open, honest, and vulnerable in all interactions.

Advice for someone beginning an HR career...
Be open and enthused about learning HR from the bottom up. HR impacts the entire organization, so make sure to learn as much as you can about other departments as well.

Total Rewards

What Do I Need to Know? After reading this chapter, you should be able to:

1. Discuss how organizations implement a "total rewards" approach to compensating and rewarding employees.

2. Identify the kinds of decisions and influences involved in providing base pay to employees.

3. Describe alternatives to job-based pay.

4. Describe how organizations recognize individual, team, and organizational performance through the use of incentives.

5. Discuss the role of benefits as part of employee total rewards.

6. Summarize the types of employee benefits offered by employers.

7. Discuss the importance of effectively communicating the organization's approach to total rewards.

8. Discuss issues related to compensating and rewarding executives.

LO1 - Discuss how organizations implement a "total rewards" approach to compensating and rewarding employees.

Introduction

Markham, Ontario–based business automation software company InSystems has been transforming its employee compensation and rewards system through the adoption of a total rewards approach. Some parts of the total rewards package may be considered intangibles, but Laurie McRae, vice-president of human resources, says the goal is to turn those intangibles into hard data.

The guiding philosophy is: Anything that employees take into account when considering the value of working at InSystems is part of the total rewards package. The shift to total rewards at InSystems was precipitated by an employee survey.

"The [employee satisfaction] scores weren't low, but then again I have some lofty goals for employee satisfaction," McRae says. The survey also revealed a few areas of the traditional rewards programs that could, in the minds of employees stand some improvement. "They made comments about our incentive plan, about the way it was designed and structured. From their perspective it was too complex," she says. Employees wanted high performance to be recognized, but it often wasn't clear why some employees were getting incentives while others weren't. "They wanted to see these types of direct financial awards really differentiate high performance, so people who were high performers could get more sizable rewards." Employees only singled out a few issues for improvement, but McRae wanted to reexamine everything that the employee proposition comprised. "You have to step back and say we need to balance the cost and the effectiveness of these programs. We have to manage it as a whole portfolio."

Laurie McRae, vice-president of HR at InSystems, says HR needs to bundle and market employee offerings.

Before then, compensation and rewards were managed in isolation. Therefore, it was difficult for employees to understand exactly what they were getting from their employer. After recognizing improvements were possible, and with the objective of ultimately improving corporate performance, the HR team set to work with external help to overhaul employee rewards. "We went right back to the drawing board," says McRae. A new job evaluation methodology was created to ease market salary comparisons, a retirement savings program was introduced for the first time, incentive programs were tweaked, and new recognition programs introduced. A total rewards package also makes it easier for employees to make comparisons when other opportunities arise. She is confident that the InSystems total rewards package is strong enough that when employees have a full picture of everything they get from InSystems, they won't easily be lured away.[1]

Like InSystems, many organizations are recognizing the strategic value of adopting a comprehensive approach to compensating and rewarding employees, frequently referred to as **total rewards**. Figure 9.1 shows how a total rewards strategy reflecting the organization's culture, business and HR strategy is a powerful tool to attract, motivate, and retain satsified employees while achieving desired business results.

Organizations such as InSystems and RBC are redefining their approaches to employee compensation and benefits to also take into account the "overall work experience provided to employees."[2] Organizations with this total rewards approach create a *value proposition* for current and prospective employees that considers the total value they receive for contributing their time and energy to the company. Because compensation, benefits, and the work experience have a major impact on employee attitudes and behaviours, total rewards influence what kinds of employees are attracted to (and remain with) the organization. In a recent Watson Wyatt survey on strategic rewards and pay practices, Canadian companies cited the primary reason for developing a total rewards strategy was to align rewards with the business strategy. As shown in Figure 9.2, other reasons Canadian companies take a total rewards approach is to focus employees on business goals, enforce consistent pay practices, optimize how reward dollars are used, and control costs.[3]

1,2,5

total rewards A comprehensive approach to compensating and rewarding employees.

FIGURE 9.1

Total Rewards Model

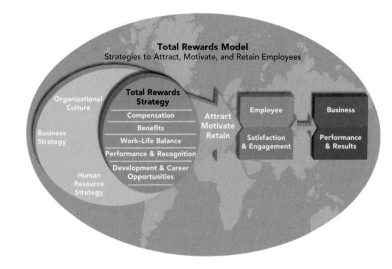

total compensation

All types of financial rewards and tangible benefits and services employees receive as part of their employment.

Employees care about policies affecting their compensation, benefits, and the work experience itself because the policies affect the employee's income, well-being, and security. Also, employees consider these elements a sign of status and success. They attach great importance to compensation and rewards when they evaluate their relationship and satisfaction with their employers. As the workforce becomes increasingly diverse, the definition of what employees expect in exchange for their work will become increasingly complex. As a result, although this chapter addresses total rewards, the primary emphasis will be on forms of **total compensation**, that is, direct and indirect compensation including base pay, incentives, and benefits received in exchange for the employee's contribution of time, talent, effort, and results.[4] Chapter 3 discussed attributes of work environments where employees are more likely to experience satisfaction and engagement, Chapter 7 explored learning and development opportunities provided employees, and Chapter 8 examined performance processes. A comprehensive "Total Rewards Inventory" checklist outlining elements that could be included in an organization's value proposition is provided in Figure 9.3, and Table 9.1 explains some generational considerations related to total rewards.

FIGURE 9.2

Why Firms Develop a Total Rewards Strategy

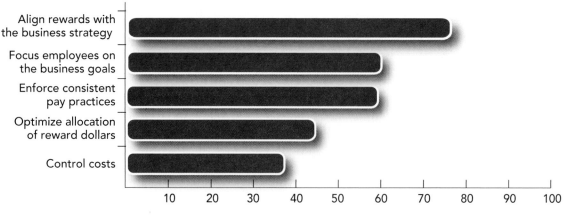

SOURCE: "Strategic Rewards in Canada: Building the Optimal Reward Plan—Watson Wyatt's 2004 Survey of Canadian Strategic Rewards and Pay Practices," in "Why Firms Develop a Total Rewards Strategy," *Canadian HR Reporter,* February 14, 2005, p. R5.

FIGURE 9.3

Total Rewards Inventory

Total Rewards Inventory

To get a comprehensive view of your organization's value proposition, simply check off the rewards your organization currently provides.

Compensation	Benefits	Work–Life		Performance & Recognition	Development & Career Opportunities

Compensation

Base Wages
- ☐ Salary Pay
- ☐ Hourly Pay
- ☐ Piece Rate Pay

Premium Pay
- ☐ Shift Differential Pay
- ☐ Weekend/Holiday Pay
- ☐ On-Call Pay
- ☐ Call-In Pay
- ☐ Hazard Pay
- ☐ Bilingual Pay
- ☐ Skill-Based Pay

Variable Pay
- ☐ Commissions
- ☐ Team-Based Pay
- ☐ Bonus Programs
  - ☐ Referral Bonus
  - ☐ Hiring Bonus
  - ☐ Retention Bonus
  - ☐ Project Completion Bonus
- ☐ Incentive Pay
  Short-Term:
  - ☐ Profit Sharing
  - ☐ Individual Performance–Based Incentives
  - ☐ Performance-Sharing Incentives
  Long-Term:
  - ☐ Restricted Stock
  - ☐ Performance Shares
  - ☐ Performance Units
  - ☐ Stock Options/Grants

Benefits

Legally Required/Mandated
- ☐ Unemployment Insurance
- ☐ Worker's Compensation Insurance
- ☐ Social Security Insurance
- ☐ Medicare
- ☐ State Disability Insurance (if applicable)

Health & Welfare
- ☐ Medical Plan
- ☐ Dental Plan
- ☐ Vision Plan
- ☐ Prescription Drug Plan
- ☐ Flexible Spending Accounts (FSAs)
- ☐ Health Reimbursement Accounts (HRAs)
- ☐ Health Savings Accounts (HSAs)
- ☐ Mental Health Plan
- ☐ Life Insurance
- ☐ Spouse/Dependent Life Insurance
- ☐ AD&D Insurance
- ☐ Short-Term/Long-Term Disability Insurance

Retirement
- ☐ Defined Benefit Plan
- ☐ Defined Contribution Plan
- ☐ Profit-Sharing Plan
- ☐ Hybrid Plan

Pay for Time Not Worked
- ☐ Vacation
- ☐ Holiday
- ☐ Sick Leave
- ☐ Bereavement Leave
- ☐ Leaves of Absence (military, personal, medical, family medical)

Work–Life

Workplace Flexibility/Alternative Work Arrangements
- ☐ Flextime
- ☐ Flexible Schedules
- ☐ Telecommuting
- ☐ Alternative Work Sites
- ☐ Compressed Workweek
- ☐ Job Sharing
- ☐ Part-Time Employment
- ☐ Seasonal Schedules

Paid and Unpaid Time Off
- ☐ Maternity/Paternity Leave
- ☐ Adoption Leave
- ☐ Sabbaticals

Health and Wellness
- ☐ Employee Assistance Programs
- ☐ On-Site Fitness Facilities
- ☐ Discounted Fitness Club Rates
- ☐ Preventive Care Programs
- ☐ Weight Management Programs
- ☐ Smoking Cessation Assistance
- ☐ On-Site Massages
- ☐ Stress Management Programs
- ☐ Voluntary Immunization Clinics
- ☐ Wellness Initiatives
- ☐ Health Screenings
- ☐ Nutritional Counseling
- ☐ On-Site Nurse
- ☐ Business Travel Health Services
- ☐ Occupational Health Programs
- ☐ Disability Management
- ☐ Return-to-Work Programs
- ☐ Reproductive Health/Pregnancy Programs

Community Involvement
- ☐ Community Volunteer Programs
- ☐ Matching Gift Programs
- ☐ Shared Leave Programs
- ☐ Disaster Relief Funds
- ☐ Sponsorships/Grants
- ☐ In-Kind Donations

Caring for Dependents
- ☐ Dependent Care Reimbursement Accounts
- ☐ Dependent Care Travel-Related Expense Reimbursement
- ☐ Dependent Care Referral and Resource Services
- ☐ Dependent Care Discount Programs or Vouchers
- ☐ Emergency Dependent Care Services
- ☐ Childcare Subsidies
- ☐ On-Site Caregiver Support Groups
- ☐ On-Site Dependent Care
- ☐ Adoption Assistance Services
- ☐ After-School Care Programs
- ☐ College/Scholarship Information
- ☐ Scholarships
- ☐ Mother's Privacy Rooms
- ☐ Summer Camps and Activities

Financial Support
- ☐ Financial Planning Services and Education
- ☐ Adoption Reimbursement
- ☐ Transit Subsidies
- ☐ 529 Plans
- ☐ Savings Bonds

Voluntary Benefits
- ☐ Long-Term Care
- ☐ Auto/Home Insurance
- ☐ Pet Insurance
- ☐ Legal Insurance
- ☐ Identity Theft Insurance
- ☐ Employee Discounts
- ☐ Concierge Services
- ☐ Transit Passes
- ☐ Parking

Culture Change Initiatives
- ☐ Work Redesign
- ☐ Team Effectiveness
- ☐ Diversity/Inclusion Initiatives
- ☐ Women's Advancement Initiatives
- ☐ Work Environment Initiatives

Performance & Recognition

Performance
- ☐ Manager/Employee 1:1 Meetings
- ☐ Performance Reviews
- ☐ Project Completion/Team Evaluations
- ☐ Performance Planning/Goal-Setting Sessions

Recognition
- ☐ Service Awards
- ☐ Retirement Awards
- ☐ Peer Recognition Awards
- ☐ Spot Awards
- ☐ Managerial Recognition Programs
- ☐ Organization-Wide Recognition Programs
- ☐ Exceeding Performance Awards
- ☐ Employee of the Month/Year Awards
- ☐ Appreciation Luncheons, Outings, Formal Events
- ☐ Goal-Specific Awards (quality, efficiency, cost savings, productivity, safety)
- ☐ Employee Suggestion Programs

Development & Career Opportunities

Learning Opportunities
- ☐ Tuition Reimbursement
- ☐ Tuition Discounts
- ☐ Corporate Universities
- ☐ New Technology Training
- ☐ On-the-Job Learning
- ☐ Attendance at Outside Seminars and Conferences
- ☐ Access to Virtual Learning, Podcasts, Webinars
- ☐ Self-Development Tools

Coaching/Mentoring
- ☐ Leadership Training
- ☐ Exposure to Resident Experts
- ☐ Access to Information Networks
- ☐ Formal or Informal Mentoring Programs

Advancement Opportunities
- ☐ Internships
- ☐ Apprenticeships
- ☐ Overseas Assignments
- ☐ Internal Job Postings
- ☐ Job Advancement/Promotion
- ☐ Career Ladders and Pathways
- ☐ Succession Planning
- ☐ On/Off Ramps Through Career Lifecycle
- ☐ Job Rotations

SOURCE: "Your Total Rewards Inventory," p. 4, WorldatWork website, retrieved May 5, 2008.

TABLE 9.1

Generational Emphasis Within Total Rewards

Traditionalist (1922–1945)	Incentives and stocks, promotions, health benefits (life/disability), pensions, stability, formal recogntion, community involvement
Baby Boomers (1946–1964)	High-visibility projects, promotions, support around work–life issues, personal learning and development, onsite facilities, industry recognition
Gen-X (1965–1980)	Training and development, challenging tasks/stretch assignments, independent work environment, project variety, work–life balance, flexible work arrangements, variable pay
Gen-Y (1981–2000)	Meaningfulness of work/projects, manager feedback, casual work environment, daily work–life balance, access to senior leaders, mentoring, social activities, community involvement, flextime

SOURCE: Adapted from Adwoa K. Buahene and Giselle Kovary, "The Great Divide," *HR Professional*, October/November 2007, p. 27.

direct compensation
Financial rewards employees receive in exchange for their work.

indirect compensation
The benefits and services employees receive in exchange for their work.

This chapter opens by describing the role of **direct compensation**, all types of financial rewards employees receive as part of their employment, and defines the kinds of influences on managers making pay level decisions. We describe methods of evaluating jobs and market data to develop effective pay structures. Next, we look at the elements of incentive pay systems. The many kinds of incentive pay fall into three broad categories: incentives linked to individual, group, or organizational performance. Choices from these categories should consider not only their strengths and weaknesses, but also their fit with the organization's goals. This chapter also looks at **indirect compensation**, the benefits and services employees receive in exchange for their work, including the important role benefits play. The chapter also covers why and how organizations should effectively communicate with employees about their total rewards. Finally, this chapter looks at an issue also linked to organizational performance—executive compensation. In summary, Figure 9.4 illustrates how total rewards are allocated in 294 organizations surveyed by the Conference Board of Canada.

FIGURE 9.4

The Total Rewards Dollar

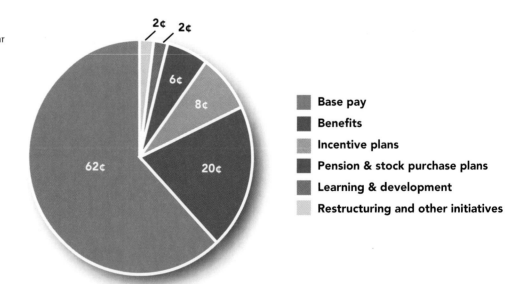

- Base pay
- Benefits
- Incentive plans
- Pension & stock purchase plans
- Learning & development
- Restructuring and other initiatives

SOURCE: "Compensation Planning Outlook 2005, Conference Board of Canada," *Canadian HR Reporter*, February 14, 2005, p. R5.

Decisions About Base Pay

Because pay is important both in its effect on employees and on account of its cost, organizations need to plan what they will pay employees in each job. An unplanned approach, in which each employee's pay is independently negotiated, will likely result in unfairness, dissatisfaction, and rates that are either overly expensive or so low that positions are hard to fill. Organizations therefore make decisions about two aspects of pay structure: job structure and pay level. **Job structure** consists of the relative pay for different jobs within the organization. It establishes relative pay among different functions and different levels of responsibility. For example, job structure defines the difference in pay between an entry-level accountant and an entry-level assembler, as well as the difference between an entry-level accountant, the accounting department manager, and the organization's comptroller. **Pay level** is the average amount (including wages, salaries, and incentives) the organization pays for a particular job. Together, job structure and pay levels establish a **pay structure** that helps the organization achieve goals related to employee motivation, cost control, and the ability to attract and retain talented human resources.

The organization's job structure and pay levels are policies of the organization, rather than the amount a particular employee earns. For example, an organization's pay structure could include the range of pay that a person may earn in the job of entry-level accountant. an individual accountant could be earning an amount anywhere within that range. Typically, the amount a person earns depends on the individual's qualifications, accomplishments, and experience. The individual's pay may also depend partly on how well the organization performs.

Especially in an organization with hundreds or thousands of employees, it would be impractical for managers and the human resource department to make an entirely unique decision about each employee's pay. The decision would have to weigh so many factors that this approach would be expensive, difficult, and often unsatisfactory. Establishing a pay structure simplifies the process of making decisions about individual employees' pay by grouping together employees with similar jobs. As shown, in Figure 9.5,

LO2 - Identify the kinds of decisions and influences involved in providing base pay to employees.

5

job structure
The relative pay for different jobs within the organization.

pay level
The average amount (including wages, salaries, and bonuses) the organization pays for a particular job.

pay structure
The pay policy resulting from job structure and pay-level decisions.

| Legal Requirements | Market Forces
• Product markets
• Labour markets | Organization's Goals
• High-quality workforce
• Cost control
• Equity and fairness
• Legal compliance |

Pay Level Decision
Job Structure Decision
Pay Structure Decisions
• Pay rates
• Pay grades
• Pay ranges
• Pay differentials

FIGURE 9.5

Issues in Developing a Pay Structure

human resource professionals develop this pay structure based on legal requirements, market forces, and the organization's goals, such as attracting a high-quality workforce and meeting principles of fairness.

1,5

Legal Requirements

All of an organization's decisions about compensation should comply with the applicable laws. Although these laws differ across federal, provincial, and territorial jurisdictions, a common core of legal requirements exists.

Human Rights Legislation

Under human rights legislation, described in Chapter 2, employers may not base differences in pay on an employee's age, sex, race, or other prohibited grounds of discrimination. Any differences in pay must instead be tied to such business-related considerations as job responsibilities or performance. Job descriptions, job structures, and pay structures can help organizations demonstrate that they are upholding these laws.

Employment/Labour Standards Acts

The Canada Labour Code and the relevant provincial and territorial laws include minimum requirements for wages, hours of work, overtime pay, vacation, statutory holidays, as well as other specific provisions. Executives, professionals, administrative, and outside sales employees are usually considered "exempt" employees and are not eligible for certain provisions such as overtime pay that "non-exempt" employees receive.

Two employees who do the same job cannot be paid different wages because of gender, race, or age. It would be illegal to pay these two employees differently because one is male and the other is female. Only if there are differences in their experinece, skills, seniority, or job performance are there legal reasons why their pay might be different.

Pay Equity Acts

As discussed in Chapter 2, pay equity legislation exists federally and in several provincial jurisdictions, and it attempts to address the wage gap between female and male-dominated jobs to ensure that jobs of equal value within the organization receive similar rates of pay. Organizations use job evaluation (described later in the chapter) to establish the worth of an organization's jobs in terms of such criteria as their difficulty and their importance to the organization. The employer then compares the evaluation points awarded to each job with the pay for each job. If jobs have the same number of evaluation points, they should be paid equally. If they are not, pay of the lower-paid job is raised to meet the comparable worth of the male-dominated job.

2,3,4,5

Economic Influences on Pay

An organization cannot make spending decisions independently of the economy. Organizations must keep costs low enough that they can sell their products profitably, yet they must be able to attract workers in a competitive labour market. Decisions about how to respond to the economic forces of product markets and labour markets limit an organization's choices about pay structure.

Product Markets

Pressure to be globally competitive influences compensation and rewards. Companies increasingly recognize that increases in employees' pay needs to be linked to corresponding increases in productivity. To protect Canadian jobs from being outsourced to nations with lower labour costs, organizations are also focusing on cost containment.[5] Organizations under pressure to cut labour costs may respond by reducing staff levels, freezing pay levels, postponing hiring decisions, or requiring employees to bear more of the cost of benefits such as insurance premiums.

Pay Level: Deciding What to Pay

Although legal requirements and economic influences limit organizations' choices about pay levels, there is a range within which organizations can make decisions.[6] The size of this range depends on the details of the organization's competitive environment. If many workers are competing for a few jobs, employers will have more choice. Similarly, employers can be more flexible about pay policies if they use technology and work design to get better results from employees than their competitors do.

When organizations have a broad range in which to make decisions about pay, they can choose to pay at, above, or below the rate set by market forces. Economic theory holds that the most profitable level, all things being equal, would be at the market rate. Often, however, all things are *not* equal from one employer to another. For instance, an organization may gain an advantage by paying above the market rate if it uses the higher pay as one means to attract top talent and then uses these excellent employees' knowledge to be more innovative, produce higher quality, or work more efficiently.

This approach is based on the view of employees as resources. Higher pay may be an investment in superior human resources. Having higher labour costs than your competitors is not necessarily bad if you also have the best and most effective workforce, which produces more products of better quality. Pay policies are one of the most important human resource tools for encouraging desired employee behaviours and discouraging undesired behaviours. Therefore, organizations must evaluate pay as more than a cost, but also as an investment that can generate returns in attracting, retaining, and motivating a high-quality workforce. Of course, employers do not always have this much flexibility. Some companies are under intense pressure to charge low prices for their products, and some companies are trying to draw workers from a pool that is too small to satisfy all employers' needs.

Gathering Information About Market Pay

To compete for talent, organizations use **benchmarking**, a procedure in which an organization compares its own practices against those of successful competitors. Benchmarking involves the use of pay surveys. These provide information about the going rates of pay at competitors in the organization's product and labour markets. An organization can conduct its own surveys, but the federal government and other organizations make a great deal of data available already.

For example, the federal government's Job Futures website (www.jobfutures.ca) provides average hourly earnings data for occupations listed in the National Occupational Classification (NOC) discussed in Chapter 4. Many industry, trade, and professional groups also collect wage and salary data. Employers should check with the relevant groups to see what surveys are available. Consulting firms also will provide data, including the results of international surveys, and can tailor data to the organization's particular needs.

benchmarking
A procedure in which an organization compares its own practices against those of successful competitors.

Human resource professionals need to determine whether to gather data focusing on particular industries or on job categories. Industry-specific data is especially relevant for jobs with skills that are specific to the type of product. For jobs with skills that can be transferred to companies in other industries, surveys of job classifications will be more relevant.

4,5

Employee Judgments About Pay Fairness

In developing a pay structure, it is important to keep in mind employees' opinions about fairness. If employees perceive their pay as unfair they may experience pay dissatisfaction and be less motivated to achieve organizational goals.

Judging Fairness

Employees evaluate their pay relative to the pay of other employees. Social scientists have studied this kind of comparison and developed *equity theory* to describe how people make judgments about fairness.[7] According to equity theory, people measure outcomes such as pay in terms of their inputs. For example, an employee might think of her pay in terms of her master's degree, her 12 years of experience, and her 60-hour workweeks. To decide whether a certain level of pay is equitable, the person compares her ratio of outcomes and inputs with other people's outcome/input ratios, as shown in Figure 9.6. The person in the previous example might notice that an employee with less education or experience is earning more than she is (unfair) or that an employee who works 80 hours a week is earning more (fair). In general, employees compare their pay and contributions using several considerations:

- What they think employees in other organizations earn for doing the same job
- What they think other employees holding different jobs within the organization earn for doing work at the same or different levels
- What they think other employees in the organization earn for doing the same job as theirs

How employees respond to their impressions about equity can have a great impact on the organization. Typically, if employees see their pay as equitable, their attitudes and behaviour continue unchanged. If employees see themselves as receiving an advantage, they usually rethink the situation to see it as merely equitable. But if

FIGURE 9.6

Opinions About Pay Fairness

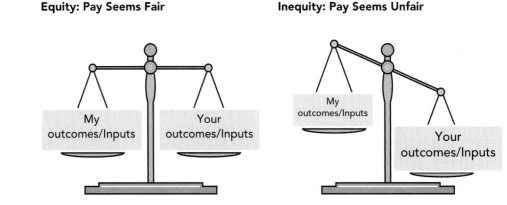

employees conclude that they are underrewarded, they are likely to make up the difference in one of three ways. They might put forth less effort (reducing their inputs), find a way to increase their outcomes (e.g., asking for a raise), or withdraw by leaving the organization or refusing to cooperate. Employees' beliefs about fairness also influence their willingness to accept transfers or promotions. For example, if a job change involves more work, employees will expect higher pay.

Job Structure: Relative Value of Jobs

2,5

Along with market forces and principles of fairness, organizations consider the relative contribution each job should make to the organization's overall performance. In general, an organization's top executives have a great impact on the organization's performance, so they tend to be paid much more than entry-level workers. Executives at the same level of the organization—for example, the vice-president of marketing and the vice-president of information systems—tend to be paid similar amounts. Creation of a pay structure requires that the organization develop an internal structure showing the relative contribution of its various jobs.

One typical way of doing this is with a **job evaluation**, an administrative procedure for measuring the relative internal worth of the organization's jobs. Usually, the organization does this by assembling and training a job evaluation committee, consisting of people familiar with the jobs to be evaluated. The committee often includes a human resource specialist and, if its budget permits, may hire an outside consultant.

job evaluation
An administrative procedure for measuring the relative internal worth of the organization's jobs.

To conduct a job evaluation, the committee identifies each job's *compensable factors*, meaning the characteristics of a job that the organization values and chooses to pay for. As shown in Table 9.2, an organization might consider the effort required and skill requirements of people performing computer-related jobs. Other compensable factors might include working conditions and responsibility. Based on the job attributes defined by job analysis (discussed in Chapter 4), the jobs are rated for each factor. The rater assigns each factor a certain number of points, giving more points to factors when they are considered more important and when the job requires a high level of that factor. Often the number of points comes from one of the *point manuals* published by trade groups and management consultants. If necessary, the organization can adapt the scores in the point manual to the organization's situation or even develop its own point manual. As in the example in Table 9.2, the scores for each factor are totalled to arrive at an overall evaluation for each job.

Job evaluations provide the basis for decisions about relative internal worth, that is, value of the job within the organization. According to the sample assessments in Table 9.2, the job of systems analyst is worth more to this organization than the job of

JOB TITLE	COMPENSABLE FACTORS				
	SKILL	EFFORT	RESPONSIBILITY	WORKING CONDITIONS	TOTAL
Data entry clerk	20	40	20	30	**110**
Computer programmer	80	60	50	20	**210**
Systems analyst	110	70	70	20	**270**

TABLE 9.2

Job Evaluation of Three Jobs

data entry clerk. Therefore, the organization would be willing to pay significantly more for the work of a systems analyst than it would for the work of a data entry clerk.

The organization may limit its pay survey to jobs evaluated as *key jobs*. These are jobs that have relatively stable content and are common among many organizations, so it is possible to obtain survey data about what people earn in these jobs. Organizations can make the process of creating a pay structure more practical by defining key jobs. Research for creating the pay structure is limited to the key jobs that play a significant role in the organization. Pay for the key jobs can be based on survey data, and pay for the organization's other jobs can be based on the organization's job structure. A job with a higher evaluation score than a particular key job would receive higher pay than that key job.

Pay Structure: Putting It All Together

As we described in the first section of this chapter, the pay structure reflects decisions about how much to pay (pay level) and the relative value of each job (job structure). The organization's pay structure should reflect what the organization knows about market forces, as well as its own unique goals and the relative contribution of each job to achieving the goals. By balancing this external and internal information, the organization's goal is to set levels of pay that employees will consider motivating. Organizations typically apply the information by establishing some combination of pay rates, pay grades, and pay ranges. Within this structure, they may state the pay in terms of a rate per hour, commonly called an **hourly wage**, a rate of pay for each unit produced, known as a **piecework rate**, or a rate of pay per month or year, called a **salary**.

Pay Rates

If the organization's main concern is to match what people are earning in comparable jobs, the organization can base pay directly on market research into as many of its key jobs as possible. To do this, the organization looks for survey data for each job title. If it finds data from more than one survey, it must weight the results according to their quality and relevance. The final number represents what the competition pays. In light of that knowledge, the organization decides what it will pay for the job.

The next step is to determine salaries for the nonkey jobs, for which the organization has no survey data. Instead, the person developing the pay structure creates a graph like the one in Figure 9.7. The vertical axis shows a range of possible pay rates, and the horizontal axis measures the points from the job evaluation. The analyst plots points according to the job evaluation and pay rate for each key job. Finally, the analyst fits a line, called a **pay policy line**, to the points plotted. (This can be done statistically on a computer, using a procedure called regression analysis.) Mathematically, this line shows the relationship between job evaluation and rate of pay. Using this line, the analyst can estimate the market pay level for a given job evaluation. Looking at the graph gives approximate numbers, or the regression analysis will provide an equation for calculating the rate of pay.

The pay policy line reflects the pay structure in the market, which does not always match rates in the organization (see key job F in Figure 9.7). Survey data may show that people in certain jobs are actually earning significantly more or less than the amount shown on the pay policy line. For example, some kinds of expertise are in short supply. People with that expertise can command higher salaries, because they

hourly wage
Rate of pay for each hour worked.

piecework rate
Rate of pay for each unit produced.

salary
Rate of pay for each week, month or year worked.

pay policy line
A graphed line showing the mathematical relationship between job evaluation points and pay rate.

FIGURE 9.7

Pay Policy Lines

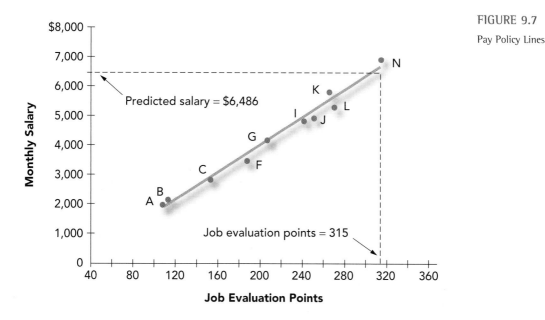

can easily leave one employer to get higher pay somewhere else. Suppose, in contrast, that local businesses have laid off many warehouse employees. Because so many of these workers are looking for jobs, organizations may be able to pay them less than the rate that job evaluation points would suggest.

When job structure and market data conflict in these ways, organizations have to decide on a way to resolve the two. One approach is to stick to the job evaluations and pay according to the employees' worth to the organization. Organizations that do so will be paying more or less than they have to, so they will likely have more difficulty competing for customers or employees. A way to moderate this approach is to consider the importance of each position to the organization's goals.[8] If a position is critical for meeting the organization's goals, paying more than competitors pay may be worthwhile.

At the other extreme, the organization could base pay entirely on market forces. However, this approach also has some practical drawbacks. One is that employees may conclude that pay rates are unfair. Two vice-presidents or two supervisors will expect to receive similar pay because their responsibilities are similar. If the differences between their pay are large, because of different market rates, the lower-paid employee will likely be dissatisfied. Also, if the organization's development plans include rotating managers through different assignments, the managers will be reluctant to participate if managers in some departments receive lower pay. Organizations therefore must weigh all the objectives of their pay structure to arrive at suitable rates.

Pay Grades

A large organization could have hundreds or even thousands of different jobs. Setting a pay rate for each job would be extremely complex. Therefore, many organizations group jobs into **pay grades**—sets of jobs having similar worth or content, grouped together to establish rates of pay. For example, the organization could establish five pay grades, with the same pay available to employees holding any job within the same grade.

pay grades
Sets of jobs having similar worth or content, grouped together to establish rates of pay.

A drawback of pay grades is that grouping jobs will result in rates of pay for individual jobs that do not precisely match the levels specified by the market and the organization's job structure. Suppose, for example, that the organization groups together its senior accountants (with a job evaluation of 255 points) and its senior systems analysts (with a job evaluation of 270 points). Surveys might show that the market rate of pay for systems analysts is higher than that for accountants. In addition, the job evaluations give more points to systems analysts. Even so, for simplicity's sake, the organization pays the same rate for the two jobs, because they are in the same pay grade. The organization would have to pay more than the market requires for accountants or pay less than the market rate for systems analysts (so it would probably have difficulty recruiting and retaining them).

Pay Ranges

pay ranges
A set of possible pay rates defined by a minimum, maximum, and midpoint of pay for employees holding a particular job or a job within a particular pay grade or band.

Usually, organizations want some flexibility in setting pay for individual jobs. They want to be able to pay the most valuable employees the highest amounts and to give rewards for performance. Flexibility also helps the organization balance conflicting information from market surveys and job evaluations. Therefore, pay structure usually includes a **pay range** for each job or pay grade. In other words, the organization establishes a minimum, maximum, and midpoint of pay for employees holding a particular job or a job within a particular pay grade or band. Employees holding the same job may receive somewhat different pay, depending on where their pay falls within the range.

A typical approach is to use the market rate or the pay policy line as the midpoint of a range for the job or pay grade. The minimum and maximum values for the range may also be based on market surveys of those amounts. Figure 9.8 shows an example of pay ranges based on the pay policy line in Figure 9.7. Notice that the jobs are

FIGURE 9.8

Sample Pay Grade Structure

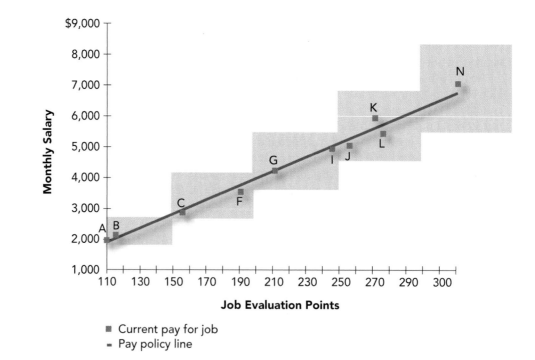

grouped into five pay grades, each with its own pay range. In this example, the range is widest for employees who are at higher levels in terms of their job evaluation points. That is because the performance of these higher-level employees will likely have more effect on the organization's performance, so the organization needs more latitude to reward them. For instance, as discussed earlier, the organization may want to select a higher point in the range to attract an employee who is more critical to achieving the organization's goals.

Usually pay ranges overlap somewhat, so that the highest pay in one grade is somewhat higher than the lowest pay in the next grade. Overlapping ranges gives the organization more flexibility in transferring employees among jobs, because transfers need not always involve a change in pay. On the other hand, the less overlap, the more important it is to earn promotions in order to keep getting raises. When the organization develops a pay structure, it may find that a few employees are being paid at rates that are above or below the range for their jobs. For example, an employee with exceptionally high seniority might earn above his range. Rates above the range are often called **red-circle rates**. In some cases, employees earning red-circle rates would receive no pay increases until they receive a promotion or until cost-of-living adjustments raise the pay range to include their pay rate. At the other extreme are **green-circle rates**, that is, rates below the pay range for a job. These employees usually would receive raises when the pay structure is put into practice; otherwise, their current pay rate signals that they are being paid less than their worth to the organization.

red-circle rate
Pay at a rate that falls above the pay range for the job.

green-circle rate
Pay at a rate that falls below the pay range for the job.

Alternatives to Job-Based Pay

The traditional and most widely used approach to developing a pay structure focuses on setting pay for jobs or groups of jobs.[9] This emphasis on jobs has some limitations. The precise definition of a job's responsibilities can contribute to an attitude that some activities "are not in my job description," at the expense of flexibility, innovation, quality, and customer service. Organizations may avoid change because it requires repeating the time-consuming process of creating job descriptions and related paperwork. Another change-related problem is that when the organization needs a new set of competencies, the existing pay structure may be rewarding the wrong behaviours. Finally, a pay structure that rewards employees for winning promotions may discourage them from gaining valuable experience through lateral career moves.

Organizations have responded to these problems with a number of alternatives to job-based pay structures. Some organizations have found greater flexibility through **broadbanding**, or reducing the number of levels in the organization's job structure. By combining more assignments into a single layer, organizations give managers more flexibility in making assignments and awarding pay increases. These broader groupings often are called *broad bands*. IBM recently changed from a pay structure with 5,000 job titles and 24 salary grades to one with 1,200 jobs and 10 bands. Broad bands reduce the opportunities for promoting employees, so organizations that eliminate layers in their job descriptions must find other ways to reward employees.

Another way organizations have responded to the limitations of job-based pay has been to move away from the link to jobs and toward pay structures that reward employees based on their competencies.[10] **Competency-based pay systems** are pay structures that set pay according to the employees' level of skill or knowledge and what they are capable of doing. Paying for competencies makes sense at organizations

L03 - Describe alternatives to job-based pay.

broadbanding
Reducing the number of levels in the organization's job structure.

competency-based pay systems
Pay structures that set pay according to the employees' levels of skill or knowledge and what they are capable of doing.

where changing technology requires employees to continually widen and deepen their knowledge. Competency-based pay also supports efforts to involve employees and enrich jobs because it encourages employees to add to their knowledge so they can make decisions in many areas. In this way, competency-based pay helps organizations become more flexible and innovative. More generally, competency-based pay can encourage a climate of learning and adaptability and give employees a broader view of how the organization functions.

Of course, competency-based pay has its own disadvantages.[11] It rewards employees for acquiring skills but does not provide a way to ensure that employees can use their new skills. The result may be that the organization is paying employees more for learning skills that the employer is not benefiting from. The challenge for HRM is to design work so that the work design and pay structure support one another.

2,5

LO4 - Describe how organizations recognize individual, team, and organizational performance through the use of incentives.

incentive (variable) pay
Forms of pay linked to an employee's performance as an individual, group member, or organization member.

Incentive (Variable) Pay

The first part of this chapter discussed the framework for total rewards and setting pay for jobs. Now we focus on using pay to recognize and reward employees' contributions to the organization's success.

In contrast to decisions about pay structure, organizations have wide discretion in setting performance-related pay, called **incentive (variable) pay** or *pay for performance*. Organizations can tie incentive pay to individual performance, profits, or many other measures of success. They select incentives based on their costs, expected influence on performance, and fit with the organization's broader HR and company policies and goals. These decisions are significant. A study of 150 organizations found that the way organizations paid employees was strongly associated with their level of profitability.[12]

Along with wages and salaries, many organizations offer *incentive pay*—that is, pay specifically designed to energize, direct, or influence employees' behaviour. According to the Conference Board of Canada, 83 percent of Canadian organizations have at least one annual variable pay plan. These plans are particularly popular in the private sector—93 percent of companies reported having one or more plans. Fifty-six percent of public sector organizations also have one or more variable pay plans.[13] Incentive pay is influential because the amount paid is linked to certain predefined behaviours or outcomes. For example, an organization can pay a salesperson a *commission* for closing a sale, or the members of a production department can earn a *bonus* for meeting a monthly production goal. Knowing they can earn extra money for closing sales or meeting departmental goals, the employees often try harder or get more creative than they might without the incentive pay. In addition, the policy of offering higher pay for higher performance may make an organization attractive to high performers when it is trying to recruit and retain these valuable employees.[14]

For incentive pay to motivate employees to contribute to the organization's success, the pay plans must be well designed. According to a recent study by Hewitt Associates, a global HR consulting firm, approximately 83 percent of companies using incentive pay say "this approach is only somewhat successful or not successful at all."[15] In designing incentive pay plans, organizations should consider whether the pay encourages the kinds of behaviour that are most needed, whether employees believe they have the ability and resources to meet the performance standards, and whether they value the rewards and think the pay plan is fair.

Since incentive pay is linked to particular outcomes or behaviours, the organization is encouraging them to demonstrate those desired outcomes and behaviours. As obvious as that may sound, the implications are more complicated. If incentive pay is extremely rewarding, employees may focus on only the performance measures rewarded under the plan and ignore measures that are not rewarded. Many call centres pay employees based on how many calls they handle, as an incentive to work quickly and efficiently. However, speedy call handling does not necessarily foster good customer relationships. Organizations may combine a number of incentives so employees do not focus on one measure to the exclusion of others.

Another criticism is the concern that individual pay for performance can "foster an individualistic culture or a culture of entitlement."[16] Employees must also believe they have the ability and resources to meet the performance standards and that the performance standards are under their control. As we will discuss in the section on rewards for organizational performance, this is a challenge in the case of incentives based on an organization's profits or stock price. Employees at lower levels of the organization may doubt that they have much influence over these performance measures. Therefore, these incentives likely will not have much effect on these employees' behaviour, at least in large companies.

Other attitudes that influence the success of incentive pay include whether employees value the rewards and think the pay plan is fair. Most, if not all, employees value pay, but it is important to remember that earning money is not the only reason people try to do a good job. As discussed in other chapters (see Chapters 3, 7, and 12), people also want interesting work, appreciation for their efforts, flexibility, and a sense of belonging to the work group—not to mention the inner satisfaction of work well done. Therefore, a complete plan for compensating and rewarding employees has many components, from pay to work design to developing managers so they can exercise positive leadership.

We will now identify elements of incentive pay systems. We consider each option's strengths and limitations with regard to these principles. The many kinds of incentive pay fall into three broad categories: incentives linked to individual, group, or organizational performance. Choices from these categories should consider not only their strengths and weaknesses, but also their fit with the organization's goals. The choice of incentive pay may affect not only the level of motivation, but also the kinds of employees who are attracted to and stay with the organization. For example, there is some evidence that organizations with team-based rewards will tend to attract employees who are more team-oriented.[17]

Pay for Individual Performance

Organizations may reward individual performance with incentives such as piecework rates, standard hour plans, merit pay, individual bonuses, and sales commissions. These alternatives are summarized in Figure 9.9.

Piecework Rates

As an incentive to work efficiently, some organizations pay production workers a piecework rate, a wage based on the amount they produce. This rate is often paid in addition to employees' base pay. The amount paid per unit is set at a level that rewards employees for above-average production volume. For example, suppose that on

FIGURE 9.9

Types of Pay for Individual Performance

| Piecework Rates | Standard Hours Plan | Merit Pay | Performance Bonus | Sales Commissions |

average, assemblers can finish ten components in an hour. If the organization wants to pay its average assemblers $12 per hour, it can pay a piecework rate of $12 per hour divided by ten components/hour, or $1.20 per component. An assembler who produces the average of ten components per hour earns an amount equal to $12 per hour. An assembler who produces 12 components in an hour would earn $1.20 × 12, or $14.40 each hour.

An obvious advantage of piece rates is the direct link between how much work the employee does and the amount the employee earns. In spite of their advantages, piece rates are relatively rare for several reasons.[18] Most jobs, including those of managers, have no physical output, so it is hard to develop an appropriate performance measure. This type of incentive is most suited for very routine, standardized jobs with output that is easy to measure. For complex jobs or jobs with hard-to-measure outputs, piecework plans do not apply very well. Also, unless a plan is well designed to include performance standards, it may not reward employees for focusing on quality or customer satisfaction if it interferes with the day's output. (See Figure 9.10.)

FIGURE 9.10

How Incentives Sometimes "Work"

SOURCE: DILBERT, reprinted by permission of United Features Syndicate, Inc.

Standard Hour Plans

Another quantity-oriented incentive for production workers is the **standard hour plan**, an incentive plan that pays workers extra for work done in less than a preset "standard time." The organization determines a standard time to complete a task, such as tuning up a car engine. If the mechanic completes the work in less than the standard time, the mechanic receives an amount of pay equal to the wage for the full standard time. Suppose the standard time for tuning up an engine is two hours. If the mechanic finishes a tuneup in 1½ hours, the mechanic earns two hours' worth of pay in 1½ hours. Working that fast over the course of a week could add significantly to the mechanic's pay.

In terms of their pros and cons, standard hour plans are much like piecework plans. They encourage employees to work as fast as they can, but not necessarily to care about quality or customer service. Also, they only succeed if employees want the extra money more than they want to work at a pace that feels comfortable.

standard hour plan
An incentive plan that pays workers extra for work done in less than a preset "standard time."

Merit Pay

Almost all organizations have established some program of **merit pay**—a system of linking pay increases to ratings on performance appraisals. (Chapter 8 described the content and use of performance appraisals.) Merit pay is most common for management and professional employees.

An advantage of merit pay is that it provides a method for rewarding performance in all of the dimensions measured in the organization's performance management system. If that system is appropriately designed to measure all the important job behaviours, then the merit pay is linked to the behaviours the organization desires. This link seems logical, although so far there is little research showing the effectiveness of merit pay.[19]

A drawback of merit pay, from the employer's standpoint, is that it can quickly become expensive. Managers at a majority of organizations rate most employees' performance in the top two categories (out of four or five).[20] Therefore, the majority of employees are eligible for the biggest merit increases, and their pay rises rapidly. This cost is one reason that some organizations have established guidelines about the percentage of employees that may receive the top rating, as discussed in Chapter 8.

Another drawback of merit pay is that it makes assumptions that may be misleading. Rewarding employees for superior performance ratings assumes that those ratings depend on employees' ability and motivation. But performance may actually depend on forces outside the employee's control, such as managers' rating biases, the level of cooperation from coworkers, or the degree to which the organization gives employees the authority, training, and resources they need. Under these conditions, employees will likely conclude that the merit pay system is unfair. The HR How-To box suggests ways to set up a merit pay system so that is maximizes the advantages of this type of pay while minimizing the drawbacks.

merit pay
A system of linking pay increases to ratings on performance appraisals.

Performance Bonuses

Like merit pay, performance bonuses reward individual performance, but bonuses are not rolled into base pay. The employee must re-earn them during each performance

HR   HOW-TO

Implementing a Merit Pay Program

Increasingly, companies are linking bonuses and pay increases to employees' performance. This means employees will see the money only if they can show they have met or exceeded goals. One reason is that in times of low growth and low inflation, the budgets available to reward employees are smaller. For the pay to have an impact, companies need to ensure that the money is directed toward the best performers.

An important requirement for merit pay is that the employees understand what they have to do to receive it. Employers should provide frequent written information about the company's merit pay. Employees and their supervisors should be sure they understand how to define excellent performance. They also need to know when failure to meet standards will result in their receiving no pay increase. When the measures are clear, managers are better able to withstand the temptation to reward everyone in order to avoid the discomfort of telling certain employees that they will not be receiving merit pay. At the same time, the employees can see that the system is fair.

Throughout the year, employees should be able to see whether they are making progress toward meeting those requirements. For individual performance, managers need to provide frequent personal feedback. In organizations that reward team performance, managers can post charts showing both goals and progress toward those goals. This feedback gives employees a chance to improve before merit pay decisions are made.

When pay increases or bonuses are awarded, employees should not be surprised. A surprise means the communication throughout the year was not adequate. At the time employees receive information about merit pay awards, they should be fully aware of what their goals were, whether they were meeting goals, and what the link between goal achievement and merit pay is.

Even when an organization clearly communicates its expectations and when managers give frequent feedback, it still feels uncomfortable to tell a poorly performing employee that he or she will not receive any pay raise that year. So, a merit pay system will be more successful if the company also provides managers with training and coaching in how to deliver bad news. For example, role-playing exercises can help managers develop skills in navigating difficult conversations. The company may also give managers flexibility—for example, allowing them to delay a pay increase for several months, to give the employee a chance to improve.

SOURCE: Jeff D. Opdyke, "Getting a Bonus Instead of a Raise," *The Wall Street Journal*, December 29, 2004, pp. D1–D2; and Susan J. Wells, "No Results, No Raise, *HR Magazine*, May 2005, http://web6.infotrac.galegroup.com.

period. In some cases, the bonus is a one-time reward. Bonuses may also be linked to objective performance measures rather than subjective ratings. Bonuses for individual performance can be extremely effective and give the organization great flexibility in deciding what kinds of behaviour to reward.

Many salespeople in the auto industry earn a straight commission, meaning that 100 percent of their pay comes from commission instead of a salary. What type of individual might enjoy a job like this?

Sales Commissions

A variation on piece rates and bonuses is the payment of **commissions**, or pay calculated as a percentage of sales. For instance, a furniture salesperson might earn commissions equalling 6 percent of the price of the furniture the person sells during the period. Selling a $2,000 sofa would add $120 to the salesperson's commissions for the period. At most organizations today, commissions range from 5 to 20 percent of sales.[21] In a growth-oriented organization, sales commissions need not be limited to salespeople. Many of the technical experts at Scientific & Engineering Solutions are eligible for commissions and bonuses tied to the profitability of the sales they help to close. The HR How-To box provides additional suggestions for incentive pay.

commissions
Incentive pay calculated as a percentage of sales.

Pay for Team Performance

Employers may address the drawbacks of individual incentives by including team incentives in the organization's compensation plan. To earn team incentives, employees must cooperate and share knowledge so that the entire group can meet its performance targets. As shown in Figure 9.11, common team incentives include gainsharing, bonuses, and team awards.

Gainsharing

Organizations that want employees to focus on efficiency may adopt a **gainsharing** program, which measures increases in productivity and effectiveness and distributes a portion of each gain to employees. For example, if a factory enjoys a productivity gain worth $30,000, half the gain might be the company's share. The other $15,000 would be distributed among the employees in the factory. Knowing that they can

gainsharing
Group incentive program that measures improvements in productivity and effectiveness and distributes a portion of each gain to employees.

FIGURE 9.11

Types of Pay for Team Performance

Gainsharing   Bonuses   Team Awards

enjoy a financial benefit from helping the company be more productive, employees supposedly will look for ways to work more efficiently and improve the way the factory operates.

Gainsharing addresses the challenge of identifying appropriate performance measures for complex jobs. Even for simpler jobs, setting acceptable standards and measuring performance can be complicated. Gainsharing frees employees to determine how to improve their own and their group's performance. It also broadens employees' focus beyond their individual interests. But in contrast to profit sharing, discussed later, it keeps the performance measures within a range of activity that most employees believe they can influence. Organizations can enhance the likelihood of a gain by providing a means for employees to share knowledge and make suggestions, as we will discuss later in this chapter.

Gainsharing is most likely to succeed when organizations provide the right conditions. Among the conditions identified, the following are among the most common:[22]

- Management commitment
- Need for change or strong commitment to continuous improvement
- Management acceptance and encouragement of employee input
- High levels of cooperation and interaction
- Employment security
- Information sharing on productivity and costs
- Goal setting
- Commitment of all involved parties to the process of change and improvement
- Performance standard and calculation that employees understand and consider fair and that is closely related to managerial objectives
- Employees who value working in groups

Happy sales staff look forward to getting their one-time bonus cheques, along with most of The Brick's 5,700 employees across Canada.

The Brick, the Edmonton-based furniture chain, recently surprised and delighted its employees by announcing a one-time bonus to almost all of its 5,700 Canadian employees. The bonuses will be based on years of service and were announced by the Brick's chairman, Bill Comrie. "[Comrie] knows it's the people around him who helped make him who he is." "He wants all of his team to be winners."[23]

Team Bonuses and Awards

In contrast to gainsharing plans, which typically reward the performance of all employees at a facility, bonuses for team performance tend to be for smaller work groups.[24] These bonuses reward the members of a group for attaining a specific goal, usually measured in terms of physical output. Team awards are similar to team bonuses, but they are more likely to use a broad range of performance measures, such as cost savings, successful completion of a project, or even meeting deadlines.

Both types of incentives have the advantage that they encourage group or team members to cooperate so that they can achieve their goal. However, depending on the reward system, competition among individuals may be replaced by competition among teams. Competition may be healthy in some situations, as when teams try to outdo one another in satisfying customers. On the downside, competition may also prevent necessary cooperation among teams. To avoid this, the organization should carefully set the performance goals for these incentives so that concern for costs or sales does not obscure other objectives, such as quality, customer service, and ethical behaviour.

Team members that meet a sales goal or a product development team that meets a deadline or successfully launches a product may be rewarded with a bonus for team performance. What are some advantages and disadvantages of team bonuses?

2,5

Pay for Organizational Performance

Two important ways organizations measure their performance are in terms of their profits and their stock price. In a competitive marketplace, profits result when an organization is efficiently providing products that customers want at a price they are willing to pay. Stock is the owners' investment in a corporation; when the stock price is rising, the value of that investment is growing. Rather than trying to figure out what performance measures will motivate employees to do the things that generate high profits and a rising stock price, many organizations offer incentive pay tied to those organizational performance measures. The expectation is that employees will focus on what is best for the organization.

These organization-level incentives can motivate employees to align their activities with the organization's goals. Linking incentives to the organization's profits or stock price exposes employees to a high degree of risk. Profits and stock price can soar very high very fast, but they can also fall, as witnessed by many wary investors. The result is a great deal of uncertainty about the amount of incentive pay each employee will receive in each period. Therefore, these kinds of incentive pay are likely to be most effective in organizations that emphasize growth and innovation, which tend to need employees who thrive in a risk-taking environment.[25]

Profit Sharing

profit sharing
Incentive pay in which payments are a percentage of the organization's profits and do not become part of the employees' base salary.

Under **profit sharing**, payments are a percentage of the organization's profits and do not become part of the employees' base salary. Organizations use profit sharing for a number of reasons. It may encourage employees to think more like owners, taking a broad view of what they need to do in order to make the organization more effective. They are more likely to cooperate and less likely to focus on narrow self-interest. Also, profit sharing has the practical advantage of costing less when the organization is experiencing financial difficulties. If the organization has little or no profit, this incentive pay is small or nonexistent, so employers may not need to rely as much on layoffs to reduce costs.[26]

An organization setting up a profit-sharing plan should consider what to do if profits fall. If the economy slows and profit-sharing payments disappear along with profits, employees may become discouraged or angry. One way to avoid this kind of problem is to design profit-sharing plans to reward employees for high profits but not penalize them when profits fall. This solution may be more satisfactory to employees but does not offer the advantage of reducing labour costs without layoffs during economic downturns.

Given the limitations of profit-sharing plans, one strategy is to use them as a component of a pay system that includes other kinds of pay more directly linked to individual behaviour. This increases employees' commitment to organizational goals while addressing concerns about fairness.

Stock Ownership

While profit-sharing plans are intended to encourage employees to "think like owners," a stock ownership plan actually makes employees part owners of the organization. Like profit sharing, employee ownership is intended as a way to encourage employees to focus on the success of the organization as a whole. The drawbacks of stock ownership as a form of incentive pay are similar to those of profit sharing. Specifically, it may not have a strong effect on individuals' motivation. Employees

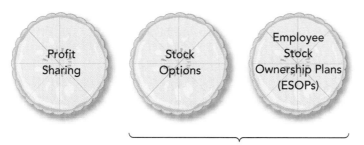

FIGURE 9.12

Types of Pay for
Organizational
Performance

may not see a strong link between their actions and the company's stock price, especially in larger organizations. The link between pay and performance is even harder to appreciate because the financial benefits mostly come when the stock is sold—typically when the employee leaves the organization.

Ownership programs usually take the form of *stock options* or *employee stock ownership plans*. These are illustrated in Figure 9.12.

Stock Options

One way to distribute stock to employees is to grant them **stock options**—the right to buy a certain number of shares of stock at a specified price. (Purchasing the stock is called *exercising* the option.) Suppose that in 2009 a company's employees received options to purchase the company's stock at $10 per share. The employees will benefit if the stock price rises above $10 per share, because they can pay $10 for something (a share of stock) that is worth more than $10. If in 2012 the stock is worth $30, they can exercise their options and buy stock for $10 a share. If they want to, they can sell their stock for the market price of $30, receiving a gain of $20 for each share of stock. Of course, stock prices can also fall. If the 2012 stock price is only $8, the employees would not bother to exercise the options.

Traditionally, organizations have granted stock options to their executives. In recent years, many organizations pushed eligibility for options further down in the organization's structure. For example, it is estimated there are 1,000 Google employees who have become millionaires from stock grants and options.[27] The share of companies granting stock options to at least half of their employees has grown from less than one-quarter to more than half. Some studies suggest that organizations perform better when a large percentage of top and middle managers are eligible for long-term incentives such as stock options. This evidence is consistent with the idea of encouraging employees to think like owners.[28]

Recent scandals have drawn attention to another challenge of using stock options as incentive pay. As with other performance measures, employees may focus so much on stock price that they lose sight of other goals, including ethical behaviour. Ideally, managers would bring about an increase in stock price by adding value in terms of efficiency, innovation, and customer satisfaction. But there are other, unethical ways to increase stock price by tricking investors into thinking the organization is more valuable and more profitable than it actually is. Hiding losses and inflating the recorded value of revenues are just two ways some companies have boosted stock prices, enriching managers until these misdeeds come to light. The bankruptcy of WorldCom demonstrated on a massive scale that the short-term benefits of an inflated stock price may not be in a company's long-term best interests. Criticism has also been aimed at Nortel Networks' former CEO, John Roth, who received stock

stock options
Rights to buy a
certain number of
shares of stock at a
specified price.

option grants that "allowed him to walk away fabulously wealthy while millions of Canadians tossed their retirement plans in the fire."[29]

Employee Stock Ownership Plans

employee stock ownership plan (ESOP)
An arrangement in which the organization distributes shares of stock to all its employees by placing it in a trust.

While stock options are most often used with top management, a broader arrangement is the **employee stock ownership plan (ESOP)**. In an ESOP, the organization distributes shares of stock to its employees by placing the stock into a trust managed on the employees' behalf. Employees receive regular reports on the value of their stock, and when they leave the organization, they may sell the stock to the organization or (if it is a publicly traded company) on the open market.

For example, WestJet's Share Purchase Program enables WestJetters to receive up to 20 percent of their salaries in WestJet shares. Shares can be purchased as common shares or can be directed into RRSPs with WestJet matching the employee's contributions.[30]

ESOPs are the most common form of employee ownership. ESOPs raise a number of issues. On the negative side, they carry a significant risk for employees. Problems with the company's performance therefore can take away significant value from the ESOP. Many companies set up ESOPs to hold retirement funds, so these risks directly affect employees' retirement income.

Still, ESOPs can be attractive to employers. Along with tax and financing advantages, ESOPs give employers a way to build pride in and commitment to the organization. Employees have a right to participate in votes by shareholders (if the stock is registered on a national exchange, such as the TSX).[31] This means employees participate somewhat in corporate-level decision making.

Refer to Table 9.3 for a summary of the advantages and disadvantages of individual, team, and organizational incentives.

TABLE 9.3

An Overview of Incentive Pay

CRITERION	INCENTIVES	ADVANTAGES	DISADVANTAGES
Individual performance	Piecework rates, sales commissions	Exert most powerful impact on productivity.	Do not promote teamwork or ensure a corresponding increase in product quality. May be difficult to measure.
Team performance	Gainsharing, team-based incentive plans	Encourage teamwork.	Yield a moderate impact on productivity.
Organizational performance	Profit sharing and stock sharing, including stock ownership, stock options, and employee stock ownership plan	Increase shareholder returns and company profit.	Generate only a small increase in productivity.

SOURCE: "Implementing Total Rewards Strategies," *SHRM Foundation*, p. 6, www.shrm.org/FOUNDATION/07RewardsStratReport.pdf, retrieved May 6, 2008.

Processes That Make Incentives Work

Communication and employee participation can contribute to a belief that the organization's pay structure is fair. In the same way, the process by which the organization creates and administers incentive pay can help it use incentives to create a motivational work environment. The monetary rewards of gainsharing, for example, can improve productivity,[32] but the organization can set up the process to be even more effective. In a study of an automotive parts plant, productivity rose when the gainsharing plan added employee participation in the form of monthly meetings with managers to discuss the gainsharing plan and ways to increase productivity. A related study asked employees what motivated them to participate actively in the plan (e.g., by making suggestions for improvement). According to employees, other factors besides the pay itself were important—especially the ability to influence and control the way their work was done.[33]

Participation in Decisions

Employee participation in incentive-related decisions can be part of a general move toward employee involvement. If employees are involved in decisions about incentive pay plans and employees' eligibility for incentives, the process of creating and administering these plans can be more complex.[34] There is also a risk that employees will make decisions that are in their interests, at the expense of the organization's interests. However, employees have hands-on knowledge about the kinds of behaviour that can help the organization perform well, and they can see whether individuals are displaying that behaviour.[35] Therefore, in spite of the potential risks, employee participation can contribute to the success of an incentive plan. This is especially true when monetary incentives encourage the monitoring of performance and when the organization fosters a spirit of trust and cooperation.

Providing Employee Benefits

Hewitt Associates signals to its employees that it cares about them, body, mind, and spirit. Employees participate in plans that help them pay for medical, dental, and vision care expenses, stop-smoking programs, and care expenses for sick children. Employees who travel on business can receive reimbursement for overnight dependant care and overnight care for their pets. Employees enjoy paid time off for vacations and holidays, plus additional "Splash" time off in their fifth year of service and every five years after that. Through the LifeWorks referral service, Hewitt employees can find help with family, education, legal, and financial issues. A tuition reimbursement program pays 85 percent of employees' tuition for approved courses. The company also encourages employees to participate in charitable activities. Employees who wish to volunteer time in their communities can receive up to two days of paid time off. These and other benefits attract qualified employees and keep them loyal to Hewitt.[36]

Like Hewitt's employees, employees at almost every organization receive more than dollars and cents in exchange for their efforts. They also receive a package of **employee benefits** compensation in forms other than cash. Besides the use of corporate fitness centres, examples include paid vacation time, employer-paid health insurance, and pension plans, among a wide range of possibilities.

employee benefits
Compensation in forms other than cash.

The following section describes the content of an employee benefits and services package and the way organizations administer these employee benefits and services. We begin by discussing the important role of benefits as a part of employee rewards.

The Role of Employee Benefits

As part of the total rewards provided to employees, benefits serve functions similar to pay. Benefits contribute to attracting, retaining, and motivating employees. Different employees look for different types of benefits. Employers need to examine their benefits package regularly to see whether they still meet employees' needs and expectations. At the same time, benefits packages are more complex than pay structures, so benefits are harder for employees to understand and appreciate. Even if employers spend large sums on benefits and services, if employees do not understand how to use them or why they are valuable, the cost of the benefits will be largely wasted.[37] Employers need to communicate effectively so that the benefits succeed in motivating employees.

Employees have come to expect that benefits will help them maintain economic security. Canada Pension/Quebec Pension, company pension plans, and retirement savings plans help employees prepare for their retirement. Insurance plans help to protect employees from unexpected costs such as prescription drugs. This important role of benefits is one reason that some benefits are subject to government regulation. Benefits, such as Employment Insurance, are required by law.

Even though many kinds of benefits are not required by law, they have become so common that today's employees expect them. Many employers find that attracting qualified workers requires them to provide health and retirement benefits of some sort. A large employer without such benefits would be highly unusual and would have difficulty competing in the labour market. A national survey conducted by Ipsos-Reid found that Canadian employees value their health benefits. As reported by Benefits Canada, 91 percent of survey respondents said that other than salary, a "good job" was defined as having a good benefits package—"benefits are serving as a proxy or a marker for a good workplace."[38]

Like other forms of compensation and rewards, benefits impose significant costs. The number one concern of Canadian employee benefit specialists, according to Deloitte's *Top Five Total Rewards Priorities Survey for 2008*, "the mounting cost of total rewards still remains a high priority for survey respondents, particularly health care benefits."[39] An organization managing its labour costs must pay careful attention to the cost of its employee benefits.

Overall, employers are concerned about balancing various issues related to benefits provided to employees. Several forces have made benefits and services a significant part of compensation packages. One is that laws require employers to provide certain benefits, such as contributions to Canada Pension Plan and Employment Insurance. Also, tax laws can make benefits favourable. For example, employees do not pay income taxes on most benefits they receive, but they pay income taxes on cash compensation. Therefore, an employee who receives a $1,000 raise "takes home" less than the full $1,000, but an employee who receives an additional $1,000 worth of benefits receives the full benefits. Another cost advantage of paying benefits is that employers, especially large ones, often can get a better deal on insurance or other programs than employees can obtain on their own. Finally, some employers assemble creative benefits packages that set them apart in the competition for talent—for example, InSystems, described at the beginning of this chapter.

1,5

Benefits Required by Law

Governments require various forms of security to protect workers from the financial hardships of being out of work. In general, the Canada Pension Plan/Quebec Pension Plan provides support for retired workers, Employment Insurance assists workers who are unemployed involuntarily, and workers' compensation provides benefits and services to workers injured on the job. Employers must also provide unpaid leave for certain family and medical needs. Because these benefits are required by law, employers cannot gain an advantage in the labour market by offering them, nor can they design the nature of these benefits. Rather, the emphasis must be on complying with the details of the law.

LO6 - Summarize the types of employee benefits offered by employers.

Canada Pension Plan (CPP)/Quebec Pension Plan (QPP)

The **Canada Pension Plan (CPP)** and the **Quebec Pension Plan (QPP)** (in Quebec), established in 1966, cover all workers in Canada who are age 18 and older and have annual income exceeding $3,500. CPP/QPP is a mandatory **contributory plan** that provides retirement pensions, disability benefits, and survivor benefits.

Workers who meet eligibility requirements receive the retirement benefits according to their age and earnings history. If they elect to begin receiving benefits at age 65, they can receive full benefits, or if eligible to begin receiving benefits at age 60, they receive benefits at a permanently reduced level. For example, if the individual elects to commence their pension at age 60, they will receive 30 percent less than they would receive if they started receiving their pension at age 65. In 2008, the maximum monthly CPP benefit was $884.58.[40]

Canada Pension Plan (CPP)/Quebec Pension Plan (QPP)
A contributory, mandatory plan that provides retirement pensions, disability benefits, and survivor benefits.

contributory plan
All costs of the plan are funded by employees, employers, and the plan's own investments.

Employment Insurance (EI)

The **Employment Insurance (EI)** program provides temporary financial assistance to unemployed workers who have lost their jobs through no fault of their own, while they look for another job or upgrade their skills. Coverage is also extended to eligible workers who are sick, are pregnant, or are caring for a newborn or adopted child. In addition, EI can assist employees when they are caring for a gravely ill family member.

Employment Insurance (EI)
A federally mandated program to provide temporary financial assistance to unemployed Canadians.

Workers' Compensation

Decades ago, workers who suffered work-related injury or illness had to bear the cost unless they won a lawsuit against their employer. Those who sued often lost the case because of the defences available to employers. Today, the provinces have passed **Workers' Compensation Acts**, which help workers with the expenses resulting from job-related accidents and illnesses.[41] These laws operate under a principle of *no-fault liability*, meaning that an employee does not need to show that the employer was grossly negligent in order to receive compensation, and the employer is protected

Workers' Compensation Acts
Provincial programs that provide benefits to workers who suffer work-related injuries or illnesses.

from lawsuits. The employer loses this protection if it intentionally contributes to a dangerous workplace. The benefits fall into three major categories:

1. Wage loss benefits
2. Medical services
3. Rehabilitative services

Compensation varies from province to province but is typically 80 percent of the worker's earnings before the disability. The benefits are tax-free; however, the person receiving the benefits must report them to the Canada Revenue Agency.

Workers' compensation laws are intended to protect the incomes of workers injured on the job, without the workers having to sue or the employers having to admit responsibility.

Workers' compensation is entirely funded by employers—neither workers nor the government contribute. The amount employers pay depends on the industry and kinds of occupations involved as well as the size of the employer's payroll. Organizations can minimize the cost of this benefit by keeping workplaces safe and making employees and their managers conscious of safety issues, as discussed in Chapter 3. Benefits continue as long as the employee is unable to work.

Optional Benefits Programs

Other types of benefits are optional. These include various kinds of insurance, retirement plans, and paid leave. Part-time workers often receive fewer benefits than full-time employees. The most widely offered benefits are paid leave for vacations and holidays (that exceed the legally required minimums specified in employment/labour standards legislation), life and medical insurance, and retirement plans. In general, benefits packages at smaller companies are more limited than at larger companies. The extent to which the employer pays for the benefit varies widely among organizations. Some organizations require employees to pay a significant percentage of the premiums for insurance plans such as dental coverage. Other organizations pick up 100 percent of the premiums.

Benefits such as health insurance usually extend to employees' dependants. Today, to ensure an employer does not face a charge of discrimination where the relevant jurisdiction includes sexual orientation and/or marital status as a protected ground of discrimination, employers cover domestic partners. Typically, a domestic partner is an adult non-relative who lives with the employee in a relationship defined as permanent and financially interdependent.

As organizations continue to contain the increasing costs of providing employee benefits a variety of alternatives may be considered. As is outlined in Table 9.4, many Canadian organizations are considering increasing employee contributions (premiums) or increasing deductibles and/or requiring co-payment of associated costs.

Paid Leave

Employment/labour standards legislation outlines minimum vacation entitlements and paid holidays. Many employers provide vacation and holidays in addition to the minimum legislated requirements. Some organizations also offer additional days off for personal reasons or to contribute their time to a charitable organization.

TABLE 9.4

Keeping the Lid on Benefits

Respondents from survey of 130 Canadian organizations were asked what cost reduction measures they are using or considering. The following table provides their answers, in percentages:

BENEFIT	BEING CONSIDERED	NOT BEING CONSIDERED
Eliminated or reduced coverage	15	78
Increased employee contributions	18	62
Increased deductible and/ or co-payments	18	65
Implementation or expansion of a disability management program	21	65

SOURCE: Hewitt Associates, "HR's Cost Control," *Canadian HR Reporter,* May 31, 2004, p. 2.

Sick leave programs pay employees for days not worked because of illness. The amount of sick leave is often based on length of service, so that it accumulates over time—for example, one day added to sick leave for each month of service. Employers have to decide how many sick days to grant and whether to let them continue accumulating year after year. If sick days accumulate without limit, employees can "save" them in case of disability. Some employers let sick days accumulate for only a year, and unused sick days "disappear" at year-end. This may provide an unintended incentive to use up sick days. Some healthy employees may call in sick near the end of the year so that they can obtain the benefit of the paid leave before it disappears.

An organization's policies for time off may include other forms of paid and unpaid leave. For a workforce that values flexibility, the organization may offer paid *personal days*, days off that employees may schedule according to their personal needs, with the supervisor's approval. Typically, organizations offer a few personal days in addition to sick leave. *Floating holidays* are paid holidays that vary from year to year. The organization may schedule floating holidays so that they extend a Tuesday or Thursday holiday into a long weekend. Organizations may also give employees discretion over the scheduling of floating holidays. Employers should establish policies for leaves without pay—for example, leaves of absence to pursue nonwork goals or to meet family needs. Unpaid leave is an employee benefit because the employee usually retains seniority and benefits during the leave.

Group Insurance

As we noted earlier, rates for group insurance are typically lower than for individual policies. Also, insurance benefits are not subject to income tax, as wages and salaries are. When employees receive insurance as a benefit, rather than higher pay so they can buy their own insurance, employees can get more for their money. Because of this, most employees value group insurance. The most common types of insurance offered as employee benefits are medical, life, and disability insurance.

Medical Insurance

For many employees, the most important benefit is medical insurance. The policies typically cover medical expenses that are incurred over and above provincially funded medical coverage. Some employers offer additional coverage, such as dental care, vision care, and prescription drug programs. As is discussed in this chapter's Thinking Ethically feature, employers must also make choices about coverage of so-called "lifestyle drugs," that is, drugs considered "cosmetic" or "discretionary." Examples are medical treatments for obesity, infertility, erectile dysfunction, male pattern baldness, and smoking cessation.[42]

Health Spending Accounts

health spending account
A specific amount of money set aside per employee by the employer to cover health-related costs.

Another alternative to traditional employer-provided insurance is a **health spending account**, also known as a medical savings account, in which an employer puts aside a specific amount of money per employee to cover health-related costs. Employees decide what health care services they will purchase with their allocation. Major insurers, such as Great-West Life, administer the health spending account, usually for a fixed percentage fee. Health spending accounts are particularly attractive to small companies because the cost to the employer for employee benefits and administration is capped.[43]

Wellness Programs

employee wellness program
A set of communications, activities, and facilities designed to change health-related behaviours in ways that reduce health risks.

Another way to lower the cost of health insurance is to reduce employees' need for health care services. Employers may try to do this by offering an **employee wellness program**, a set of communications, activities, and facilities designed to change health-related behaviours in ways that reduce health risks. Typically, wellness programs aim at specific health risks, such as high blood pressure, high cholesterol levels, smoking, and obesity, by encouraging preventive measures such as exercise and good nutrition. However, many organizations are adopting an integrated strategic approach to wellness that promotes a corporate culture to support employees in taking responsibility

Dofasco Inc. operates a 100-acre recreational facility park in Hamilton, Ontario, for employees, retirees, and their families. These facilities include double NHL-size ice surfaces, a twin gymnasium complex, track, golf driving range, miniputt, tennis courts, kids' playground, and baseball diamonds. Can you think of other organizations that offer unique benefits and services?

for their health and overall wellness. Many organizations are also using incentives to create more interest in their program. "Incentives create more interest in the program and inspire people who aren't usually active to get involved," says Kathleen Jones, business solutions manager at Fraser & Hoyt Incentives in Halifax. "Examples of wellness incentives include exercise-themed prizes like yoga mats, iPods, and even big-ticket items like trips and flat-screen TVs.[44]

Organizations that place a strategic emphasis on corporate wellness achieve economic benefits including reduced injury and disability insurance costs, enhanced productivity and service, and reduced costs due to a reduction in employee absenteeism and turnover.[45]

Wellness programs are either *passive* or *active*. Passive programs provide information and services, but no formal support or motivation to use the program. Examples include health education (such as lunchtime courses) and fitness facilities. These programs are considered passive because they rely on employees to identify the services they need and act on their own to obtain the services, such as participating in classes. Active wellness programs assume that behaviour change requires support and reinforcement along with awareness and opportunity. These programs provide for outreach and follow-up. For example, the program may include counsellors who tailor programs to individual employees' needs, take baseline measurements (e.g., blood pressure and weight), and take follow-up measures for comparison to the baseline. Active programs often set goals and provide symbolic rewards as individuals make progress toward meeting their goals. In general, passive health education programs cost less than active wellness programs.[46] All these variations have had success in reducing risk factors associated with cardiovascular disease (obesity, high blood pressure, smoking, lack of exercise), but the follow-up method is most successful.

Employee Assistance Program (EAP)

An **employee assistance program (EAP)** provides confidential counselling services to employees experiencing personal problems. Many organizations also extend these services to family members. Left untreated, personal problems may cause an employee to their ability to cope and work performance will suffer. Employees must be able to feel confident the program respects their confidentiality. Other considerations include the range of offerings provided (some EAP providers offer a very broad range of services that may overlap with health, wellness and lifestyle-related services), proximity to counsellors, client references, and availability of effectiveness reporting measures.[47]

**employee
assistance program
(EAP)**
Confidential
counselling services
for employees
experiencing
personal problems.

Life Insurance

Employers may provide life insurance to employees or offer the opportunity to buy coverage at low group rates. With a *term life insurance* policy, if the employee dies during the term of the policy, the employee's beneficiaries receive a payment called a *death benefit*. In policies purchased as an employee benefit, the usual death benefit is a multiple of the employee's yearly pay. The policies may provide additional benefits for accidental death and dismemberment. Along with a basic policy, the employer may give employees the option of purchasing additional coverage, usually at a nominal cost.

Disability Insurance

short-term disability insurance
Insurance that pays a percentage of a disabled employee's salary as benefits to the employee for six months or less.

long-term disability insurance
Insurance that pays a percentage of a disabled employee's salary after an initial period and potentially for the rest of the employee's life.

Employees risk losing their incomes if a disability makes them unable to work. Disability insurance provides protection against this loss of income. Typically, **short-term disability insurance** provides benefits for six months or less. **Long-term disability insurance** provides benefits after that initial period, potentially for the rest of the disabled employee's life. Disability payments are a percentage of the employee's salary—typically 50 to 70 percent. Payments under short-term plans may be higher. Often the policy sets a maximum amount that may be paid each month. Because its limits make it more affordable, short-term disability coverage is offered by more employers. Fewer than half of employers offer long-term plans. An additional key issue facing disability management programs is the increasing number of multiple-issue (psychological and medical) claims, resulting in increased organizational costs.

In planning an employee benefits package, the organization should keep in mind that CPP and QPP includes some long-term disability benefits. To manage benefits costs, the employer should ensure that the disability insurance is coordinated with CPP/QPP and any other programs that help workers who become disabled.

Retirement Plans

Employers have no obligation to offer retirement plans beyond the protection of CPP/QPP security, but many offer some form of pension or retirement savings plan. About half of employees working for private businesses (i.e., nongovernment jobs) have employer-sponsored retirement plans. These plans are most common for higher-earning employees. Among employees earning the top one-fifth of incomes, almost three-quarters have a pension plan, and about one out of six employees in the bottom fifth have pensions.[48] Retirement plans may be *contributory plans*, meaning they are funded by contributions from the employer and employee, or *noncontributory plans*, meaning all the contributions come from the employer. As is illustrated in Figure 9.13, 88 percent of organizations offer at least one type of pension plan, and many offer both.

FIGURE 9.13

Defined Benefit Pension Plans Still as Prevalent as Defined Contribution Plans

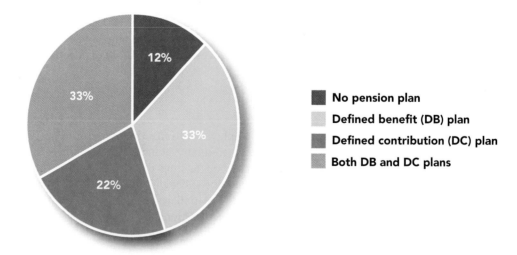

- No pension plan
- Defined benefit (DB) plan
- Defined contribution (DC) plan
- Both DB and DC plans

Defined Benefit Plans

Employers have a choice of using retirement plans that define the amount to be paid out after retirement or plans that define the amount the employer will invest each year. A **defined benefit plan** guarantees a specified level of retirement income. Usually the amount of this defined benefit is calculated for each employee based on the employee's years of service, age, and earnings level (e.g., the average of the employee's five highest-earnings years). These calculations typically result in pension payments that may provide 70 percent of pre-retirement income for a long-service employee. Using years of service as part of the basis for calculating benefits gives employees an incentive to stay with the organization as long as they can, so it can help to reduce voluntary turnover.

For employees under federal legislation, defined benefit plans must meet the funding requirements of the Pension Benefits Act. With a defined benefit plan, the employer sets up a pension fund to invest the contributions. The employer and/or employee must contribute enough for the plan to cover all the benefits to be paid out to retirees. Defined benefit plans are intended to protect employees from the risk that the pension fund will not earn as much as expected. If the pension fund earns less than expected, the employer is required to make up the difference from other sources. Many defined benefit plans are underfunded, leading to concerns about the future retirement security of today's workforce. Approximately one-half of chief financial officers surveyed by the Conference Board agree there is a pension funding crisis in Canada, but this figure has dropped from 61 percent in 2006.[49]

defined benefit plan
A pension plan that guarantees a specified level of retirement income.

Defined Contribution Plans

An alternative to defined benefits is a **defined contribution plan**, which sets up an individual account for each employee and specifies the size of the investment into that account, rather than the amount to be paid out upon retirement. The amount the retiree receives will depend on the account's performance. These plans free employers from the risks that investments will not perform as well as expected. They put the responsibility for wise investing squarely on the shoulders of each employee. A defined contribution plan is also easier to administer. Considering the advantages to employers, it is not surprising that a growing share of retirement plans are defined contribution plans, especially at relatively small organizations.

When retirement plans make individual employees responsible for investment decisions, the employees need information about retirement planning. Retirement savings plans often give employees much control over decisions about when and how much to invest.

Defined contribution plans also offer an advantage to employees in today's highly mobile workforce. They do not penalize employees for changing jobs. With these plans, retirement earnings are less related to the number of years an employee stays with a company.

An additional issue facing employers' approaches to retirement plans is a growing interest in **phased retirement**, a gradual transition into full retirement by reducing hours or job responsibility.[50] Employers are facing an increasing demand for phased retirement programs from employees who are healthier, living longer, and have personal or financial reasons to continue working in some capacity. Employers also benefit from retaining older workers with valued skills and experience who wish to

defined contribution plan
A retirement plan in which the employer sets up an individual account for each employee and specifies the size of the investment into that account.

phased retirement
A gradual transition into full retirement by reducing hours or job responsibility.

Many organizations provide an extensive range of family-friendly benefits. What types of benefits would help to alleviate stress at the workplace?

retire gradually. Phased retirement also provides the employer with more time to transfer knowledge and skills to younger employees[51]; however, many employers are worried about the implications and costs of providing benefits coverage to 65+-year-old employees.

Family-Friendly Benefits and Services

As employers have recognized the importance of employees' need to balance their work and outside commitments including the care of family members, pursuit of education, personal development, and volunteer activities, many have implemented "family-friendly" HR practices. Options such as flextime and telework were discussed in Chapter 3. In addition, some organizations provide benefits and services including child and/or elder care, parental leave top-up, and adoption assistance. For example, the University Health Network, Canada's largest health care employer, provides onsite subsidized daycare, top-up to 75 percent of salary for the first 25 weeks of parental leave, telecommuting, and flextime.[52] Ernst & Young LLP's family-friendly benefits include access to a nearby daycare facility, parental leave salary top up to 100 percent for the first 17 weeks of leave, and adoption benefits of up to $5,000 per child in addition to telecommuting, flextime, and reduced summer hours.[53]

Statistics Canada recently released the results of the study related to the "sandwich generation"—approximately 712,000 Canadians with the dual responsibility of raising children and providing care for aging parents or relatives. Due to the aging of the baby boomers and their delay in having children the sandwich generation is expected to grow, resulting in increased stress and demands on employees.[54] Some employers have responded by providing benefits and services including access to counselling, flexible schedules, referral services, and access to information and other resources available in the community or region.

The value of these family-friendly benefits accrue to not only employees but to employers as well in the form of increased productivity, enhanced commitment, and reduced stress.[55]

2,3,5

Other Benefits

The scope of possible employee benefits is limited only by the imagination of the organization's decision makers. Figure 9.14 outlines emerging benefits expected to be the most popular over the next few years. Organizations have developed a wide variety of benefits to meet the needs of employees and to attract and keep the kinds of workers who will be of value to the organization. Traditional extras include subsidized cafeterias, onsite health care for minor injuries or illnesses, and moving expenses for newly hired or relocating employees. Stores and manufacturers may offer employee discounts on their products.

To encourage learning and attract the kinds of employees who wish to develop their knowledge and skills, many organizations offer *tuition reimbursement* programs.

FIGURE 9.14

Emerging Benefits, Expected by 2009

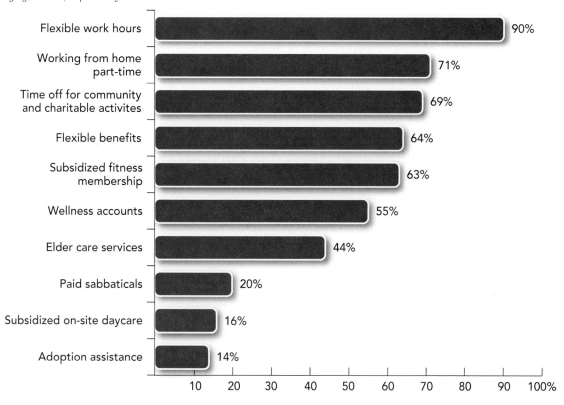

Benefit	Percentage
Flexible work hours	90%
Working from home part-time	71%
Time off for community and charitable activites	69%
Flexible benefits	64%
Subsidized fitness membership	63%
Wellness accounts	55%
Elder care services	44%
Paid sabbaticals	20%
Subsidized on-site daycare	16%
Adoption assistance	14%

SOURCE: Hewitt Associates, "Emerging Benefits Focus on Flexibility," *Canadian HR Reporter,* December 17, 2007, pp. 20, 27; Kira Vermond, "Sabbaticals: Time Out for the Burned Out," *Globe and Mail Update,* November 2, 2007, www.theglobeandmail.com, retrieved November 8, 2007.

A typical program covers tuition and related expenses for courses that are relevant to the employee's current job or future career at the organization. Employees are reimbursed for these expenses after they demonstrate they have completed an approved course. The Best Practices box discusses tuition reimbursement as an imporant perk at many organizations on top employer lists.

Especially for demanding, high-stress jobs, organizations may look for benefits that help employees put in the necessary long hours and alleviate stress. Recreational activities such as onsite basketball courts or company-sponsored softball teams provide for social interaction as well as physical activity. As employers try to come up with ways to help employees find relief, a growing craze has been "the perk of an onsite massage." Companies offering onsite massage therapy include Research in Motion, TD Canada Trust, Reebok

Hill and Knowlton has received recognition as a top employer and for its travelling refreshment cart.

BEST PRACTICES

Tuition Reimbursement Can Put Employees at the Top

Mandy Webster arrived at the Vancouver Fraser Port Authority (VFPA) as a temporary employee in a low skill job. Personal issues had forced her to leave university a few years before, with only a handful of credits and few career opportunities. Today, she is the document support analyst at VFPA and on her way to completing a bachelor of arts degree. The VFPA is picking up the tab for her $15,000 tuition fees, plus her books and supplies. On top of that, Webster has been given "education days" to cover some of the time she needs for classes.

"It's almost too good to be true," she says. "To me it was a no-brainer. I can take care of my unfinished business and do it without missing a mortgage payment. "She applied for a tuition reimbursement last year reasoning, "it was time to make a move or I would get too comfortable." Webster uses words such as "invigorating" and "rejuvenating" to describe the return to education—even though a BA will have little value in her current role. "There was a time when I was sinking a bit," she says. "I feel a new sense of ambition and excitement and I feel like I'm accomplishing something."

Canadian studies on how much firms spend on tuition reimbursement for courses unrelated to an employee's current role—or the return on investment—are hard to come by. However, this is an important perk at many organizations on top employer lists.

Christine Dioszeghy, director of human resources with the VFPA and the person who approved Webster's application, doesn't need numbers to tell her the story. "We want to hire continuous learners," she says. "Even if these skills are not related, they're still somebody broadening their business acumen."

Some organizations are willing to pay for courses not directly related to a specific job as long as they will contribute to the organization in some way. At VFPA, the employee has to make a formal application that makes a case for the course and a reason for the company to foot the bill.

Christie Digital, a Waterloo, Ontario–based video projection design and manufacturing firm, offers a similar program.

Kimberley Hogan, vice-president of HR, says most employees apply to upgrade their education—such as a technologist with a college diploma who wants to earn a university degree-but there are those who simply want to try something new. "At the end of the day, anybody going out and learning and taking that initiative to learn new things, to learn new technologies—all of that is going to benefit Christie," she says. "Somebody who is working as a young technician on the floor and wants to get his engineering degree, it's not pertinent today but, in the future, he'll be somebody we can move into our engineering organization."

In the long term, Hogan says investing in training now, even if it's unrelated, offsets future recruitment costs. "To hire one engineer, if we go outside and we use a recruiting firm, on average we're going to spend $30,000 a year," she says. "If I can keep them and upgrade their skills and I can grow the future managers of the company, that's good."

SOURCE: Danielle Harder, "Tuition Reimbursement Can Put Employees at the Top," *Canadian HR Reporter*, March 24, 2008. pp. 17, 21.

Canada, HSBC Bank Canada, and 1-800-GOT-JUNK?[56] And at public relations firm and top employer, Hill & Knowlton Canada, a travelling refreshment cart winds through the office to celebrate the end of the week.[57]

Selecting Employee Benefits

2,3,4,5

Although the government requires certain benefits, employers have wide latitude in creating the total benefits package they offer employees.[58] Decisions about which benefits to include should take into account the organization's goals, its budget, and the expectations of the organization's current employees and those it wishes to recruit in the future. Employees have come to expect certain things from employers. An organization that does not offer the expected benefits will have more difficulty attracting and keeping talented workers. Also, if employees believe their employer feels no commitment to their welfare, they are less likely to feel committed to their employer.

Organization's Objectives

A logical place to begin selecting employee benefits is to establish objectives for the benefits package. This helps an organization select the most effective benefits and monitor whether the benefits are doing what they should. Unfortunately, research suggests that most organizations do not have written objectives for benefits.

Intuit Canada, the Edmonton-based company that develops small business, accounting, and tax software (Quicken), offers employees a set of benefits intended to attract and retain loyal and high-performing employees. The bottom line for Glenn McGillivray, senior human resources specialist at Intuit, is attracting and retaining the best people. "Top notch people in any specific field have a lot of choices. So we want to make sure we are the choice they're going to make and this is the type of place they want to work."[59] McGillivray adds that turnover is low at Intuit, "fluctuating between 3 and 6 percent."[60] Intuit Canada picks up 100 percent of most health and benefit plan premiums, offers stock options and an employee stock purchase plan, pays 100 percent of Alberta Health Care Benefit premiums, reimburses home Internet access, supplies interest-free loans to purchase computer equipment, includes towel service in the onsite gym and fitness centre, and provides nap rooms.[61]

Employees' Expectations and Values

To meet employees' expectations about benefits, it can be helpful to see what other organizations offer. Employers should also consider that the value employees place on various benefits is likely to differ from one employee to another. At a broad level, basic demographic factors such as age and sex can influence the kinds of benefits employees want. An older workforce is more likely to be concerned about (and use) medical coverage, life insurance, and pensions. A workforce with a high percentage of employees in their 20s–40s may care more about disability or family leave. Young, unmarried men and women often place more value on pay than on benefits. However, these are only general observations; organizations should check which considerations apply to their own employees and identify more specific needs and differences.

The choice of benefits may influence current employees' satisfaction and may also affect the organization's recruiting, in terms of both the ease of recruiting and the kinds of employees attracted to the organization.

Flexible Benefits

Organizations can address differences in employees' needs and engage their employees by offering **flexible benefits plans** in place of a single benefits package for all employees. These plans, often called flexible benefits or "flex benefits," offer employees

flexible benefits plan
A benefits plan that offers employees a set of alternatives from which they can choose the types and amounts of benefits they want.

a set of alternatives from which they can choose the types and amounts of benefits they want. The plans vary. Some impose minimum levels for certain benefits, such as health care coverage; some allow employees to receive money in exchange for choosing a "light" package; and some let employees pay extra for the privilege of receiving more benefits. For example, some plans let employees give up vacation days for more pay or to purchase extra vacation days in exchange for a reduction in pay.

Flexible benefits plans have a number of advantages.[62] The selection process can make employees more aware of the value of the benefits, particularly when the plan assigns each employee a sum of money to allocate to benefits. Also, the individual choice in a flexible benefits plan enables each employee to match his or her needs to the company's benefits, increasing the plan's actual value to the employee. Superior Propane, a Calgary-based Canadian marketer of propane and appliances, switched to a flex benefits plan for its 1,800 employees. Terry Gill, vice-president of human resources, says that Superior Propane changed to flex benefits to "attract a more diverse group of employees to fit in with our new performance-based culture. We realized that most employees wanted opportunity and choice—a 'one-size-fits-all' plan wouldn't work."[63]

A drawback of flexible benefits plans is that they have a higher administrative cost, especially in the design and startup stages. Organizations can avoid some of the higher cost, however, by using software packages and standardized plans that have been developed for employers wishing to offer flexible benefits. Another possible drawback is that employee selection of benefits will increase rather than decrease costs, because employees will select the kinds of benefits they expect to need the most. For example, an employee expecting to need a lot of dental work is more likely to sign up for a dental plan. The heavy use of the dental coverage would then drive up the employer's premiums for that coverage. Costs can also be difficult to estimate when employees select their benefits. Organizations frequently respond by requiring employees to share in the costs of benefits.

L07 - Discuss the importance of effectively communicating the organization's approach to total rewards.

Communicating Total Rewards to Employees

"Communication is often a weak link. An average program well-communicated will do better than an outstanding program poorly communicated."[64] A comprehensive communications strategy is required to help employees understand the total value the organization is investing in its approach to compensating and rewarding employees. This is essential so that total rewards can achieve their objectives including focusing employees on organizational goals, attracting and retaining employees, and creating a motivating environment.

Because they interact with their employees each day, managers play a significant role in communication. The HR department should prepare them to explain to their employees why the organization's approach to compensating and rewarding employees is designed as it is, and to determine whether employee concerns indicate a need for change. Employees are interested in their compensation and rewards and they need a great deal of detailed information. It follows that technology such as the Internet and supporting databases can play a significant role. More employers are using technology to provide employees with tools and information related to both communication and administration of employee compensation and rewards. According to a recent survey, 56 percent of employers communicate benefit plan details to employees online, up from 30 percent in 2001.[65] The e-HRM box discusses how Canada Post

E- HRM

Instant Information at Everyone's Fingertips—Canada Post

Canada Post has 70,000 employees spread across every province and territory. Until recently, Canada Post had been using a home-grown technology system that was only accessible by a handful of HR professionals. Line managers had no instant access to basic information on their employees. If a manager needed to know how many vacation days a particular employee was entitled to, he/she usually had to pick up the phone or navigate an unfriendly, unreliable patchwork of systems.

Now Canada Post is on the leading edge of HR technology. One of the most useful features of the new system at Canada Post is self-service for both employees and managers. Through self-service, Canada Post has been able to decentralize its HR data collection and maintenance, putting information at the fingertips of every employee.

Managers can now access everything about the organization on their computers, including:

- How much employees are being paid
- What leave days employees have
- What benefits they are entitled to

With self-service, every employee across the country can log on to:

- Change an address
- Change banking information
- View benefits entitlement
- View vacation time

Canada Post employees can access self-service through computers at work or through their home Internet connection.

SOURCE: Todd Humber, "Through Wind, and Sleet and the Internet," *Guide to HR Technology—Supplement to Canadian HR Reporter*, November 8, 2004, pp. G1, G8.

is using technology to provide employees with information related to compensation and rewards.

In fact, employees and job applicants often lack a clear sense of the market value of total rewards that an organization offers. For example, research asking employees about their benefits has shown that employees significantly underestimate the cost and value of their benefits.[66] Probably a major reason for their lack of knowledge is a lack of communication from employers. When New Brunswick Power teamed up with its union to communicate the benefits of the move to a flexible benefits plan, the objective was to "get the message out to workers that this was their plan, they owned it, and they needed to get an understanding of how it worked." The company provided training sessions, and gave every employee a video to take home and watch and discuss with their families.[67]

Employers have many options for communicating information about benefits. To increase the likelihood that employees will receive and understand the messages, employers can combine several media, such as videos, brochures, question-and-answer meetings, online total rewards statements, intranet pages, memos, presentations, and email. An investment of creativity in employee communication can reap great returns in the form of committed, satisfied employees, and the achievement of organizational objectives.

LO8 - Discuss issues related to compensating and rewarding executives.

2,4,5

Executive Compensation and Rewards

The media have drawn public attention to the issue of executive compensation and rewards. The issue attracts notice because of the very high pay that the top executives of major North American companies have received in recent years. A significant part of executive compensation comes in the form of company stock. For example, Peter Godsoe, retired chairman of the Bank of Nova Scotia, received $1.35 million in salary and a $2.6 million bonus in his final year with the company. In total, however, he will have amassed approximately $122 million worth of shares and securities in the company after 37 years of service. In addition, he will receive an annual pension of $2.5 million.[68]

Although high amounts like this apply to only a small proportion of the total workforce, the issue of executive pay is relevant to pay structure in terms of equity theory. As we discussed earlier in the chapter, employees draw conclusions about the fairness of pay by making comparisons among employees' inputs and outcomes. By many comparisons, CEOs pay is high. In 2006, Canada's 100 best-paid CEOs made an average of $8,528,304. For Canada's best-paid CEOs, pay ranged from $54,709,465 to $3,059,604 in total compensation.[69] Overall, executive compensation and rewards are complicated due to the increased number of items included, for example, direct pay, short- and long-term incentives, stock options, and benefits. Top executives help to set the tone or culture of the organization, and employees at all levels are affected by behaviour at the top. As a result, the equity of executive compensation and rewards can affect more employees than, say, the compensation and rewards received by warehouse workers or sales clerks. Another way to think about the equity of CEO pay is to compare it with the pay of other employees in the organization. Again, equity theory would consider not only the size of the executive pay relative to pay for other employees but also the amount the CEOs contribute. For example, Canadians will work full-time all 2008 to earn an average wage of $38,998. But by 10:33 a.m. January 2, 2008, the 100 best-paid CEOs of public companies had already earned that amount. And they will continue to earn the average Canadian wage every nine hours and 33 minutes for the rest of the year.[70]

Executive Incentives

Because executives have a much stronger influence over the organization's performance than other employees do, incentive pay for executives warrants special attention. Assuming that incentives influence performance, decisions about incentives for executives should have a great impact on how well the executives and the organization perform. Along with overall pay levels for executives, organizations need to create incentive plans for this small but important group of employees.

To encourage executives to develop a commitment to the organization's long-term success, executive compensation often combines short-term and long-term incentives. *Short-term incentives* include bonuses based on the year's profits, return on investment, or other measures related to the organization's goals. Sometimes, to gain tax advantages, the actual payment of the bonus is deferred (e.g., by making it part of a retirement plan). *Long-term incentives* include stock options and stock purchase plans. The rationale for these long-term incentives is that executives will want to do what is best for the organization because that will cause the value of their stock to grow.

According to a recent study released by Watson Wyatt Worldwide, "CEOs of high-performing Canadian companies earned significantly more compensation than their counterparts at low-performing organizations."[71] This study concluded that a strong link exists between an organization's financial performance and executive compensation. Companies that provided above-median increases in total direct compensation for executives (i.e., base salary plus annual bonuses, and long-term incentives including stock option rewards) also "provided significantly higher performance for their shareholders."[72]

Ed Clark, TD Canada Trust's CEO was rewarded for a strong year, when TD avoided the pitfalls of most of its peers. Clark's total compensation was $14.2 million, up from $12 million the previous year and his cash bonus was boosted to $2.25 million, up from $1.88 million a year earlier, the biggest total compensation package any Canadian bank executive received.[73]

A corporation's shareholders—its owners—want the corporation to encourage managers to act in the owners' best interests. They want managers to care about the company's profits and stock price, and incentive pay can encourage this interest. One way to achieve these goals is to tie a large share of executives' pay to performance. Another study has found that relying on such long-term incentives is associated with greater profitability.[74] In Canada, 96 percent of companies offer their executives stock options.[75]

Performance Measures for Executives

The balanced-scorecard approach is useful in designing executive pay. Whirlpool, for example, has used a balanced scorecard that combines measures of whether the organization is delivering value to shareholders, customers, and employees. These measures are listed in Table 9.5.

Regulators and shareholders have pressured companies to do a better job of linking executive pay and performance. The Ontario Securities Commission requires companies to disclose executive compensation levels and the company's performance relative to that of compensation.[76] These reporting requirements shine a light on situations where executives of poorly performing companies receive high pay, so companies feel more pressure to link pay to performance.

TYPE OF MEASURES	VALUE CREATION
Shareholder value	Economic value added
	Earnings per share
	Cash flow
	Total cost productivity
Customer value	Quality
	Market share
	Customer satisfaction
Employee value	High-performance culture index
	High-performance culture deployment
	Training and development diversity

TABLE 9.5

Balanced Scorecard for Whirlpool Executives

SOURCE: E. L. Gubman, *The Talent Solution* (New York: McGraw-Hill, 1998).

Ethical Issues

Incentive pay for executives lays the groundwork for significant ethical issues. When an organization links pay to its stock performance, executives need the ethical backbone to be honest about their company's performance even when dishonesty or clever shading of the truth offers the tempting potential for large earnings. As recent scandals involving WorldCom, Enron, Nortel Networks, and other companies have shown, the results can be disastrous when unethical behaviour comes to light.

Among these issues is one we have already touched on in this chapter: the difficulty of setting performance measures that encourage precisely the behaviour desired. In the case of incentives tied to stock performance, executives may be tempted to inflate the stock price in order to enjoy bonuses and valuable stock options. The intent is for the executive to boost stock value through efficient operations, technological innovation, effective leadership, and so on. Unfortunately, individuals at some companies determined that they could obtain faster results through accounting practices that stretched the norms in order to present the company's performance in the best light. When such practices are discovered to be misleading, stock prices plunge and the company's reputation is damaged, sometimes beyond repair.

A related issue when executive pay includes stock or stock options is insider trading. When executives are stockholders, they have a dual role as owners and managers. This places them at an advantage over others who want to invest in the company. An individual, a pension fund, or other investors have less information about the company than its managers do—for example, whether product development is proceeding on schedule, whether a financing deal is in the works, and so on. An executive who knows about these activities could therefore reap a windfall in the stock market by buying or selling stock based on his or her knowledge about the company's future. Although regulators place strict limits on this "insider trading," some executives have violated these limits. In the worst cases executives have sold stock, secretly knowing their company was failing, before the stock price collapsed. The losers are the employees, retirees, and other investors who hold the now-worthless stock.

As recent news stories have reminded us, linking pay to stock price can reward unethical behaviour, at least in the short term and at least in the minds of a handful of executives. Yet, given the motivational power of incentive pay, organizations cannot afford to abandon incentives for their executives. These temptations are among the reasons that executive positions demand individuals who maintain high ethical standards.

As well as legally required benefits and the benefits extended to other employees in the organization, executives often receive extra benefits and services. These executive benefits and services may include such far-reaching benefits as use of corporate aircraft, company-provided or -subsidized homes, memberships and tickets to sporting and cultural events, in addition to benefits such as company cars, cellphones, home computers, PDAs, sabbaticals, and extended vacations. For example, Donald Guloien, the chief investment officer at Manulife Financial, received $82,310 for personal expenditures, including car payments and club memberships, last year, and Royal Bank head Gordon Nixon received $77,963 for car leases.[77]

THINKING ETHICALLY

Should "Lifestyle" Be Covered?

In recent years a variety of widely-publicized "lifestyle" drugs to treat conditions such as obesity, male erectile dysfunction, infertility, and male pattern baldness have become available. As a result, the line between the medical and social dimensions of health is blurring. Although some employers consider these drugs "cosmetic" or "discretionary" and refuse to include them in their health care plans, other employers are willing to share or fund the coverage. According to a Hewitt Associates' survey, more than one-half of employers provide coverage for infertility treatments, and smoking cessation medication. However, only one-third of employers covered drugs to treat obesity and only 5 percent of employers were willing to pay for drugs to treat male pattern baldness. Employers that provide coverage for "lifestyle" drugs often put in cost-control measures—for example, annual or lifetime dollar maximums, or capping coverage for smoking cessation medications at $825 (lifetime) and for obesity drugs at $1,325 (annually).

SOURCE: Sarah Beech, "Lifestyle Choices," *Benefits Canada*, March 2008, p. 45; Sarah Beech, "Rethinking Coverage for 'Lifestyle' Drugs," *Benefits Canada*, October 10, 2007, www .benefitscanada.com, retrieved October 18, 2008; Joel Lexchin, "Lifestyle Drugs: Issues for Debate," *CMAJ*, May 15, 2001, p. 164, www .cmaj.ca/cgi/content/full/164/10/1449, retrieved May 8, 2008.

Questions

1. Should "lifestyle drugs" be included in an organization's benefits coverage? Why or why not?
2. Should an employer be able to intervene in the physician–patient relationship to assess whether a treatment is "medically necessary"?
3. Would your answer to question 1 be different if the treatment in question were for easing the suffering of a cancer patient rather than treating male pattern baldness or obesity?

SUMMARY

L01 Discuss how organizations implement a "total rewards" approach to compensating and rewarding employees.

- Many organizations are recognizing the strategic value of taking a comprehensive approach to compensating and rewarding employees. This "total rewards" approach frequently involves creating a value proposition for current and prospective employees that clearly identifies all of the aspects that are valued by employees in exchange for their time and expertise.

- Canadian companies take a total rewards approach to attract and retain valued employees and improve capacity to meet organizational goals.

L02 Identify the kinds of decisions and influences involved in providing base pay to employees.

- Organizations make decisions to define a job structure, or relative pay for different jobs within the organization. They establish relative pay for different functions and different levels of responsibility for each function.

- Organizations must also establish pay levels, or the average paid for the different jobs. These decisions are based on the organization's goals, market data, legal requirements, and principles of fairness. Together job structure and pay level establish a pay structure policy.

- Organizations typically begin with a job evaluation to measure the relative worth of their jobs. The organization then creates a pay structure that includes pay grades or pay ranges for each job in the organization.

LO3 Describe alternatives to job-based pay.

- To obtain more flexibility, organizations may reduce the levels in the organization's job structure. This process of delayering or broadbanding involves creating broad bands of jobs within pay ranges.
- Other organizations reward employees according to their competencies. They establish competency-based pay systems, or structures that set pay according to the employees' level of knowledge and what they are capable of doing.

LO4 Describe how organizations recognize individual, team, and organizational performance through the use of incentives.

- Organizations may recognize individual performance through such incentives as piecework rates, merit pay, sales commissions, and bonuses for meeting individual performance objectives.
- Common team incentives include gainsharing, bonuses, and team awards.
- Incentives for meeting organizational objectives include profit sharing and stock ownership.

LO5 Discuss the role of benefits as part of employee total rewards.

- Like pay, benefits and services help employers attract, retain, and provide a source of motivation for employees. Employees expect at least a minimum level of benefits, and providing more than the minimum helps an organization compete in the labour market.
- Benefits and services are also a significant expense, but employers provide benefits and services because employees value them and many are required by law.

LO6 Summarize the types of employee benefits offered by employers.

- Employers must contribute to the Canada Pension Plan/Quebec Pension Plan, Employment Insurance, and Workers' Compensation. In addition, employers offer various kinds of insurance, retirement plans, and paid leave.
- Due to the increasing costs of providing employee benefits, many Canadian organizations are seeking ways to hold back the costs. Many employers have responded to work–life role conflicts by offering family-friendly benefits.
- Organizations need to establish objectives and select benefits that support those objectives. Flexible benefits are a means to give employees control over the benefits they receive.

LO7 Discuss the importance of effectively communicating the organization's approach to total rewards.

- A comprehensive communications strategy is needed to help employees understand and value all the components in an organization's approach to total rewards. Managers and the human resource department share responsibility for this important requirement.
- Technology can provide employees access to information and other tools associated with administration of compensation and rewards.
- Employers have many options for communicating information about total rewards. Using a combination of media increases employees' understanding.

LO8 Discuss issues related to compensating and rewarding executives.

- Executive compensation has drawn public scrutiny because top executive compensation is much higher than average workers' pay.
- Chief executive officers have an extremely large impact on the organization's performance, but critics complain that when performance falters, executive pay does not decline as fast as the organization's profits or stock price.
- Performance measures should encourage behaviour that is in the organization's best interests, including ethical behaviour.

REVIEW AND DISCUSSION QUESTIONS

1. Some individuals evaluate prospective employers' job offers based only on direct pay considerations. What additional factors should be considered when evaluating job offers from employers?

2. Why might an organization choose to pay employees more than the market rate? Why might it choose to pay less? What are the consequences of paying more or less than the market rate?

3. What are the advantages of establishing pay ranges, rather than specific pay levels, for each job? What are the drawbacks of this approach?

4. Suppose a small startup business wants to establish a competency-based pay structure. What would be some advantages of this approach? List the issues the company should be prepared to address in setting up this system. Consider the kinds of information you will need and the ways employees may react to the new pay structure.

5. With some organizations and jobs, pay is primarily wages or salaries, and with others, incentive pay is more important. For each of the following jobs, state whether you think the pay should emphasize base pay (wages and salaries) or incentive pay (bonuses, profit sharing, and so on). Give a reason for each.

   a. An accountant at a manufacturing company
   b. A salesperson for a software company
   c. A mechanic for a major airline
   d. A marketing manager for a consumer packaged-goods firm
   e. A recruitment specialist for the federal government

6. Why do some organizations link incentive pay to the organization's overall performance? Is it appropriate to use stock performance as an incentive for employees at all levels? Why or why not?

7. Why do employers provide employee benefits, rather than providing all compensation in the form of pay and letting employees buy the services they want?

8. Of the benefits discussed in this chapter, list the ones you consider essential—those benefits you would require in any job offer. Why are these benefits important to you?

9. Why is it important to communicate information about total rewards? Suppose you work in the HR department of a company that has decided to add new elements to its total rewards—onsite massage plus an increased budget to support learning and development opportunities for all employees. How would you recommend communicating this change? What information should your messages include?

10. Do you think executive total compensation is too high? Why or why not?

WHAT'S YOUR HR IQ?

The Online Learning Centre offers more ways to check what you've learned so far. Find experiential exercises as well as Test Your Knowledge Quizzes, Videos, and many other resources at www.mcgrawhill.ca/olc/steen.

Excalibur Case:
Smith Rubber

Located in the Eastern Townships region of Quebec, Smith Rubber grew from a small family-owned business into a medium-sized company. The organization is now facing a great deal of competition within Quebec and across North America. Its success has always been tied to its ability to compete with Japanese and Mexican companies that also supply the automobile industry.

Steve Smith Jr. is now president of Smith Rubber. At the time of his promotion some years ago, the company was not unionized. During this period he wondered how to best recognize employees and reward their performance while encouraging them to increase productivity. He hesitated about increasing wages because he feared losing his competitive edge if his fixed costs rose.

Three years ago, Smith Rubber had a particularly good year in terms of sales and profits. As a result, Steve

thought that a Christmas bonus would be the best way to reward employees. In fact, he told David Sanders, his human resource manager, "There is nothing like cold hard cash to make employees work harder." He set out his bonus system as follows:

Compensation	Bonus
$30,000 and under	$2,500
$30,001–$35,000	$3,000
$35,001–$40,000	$3,500
$40,001–$45,000	$4,000
$45,001–$50,000	$4,500
$50,001 or higher	10% of salary

The bonuses were a hit. Many employees thanked the president personally. Moreover, in February, David Sanders received many positive comments from supervisors, saying that employees were working harder.

The following year there was a slump in the automobile industry, and competitors abroad made dramatic cuts in their costs by using robots in their assembly lines. It was difficult for Smith Rubber to compete and sales dropped by 5 percent, while profits plunged by 15 percent. Steve decided he could not offer the same bonuses as the previous year. The company, therefore, set out the following plan:

Compensation	Bonus
$30,000 and under	$1,250
$30,001–$35,000	$1,500
$35,001–$40,000	$1,750
$40,001–$45,000	$2,000
$45,001–$50,000	$2,250
$50,001 or higher	5% of salary

This time around, David Sanders did not receive any favourable comments from supervisors on the subject of increased productivity. In fact, he asked Jim Rolland, a supervisor, how employees had reacted.

Jim: To tell you the truth, morale is low. Many people worked hard this year. Some of them were hoping to get the same bonus, or even more. So they bought Christmas presents with the old bonus in mind. When they got the letter from the president telling them that he had cut their bonuses in half,

they were in a sour mood and lost their motivation. Some of my employees have never been so unproductive.

David: But that's not right. We never even had bonuses before. They should have been happy just getting something this year.

Jim: That's not how they see it.

David Sanders decided that he would not discuss the matter with Steve for fear of upsetting him.

Eleven months passed, bringing increased stagnation. Sales were steady, but not on par with the levels of previous years. Profits were modest, and the board of directors cut the dividend. On December 1, Steve had a meeting with David and told him, "David, I don't know how I can pay out any bonuses this year. Do you think we can hold back without damaging the morale of our troops?"

NOTE: This case study was used in the 17th edition (2003) of Excalibur (the Canadian University Tournament of Human Resources).

SOURCE: Richard Matte, CHRP, "Matte groupe conseil," www.rhri.org/excalibur/en/case_study.

Questions

You are David Sanders:

1. What would you advise Steve Smith to do? (Two lines)
2. What are the pros and cons of the proposed bonus plan? (At least three)
3. What would have been the right approach from the outset of the plan? (No more than five lines)

Case:
Microsoft Abandons Stock Options

As Microsoft Corporation became hugely successful, many of its employees became rich. One important source of their wealth was incentive pay in the form of stock options. The company would issue the options to employees, and as the value of Microsoft stock rose, the employees exercised the options to receive an immediate return and then realized enormous returns over time.

Options were extremely motivating through the 1990s because they give a right to buy stock at a fixed price. The stock price at Microsoft and other technology companies rose so fast that exercising options was extremely profitable. But when stock prices dropped in 2000 and afterward, options became worthless. It doesn't pay to exercise an option if the stock price is less than the exercise price; you would lose money on the deal.

From a high of $59.56 near the end of 1999, share prices for Microsoft tumbled during the following year to a price near $20 per share. Since then, prices have roughly ranged between $25 and $30 a share. In response to this situation, Microsoft in 2003 announced that it

would no longer reward employees with stock options. Instead, it began using restricted stock, earning shares of stock that employees could sell only at a specified point in the future and only if they still worked for Microsoft. The use of stock instead of stock options avoids the risk of options being worthless if stock prices don't rise fast enough to make the exercise price profitable. The move away from stock options signals that the company does not expect a return to the fast-growth 1990s. In the words of Microsoft's chief financial officer John Conners, "If you think what happened in the nineties is going to happen again—it's not."

Recognizing that the personal computer industry in general and Microsoft in particular have left the early fast-growth days behind, the company's management believes that stock options no longer have a place in the company's performance-based pay. By replacing the stock options with stock grants, the company hopes that employees will continue to be rewarded by the now-mature company's long-term growth and profits.

Because Microsoft, with over 50,000 employees and revenues of almost $37 billion, is such a dominant player in the technology sector, the decision to abandon stock options signals a major change in how technology companies compensate their employees. Exceptions might be startup companies that expect to grow fast and enjoy rapid growth in their earnings and stock prices. Despite those exceptions, in the time since Microsoft announced its decision, the use of stock options has been declining in every industry sector. The trend has been accelerated by a recent federal government requirement that companies treat stock options as an expense, an accounting change that reduces a company's reported profits when it issues stock options. For example, Microsoft said that if it had counted stock options as an expense during the nine months ending March 32, 2003, its profits would have been one-fourth less than it had reported. Thus, the new regulations governing stock options can have a major impact on companies' financial reports.

Are stock options just a good idea whose time has passed? One person who evidently disagrees is Microsoft's own former chairman, Bill Gates, who recently told a *BusinessWeek* reporter, "I actually regret that we ever used [stock options]. There's some benefit, but the approach we're taking now is just a better approach."

SOURCE: Robert A. Guth and Joann S. Lublin, "Microsoft Ushers Out Golden Era of Options," *The Wall Street Journal*, July 9, 2003; "MSFT Stock Chair," MSN *Money*, http://moneycentral.msn.com, accessed May 31, 2005; Microsoft Corporation, "Microsoft Reports Strong Fourth Quarter Earnings," news release, July 22, 2004, www.microsoft.com; Ira Sager, "Gates Good Riddance to Options," *BusinessWeek*, May 16, 2055, p. 10; and Louis Lavelle "Are Options Headed for Extinction?," *BusinessWeek*, May 2, 2005, http://web3.infotrac.galegroup.com.

Questions

1. In general, stock options are most valuable if the stock price rises above the exercise price during the life of the option, and stock grants are most valuable if the stock's value rises during the entire time the person owns the stock. From the point of view of an employee receiving stock options or stock grants, is this difference significant? Would this difference affect the kind of motivation provided to Microsoft's employees?
2. Why do you think Bill Gates expressed "regret" for issuing stock options to reward employees? What drawbacks of stock options might he have been thinking about?
3. In terms of skills, abilities, and other qualities, what kinds of employees would be most valuable for Microsoft? Besides stock, what other rewards would you recommend Microsoft use to attract and keep the kinds of people you identified?

VIDEO CASE

CBC ⦿

Work–Life Balance

CBC Venture explores a crisis in the Canadian workforce—a crisis that is costly to business in terms of absenteeism, health costs, and lost productivity. Canadians are under more stress than ever. From children to work to parents, the list of Canadians' responsibilities is growing—and so are workers' stress levels. A major study, "Voice of Canadians," representing the views of 33,000 Canadians from coast to coast, reveals that Canada's workforce is cracking under the strain of balancing work, family, and lifestyle responsibilities. For example, more employees are working 50-hour weeks, health care benefit costs are growing, and absenteeism is a $3 billion annual drain on the economy.

There is some hope that corporate Canada is waking up to the costs of overwork and recognizing that finding balance between work and life is a way to attract and retain employees. However, concerns are expressed that although many organizations talk about human capital and the importance of balancing work and family, disconnects between words and actions exist in many organizations.

SOURCE: Based on CBC, "Work–Life Balance," *Venture* 863, January 19, 2003.

Questions

1. What concerns did employees express about using the family-friendly benefits and services offered by employers?

2. Do you expect to utilize employer-provided family-friendly benefits and services during your career? Why or why not?

3. Describe the work environment at Davies-Howe Partners, the law firm in the video. How does the work environment contribute to the success of the firm? How important is work environment relative to pay and incentives when choosing an employer? Why?

Part 5

Meeting Other HR Goals

Real People in HR

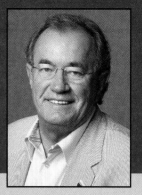

...Basil "Buzz" Hargrove, National President (Ret.), CAW-Canada

Basil "Buzz" Hargrove is perhaps the most public and recognizable figure in Canadian Labour. Buzz has held leadership positions in the Canadian Auto-workers' Union, Canada's largest private-sector union, for over three decades, and was president of the union for 16 years, retiring in 2008. He is also a vice-president on the executive committee of the Canadian Labour Congress and a published author. He is regularly called upon to appear on television and radio, and as a guest lecturer at colleges and universities.

Name...
Basil "Buzz" Hargrove.

Job...
National President (Retired), CAW-Canada.

Adjective people would use to describe you...
There are a few, I think. Most likely—skilled negotiator with a strong social commitment.

First job...
Picking potatoes in New Brunswick.

First union role...
Shop steward.

Most challenging/most rewarding aspect of your job...
Working with so many different people, both union and management and government.

Four essential attributes that make someone an effective union leader...
Integrity, excellent communication skills, an openness and willingness to challenge the status quo, and you need to be prepared to work hard.

If you had to pick an alternative career...
Teaching. In fact, in retirement, that is what I hope to do.

Advice to new employees...
Social, economic, and political justice are more relevant today than ever. Unions are a vehicle for working people to have a say in their workplaces, in establishing standards, and in playing an active role in their communities.

Best career advice that you ever received...
Protect your job!

Advice for someone beginning an HR career...
Always be open to change and make sure to communicate with your workplace partners.

Chapter 10

Labour Relations

What Do I Need to Know? After reading this chapter, you should be able to:

1. Define unions and labour relations and their role in organizations.

2. Identify the labour relations goals of management, labour unions, and society.

3. Summarize laws and regulations that affect labour relations.

4. Describe the union organizing process.

5. Explain how management and unions negotiate collective agreements.

6. Summarize the practice of collective agreement administration.

7. Describe more cooperative approaches to labour–management relations.

Introduction

After maintaining a mostly union-free workplace for more than 50 years, Aurora, Ontario–based automotive parts giant Magna International announced a peace agreement with the Canadian Auto Workers (CAW) that could bring about wide-scale unionization of 18,000 employees at 45 Magna plants in Ontario. By adopting the agreement, known as the "Framework of Fairness Agreement" (FFA), the CAW gave up the ability to strike in exchange for an immediate $3-per-hour wage increase for production workers (with annual improvements), layoff and job security protections, paid educational leave, and a skilled trades program.

In a press release, Magna founder Frank Stronach said the "traditional, confrontational model of labour relations is unproductive and wastes energy that would be better focused on creating the conditions [that] would be fair to employees and would ensure that Magna remains competitive in the global automotive industry."

Stronach calls the FFA a "new, innovative, flexible, and efficient model of labour relations." Although the deal has generated criticism from some within the Canadian labour movement, former CAW national president Buzz Hargrove says "that having Magna onside will boost the union's lobbying power when it goes to governments with concerns about trade deals and the Canadian auto industry."[1]

Frank Stronach (left), chairman of the Board of Magna, and Buzz Hargrove, former president of the Canadian Auto Workers union.

This chapter explores human resource activities in organizations where employees belong to unions or where employees are seeking to organize unions. We begin by formally defining unions and labour relations, then describe the history and scope and impact of union activity. We next summarize government laws and regulations affecting unions and labour relations. The following three sections detail types of activities involving unions: union organizing, collective agreement negotiation, and collective agreement administration. Finally, we identify ways in which unions and management are working together in arrangements that are more cooperative than the traditional labour–management relationship.

Role of Unions and Labour Relations

In Canada today, most workers act as individuals to select jobs that are acceptable to them and to negotiate pay, benefits, flexible hours, and other work conditions. Especially when there is stiff competition for labour and employees have hard-to-replace skills, this arrangement produces satisfactory results for most employees. At times, however, workers have believed their needs and interests do not receive enough consideration from management. One response by workers is to act collectively by forming and joining labour **unions**, organizations formed for the purpose of representing their members' interests and resolving conflicts with employers.

Unions have a role because some degree of conflict is inevitable between workers and management.[2] For example, managers can increase profits by lowering workers' pay, but workers benefit in the short term if lower profits result because their pay is higher. Still, this type of conflict is more complex than a simple tradeoff, such as wages versus profits. Rising profits can help employees by driving up profit sharing or other benefits, and falling profits can result in layoffs and a lack of investment. Although employers can use programs like profit sharing to help align employee interests with their own, some remaining divergence of interests is inevitable. Labour unions represent worker interests and the collective bargaining process provides a way to manage the conflict. In other words, through systems for hearing complaints and negotiating agreements, unions and managers resolve conflicts between employers and employees.

As unionization of workers became more common, universities and colleges developed training in how to manage union–management interactions.[3] This specialty, called **labour relations**, emphasizes skills that managers and union leaders can use to foster effective labour–management cooperation, minimize costly forms of conflict (such as strikes), and seek win-win solutions to disagreements. Labour relations involves three levels of decisions:[4]

L01 - Define unions and labour relations and their role in organizations.

1,2,4

unions
Organizations formed for the purpose of representing their members' interests in dealing with employers.

labour relations
A field that emphasizes skills managers and union leaders can use to minimize costly forms of conflict (such as strikes) and seek win-win solutions to disagreements.

1. *Labour relations strategy.* For management, the decision involves whether the organization will work with unions or develop (or maintain) nonunion operations. This decision is influenced by outside forces such as public opinion and competition. For unions, the decision involves whether to resist changes in how unions relate to the organization or accept new kinds of labour–management relationships.

2. *Negotiating contracts.* As we will describe later in the chapter, collective agreement negotiations in a union setting involve decisions about pay structure, job security, work rules, workplace safety, and many other issues. These decisions affect workers' and the employer's situation for the term of the contract.

3. *Administering collective agreements.* These decisions involve day-to-day activities in which union members and the organization's managers may have disagreements. Issues include complaints of work rules being violated or workers being treated unfairly in particular situations. A formal grievance procedure is typically used to resolve these issues.

Later sections in this chapter describe how managers and unions carry out the activities connected with these levels of decisions, as well as the goals and legal constraints affecting these activities.

National and International Unions

Most union members belong to a national or international union. Figure 10.1 shows the membership of the largest national unions in Canada. Half of these have memberships of over 200,000 workers.

craft union
Labour union whose members all have a particular skill or occupation.

These unions may be either craft or industrial unions. The members of a **craft union** all have a particular skill or occupation. Examples include the International Brotherhood of Electrical Workers for electricians and the United Brotherhood of Painters and Allied Trades for painters. Craft unions are often responsible for training their members through apprenticeships and for supplying craft workers to employers. For example, an employer would send requests for electricians to the union, which would decide which electricians to send out. In this way, craft workers may work for many employers over time but have a constant link to the union. A craft union's bargaining power depends greatly on its control over the supply of its workers.

industrial union
A labour union whose members are linked by their work in a particular industry.

In contrast, **industrial unions** consist of members who are linked by their work in a particular industry. Examples include the Canadian Union of Public Employees and the Communications Energy and Paperworkers Union of Canada. Typically, an industrial union represents many different occupations. Membership in the

union is the result of working for a particular employer in the industry. Changing employers is less common than it is among craft workers, and employees who change employers remain members of the same union only if they happen to move to other employers covered by that union. Another difference is that whereas a craft union may restrict the number of skilled craftspeople—say, carpenters—to maintain higher wages, industrial unions try to organize as many employees in as wide a range of skills as possible.

Canadian Labour Congress (CLC)
An association that seeks to advance the shared interests of its member unions at the national level.

Kenneth Georgetti, president of the Canadian Labour Congress (CLC). Most national unions are affiliated with the CLC.

Most national unions are affiliated with the **Canadian Labour Congress (CLC)**. The CLC is not a labour union but an association that seeks to advance the shared interests of its member unions at the national level, much

FIGURE 10.1

Labour Organizations with Largest Membership

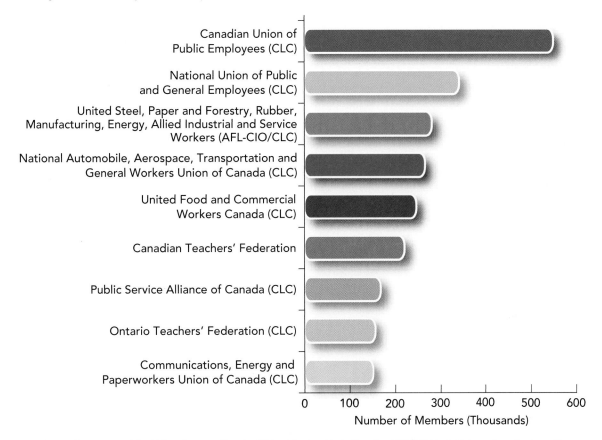

SOURCE: Human Resources and Social Development Canada, "Union Membership in Canada—2007," Table 2, "Labour Organizations with Largest Membership—2007," www.hrsdc.gc.ca/en/lp/wid/unionmembership.shtml, retrieved September 21, 2008. Reproduced with the permission of the Minister of Public Works and Government Services Canada, 2008.

as the Chamber of Commerce does for its member employers. Approximately three million workers are affiliated with the CLC. An important responsibility of the CLC is to represent labour's interests in public policy issues such as labour law, social equality, economic policy, and occupational safety and health. The organization also provides information and analysis that member unions can use in their activities. Some international unions, such as the International Brotherhood of Teamsters, are also associated with the **American Federation of Labor and Congress of Industrial Organizations (AFL-CIO)**, which advances member interests at the international level, that is, headquartered in the United States but with members in Canada.

Local Unions

Most national unions consist of multiple local units. Even when a national union plays the most critical role in negotiating the terms of a collective bargaining agreement, negotiation occurs at the local level for work rules and other issues that are locally determined. In addition, administration of the agreement largely takes place at the local union level. As a result, most day-to-day interaction between labour and management involves the local union.

RPC

4

American Federation of Labor and Congress of Industrial Organizations (AFL-CIO)
An association that seeks to advance the shared interests of its member unions at the international level.

Membership in the local union depends on the type of union. For an industrial union, the local may correspond to a single large facility or to a number of small facilities. In a craft union, the local may cover a city or a region.

Typically, the local union elects officers, such as president, vice-president, and treasurer. The officers may be responsible for contract negotiation, or the local may form a bargaining committee for that purpose. When the union is engaged in bargaining, the national union provides help, including background data about other settlements, technical advice, and the leadership of a representative from the national office.

union steward
An employee elected by union members to represent them in ensuring that the terms of the collective agreement are enforced.

Individual members participate in local unions in various ways. At meetings of the local union, they elect officials and vote on resolutions to strike. Most of workers' contact is with the **union steward**, an employee elected by union members to represent them in ensuring that the terms of the agreement are enforced. The union steward helps to investigate complaints and represents employees to supervisors and other managers when employees file grievances alleging contract violations.[5] When the union deals with several employers, as in the case of a craft union, a *business representative* performs some of the same functions as a union steward. Because of union stewards' and business representatives' close involvement with employees, it is to management's advantage to cultivate positive working relationships with them.

History and Trends in Union Membership

Labour unions have existed in Canada as early as 1812. Unionism in Canada had early ties to Britain, as tradesmen active in the British trade union movement immigrated to Canada and settled in the Maritimes. The first national labour organization, a forerunner of the Canadian Labour Congress, was formed in 1873. During the early 1900s labour activities escalated as workers demanded better wages, shorter workdays, and improved working conditions. Strikes involving large numbers of workers were frequent, with the Winnipeg General Strike in 1919 being one of the largest. As labour politics developed, unionization was supported by the Co-operative Commonwealth Federation (CCF Party), which later became the New Democratic Party (NDP). Collective bargaining was first recognized in 1937. Post–World War II, U.S. unions began to spread into Canada and influenced Canada's labour legislation. Unionization levels continued to grow in both the private and public sectors until the mid-1990s despite pressures on unions that labour costs had not kept pace with productivity.[6]

Union membership in Canada peaked in 1994, reaching 36.1 percent of employees.[7] The total number of unionized employees has increased from 2.8 million in 1977 to over 4.4 million in 2007;[8] however, this growth did not keep up with increased employment. As a result, the rate of unionization has gradually declined to 30.3 percent of nonagricultural paid workers.[9]

As is illustrated in Figure 10.2, union membership is concentrated in public-sector jobs (70 percent), and education, health care, and social services (62 percent). Manufacturing is also highly unionized. Among the least unionized sectors are retail trade (16 percent), financial services (9 percent), and the food and accommodation industry (9 percent).

Figure 10.3 illustrates the significant variation in rates of union membership among the provinces. Quebec (40 percent) and Newfoundland (39 percent) have the highest rates of unionization. Alberta (24 percent) and Ontario (28 percent) have the lowest rates of union density. Unionization also varies by firm size. Unionization is most common in large organizations.

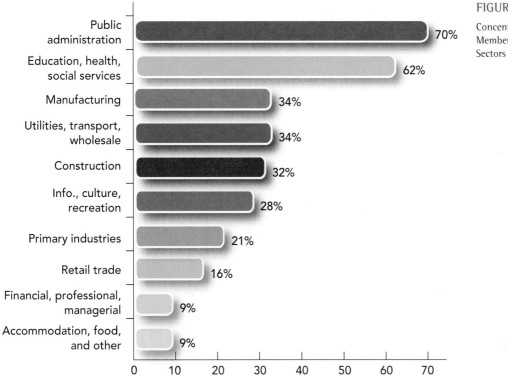

FIGURE 10.2

Concentration of Union
Membership Across Job
Sectors

SOURCE: Work Network of Canadian Policy Research Networks, www.jobquality.ca/indicator_e/enlarge/
uni001cc.htm, retrieved November 5, 2004.

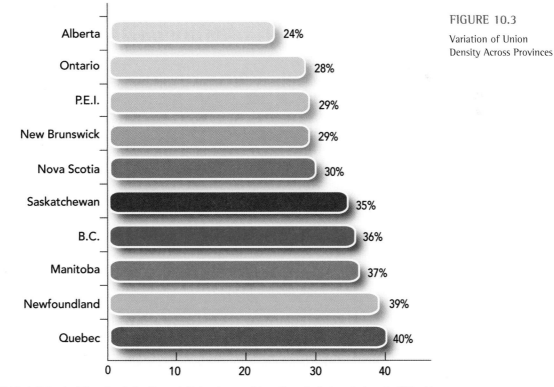

FIGURE 10.3

Variation of Union
Density Across Provinces

SOURCE: Work Network of Canadian Policy Research Networks, www.jobquality.ca/indicator_e/enlarge/uni001cc.htm.
Retrieved November 5, 2004.

The decline in union membership has been attributed to several factors.[10] The factor cited most often seems to be change in the structure of the economy. Much recent job growth has occurred among women and youth in the service sector of the economy, while union strength has traditionally been among urban blue-collar workers, especially middle-aged workers.

Another force working against union membership is management efforts against union organizing. In a survey, almost half of large employers said their most important labour goal was to be union-free. Efforts to control costs have contributed to employer resistance to unions.[11] On average, unionized workers receive higher pay than their nonunionized counterparts, and the pressure is greater because of international competition. In the past, union membership across an industry such as automobiles or steel resulted in similar wages and work requirements for all competitors. Today, North American producers have to compete with companies that have entirely different pay scales and work rules, often putting the North American companies at a disadvantage. Another way management may be contributing to the decline in union membership is by adopting human resource practices that increase employees' commitment to their job and employer. Competition for scarce human resources can lead employers to offer much of what employees traditionally sought through union membership. Government regulations, too, can make unions seem less important. Stricter regulation in such areas as workplace safety and human rights leaves fewer areas in which unions can show an advantage over what employers already have to offer.

Unions have made strategic decisions in recent years to organize the growing private-service sector. This sector includes workers employed in hotels, home care agencies, and offices. Often, these employees are women. This extension of union activity into the service sector has been one reason for the most significant transformation in union membership, that is, the mix of men and women. In 1977, women represented only 12 percent of total union membership, however, in 2007 for the first time in Canadian history, there were more women than men belonging to unions. As reported by Statistics Canada, 2,248,000 women were represented by unions—50.1 percent of the unionized workforce.[12] Reasons for the increase in women membership in unions can be attributed to the increasing

- Number of women in the paid workforce
- Number of women in the highly unionized public sector
- Unionization of part-time employees (many of whom are women)
- Number of women employed in nontraditional male-dominated occupations and industries[13]

Unions active in organizing workers in the private-service sector include the United Steelworkers of America (USWA), which organized Pinkerton's security guards, and the Canadian Autoworkers (CAW), which organized more than 50 Kentucky Fried Chicken outlets in British Columbia.[14] The Ontario Public Service Employees Union (OPSEU) have launched a campaign to unionize more than 12,500 part-time and sessional employees working in Ontario's community colleges.[15]

The mindset with respect to collective action and unionization is also an important consideration of union leaders. Union density among employees aged 15 to 24 years of age is only 13.3 percent—well below the national average.[16] CLC president Georgetti emphasized the group-minded nature of Generation Y: "We have noted that Generation Y travels in packs" and "this bodes well for selling this group of workers on the notion of collective action."[17] However, Prem Benimadhu with the Conference

Board of Canada, suggests that younger workers are less likely to want or need union representation— "Once workers figure out that they can negotiate successfully on their own behalf, it will be hard for unions to convince them to join up and pay dues for the same service," he concludes.[18] An example of a recent initiative likely to appeal to younger work-

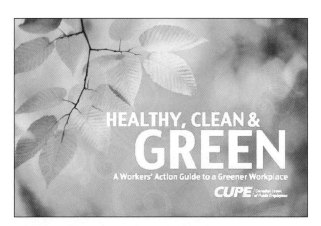

ers is CUPE's new workplace environmental guide "Healthy, Clean & Green: A Workers' Action Guide to a Greener Workplace," which shows workers ways to tackle environmental problems such as climate change.[19]

As Figure 10.4 indicates, the percentage of Canadian workers who belong to unions, although much higher than in the United States, is lower than in many countries. More dramatic is the difference in "coverage"—the percentage of employees whose terms and conditions of employment are governed by a union contract, whether or not the employees are technically union members. In western Europe, it is common to have coverage rates of 80 to 90 percent, so the influence of labour unions far outstrips what membership levels would imply.[20] Also, employees in western Europe tend to have a larger formal role in decision making than in Canada. This role, including worker representatives on boards of directors, is often mandated by the government. But as markets become more and more global, pressure to cut labour costs and increase productivity is likely to be stronger in every country. Unless unions can help companies improve productivity or organize new production facilities opened in lower-wage countries, union influence may decline in countries where it is now strong.

Impact of Unions on Company Performance

Organizations are concerned about whether union organizing and bargaining will hurt their performance, in particular unions' impact on productivity, profits, and stock performance. Researchers have studied the general relationship between unionization and these performance measures. Through skillful labour relations, organizations can positively influence outcomes.

2,4

There has been much debate regarding the effects of unions on productivity.[21] The view that unions decrease productivity is based on work rules and limits on workloads set by union contracts and production lost to such union actions as strikes and work slowdowns. At the same time, unions can have positive effects on productivity.[22] They can reduce turnover by giving employees a route for resolving problems.[23] Unions emphasize pay

Harley-Davidson and the International Association of Machinists and Aerospace Workers have cooperated to produce good results. In general, though, companies wishing to become more competitive need to continually monitor their labour relations strategies.

FIGURE 10.4

Union Membership Rates
and Coverage in Selected
Countries

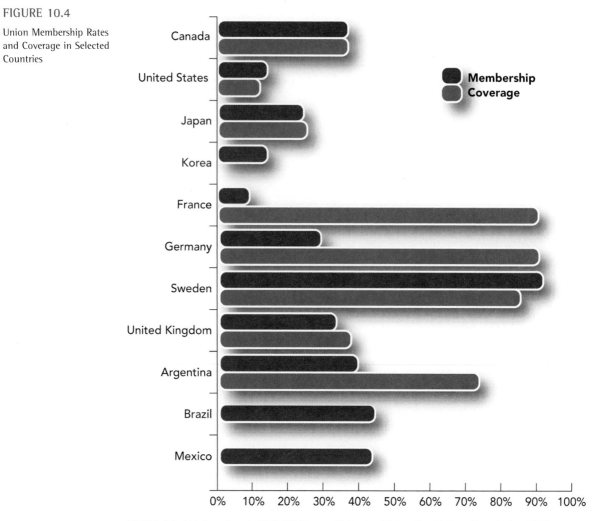

SOURCE: "World Labour Report, 1997–98" (Geneva, Switzerland: International Labour Organization, 2008),
www.oit.org/public/english/dialogue/ifpdial/publ/wlr97/annex/notes.htm, retrieved September 21, 2008.

systems based on seniority, which remove incentives for employees to compete rather
than cooperate. The introduction of a union also may force an employer to improve
its management practices and pay greater attention to employee ideas.

Although there is evidence that unions have both positive and negative effects
on productivity, most studies have found that union workers are more productive
than nonunion workers. Are highly productive workers more likely to form unions,
or does a union make workers more productive? The answer is unclear. In theory, if
unions caused greater productivity, we would expect union membership to be rising,
not falling as it has been.[24]

Even if unions do raise productivity, a company's profits and stock performance
may still suffer if unions raise wage and benefits costs by more than the productivity
gain. On average, union members receive higher wages and more generous benefits
than nonunion workers, and evidence shows that unions have a large negative effect
on profits. Also, union coverage tends to decline faster in companies with a lower return to shareholders.[25] In summary, companies wishing to become more competitive
need to continually monitor their labour relations strategy.

These studies look at the average effects of unions, not at individual companies or innovative labour relations. Some organizations can report success stories in labour relations. Harley-Davidson, for example, has developed a cooperative relationship with the International Association of Machinists and Aerospace Workers (IAM).[26] The two parties negotiated a contract that provides for employment security and joint labour–management decision making in many areas. The company shares technical and financial information and expects a high level of participation in improving productivity and satisfying customers. The IAM's Lou Kiefer explains, "We know that if we increase productivity and lower costs, we're not working ourselves out of a job."

Goals of Each Group

Resolving conflicts in a positive way is usually easiest when the parties involved understand each other's goals. Although individual cases vary, we can draw some general conclusions about the goals of labour unions and management. Society, too, has goals for labour and business, given form in the laws regulating labour relations.

LO2 - Identify the labour relations goals of management, labour unions, and society.

Goals of Management

Management goals are to increase the organization's profits and/or increase productivity. Managers tend to prefer options that lower costs and raise output. When deciding whether to discourage employees from forming a union, a concern is that a union will create higher costs for wages and benefits, as well as raise the risk of work stoppages. Managers may also fear that a union will make managers and workers into adversaries or limit management's discretion in making business and employment decisions.

When an employer has recognized a union, management's goals continue to emphasize restraining costs and improving output. Managers continue to prefer to keep the organization's operations flexible, so they can adjust activities to meet competitive challenges and customer demands. Therefore, in their labour relations managers prefer to limit increases in wages and benefits and to retain as much control as they can over work rules and schedules. In addition, globalization and the need to compete with lower-cost competitors influences management's goals to remain competitive and productive.

Goals of Labour Unions

Labour unions have the goals of obtaining pay, job security, and working conditions that satisfy their members and of giving members a voice in decisions that affect them. Traditionally, they obtain these goals by gaining power in numbers. The more workers who belong to a union, the greater the union's power. More members translates into greater ability to halt or disrupt production. Larger unions also have greater financial resources for continuing a strike; the union can help to make up for the wages the workers lose during a strike. The threat of a long strike—stated or implied—can make an employer more willing to meet the union's demands.

Statistics Canada reported that unionized workers received on average, hourly earnings 26 percent higher than the average nonunion worker did. Union membership has an even greater impact on part-time workers. Unionized part-time workers averaged 65 percent higher earnings than nonunion part-time workers.[27]

social unionism
A type of unionism that attempts to influence social and economic policies of government.

Unions typically want to influence the *way* pay and promotions are determined. Unlike management, which tries to consider employees as individuals so that pay and promotion decisions relate to performance differences, unions try to build group solidarity and avoid possible arbitrary treatment of employees. To do so, unions try to have any pay differences based on seniority, on the grounds that this measure is more objective than performance evaluations. As a result, where workers are represented by a union, it is common for all employees in a particular job classification to be paid at the same rate. As well as working to advance the interests of members, unions often engage in **social unionism**, that is, activities intended to influence social and economic policies of government. For example, CAW, Canada's largest private-sector union, is actively involved in antiracism programs, creating safer workplaces for LGBT (lesbian, gay, bisexual, and transgender) union members, and supporting work and family balance initiatives.

Rand Formula
A union security provision that makes payment of labour union dues mandatory even if the worker is not a member of the union.

However, the survival and security of a union ultimately depends on its ability to ensure a regular flow of new members and member dues to support the services it provides. In 1946, Supreme Court of Canada Justice Ivan Rand brought down a significant decision that affected union financial security in Canada. The case came about as part of an arbitrated settlement of the labour dispute between the Ford Motor Company and the United Auto Workers. The **Rand Formula** is a union security provision that makes the payment of labour union dues mandatory even if the worker is not a member of the union. The rationale for the principle was that every employee benefits from union representation.[28] Unions typically place high priority on negotiating two types of contract provisions with an employer that are critical to a union's security and viability: checkoff provisions and provisions relating to union membership or contribution.

checkoff provision
A requirement that the employer, on behalf of the union, automatically deducts union dues from employees' paycheques.

Under a **checkoff provision**, the employer, on behalf of the union, automatically deducts union dues from employees' paycheques.

The strongest union security arrangement is a **closed shop**, under which a person must be a union member before being hired or the **union shop**, an arrangement that requires an employee to join the union within a certain time after beginning employment.

These provisions are ways to address unions' concern about "free riders"—employees who benefit from union activities without belonging to a union. By law, all members of a bargaining unit, whether union members or not, must be represented by the union. If the union is required to offer services to all bargaining unit members even though some of them do not pay dues, it may not have enough financial resources to operate successfully.

closed shop
A union security arrangement under which a person must be a union member before being hired.

union shop
A union security arrangement that requires employees to join the union within a certain amount of time after beginning employment.

Goals of Society

The activities of unions and management take place within the context of society, with society's values driving the laws and regulations that affect labour relations. As long ago as the late 1800s and early 1900s, industrial relations scholars saw unions as a way to make up for individual employees' limited bargaining power.[29] At that time, clashes between workers and management could be violent, and many people hoped that unions would replace the violence with negotiation. Since then, observers have expressed concern that unions in certain industries have become too strong, achieving their goals at the expense of employers' ability to compete or meet other objectives. Overall, however, societal goals for government include ensuring that neutral rules exist to ensure balance is maintained between the powers of unions and employers. For example, Ontario recently introduced labour law changes intended to "restore greater fairness and balance to labour relations in Ontario."[30]

Rather than being left to the activities of unions and management, many societal goals are also enforced through laws and regulations. As discussed in Chapter 2, human rights, pay equity, employment equity, privacy and other types of legislation determine how workers are treated by their employers. In addition, as we will see in the next section, a set of laws and regulations also exists to give workers the right to choose to join unions.

Laws and Regulations Affecting Labour Relations

LO3 - Summarize laws and regulations that affect labour relations.

The laws and regulations pertaining to labour relations affect unions' size and bargaining power, so they significantly affect the degree to which unions, management, and society achieve their varied goals. These laws and regulations set limits on union structure and administration and the ways in which unions and management interact.

Canada's overall labour relations legal framework is decentralized and relatively complex. Since a ruling of the Supreme Court of Canada in 1925, responsibility for labour relations is primarily a provincial/territorial responsibility. Which organizations fall under federal versus provincial/territorial legislation was discussed in Chapter 2. Federally regulated private-sector employees are regulated by the Canada Labour Code (Part 1—Industrial Relations). In addition, private-sector employees in Nunavut, the Yukon, and the Northwest Territories are also regulated by the Canada Labour Code. Each province and territory has its own distinct labour laws. Each jurisdiction—federal, provincial, and territorial—also has laws governing public-sector employees. There are additional labour statutes that apply to specific occupations determined to be essential services, for example, teachers, law enforcement officers, firefighters, and health care employees. For example, in Alberta, health care workers are not allowed to take job action. However, the right to strike will likely be revisited soon due to a Supreme Court of Canada ruling that access to collective bargaining constitutes a protected right under Canada's Charter of Rights and Freedoms. As a result of this ruling, labour leaders expect that governments will be markedly less able to restrict the right of essential services workers to bargain and take job action.[31] One of the chapter-ending case studies explores this issue in more detail. The Human Resources and Social Development Canada website provides links to all industrial relations legislation in Canada (www.hrsdc.gc.ca).

Although some differences exist among jurisdictions, the main features of labour legislation in Canada can be summarized as follows:

- Methods to certify a union that will represent a group of employees
- Requirement of the employer to recognize the union chosen by the majority of its employees and to accept the union as the employees' exclusive representative for bargaining purposes
- Responsibility to bargain in good faith with the intention to reach an agreement
- Requirement of the employer to deduct union dues from employees
- Minimum length of a collective agreement (at least one year)
- Regulation of strike and lockout activities
- Creation of a labour relations board (or specialized tribunal) to interpret and enforce the labour laws in their jurisdiction
- Prohibition of identified **unfair labour practices** by management and labour (see the HR How-To box)

unfair labour practice
A prohibited conduct of an employer, union, or individual under the relevant labour legislation.

HR HOW-TO

Avoiding Unfair Labour Practices

A common core of labour legislation prohibits employers, unions, and individuals from engaging in unfair labour practices. Each jurisdiction in Canada has specific provisions dealing with unfair labour practices by management. Here are some of the most common examples of unfair labour practices that management must avoid:

- Interfering in the formation of a union or contributing to it financially (although, there have been allowances for the providing of an office for the union to conduct business and for paid leave for union officials conducting union business)
- Discriminating against an employee because the

individual is or is not a member of a union
- Discriminating against an employee because the individual chooses to exercise rights granted by labour law
- Intimidating or coercing an employee to become or not become a member of a union

Unfair labour practices by unions are also prohibited. While each jurisdiction has laws regulating union conduct, important examples of unfair labour practices that unions must avoid include

- Seeking to compel an employer to bargain collectively with the union if the union is not the certified bargaining agent

- Attempting at the workplace and during working hours to persuade an employee to become or not become a union member
- Intimidating, coercing, or penalizing an individual because he or she has filed a complaint or testified in any proceeding pursuant to the relevant labour law
- Engaging in, encouraging, or threatening illegal strikes
- Failing to represent employees fairly

SOURCE: Hermann Franz Schwind, Hari Das, and Terry H. Wagar, *Canadian Human Resource Management*, 7th ed. (Toronto: McGraw-Hill Ryerson, 2005), p. 604.

Labour Relations Board (LRB)
A specialized tribunal with authority to interpret and enforce the labour laws in their jurisdiction.

There is a **Labour Relations Board (LRB)** (or similar structure) in each jurisdiction that serves as a specialized quasi-judicial tribunal with authority to interpret and enforce the labour laws in their jurisdiction. The **Canada Industrial Relations Board (CIRB)** has jurisdiction for federally regulated employees as well as private-sector employees in Nunavut, the Yukon, and the Northwest Territories. As described in the e-HRM box, the Ontario Labour Relations Board offers access to tools and resources on its interactive website.

Canada Industrial Relations Board (CIRB)
A quasi-judicial tribunal responsible for the interpretation and enforcement of the Industrial Relations section of the Canada Labour Code.

Prevention of Unfair Labour Practices

When someone believes that an unfair labour practice has taken place, he or she may file a complaint with the appropriate Labour Relations Board for the jurisdiction. There are deadlines for filing complaints. For example, the deadline for filing a complaint with the Canada Industrial Relations Board (CIRB) for employees falling under the Canada Labour Code is no later than the 90th day after the individual knew, or in the Board's opinion should have known, of the events in question.[32] All parties are provided a copy of the complaint and the process usually involves the Labour Relations Board conducting a preliminary investigation to determine if the

E-HRM

The OLRB's Interactive Website

HR professionals can now access a comprehensive range of tools and resources on a self-service basis. The Ontario Labour Relations Board has advanced the use of technology to clients and stakeholders through the implementation of an interactive website (www. olrb.gov.on.ca). OLRB Online provides access to the full text of OLRB decisions from January 1, 2000 (as well as some prior decisions) from their link to the Canadian

Legal Information Institute (www.canlii.org). The site also provides access to key processes such as rules of procedure, making an application, mediation, and adjudication, and to its bimonthly collection of significant decisions and featured "decisions of interest."

In addition, all forms that relate to labour relations in Ontario are made accessible, alphabetically or by application. For example, all forms, information bulletins,

and schedules related to certification of a union in the construction industry are grouped to ensure clients and stakeholders can retrieve all relevant forms and information from a single point of self-directed contact.

SOURCES: Ontario Labour Relations Board website, www.olrb.gov.on.ca; "A Look Ahead—Technology at the OLRB," *OLRB Annual Report 2000–2001*, p. 42, www.olrb.gov .on.ca/english/Public.htm, retrieved November 6, 2004; Canadian Legal Information Institute website, www.canlii.org/on/cas/onlrb.

complaint has merit and if it may be possible for the parties to resolve the complaint themselves. If the Labour Relations Board finds the complaint has merit and determines the complaint cannot be resolved through the parties, the Labour Relations Board will conduct a formal hearing with the parties present. Either the case can be dismissed at this point or the Labour Relations Board has the authority to issue cease-and-desist orders to halt unfair labour practices. If the union or employer does not comply with the Labour Relations Board order, the order can be referred to a court of law for enforcement.

Union Organizing

LO4 - Describe the union organizing process.

Unions begin their involvement with an organization's employees by conducting an organizing campaign. To meet its objectives, a union needs to convince a majority of workers that they should receive better pay or other employment conditions and that the union will help them do so. The employer's objectives will depend on its strategy—whether it seeks to work with a union or convince employees that they are better off without union representation.

The Process of Organizing

The organization process begins with a membership application such as the one shown in Figure 10.5. Union representatives contact employees, present their message about the union, and invite them to sign an application for membership. By signing the application and paying a nominal fee in some jurisdictions (e.g., for

FIGURE 10.5

Example of an
Application for
Membership

APPLICATION FOR MEMBERSHIP

Ontario Public Service Employees Union, 100 Lesmill Road, Toronto, ON M3B 3P8

I hereby apply for and accept membership in, and authorize OPSEU, its agents or representatives, to act for me as my exclusive representative in collective bargaining, in respect to all the terms and conditions of my employment and to negotiate contracts with my employer covering all such matters.

X_____ Date_____
(Signature of applicant)

On behalf of the above organization, I hereby accept this application.

X_____ Date_____
(Signature of recruiter)

Last name (please print)_____

First name (please print)_____

Address_____ Apt. #_____

City_____ Prov._____ Postal code_____

Phone (home)_____ Phone (work)_____

Employed by (name of college)_____

Campus_____ Department _____

First name (please print)_____

☐ Faculty: ☐ Faculty: ☐ Support: ☐ Support:
   Part-time   Sessional   Part-time   Non-recurring project

Home or secure e-mail address _____

SOURCE: Ontario Public Service Employees Union website, www.opseu.org/caat/parttime/pdf/FaxformNov2907.pdf, retrieved May 14, 2008.

private-sector employees under federal jurisdiction the fee is $5) the employee indicates they want the union to represent them.

When the necessary number of employees have signed membership applications, the union will apply to the appropriate Labour Relations Board for certification. Requirements differ among jurisdictions. For example, if your employer is in the private sector and falls under federal jurisdiction, the local can be certified without a vote if more than 50 percent of employees sign applications. If fewer than 50 percent of employees signed, the Canada Industrial Relations Board will conduct an election among the employees. For the union to be certified, at least 35 percent of employees in the work group must vote and more than 50 percent of these voting employees must vote in favour of unionizing.[33]

Management Strategies

Sometimes an employer will recognize a union after a majority of employees have signed membership applications. More often, there is a hotly contested election campaign. During the campaign, unions try to persuade employees that their wages,

Wal-Mart Canada closed its store in Jonquière, Quebec, six months after workers obtained union certification.

benefits, treatment by employers, and chances to influence workplace decisions are too poor or small and that the union will be able to obtain improvements in these areas. Management typically responds with its own messages providing an opposite point of view. Management messages say the organization has provided a valuable package of wages and benefits and has treated employees well. Management also argues that the union will not be able to keep its promises but will instead create costs for employees, such as union dues and lost income during strikes. For example, the CAW organized about 140 Starbucks workers at ten stores in Vancouver. Susan Spratt, lead union negotiator with Starbucks, "alleges the company has fought off further organizing in part by removing managers and promising better conditions at stores where the union has tried to sign up members."[34]

Employers use a variety of methods to avoid unionization in organizing campaigns.[35] Their efforts range from hiring consultants to distributing leaflets and letters to presenting the company's viewpoint at meetings of employees. Some management efforts go beyond what the law permits, especially in the eyes of union organizers. This impression is supported by an increase in charges of employer unfair labour practices and awards of back pay since the late 1960s.[36] Why would employers break the law? One explanation is that the consequences, such as reinstating workers with back pay, are small compared to the benefits.[37] If coercing workers away from joining a union saves the company the higher wages, benefits, and other costs of a unionized workforce, management may feel an incentive to accept costs like back pay.

Supervisors have the most direct contact with employees. Thus, as Table 10.1 indicates, it is critical that they establish good relationships with employees even before there is any attempt at union organizing. Supervisors also must know what *not* to do if a union drive takes place. They should be trained in the legal principles discussed earlier in this chapter.

Decertifying a Union

Union members' right to be represented by unions of their own choosing also includes the right to vote out an existing union. The action is called *decertifying* the union. Decertification follows the same process as a representation election. An application to decertify a union may not be acted upon during a legal strike or lockout. In some jurisdictions

TABLE 10.1

What Supervisors Should and Should Not Do to Reduce the Likelihood of Unionization

WHAT TO DO
Report any direct or indirect signs of union activity to a core management group.
Deal with employees by carefully stating the company's response to pro-union arguments. These responses should be coordinated by the company to maintain consistency and to avoid threats or promises. Take away union issues by following effective management practices all the time: • Deliver recognition and appreciation. • Solve employee problems. • Protect employees from harassment or humiliation. • Provide business-related information. • Be consistent in treatment of employees. • Accommodate special circumstances where appropriate. • Ensure due process in performance management. • Treat all employees with dignity and respect.

WHAT TO AVOID
Threatening employees with harsher terms and conditions of employment or employment loss if they engage in union activity.
Interrogating employees about pro-union or anti-union sentiments that they or others may have or reviewing union authorization cards or pro-union petitions.
Promising employees that they will receive favourable terms or conditions of employment if they forgo union activity.
Spying on employees known to be, or suspected of being, engaged in pro-union activities.

SOURCE: J. A. Segal, "Unshackle Your Supervisors to Stay Union Free," *HR Magazine*, June 1998. Copyright 1998 by Society for Human Resource Management. Reproduced with permission of Society for Human Resource Management via Copyright Clearance Center.

(e.g., Ontario) when a collective agreement is in place, decertification applications may only be filed during specified "open periods." Laws in some jurisdictions require the employer to post and annually circulate information related to union decertification.

LO5 - Explain how management and unions negotiate collective agreements.

collective bargaining
Negotiation between union representatives and management representatives to arrive at an agreement defining conditions of employment for the term of the agreement and to administer that agreement.

Collective Bargaining

When a union has been certified, that union represents employees during contract negotiations. In **collective bargaining**, a union negotiates on behalf of its members with management representatives to arrive at a contract defining conditions of employment for the term of the contract and to resolve differences in the way they interpret the contract. Typical collective agreements include provisions for pay, benefits, work rules, and resolution of workers' grievances. Table 10.2 shows typical provisions negotiated in collective agreements.

Collective bargaining differs from one situation to another in terms of *bargaining structure*—that is, the range of employees and employers covered by the contract. An agreement may involve a narrow group of employees in a craft union or a broad group in an industrial union. Agreements may cover one or several facilities of the same employer, or the bargaining structure may involve several employers. Many more interests must be considered in collective bargaining for an industrial union with a bargaining structure that includes several employers than in collective bargaining for a craft union in a single facility.

TABLE 10.2

Typical Provisions
in Collective
Agreements

Rights of Parties	*Recognition of Union Security* • Union membership • Union security • Leave for union business • Restrictions on contracting out *Management Rights to Test* • Drug and alcohol testing • Intelligence and aptitude testing • Electronic surveillance • Internet/telephone monitoring • Medical examinations • Other tests *Employee Rights/Security* • Harassment • Employment Equity Program • Assistance programs, e.g., substance abuse
Organization of Work	*Technological Change* • Advance notice • Obligation to provide training, instruction, or retraining • Layoff protection • Wage protection • Special leaves, severance pay, and/or retirement offers *Distribution of Work* • Flexibility in work assignment • Job rotation • Semi-autonomous work groups or teams • Job sharing
Labour Relations	*Labour Relations* • Grievance procedures • Bargaining method or approach • Application of the agreement • Job evaluation (position evaluation) • Joint committees • Participation (other than committees)
Education, Training, and Development	*Education, Training, and Employee Development* • Leave • Reimbursement for tuition fees and books • Multiskilling, i.e., flexibility for the employee • Contribution to a training fund • Apprenticeship programs
Conditions of Work	*Work Schedule* • Normal hours of work • Type of work schedules • Special provisions *Overtime* • Clause limiting the use of overtime • Compensatory days in lieu of pay (banking) • Overtime pay • Meal allowance (overtime)

(continued)

Job Security and Termination
- No layoffs while the agreement is in effect
- Layoffs by seniority
- Bumping rights
- Retention of seniority
- Work sharing (reduction in hours to avoid layoffs)
- Education/training with pay
- Supplementary employment insurance benefit

Pay
- Cost-of-living allowance
- Wage guarantees

Leaves and Vacations
- Paid holidays
- Annual vacation
- Family leave
- Paid sick leave plan

Benefits
- Private group insurance plans
- Pension plans (funding, administration)

Provisions Relating to Part-Time Workers
- Maximum hours of work normally allowed
- Ratio of part-time to full-time workers
- Holidays, vacations, sick leave, benefits, pension plan, seniority

SOURCE: "Collective Agreement Provisions," Human Resources and Skills Development website, www.hrsdc.gc.ca, retrieved November 2, 2004. Reproduced with the permission of the Minister of Public Works and Government Services, 2005.

The majority of collective agreement negotiations take place between unions and employers that have been through the process before. In the typical situation, management has come to accept the union as an organization it must work with. The situation can be very different when a union has just been certified and is negotiating its first collective agreement.

As part of its programming, the Labour Relations Board British Columbia makes available a free-of-charge information session that is offered to an employer or union either jointly or separately as requested to help reach a first collective agreement.[38] Due to the recognized difficulties associated in reaching a first agreement, the legislation in some jurisdictions provides a process to ensure a first agreement can be reached. Under the Canada Labour Code, the federal Minister of Labour can direct the Canada Industrial Relations Board to establish the terms and conditions of a first collective agreement for the parties. This process would require the use of arbitration, which is discussed later in this chapter.[39]

Bargaining over New Collective Agreements

Clearly, the outcome of collective agreement negotiations can have important consequences for labour costs, productivity, and the organization's ability to compete. Therefore, unions and management need to prepare carefully for collective bargaining. Preparation includes establishing objectives for the agreement, reviewing the old agreement, gathering data (such as compensation paid by competitors and the company's ability to survive a strike), predicting the likely demands to be made, and establishing the cost of meeting the demands.[40] This preparation can help negotiators develop a plan for how to negotiate. Different situations and goals call for different approaches to bargaining, such as the following alternatives proposed by Richard Walton and Robert McKersie:[41]

- *Distributive bargaining* divides an economic "pie" between two sides—for example, a wage increase means giving the union a larger share of the pie.

- *Integrative (mutual-gains) bargaining* looks for win-win solutions, or outcomes in which both sides benefit. If the organization's labour costs hurt its performance, integrative bargaining might seek to avoid layoffs in exchange for work rules that improve productivity.

- *Attitudinal structuring* focuses on establishing a relationship of trust. The parties are concerned about ensuring that the other side will keep its part of any bargain.

- *Intraorganizational bargaining* addresses conflicts within union or management groups or objectives, such as between new employees and workers with high seniority or between cost control and reduction of turnover.

The collective bargaining process may involve any combination of these alternatives.

Negotiations go through various stages.[42] In the earliest stages, many more people are often present than in later stages. On the union side, this may give all the various internal interest groups a chance to participate and voice their goals. Their input helps communicate to management what will satisfy union members and may help the union achieve greater solidarity. At this stage, union negotiators often present a long list of proposals, partly to satisfy members and partly to introduce enough issues that they will have flexibility later in the process. Management may or may not present proposals of its own. Sometimes management prefers to react to the union's proposals.

During the middle stages of the process, each side must make a series of decisions, even though the outcome is uncertain. How important is each issue to the other side? How likely is it that disagreement on particular issues will result in a strike? When and to what extent should one side signal its willingness to compromise?

In the final stage of negotiations, pressure for an agreement increases. Public negotiations may be only part of the process. Negotiators from each side may hold one-on-one meetings or small-group meetings where they escape some public relations pressures. A neutral third party may act as a go-between or facilitator. In some cases, bargaining breaks down as the two sides find they cannot reach a mutually acceptable agreement. The outcome depends partly on the relative bargaining power of each party. That power, in turn, depends on each party's ability to withstand a strike, which costs the workers their pay during the strike and costs the employer lost production and possibly lost customers.

When Bargaining Breaks Down

The intended outcome of collective bargaining is an agreement with terms acceptable to both parties. If one or both sides determine that negotiation alone will not produce such an agreement, bargaining breaks down. To bring this impasse to an end, the union may strike, or the parties may bring in outside help to resolve their differences.

Strikes and Lockouts

strike
A collective decision by union members not to work or to slow down until certain demands or conditions are met.

lockout
A closure of a place of employment or refusal of the employer to provide work as a way to compel employees to agree to certain demands or conditions.

A **strike** is a collective decision of the union members not to work or to slow down until certain demands or conditions are met. The union members vote, and if the majority favours a strike, they all go on strike at that time or when union leaders believe the time is right. Strikes are typically accompanied by *picketing*—the union stations members near the work site with signs indicating the union is on strike. During the strike, the union members do not receive pay from their employer, but the union may be able to make up for some of the lost pay. The employer loses production unless it can hire replacement workers, and even then, productivity may be reduced. Often, other unions support striking workers by refusing to cross their picket line—for example, refusing to make deliveries to a company during a strike. A **lockout** on the other hand, is initiated by the employer. A lockout is a closure of a place of employment or refusal of the employer to provide work as a way to compel employees to agree to certain demands or conditions.

Although the vast majority of labour–management negotiations do not result in a strike or lockout, Figure 10.6 shows a chronological perspective of work stoppages. The year 2006 set a record and was uncharacteristic in having very few work disruptions. As shown in Figure 10.7, Canada lost only 0.02 percent of total working time to strikes and lockouts in 2006 in contrast to 0.12 percent in 2005. The estimated number of person-days lost through strikes and lockouts more than doubled from 1.7 million in 2003 to 4.1 million in 2005. In 2006, however, the number dropped sharply to 813,000.[43] Not only do workers lose wages and employers lose production, but the negative experience of a strike or lockout can make future interactions more difficult. When strikes or lockouts do occur, the conduct of each party during the strike can do lasting harm to labour–management relations. Violence by either side or threats of job loss or actual job loss because jobs went to replacement workers can make future relations difficult. One of the chapter-ending case studies looks at the TA strike at McGill from this perspective.

FIGURE 10.6

Number of Strikes and Lockouts; Workers Involved (000s), 1982–2006

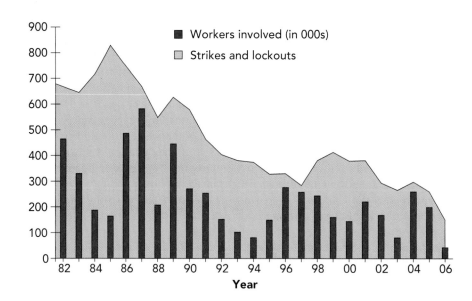

SOURCE: Adapted from Statistics Canada, "Estimated Time Lost to Strikes and Lockouts, 1982–2006," *Perspectives on Labour and Income*, Catalogue No. 75-001, 8, no. 8, April 2007, www.statcan.ca/bsolc/english/bsolc?catno=75-001-X, retrieved May 21, 2008.

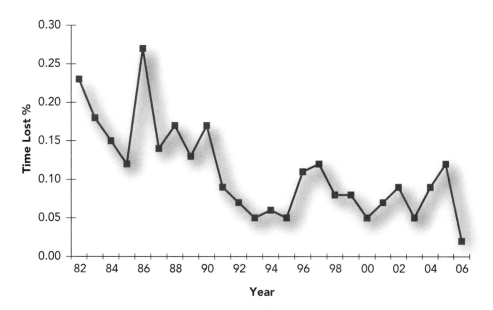

FIGURE 10.7

Estimated Working
Time Lost to Strikes and
Lockouts, 1982–2006
(percent)

SOURCE: Adapted from Statistics Canada, "Estimated Time Lost to Strikes and Lockouts, 1982–2006," *Perspectives on Labour and Income*, Catalogue No. 75-001, 8, no. 8, April 2007, www.statcan.ca/bsolc/english/bsolc?catno=75-001-X, retrieved May 21, 2008.

Alternatives to Strikes and Lockouts

Because strikes and lockouts are so costly and risky, unions and employers generally prefer other methods for resolving conflicts. Three of the most common alternatives are mediation, conciliation, and arbitration. All of these rely on a neutral third party, who usually is appointed by the federal or provincial Minister of Labour.

The least formal and most widely used of these procedures is **mediation**, in which a third party or *mediator* hears the views of both sides and facilitates the negotiation process. He or she has no formal authority to impose a resolution, so a strike remains a possibility. In a survey studying negotiations between unions and large businesses, mediation was used in almost four out of ten negotiation efforts.[44]

Conciliation, most often used for negotiations with governmental bodies, typically reports on the reasons for the dispute, the views and arguments of both sides, and (sometimes) a recommended settlement, which the parties may decline. The public nature of these recommendations may pressure the parties to reach a settlement. Even if they do not accept the conciliator's recommended settlement, the hope of this process is that the conciliator will identify or frame issues in a way that makes agreement easier. Sometimes merely devoting time to this process gives the parties a chance to reach an agreement. In most jurisdictions in Canada, conciliation is mandatory before a strike or lockout can be called. Again, however, there is no guarantee that a strike or lockout will be avoided.

mediation
Conflict resolution procedure in which a mediator hears the views of both sides and facilitates the negotiation process but has no formal authority to dictate a resolution.

conciliation
Conflict resolution procedure in which a third party to collective bargaining reports the reasons for a dispute, the views and arguments of both sides, and possibly a recommended settlement, which the parties may decline.

Striker demonstrates a heated reaction to people crossing the picket line at Aliant's main office.

arbitration
Conflict resolution procedure in which an arbitrator or arbitration board determines a binding settlement.

The most formal type of outside intervention is **arbitration**, under which an arbitrator or arbitration board determines a settlement that is *binding*, meaning the parties have to accept it. There is wide acceptance of "rights arbitration," which focuses on enforcing or interpreting agreement terms, but arbitration in the writing of collective agreements or setting of agreement terms has traditionally been reserved for special circumstances such as negotiations between unions and government agencies, where strikes may be illegal or especially costly. Occasionally, arbitration has also been used with businesses in situations where strikes have been extremely damaging. Arbitration is uncommon in the private sector, and one reason is the general opinion that union and management representatives are in the best position to resolve conflicts themselves because they are closer to the situation than an arbitrator can be. A notable exception is in the case of first-agreement arbitration, mentioned previously in the context of ensuring a first collective agreement is reached in a timely manner.

L06 - Summarize the practice of collective agreement administration.

Collective Agreement Administration

Although the process of negotiating a collective agreement (including the occasional strike) receives the most publicity, other union–management activities occur far more often. Bargaining over a new contract typically occurs only about every three years, but administering labour agreements goes on day after day, year after year. The two activities are linked, of course. Vague or inconsistent language in the agreement can make administering the agreement more difficult. The difficulties can create conflict that spills over into the next round of negotiations.[45] Events during negotiations—strikes, the use of replacement workers, or violence by either side—also can lead to difficulties in working successfully under a conflict.

grievance procedure
The process for resolving union–management conflicts over interpretation or violation of a collective agreement.

Collective agreement administration includes carrying out the terms of the agreement and resolving conflicts over interpretation or violation of the agreement. Under a labour agreement, the process for resolving these conflicts is called a **grievance procedure**. This procedure has a key influence on success in collective agreement administration. A grievance procedure may be started by an employee or discharged employee who believes the employer violated the agreement or by a union representative on behalf of a group of workers or union representatives.

For grievances launched by an employee, a typical grievance procedure follows the steps shown in Figure 10.8. The grievance may be settled during any of the four steps. In the first step, the employee talks to his or her supervisor about the problem. If this conversation is unsatisfactory, the employee may involve the union steward in further discussion. The union steward and employee decide whether the problem has been resolved and, if not, whether it is an agreement violation. If the problem was not resolved and does seem to be an agreement violation, the union moves to step 2, putting the grievance in writing and submitting it to a line manager. The union steward meets with a management representative to try to resolve the problem. Management consults with the labour relations staff and puts its response in writing too at this second stage. If step 2 fails to resolve the problem, the union appeals the grievance to top line management and representatives of the labour relations staff. The union may involve more local or national officers in discussions at this stage (see step 3 in Figure 10.8). The decision resulting from the appeal is put into writing. If the grievance is still not resolved, the union may decide (step 4) to appeal the grievance to an arbitrator. If the grievance involves a discharged employee, the process may begin at

FIGURE 10.8

Steps in an Employee-Initiated Grievance Procedure

Step 1

- Employee (and union steward) discusses problem with supervisor.
- Union steward and employee decide whether problem was resolved.
- Union steward and employee decide whether contract was violated.

Step 2

- Written grievance is submitted to production superintendent, another line manager, or labour relations representative.
- Steward and manager discuss grievance.
- Management puts response in writing.

Step 3

- Union appeals grievance to top line management and senior labour relations staff.
- Additional local or national union officers may be involved.
- Decision resulting from appeal is put into writing.

Step 4

- Union decides whether to refer unresolved grievance to arbitration.
- Union appeals grievance to arbitration for binding decision.

SOURCE: Adapted from T. A. Kochan, *Collective Bargaining and Industrial Relations* (Homewood, IL: Richard D. Irwin, 1980), p. 395; J. A. Fossum, *Labour Relations* (Boston: McGraw-Hill/Irwin, 2002), pp. 448–52.

step 2 or 3, however, and the time limits between steps may be shorter. Grievances filed by the union on behalf of a group may begin at step 1 or step 2.

The majority of grievances are settled during the earlier steps of the process. This reduces delays and avoids the costs of arbitration. If a grievance does reach arbitration, the arbitrator makes the final ruling in the matter.

From the point of view of employees, the grievance procedure is an important means of getting fair treatment in the workplace. Its success depends on whether it provides for all the kinds of problems that are likely to arise (such as how to handle a business slowdown), whether employees feel they can file a grievance without being punished for it, and whether employees believe their union representatives will follow through. Too many grievances may indicate a problem—for example, the union members or line managers do not understand how to uphold the collective agreement or have no desire to do so. At the same time, a very small number of grievances may also signal a problem. A very low grievance rate may suggest a fear of filing a grievance, a belief that the system does not work, or a belief that employees are poorly represented by their union.

Labour–Management Cooperation

The traditional understanding of union–management relations is that the two parties are adversaries, meaning each side is competing to win at the expense of the other. There have always been exceptions to this approach. And since at least the 1980s, there seems to be wider acceptance of the view that greater cooperation can increase employee commitment and motivation while making the workplace more flexible.[46] Also, evidence suggests that employees who worked under traditional labour relations systems and then under the new, more cooperative systems prefer the cooperative approach.[47]

Cooperation between labour and management may feature employee involvement in decision making, self-managing employee teams, joint labour–management committees, broadly defined jobs, and sharing of financial gains and business information with employees.[48] The search for a win-win solution requires that unions and their members understand the limits on what an employer can afford in a competitive marketplace. Finding common ground may be part of an ongoing trend at least in parts of the private sector. As outlined in the Conference Board of Canada's *Industrial Relations Outlook:* "Many unions recognize they have a stake in their organizations' competitiveness."[49]

For example, Bombardier Inc. and the union representing Montreal-area workers reached a deal aimed at ensuring that Bombardier Aerospace will build its new series of C-Series passenger jets in the province (other locations in the running for the new plant that would employ 2,500 workers were Toronto, Belfast in Northern Ireland, and New Mexico).[50] Union members voted in favour of a six-year labour agreement that includes reducing overtime costs by using flextime scheduling and accepting a one-year wage freeze.[51] Although some might say the union members provided concessions to management, others argue the agreement is a mutual-gains solution, that is, jobs in the aerospace industry are retained in Quebec. The Best Practices box describes the *Toronto Star*'s collaborative efforts.

Without the union's support, efforts at employee involvement are less likely to survive and less likely to be effective if they do survive.[52] Unions have often resisted employee involvement programs, precisely because the programs try to change workplace relations and the role that unions play. Union leaders have often feared that such programs will weaken unions' role as independent representatives of employee interests.

An effective day-to-day relationship between labour and management is critical to achieving cooperation. In an adversarial type of environment, union–management communication consists of dealing with grievances; however, a cooperative model requires effective communication, trust, and mutual respect as the foundation for the day-to-day relationship. Many management and union leaders recognize that new approaches are needed to handle mutual concerns. "A sense of shared purpose is required to increase the effectiveness of the organization"[53] and methods are needed to benefit from the insights and skills of employees. Joint labour–management committees provide a relatively flexible approach to labour–management cooperation in the workplace.

Over the past two decades, the use of *joint labour–management committees* has been growing. More than 80 percent of labour and management respondents to a recent study conducted by the Conference Board of Canada reported that they have experience in using joint labour–management committees. The most common issues that such committees deal with are summarized in Table 10.3.

Employers build cooperative relationships by the way they treat employees—with respect and fairness, in the knowledge that attracting talent and minimizing turnover

BEST PRACTICES

Responding to Change with Union Support

Toronto Star Newspapers, like other major metropolitan newspapers, has a problem: the market for its traditional product, the print newspaper, is disappearing. While the newspaper is still being read by an increasingly limited demographic (people who tend to be older), younger people are turning to the Internet as their source of news and ideas—and to access classified advertisements. As a consequence, Toronto Star Newspapers is losing precious advertising revenue.

In response to these developments, Toronto Star Newspapers has had to make substantial changes to many facets of its business. "We used to focus primarily on our daily print newspapers in Toronto and its surrounding communities, but we have had to diversity our business to reach new readers," explains Alan Bower, Director, Industrial Relations. Efficiency is also a key facet of the Toronto Star Newspapers' bid for renewal. The organization has invested in its facilities to boost productivity and lower its operating costs. To bring about these critical changes, Toronto Star Newspapers needed to do more than tinker with its print model. With four unions representing the majority of its 1,700-employee workforce, management requires union support. This is something that is definitely easier said than done. Just how does management gain the support of unions for change, particularly large-scale change?

"You need to demonstrate to your unions how your world has changed," explains Bower. This includes helping union leaders to objectively understand how circumstances have changed for the organization, as well as why it is necessary to take action. Bower points out, however, that collective bargaining may not always be the best forum for this kind of communication. "I have my serious doubts that traditional bargaining is the right tool to discuss the need for such significant change," he reflects. "Often, change happens when the parties are not bargaining. What do unions and management do then? Some employers are establishing joint committees of management and unions to discuss ongoing and late-breaking issues. The advantages of inter-bargaining committees are twofold: they allow the parties to deal with important issues in a timely way, and the tension that often accompanies bargaining is not present to the same degree. "It is much easier to talk about high-level issues with your union counterparts when there is no strike deadline ticking away in the background," affirms Bower.

Inter-bargaining committees and joint tours aside, bargaining is still an effective means to bring about change. Bower points out that the Toronto Star's printing press plant would not have achieved its current production capacity had the company not successfully negotiated work-rule changes with the Teamsters. Negotiating big changes at the Toronto Star was not easy, however, so the employer enlisted help. "The Toronto Star and union agreed to bring in an experienced mediator to help us through our discussions," Bower explains. The parties used a mediation and bargaining process that focused on common problems and shared interests and removed much of the potential for interpersonal conflict. By doing so, the employer was able to demonstrate to the union that it too had a vested interest in change. "The union looked at our business and came to the same conclusion we had—the plant needed to become much more efficient if it was going to remain viable." Rather than wait for the employer to lose money, the union and employer agreed to work-rule changes that enhanced the prospects for the plant's long-term viability.

SOURCE: Christopher Hallamore, "Industrial Relations Outlook 2008," *The Conference Board of Canada*, pp. 6–8.

are in the employer's best interests. "In the end we must look for opportunities to create a more collaborative culture in Canadian workplaces to ensure the long-term sustainability of our businesses."[54]

TABLE 10.3

Most Common Joint Labour–Management Committees

1. Pay, benefits, pensions
2. Business issues/updates
3. General labour relations
4. Training/apprenticeships
5. Job evaluation/classifications/postings
6. Operations/technology
7. Hours of work/scheduling

SOURCE: Judith Lendvay-Zwicki, "The Canadian Industrial Relations System: Current Challenges and Future Options," Conference Board Document, April 2004, p. 17, www.conferenceboard.ca, retrieved April 19, 2004.

THINKING ETHICALLY

Is the Seniority System Fair?

Traditionally, union contracts have called for pay and promotion systems that reward employees with higher pay and advancement as they achieve greater seniority, that is, more years on the job. In a company, with a unionized workforce, employees with comparable amounts of experience would have comparable earnings. Employees with greater seniority would earn more than newer employees and employees with the most seniority would be promoted if they met the minimum requirements of the job opportunity.

Some people have questioned whether tying pay and advancement to seniority is effective or even fair. For example, a top-performing, recently hired employee with educational qualifications that exceed the requirements of a desired job may become frustrated when he/she is not even selected for an interview because many employees with greater seniority applied. However, union leaders view the seniority clause as the means to ensure fairness in how employees are rewarded in an organization.

In a survey of Canadian organizations, consulting firm Watson Wyatt found that one of the top five reasons that employees quit their jobs is dissatisfaction with promotional opportunities.

SOURCE: Virginia Galt, "Stress, Not Money, Main Cause of Turnover," *The Globe and Mail*, December 15, 2007, p. B10.

Questions

1. Why do you think unions have traditionally favoured a system of linking pay and advancement to seniority? Who benefits? Why do you think management might favour a system of linking pay and advancement to performance? Who benefits?
2. What employee rights does seniority-based pay fulfill? What standards for ethical behaviour does it meet? (See Chapter 1 to review a description of employee rights and ethical standards.)
3. What employee rights does a performance-based pay and promotion system fulfill? What standards for ethical behaviour does it meet?

SUMMARY

L01 Define unions and labour relations and their role in organizations.

- A union is an organization formed for the purpose of representing its members in resolving conflicts with employers.
- Labour relations is the management specialty emphasizing skills that managers and union leaders can use to minimize costly forms of conflict and to seek win-win solutions to disagreements.
- In Canada, union membership has declined marginally from a peak in 1994. Unionization is associated with more generous compensation and higher productivity but lower profits. Unions may reduce a business's flexibility and economic performance.

L02 Identify the labour relations goals of management, labour unions, and society.

- Management goals are to increase the organization's profits and/or productivity. Managers generally expect that unions will make these goals harder to achieve.
- Unions have the goal of obtaining pay and working conditions that satisfy their members.
- Society's values have included the hope that the existence of unions will replace conflict or violence between workers and employers with fruitful negotiation.

L03 Summarize laws and regulations that affect labour relations.

- Laws and regulations affect the degree to which management, unions, and society achieve their varied goals.
- Canada's overall labour relations legal framework is decentralized with responsibility for labour relations shared between the federal, provincial, and territorial governments.
- A common core of labour legislation exists that includes prohibiting unfair labour practices by management and labour. Labour Relations Boards or similar quasi-judicial tribunals exist within each jurisdiction to administer and enforce labour laws.

L04 Describe the union organizing process.

- Organizing begins when union representatives contact employees and invite them to sign a membership application. When the required numbers of employees have signed membership applications, the union will apply to their appropriate Labour Relations Board for certification.
- Requirements for certification differ among federal, provincial, and territorial jurisdictions.

L05 Explain how management and unions negotiate collective agreements.

- Negotiations take place between representatives of the union and the management bargaining unit.
- The process begins with preparation, including research into the other side's strengths and demands. The union presents its demands, and management sometimes presents demands as well. Then the sides evaluate the demands and the likelihood of a strike.
- In the final stages, pressure for an agreement increases, and a neutral third party may be called on to help reach a resolution. If bargaining breaks down, the impasse may be broken with a strike, lockout, mediation, conciliation, or arbitration.

L06 Summarize the practice of collective agreement administration.

- Collective agreement administration is a daily activity under the collective agreement. It includes carrying out the terms of the agreement and resolving conflicts over interpretation or violation of the agreement.
- Conflicts are resolved through a grievance procedure that begins with an employee talking to his or her supervisor about the problem and possibly involving the union steward. If this does not resolve the conflict, the union files a written grievance and union and management representatives meet to discuss the problem. If this effort fails, the union appeals the grievance to top line management and ultimately the use of an arbitrator may be required for final resolution.

L07 Describe more cooperative approaches to labour–management relations.

- In contrast to the traditional view that labour and management are adversaries, some organizations and unions work more cooperatively.

- Cooperation may feature employee involvement in decision making, self-managing employee teams, joint labour–management committees, broadly defined jobs, and sharing of financial gains and business information with employees. Cooperative labour relations seem to contribute to an organization's success.

REVIEW AND DISCUSSION QUESTIONS

1. Why do employees join unions? Did you ever belong to a union? If you did, do you think union membership benefited you? If you did not, do you think a union would have benefited you? Why or why not?

2. Why do managers at most companies prefer that unions not represent their employees? Can unions provide benefits to an employer? Explain.

3. How has union membership in Canada changed over the past few decades? How does union membership in Canada compare with union membership in other countries? How might these patterns in union membership affect the HR decisions of an international company?

4. What legal responsibilities do employers have regarding unions? What are the legal requirements affecting unions?

5. Suppose you are the HR manager for a chain of clothing stores. You learn that union representatives have been encouraging the stores' employees to sign an application for membership. What events can follow in this process of organizing? Suggest some ways that you might respond in your role as HR manager.

6. If the parties negotiating a collective agreement are unable to reach a settlement, what actions can resolve the situation?

7. Why are most negotiations settled without a strike or lockout? Under what conditions might management choose to accept a strike?

8. What are the usual steps in a grievance procedure? What are the advantages of resolving a grievance in the first step? What skills would a supervisor need so grievances can be resolved in the first step?

9. The Best Practices box in this chapter gives an example of union–management cooperation at the *Toronto Star*. What does the employer gain from this effort? What do workers gain? Do you think the cooperative effort eliminates the union's role for the *Star*? Explain.

WHAT'S YOUR HR IQ?

The Online Learning Centre offers more ways to check what you've learned so far. Find experiential exercises as well as Test Your Knowledge Quizzes, Videos, and many other resources at www.mcgrawhill.ca/olc/steen.

Case:
Wal-Mart Reacts to Unionization

Wal-Mart Canada Corp. dealt a decisive blow to union forces, announcing it will shut down the first Wal-Mart store to successfully certify in North America in almost a decade. "We honestly were hoping we could avoid this—it's a sad day for us," Wal-Mart spokesperson Andrew Pelletier said of the decision to shutter the four-year-old outlet in Jonquière, Quebec, which the retailer says was losing money. "Despite nine days of meeting with the union over more than a three-month period, we have been unsuccessful in reaching an agreement that would allow the store to operate efficiently and, ultimately, profitably."

"We're all in shock," said one employee reached the next day at the Jonquière store. Michael Fraser, the United Food and Commercial Workers Union president, was not available for comment. The store's 190 workers will be offered "generous" severance packages and career counselling," Mr. Pelletier said.

While the big-box giant has never before closed a store in this country for economic reasons, the news does not come as a surprise. The announcement of the closure of the Jonquière store was the latest event in a longstanding fight between the world's biggest retailer and unions determined to organize the corporation's workers throughout North America. Wal-Mart insists it does not promote an anti-union agenda. "We bargained in good faith," Mr. Pelletier said.

However, union organizers and some industry analysts say otherwise. "Wal-Mart, like a lot of other companies with a nonunionized workforce, is scared to death of unions," said David Abella, an analyst at New-York based Rochdale Investment Management. Even if they could manage that store with the union, it could lead to a domino effect across Canada and the United States. The UFCW scored a minor victory recently when a Saskatchewan appeal overturned a decision barring the province's labour board from accessing internal Wal-Mart documents, among them one titled "Wal-Mart: A Manager's Tool Box to Remaining Union-Free." Jonquière's certification was viewed as a big win for the UFCW, one that has not been realized since 1996, when the Ontario Labour Relations Board unionized a Wal-Mart in Windsor, Ontario. The store was later decertified after a high-profile campaign by anti-union employees, which included allegations of union misconduct.

"Shutting down the Jonquière store for any reason is completely legal," said Anil Verna, a professor of industrial relations at the University of Toronto. "Any business can open or close as they see fit. Most of the time it is about whether the operations are profitable or not. In this case, the timing kind of looks suspicious, but not knowing the numbers for the store, it's difficult to make a conclusive inference that [unionization] had anything to do with it."

SOURCE: Hollie Shaw, "Wal-Mart Closes First Union Store in Quebec," *Financial Post*, February 10, 2005, pp. A1, A9. Material reprinted with permission of The National Post Company, a Can West Partnership.

Questions

1. Do you believe that Wal-Mart is "anti-union"? Explain your response.
2. What would you expect to happen if Wal-Mart employees were able to join unions?
3. Would you be willing to pay more for products from a unionized Wal-Mart? Explain.

Case:
McGill's Teaching Assistants on Strike

McGill's 1,100 unionized teaching assistants voted to go on strike April 7, 2008, when talks with administration broke down. The TAs were seeking a $5 to $6 per hour increase over the next three years to their current average hourly salary of $22 per hour. Other issues include capping the size of discussion groups, and meeting spaces. On April 8, 2008 the TAs launched a strike.

During a visit to a McGill chemistry lab the following week, Labour Department investigator Thomas Hayden said he found a non-managerial employee, an assistant chemistry professor, overseeing the lab. That person openly said he was doing work usually performed by a teaching assistant. This, Hayden indicated, was a violation of the Labour Code and said that a hearing would be required to "reconcile differences of interpretation between McGill and its teaching assistants on their respective roles." According to McGill, professors "are responsible for everything that happens in their courses, including marking exams, and supervising labs." However, the TAs' union claims that certain types of work "belongs to its members."

Edith Zorychta, president of the McGill Association of University Teachers (MAUT), said, "MAUT is aware of the difficult situation many faculty members are currently experiencing with regard to the strike by the teaching assistants, particularly in view of the conflicting interpretations of the Quebec Labour Code being circulated."

McGill was accused of "nastiness" when 72 students who belonged to the TA union but were performing unrelated jobs such as invigilators and exam supervisors (jobs outside the union) were fired. Sessional lecturers who belonged to the union have also received notice from the university that they will not be required to teach scheduled summer classes. "It seems like retribution," says Scott Matter, a Ph.D. candidate in anthropology. He had signed a contract with McGill on March 17, 2008 to teach a summer anthropology course starting in June; however, he later received an email that his contract was being cancelled. "I really feel my rights are being infringed upon. McGill is trying to punish me for being part of a union," said Matter, who has filed a grievance. "I'm spending the afternoon arranging a student line of credit, because otherwise I'm not going to be able to get through the rest of the summer."

SOURCES: Carson Jerema, "Can Professors Be Scabs?" *Macleans.ca on Campus*, April 30, 2008, http://oncampus.macleans.ca, retrieved May 13, 2008; Peggy Curran, "Tough Learning Experience for McGill TAs," *The Gazette*, April 22, 2008, www.canadacom/montrealgazette, retrieved May 13, 2008; Peggy Curran, "Inspector Finds Violations in McGill Strike," *The Gazette*, April 17, 2008, www.canadacom/montrealgazette, retrieved May 13, 2008; "McGill Teaching Assistants Vote to Go on Strike," *The Gazette*, April 7, 2008, www.canadacom/montrealgazette, retrieved May 13, 2008.

Questions

1. What is your analysis of the situation faced by McGill and its stakeholders—for example, students, professors, teaching assistants, managers, and other employees at McGill? How do you think the timing of the strike, that is, around final exams, may have influenced the actions of the parties to the labour dispute?
2. How would you recommend McGill solve their labour dispute? What is your advice to university administration? To the union representing the TAs?
3. What effect might the actions of McGill's administration and the TAs' union have on labour-management relations at McGill in the future?

Chapter **11**

Managing Human Resources Globally

What Do I Need to Know? After reading this chapter, you should be able to:

1. Summarize how the growth in international business activity affects human resource management.

2. Identify the factors that most strongly influence HRM in international markets.

3. Discuss how differences among countries affect HR planning at organizations with international operations.

4. Describe how companies select and train human resources in a global labour market.

5. Discuss challenges related to compensating and rewarding employees from other countries.

6. Explain how employers prepare employees for international assignments and for their return home.

Introduction

Research in Motion (RIM) is a leading designer, manufacturer, and marketer of innovative wireless solutions for the worldwide mobile communications market. RIM's portfolio of award-winning products, including the BlackBerry, is used by organizations and individuals around the world. The company, founded in 1984 and based in Waterloo, Ontario, continues to grow rapidly and is a significant player in the global market. RIM's core Asia Pacific contact centre is in Singapore, but is expanding with a presence in Hong Kong, China, Australia, and India. RIM's European headquarters are based in London and current expansion includes France, Germany, Poland, the

374

Netherlands, Belgium, Hungary, Italy, Spain, and South Africa. Operations in the Americas include several offices in the United States, including ones in Chicago, Dallas, and Seattle, and in Mexico and the Caribbean. A search of the "Careers" area of RIM's website provides some insight about the extent of globalization of RIM's business structure and operations. For example, at the time of this writing, 1,043 job openings were listed for RIM's worldwide operations. This included openings for Manager of Compensation & Benefits in the UK, Business Development Manager in Hong Kong, Field Marketing and Training Specialist in Mexico, Facilities Manager in Fort Lauderdale, and a Public Relations Manager based in Sydney, Australia.[1]

Mike Lazaridis and Jim Balsillie of Research in Motion. RIM is headquartered in Canada and has offices in Europe, Asia Pacific, and the United States.

According to a survey of almost 3,000 line executives and HR executives from 12 countries, international competition is the number one factor affecting human resource management. The globalization of business structures and globalization of the economy ranked fourth and fifth, respectively.[2] Business decisions such as whether to enter foreign markets or set up operations in other countries are complex, and in the course of moving and executing them many human resource issues surface.

This chapter discusses the HR issues that organizations must address in a world of global competition. We begin by describing how the global nature of business is affecting human resource management in modern organizations. Next, we identify how global differences among countries affect the organization's decisions about human resources. In the following sections we explore workforce planning, selection, training, and compensation practices in international settings. Finally, we examine guidelines for managing employees on international assignments.

HRM in a Global Environment

The environment in which organizations operate is rapidly becoming a global one. More and more companies are entering international markets by exporting their products, building facilities in other countries, and entering into alliances with foreign companies. At the same time, companies based in other countries are investing and setting up operations in Canada. Indeed, most organizations now function in the global economy. The HRM function needs to continuously reexamine its role in supporting this expanding pace of business globalization. This requires HRM to

- Align HRM processes and functions with global requirements
- Adopt a global mindset including a thorough understanding of the global environment and the impact on managing people worldwide
- Enhance its own capabilities and competencies to become a business partner in acting on global business opportunities[3]

What is behind the trend toward expansion into global markets? Foreign countries can provide a business with new markets in which there are millions or billions of new customers; developing countries often provide such markets, but developed

LO1 - Summarize how the growth in international business activity affects human resource management.

1,2

countries do so as well. Companies set up operations overseas because they can operate with lower labour costs. As discussed in Chapter 1, outsourcing jobs to lower-cost nations will continue to increase. For example, countries such as the "BRICs" (Brazil, Russia, India, and China) are particularly attractive, because they offer both low-cost labour and fast-growing economies. Turkey, Vietnam, South Korea, the United Arab Emirates, and emerging central and eastern European countries such as Hungary, Romania, and Slovenia have also been identified as hot new labour markets.[4]

Global activities are simplified and encouraged by trade agreements among nations; for example, most countries in Western Europe belong to the European Union (EU) and share a common currency, the euro. Canada, Mexico, and the United States have encouraged trade among themselves with the North American Free Trade Agreement (NAFTA). The World Trade Organization (WTO) resolves trade disputes among more than 100 participating nations.

As companies in Canada and the United States cut software jobs and outsource to other countries in order to drive down costs, countries such as India continue to see employment rates rise.

As these trends and arrangements encourage international trade, they increase and change the demands on human resource management. According to a recent study from Hewitt Associates, a global human resource consulting firm, organizations must do a better job of addressing human capital costs and issues.[5] Organizations with customers or suppliers in other countries need employees who understand those customers or suppliers. Organizations that operate facilities in foreign countries need to understand the laws and customs that apply to employees in those countries. They may have to prepare managers and other employees to take international assignments. They have to adapt their human resource plans and policies to different settings. Even if some practices are the same worldwide, the company now has to communicate them to its international workforce. A variety of international activities require managers to understand HRM principles and practices prevalent in global markets.

5

Employees in an International Workforce

home country
The country in which an organization's headquarters is located.

When organizations operate globally, their employees are very likely to be citizens of more than one country. Employees may come from the employer's home country, a host country, or a third country. The **home country** is the country in which the organization's headquarters is located. For example, Canada is the home country of Fairmont Hotels and Resorts, because Fairmont's headquarters are in Toronto.

A Fairmont employee who is a Canadian citizen and works at Fairmont's headquarters or one of its Canadian properties is therefore a *home-country national*.

A **host country** is a country (other than the home country) in which an organization operates a facility. Barbados is a host country of Fairmont because Fairmont has operations there. Any Barbadian workers hired to work at Fairmont's Barbados property would be *host-country nationals*, that is, employees who are citizens of the host country.

A **third country** refers to a country that is neither the home country nor the host country. (The organization may or may not have a facility in the third country.) In the example of Fairmont's operations in Barbados, the company could hire an Australian manager to work there. The Australian manager would be a *third-country national*, because the manager is neither from the home country (Canada) nor from the host country (Barbados).

When organizations operate globally, they need to decide whether to hire home-country nationals, host-country nationals, or third-country nationals for the overseas operations. Usually, they hire a combination of these. In general, employees who take assignments in other countries are called **expatriates**. In the Fairmont example, the Canadian and Australian managers working in Barbados would be expatriates during those assignments.

The extent to which organizations use home-country, host-country, or third-country nationals varies. In Japan, Canon is keeping the majority of its production facilities in the home country as a way to foster close ties between product development and production teams. The goal is for designers and production engineers to collaborate on improving quality and efficiency. In China, a challenge for companies is the limited supply of people with management expertise, so Chinese companies often recruit managers working in Canada and the United States. These managers may be Canadian or U.S. citizens, Chinese citizens gaining experience in North America, or third-country nations, including Malaysians (many of whom are ethnic Chinese and able to communicate in their employer's language).[6] In all of these situations, human resource management across national borders is complex, but modern technology is helping. The e-HRM box describes online recruiting services in China.

Employers in the Global Marketplace

Just as there are different ways for employees to participate in international business—as home-country, host-country, or third-county nationals—so there are different ways for employers to do business globally, ranging from simply shipping products to customers in other countries to transforming the organization into a truly global one, with operations, employees, and customers in many countries. Figure 11.1 shows the major levels of global participation.

Most organizations begin by serving customers and clients within a domestic marketplace. Typically, a company's founder has an idea for serving a local, regional, or national market. The business must recruit, hire, train, and compensate employees to produce the product, and these people usually come from the business owner's local labour market. Selection and training focus not only on employees' technical abilities but also on other competencies such as interpersonal skills. Pay levels reflect local labour conditions. If the product succeeds, the company might expand operations to other domestic locations, and HRM decisions become more complex as the organization draws from a larger labour market and needs systems for training and engaging employees in several locations. As the employer's workforce grows, it is also likely to become more diverse. Even in small domestic organizations, a significant

host country
A country (other than the home country) in which an organization operates a facility.

third country
A country that is neither the home country nor the host country of an employer.

expatriates
Employees who take assignments in other countries.

2

E- HRM

Monster Advancing into China

By now, most North American companies realize the advantages of recruiting online, where they can quickly sort through résumés from applicants who have expressed interest in their industry and location. What about companies that have operations overseas? The search for applicants in another country is even more complicated, so the need for Web-based recruiting tools is that much greater.

In China, where economic growth is strong and the potential for the future even stronger, Internet recruiting services are already playing an important role. Recently, Monster Worldwide, one of

the dominant players in North American recruiting sites, acquired 40 percent ownership of ChinaHR.com, a Chinese job search site. The acquisition gives Monster an opening into the massive—population 1.3 billion—market and helps ChinaHR.com improve its methods.

The challenges for expansion into China are greater than in another hot spot, India, where the business language is English. Most of the job postings and résumés on ChinaHR.com are in Chinese characters, so the information cannot easily be shared with non-Chinese websites. As a result, recruiters need to

be able to read and write in Chinese characters. They also should consider including company logos in their listings, as a way to communicate their identity across language systems. Finally, recruiters need to understand that Chinese employees with strong technical skills may lack knowledge or skill in preparing English-language résumés. Matching key terms may be more important than looking for the fine details of a well-crafted résumé.

SOURCE: John Zappe, "Monster Makes a Play for the Chinese Market," *Workforce Management*, March 2005, http://web5.infotrac.galegroup.com.

share of workers may be immigrants. In this way, even domestic companies are affected by issues related to the global economy.

As organizations grow, they often begin to meet demand from customers in other countries. The usual way that a company begins to enter foreign markets is by *exporting*, or shipping domestically produced items to other countries to be sold there. For example, Loewen, the Steinbach, Manitoba–based manufacturer of premium doors

FIGURE 11.1

Levels of Global Participation

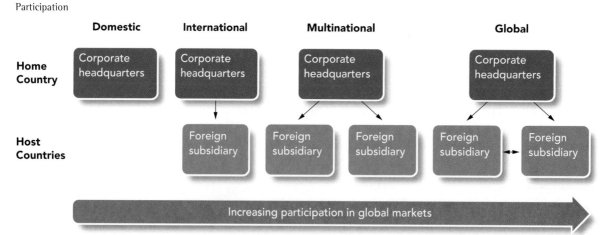

and windows, produces all of its products in its 587,000 square-foot plant in Steinbach but sells products to 15 countries including the United States, Japan, and Mexico.[7] Eventually, it may become economically desirable to set up operations in one or more foreign countries. An organization that does so becomes an **international organization**. The decision to participate in international activities raises a host of HR issues, including the basic question of whether a particular location provides an environment where the organization can successfully acquire and manage human resources. Canada's largest hardware retailer, Canadian Tire, has had an office in Hong Kong for more than 25 years. Canadian Tire also has offices in Seoul, Taipei, and Shanghai.[8] CN Rail opened its office in China "to try and capture a larger share of the growing freight market for Canadian commodities shipped to China as well as consumer goods coming from China to North America."[9] The Bank of Nova Scotia has taken over the fourth-largest bank in El Salvador, a Central American country of 6.6 million people, and will merge Banco de Comercio (assets of US$1.1 billion) with Scotiabank El Salvador. Scotiabank also owns the seventh-largest bank in Mexico and the largest bank in the Caribbean.[10]

While international companies build one or a few facilities in another country, **multinational companies** expand on a broader scale. They build facilities in a number of different countries as a way to keep production and distribution costs to a minimum. In general, when organizations become multinationals, they move production facilities from relatively high-cost locations to lower-cost locations. The lower-cost locations may have lower average wage rates, or they may reduce distribution costs by being nearer to customers. The HRM challenges faced by a multinational company are similar but larger than those of an international organization, because more countries are involved. More than ever, the organization needs to hire people who can function in a variety of settings, give them necessary training, and provide flexible compensation systems that take into account the different pay rates, tax systems, and costs of living from one country to another.

At the highest level of involvement in the global marketplace are **global organizations**. These flexible organizations compete by offering top products tailored to segments of the market while keeping costs as low as possible. A global organization locates each facility on the basis of the ability to effectively, efficiently, and flexibly produce a product or service, using cultural differences as an advantage. Rather than treating differences in other countries as a challenge to overcome, a global organization treats different cultures as a source of competitive advantage. It may have multiple headquarters spread across the globe, so decisions are more decentralized. BP is one of the largest integrated oil and gas companies in the world. BP has global sales and operating revenues of $284 billion, employs 97,600 employees worldwide, and produces 2.4 million barrels of oil every day. BP Canada Energy Company, headquartered in Calgary, employs more than 1,500 Canadians.[11] This type of organization needs HRM practices that encourage flexibility and are based on an in-depth knowledge of differences among countries. Global organizations must be able to recruit, develop, retain, and fully utilize employees who can get results across national boundaries.

A global organization needs a **transnational HRM system**[12] that features decision making from a global perspective, managers from many countries, and ideas contributed by people from a variety of cultures. Decisions that are the outcome of a transnational HRM system balance uniformity (for fairness) with flexibility (to account for cultural and legal differences). This balance and the variety of perspectives should work together to improve the quality of decision making. The participants from various countries and cultures contribute ideas from a position of equality, rather than the home country's culture dominating.

international organization
An organization that sets up one or a few facilities in one or a few foreign countries.

multinational company
An organization that builds facilities in a number of different countries in an effort to minimize production and distribution costs.

global organization
An organization that chooses to locate a facility based on the ability to effectively, efficiently, and flexibly produce a product or service, using cultural differences as an advantage.

transnational HRM system
Type of HRM system that makes decisions from a global perspective, includes managers from many countries, and is based on ideas contributed by people representing a variety of cultures.

LO2 - Identify the factors that most strongly influence HRM in international markets.

Factors Affecting HRM in International Markets

Whatever their level of global participation, organizations that operate in more than one country must recognize that the countries are not identical and differ in terms of many factors. To simplify this discussion, we focus on four major factors: culture, education, economic systems, and political-legal systems. These influences on human resource management are shown in Figure 11.2.

Culture

By far the most important influence on international HRM is the culture of the country in which a facility is located. *Culture* is a community's set of shared assumptions about how the world works and what ideals are worth striving for.[13] Cultural influences may be expressed through customs, languages, religions, and so on.

Culture is important to HRM for two reasons. First, it often determines the other three international influences. Culture can greatly affect a country's laws, because laws often are based on the culture's definitions of right and wrong. Culture also influences what people value, so it affects people's economic systems and efforts to invest in education.

Even more important for understanding human resource management, culture often determines the effectiveness of various HRM practices. Practices that are effective in Canada, for example, may fail or even backfire in a country with different beliefs and values.[14] Consider the five dimensions of culture that Geert Hofstede identified in his classic study of culture:[15]

1. *Individualism/collectivism* describes the strength of the relation between an individual and other individuals in the society. In a culture that is high in individualism, such as Canada, Great Britain, and the Netherlands, people tend to think and act as individuals rather than as members of a group. People in these countries are expected to stand on their own two feet, rather than be protected by the group. In a culture high in collectivism, such as Colombia, Pakistan, and Taiwan, people think of themselves mainly as group members. They are expected to devote themselves to the interests of the community, and the community is expected to protect them when they are in trouble.
2. *Power distance* concerns the way the culture deals with unequal distribution of power and defines the amount of inequality that is normal. In countries with large power distances, including India and the Philippines, the culture defines it as normal to maintain large differences in power. In countries with lower power distances, such as Denmark and Israel, people try to eliminate inequalities.

FIGURE 11.2

Factors Affecting Human Resource Management in International Markets

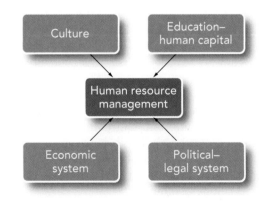

One way to see differences in power distance is in the way people talk to one another. In the high-power-distance countries of Mexico and Japan, people address one another with titles (Señor Smith, Smith-san). At the other extreme, in Canada, in most situations people use one another's first names—behaviour that would be disrespectful in some other cultures.

3. *Uncertainty avoidance* describes how cultures handle the fact that the future is unpredictable. High uncertainty avoidance refers to a strong cultural preference for structured situations. In countries such as Greece and Portugal, people tend to rely heavily on religion, law, and technology to give them a degree of security and clear rules about how to behave. In countries with low uncertainty avoidance, including Singapore and Jamaica, people seem to take each day as it comes.

4. *Masculinity/femininity* is the emphasis a culture places on practices or qualities that have traditionally been considered masculine or feminine. A "masculine" culture is a culture that values achievement, money making, assertiveness, and competition. A "feminine" culture is one that places a high value on relationships, service, care for the weak, and preserving the environment. In this model, Germany and Japan are examples of masculine cultures, and Sweden and Norway are examples of feminine cultures.

5. *Long-term/short-term orientation* suggests whether the focus of cultural values is on the future (long term) or the past and present (short term). Cultures with a long-term orientation value saving and persistence, which tend to pay off in the future. Many Asian countries, including Japan and China, have a long-term orientation. Short-term orientations, as in the cultures of Canada, Russia, and West Africa, promote respect for past tradition, and for fulfilling social obligations in the present. Figure 11.3 summarizes these five cultural dimensions.

Such cultural characteristics as these influence the ways members of an organization behave toward one another, as well as their attitudes toward various HRM practices. For instance, cultures differ strongly in their opinions about how managers should lead, how decisions should be handled, and what motivates employees. In Germany, managers achieve their status by demonstrating technical skills, and employees look to managers to assign tasks and resolve technical problems. In the Netherlands, managers focus on seeking agreement, exchanging views, and balancing

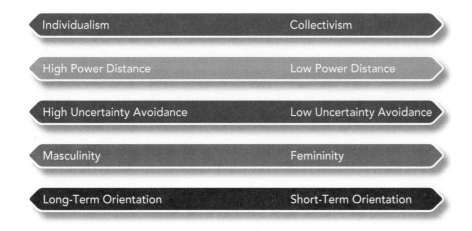

FIGURE 11.3

Five Dimensions of Culture

SOURCE: G. Hofstede, "Dimensions of National Cultures in Fifty Countries and Three Regions," in *Expectations in Cross-Cultural Psychology*, J. Deregowski, S. Dziurawiec, and R. C. Annis, eds. (Lisse, Netherlands: Swets and Zeitlinger, 1983); G. Hofstede, "Cultural Constraints in Management Theories," *Academy of Management Executive* 7 (1993), pp. 81–90.

the interests of the people affected by a decision.[16] Clearly, differences like these would affect how an organization selects and trains its managers and measures their performance.

Cultures strongly influence the appropriateness of HRM practices. For example, the extent to which a culture is individualist or collectivist will affect the success of a compensation program. Compensation tied to individual performance may be seen as fairer and more motivating by members of an individualist culture; a culture favouring individualism will be more accepting of great differences in pay between the organization's highest- and lowest-paid employees. Collectivist cultures tend to have much flatter pay structures.

Job design aimed at employee involvement can be problematic in cultures with high "power distance." In a Mexican slipper-manufacturing plant, an effort to expand the decision-making authority of production workers stumbled when the workers balked at doing what they saw as the supervisor's proper responsibility.[17] Realizing they had moved too quickly, the plant's managers narrowed the scope of the workers' decision-making authority so they could adapt to the role. On the other hand, a factor in favour of involvement at that plant was the Mexican culture's high collectivism. The workers liked discussing team-related information and using the information to benefit the entire team. As in this example, a culture does not necessarily rule out a particular HRM practice, such as employee involvement, but it should be a consideration in deciding how to carry out the practice. Imran Qureshi, international practice leader at Watson Wyatt Worldwide agrees one of the biggest challenges and payoffs for Canadian companies doing business globally is "understanding and tailoring strategies based on cultural differences." He cautions that companies should not be afraid of imposing certain standards or ways of business that define their own business culture, perspective, ethics or business processes. "You do need to be sensitive to environment but you also have to say what's important to [you] as a company. There may be a certain internal business cultural consideration that you really need to export."[18] Despite cultural differences, the factors that engage workers are relatively similar across cultures. Table 11.1 provides a look at what engages employees in four countries.

Finally, cultural differences can affect how people communicate and how they coordinate their activities. In collectivist cultures, people tend to value group decision making, as in the previous example. When a person raised in an individualistic culture has to work closely with people from a collectivist culture, communication problems and conflicts often occur. People from the collectivist culture tend to collaborate heavily and may evaluate the individualistic person as unwilling to cooperate and share information with them. Cultural differences in communication affected the way an agricultural company embarked on employee involvement at its facilities in North America and Brazil.[19] Employee involvement requires information sharing, but in Brazil, high power distance leads employees to expect managers to make decisions, so they do not desire information appropriately held by managers. Involving the Brazilian employees required involving managers directly in giving and sharing information to show that this practice was in keeping with the traditional chain of command. Also, because uncertainty avoidance is another aspect of Brazilian culture, managers explained that greater information sharing would reduce uncertainty about their work. At the same time, greater collectivism in Brazil made employees comfortable with the day-to-day communication of teamwork. The individualistic North American employees needed to be sold more on this aspect of employee involvement.

Because of these challenges, organizations need to prepare employees to recognize and handle cultural differences. They may recruit managers with knowledge of other

UNITED STATES	CHINA
• Confidence they can achieve career objectives	• Sense of personal accomplishment
• Sense of personal accomplishment	• Fair pay, given performance
• Confidence organization will be successful	• Comparable benefits to industry
• Quality is a high priority	• Confidence in senior management
• Opportunity for growth and development	• IT systems support business needs
• Information and assistance to manage career	• Opportunities for training
UNITED KINGDOM	**BRAZIL**
• Sense of personal accomplishment	• Sense of personal accomplishment
• Confidence in senior management	• Confidence in senior management
• Opportunities for training	• Opportunities for training
• Fair pay, given performance	• Fair pay, given performance
• Good reputation for customer service	• Good reputation for customer service
• Regular feedback on performance	• Comparable benefits to industry

TABLE 11.1

What Keeps Foreign Workers Engaged

SOURCE: Mercer HR Consulting, *Engaging Employees to Drive Global Business Success: Insight from Mercer's What's Working Research,* www.mercer.com/referencecontent.htm?idContent= 1288115, retrieved September 14, 2008, quoted in Lesley Young, "Attracting, Keeping Employees Overseas," *Canadian HR Reporter,* April 7, 2008, www.hrreporter.com, retrieved May 26, 2008.

cultures or provide training, as described later in the chapter. For expatriate assignments, organizations may need to conduct an extensive selection process to identify individuals who can adapt to new environments.

Education and Skill Levels

Countries also differ in the degree to which their labour markets include people with education and skills of value to employers. As discussed in Chapter 1, Canada suffers from a shortage of skilled workers in many occupations, and the problem is expected to increase. On the other hand, the labour markets in many countries are very attractive because they offer high skills and low wages.

Educational opportunities also vary from one country to another. In general, spending on education is greater per student in high-income countries than in poorer countries.[20] In the Netherlands, government funding of school systems allows students to go all the way through graduate school without paying.[21] Similarly, the free education provided to citizens in the former Soviet bloc resulted in a highly educated workforce, in spite of the region's economic difficulties. Some Third World countries, such as Nicaragua and Haiti, have relatively low educational levels because those countries have not invested in education.

Companies with foreign operations locate in countries where they can find suitable employees. The education and skill levels of a country's labour force affect how and the extent to which companies want to operate there. In countries with a poorly educated population, companies will limit their activities to low-skill, low-wage jobs. In contrast, India's large pool of well-trained technical workers is one reason the country has become a popular location for outsourcing computer programming jobs.

2

Economic System

A country's economic system whether capitalist or socialist, as well as the government's involvement in the economy through taxes or compensation, price controls, and other activities, influences human resource management practices in a number of ways.

As with all aspects of a region's or country's life, the economic system and culture are likely to be closely tied, providing many of the incentives or disincentives for developing the value of the labour force. Socialist economic systems provide ample opportunities for educational development because the education system is free to students. At the same time, socialism may not provide economic rewards (higher pay) for increasing one's education. In capitalist systems, students bear more of the cost of their education, but employers reward those who invest in education.

The health of an economic system affects human resource management. In developed countries with great wealth, labour costs are relatively high. Such differences show up in compensation systems and in recruiting and selection decisions.

Students at the University of Warsaw in Poland are provided with a government-supported education. In general, former Soviet bloc countries tend to be generous in funding education, so they tend to have highly educated and skilled labour forces. Countries such as Canada and the United States generally leave higher education up to individual students to pay for, but the labour market rewards students who earn a college diploma or university degree.

In general, socialist systems take a higher percentage of each worker's income as the worker's income increases. Capitalist systems tend to let workers keep more of their earnings. In this way, socialism redistributes wealth from high earners to the poor, while capitalism apparently rewards individual accomplishments. In any case, since the amount of takehome pay a worker receives after taxes may thus differ from country to country, in an organization that pays two employees in two countries $100,000 each, the employee in one country might take home more than the employee in the other country. Such differences make pay structures more complicated when they cross national boundaries, and they can affect recruiting of candidates from more than one country.

Political-Legal System

A country's political-legal system—its government, laws, and regulations—strongly impinges on human resource management. The country's laws often dictate the requirements for certain HRM practices, such as training, compensation, selection, and labour relations. As we noted in the discussion of culture, the political-legal system arises to a large degree from the culture in which it exists, so laws and regulations reflect cultural values.

For example, Canada has been a leader in eliminating discrimination in the workplace. Because the value of diversity is important in Canadian culture, legal safeguards such as human rights laws discussed in Chapter 2 exist, which affect hiring and other HRM decisions. As a society, Canada also has strong beliefs regarding the fairness of pay systems. Thus, pay equity legislation (discussed in Chapter 2), provides for equal pay for work of equal value. Other laws and regulations dictate much of the process of negotiation between unions and management. All these are examples of laws and regulations that affect the practice of HRM in Canada. When Canadian companies employ workers in other countries, the workers are usually covered by the employment laws in their own countries. Employment laws in many countries offer workers less protection than Canadian legislation provides.

Laws and regulations in other countries reflect the norms of their cultures. In Germany employees have a legal right to "codetermination" at the level of the company, facility, and individual. At the company level, an organization's employees have direct influence on the important decisions that affect them, such as large investments or new strategies. This influence comes from employee representatives on each company's supervisory council. At the level of each facility, codetermination exists through work councils. The councils have no rights in the economic management of the company, but they can influence HRM policies on issues such as working hours, payment methods, hirings, and transfers. Finally, at the individual level, employees have contractual rights, such as the right to read their employee files and the right to be informed about how their pay is calculated.[22]

As this example suggests, an organization that expands internationally must gain expertise in the host country's legal requirements and ways of dealing with its legal system, often leading organizations to engage an international relocation consulting firm or hire one or more host-country nationals to help in the process. Some countries have laws requiring that a certain percentage of the employees of any foreign-owned subsidiary be host-country nationals, and in the context of our discussion here, this legal challenge to an organization's HRM may hold an advantage if handled creatively.

Workforce Planning in a Global Economy

As economic and technological change creates a global environment for organizations, workforce planning is involved in decisions about participating as an exporter or as an international, multinational, or global company. Even purely domestic companies may draw talent from the international labour market. For example, officials from Saskatchewan's five health regions and the provincial health recruitment agency recently traveled to the Philippines to recruit 300 registered nurses.[23] As organizations consider decisions about their level of international activity, HR professionals should provide information about the relevant human resource issues, such as local market pay rates and labour laws. When organizations decide to operate internationally or globally, workforce planning involves decisions about where and how many employees are needed for each international facility.

Decisions about where to locate include HR considerations such as the cost and availability of qualified workers. In addition, HR specialists have to work with other members of the organization to weigh these considerations against financial and

LO3 - Discuss how differences among countries affect HR planning at organizations with international operations.

3

operational requirements. Other location decisions involve outsourcing, described in Chapter 1. Many companies have boosted efficiency by arranging to have specific functions performed by outside contractors.

In Chapter 4, we saw that workforce planning includes decisions to hire and lay off workers to prepare for the organization's expected needs. Compared with other countries, Canada allows employers wide latitude in reducing their workforce, giving Canadian employers the option of hiring for peak needs, then laying off employees if needs decline. Other governments put more emphasis on protecting workers' jobs. European countries tend to be very strict in this regard.

Until recently, Japanese law and culture supported the concept of "lifetime employment," but this practice changed to help companies weather a difficult recession.[24]

LO4 - Describe how companies select and train human resources in a global labour market.

Selecting Employees in a Global Labour Market

Many companies such as Fairmont have headquarters in Canada plus facilities in locations around the world. To be effective, employees in Fairmont's Mexico operations need to understand that region's business and social culture. Organizations often meet this need by hiring host-country nationals to fill most of their foreign positions.[25] A key reason is that a host-country national can more easily understand the values and customs of the local workforce than someone from another part of the world can. Also, training for and transporting families to foreign assignments is more expensive than hiring people in the foreign country. Employees may be reluctant to take a foreign assignment because of the difficulty of relocating internationally. Sometimes the move requires the employee's partner to quit a job, and some countries will not allow the employee's partner to seek work, even if jobs might be available.

Qualities associated with success in foreign assignments are the ability to communicate in the foreign country, flexibility, enjoying a challenging situation, and support from family members. What would persuade you to take an international assignment?

Even so, organizations fill many key foreign positions with home-country or third-country nationals. Sometimes a person's technical and human relations skills outweigh the advantages of hiring locally. In other situations, such as the shortage of North American knowledge workers, the local labour market simply does not offer enough qualified people. At organizations located where needed skills are in short supply, hiring immigrant employees may be part of an effective recruitment and selection strategy.[26]

Whether the organization is hiring immigrants or selecting home-country or third-country nationals for international assignments, some basic principles of selection apply. Selection of employees for international assignments should reflect criteria that have been associated with success:

- Competency in the employee's area of expertise
- Ability to communicate verbally and nonverbally in the foreign country
- Flexibility, tolerance of ambiguity, and sensitivity to cultural differences
- Motivation to succeed and enjoyment of challenges
- Willingness to learn about the foreign country's culture, language, and customs
- Support from family members[27]

In research conducted a number of years ago, the factor most strongly influencing whether an employee completed a foreign assignment was the comfort of the employee's spouse and family.[28] Providing "trailing partner" career transition services may make the difference whether or not an international assignment will be accepted. Personality may also be important. Research has found successful completion of international assignments to be most likely among employees who are extroverted (outgoing), agreeable (cooperative and tolerant), and conscientious (dependable and achievement oriented).[29]

Qualities of flexibility, motivation, agreeableness, and conscientiousness are so important because of the challenges involved in entering another culture. The emotions that accompany an international assignment tend to follow a cycle like that in Figure 11.4. For a month or so after arriving, the foreign worker enjoys a "honeymoon" of fascination and euphoria as the employee enjoys the novelty of the new culture and compares its interesting similarities to or differences from the employee's own culture. Before long, the employee's mood declines as he or she notices more unpleasant differences and experiences feelings of isolation, criticism, stereotyping, and even hostility. As the mood reaches bottom, the employee is experiencing **culture shock**, the disillusionment and discomfort of ideas that occur during the process of adjusting to a new culture and its norms, values, and perspectives. Eventually, if employees persist and continue learning about their host country's culture, they develop a greater understanding and a support network. As the employee's language skills and comfort increase, the employee's mood should improve as well. Eventually, the employee reaches a stage of adjustment in which he or she accepts and enjoys the host country's culture.

Even if the organization determines that the best candidate for a position is someone from another country, employers often have difficulty persuading candidates to accept foreign assignments. Not only do the employee and employee's family have to contend with culture shock, but the employee's partner commonly loses a job when an employee makes an international move. Some organizations solve this problem with a compromise: the use of **virtual expatriates**, or employees who manage an operation abroad without locating permanently in that country.[30] They take frequent trips to the foreign country, and when they are home, they use technologies such as videoconferencing and electronic collaboration tools to stay in touch. An assignment as a virtual expatriate may be less inconvenient to family members and less costly to the employer. The arrangement, sometimes referred to as a "commuter assignment" does have disadvantages. Most notably, by limiting personal contact to sporadic trips, the virtual expatriate will likely have a harder time building relationships. These short-term assignments are also growing in popularity. According to a recent study involving more than 200 multinational organizations, 100 percent of North American companies reported using short-term assignments.[31] These types of assignments generally last six to twelve months, avoiding the move of the whole family. Short-term and commuter assignments are gaining increasing acceptance by employees and decrease the risk of assignment failure, which provides a win-win for both the employee and the employer.[32]

culture shock
Disillusionment and discomfort that occur during the process of adjusting to a new culture.

virtual expatriates
Employees who manage an operation abroad without permanently locating in the country.

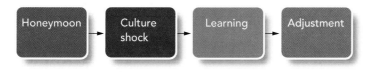

FIGURE 11.4

Emotional Cycle Associated with a Foreign Assignment

SOURCE: Adapted from C. Lachnit, "Low-Cost Tips for Successful Inpatriation," *Workforce*, August 2001, p. 44.

Training and Developing a Global Workforce

In an organization whose employees come from more than one country, some special challenges arise with regard to training and development:

1. Training and development programs should be effective for all participating employees, regardless of their background.
2. When organizations hire employees to work in a foreign country or transfer them to another country, the employer needs to provide training in how to handle the challenges of working there.

Training Programs for an International Workforce

Developers of effective training programs for an international workforce must ask certain questions.[33] The first is to establish the objectives for the training and its content. Decisions about the training should support those objectives. The developers should next ask what training techniques, strategies, and media to use. Some will be more effective than others, depending on the learners' language and culture, as well as the content of the training. For example, in preparation for training, Canadian employees might expect to discuss and ask questions about the training content, whereas employees from other cultures might consider this level of participation to be disrespectful, so for them some additional support might be called for. Language differences will require translations and perhaps an interpreter at training activities. Next, the developers should identify any other interventions and conditions that must be in place for the training to meet its objectives. For example, training is more likely to meet its objectives if it is linked to performance management and has the full support of management. Finally, the developers of a training program should identify who in the organization should be involved in reviewing and approving the training program.

The plan for the training program must consider international differences among trainees. For example, economic and educational differences might influence employees' access to and ability to use web-based training. Cultural differences may influence whether they will consider it appropriate to ask questions and whether they expect the trainer to spend time becoming acquainted with employees or to get down to business immediately. Table 11.2 provides examples of how cultural characteristics can affect training design. These differences may call for extra planning and creativity on the part of the training program's developer. To meet the needs of trainees in China, for instance, the training program should take into account that culture's high power distance.[34] The instructor needs to encourage audience feedback, perhaps by inviting the group's senior member to speak. If the instructor gives other trainees a chance to forward questions to this person, they can avoid embarrassing a high-status participant by asking a better question. Also, extra time is needed to prepare translations and practice delivering presentations with a translator.

When working internationally, there may also be times when an employee requires immediate training or coaching to perform the job in a remote location. Schlumberger, one of the world's largest oilfield services providers, employs approximately 80,000 people in 80 countries, representing 140 nationalities. Schlumberger recently introduced technology that provides field engineers immediate access to training needed to perform their jobs. For example, a field engineer working on a drilling project in a far-flung corner of Asia, notices an unexpected response and is uncertain what is causing the problem or how to proceed. The engineer receives on-the-spot training and expert advice by putting on a pair of headphones and a specially designed pair

CULTURAL DIMENSION	IMPACT ON TRAINING
Individualism	Culture high in individualism expects participation in exercises and questioning to be determined by status in the company or culture.
Uncertainty avoidance	Culture high in uncertainty avoidance expects formal instructional environments. Less tolerance for impromptu style.
Masculinity	Culture low in masculinity values relationships with fellow trainees. Female trainers less likely to be resisted in low-masculinity cultures.
Power distance	Culture high in power distance expects trainer to be expert. Trainers expected to be authoritarian and controlling of session.
Time orientation	Culture with a long-term orientation will have trainees who are likely to accept development plans and assignments.

TABLE 11.2

Effects of Culture on Training Design

SOURCE: Based on B. Filipczak, "Think Locally, Act Globally," *Training*, January 1997, pp. 41–48.

of glasses, fitted with a webcam, a small screen, and a two-way microphone. Using a wireless laptop, the engineer walks around the site demonstrating where the problem lies, and gets immediate on-the-job training from an expert (who may be based several thousand miles away) on how to diagnose and deal with the situation.[35]

Cross-Cultural Preparation

When an organization selects an employee for a position in a foreign country, it must prepare the employee for the foreign assignment. This kind of training is called **cross-cultural preparation**, preparing employees to work across national and cultural boundaries, and it often includes family members who will accompany the employee on the assignment. The training is necessary for all three phases of an international assignment:

1. *Preparation for departure.* Language instruction and an orientation to the foreign country's culture.
2. *The assignment itself.* Some combination of a formal program and mentoring relationship to provide ongoing further information about the foreign country's culture.
3. *Preparation for the return home.* Providing information about the employee's community and home-country workplace (from company newsletters, local newspapers, and so on).

cross-cultural preparation
Training to prepare employees and their family members for an assignment in a foreign country.

Methods for providing this training may range from lectures for employees and their families to visits to culturally diverse communities.[36] Employees and their families may also spend time visiting a local family from the country where they will be working. In many organizations, cross-cultural training is mandatory. In the later section on managing expatriates, we provide more detail about such preparation. Canadian-based companies sometimes need to be reminded that foreign-born employees who come to Canada—*inpatriates*—need cross-cultural preparation as much as Canadian employees sent on foreign assignments.[37] In spite of the many benefits of living in Canada, relocation can be challenging for inpatriates. As with expatriates, organizations can prepare inpatriate employees by providing information about getting the resources they need to live safely and comfortably in their new surroundings.

Global Employee Development

At global organizations, international assignments are a part of many career paths. The organization benefits most if it applies the principles of employee development in deciding which employees should be offered jobs in other countries. Career development helps expatriate and inpatriate employees make the transitions to and from their assignments and helps the organization apply the knowledge the employees obtain from these assignments. An example of a company with a strong program for global employee development is Deloitte, described in the Best Practices box.

BEST PRACTICES

Deloitte Develops a Global Workforce

Deloitte is an accounting and consulting firm whose 95,000 employees work in 700 offices located in 140 different countries around the world. An organization like that has the human resources to know the ins and outs of international business—but only if it gives employees international experience. Deloitte does just that with its Global Development Program.

The program, based on a curriculum developed by the human resource department, identifies mid-career employees in Deloitte's worldwide locations and assigns them to work in other countries. HR coordinators work with applicants to identify countries that offer experiences likely to be relevant to future work in the applicants' own countries. Often, employees wind up working with the same multinational client but in another country where that client operates. Through the

program, these employees learn the languages, business practices, and cultures of the countries where they are assigned. They also have plenty of opportunity to interact with other expatriate employees.

For example, Fabian Gomez left Mexico for a year and a half at Deloitte's New York office. When he returned to León, a city northwest of Mexico City, Gomez was well prepared to serve an international clientele as an audit partner. Explains Gomez, "A lot of our business is serving Mexican subsidiaries of international companies, and the executives usually come from other places" as far from Mexico as Japan.

Hundreds of employees and Deloitte offices in 50 countries participate in the Global Development Program. Executives give the program some of the credit for the firm's growth in global revenue. The company expects further benefits down the road, as Deloitte increases its ability to

serve the multinational needs of its clients.

The participants praise the program, too. Gomez says, "People are very excited about [the Global Development Program], because they know that if they have international experience, both they and the company are going to get ahead."

Canadian Pam McLaughlin trained with a Big Four firm and qualified with Deloitte's Ottawa office in September 2002. Six weeks later, Pam joined Deloitte's Bermuda office as an audit senior with the insurance group. Pam was promoted to manager in July 2004, and is now serving one of Bermuda's largest insurance clients. Pam is an active participant in softball and sailing and is a volunteer little-league coach on the weekends.

SOURCES: P. J. Kiger, "How Deloitte Builds Global Expertise," *Workforce*, June 2002, pp. 62–64, 66; "Looking for a New Experience?" *Leader-Post*, March 5, 2005, p. D1.

Performance Management Across National Boundaries

The general principles of performance management may apply in most countries, but the specific methods that work in one country may fail in another. Therefore, organizations have to consider legal requirements, local business practices, and national cultures when they establish performance management methods in other countries. Differences may include which behaviours are rated, how and the extent to which performance is measured, who performs the rating, and how feedback is provided.[38]

For example, National Rental Car uses a behaviourally based rating scale for customer service representatives. To measure the extent to which customer service representatives' behaviours contribute to the company's goal of improving customer service, the scale measures behaviours such as smiling, making eye contact, greeting customers, and solving customer problems. Depending on the country, different behaviours may be appropriate. In Japan, culturally defined standards for polite behaviour include the angle of bowing as well as proper back alignment and eye contact. In Ghana and many other African nations, appropriate measures would include behaviours that reflect loyalty and repaying of obligations as well as behaviours related to following regulations and procedures.

The extent to which managers measure performance may also vary from one country to another. In rapidly changing regions, such as Southeast Asia, the organization may have to update its performance plans more often than once a year.

Feedback is another area in which differences can occur. Employees around the world appreciate positive feedback, but Canadian employees are much more used to direct feedback than are employees in other countries. In Mexico, managers are expected to provide positive feedback before focusing the discussion on behaviours the employee needs to improve.[39] At the Thai office of Singapore Airlines, managers resisted giving negative feedback to employees because they feared this would cause them to have bad karma, contributing to their reincarnation at a lower level in their next life.[40] The airlines therefore allowed the managers to adapt their feedback process to fit local cultures.

Compensating and Rewarding an International Workforce

L05 - Discuss challenges related to compensating and rewarding employees from other countries.

Chapter 9 explained that total rewards includes decisions about pay structure, incentive pay, and employee benefits and services. All these decisions become more complex when an organization has an international workforce. In a recent survey of employers with international operations, 85 percent said they have a global compensation strategy to guide compensation decisions for employees at all levels and in all countries where they operate.[41] Still, HR specialists may need to make extra efforts to administer these systems effectively. In half of the companies surveyed, the person in charge of HRM in one country reports to the head of that company's operations, rather than to the leader of HRM at headquarters.

Pay Structure

As Figure 11.5 shows, market pay structures can differ substantially across countries in terms of both pay level and the relative worth of jobs. For example, compared with the labour markets in Frankfurt, Germany, the markets in Budapest, Hungary, and in

FIGURE 11.5

Earnings in Selected Occupations in Seven Cities

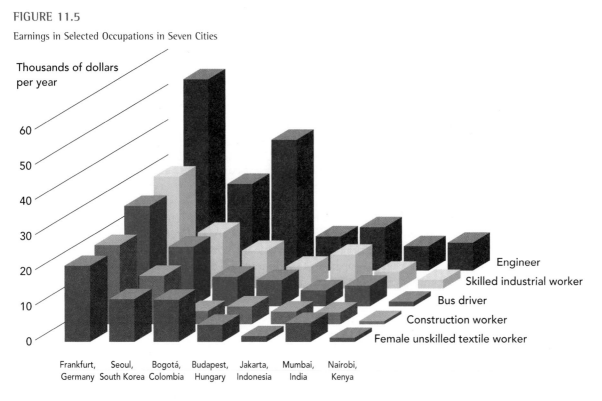

NOTE: Earnings are adjusted to reflect purchasing power.

SOURCE: From World Bank, *World Development Report 1995: Workers in an Integrating World*. Copyright 1995 by World Bank. Reprinted with permission of World Bank via Copyright Clearance Center.

Mumbai, India, provide much lower pay levels overall. The latter two labour markets also exhibit less of a pay difference for jobs requiring greater skill and education.

Differences such as these create a dilemma for global companies: Should pay levels and differences reflect what workers are used to in their own countries? Or should they reflect the earnings of colleagues in the country of the facility, or earnings at the company headquarters? For example, should a German engineer posted to Mumbai be paid according to the standard in Germany or the standard in Mumbai? If the standard is Germany, the engineers in Mumbai will likely see the German engineer's pay as unfair. If the standard is Mumbai, the company will likely find it impossible to persuade a German engineer to take an assignment in Mumbai. Dilemmas such as these make a global compensation strategy important as a way to show employees that the pay structure is designed to be fair and related to the value that employees bring to the organization.

These decisions affect a company's costs and ability to compete. The average hourly labour costs in industrialized countries such as Canada, the United States, Germany, and Japan are far higher than these costs in newly industrialized countries such as Mexico, Hong Kong, and Korea.[42] As a result, we often hear that Canadian labour costs are too high to allow Canadian companies to compete effectively unless the companies shift operations to low-cost foreign subsidiaries. That conclusion oversimplifies the situation for many companies. Merely comparing wages ignores differences in education, skills, and productivity.[43] If an organization gets more or higher-quality output from a higher-wage workforce, the higher wages may be worth the cost. Besides this, if the organization has many positions requiring highly skilled workers, it may need to operate in (or hire immigrants from) a country with a strong educational system, regardless of labour costs. Finally, labour costs may be outweighed by other factors, such as transportation costs or access to resources or customers. When a production process is highly automated, differences in labour costs may not be significant.

At the same time, the challenge of competing with organizations in low-wage countries can be very difficult. China, for example, has invested in vocational schools, which provide training for skilled factory jobs. Chinese universities graduate a much larger share of engineers than Canadian universities. These schools are flooding the Chinese labour market with talent, so that even as high-tech manufacturing spreads to many Chinese cities, the need for workers is easy to fill. China had 5.6 million university graduates in 2008, up from less than 5 million in 2007.[44] For Chinese workers, even with a university degree and experience, the result is that pay is growing but remains low compared to rates in other countries. An example is Li Guangxiang, a senior engineer and assistant manager at a Flextronics International computer parts factory, who earns just $10,000 a year.[45]

A large number of journalists found shelter in the old building of the French nongovernmental organization in Afghanistan. Taking an overseas assignment, especially in a harsh or potentially dangerous climate, requires the challenge of adjusting to life in a new country, so many companies pay employees higher salaries to compensate for this hardship.

Incentive Pay

Besides setting a pay structure, the organization must make decisions with regard to incentive pay, such as bonuses and stock options. International labour laws vary. For example, in Mexico, profit sharing is mandatory. Employers are required by law to distribute 10 percent of pre-tax earnings among employees other than senior managers.[46] Although stock options became a common form of incentive pay in North America during the 1990s, European businesses did not begin to embrace this type of compensation until the end of that decade. European companies with North American operations have felt the greatest pressure to join the stock option "club."[47] For instance, executives at Alcatel, a French manufacturer of telecommunications equipment, recently realized they needed to broaden the scope of their compensation when they began to acquire North American firms such as Canada's Newbridge Networks. Afraid that failure to offer stock options would result in a loss of qualified employees, Alcatel announced a plan that would award options to over one-third of its engineers and middle managers.

Canada and Europe differ in the way they award stock options. European companies usually link the options to specific performance goals, such as the increase in a company's share price compared with that of its competitors. German law actually requires this, and British firms such as Barclays are beginning to enforce stricter guidelines. Belgium and Switzerland still discourage the use of stock options by imposing high taxes on this form of compensation. Italy and Norway have passed laws and tax changes that make stock options more attractive to employers and employees. As competition in European labour markets increases, experts predict that companies not offering options will have a harder time recruiting the best employees.

Employers are adding incentives to compensate employees working in high-risk parts of the world such as the Middle East. The list of dangerous hot spots in the world is long—"Iraq, Somalia, Afghanistan, Sudan, Chad, and Lebanon are just a few of the countries where employees can encounter myriad problems including disease, a higher incidence of crime, civil unrest, and war."[48] A recent study conducted by Watson Wyatt, found that many companies are offering added incentives to reward staff for working in high-risk areas.[49] For example, a "major U.S. engineering and construction company with federal contracts to rebuild Iraq compensates for the hazardous duty by offering each typical $130,000-a-year expatriate an extra $75,000 tax-free a year in foreign service, hardship and danger allowance."[50] Oil and gas companies, have adopted a "total security" approach to keep employees safe from harm that includes keeping employees "informed and isolated from the general population and surrounding them with total security when they venture beyond their secure, well-protected enclaves. This approach is effective—and expensive."[51]

Employee Benefits

As in Canada, compensation packages in other countries include benefits. Decisions about benefits and services must take into account the laws of each country involved, as well as employees' expectations and values in those countries. Some countries require paid parental leave, and some countries, in addition to Canada, have nationalized health care systems, which would affect the value of private health insurance in a reward package. Availability of partner relocation assistance is a differentiator for many organizations in attracting employees to global assignments. For example, some organizations provide the "trailing partner" with educational and career assistance. Pension plans are more widespread in parts of Western Europe than in Canada, the United States, or Japan. Over 90 percent of workers in Switzerland have pension plans, as do all workers in France. Among workers with pension plans, Canadian workers are significantly less likely to have defined benefit plans than workers in Japan or Germany.

Paid vacation, also discussed in Chapter 9, tends to be more generous in Western Europe than in North America. Figure 11.6 compares the number of hours the average manufacturing employee works in various countries. Of these countries, only in the Czech Republic, South Korea, and the United States do manufacturing workers put in more hours than Canadian workers—up to 400 more hours per year. In Brazil, Great Britain, and Germany, the norm is to work 150 to 400 hours less than a Canadian worker over the course of a year.

FIGURE 11.6

Normal Annual Hours Worked in Manufacturing Relative to Canada

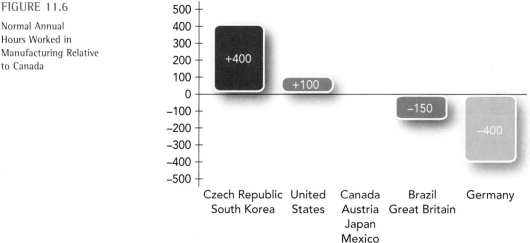

SOURCE: *Key Indicators of the Labor Market 2001–2002* (Geneva, Switzerland: International Labor Office, 2001).

International Labour Relations

In some industries, unions are forming global labour alliances. For example, the United Steelworkers of America and Mexico's Miners and Metalworkers Union (250,000 members) want to create a coalition of metals and mining industry unions throughout the Western Hemisphere.[52]

Companies that operate across national boundaries will increasingly need to work with unions in more than one country. Organizations establish policies and goals for labour relations, overseeing labour agreements, and monitoring labour performance (e.g., output and productivity).[53] The day-to-day decisions about labour relations are usually handled by each foreign subsidiary. The reason is that labour relations on an international scale involve differences in laws, attitudes, and economic systems, as well as differences in negotiation styles.

At least in comparison with European organizations, North American organizations exert more centralized control over labour relations in the various countries where they operate.[54] Management therefore must recognize differences in how various countries understand and regulate labour relations. For example, in Canada, collective bargaining usually involves negotiations between a union local and an organization's management, but in Sweden and Germany, collective bargaining generally involves negotiations between an employers' organization and a union representing an entire industry's employees.[55] Legal differences range from who may form a union to how much latitude an organization is allowed in laying off workers. In China, for example, efforts at economic reform resulted in many thousands of layoffs. As many as 20,000 workers at a time have rallied to protest layoffs by PetroChina, angry that early-retirement packages did not include expected medical insurance and social security payments. The workers resort to public protest, because the country's legal and economic system allows only government-controlled unions and does not provide them with recourse when the government does not support their position.[56] In Germany, because labour representatives participate on companies' boards of directors, the way management handles labour relations can affect a broad range of decisions.[57] Management therefore has an incentive to build cooperative relationships.

International labour relations must also take into account that negotiations between labour and management take place in a different social context, not just different economic and legal contexts. Cultural differences that affect other interactions come into play in labour negotiations as well. Negotiators will approach the process differently depending on whether the culture views the process as primarily cooperative or competitive and whether it is local practice to negotiate a deal by starting with the specifics or agreeing on overall principles.[58] Working with host-country nationals can help organizations navigate such differences in negotiation style.

Managing Expatriates

At some point, most international and global organizations assign employees to foreign posts. According to Statistics Canada, there are "about 68,000 Canadians working abroad at any given time and, with more companies active in the global marketplace, this number is expected to increase."[59] In addition, "North American companies are relying on more women to pursue international business opportunities—about four times as many as in 2001."[60] These assignments give rise to significant human resource challenges, from selecting employees for these assignments to preparing them, compensating them, helping them adjust, remain safe, providing support and preparing for return home. In a global marketplace, expatriate assignments are important, but evidence suggests that North American companies have not yet learned to select and use expatriates effectively. Out of every 100 expatriates, between 16 and 40 return before their assignment is complete, a rate about two to three times that of foreign nationals.[61] Other research found that between one-third and one-half of expatriates perform at a level that, according to employers' evaluations, is either ineffective or marginally effective.[62] The same kinds of HRM principles that apply to domestic positions can help organizations avoid mistakes in managing expatriates: planning and goal setting, selection aimed at achieving the HR goals, and performance management that includes evaluation of whether the overseas assignment delivered value relative to the costs involved.[63] The HR How-To box provides a summary of HRM practices that support expatriates.

Selecting Expatriates

The challenge of managing expatriates begins with determining which individuals in the organization are most capable of handling an assignment in another country. Expatriates need technical competence in the area of operations, in part to help

---

HR HOW-TO

Ensuring Success of Expatriates

The following HRM practices support the effectiveness of expatriates.

Staffing and Selection

- Communicate the value of international assignments for the company's global mission.
- Ensure that those with the highest potential move internationally.
- Provide short-term assignments to increase the pool of employees with international experience.
- Recruit employees who have lived or who were educated abroad.

Training and Career Development

- Make international assignment planning a part of the career development process.
- Encourage early international experience.
- Create learning opportunities during the assignment.
- Use international assignments as a leadership development tool.

Performance Appraisal and Compensation

- Differentiate performance management on the basis of expatriate roles.
- Align incentives with objectives for expatriation.
- Tailor benefits to the expatriate's needs.
- Focus on equality of opportunities, not cash.
- Emphasize rewarding careers rather than short-term outcomes.

Expatriation and Repatriation Activities

- Involve the family in the orientation program at the beginning and the end of the assignment.
- Establish mentor relationship between expatriates and executives from the home country.
- Provide support for dual careers.
- Secure opportunities for the returning manager to use knowledge and skills learned while on the international assignment.

SOURCE: P. Evans, V. Pucik, and J. Barsoux, *The Global Challenge: Framework for International Human Resource Management* (Boston: McGraw-Hill/Irwin, 2002). Copyright 2002 The McGraw-Hill Companies, Inc. Reprinted with permission.

them earn the respect of employees. Of course, many other skills are also necessary for success in any new job, especially one that involves working overseas. Depending on the nature of the assignment and the culture where it is located, the organization should consider each candidate's skills, learning style, and approach to problem solving. Each of these should be related to achievement of the organization's goals, such as solving a particular problem, transferring knowledge to host-country employees, or developing future leaders for the organization.[64]

A successful expatriate must be sensitive to the host country's cultural norms, flexible enough to adapt to those norms, and strong enough to survive the culture shock of living in another culture. In addition, if the expatriate has a family, the family members must be able to adapt to a new culture. Adaptation requires three kinds of skills:[65]

1. Ability to maintain a positive self-image and feeling of well-being
2. Ability to foster relationships with the host-country nationals
3. Ability to perceive and evaluate the host country's environment accurately

In a study that drew on the experience of people holding international assignments, expatriates told researchers that the most important qualities for an expatriate are, in order of importance, family situation, flexibility and adaptability, job knowledge and motivation, relational skills, and openness to other cultures.[66] To assess candidates' ability to adapt to a new environment, interviews should address topics such as the ones listed in Table 11.3. The interviewer should be certain to give candidates a clear and complete preview of the assignment and the host-country culture. This helps the candidate evaluate the assignment and consider it in terms of his or her family situation, so the employer does not violate the employee's privacy.[67]

TABLE 11.3

Topics for Assessing Candidates for Global Assignments

Motivation
- Investigate reasons and degree of interest in wanting to be considered.
- Determine desire to work abroad, verified by previous concerns such as personal travel, language training, reading, and association with foreign employees or students.
- Determine whether the candidate has a realistic understanding of what working and living abroad requires.
- Determine the basic attitudes of the spouse/partner toward an overseas assignment.

Health
- Determine whether any medical problems of the candidate or candidate's family might be critical to the success of the assignment.
- Determine whether the candidate is in good physical and mental health.

Language Ability
- Determine potential for learning a new language.
- Determine any previous language(s) studied or oral ability (judge against language needed on the overseas assignment).
- Determine the ability of the spouse/partner to meet the language requirements.

Family Considerations
- How many moves have been made in the past among different cities or internationally?
- What problems were encountered?

(continued)

TABLE 11.3 (concluded)

Family Considerations (*continued*)
- How recent was the last move?
- What is the spouse/partner's goal in this move?
- What family responsibilities—for example, child care, elder care—does the candidate have?
- Are there any special adjustment problems that you would expect?
- How is each member of the family reacting to this possible move?
- Do special educational problems exist within the family?

Resourcefulness and Initiative
- Can the candidate make and stand by decisions and judgments?
- Does the candidate have the intellectual capacity to deal with several dimensions simultaneously?
- Is the candidate able to reach objectives and produce results with whatever people and facilities are available, regardless of the limitations and barriers that might arise?
- Is the candidate able to operate without a clear definition of responsibility and authority on a foreign assignment?
- Will the candidate be able to explain the aims and company philosophy to the local managers and workers?
- Does the candidate possess sufficient self-discipline and self-confidence to overcome difficulties or handle complex problems?
- Can the candidate work without supervision?
- Can the candidate operate effectively in a foreign environment without normal communications and supporting services?

Adaptability
- Is the candidate sensitive to others, open to the opinions of others, cooperative, and able to compromise?
- What are the candidate's reactions to new situations, and efforts to understand and appreciate differences?
- Is the candidate culturally sensitive, aware, and able to relate across the culture?
- Does the candidate understand his or her own culturally derived values?
- How does the candidate react to criticism?
- What is the candidate's understanding of the government system?
- Will the candidate be able to make and develop contacts with peers in the foreign country?
- Does the candidate have patience when dealing with problems?
- Is the candidate resilient; can he or she bounce back after setbacks?

Career Planning
- Does the candidate consider the assignment more than a temporary overseas trip?
- Is the move consistent with the candidate's career goals and aspirations?
- Is the employee's career planning realistic?
- What is the candidate's basic attitude toward the company?
- Is there any history or indication of interpersonal problems with this employee?

Financial
- Are there any current financial and/or legal considerations that might affect the assignment?
- Are financial considerations negative factors? Will undue pressures be brought to bear on the employee or family as a result of the assignment?

SOURCE: Adapted from D. M. Noer, *Multinational People Management*, pp. 55–57. © 1989 by the Bureau of National Affairs, Inc., Washington, DC, 20037.

Of course, selection decisions are not just about finding employees who can do the job; the organization needs to select people who *want* an expatriate assignment. It is nothing new that many people are reluctant to move to a foreign country. A final issue with regard to selecting expatriates is the employment of women in international assignments. For a long time, many firms believed that women would have little success as in countries where women have not traditionally been promoted to management positions (such as in Japan and other Asian countries). However, Robin Abrams, working for Apple Computer in Hong Kong, found that nobody cares whether "you are wearing trousers or a skirt if you have demonstrated core competencies." Some female expatriates' experience has been that the novelty of being a woman in a group of men gives them an extra sort of credibility with host-country nationals.[68] As mentioned previously in this chapter, the number of female expatriates is increasing—the percentage of female expatriates is currently 18 percent of the overall expatriate population.[69]

Preparing Expatriates

Once the organization has selected an employee for an overseas assignment, it is necessary to prepare that person through training and development. Because expatriate success depends so much on the entire family's adjustment, the employee's partner should be included in the preparation activities. Employees selected for expatriate assignments already have job-related skills, so preparation for expatriate assignments often focuses on cross-cultural training—that is, training in what to expect from the host country's culture. The general purpose of cross-cultural training is to create an appreciation of the host country's culture so expatriates can behave appropriately.[70] Paradoxically, this requires developing a greater awareness of one's own culture, so that the expatriate can recognize differences and similarities between the cultures and, perhaps, home-culture biases.

On a more specific level, cross-cultural training for foreign assignments includes the details of how to behave in business settings in another country—the ways people behave in meetings, how employees expect managers to treat them, and so on. As an example, Germans value promptness for meetings to a much greater extent than do Latin Americans—and so on. How should one behave when first meeting one's business counterparts in another culture? The "outgoing" personality style so valued in North America may seem quite rude in other parts of the world.[71]

Employees preparing for a foreign assignment also need information about such practical matters as housing, schools, recreation, shopping, and health care facilities in the country where they will be living. This is a crucial part of the preparation.

Communication in another country often requires a determined attempt to learn a new language. Some employers try to select managers who speak the language of the host country, and a few provide language training. Most companies assume that employees in the host country will be able to speak the host country's language. Even if this is true, host country nationals are not likely to be fluent in the home country's language, so language barriers often remain.

Along with cross-cultural training, preparation of the expatriate should include career development activities. Before leaving for a foreign assignment, expatriates should discuss with their managers how the foreign assignment fits into their career plans and what types of positions they can expect upon their return. This prepares the expatriate to develop valuable skills during the overseas assignment and eases the return home when the assignment is complete.

LO6 - Explain how employers prepare employees for international assignments and for their return home.

6

When the employee leaves for the assignment, the preparation process should continue.[72] Employees need a chance to discuss their experiences with other expatriates, so they can learn from their failures and successes. The organization may provide a host-country mentor or "assimilator" to help expatriates understand their experiences. Successful expatriates tend to develop a bicultural or multicultural point of view, so as they spend more time in the host country, the value of their connections to other expatriates may actually increase.

5

Compensating and Rewarding Expatriates

One of the greatest challenges of managing expatriates is determining the compensation package. Most organizations use a *balance sheet approach* to determine the total amount of the package. This approach adjusts the employee's compensation so that it gives the employee the same standard of living as in the home country plus extra pay for the inconvenience of locating globally. As is shown in Figure 11.7, the balance sheet approach begins by determining the purchasing power of compensation for the same type of job in the employee's own country—that is, how much a person can buy, after taxes, in terms of housing, goods and services, and a reserve for savings. Next, this amount is compared with the cost (in dollars, for a Canadian company) of these same expenses in the foreign country. In Figure 11.7, the greater size of the second column means the costs for a similar standard of living in the foreign country are much higher

FIGURE 11.7

The Balance Sheet for Determining Expatriate Compensation

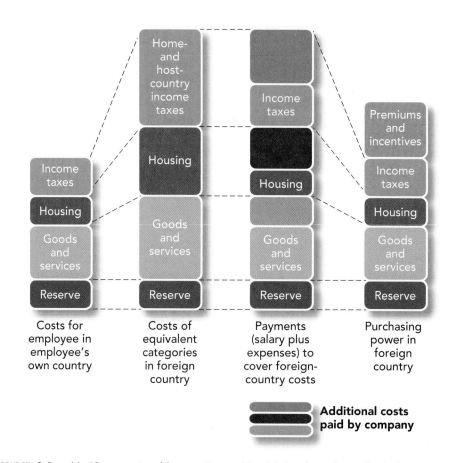

SOURCE: C. Reynolds, "Compensation of Overseas Personnel," in J. J. Famularo, ed., *Handbook of Human Resource Administration*, 2nd ed. (New York: McGraw-Hill, 1986), p. 51. Reprinted with permission.

in every category except the reserve amount. For the expatriate in this situation, the employer would pay the additional costs, as shown by the third column. Finally, the expatriate receives additional purchasing power from premiums and incentives. Because of these added incentives, the expatriate's purchasing power is more than what the employee could buy at home with the salary for an equivalent job. (Compare the fourth column with the first.) In practice, the total cost of an international assignment is often three to five times the employee's salary in the host country.[73]

After setting the total pay, the organization divides this amount into the four components of a total compensation package. First, there is a base salary. Determining the base salary is complex because different countries use different currencies (dollars, yen, euros, and so on). The exchange rate—the rate at which one currency may be exchanged for another—constantly shifts in response to a host of economic forces, so the real value of a salary in terms of dollars is constantly changing. Also, as discussed earlier, the base salary may be comparable to the pay of other managers at headquarters or comparable to other managers at the foreign subsidiary. Because many organizations pay a salary premium as an incentive to accept an overseas assignment, expatriates' salaries are often higher than pay for staying at headquarters.

A second component of total pay is a *tax equalization allowance*. "Tax equalization holds that the worker neither gains nor loses with regards to tax liability as a result of an international assignment."[74] Countries have different systems for taxing income, and in some countries, tax rates are higher than in Canada. Usually, the employer of an expatriate withholds the amount of tax to be paid in the home country, then pays all of the taxes due in the country where the expatriate is working.

A third component, benefits, presents additional challenges. Most of these have to do with whether an employee can use the same benefits in the foreign country. For example, if an expatriate has been contributing to a pension plan in Canada, does this person have a new pension plan in the foreign country? Or can the expatriate continue to contribute to the Canadian pension plan? Similarly, health benefits may involve receiving care at certain health facilities. While the person is abroad, does the same health plan cover services received in the foreign country? In one case, flying an employee back to Canada for certain procedures actually would have cost less than having the procedures done in the country where the person was working. But the company's health plans did not permit this alternative. Expatriates may also have access to resources that domestic employees do not have, including international employee and family assistance plans and personal crisis or risk services.[75]

An employer may offer expatriates additional benefits to address the problem of uprooting a partner when assigning an employee overseas. Pfizer, a pharmaceutical company, provides a $10,000 allowance that the partner can use in many different ways.[76] A person in the foreign country helps the partner with professional development and locating educational or other resources. In countries where the partner is allowed to work, Pfizer tries to find him or her a job within the company. Pfizer also provides cross-cultural counselling and language assistance and tries to connect the family with the area's expatriate community.

The final component of the total compensation packages is some set of allowances to make a foreign assignment more attractive. Cost-of-living allowances make up the differences in expenses for day-to-day needs. Housing allowances ensure that the expatriate can maintain the same standard of living as in Canada. Education allowances reimburse expatriates who pay tuition for their children to attend private schools. Relocation allowances cover the expenses of making the move to the foreign country, including transportation, shipping or storage of possessions, and expenses for temporary housing until the employee can rent or purchase a home.

4

repatriation
The process of preparing expatriates to return home from a foreign assignment.

Helping Expatriates Return and Minimizing Turnover

As the expatriate's assignment nears its end, the human resource department faces a final challenge: helping the expatriate make the transition back to his or her home country. The process of preparing expatriates to return home from a foreign assignment is called **repatriation**. According to a recent study by a partnership between PricewaterhouseCoopers and Cranfield University School of Management, more than 25 percent of repatriated employees leave the company within one year after an international assignment ends.[77] Companies are increasingly discussing repatriation/reentry. Presently, 86 percent of organizations discuss repatriation with employees.[78] Often, repatriation issues are discussed, at least informally, even before the candidate accepts an international assignment. The use of a well-written *international assignment letter* is a helpful means to clarify the rights and responsibilities of both the employer and employee for a relocation and subsequent return. Table 11.4 describes what to include in an international assignment letter. Reentry is not as simple as it

TABLE 11.4

What to Include in an International Assignment Letter

Assignment	• Location • Duration of assignment
Remuneration	• Base salary • Incentives and benefits • Pension plans • Currency of payment
Tax Issues	• Tax equalization • Tax advice • Tax reporting
Host Country	• Housing
Relocation Program	• Home and automobile sale • Family allowances (if family doesn't relocate) • House hunting • Moving • Schooling • Elder care • Language training • Cultural acclimatization programs
Vacation and Home Leave	• Number of trips • Emergency and compassionate travel provisions
Repatriation	• Timing (e.g., to coincide with family needs such as school terms) • Employment opportunities upon the employee's return • Assignment debriefing • Financial counselling • Dealing with dismissal or resignation

SOURCE: Joyce Head, "How Paper Can Protect International Relocations," *Canadian HR Reporter*, March 13, 2006, p. 14; Margaret Sim and Liam Dixon, "Unraveling Comp, Benefits for Expatriates," *Canadian HR Reporter*, December 3, 2007, p. 23.

might sound. Culture shock takes place in reverse. The experience has changed the expatriate, and the company's and expatriate's home culture may have changed as well. Also, because of differences in economies and compensation levels, a returning expatriate may experience a decline in living standards. The standard of living for an expatriate in many countries includes household help, a limousine or driver, private schools, and clubs.

Companies are increasingly making efforts to help expatriates through this transition and take steps to ensure expatriates stay with the company after their return. Expatriates are more likely to stay with a company that provides them opportunities to use their international experience.[79] Two activities help the process along: *communication* and *validation*.[80] Communication refers to the expatriate receiving information and recognizing changes while abroad. The more the organization keeps in contact with the expatriate, the more effective and satisfied the person will be upon return. The expatriate plays a role in this process as well. Expatriates should work at maintaining important contacts in the company and industry. Communication related to performance and career development before and during the international assignment also should help the employee return to a choice of positions that are challenging and interesting. Validation means giving the expatriate recognition for the international service when this person returns home. Expatriates who receive family repatriation support and recognition from colleagues and top managers for their international service and future contribution have fewer troubles with reentry than those whose contributions are disregarded. Validation should also include planning for how the returning employee will contribute to the organization. What skills will this person bring back? What position will he or she fill? The new skills may be much more than knowledge of a particular culture. For example, the person may have learned how to lead or negotiate with a diverse group of people.[81]

THINKING ETHICALLY

Carrying Ethics Standards Abroad

For many companies, the political, cultural, and economic realities of a host country may be extremely different from those of the home country, causing ethical dilemmas.

Consider companies that market clothing in Canada manufactured in low-wage countries where living standards are far from those in Canada. Critics have objected to the practice of selling goods made in "sweatshops," factories where working conditions are unhealthy and unsafe. Typically, the North American marketer doesn't hire its own manufacturing employees, but instead contracts with manufacturing firms in low-wage countries, so the North American company has limited direct control over working conditions. Nike has addressed the criticism by joining the Fair Labour Association, an international group that monitors factory conditions, and issues reports of working conditions. For example, in 2005, the company published a report indicating, for example, that abuses of employees occurred in one-fourth of its factories in South Asia and that over one-fourth of those factories restricted access to toilets and drinking water during the workday. The Gap has issued similar reports

(continued)

THINKING ETHICALLY

about working conditions in the factories of its suppliers. The retailer conducts initial evaluations of potential suppliers and has reported that about 90 percent fail that evaluation. The Gap also trains suppliers in its requirements for working conditions, and it helps them set up compliance programs.

Paul Fireman, the chair and chief executive officer of Reebok International, says

disclosing information is not always sufficient in extreme situations. He notes that human rights in Burma are in a deplorable state under its current rulers. Noting that the Burmese government's record includes the use of slave labour, removal of over a million people from their homelands, and rape as a weapon of war. Fireman urges companies to uphold ethical standards by publicly refusing to operate

in Burma, as a way to force political change in that country. Companies that have joined Reebok in making that decision include IKEA, and BP.

SOURCE: David Teaher, "Nike Lists Abuses at Asian Factories," The Guardian, April 14, 2005, www .guardian.co.uk; Amy Merrick, "Gap Offers Unusual Look at Factory Conditions," The Wall Street Journal, May 12, 2004, pp. A1, A12; and Paul Fireman, "What We Can Do about Burma," The Wall Street Journal, June 7, 2007, http://online.wsj.com.

Questions

1. Does a company bear responsibility for the ethical practices of its suppliers? Why or why not?
2. Suppose you work in the HR department of Nike or The Gap. How does the decision to publicize information about working conditions in overseas factories affect HRM at your company? How can your department support the principles behind this decision?
3. How is HRM affected when a company such as Reebok takes an ethics-based position not to operate in certain countries? Will it be easier or harder to find and keep talented people? Why?

SUMMARY

L01 Summarize how the growth in international business activity affects human resource management.

- More and more companies are entering international markets by exporting and operating foreign facilities. To do this organizations may hire a combination of home-country, host-country, and third-country nationals.
- They may operate on the scale of an exporter or an international, global, or multinational organization.
- A global organization needs a transnational HRM system, which makes decisions from a global perspective, includes employees from many countries, and is based on ideas contributed by people representing a variety of cultures.

L02 Identify the factors that most strongly influence HRM in international markets.

- By far the most important influence is the culture of each market—its set of shared assumptions about how the world works and what ideals are worth striving for.

- Countries also differ in the degree to which their labour markets include people with education and skills of value to employers. Another influence on international HRM is the foreign country's political-legal system—its government, laws, and regulations.

- Finally, a country's economic system, capitalist or socialist, as well as the government's involvement in the country's economy, such as through taxes and price controls, is a strong factor determining HRM practices.

LO3 | **Discuss how differences among countries affect HR planning at organizations with international operations.**

- As organizations consider decisions about their level of international activity, HR professionals should provide information about the relevant human resource issues.

- When organizations decide to operate internationally or globally, workforce planning involves decisions about where and how many employees are needed for each international facility. Some countries allow employers more flexibility in meeting human resource needs. HRM professionals need to be conversant with such differences.

LO4 | **Describe how companies select and train human resources in a global labour market.**

- Many organizations with international operations fill most positions with host-country nationals. These employees can more easily understand the values and customs of the local workforce, and hiring locally tends to be less expensive than moving employees to new locations.

- Organizations also fill foreign positions with home-country and third-country nationals who have human relations skills associated with success in international assignments. They also may use "virtual expatriates," who do not go abroad for an extended period.

- When sending employees on international assignments, organizations prepare the employees (and often their families) through cross-cultural training.

LO5 | **Discuss challenges related to compensating and rewarding employees from other countries.**

- Pay structures can differ substantially among countries in terms of pay level and the relative worth of jobs. Organizations have to decide whether to set pay levels and differences in terms of what workers are used to in their own countries or in terms of what employees' colleagues earn at headquarters.

- These decisions affect the organization's costs and ability to compete, so organizations consider local labour costs in their location decisions. Along with the basic pay structure, organizations must make decisions regarding incentive pay, such as bonuses and stock options.

- Laws may dictate differences in benefit packages, and the value of benefits will differ if a country requires them or makes them a government service.

LO6 | **Explain how employers prepare employees for international assignments and for their return home.**

- When an organization has selected an employee for an international assignment, it must prepare the person for the experience. In cross-cultural training, the soon-to-be-expatriate learns about the foreign culture he or she is heading to, and studies her or his own home-country culture as well for insight.

- Preparation of the expatriate should also include career development activities to help the individual acquire valuable career skills during the international assignment and at the end of the assignment to handle repatriation successfully.

- Communication of changes at home and validation of a job well done abroad help the expatriate through the repatriation process.

REVIEW AND DISCUSSION QUESTIONS

1. Identify the home country, host country(ies), and third country(ies) in the following example: A global soft-drink company called Cold Cola has headquarters in Halifax, Nova Scotia. It operates production facilities in the United States, and in Jakarta, Indonesia. The company has assigned a manager from Moncton to head the U.S. facility and a manager from Hong Kong to manage the Jakarta facility.

2. What are some HRM challenges that arise when a Canadian company expands from domestic markets by exporting? When it changes from simply exporting to operating as an international company? When an international company becomes a global company?

3. In recent years, many North American companies have invested in Russia and sent Canadian managers there in an attempt to transplant North American-style management. According to Hofstede (see Figure 11.3), Canadian culture has low power distance, uncertainty avoidance, and long-term orientation, and high individuality and masculinity. Russia's culture has high power distance and uncertainty avoidance, low masculinity and long-term orientation, and moderate individuality. In light of what you know about cultural differences, how well do you think Canadian managers can succeed in each of the following North American-style HRM practices? (Explain your reasons.)
   a. Selection decisions based on extensive assessment of individual abilities
   b. Appraisals based on individual performance
   c. Systems for gathering suggestions from workers
   d. Self-managing work teams

4. Besides cultural differences, what other factors affect human resource management in an organization with international operations?

5. Suppose you work in the HR department of a company that is expanding into a country where the law and culture make it difficult to lay off employees. How should your knowledge of that difficulty affect workforce planning for the overseas operations?

6. Why do multinational organizations hire host-country nationals to fill most of their foreign positions, rather than sending expatriates for most jobs?

7. Suppose an organization decides to improve collaboration and knowledge sharing by developing an intranet to link its global workforce. It needs to train employees in several different countries to use this system. List the possible cultural issues you can think of that the training program should take into account.

8. For an organization with operations in three different countries, what are some advantages and disadvantages of setting compensation according to the labour markets in the countries where the employees live and work? What are some advantages and disadvantages of setting compensation according to the labour market in the company's headquarters? Would the best arrangement be different for the company's top executives and its production workers? Explain.

9. What abilities make a candidate more likely to succeed in an assignment as an expatriate? Which of these abilities do you have? How might a person acquire these abilities?

10. In the past, a large share of expatriate managers from Canada have returned home before successfully completing their international assignments. Suggest some possible reasons for the high failure rate. What can HR departments do to increase the success of expatriates?

WHAT'S YOUR HR IQ?

Online LearningCentre   The Online Learning Centre offers more ways to check what you've learned so far. Find experiential exercises as well as Test Your Knowledge Quizzes, Videos, and many other resources at www.mcgrawhill.ca/olc/steen.

BusinessWeek Case:
China Unchains Ad Agencies

BusinessWeek

The ad campaign left shoemaker Nike Inc. flatfooted. The company's "Chamber of Fear" spot feature LeBron James of the NBA's Cleveland Cavaliers battling—and defeating—a computer-generated Kung Fu master. It might not have raised eyebrows elsewhere, but Chinese consumers found the concept insulting, and Beijing banned the ad in 2004.

The bad news for Nike, though, was great news for advertisers. The fact that the ad ignited a national debate highlighted the growing power of advertising in China. The industry has grown from virtually nothing in 1979, when the communist government lifted a ban on ads, to as much as $16 billion in 2004—an increase of at least 20 percent over the year before, according to MindShare, a media buying company. China is forecasted to soon be the third-largest ad market in the world as the nation gears up for the 2008 Beijing Olympics.

The potential has international ad agencies scrambling for position. Since the market opened more than a quarter-century ago, virtually every major industry player has set up shop in China. Until now they have been confined to operating joint ventures with local partners. That restriction, though was lifted at the end of 2005 under commitments China made when it joined the World Trade Organization. While some agencies have good relationships with their local partners and value the cultural background they provide, others feel constrained by the regulations. The rule change "will be liberating for a lot of [agencies] that have been boxed in with a bad or mediocre partner," says David Droga, global creative director for Publicis Group, the giant ad agency conglomerate.

International ad agencies control the biggest accounts, but there's plenty of local competition. The country has some 80,000 ad shops doing everything from designing fliers and renting space on local taxis to placing ads on the Internet—and charging cutthroat prices for their services. The best of those agencies—and myriad companies in other industries hungry for experienced marketing hands—are also attracting many of the young Chinese execs that the global giants have schooled. "The biggest problem we have is finding more people to hire and keeping the ones we train," says Shelly Lazarus, chairman of New-York-based Ogilvy & Mather Worldwide, which has 1,000 employees in four cities in China.

One challenge for global agencies is tailoring ads to the regional sensibilities of China's 1.3 billion citizens. As the divide between the rich coastal cities and the poorer interior grows, companies must make sure their messages fit the audience. "In Shanghai, where women are more cosmopolitan and sophisticated, we cater to a daily regimen of skin care with Oil of Olay," says Alfonso de Dios, media director for Greater China at consumer-goods giant Proctor & Gamble Company. "But in Urumqi we sell women Safeguard soap and Crest first. It's a question of needs."

Those concerns have spurred big foreign agencies to seek out local expertise. J. Walter Thompson Company has taken a 30 percent stake in Guangzhou's Newsun Insight, where Ogilvy & Mather bought Fujian Effort Advertising.

While multinationals have driven the market until now—P&G's Oil of Olay skin cream was the most advertised brand in China last year—local clients are coming on strong. Last year four local brands were among the top ten advertisers in China. J. Walter Thompson gets about 35 percent of its billings from Chinese companies, as it has signed up the likes of computer maker Lenovo, cellular carrier China Mobile, and TV manufacturer Konka.

China's advertising industry may remain decades behind the West in sophistication and creativity, but most Chinese put the highest value on low price and reliability, so ads need a straightforward message that tells the consumer exactly what to expect. That helps explain the tremendous success of products such as Gai Zhong Gai, a brand of calcium tablets. Although many in the industry pooh-poohed Gai Zhong Gai's simplistic approach and constant repetition of the same message, "they did everything that an advertising textbook in North America would tell you not to do, but it worked," says Quinn Taw, managing partner of Mind-Share. "They created a whole awareness about calcium and bones."

And what works elsewhere in the world doesn't always translate well in china. Nike's "Just Do It" campaign doesn't work, because it emphasizes individualistic youthful irreverence—a no-no in Confucian China. Instead, Nike runs ads such as a ten-second spot that features a school kid impressing classmates by spinning the globe on his finger. While the ad expresses playfulness and a certain bravado, "there's no rebellion," says Tom Doctoroff, CEO of Greater China for J. Walter Thompson, which made the spot.

SOURCE: Adapted from Frederik Balfour and David Kiley, "China Unchains Ad Agencies," *BusinessWeek,* April 25, 2005, www.businessweek.com.

Questions

1. If you worked for an international advertising agency and were involved in workforce planning for positions that involve serving the Chinese market, would you recommend that the firm look for home-country nationals, host-country nationals, or third-country nationals? Explain.
2. What qualifications are necessary in an employee who creates advertising for a Chinese audience?
3. Imagine that you are sending a manager from your advertising agency's headquarters to set up an office in China. Suggest several ways to prepare the manager for this assignment.

Case:
Foreign Assignments Increasing, Along with Employee Resistance

Canadians are working outside the country in increasing numbers. Data from Statistics Canada show that about 68,000 Canadians had a place of work outside the country. In addition, as Canada continues to play a growing role in an expanding global marketplace, there is every expectation the need for Canadian talent to work abroad will grow.

In the Canadian Employee Relocation Council's recent Survey of Corporate Relocation Policies, more than two-thirds of the 88 firms surveyed had transferred staff overseas. In the same survey, family issues ranked as the number one challenge for an overseas assignment.

While working in foreign lands may hold appeal, it is clearly not for everybody. There are many barriers to overcome for both the organization and its employees when it comes to a foreign posting. Partly in response to the personal realities that individuals are coping with as well as to rapidly changing business opportunities, shorter-term assignments, lasting from six months to three years, are becoming more common.

Whether it's a short- or long-term assignment, many of the challenges remain the same: getting the right people in the right job, at the right place, and at the right time.

Today, most Canadian families have both partners working, so when it comes to taking on a foreign assignment, it's no surprise that family issues are top of mind. Statistics Canada also reports a 40-percent increase in the number of female managers since 1990. Today, their careers are an even more important consideration than perhaps was the case ten or so years ago. The bottom line: moving is a far more complex undertaking than ever before.

"Moving people is a very expensive undertaking for the company," says Sue Irwin, responsible for international HR and relocations with ConocoPhillips Canada in Calgary. "It can cost three times as much to move somebody from say Houston than it does to hire a local person in Calgary and so it has to be the right fit."

Irwin manages a portfolio of both inpatriates (people coming to work in Canada) as well as expatriates. "While shorter-term assignments meet business needs, they also provide the much-needed career development and experience to the best talent in the organization," she says. "And it's not just about getting the right technical talent. Equally important is the ability to work with people with varied skill sets and from different backgrounds." All are critical skills on the global stage.

Terri Lynn Oliver, international HR advisor with Siemens Canada, notes that at Siemens, "the selection of high potentials [for international assignment] is part of the overall corporate approach for succession planning and career development."

With a global workforce of 420,000, of which 6,600 are in Canada, there is no shortage of foreign opportunities. At Siemens the process for selection is structured and the company maintains a pool of potential talent to draw from as opportunities arise. The challenge from a corporate perspective, says Oliver, is managing the expectation and linking the move to a strategic objective. "People want to know, 'What position will I come back to?' In most situations it's impossible to give a guarantee about opportunities on the completion of the assignment. And so people will often opt for the domestic promotion."

When it comes to individuals accepting an assignment, family and career issues dominate. "The spouse's career is a major consideration particularly on a longer assignment," says Oliver. "Schooling is also a challenge and Siemens tries to be innovative for both its inpatriates and expatriates in finding workable solutions within budget."

Schooling issues are echoed by Irwin who adds, "There are many students in gifted and extracurricular programs, people just don't want to uproot their families."

Thomas Vulpe, with the Canadian Foreign Service Institute, an agency within the Department of Foreign Affairs and International Trade, says family issues can predict the successful completion of an international assignment.

"Various studies have shown family issues to be the single most important issue in early repatriation," he says. These subtleties may not be readily apparent before the move, but culture shock and the inability to work in a foreign location can often be too much for the trailing spouse, leading to an early return.

"Companies are becoming more concerned about these soft issues," says Mike Watters, vice-president of sales with moving firm Allied International. These are not just Canadian problems, he adds. He tells the story of the wife of a French company executive who was "abandoned" in the Toronto-area, without access to any support. "She couldn't speak a word of English and left saying it was the worst two years of her life."

While family issues are the main barriers to individuals taking on a foreign assignment, safety is an escalating concern. Canada is a safe country to live and raise a family in. Many of the countries where Canadians are working are becoming more dangerous it seems with each passing day.

"One of the key parts of safety training for foreign-aid workers in hot spots like Columbia, Bolivia, and Afghanistan, includes looking under their vehicles with a mirror to check for bombs," Vulpe says. Not a pleasant routine, as you're also trying to comfort children who are used to walking to school. These issues are compounded by the fact the "megalopolises where people are being posted are becoming more polluted, and access to quality health care is a concern. Ten years ago it wasn't such a big issue, but today it's a big decision," he adds.

Perhaps that's why Terri Lynn Oliver says, "flexibility to shorten an assignment and planning for the worst," are a key part in the development of any foreign assignment.

SOURCE: Stephen Cryne, "Foreign Assignments Increasing, Along with Employee Resistance," *Canadian HR Reporter,* September 27, 2004, www.hrreporter.com, retrieved April 15, 2005. © *Canadian HR Reporter,* September 27, 2004, by permission of Carswell, Toronto, Ontario, 1-800-387-5164, www.hrreporter.com.

Questions

1. What are some of the human resource challenges associated with relocating employees to jobs and work assignments outside Canada?
2. Would you be interested in working outside Canada? Why or why not? If you would consider working outside Canada at some point in your career, at what life/career stage would a global assignment be most appealing?

Chapter 12

Creating and Maintaining High-Performance Organizations

What Do I Need to Know? After reading this chapter, you should be able to:

1. Define high-performance work systems and identify the elements of such a system.

2. Summarize the outcomes of a high-performance work system.

3. Describe the conditions that create a high-performance work system.

4. Explain how human resource management can contribute to high performance.

5. Discuss HRM's role in successful mergers and acquisitions.

6. Discuss the role of HRM technology in high-performance work systems.

7. Summarize ways to measure the effectiveness of human resource management.

Introduction

"It is the world's most spectacular and unifying event. Literally billions of people stop what they're doing to watch it. The attention of those billions will focus on British Columbia and Canada as we celebrate the Vancouver 2010 Olympic & Paralympic Games. The planning and staging of this extraordinary event will require the harmonized efforts and passions of thousands of people. It will become an intricate, split second ballet of planning, construction, revenue generation, relationship building, coordination, and leadership. It will attract the best and the brightest as the clock ticks down to the opening ceremonies, then twenty-seven days of unprecedented athletic achievement, international goodwill, arts and cultural events. It will be the time of our lives!"[1]

The Vancouver Organizing Committee for the 2010 Olympic & Paralympic Games has a mandate of high performance, and Donna Wilson, Executive Vice-President, Human Resources, Sustainability, and International Client Services, has a key role to play.

To achieve this mandate of high performance, the leadership team of the Vancouver Organizing Committee for the 2010 Olympic & Paralympic Games (Vancouver 2010) includes Donna Wilson in the key role of Executive Vice-President, Human Resources, Sustainability, and International Client Services. Wilson sums up her broad scope of responsibilities in a short sentence: "I'm responsible for everything that has to do with people, relationships, and lasting legacy." Her Human Resources division's mission is to "plan, deliver, train and retain high quality, volunteer and paid staff and contractors necessary to stage the 2010 Olympic and Paralympic Winter Games. Human Resources (HR) practices will be fair, equitable and transparent while being guided by best HR management practices and lessons learned from previous organizing committees."[2]

1,2

Although few occupy roles as visible as that of Donna Wilson, HR professionals are increasingly engaged in strategic roles responsible for creating and maintaining high-performance organizations.

This chapter summarizes the role of human resource management in creating an organization that achieves a high level of performance, measured in such terms as long-term profits, quality, and customer satisfaction. We begin with a definition of *high-performance work systems* and a description of these systems' elements and outcomes. Next, we identify the conditions that contribute to high performance. We explain how the various HRM functions can contribute to high performance. Finally, we introduce ways to measure the effectiveness of human resource management.

High-Performance Work Systems

The challenge facing managers today is how to make their organizations into **high-performance work systems** with the right combination of people, technology, and organizational structure to make full use of resources and opportunities in achieving their organizations' goals. To function as a high-performance work system, each of these elements must fit well with the others in a smoothly functioning whole. Many manufacturers use the latest in processes including flexible manufacturing technology and just-in-time inventory control (meaning parts and supplies are automatically restocked as needed), but, of course, these processes do not work on their own; they must be run by qualified people. Organizations have to determine what kinds of people fit their needs, and then locate, train, and motivate those special people.[3] According to research, organizations that introduce integrated high-performance work practices usually experience increases in productivity and long-term financial performance.[4]

Creating a high-performance work system contrasts with traditional management practices. In the past, decisions about technology, organizational structure, and human resources were treated as if they were unrelated. An organization might acquire a new information system, restructure jobs, or add an office in another country without considering the impact on its people.[5] More recently, managers have realized that success depends on how well all the elements work together.

SGCI, a marketing communications company based in Sackville, New Brunswick (www.sgcicom.com), is an example of an organization that has effectively integrated all the elements of a high-performance work system. Harvey Gilmour, Director of Development, Acadia University, describes SGCI as a

> collection of wonderfully creative individuals, working as a team. They have supported Acadia University since 1995 with work that has been unparalleled. We know—we have tested their quality of work, dedication to their client, their enthusiasm, willingness to go the extra mile and their philanthropy—against many others in New Brunswick and Nova Scotia. SGCI always comes out ahead. We rely on SGCI greatly and they share in our success at Acadia.[6]

**high-performance
work system**
The right
combination of
people, technology,
and organizational
structure that
makes full use of
the organization's
resources and
opportunities in
achieving its goals.

SGCI, the Sackville,
New Brunswick–
based marketing
communications
company, serves diverse
and clients, including
Aliant Mobility, Mount
Allison University, and
the Royal Canadian
Mint—introducing the
country to the infamous
"toonie." SGCI is
legendary for providing
a caring, appreciative,
family-oriented
environment.

SGCI's work environment is described by Nelson Cabral, creative director, like this: "We work in a house that we fill with family. We have a chef. Egos are rare but sentiment is frequent."[7]

Elements of a High-Performance Work System

As is shown in Figure 12.1, in a high-performance work system, the elements that must work together include organizational structure, task design, people (the selection, training, and development of employees), reward systems, and information systems, and human resource management plays an important role in establishing all these.

Organizational structure is the way the organization groups its people into useful divisions, departments, and reporting relationships. The organization's top management makes most decisions about structure, for instance, how many employees report to each supervisor, and whether employees are grouped according to the functions they carry out or the customers they serve. Such decisions affect how well employees coordinate their activities and respond to change. In a high-performance work system, organizational structure promotes cooperation, learning, and continuous improvement.

Task design determines how the details of the organization's necessary activities will be grouped, whether into jobs or team responsibilities. In a high-performance work system, task design makes jobs efficient while encouraging high-quality results. In Chapter 4, we discussed how to carry out this HRM function through job analysis and job design.

The right *people* are a key element of high-performance work systems. HRM has a significant role in providing people who are well suited and well prepared for their jobs. Human resource professionals help the organization recruit and select people with the needed qualifications. Training, development, and career management ensure that these people are able to perform their current and future jobs and "fit" with the culture of the organization.

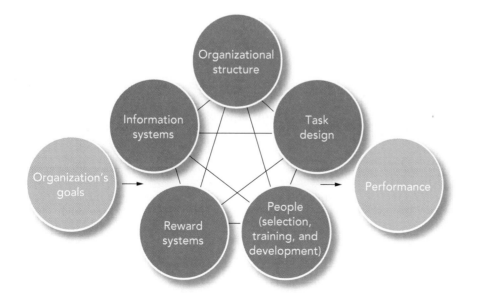

FIGURE 12.1

Elements of a High-Performance Work System

In a high-performance work system, all the elements—people, technology, and organizational structure—work together for success.

Reward systems contribute to high performance by encouraging people to strive for objectives that support the organization's overall goals. Reward systems include the performance measures by which employees are assessed, the methods of measuring performance, and the incentive pay and other rewards linked to success. Human resource management plays an important role in developing and administering reward systems, as we saw in Chapters 8 and 9.

The final element of high-performance work systems is the organization's *information systems*. Managers make decisions about the types of information to gather and the sources of information. They also must decide who in the organization should have access to the information and how they will make the information available. Modern information systems, including the Internet, have enabled organizations to share information widely. HR departments take advantage of this technology to give employees access to information about benefits, training opportunities, job openings, and more, as we will describe later in this chapter.

L02 - Summarize the outcomes of a high-performance work system.

Outcomes of a High-Performance Work System

Consider the practices of steel minimills (which produce steel to make a limited quantity of products for the construction industry). Some minimills have strategies based on keeping their costs below competitors' costs; low costs let them operate at a profit while winning customers with low prices. Other steel minimills focus on "differentiation," meaning they set themselves apart in some way other than low price—for example, by offering higher quality or unusual product lines. Research has found that the minimills with cost-related goals tend to have highly centralized structures, so managers can focus on controlling through a tight line of command. These organizations have low employee participation in decisions, relatively low wages and benefits, and pay highly contingent on performance.[8] At minimills that focus on differentiation, structures are more complex and decentralized, so authority is more spread out. These minimills encourage employee participation and have higher wages and more generous benefits. They are high-performance work systems. In general, these differentiator mills enjoy higher productivity, lower scrap rates, and lower employee turnover than the mills that focus on low costs.

Outcomes of a high-performance work system thus include higher productivity and efficiency. These outcomes contribute to higher profits. A high-performance work system may have other outcomes, including high product quality, great customer satisfaction, and low employee turnover. Some of these outcomes meet intermediate goals that lead to higher profits (see Figure 12.2). For example, high quality contributes to customer satisfaction, and customer satisfaction contributes to growth of the business. Likewise, improving productivity lets the organization do more with less, which satisfies price-conscious customers and may help the organization win over customers from its competitors. Other ways to lower cost and improve quality are to reduce absenteeism and turnover, providing the organization with a steady supply of experienced workers. In the previous example of minimills, some employers

FIGURE 12.2

Outcomes of a High-Performance Work System

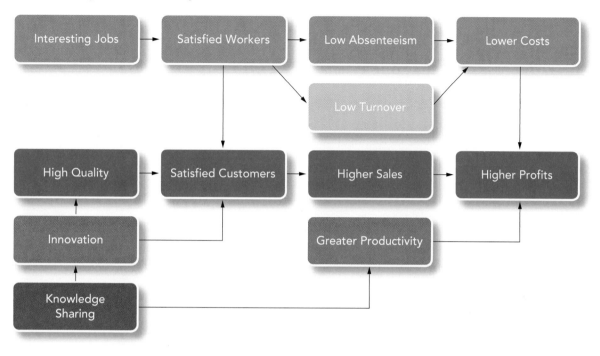

keep turnover and scrap rates low. Meeting those goals helps the minimills improve productivity, which helps them earn more profits.

In a high-performance work system, the outcomes of each employee and work group contribute to the system's overall high performance. The organization's individuals and groups work efficiently, provide high-quality goods and services, and so on, and in this way, they contribute to meeting the organization's goals. When the organization adds or changes goals, people are flexible and make changes as needed to meet the new goals.

Conditions That Contribute to High Performance

LO3 - Describe the conditions that create a high-performance work system.

Certain conditions underlie the formation of a high-performance work system. Common practices in high-performing organizations, such as those involving rewards, employee empowerment, and jobs with variety, contribute to high performance by giving employees skills, incentives, knowledge, autonomy—as well as satisfaction and engagement—conditions associated with high performance. Table 12.1 shows examples of such conditions. Finally, ethical behaviour is a necessary condition of high performance because it contributes to good long-term relationships with employees, customers, and the public.

Teamwork and Empowerment

Today's organizations empower employees. They expect employees to make more decisions about how they perform their jobs. One of the most popular methods of **employee empowerment** is to design work so that it is performed by teams. On a

employee empowerment
Giving employees responsibility and authority to make decisions regarding all aspects of product development or customer service.

TABLE 12.1

Conditions for High
Performance

- Teams perform work.
- Employees participate in selection.
- Employees receive formal performance feedback and are actively involved in the performance improvement process.
- Ongoing training is emphasized and rewarded.
- Employees' rewards and compensation relate to the company's financial performance.
- Equipment and work processes are structured and technology is used to encourage maximum flexibility and interaction among employees.
- Employees participate in planning changes in equipment, layout, and work methods.
- Work design allows employees to use a variety of skills.
- Employees understand how their jobs contribute to the finished product or service.
- Ethical behaviour is encouraged.

SOURCE: Based on J. A. Neal and C. L. Tromley, "From Incremental Change to Retrofit: Creating High-Performance Work Systems," *Academy of Management Executive* 9 (1995), pp. 42–54; M. A. Huselid, "The Impact of Human Resource Management Practices on Turnover, Productivity, and Corporate Financial Performance," *Academy of Management Journal* 38 (1995), pp. 635–72.

work team, employees bring together various skills and experiences to produce goods or provide services. The organization may charge the team with making decisions traditionally made by managers, such as hiring team members and planning work schedules. Teamwork and empowerment contribute to high performance when they improve job satisfaction and give the organization fuller use of employees' ideas and expertise.

At Cognos Inc., an Ottawa-based software company, managers worldwide are required to attend workshops on how to recognize individual achievements and keep employees challenged and motivated to stay. According to Beverly Kaye, a California-based author and consultant whose theories form the basis of the Cognos program, the most consistent reason that people left their previous job was "my boss was a jerk." When asked, "What do you mean by jerk?" most of the responses came down to "lack of appreciation, or their manager's desire to always be in control."[9]

For employee empowerment to succeed, managers must serve in linking and co-ordinating roles[10] and providing the team with the resources it needs to carry out its work. The manager should help the team and its members interact with employees from other departments or teams and should make sure communication flows in both directions—the manager keeps the team updated on important issues and ensures that the team shares information and resources with others who need them. Along with these efforts at coordination, the team's manager should help team members resolve problems as needed. To provide such help, the manager may have to refer team members to resources outside the team or organization. Several academic studies on employee engagement and organizational performance have concluded that an employee's immediate manager has a profound effect on his or her level of job satisfaction. In a recent survey of 2,687 working-age Canadians, Monster Canada reported, "there is no doubt that bosses typically are seen as the primary reason for people either loving or leaving their jobs." Monster reported that only 16 percent of the survey participants had quit a job for reasons *unrelated* to a boss.[11]

Knowledge Sharing

For more than a decade, managers have been interested in creating a **learning organization**, that is, an organization in which the culture values and supports lifelong learning by enabling all employees to continually acquire and share knowledge. The people in a learning organization have resources for training, and they are encouraged to share their knowledge with colleagues. Managers take an active role in identifying training needs and encouraging the sharing of ideas.[12] An organization's information systems, discussed later in this chapter, have an important role in making this learning activity possible. Information systems capture knowledge and make it available even after individual employees who provided the knowledge have left the organization. Ultimately, people are the essential ingredients in a learning organization. They must be committed to learning and willing to share what they have learned. A learning organization has the key features identified in Figure 12.3: continuous learning, generating and sharing of knowledge, thinking that is critical and systemic, a culture that values learning, encouraging flexibility and experimentation, and appreciating the value of each employee.

Continuous learning is each employee's and each group's ongoing efforts to gather information and apply the information to their decisions. In many organizations, the process of continuous learning is aimed at improving quality. To engage in continuous learning, employees must understand the entire work system they participate in, the relationships among jobs, their work units, and the organization as a whole. Employees who continuously learn about their work system are adding to their ability to improve performance.

Knowledge is most valuable to the organization when it is *shared*. Therefore, to create a learning organization, one challenge is to shift the focus of training away from merely teaching skills and toward a broader focus on generating and sharing knowledge.[13] In this view, training is an investment in the organization's human resources; it increases employees' value to the organization. Also, training content should be related to the organization's goals. Human resource departments can

6

learning organization
An organization that supports lifelong learning by enabling all employees to acquire and share knowledge.

continuous learning
Each employee's and each group's ongoing efforts to gather information and apply the information to their decisions.

FIGURE 12.3

Key Features of a Learning Organization

Continuous learning

Critical, systemic thinking

Knowledge-generating and -sharing

Learning Organization

Encourging flexibility and experimentation

Valuing employees

Learning culture

SOURCE: Adapted from M. A. Gephart, V. J. Marsick, M. E. Van Buren, and M. S. Spiro, "Learning Organizations Come Alive," *Training and Development* 50 (1996), pp. 34–45.

support the creation of a learning organization by planning training programs that meet these criteria, and they can help to create systems for creating, capturing, and sharing knowledge.

Critical, systemic thinking occurs when organizations encourage employees to see relationships among ideas and to test assumptions and observe the results of their actions. Reward systems can be set up to encourage employees and teams to think in new ways.

A *learning culture* is an organizational culture in which learning is rewarded, promoted, and supported by managers and organizational objectives. This culture may be reflected in performance management systems and pay structures that reward employees for gathering and sharing more knowledge. A learning culture creates the conditions in which managers encourage *flexibility* and *experimentation*. The organization should encourage employees to take risks and innovate, which means it cannot be quick to punish ideas that do not work out as intended.

Finally, in a learning organization, *employees are valued*. The organization recognizes that employees are the source of its knowledge. It therefore focuses on ensuring the development and well-being of each employee.

An example of a learning organization is Viant, a consulting firm that specializes in building e-businesses.[14] When employees join the company, they start in the home office, where they learn team skills, the company's consulting strategy, and the organization's culture. There they meet members of upper management. On the job, Viant employees work in settings that encourage interaction; no walls separate desks, and snack areas are located conveniently nearby. Performance reviews emphasize growth in employees' skills, and the company rewards knowledge sharing with incentives in the form of stock options. Before each project, consultants complete a brief document describing the knowledge they need, the knowledge they can use from other projects, what they need to create, and what they hope to learn that they can share with their colleagues. These documents are posted on Viant's internal website. Every six weeks, Viant's knowledge management group posts an online summary of what has been learned.

Employee Satisfaction and Engagement

As discussed in Chapter 3, a condition underpinning any high-performance organization is that employees experience job satisfaction—they experience their jobs as fulfilling or allowing them to fulfill important values. Research supports the idea that employees' job satisfaction and job performance are related.[15] Higher performance at the individual level should contribute to higher performance for the organization as a whole.

Chapter 3 described a number of ways that organizations can promote job satisfaction. They include making jobs more interesting, setting clear and challenging goals, and providing valued rewards that are linked to performance in a performance management system that employees consider fair. Effective promotion of employee satisfaction can distinguish an organization from its competitors. As was recently reported by Monster Worldwide, there are many organizations at which employees feel dissatisfied and overstressed. Figure 12.4 suggests there is plenty of room for organizations that want to carve out a niche for themselves as desirable employers. Still, it's important to remember that these numbers come from online pools of visitors to Monster's website, presumably, employees satisfied with their positions are less likely to visit the site.[16]

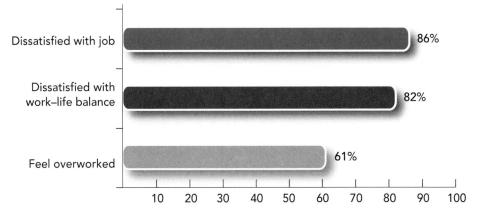

FIGURE 12.4

Employee Satisfaction Is
Weak by Some Measures

SOURCE: Monster Worldwide, "61 Percent of Americans Consider Themselves Overworked and 86 Percent Are
Not Satisfied with Their Job, According to Monster's 2004 Work/Life Balance Survey," news release, August 3,
2004, http://pr.monsterworldwide.com.

As is discussed in Chapter 3, some organizations are moving beyond concern with
mere job satisfaction and are trying to foster employee engagement and *passion* for
their work. Passionate people are fully engaged with something so that it becomes
part of their sense of who they are. Feeling this way about one's work has been
called *occupational intimacy*.[17] People experience occupational intimacy when they
love their work, when they and their co-workers care about one another, and when
they find their work meaningful. Human resource managers have a significant role
in creating these conditions. For example, they can select people who care about
their work and customers, provide methods for sharing knowledge, design work to
make jobs interesting, and establish policies and programs that show concern for
employees' needs. Such efforts may become more and more important as the business
world increasingly uses employee empowerment, teamwork, and knowledge sharing
to build flexible organizations.[18]

These trends rely on positive employee relationships. Perhaps that is why, when
the Gallup Organization studied more that 105,000 employees, it found that one of
the 12 circumstances associated with high productivity was "having a best friend at
work." A case in point is David Liggett, who developed important friendships at work.
Those friends encouraged him, provided helpful feedback, and pitched in whenever
one of the friends needed help to meet a deadline. Fifteen years after meeting, the
friends continue to get together. An organization's capacity to manage employee
engagement is closely related to its ability to achieve superior results.

Ethics

In the long run, a high-performance organization meets high ethical standards.
Ethics, defined in Chapter 1, and discussed in more detail in Chapter 3 in the context
of employee engagement, establishes fundamental principles for behaviour, such as
honesty and fairness. Organizations and their employees must meet these standards
if they are to maintain positive long-term relationships with their customers and
their community. The most recent annual *Best Employers in Canada* survey gauged
the degree to which co-workers and managers demonstrated ethical conduct. Eighty
percent of employees working for "best employers," that is, those with high levels
of employee engagement, believed their co-workers displayed integrity and acted

LO4 - Explain how
human resource
management can
contribute to high
performance.

ethically, in contrast with 68 percent at moderate- and 61 percent at low-engagement employers. Most telling was the difference in employee opinions with respect to the integrity of senior leaders. At low-engagement organizations, only 49 percent of employees agreed or strongly agreed that leaders displayed ethical conduct, whereas 82 percent did so at the best employers.[19]

1,2

HRM'S Contribution to High Performance

Management of human resources plays a critical role in determining companies' success in meeting the challenges of a rapidly changing, highly competitive environment.[20] Compensation, staffing, training and development, performance management, and other HRM practices are investments that directly affect employees' motivation and ability to provide products and services that are valued by customers. A study by Watson Wyatt Worldwide found that significant improvements in major HR practices, including reward systems, recruitment, and employee retention, led to significant increases in the value of a company's stock.[21] Table 12.2 lists examples of HRM practices that contribute to high performance.

Research suggests that it is more effective to improve HRM practices as a whole than to focus on one or two isolated practices, such as the organization's pay structure or selection system.[22] Also, to have the intended influence on performance, the HRM practices must fit well with one another and the organization as a whole.[23] An example of an organization that has achieved this fit is SYSCO Corporation, described in the Best Practices box.

3

Job Design

For the organization to benefit from teamwork and employee involvement, jobs must be designed appropriately. Often, a high-performance work system places employees in work teams where employees collaborate to make decisions and solve problems. Individual employees also may be empowered to serve on teams that design jobs and work processes. For example, the members of the staff at a health clinic evaluated the process of office visits, looking for a way to shrink the average length of a visit

TABLE 12.2

HRM Practices That Can Help Organizations Achieve High Performance

• HRM practices match organization's goals.	• Performance management system measures customer satisfaction and quality.
• Individuals and groups share knowledge.	• Organization monitors employees' satisfaction.
• Work is performed by teams.	• Discipline system is progressive.
• Organization encourages continuous learning.	• Pay systems reward skills and accomplishments.
• Work design permits flexibility in where and when tasks are performed.	• Skills and values of a diverse workforce are valued and used.
• Selection system is job-related and legal.	• Technology reduces time and costs of tasks while preserving quality.

BEST PRACTICES

SYSCO Serves Up HRM That's Well Worth the Price

Hamburgers don't just deliver themselves, and SYSCO Corporation has prospered by capitalizing on this fact. Founded in 1970, SYSCO has become North America's leading food-service provider, with approximately 400,000 customers from mom-and-pop diners to large chains like Hilton Hotels and Wendy's International.

Several factors explain SYSCO's success. One is its principle of "Earned Autonomy," in which each of the company's 150 businesses operates independently as long as it is successful. SYSCO also tries to keep its people close to their customers by limiting the size of each business unit. When a unit approaches 700 employees, SYSCO splits it into separate businesses. The result is a corporation with a decentralized structure in which many managers have a significant degree of control, so they can encourage innovation and customer service. The company also empowers its sales force by making employees more than salespeople. These "marketing associates" not only take orders but also help customers with food handling, inventory management, and recipe ideas.

In such a decentralized company with so many individuals empowered to act creatively, running an HRM organization presents a host of challenges. Ken Carrig, SYSCO's vice-president of human resources, wants his staff to provide services that contribute to high performance. But his group cannot simply design one set of services to force on the other business units.

So Carrig developed what he calls "market-based" human resource management. This approach treats SYSCO as a market and its business unit leaders as customers, who are free to select the HRM services they actually pay for, on the basis of their decisions about which services are valuable. For example, if a business unit wants to conduct a survey of employees, that unit has a choice between using the company's own HRM staff or the research capabilities of an outside firm. Corporate HRM, as a result, has an incentive to ensure that its services are effective and reasonably priced.

Under Carrig's leadership, HRM at SYSCO has focused on identifying and providing the services the company's business units want. It also focuses on collecting data that help the HRM team learn how it can help business units succeed.

Carrig and his associates study the company's most successful business units to learn what they are doing that other units might copy. They also collect data on HR programs so that they can demonstrate to business unit leaders the value provided by their services. For example, HR programs have boasted a 30 percent reduction in claims for workers' compensation—saving $10 million a year—and 20 percent improvement in retention of night-shift warehouse employees—saving about $15 million a year.

Executives can look up such performance data on the company's intranet to learn about the programs that are producing results in SYSCO's business units. The readily available database informs decision making all the way to the top of SYSCO. The company's chief executive, Richard J. Schnieders, tracks data from the company's workplace climate survey, which has shown a strong link with units' profits.

SOURCE: R. Stoltz, "Ah, to Be Strategic," *Human Resource Executive*, November 2003, pp. 1, 20–30; P. Kiger, "HR Proves Its Value," *Workforce*, March 2002, pp. 28–33; and Richard F. Stolz, "CEOs Who 'Get It,'" *Human Resource Executive*, March 16, 2005, pp. 1, 18–29, 22–24.

from an hour to 30 minutes. They drew a chart showing the typical steps involved in serving a patient with pneumonia, and discovered that of the 68 steps identified, only 17 were considered valuable. They determined that instead of requiring patients to walk down the hall to a laboratory to have blood drawn, they could have a technician visit the examination room to draw blood. Changes such as these cut patients' waiting time from 30 minutes to just 9. The nature of certain jobs also changed. Six assistants had been assigned to work with individual doctors; in the redesigned process, these assistants were pooled to work wherever they were needed most.[24]

Recruitment and Selection

At a high-performance organization, recruitment and selection aim at obtaining the kinds of employees who can thrive in this type of setting. These employees are enthusiastic about and able to contribute to teamwork, empowerment, and knowledge sharing. Qualities such as creativity and ability to cooperate as part of a team may play a large role in selection decisions. High-performance organizations need selection methods that identify more than technical skills like ability to perform accounting and engineering tasks. Employers may use group interviews, open-ended questions, and psychological tests to find employees who innovate, share ideas, and take initiative.

Training and Development

When organizations base hiring decisions on qualities like decision-making and teamwork skills, training may be required to teach employees the specific skills they need to perform the duties of their job. Extensive training and development also are part of a learning organization, described earlier in this chapter. And when organizations delegate many decisions to work teams, the members of those teams likely will benefit from participating in team development activities that prepare them for their roles as team members.

Employee development is an important factor in IBM's top ranking in a study of the "Top 20 Companies for Leaders," jointly conducted by Hewitt Associates and *Chief Executive* magazine. According to Randall MacDonald, IBM's senior vice-president of human resources, IBM had determined that leadership was one of four areas it had to focus on to achieve high performance. So the company charged all its existing leaders with developing future leaders. Once a year, IBM calls together its top managers to select candidates for leadership development, and they work with the candidates to create a development plan that meets their personal goals. By making leadership development a part of the company's routine processes, IBM removes the fear that coaching one's replacement threatens one's own career. MacDonald points out that planning for leadership is at least as important as other types of planning: "The [chief financial officer], when he gives one of our line guys $3 billion to go build a new plant, he doesn't say, 'Go build the plant and do what you want with it.' No, that CFO and that line person are going to manage that asset . . . . Whatever happened to the concept of people being our most important asset? Well if they are, we ought to manage them."[25]

Business Development Bank of Canada (BDC) demonstrates its commitment to training and development by investing approximately 5 percent of payroll into learning annually. The Crown corporation, based in Montreal, offers financing, business loans, consulting, and venture capital to businesses and is participating in a project sponsored by the federal government to substantiate the return on investment of training. "We know there's a declining investment in training overall in Canada. And we know that has a big impact on growth productivity, so it's sort of a win-win type of project to learn ourselves what a return-on-investment (ROI) project is all about," said Jacinthe Higgs, director of learning strategies at Montreal-based BDC.[26]

Performance Management

2

In a high-performance organization, employees know the organization's goals and what they must do to help achieve those goals. HR departments can contribute to this ideal through the design of the organization's performance management system. As we discussed in Chapter 8, performance management should be related to the organization's goals. For example, teamwork is central to the success of a joint venture between General Electric and FANUC Ltd. Of Japan. The company organized its workforce into more than 40 self-directed work teams to encourage employees to contribute their ideas. Therefore, managers must support their teams, and support of teamwork is one performance measure in the managers' performance evaluations.[27] At Extreme Logic, high performance comes from clear communication about what kinds of behaviour are needed. On its intranet, the software company publishes attributes and behaviours associated with success in each job, as well as the performance standard for each attribute and behaviour. Employees can go online at any time to gauge whether they are meeting those standards.[28]

To set up a performance management system that supports the organization's goals, managers need to understand the process of employee performance. As is shown in Figure 12.5, individual employees bring a set of skills and abilities to the job, and by applying a set of behaviours, they use those skills to achieve certain results. But success is more than the product of individual efforts. The organization's goals should influence each step of the process. The organization's culture and other factors influence the employees' abilities, behaviours, and results. Sometimes uncontrollable forces such as the current economic conditions enter the picture, it mustn't be forgotten—for example, a salesperson can probably sell more during an economic expansion than during an economic slowdown.

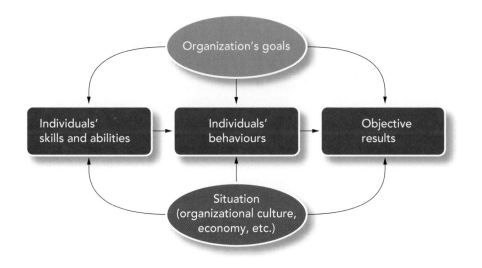

FIGURE 12.5

Employee Performance as a Process

To develop future leaders, new IBM managers participate in IBM's Basic Blue program for an intensive nine-month training program. IBM is considered one of the best companies in the development of future leaders.

This model suggests some guidelines for performance management. First, every aspect of performance management should be related to the organization's goals. Business goals should influence the kinds of employees selected and their training, the requirements of each job, and the measures used for evaluating results. Generally, this means the organization identifies what each department needs to do to achieve the desired results, then defines how individual employees should contribute to their department's goals. More specifically, the following guidelines describe how to make the performance management system support organizational goals:[29]

- *Define and measure performance in precise terms.* Focus on outcomes that can be defined in terms of how frequently certain behaviours occur. Include criteria that describe ways employees can add value to a product or service (such as through quantity, quality, or timeliness). Include behaviours that go beyond the minimum required to perform a job (such as helping co-workers).

- *Link performance measures to meeting customer needs.* "Customers" may be the organization's external customers, or they may be internal customers (employees receiving services from a co-worker). Service goals for internal customers should be related to satisfying external customers.

- *Measure and correct for the effect of situational constraints.* Monitor economic conditions, the organization's culture, and other influences on performance. Measures of employees' performance should take these influences into account.

This approach gives employees the information they need to behave in ways that contribute to high performance. In addition, organizations should help employees identify and obtain the abilities they need to meet their performance goals.

Compensation and Rewards

Organizations can reinforce the impact of this kind of performance management by linking employee rewards in part to performance measures. Chapter 9 described a number of methods for doing this, including merit pay, gainsharing, and profit sharing. A small manufacturer called Headsets.com improved productivity by linking bonuses to sales volume; employees share a fixed percentage of the company's total sales.[30] Employees at Headsets.com can see that if the company grows by hiring more workers, rather than by using the same number of workers to produce and sell more, the bonus will be divided among more people. They can earn a bigger bonus if they get the same results by working more efficiently. Since starting this bonus plan, Headsets.com has been able to grow more profitably. Compensation systems also can help to create the conditions that contribute to high performance, including teamwork, involvement, and job satisfaction. For example, as discussed in Chapter 9, compensation can be linked to achievement of team objectives.

Organizations can increase employee empowerment, satisfaction, and engagement by including employees in decisions about compensation and by communicating the basis for decisions about pay. When the organization designs a pay structure, it can set up a task force that includes employees with direct experience in various types of jobs. Some organizations share financial information with their employees and invite them to recommend pay increases for themselves, on the basis of their contributions. Employees may also participate in setting individual or group goals for which they can receive bonuses. Research has found that employee participation in decisions about pay policies is linked to greater satisfaction with the pay and the job.[31] And as we discussed in Chapter 9, when organizations explain their pay structures to employees, the communication can enhance employees' satisfaction and belief that the system is fair.

Mergers and Acquisitions

L05 - Discuss HRM's role in successful mergers and acquisitions.

Mergers and acquisitions dominate the business landscape. But the risks are high. It is estimated that 80 percent of mergers and acquisitions actually reduce shareholder value due to a combination of business and people issues. Reasons for these failures include

- Combining strategic weaknesses rather than strategic strengths
- Top management conflict
- Failure to win employee support
- Loss of competitive position due to extended time to complete the deal[32]

1,2

HRM's Role in Mergers and Acquisitions

"In the past, HR issues might have been an afterthought in mergers and acquisitions (M&As), with the HR department only stepping in and playing a role once the deal was done. But there is growing recognition HR can and should contribute right from the start."[33] According to a recent survey, conducted by Towers Perrin, a global consulting organization, and the Society for Human Resource Management Foundation, "there is a direct correlation between involvement by human resources and successful mergers and acquisitions."[34]

Josee Dykun, vice-president of HR at Montreal-headquartered Yellow Pages Group, says that she gets involved "right at the start of the process, when the company decides to purchase another business."[35] At this early stage, often referred to as *due diligence*, her work involves "identifying potential risks and liabilities and any potential integration issues in terms of alignment of things like working conditions, benefits, and pensions."[36] Sandra Munteanu, TELUS's director of mergers and acquisitions describes the importance of HR work during this due diligence phase. "We have a very comprehensive list of questions. We assess market culture, management team skills, key employees and potential cultural gaps. We collect data on everything," said Munteanu.[37]

The change and upheaval that accompanies a merger or acquisition is a key opportunity for HR to demonstrate its expertise to line executives and serve as a trusted advisor. The key areas of HR due diligence are outlined in Table 12.3. One of the chapter-ending cases also takes a closer look at a merger between two rival Canadian mining operations.

TABLE 12.3

Key Areas of HR
Due Diligence
in Mergers and
Acquisitions

KEY M&A CONSIDERATIONS	HR'S ROLE
Culture	• Assess the similarities and differences between the two companies with respect to issues such as where authority lies and how decisions are made. • Assess the emotional element of how employees feel about the company, leaders, and their openness to the change. • Map out differences between the acquiring company and the target company including how to bridge the gaps. • Create and execute a comprehensive communication plan to share a vision of the future and engage employees.
Analysis and retention of talent	• Ensure leadership talent is in place to lead and implement the transition. • Assess each key individual relative to competencies aligned to the needs of the new group. • Identify key people and take steps to retain them. • Put people in the right roles during the merger/acquisition. • Discuss individual job and career options.
Rewards structure	• Examine rewards and work environment factors.
Legal issues, e.g., outstanding human rights challenges	• Assess all outstanding legal issues including timetable for resolution and stakeholders involved.
Union issues, e.g., collective agreements	• Identify key stakeholders including history of relationship, and develop an integration timetable.

SOURCE: Adapted from "Ruth N. Bramson, "HR's Role in Mergers and Acquisitions—Human Resource Management," http://findarticles.com, retrieved June 10, 2008; Uyen Vu, "HR's Role in Mergers, Acquisitions," *Canadian HR Reporter*, December 4, 2006, pp. 17, 21.

LO6 - Discuss the role of HRM technology in high-performance work systems.

HRM Technology

Human resource departments can improve their own and their organization's performance by appropriately using new technology. New technology usually involves *automation*—that is, using equipment and information processing to perform activities that had been performed by people. Over the last few decades, automation has improved HRM efficiency by reducing the number of people needed to perform routine tasks. Using automation can free HRM experts to concentrate on ways to determine how human resource management can help the organization meet its goals, so technology also can make this function more valuable.[38] Information technology also provides ways to build and improve systems for knowledge generation and sharing, as part of a learning organization. The HR How-To box describes some ways of using information technology to create and share knowledge.

HR HOW-TO

Using Information Systems in a Learning Organization

A learning organization uses information technology to encourage employees to share information with each other, and HR professionals can help establish these applications. Here are some ideas:

- Set up an intranet that allows employees to store and share knowledge through Web pages and email.
- Publish directories listing what employees do, what kinds of knowledge they have, and how to contact them.

- Develop "informational maps" or charts that identify where specific knowledge is stored in the organization.
- Create the position of chief information officer, which includes the responsibility for cataloguing information and enabling the sharing of information within the organization.
- When employees attend training programs, require that they give their co-workers presentations or post summaries on the

intranet of what they have learned in the programs.
- Establish policies for sabbaticals, attendance at training programs, and other time away from the workplace for learning, and communicate these on the intranet.
- Create an online library of learning resources, such as journals, technical manuals, training opportunities, and seminars. These can be available through the organization's intranet.

HRM Applications

New technologies continue to be introduced. In fact, so many HRM applications are developed for use on personal computers that publications serving the profession (such as *HR Magazine* and *Workforce*) devote annual issues to reviewing this software. Some of the technologies that have been widely adopted are transaction processing, decision support systems, and expert systems.[39]

Transaction processing refers to computations and calculations involved in reviewing and documenting HRM decisions and practices. It includes documenting decisions and actions associated with employee relocation, training expenses, and enrolments in courses and benefit plans. Transaction processing also includes the activities required to meet government reporting requirements, such as filling out employment equity reports on which employers report information about employment equity group participation rates. Computers enable companies to perform these tasks more efficiently. Employers can fill out computerized forms and store HRM information in databases, so that it is easier to find, sort, and report.

Decision support systems are computer software systems designed to help managers solve problems. They usually include a "what if?" feature that managers can use to enter different assumptions or data and see how the likely outcomes will change. This type of system can help managers make decisions for workforce planning. The manager can, for example, try out different assumptions about turnover rates to see how those assumptions affect the number of new employees needed. Or the manager can test a range of assumptions about the availability of a certain skill in the labour market, looking at the impact of the assumptions on the success of different recruiting plans. Possible applications for a decision support system include forecasting (discussed in Chapter 4) and succession planning (discussed in Chapter 7).

transaction processing
Computations and calculations involved in reviewing and documenting HRM decisions and practices.

decision support systems
Computer software systems designed to help managers solve problems by showing how results vary when the manager alters assumptions or data.

expert systems
Computer systems that support decision making by incorporating the decision rules used by people who are considered to have expertise in a certain area.

Expert systems are computer systems that incorporate the decision rules used by people who are considered to have expertise in a certain area. The systems help users make decisions by recommending actions based on the decision rules and the information provided by the users. An expert system is designed to recommend the same actions that a human expert would in a similar situation. For example, an expert system could guide an interviewer during the selection process. Some organizations use expert systems to help employees decide how to allocate their money for benefits (as in a flexible plan) and help managers schedule the labour needed to complete projects. Expert systems can deliver both high quality and lower costs. By using the decision processes of experts, an expert system helps many people to arrive at decisions that reflect the expert's knowledge. It helps avoid the errors that can result from fatigue and decision-making biases, such as biases in appraising employee performance, described in Chapter 8; and it can increase efficiency by enabling fewer or less-skilled employees to do work that otherwise would require many highly skilled employees.

In proactive HR departments, transaction processing, decision support systems, and expert systems are often part of a human resource information system. Also, these technologies may be linked to employees through a network such as an intranet. The e-HRM box describes how Labatt Breweries have created a dynamic HR portal that serves a variety of applications. Information systems and networks have been evolving rapidly; the following descriptions provide a basic introduction.

Human Resource Information Systems

A standard feature of a modern HRIS is the use of *relational databases*, which store data in separate files that can be linked by common elements. These common elements are fields identifying the type of data. Commonly used fields for an HR database include name, social insurance number, job status (full- or part-time), hiring date, position, title, rate of pay, job history, job location, mailing address, birth date, and emergency contacts. A relational database lets a user sort the data by any of the fields. For example, depending on how the database is set up, the user might be able to look up tables listing employees by location, rate of pay for various jobs, or training courses employees have completed. This system is far more sophisticated than the old-fashioned method of filing employee data by name, with one file per employee.

The ability to locate and combine many categories of data has a multitude of uses in human resource management. Databases have been developed to track employee benefit costs, training courses, and compensation. The system can meet the needs of line managers as well as the HR department. On an oil rig, for example, management might look up data listing employee names along with safety equipment issued and appropriate skill certification. HR managers at headquarters might look up data on the same employees to gather information about wage rates or training programs needed. Another popular use of an HRIS is applicant tracking, or maintaining and retrieving records of job applicants. This is much faster and easier than trying to sort through stacks of résumés. With relational databases, HR staff can retrieve information about specific applicants or obtain lists of applicants with specific skills, career goals, work history, and employment background. Such information is useful for HR planning, recruitment, succession planning, and career development. Taking the process a step further, the system could store information related to hiring and terminations. By analyzing such data, the HR department could measure the long-term success of its recruiting and selection processes.

E- HRM

From Filling In Forms to Brainstorming the Firm's Next Big Innovation

Vacation. Illness. Promotions. Many roads lead to the human resources department. But with the evolution of technology, more and more of these roads are leading employees to an HR portal. Every organization needs to manage employee information effectively to make the most of its diverse talents, services, and information. Originally designed to disseminate information quickly, the employee intranet has become a common feature of many workplaces.

Over time, this type of intranet has evolved from a static repository of company information to a collaborative meeting place where employees can ask HR-related questions and find the appropriate, up-to-date answers, fill in and file administrative forms, and further develop their skills.

Through a dynamic HR portal, employees can find and communicate with key contacts and experts, by email and with instant messaging. Site content can be easily searched, and employees can receive alerts to tell them about changes or new information and documents on the portal. The online portal also allows for

anonymity, which can be helpful to employees searching for sensitive information. Through a portal, employees can quickly and easily share their ideas and contribute to projects, accessing the sites through the office intranet or outside work through a Web browser.

Labatt Breweries of Canada set up an intranet called "The Pub." Its goals were to improve overall communication with employees located in eight breweries from coast to coast, and eliminate silos of information between business units. Using the portal, Labatt was able to improve employee communications significantly and now 70 percent of its employees frequently visit The Pub. The Pub has also turned into a home for more than 30 team workspaces, where employees share information and collaborate on documents. With the new workspaces, various business units have a common point of access for project or departmental information, including documents, contacts, tasks, and discussions.

"Employee response to The Pub has been extremely positive," says Jonathan Starkey, data architecture centre of excellence manager

at Labatt. "Through our intranet, we've been able to deliver immense value to our employees by providing tools that enable them to make better informed decisions and increase their productivity. The business value of bringing employees closer together is apparent when you look at the individual contributions and recommendations for greater innovation that come in through The Pub."

Team building through virtual communities of interest created through the HR portal can also translate directly into improvements in the day-to-day functioning of a company. Work teams that may have members too busy to meet with the rest of the team, or perhaps even working from a different location, can meet online. This allows teams to be efficient and productive and ensures every individual on the team can meaningfully contribute to a project, increasing overall employee satisfaction.

SOURCE: Michael Bulmer, "From Filling In Forms to Brainstorming the Firm's Next Big Innovation," *Guide to HR Technology*, in *Canadian HR Reporter*, March 8, 2004, p. G2. © Canadian HR Reporter, March 8, 2004, by permission of Carswell, Toronto, Ontario, 1-800-387-5164, www.hrreporter.com.

Cara Operations Ltd.'s career home page. Online recruiting offers many benefits to the company and the potential employee. Companies are able to easily post job openings, retrieve résumés, and, most importantly, voice the message of their company. Potential employees also benefit by having the ability to research the company, search for job openings, and submit their résumé. The Internet has become an excellent source for recruiting.

Human Resource Management Online: e-HRM

During the past decade or so, organizations have seen the advantages of sharing information in computer networks. At the same time, the widespread adoption of the Internet has linked people around the globe. As we discussed in Chapter 1, more and more organizations are engaging in e-HRM, providing HR-related information over the Internet. Because much human resource information is confidential, organizations may do this with an intranet, which uses Internet technology but allows access only to authorized users (such as the organization's employees). For HR professionals, Internet access also offers a way to research new developments, post job openings, trade ideas with colleagues in other organizations, and obtain government documents. In this way, e-HRM combines company-specific information on a secure intranet with links to the resources on the broader Internet.

Increasingly, organizations are enhancing their HR technology to provide for **employee self-service (ESS)**, which is a growing trend in human resource management that allows an employee to handle many job-related tasks (such as applications for reimbursement, updates to personal information, and access to company information) that otherwise would have fallen to HR, management, or administrative staff. An ESS application may be made available over the company's intranet or portal, or through specialized kiosks, and may be confined to a company's private network or may be part of a Web self-service solution for customers, employees and managers.[40] With self-service, employees are responsible for keeping their personal information up to date, thus freeing up the time of HR and increasing the accuracy of employee data. Ninety-eight percent of organizations responding to a recent survey of HR service delivery trends indicate they offer online benefit enrolment. Thomas Keebler, leader of Towers Perrin's global HR technology practice that conducted the surveys, says, "The benefits of ESS are widespread and include a more empowered workforce that is more apt to take responsibility for its own HR and benefits decisions, greater accuracy of employee data and faster HR processes." Adds Keebler, "ESS is an area

employee self-service (ESS)
Employee self-service allows an employee to handle many job-related tasks such as applications for reimbursement and updates to personal information.

that has truly lived up to the hype of relieving HR from administrative work to focus on more strategic activities."[41]

A benefit of e-HRM including employee self-service is that employees and managers can help themselves to the information they need when they need it, instead of contacting an HR staff person. For example, employees can go online to enrol in or select benefits, submit insurance claims, or fill out employee surveys. Using these HR self-service tools can be more convenient for the employees, as well as more economical for the HR department. This access to HR information can even be completely customized for the user. For example, the delivery of HR processes may be personalized for each employee's desktop according to his or her role—employee, manager, HR professional, executive. The result is a single place to go for easy access to all the resources needed related to human resource management.[42] Similarly, at Cisco Systems, many HR activities are automated online.[43] When employees join the company, they log on, visit the "New Hire" page, and sign up for benefits. They also see that the website is the place to file expense reports, look up project information, and more. The site lets employees know when it is time for their performance review and lets them start the process with their supervisor. The employee reviews an evaluation form, studies the expected behaviours, fills in needed information, and sends the form to the supervisor. If the form requires information from someone else in the company, the supervisor clicks on a link to request that information. The supervisor receives any requested information, completes the appraisal form, and meets with the employee to discuss the review. So much of the process is automated that supervisors have more time to focus on the actual meeting with the employee.

Most administrative and information-gathering activities in human resource management can be part of e-HRM. For example, online recruiting has become a significant part of the total recruiting effort, as candidates submit résumés online. Employers go online to retrieve suitable résumés from job search sites or retrieve information from forms they post at their own websites. For selection decisions, the organization may have candidates use one of the online testing services available; these services conduct the tests, process the results, and submit reports to employers. Online appraisal systems can help managers make pay decisions consistent with company policies and employee performance. Employees and managers can update performance goals and update results. Employees can view training histories and many types of training can be conducted online, as we discussed in Chapter 7. Online surveys of employee satisfaction or engagement can be quick and easy to fill out. Besides providing a way to administer the survey, an intranet is an effective vehicle for communicating the results of the survey and management's planned response.

Not only does e-HRM provide efficient ways to carry out human resource functions, it also poses new challenges to employees and new issues for HR managers to address. The Internet's ability to link people anytime, anywhere has accelerated such trends as globalization, the importance of knowledge sharing within organizations, and the need for flexibility.[44] These trends, in turn, change the work environment for employees. For example, employees are increasingly expected to be highly committed but flexible, able to move from job to job. Employees also may be connected to the organization 24/7. In the car, on vacation, in airports, and almost anywhere, employees with BlackBerry-type devices can deal with work demands. Organizations depend on their human resource departments to help prepare employees for this changing work world through such activities as training, career development, performance management, and benefits packages that meet the need for flexibility and help employees manage stress.

LO7 - Summarize ways to measure the effectiveness of human resource management.

1

Effectiveness of Human Resource Management

In recent years, human resource management at many organizations has been taking a customer-oriented approach. For an organization's human resource division, "customers" are the organization as a whole and its other divisions. They are customers of HRM because they depend on HRM to provide a variety of services that result in a supply of talented, motivated employees. Taking this customer-oriented approach, human resource management defines its customer groups, customer needs, and the activities required to meet those needs, as shown in Figure 12.6. These definitions give an organization a basis for defining goals and measures of success.

One company that uses this approach is Whirlpool Corporation. The company's HR managers identify their customer, define the need they can satisfy or the value they can provide, and identify the methods they must use to satisfy the customer. When Whirlpool planned to start a centralized service centre, its plan called for hiring of 100 to 150 employees to process service requests from customers owning Whirlpool appliances and to schedule service calls. Whirlpool gave an HR manager the responsibility for developing a selection system for call takers. The manager determined the customer in this instance was the operations manager in charge of phone service and the need was the delivery of qualified call takers. To meet this need, the HR manager decided to use a combination of structured interviews and paper-and-pencil tests. The company can evaluate the success of this program in terms of whether it efficiently produces enough qualified call takers.

Depending on the situation, a number of techniques are available for measuring HRM's effectiveness in meeting its customers' needs. These techniques include reviewing a set of key indicators, measuring the outcomes of specific HRM activity, and measuring the economic value or ROI (return on investment) of HRM programs.

Human Resource Management Audits

HRM audit
A formal review of the outcomes of HRM functions, based on identifying key HRM functions and measures of organizational performance.

An **HRM audit** is a formal review of the outcomes of HRM functions. To conduct the audit, the HR department identifies key functions and the key measures of organizational performance and customer satisfaction that would indicate each function is succeeding. Table 12.4 lists examples of these measures for a variety of HRM functions: staffing, compensation, benefits, training, appraisal and development, and overall effectiveness. The audit may also look at any other measure associated with successful management of human resources—for instance, compliance with employment-related legislation, succession planning, maintaining a safe workplace, and positive labour relations. An HRM audit using customer satisfaction measures

FIGURE 12.6

Customer-Oriented Perspective of HRM

Who Are Our Customers?	**What Do Our Customers Need?**	**How Do We Meet Customer Needs?**
• Line managers	• Committed employees	• Qualified staffing
• Strategic planners	• Competent employees	• Performance management
• Employees		• Rewards
		• Training and development

supports the customer-oriented approach to human resource management. When HR functions are outsourced, these audits need to look at both HR functions performed internally and those that are outsourced.

TABLE 12.4

Key Measures of Success for an HRM Audit

BUSINESS INDICATORS	CUSTOMER SATISFACTION MEASURES
Staffing	
Average days taken to fill open requisitions	Anticipation of human resource needs
Ratio of acceptances to offers made	Timeliness of referring qualified workers to line supervisors
Ratio of Employment Equity target group applicant representation in local labour market	Treatment of applicants
Per capita requirement costs	Skill in handling terminations
Average years of experience/education of hires	Adaptability to changing labour market conditions
Compensation	
Per capita (average) merit increases	Fairness of existing job evaluation system
Ratio of recommendations for reclassification to number of employees	Competitiveness in local labour market
Percentage of overtime hours to regular time	Relationship between pay and performance
Ratio of average salary offers to average salary in community	Employee satisfaction with pay
Benefits	
Average workers' compensation payments	Promptness in handling claims
Benefit cost per payroll dollar	Fairness and consistency in the application of benefit policies
Percentage of sick leave to total pay	Communication of benefits to employees
	Assistance provided to line managers in reducing potential for unnecessary claims
Training	
Percentage of employees participating in training programs	Extent to which training programs meet the needs of employees and the company
Percentage of employees receiving tuition reimbursement	Communication to employees about available training opportunities
Training dollars per employee	Quality of introduction/orientation programs
Employee Appraisal and Development	
Distribution of performance appraisal ratings	Assistance in identifying management potential
Appropriate psychometric properties of appraisal forms	Organizational development activities provided by HRM department
Overall Effectiveness	
Ratio of human resource staff to employee population	Accuracy and clarity of information provided to managers and employees
Turnover rate	Competence and expertise of staff
Absenteeism rate	Working relationship between organizations and HRM department
Ratio of per capita revenues to per capita cost	
Net income per employee	

SOURCE: Reprinted with permission excerpts from Chapter 1.5, "Evaluating Human Resource Effectiveness," pp. 187–227, by Anne S. Tsui and Luis R. Gomez-Mejia, from *Human Resource Management: Evolving Roles and Responsibilities*, ed. Lee Dyer. © 1988 by The Bureau of National Affairs, Inc., Washington, DC, 20037.

After identifying performance measures for the HRM audit, the staff carries out the audit by gathering information. The information for the key business indicators is usually available in the organization's documents. Sometimes the HR department has to create new documents for gathering specific types of data. The usual way to measure customer satisfaction is to conduct surveys. Employee attitude surveys provide information about the satisfaction of these internal customers. Many organizations conduct surveys of top line executives to get a better view of how HRM practices affect the organization's business success.

Analyzing the Effect of HRM Programs

Another way to measure HRM effectiveness is to analyze specific programs or activities. The analysis can measure a program's success in terms of whether it achieved its objectives and whether it delivered value in an economic sense. Increasingly HR is being called on to measure its impact. The Conference Board of Canada identifies "measurement" as one of the "hot HR issues" and indicates that HR measures must be meaningful due to the importance of HR's role in building organizational capabilities.[45]

Senior management and other organizational stakeholders are asking for metrics or measures that relate to the value of the firm's human capital and the return on investment in that human capital. A recent report from CFO Research Services and Mercer Human Resource Consulting revealed that chief financial officers' opinions of HR are improving—most of the 180 CFOs surveyed see human capital as a value driver rather than a cost. However, the survey also showed that just 16 percent of CFOs said they knew to a "considerable" or "great" extent the return on investments in human capital.[46]

"Traditional financial numbers are an indicator of past performance, but reliable measures of human capital are much better indicators of future performance, and therefore growth, and therefore shareholder value," says Curt Coffman of the Gallup Organization.[47] The European Union is currently looking at *human capital reporting* measures. For example, Denmark requires publicly traded companies to report on the "human dimension" of their business to provide investors a background of the value of human capital and it is expected some type of reporting requirement will also be required in North America.[48]

However, caution about calculating the value of human capital is needed. "Accounting deals principally with fixed assets. Once you buy them all they do is depreciate over time," says Jac Fitz-enz, the founder of Human Capital Source. "But humans are just the opposite: they appreciate over time as they grow and develop."[49] Furthermore, the return on investment of specific, isolated HR initiatives is needed. When individual HR initiatives are evaluated in isolation on strictly quantitative terms, there may be a tendency to focus on cost containment only with a failure to consider qualitative considerations and indirect benefits. For example, if an investment in human capital, such as a training program, yields tangible results, such as an increase in product quality and a decrease in product returns, this only quantifies part of the return on investment. The ROI calculation may not fully capture the improved employee and/or customer satisfaction achieved as a result of the training. Figure 12.7 provides the math for calculating the return on investment of an investment in human capital including both direct and indirect costs and benefits.

$$ROI\% = \frac{\text{Realized direct/indirect benefits} - \text{Total direct/indirect costs} \times 100}{\text{Total direct/indirect costs}}$$

FIGURE 12.7

ROI Math

In general, HR departments should be able to improve their performance through some combination of greater efficiency and greater effectiveness. Greater efficiency means the HR department uses fewer and less-costly resources to perform its functions. According to Hewitt Associates, more than three-quarters of HR departments are experiencing pressure to reduce HR spending.[50] Greater effectiveness means that what the HR department does—for example, selecting employees or setting up a performance management system—has a more beneficial effect on employees' and the organization's performance. For example, Home Depot tracks a variety of measures to see whether it is effective at meeting goals for attracting, motivating, and keeping skilled employees. The company uses a database that includes data on job applications, career, paths, performance ratings, employee satisfaction, and attrition (employees leaving the company). Managers can analyze the data by region, district, and store, as well as compare numbers over time.[51]

HRM's potential to affect employees' well-being and the organization's performance makes human resource management an exciting field. As we have shown throughout the book, every HRM function calls for decisions that have the potential to help individuals and organizations achieve their goals. For HR managers to fulfill that potential, they must ensure that their decisions are well grounded. As an example, we discussed telework in Chapter 3, as an option for work design that many organizations have embraced to promote greater productivity and job satisfaction. At the same time, a review of the research literature shows that these assumptions about telework's benefits are largely untested.[52] Telework is but one example of an issue that can dramatically affect employees' lives and organizations' success yet remains open for future investigation. The field of human resource management provides tremendous opportunity to future researchers and managers who want to make a difference in many people's lives and contribute to the success of organizations.

THINKING ETHICALLY

Do Employers Have a Right to Know How Their Employees Feel?

As technology has advanced, so have HRM applications, and so have the questions about ethical issues such as employee privacy. Consider the case of SAS Human Capital Management, a software package that combines databases, a Web-based decision support system, and other features to create a system for maintaining and analyzing data about the organization's human resources. The system includes an advanced search feature known as data mining that lets users search for collections of characteristics and patterns.

One possible application of SAS Human Capital Management is that an organization can search for qualities associated with employees likely to leave the organization, such as education levels, salary, or length of service. The system can rank employees according

THINKING ETHICALLY

to their likelihood of quitting and can even compute the probabilities that each will leave the company. The aim is to help employers carry out workforce planning. However, some employees might worry that they would be treated unfairly by managers—who perhaps incorrectly—expect them to quit in the near future.

SOURCE: Kathleen Sibley, "SAS Says Software Can Spot Employee Angst," *Technology in Government*, January/February 2004, www.findarticles.com; and SAS, "SAS Human Capital Management," www.sas.com, retrieved June 27, 2005.

Questions

1. How might a computer system such as SAS Human Capital Management help an organization be more competitive? Can employees benefit from such a system as well?
2. Explain whether you think it is ethical for an organization to use this system in workforce planning. Under what conditions is it fair to use the information to make decisions about individual employees?
3. Imagine you work in the HR department of an organization preparing to install SAS Human Capital Management. How can you assure employees that the system will be used in an ethical manner?

SUMMARY

L01   **Define high-performance work systems and identify the elements of such a system.**

- A high-performance work system is the right combination of people, technology, and organizational structure that makes full use of the organization's resources and opportunities in achieving its goals.
- The elements of a high-performance work system are organizational structure, task design, people, reward systems, and information systems. These elements must work together in a smoothly functioning whole.

L02   **Summarize the outcomes of a high-performance work system.**

- A high-performance work system achieves the organization's goals, typically including growth, productivity, and high profits.
- On the way to achieving these overall goals, the high-performance work system meets such intermediate goals as high quality, innovation, customer satisfaction, job satisfaction, and reduced absenteeism and turnover.

L03   **Describe the conditions that create a high-performance work system.**

- Many conditions contribute to high-performance work systems by giving employees skills, incentives, knowledge, autonomy, and employee satisfaction.
- Teamwork and empowerment can make work more satisfying and provide a means for employees to improve quality and productivity.
- Organizations can improve performance by creating a learning organization, in which people constantly learn and share knowledge so that they continually expand their capacity to achieve the results they desire.

L04 Explain how human resource management can contribute to high performance.

- Jobs should be designed to foster teamwork and employee involvement. Recruitment and selection should focus on obtaining employees who have the qualities necessary for teamwork and knowledge sharing.

- Training also is important, because of its role in creating a learning organization. The performance management system should be related to the organization's goals, with a focus on meeting internal and external customers' needs.

- Total compensation and rewards should include links to performance, and employees should be included in decisions about compensation.

- Research suggests that it is more effective to improve HRM practices as a whole than to focus on one or two isolated practices.

L05 Discuss HRM's role in successful mergers and acquisitions.

- Although HR has historically been excluded from playing an early and strategic role in a merger or acquisition, there is growing evidence that when HR is involved early, the merger or acquisition is more likely to be successful.

- When HR is involved from the start some of the key roles include assessing cultural fit between the companies, analyzing and retaining talent, legal and union issues, as well as examining the rewards structure.

L06 Discuss the role of HRM technology in high-performance work systems.

- Technology can improve the efficiency of the human resource management functions and support knowledge sharing.

- HRM applications involve transaction processing, decision support systems, and expert systems, often as part of a human resource information system using relational databases, which can improve the efficiency of routine tasks and the quality of decisions.

- With Internet technology, organizations can use e-HRM to let all the organization's employees help themselves to the HR information they need whenever they need it.

L07 Summarize ways to measure the effectiveness of human resource management.

- Taking a customer-oriented approach, HRM can improve quality by defining the internal customers who use its services and determining whether it is meeting those customers' needs.

- An HRM audit is a formal review of the outcomes of HRM functions.

- Another way to measure HRM effectiveness is to analyze specific programs or activities. The analysis can measure success in terms of whether a program met its objectives, and whether it delivered value in an economic sense, such as by leading to productivity improvements and generating a return on investment.

REVIEW AND DISCUSSION QUESTIONS

1. What is a high-performance work system? What are its elements? Which of these elements involve human resource management?

2. How does your workplace compare to the conditions for high performance identified in Table 12.1? Discuss.

3. As it has become clear that HRM can help create and maintain high-performance work systems, it appears that organizations will need two kinds of human resource professionals: one focuses on identifying how HRM can contribute to high performance; the other develops expertise in particular HRM functions, such as how to administer a benefits program that complies with legal requirements. Which is more interesting to you? Why?

4. How can teamwork, involvement, knowledge sharing, satisfaction, and engagement contribute to high performance?

5. If an organization can win customers, employees, or investors through deception, why would ethical behaviour contribute to high performance?

6. How can an organization promote ethical behaviour among its employees?

7. Summarize how each of the following HR functions can contribute to high performance.
   a. Job design
   b. Recruitment and selection
   c. Training and development
   d. Performance management
   e. Compensation and rewards

8. Why do you think that a merger or acquisition is more likely to be successful when HR is involved from the start of the process?

9. How can HRM technology make a human resource department more productive? How can technology improve the quality of HRM decisions?

10. Why should human resource departments measure their effectiveness? What are some ways they can go about measuring effectiveness?

WHAT'S YOUR HR IQ?

Online Learning Centre The Online Learning Centre offers more ways to check what you've learned so far. Find experiential exercises as well as Test Your Knowledge Quizzes, Videos, and many other resources at www.mcgrawhill.ca/olc/steen.

Case:
The Timbit Affair

Tim Hortons Inc. has squelched what could have become a PR disaster over the Timbit Affair. At the same time, the company has been served a stinging lesson on how following franchise rules too zealously can stifle the ability of front-line workers to keep the customer satisfied.

The coffee and doughnut chain, one of the most valued brands in the country, rehired a London, Ont. employee just hours after she was fired for giving away one 16-cent Timbit to the restless child of a regular customer.

"When the dust settles, Tim Hortons did absolutely the right thing, which is to reconsider and say, 'if we had to do it over again, we wouldn't do it quite this way,'" said Hugh Christie, a lawyer who heads the labour and employment national group at Gowlings.

Media outlets jumped on the tale of the 27-year-old single mother of four, shunted aside by a Canadian corporate icon. Head office didn't take long to respond. Rather than go on the offensive, Tims ate humble pie. Hours after her firing, Nicole Lilliman was reinstated. But she doesn't want to go back to the same store. Ms. Lilliman will now work at a nearby location, said spokeswoman Rachel Douglas. She will be paid for the missed days.

"When something comes out of London and gets this amount of press coverage, it's a learning [experience] for the entire chain," Ms. Douglas said. "The lesson is appropriate ways to treat your staff. Using proper processes . . . and making sure everyone's aware." She stressed that the whole sorry saga was a "mistake that shouldn't have happened," and that franchises set their own policies on freebies.

Events unfolded Monday, when a long-time customer came in with a fussy toddler. Ms. Lilliman, who's worked at the store for three years, spontaneously gave the child a doughnut hole to quiet her. She thought nothing of it, according to the *London Free Press*, until Wednesday, when she was hauled into the office and told she'd been caught on video giving away free food.

The experience "was hell," she told the newspaper. "When I told my daughter I lost my job she started crying. She's only six, and she doesn't know. She said 'we won't have any food any more.'"

The fate of her manager is still being decided.

It certainly hit a nerve with the public. Globe readers posted more than 800 comments on the story yesterday, making it one of the most-talked-about stories in the history of globeandmail.com.

The Timbit Affair offers insights into how much discretion individual employees should have, and how front-line workers are the real faces of the corporate brand. "The best customer service happens when people on the front lines have decision-making power and it's assumed that they can problem-solve on the spot," said Kadi Kaljuste, senior vice-president at consultant firm Hill & Knowlton, who praised Ms. Lilliman for using common sense.

Giving employees leeway to figure out solutions isn't a new idea. U.S. fashion retailer Nordstrom Inc. and WestJet Airlines Ltd. have both won plaudits for their customer service—and handing that trust to employees is partly why, Ms. Kaljuste says.

SOURCE: Tavia Grant, "Tims Eats Humble Pie to Avert PR Catastrophe," *The Globe and Mail*, May 9, 2008, p. B1.

Questions

1. What impact might the publicity surrounding the "Timbit Affair" have on the London location's ability to achieve the desired outcomes of a high-performance work system outlined in the textbook (Figure 12.2)?

2. If you were the franchise owner of this London location what changes would you make to create a work environment that has the conditions that contribute to high performance discussed in this chapter?

Case:
Gold Standard—The Merger of Two Rival Mines

A successful merger of two organizations is many things, but how often does it involve building bridges among neighbourhoods and sports teams? Such was the challenge faced last year by Canadian gold producer Goldcorp Inc. after it took over operations of its rival Campbell Mine in Red Lake, a remote northwestern Ontario town.

Since 1949, the mine site—Canada's largest gold mine, at 700,000 ounces per year—was home to two rival and neighbouring mines: Placer Dome's Campbell Mine and Goldcorp's Red Lake Mine. The 5,000 residents of the mining town owed their livelihoods—and allegiances—to one of the operations, and it was rare when the two sides mixed.

"There was a lot of history between the two mines and there was quite a rivalry—to the extent there were separate sports teams and social events," says Goldcorp human resources VP Gerry Atkinson. People even lived in different locations depending on where they were working. The decision to merge the two mines came after Barrick bought Placer's Campbell site and then sold its entire Canadian operations to Goldcorp. Since Goldcorp already had the neighbouring Red Lake mine, "We felt there were good synergies there to bring the two mines together under one jurisdiction, physically linking them via an underground shaft," says Atkinson.

Challenges

It there were engineering challenges in linking the two mines below ground, there were also big HR challenges in merging the two workforces—and communities—above ground.

"The biggest merger challenges have definitely been on the people side," says mine general manager Dan Gagnon. "You're basically putting together two very different cultures. One mine [Red Lake] has a 50-year history with full-time employees, and the other [Campbell] was mostly contract employees. Everything was different, including wages and benefits. We had to review every HR policy with the eventual goal of creating one team and absorbing most workers as full-time employees."

In terms of organizational structure, Campbell had a large corporate structure, with local managers used to direction from head office. The Red Lake mine was more independent, with local managers entrusted with day-to-day decision making. "Today we're a little bit in between, although we still lean toward decentralization. We want the mine management to be actively involved with decisions, with some guidance from corporate—but we don't intervene on a daily basis." Unfortunately for Gagnon, choosing a management group from the two organizations was one of his harder tasks because both teams were strong. But it was this handpicked management team from both organizations that lead the way in selling the merger to Red Lake's "two solitudes."

"In terms of linking the community, there was a new corporate identity in town and we picked the management structure to make it work within the community," says Atkinson. "From the beginning, we brought in a mine general manager from one of our other Canadian mine sites because one of his particular strengths is building teams and getting them involved in the community."

Key to Success

Critical to building bridges within the community were spokespeople, chosen from both organizations to act as liaisons between management, workers, and the greater community. The spokespeople were articulate staffers with long-term links to the mines who could act as advocates and speak positively of the move. Part of their role was to meet with employees and the community and be supportive of the whole amalgamation process—answering questions and dispelling rumours.

"A big part of the merger's success was these spokespeople," says Atkinson. "They were heavily involved with communication in terms of what was happening." "The worst thing that anyone can do during periods of massive change is tell people that nothing's going to change," says Gagnon. "You have to communicate that things will change, but we're going to try to make it as painless as possible and we'll work it through with you. And the changes are positive changes for the company, the operation and the community."

SOURCE: Duff McCutcheon, "Gold Standard," *HR Professional*, June/July 2008, pp. 45–47. This article originally appeared in the June/July 2008 issue of *HR Professional Magazine*, published for the Human Resources Professional Association by Naylor (Canada) Inc.

Questions

1. What were some of the HR issues that needed to be addressed for the merger to proceed?
2. Were the "due diligence" aspects of the merger handled effectively from an HR perspective? Refer to Table 12.3 in making your assessment.
3. Do you have any additional advice or recommendations to this newly merged organization to ensure outcomes of a high-performance organization are sustained over time?

VIDEO CASE

No Wal–Mart Wages

Unions such as the United Food and Commercial Workers Union (UFCW) are fighting for their future and for the standard of living of its members. According to the Canadian president of the UFCW, the union's power at the bargaining table for the grocery industry is eroding. Employers are demanding concessions from wages to health benefits to compete with nonunionized Wal-Mart. For example, the UFCW, in negotiations with Loblaw's Real Canadian Superstore, recently made a key concession that new hires will be paid less.

Employees in the grocery industry are concerned that their jobs may no longer offer the same hope for promotions or the ability to earn a wage that will keep their families above the poverty line.

For storeowners, pressure to keep labour costs down is fierce as Wal-Mart continues to expand and compete directly in their traditional grocery business. A parallel is drawn to the loss of North American manufacturing jobs to countries with cheaper labour costs.

While companies, unions, and people are trying to hold their ground, many are hoping that Wal-Mart's workforce of more than 1 million will become unionized. An epic struggle of union against nonunion is occurring. The anti-union perspective raises the argument that a third-party intervention negatively affects a business's ability to operate successfully.

As mentioned in the video and discussed in Chapter 10, the UFCW has been working to certify Wal-Mart stores in Canada, including a store in Jonquière, Quebec. Although

this was the first Wal-Mart store to certify successfully in North America, Wal-Mart Canada recently announced the Jonquière store would be closed for economic reasons.

SOURCE: Based on CBC, "No Wal-Mart Wages," *Venture* 911, January 25, 2004.

Questions

1. Imagine you are the senior human resource manager for Wal-Mart Canada. What might be your concerns about unionization?

2. If Wal-Mart became unionized, would it be possible for the UFCW and Wal-Mart to collaborate? Explain your answer.

3. What is your reaction to Wal-Mart's announcement to close the Jonquière store? Does this violate labour legislation?

Glossary

achievement tests Tests that measure a person's existing knowledge and skills.

action learning Training in which teams get an actual problem, work on solving it and commit to an action plan, and are accountable for carrying it out.

ADR See *alternative dispute resolution.*

adventure learning A teamwork and leadership training program based on the use of challenging, structured outdoor activities.

AFL-CIO See *American Federation of Labor and Congress of Industrial Organizations.*

alternative dispute resolution (ADR) Methods of solving a problem by bringing in an impartial outsider but not using the court system.

American Federation of Labor and Congress of Industrial Organizations (AFL-CIO) An association that seeks to advance the shared interests of its member unions at the international level.

Applicant tracking system (ATS) A software application that streamlines the flow of information between job seekers, HR staff, and hiring managers.

apprenticeship A work-study training method that teaches job skills through a combination of on-the-job training and technical training.

aptitude tests Tests that assess how well a person can learn or acquire skills and abilities.

arbitration Binding process in which a professional arbitrator from outside the organization (usually a lawyer or judge) hears the case and resolves it by making a decision.

assessment Collecting information and providing feedback to employees about their behaviour, communication style, or skills.

assessment centre A wide variety of specific selection programs that use multiple selection methods to rate applicants or job incumbents on their management potential.

ATS See *Applicant tracking system.*

balanced scorecard An organizational approach to performance management that integrates strategic perspectives including financial, customer, internal business processes, and learning and growth.

BARS See *behaviourally anchored rating scale.*

behavioural interview A structured interview in which the interviewer asks the candidate to describe how he or she handled a type of situation in the past.

behavioural observation scale (BOS) A variation of BARS which uses all behaviours necessary for effective performance to rate performance at a task.

behaviourally anchored rating scale (BARS) Method of performance measurement that rates behaviour in terms of a scale showing specific statements of behaviour that describe different levels of performance.

benchmarking A procedure in which an organization compares its own practices against those of successful competitors.

BFOR See *bona fide occupational requirement.*

Bill C-45 (Westray Bill) Amendment to the Criminal Code making organizations and anyone who directs the work of others criminally liable for safety offences.

bona fide occupational requirement (BFOR) A necessary (not merely preferred) requirement for performing a job.

BOS See *behavioural observation scale.*

broadbanding Reducing the number of levels in the organization's job structure.

Canada Industrial Relations Board (CIRB) A quasi-judicial tribunal responsible for the interpretation and enforcement of the Industrial Relations section of the Canada Labour Code.

Canada Pension Plan (CPP) A contributory, mandatory plan that provides retirement pensions, disability benefits, and survivor benefits.

Canadian Human Rights Act Federal legislation that protects individuals from discrimination on the basis of 11 prohibited (protected) grounds.

Canadian Human Rights Commission (CHRC) Provides individuals under federal jurisdiction a means to resolve complaints of discrimination.

Canadian Labour Congress (CLC) An association that seeks to advance the shared interests of its member unions at the national level.

career path The identified pattern or progression of jobs or roles within an organization.

central tendency Incorrectly rating all employees at or near the middle of a rating scale.

checkoff provision A requirement that the employer, on behalf of the union, automatically deducts union dues from employees' paycheques.

CHRC See *Canadian Human Rights Commission.*

CIRB See *Canada Industrial Relations Board.*

CLC See *Canadian Labour Congress.*

closed shop A union security arrangement under which a person must be a union member before being hired.

coach A peer or manager who works with an employee to provide a source of motivation, help him or her develop skills, and provide reinforcement and feedback.

cognitive ability tests Tests designed to measure such mental abilities as verbal skills, quantitative skills, and reasoning ability.

collective bargaining Negotiation between union representatives and management representatives to arrive at an agreement defining conditions of employment for the term of the agreement and to administer that agreement.

commissions Incentive pay calculated as a percentage of sales.

compensatory model Process of arriving at a selection decision in which a very high score on one type of assessment can make up for a low score on another.

competencies Knowledge, skills, abilities, and other characteristics associated with effective job performance.

competency framework Competencies the entire organization requires to be successful.

competency-based pay systems Pay structures that set pay according to the employees' levels of skill or knowledge and what they are capable of doing.

conciliation Conflict resolution procedure in which a third party to collective bargaining reports the reasons for a dispute, the views and arguments of both sides, and possibly a recommended settlement, which the parties may decline.

concurrent validation Research that consists of administering a test to people who currently hold a job, then comparing their scores to existing measures of job performance.

construct validity Capability of a test to measure a construct such as intelligence and the relationship of this construct to successful job performance.

constructive dismissal Occurs when the employer makes a significant change to a worker's condition of employment.

content validity Consistency between the test items or problems and the kinds of situations or problems that occur on the job.

continuous learning Each employee's and each group's ongoing efforts to gather information and apply the information to their decisions in a learning organization.

contrast error Rating error caused by comparing employee's performance to co-workers rather than to an objective standard.

contributory plan All costs of the plan are funded by employees, employers, and the plan's own investments.

cooperative education A plan of higher education that incorporates paid work experience as an integral part of academic studies.

coordination training Team training that teaches the team how to share information and make decisions to obtain the best team performance.

core competency A set of knowledge and skills that provide the organization with a competitive advantage and create value for customers.

corporate social responsibility (CSR) An evolving concept generally understood to be the integration of social, environmental, and economic concerns into an organization's values, culture, decision making, strategy, and operations in a way that creates wealth and improves society.

CPP See *Canada Pension Plan.*

craft union Labour union whose members all have a particular skill or occupation.

criterion-related validity A measure of validity based on showing a substantial correlation between test scores and job performance scores.

critical-incident method Method of performance measurement based on managers' records of specific examples of the employee behaving in ways that are either effective or ineffective.

cross-cultural preparation Training to prepare employees and their family members for an assignment in a foreign country.

cross-training Team training in which team members understand and practise each other's skills so that they are prepared to step in and take another member's place.

CSR See *corporate social responsibility.*

culture shock Disillusionment and discomfort that occur during the process of adjusting to a new culture.

decision support systems Computer software systems designed to help managers solve problems by showing how results vary when the manager alters assumptions or data.

defined benefit plan A pension plan that guarantees a specified level of retirement income.

defined contribution plan A retirement plan in which the employer sets up an individual account for each employee and specifies the size of the investment into that account.

development The acquisition of knowledge, skills, and behaviours that improve an employee's ability to meet changes in job requirements and in customer demands.

differential treatment Differing treatment of individuals where the differences are based on a prohibited ground.

direct applicants People who apply for a vacancy without prompting from the organization.

direct compensation Financial rewards employees receive in exchange for their work.

direct discrimination Policies or practices that clearly make a distinction on the basis of a prohibited ground.

discrimination To treat someone differently or unfairly because of a personal characteristic.

distributed work A combination of work options, including work from the corporate office, work from home, work from a satellite office, or work from another remote location.

diversity training Training designed to change employee attitudes about diversity and/or develop skills needed to work with a diverse workforce.

downsizing The planned elimination of large numbers of personnel with the goal of enhancing the organization's competitiveness.

downward move Assignment of an employee to a position with less responsibility and authority.

duty to accommodate An employer's duty to consider how an employee's characteristic such as disability, religion, or sex can be accommodated and to take action so the employee can perform the job.

EAP See *employee assistance program.*

e-business See *electronic business.*

e-HRM See *electronic human resource management.*

EI See *Employment Insurance.*

e-learning Receiving training via the Internet or the organization's intranet.

electronic business (e-business) Any process that a business conducts electronically, especially business involving use of the Internet.

electronic human resource management (e-HRM) The processing and transmission of digitized HR information, especially using computer networking and the Internet.

employee assistance program (EAP) A referral service employees can use to seek professional treatment for emotional problems or substance abuse.

employee benefits Compensation in forms other than cash.

employee development The combination of formal education, job experiences, relationships, and assessment of personality and competencies to help employees prepare for the future of their careers.

employee empowerment Giving employees responsibility and authority to make decisions regarding all aspects of product development or customer service.

employee engagement The extent that employees are satisfied, committed to, and prepared to support what is important to the organization.

employee self-service (ESS) Employee self-service allows an employee to handle many job-related tasks such as applications for reimbursement and updates to personal information.

employee stock ownership plan (ESOP) An arrangement in which the organization distributes shares of stock to all its employees by placing it in a trust.

employee wellness program A set of communications, activities, and facilities designed to change health-related behaviours in ways that reduce health risks.

employer branding A strategic approach of attaching a visual, emotional, or cultural brand to an organization.

Employment Insurance (EI) A federally mandated program to provide temporary financial assistance to unemployed Canadians.

ergonomics The study of the interface between individuals' physiology and the characteristics of the physical work environment.

ESOP See *employee stock ownership plan.*

ESS See *employee self-service.*

ethics The fundamental principles of right and wrong.

exit interview A meeting of a departing employee with the employee's supervisor and/or human resource specialist to discuss the employee's reasons for leaving.

expatriates Employees who take assignments in other countries.

experiential programs Training programs in which participants learn concepts and apply them by simulating behaviours involved and analyzing the activity, connecting it with real-life situations.

expert systems Computer systems that support decision making by incorporating the decision rules used by people who are considered to have expertise in a certain area.

external labour market Individuals who are actively seeking employment.

externship Employee development through a full-time temporary position at another organization.

Fleishman Job Analysis System Job analysis technique that asks subject-matter experts to evaluate a job in terms of the abilities required to perform the job.

flexible benefits plan A benefits plan that offers employees a set of alternatives from which they can choose the types and amounts of benefits they want.

flexible staffing arrangements Methods of staffing other than the traditional hiring of full-time employees (e.g., use of independent contractors, on-call workers, temporary workers, and contract company workers).

flextime A scheduling policy in which full-time employees may choose starting and ending times within guidelines specified by the organization.

focus on activities Rating error when employees are assessed on how busy they appear rather than how effective they are in achieving results.

forced-distribution method Method of performance measurement that assigns a certain percentage of employees to each category in a set of categories.

forecasting The attempts to determine the supply of and demand for various types of human resources to predict areas within the organization where there will be labour shortages or surpluses.

gainsharing Group incentive program that measures improvements in productivity and effectiveness and distributes a portion of each gain to employees.

generalizable Valid in other contexts beyond the context in which the selection method was developed.

glass ceiling Circumstances resembling an invisible barrier that keep most women and other members of the employment equity target groups from attaining the top jobs in organizations.

global organization An organization that chooses to locate a facility based on the ability to effectively, efficiently, and flexibly produce a product or service, using cultural differences as an advantage.

graphic rating scale Method of performance measurement that lists competencies and provides a rating scale for each competency; the employer uses the scale to indicate the extent to which an employee displays each competency.

green-circle rate Pay at a rate that falls below the pay range for the job.

grievance procedure The process for resolving union–management conflicts over interpretation or violation of a collective agreement.

halo error Rating error that occurs when the rater reacts to one positive performance aspect by rating the employee positively in all areas of performance.

harassment Any behaviour that demeans, humiliates, or embarrasses a person, and that a reasonable person should have known would be unwelcome.

health spending account A specific amount of money set aside per employee by the employer to cover health-related costs.

high-performance work system An organization in which technology, organizational structure, people, and processes all work together to give an organization an advantage in the competitive environment.

home country The country in which an organization's headquarters is located.

horns error Rating error that occurs when the rater responds to one negative aspect by rating an employee low in other aspects.

host country A country (other than the home country) in which an organization operates a facility.

hot-stove rule Principle of discipline that says discipline should be like a hot stove, giving clear warning and following up with consistent, objective, immediate consequences.

hourly wage Rate of pay for each hour worked.

HRIS See *human resource information system.*

HRM See *human resource management.*

HRM audit A formal review of the outcomes of HRM functions, based on identifying key HRM functions and measures of organizational performance.

human capital An organization's employees, described in terms of their training, experience, judgment, intelligence, relationships, and insight.

human resource information system (HRIS) A computer system used to acquire, store, manipulate, analyze, retrieve, and distribute information related to an organization's human resources.

human resource management (HRM) The policies, practices, and systems that influence employees' behaviour, attitudes, and performance.

incentive pay Forms of pay linked to an employee's performance as an individual, group member, or organization member.

indirect compensation The benefits and services employees receive in exchange for their work.

indirect discrimination Policies or practices that appear to be neutral but have an adverse effect on the basis of a prohibited ground.

industrial engineering The study of jobs to find the simplest way to structure work in order to maximize efficiency.

industrial union A labour union whose members are linked by their work in a particular industry.

instructional design A process of systematically developing training to meet specified needs.

interactional justice A judgment that the organization carried out its actions in a way that took the employee's feelings into account.

internal labour force An organization's workers (its employees and the people who work at the organization).

internal responsibility system Philosophy of occupational health and safety whereby employers and employees share responsibility for creating and maintaining safe and healthy work environments.

international organization An organization that sets up one or a few facilities in one or a few foreign countries.

internship On-the-job learning sponsored by an educational institution as a component of an academic program.

involuntary turnover Turnover initiated by an employer (often with employees who would prefer to stay).

job A set of related duties.

job analysis The process of getting detailed information about jobs.

job description A list of the tasks, duties, and responsibilities (TDRs) that a particular job entails.

job design The process of defining the way work will be performed and the tasks that a given job requires.

job enlargement Broadening the types of tasks performed in a job.

job enrichment Engaging workers by adding more decision-making authority to jobs.

job evaluation An administrative procedure for measuring the relative internal worth of the organization's jobs.

job experiences The combination of relationships, problems, demands, tasks, and other features of an employee's jobs.

job extension Enlarging jobs by combining several relatively simple jobs to form a job with a wider range of tasks.

job hazard analysis technique Safety promotion technique that involves breaking down a job into basic elements, then rating each element for its potential for harm or injury.

job posting The process of communicating information about a job vacancy on company bulletin boards, in employee publications, on corporate intranets, and anywhere else the organization communicates with employees.

job rotation Enlarging jobs by moving employees among several different jobs.

job satisfaction A pleasant feeling resulting from the perception that one's job fulfills or allows for the fulfillment of one's important job values.

job sharing A work option in which two part-time employees carry out the tasks associated with a single job.

job specification A list of the competencies an individual must have to perform a particular job.

job structure The relative pay for different jobs within the organization.

knowledge workers Employees whose main contribution to the organization is specialized knowledge, such as knowledge of customers, a process, or a profession.

labour relations A field that emphasizes skills managers and union leaders can use to minimize costly forms of conflict (such as strikes) and seek win-win solutions to disagreements.

Labour Relations Board (LRB) A specialized tribunal with authority to interpret and enforce the labour laws in their jurisdiction.

leading indicators Objective measures that accurately predict future labour demand.

learning organization An organization that supports life-long learning by enabling all employees to acquire and share knowledge.

leniency error Rating error of assigning inaccurately high ratings to all employees.

lockout A closure of a place of employment or refusal of the employer to provide work as a way to compel employees to agree to certain demands or conditions.

long-term disability insurance Insurance that pays a percentage of a disabled employee's salary after an initial period and potentially for the rest of the employee's life.

LRB See *Labour Relations Board.*

management by objectives (MBO) A system in which people at each level of the organization set goals in a process that flows from top to bottom, so employees at all levels are contributing to the organization's overall goals; these goals become the standards for evaluating each employee's performance.

material safety data sheets (MSDSs) Detailed hazard information concerning a controlled (hazardous) product.

MBO See *management by objectives.*

mediation Conflict resolution procedure in which a mediator hears the views of both sides and facilitates the negotiation process but has no formal authority to dictate a resolution.

mentor An experienced, productive senior employee who helps develop a less experienced employee (a protégé or mentee).

merit pay A system of linking pay increases to ratings on performance appraisals.

microinequity Subtle message, sometimes subconscious, that devalues, discourages and ultimately impairs performance in the workplace.

mixed-standard scales Method of performance measurement that uses several statements describing each competency to produce a final score for that competency.

MSDSs See *material safety data sheets.*

multinational company An organization that builds facilities in a number of different countries in an effort to minimize production and distribution costs.

multiple-hurdle model Process of arriving at a selection decision by eliminating some candidates at each stage of the selection process.

National Occupational Classification (NOC) Tool created by the federal government to provide a standardized source of information about jobs in Canada's labour market.

needs assessment The process of evaluating the organization, individual employees, and employees' tasks to determine what kinds of training, if any, are necessary.

negligent hiring Legal concept where an employer may be found liable for harm that an employee causes to others when references and background checks were not performed adequately at the time of hiring.

nepotism The practice of hiring relatives.

NOC See *National Occupational Classification.*

nondirective interview A selection interview in which the interviewer has great discretion in choosing questions to ask each candidate.

OBM See *organizational behaviour modification.*

offshoring Setting up a business enterprise in another country (e.g., building a factory in China).

OJT See *on-the-job training.*

on-the-job training (OJT) Training methods in which a person with job experience and skill guides trainees in practising job skills at the workplace.

organization analysis A process for determining the appropriateness of training by evaluating the characteristics of the organization.

organizational behaviour modification (OBM) A plan for managing the behaviour of employees through a formal system of feedback and reinforcement.

orientation Training designed to prepare employees to perform their jobs effectively, learn about their organization, and establish work relationships.

outcome fairness A judgment that the consequences given to employees are just.

outplacement counselling A service in which professionals try to help dismissed employees manage the transition from one job to another.

outsourcing The practice of having another company (a vendor, third-party provider, or consultant) provide services.

paired-comparison method Method of performance measurement that compares each employee with every other one to establish rankings.

panel interview Selection interview in which several members of the organization meet to interview each candidate.

PAQ See *Position Analysis Questionnaire.*

passive job seekers Individuals who are not actively seeking a job.

pay equity Principle of nondiscrimination in wages that require men and women doing work of equal value to be paid the same.

pay grades Sets of jobs having similar worth or content, grouped together to establish rates of pay.

pay level The average amount (including wages, salaries, and bonuses) the organization pays for a particular job.

pay policy line A graphed line showing the mathematical relationship between job evaluation points and pay rate.

pay ranges A set of possible pay rates defined by a minimum, maximum, and midpoint of pay for employees holding a particular job or a job within a particular pay grade or band.

pay structure The pay policy resulting from job structure and pay-level decisions.

peer review Process for resolving disputes by taking them to a panel composed of representatives from the organization at the same levels as the people in the dispute.

performance appraisal The measurement of specified areas of an employee's performance.

performance improvement plan Summary of performance gaps and includes an action plan mutually agreed to by the employee and supervisor with specific dates to review progress.

performance management The process of ensuring that employees' activities and outputs match the organization's goals.

person analysis A process for determining individuals' needs and readiness for training.

Personal Information Protection and Electronic Documents Act (PIPEDA) Provides rules for how organizations can collect, use, or disclose information about you in the course of commercial activities.

phased retirement A gradual transition into full retirement by reducing hours or job responsibility.

piecework rate Rate of pay for each unit produced.

PIPEDA See *Personal Information Protection and Electronic Documents Act.*

Position Analysis Questionnaire (PAQ) A standardized job analysis questionnaire containing 194 questions about work behaviours, work conditions, and job characteristics that apply to a wide variety of jobs.

position The set of duties (job) performed by a particular person.

predictive validation Research that uses the test scores of all applicants and looks for a relationship between the scores and future performance of the applicants who were hired.

procedural justice A judgment that fair methods were used to determine the consequences an employee receives.

productivity The relationship between an organization's outputs (products, information or services) and its inputs (e.g., people, facilities, equipment, data, and materials).

profit sharing Incentive pay in which payments are a percentage of the organization's profits and do not become part of the employees' base salary.

progressive discipline A formal discipline process in which the consequences become more serious if the employee repeats the offence.

promotion Assignment of an employee to a position with greater challenges, more responsibility, and more authority than in the previous job, usually accompanied by a pay increase.

protean career A career that frequently changes based on changes in the person's interests, abilities, and values and in the work environment.

psychological contract A description of what an employee expects to contribute in an employment relationship and what the employer will provide the employee in exchange for those contributions.

QPP See *Quebec Pension Plan.*

Quebec Pension Plan (QPP) A contributory, mandatory plan that provides retirement pensions, disability benefits, and survivor benefits.

Rand Formula A union security provision that makes payment of labour union dues mandatory even if the worker is not a member of the union.

readiness for training A combination of employee characteristics and positive work environment that permit training.

realistic job preview Background information about a job's positive and negative qualities.

reality check Information employers give employees about their competencies and where these assets fit into the organization's plans.

recency emphasis Rating error that occurs when an annual rating is based only on most recent work performed.

recruiting Any activity carried on by the organization with the primary purpose of identifying and attracting potential employees.

recruitment The process through which the organization seeks applicants for potential employment.

red-circle rate Pay at a rate that falls above the pay range for the job.

referrals People who apply for a vacancy because someone in the organization prompted them to do so.

reliability The extent to which a measurement generates consistent results.

repatriation The process of preparing expatriates to return home from a foreign assignment.

sabbatical A leave of absence from an organization to renew or develop skills.

salary Rate of pay for each week, month or year worked.

selection The process by which the organization attempts to identify applicants with the necessary knowledge, skills, abilities, and other characteristics that will help the organization achieve its goals.

self-assessment The use of information by employees to determine their career interests, values, aptitudes, and behavioural tendencies.

severance pay Compensation that recognizes the employee's years of service and compensates the employee for loss of job-related earnings.

sexual harassment Unwelcome behaviour that is of a sexual nature or is related to a person's sex.

short-term disability insurance Insurance that pays a percentage of a disabled employee's salary as benefits to the employee for six months or less.

similar-to-me error Rating error of giving a higher evaluation to people who seem similar to oneself.

simple ranking Method of performance measurement that requires managers to rank employees in their group from the highest to the lowest performer.

simulation A training method that represents a real-life situation, with trainees making decisions resulting in outcomes that mirror what would happen on the job.

situational interviews A structured interview in which the interviewer describes a situation likely to arise on the job, then asks the candidate what he or she would do in that situation.

social unionism A type of unionism that attempts to influence social and economic policies of government.

standard hour plan An incentive plan that pays workers extra for work done in less than a preset "standard time."

stay interview A meeting with an employee to explore his or her thoughts and feelings about the job and to uncover issues in the effort to prevent that employee from becoming disgruntled.

stock options Rights to buy a certain number of shares of stock at a specified price.

strictness error Rating error of giving low ratings to all employees, holding them to unreasonably high standards.

strike A collective decision by union members not to work or to slow down until certain demands or conditions are met.

structured interview A selection interview that consists of a predetermined set of questions for the interviewer to ask.

succession planning The process of identifying and tracking high-potential employees who will be able to fill top management positions when they become vacant.

task analysis The process of identifying the tasks and competencies that training should emphasize.

task analysis inventory Job analysis method that involves listing the tasks performed in a job and rating each task according to a defined set of criteria.

teamwork The assignment of work to groups of employees with various skills who interact to assemble a product or provide a service.

technic of operations review (TOR) Method of promoting safety by determining which specific element of a job led to a past accident.

termination pay A lump-sum payment equal to the regular wages for a regular workweek that an employee would have earned during the notice period.

360-degree performance appraisal Performance measurement that combines information from the employee's managers, peers, direct reports, self, and customers.

third country A country that is neither the home country nor the host country of an employer.

TOR See *technic of operations review.*

total compensation All types of financial rewards and tangible benefits and services employees receive as part of their employment.

total rewards A comprehensive approach to compensating and rewarding employees.

training An organization's planned efforts to help employees acquire job-related competencies with the goal of applying these on the job.

transaction processing Computations and calculations involved in reviewing and documenting HRM decisions and practices.

transfer Assignment of an employee to a position in a different area of the company, usually in a lateral move.

transfer of training On-the-job use of competencies enhanced in training.

transitional matrix A chart that lists job categories held in one period and shows the proportion of employees in each of those job categories in a future period.

transnational HRM system Type of HRM system that makes decisions from a global perspective, includes managers from many countries, and is based on ideas contributed by people representing a variety of cultures.

trend analysis Constructing and applying statistical models that predict labour demand for the next year, given relatively objective statistics from the previous year.

unfair labour practice A prohibited conduct of an employer, union, or individual under the relevant labour legislation.

union shop A union security arrangement that requires employees to join the union within a certain amount of time after beginning employment.

union steward An employee elected by union members to represent them in ensuring that the terms of the collective agreement are enforced.

unions Organizations formed for the purpose of representing their members' interests in dealing with employers.

utility The extent to which something provides economic value greater than its cost.

validity The extent to which performance on a measure (such as a test score) is related to what the measure is designed to assess (such as job performance).

variable pay See *incentive pay.*

virtual expatriates Employees who manage an operation abroad without permanently locating in the country.

virtual reality A computer-based technology that provides an interactive, three-dimensional learning experience.

voluntary turnover Turnover initiated by employees often when the organization would prefer to keep them).

Westray Bill See *Bill C-45.*

work flow design The process of analyzing the tasks necessary for the production of a product or service.

Workers' Compensation Acts Provincial programs that provide benefits to workers who suffer work-related injuries or illnesses.

workforce planning Identifying the numbers and types of employees the organization will require to meet its objectives.

workforce utilization review A comparison of the proportion of employees in protected groups with the proportion that each group represents in the relevant labour market.

workplace health and safety committee A committee jointly appointed by the employer and employees at large (the union) to address health and safety issues in a workplace.

workplace literacy Prose, document, and quantitative capabilities in the languages in which business is conducted.

yield ratio A ratio that expresses the percentage of applicants who successfully move from one stage of the recruitment and selection process to the next.

Notes

Chapter 1

1. Richard Yerema, "Canada's Top 100 Employers," "What It Takes to Be One of Canada's Best Employers," Special Report, *Maclean's*, October 15, 2007, pp. 43–46; Miguel Helft, "Free Ride on Info Highway," *Financial Post*, March 19, 2007, p. FP3; www.canada stop100.com; www.google.com/support/jobs; *Fortune*'s "100 Best Companies to Work For"; http://money.cnn .com/magazines/fortune/bestcompanies/2008/full_list/index.html, retrieved March 16, 2008.

2. Janice Cooney and Allison Cowan, "Training and Development Outlook 2003: Canadian Organizations Continue to Under-Invest" (Ottawa: Conference Board of Canada, 2003), p. 1, www.conferenceboard.ca/documents.asp?rnext=548.

3. Ruth Wright, "The Strategic Value of People: Human Resource Trends and Metrics" (Ottawa: Conference Board of Canada, July 2006), p. i.

4. A. S. Tsui and L. R. Gomez-Mejia, "Evaluating Human Resource Effectiveness," in *Human Resource Management: Evolving Rules and Responsibilities*, ed. L. Dyer (Washington, DC: BNA Books, 1988), pp. 1187–227; M. A. Hitt, B. W. Keats, and S. M. DeMarie, "Navigating in the New Competitive Landscape: Building Strategic Flexibility and Competitive Advantage in the 21st Century," *Academy of Management Executive* 12, no. 4 (1998), pp. 22–42; J. T. Delaney and M. A. Huselid, "The Impact of Human Resource Management Practices on Perceptions of Organizational Performance," *Academy of Management Journal* 39 (1996), pp. 949–69.

5. Owen Parker, "It's the Journey That Matters: 2005 Strategic HR Transformation Study Tour Report 2006" (Ottawa: Conference Board of Canada, 2006), p. 1.

6. Ibid.

7. S. A. Snell and J. W. Dean, "Integrated Manufacturing and Human Resource Management: A Human Capital Perspective," *Academy of Management Journal* 35 (1992), pp. 467–504; M. A. Youndt, S. Snell, J. W. Dean Jr., and D. P. Lepak, "Human Resource Management, Manufacturing Strategy, and Firm Performance," *Academy of Management Journal* 39 (1996), pp. 836–66.

8. Charles Greer, *Strategic Human Resource Management*, 2nd ed. (New Jersey: Prentice-Hall, 2001), p. 1.

9. D. Ulrich, *Human Resource Champions* (Boston: Harvard Business School Press, 1998).

10. A. Halcrow, "Survey Shows HRM in Transition," *Workforce*, June 1998, pp. 73–80; J. Laabs, "Why HR Can Win Today," *Workforce*, May 1998, pp. 62–74; C. Cole, "Kodak Snapshots," *Workforce*, June 2000, pp. 65–72; Towers Perrin, *Priorities for Competitive Advantage: An IBM Study Conducted by Towers Perrin*, 1992.

11. David Brown, "HR Pulled in Two Directions at Once," *Canadian HR Reporter*, February 23, 2004, p. 1.

12. "How Canada Performs: A Report Card on Canada" (Ottawa: Conference Board of Canada, 2007), pp. 42–44; "Performance and Potential: Defining the Canadian Advantage" (Ottawa: Conference Board of Canada, October 2003), p. 5.

13. J. Kahn, "The World's Most Admired Companies," *Fortune*, October 26, 1998, pp. 206–26; A. Fisher, "The World's Most Admired Companies," *Fortune*, October 27, 1997, p. 232.

14. J. L. Young, "Starbucks Expansion into China Is Slated," *The Wall Street Journal*, October 5, 1998, p. B13C.

15. "2006 Census: Immigration, Citizenship, Mobility, & Immigration," *The Daily*, December 4, 2007, www.statcan.ca/Daily/English/071204/d0712049.htm, retrieved December 22, 2007.

16. www.statcan.ca/english/Pgdb/dem046a.htm, retrieved April 3, 2004.

17. www.12.statcan/ca/english/Pgdb/dem046b.htm, retrieved April 3, 2004.

18. "The Generation Bomb," *Financial Post*, March 3, 2004, p. FP6.

19. National Association of Colleges and Employers, "Job Outlook 2002," www.jobweb.com.

20. Jeff Hale, "Ask What Another Country Can Do for You," *The Globe and Mail*, February 22, 2007, p. B11.

21. Sean Silcoff, "Bombardier Examines Indian Option: 6000 Jobs Leaving?," *Financial Post*, April 13, 2004, p. FP1.

22. "Canada's Edge Eroding," *Financial Post*, April 13, 2004, p. FP6.

23. Ibid.

24. "More HR Being Outsourced," *HR Daily News*, March 1, 2002, HRnext.com.

25. Uyen Vu, "Outsourcing Calls for New HR Skills," *Canadian HR Reporter*, March 22, 2004, pp. 1, 3.

26. Andy Shaw, "Rogers Farms Out HR," *Canadian HR Reporter*, June 4, 2007, p. 1.

27. www.cchra.ca/Web/certification/content.aspx?f=29774, retrieved January 10, 2008.

28. www.cchra.ca/Web/CCHRA/content.aspx?f=29752, retrieved July 5, 2007.

29. www.cchra.ca/Web/CCHRA/content.aspx?f=29943, retrieved January 10, 2008.

30. R. Ricklees, "Ethics in America," *The Wall Street Journal*, October 31–November 3, 1983, p. 33.

31. C. O'Reilly and J. Pfeffer, *Hidden Value: How Great Companies Achieve Extraordinary Results with Ordinary People* (Cambridge, MA: Harvard Business School Press, 2000).

32. Uyen Vu, "Climate Change Sparks Attitude Shift," *Canadian HR Reporter*, March 26, 2007, p. 11.

33. J. Wiscombe, "Your Wonderful, Terrible HR Life," *Workforce*, June 2001, pp. 32–38.

34. Andrew Wahl, "Leaders Wanted," *Canadian Business*, March 1–14, 2004, p. 31.

35. "Performance and Potential 2003–2004: Defining the Canadian Advantage," Special Report (Ottawa: Conference Board of Canada, October 2003), p. 9.

36. Wahl, "Leaders Wanted," p. 32.

37. Virginia Gait, "The Generational Divide," *The Globe and Mail*, March 31, 2004, pp. C1, C6.

38. B. Wooldridge and J. Wester, "The Turbulent Environment of Public Personnel Administration: Responding to the Challenge of the Changing Workplace of the Twenty-First Century," *Public Personnel Management* 20 (1991), pp. 207–24; J. Laabs, "The New Loyalty: Grasp It. Earn It. Keep It," *Workforce*, November 1998, pp. 34–39.

39. "Employee Dissatisfaction on Rise in Last 10 Years, New Report Says," *Employee Relations Weekly* (Washington, DC: Bureau of National Affairs, 1986).

40. D. T. Hall and J. Richter, "Career Gridlock: Baby Boomers Hit the Wall," *The Executive* 4 (1990), pp. 7–22.

41. S. Shellenbarger, "Companies Must Try Harder to Attract Older Employees," *The Wall Street Journal*, Interactive Edition, May 23, 2001.

42. Kamal Dib, "Diversity Works," *Canadian Business*, March 29–April, 2004, p. 53.

43. Valerie Marchant, "The New Face of Work," *Canadian Business*, March 29–April, 2004, p. 42.

44. Andrew Wahl, "Opening Doors," *Canadian Business*, March 29–April, 2004, http://www.canadian business.com/article.jsp?content=20040329_59084_ 59084, retrieved October 20, 2008.

45. "Labour Force and Participation Rates by Sex and Age Group" (Ottawa: Statistics Canada, 2008), http://www40.statcan.ca/l01/cst01/labor05.htm, retrieved October 20, 2008.

46. BMO Financial Group 2006, *Employment Equity Report*, p. 3, www2.bmo/bmo/files/images/7/1/BMO_%202006_ %20EquityRpt.pdf, retrieved March 14, 2008.

47. "Aboriginal Identity Population by Age Groups, Median Age and Sex, 2006 Counts, for Canada, Provinces and Territories—20% Sample Data (Table)" (Ottawa: Statistics Canada, 2008); "Aboriginal Peoples Highlight Tables, 2006 Census," Catalogue No. 97-558-XWE2006002, January 15, 2008 (Ottawa: Statistics Canada, 2008), www12.statcan .ca/english/census06/data/highlights/aboriginal/ index.cfm?Lang=E, retrieved April 24, 2008.

48. www.chrc-ccdp.ca/discrimination/barrier_ freeen .asp, retrieved April 3, 2004.

49. "How Canada Performs: A Report Card on Canada" (Ottawa: Conference Board of Canada, June 2007), p. 82.

50. "Industry Report 2000," *Training*, October 2000, p. 48.

51. J. A. Neal and C. L. Tromley, "From Incremental Change to Retrofit: Creating High-Performance Work Systems," *Academy of Management Executive* 9 (1995), pp. 42–54.

52. A. Carnevale and D. Desrochers, "Training in the Dilbert Economy," *Training & Development*, December 1999, pp. 32–36.

53. www.statcan.ca/english/Pgdb/educ45.htm, retrieved November 30, 2004; "Highest Certificate, Diploma, or Degree" (Ottawa: Statistics Canada, 2008), www.12 .statcan.ca/english/census.objdata/topics, retrieved March 16, 2008.

54. Ray Turchansky, "Proof Education Is Smart Investment," *Financial Post*, March 22, 2004, p. FP13.

55. M. J. Kavanaugh, H. G. Guetal, and S. I. Tannenbaum, *Human Resource Information Systems: Development and Application* (Boston: PWS-Kent, 1990).

56. S. Greengard, "When HRMS Goes Global: Managing the Data Highway," *Personnel Journal*, June 1995, pp. 91–106.

57. This section is based on L. Grensing-Pophal, "Are You Suited for a Dot-Com?," *HR Magazine*, November 2000, pp. 75–80; and Leslie A. Weatherly, "HR Technology: Leveraging the Shift to Self-Service," *HR Magazine*, March 2005, http://web7.infotrac .galegroup.com; and Bill Roberts, "Empowerment or Imposition?," *HR Magazine*, June 2004, http://web7 .infotrac.galegroup.com.

58. Pui-Wing Tam and Nick Wingfield, "As Tech Matures, Workers File a Spate of Salary Complaints," *The Wall Street Journal*, February 24, 2005, pp. A1, A11.

59. D. M. Rousseau, "Psychological and Implied Contracts in Organizations," *Employee Rights and Responsibilities Journal* 2 (1989), pp. 121–29.

60. D. Rousseau, "Changing the Deal While Keeping the People," *Academy of Management Executive* 11 (1996), pp. 50–61; M. A. Cavanaugh and R. Noe, "Antecedents and Consequences of the New Psychological Contract," *Journal of Organizational Behavior* 20 (1999), pp. 323–40.

61. C. Tejada, "For Many, Taking Work Home Is Often a Job Without Reward," *The Wall Street Journal*, Interactive Edition, March 5, 2002.

62. www.cbc.ca/newwork/nomore9t05/234.html.

Chapter 2

1. Paul Samyn, "Tearing Down Barriers Big Job," *Winnipeg Free Press,* July 16, 2004, p. A3; Paul Egan, "He's Breaking Barriers," *Winnipeg Free Press,* July 4, 2004, pp. A1, A2; Parliament of Canada website, www2.parl.gc.ca, retrieved April 13, 2008.
2. "Anti-Discriminatory Casebook," www.chrcccdp.ca/Legis&Poli/AntiDiscriminationCasebook_Recueil DeDecisions, retrieved February 18, 2004.
3. "Bona Fide Occupational Justifications-Canadian Human Rights Act," pp. 2, 3, www.chrc-ccdp.ca/publications/BFOR, retrieved July 13, 2004.
4. www.chrc-ccdp.ca/discrimination/grounds_en.asp, retrieved July 13, 2004.
5. www.pch.gc.ca/progs/pdp-hrp/Canada/gide/overview_e.cfm?nav, retrieved February 26, 2004.
6. www.chrc-ccdp.ca/employment_equity/visibleminorities-en.asp, retrieved April 3, 2004.
7. www.chrc-ccdp.ca/employment_equity/aboriginal-en.asp, retrieved April 3, 2004.
8. www.chrc-ccdp.ca/employment_equity/disabilities-en.asp, retrieved April 3, 2004.
9. Human Resources and Social Development Canada, "Employment Equity Act: Annual Report 2006," p. 31.
10. Ibid., p. 35.
11. David Brown, "Privacy Implications for Human Resources Still Unclear," *Canadian HR Reporter,* February 24, 2003, p. 11.
12. "A Guide for Canadians: What Is the Personal Information Protection and Electronic Documents Act?," www.privcom.gc.ca/information.
13. Lesley Young, "Job-Protected Leave for Organ Donations Possible," *Canadian HR Reporter,* October 8, 2007, p. 1.
14. www.chrc-ccdp.ca/publications/employee_rights_en.asp, retrieved July 23, 2004.
15. Matthew McClearn, "Mind the Gap," *Canadian Business,* November 5, 2007, pp. 21–22.
16. Sarah Schmidt, "Report Says Male Profs Paid More Than Females," *Winnipeg Free Press,* July 17, 2004, p. A11.
17. Ibid.
18. Colin Perkel, "Female Academics Face Lower Wages, Study Says," *The Globe and Mail,* January 29, 2007, p. A7.
19. David Brown, "New Rules Proposed for Pay Equity," *Canadian HR Reporter,* May 31, 2004, pp. 1, 3.
20. Canadian Human Rights Commission, "2007 Annual Report," p. 6, www.chrc-ccdp.ca/publication/ar_2007_ra/page6-en.asp#41, retrieved April 14, 2008.
21. "Privacy Commissioner of Canada: A Guide for Canadians," www.privcom.gc.ca/information, retrieved March 21, 2004.
22. Ran LeClair, "The Evolution of Accommodation," *Canadian HR Reporter,* February 24, 2003, p. 7.
23. "Bona Fide Occupational Requirements and Bona Fide Justifications Under the Canadian Human Rights Act," pp. 4, 5, www.chrc-ccdp.ca/publications/BFOR, retrieved February 18, 2004.
24. "Mandatory Retirement in Canada," www.hrsdc.gc.ca/en/lp/spila/clli/eslc/19Mandatory_Retirement.shtml, retrieved October 20, 2008; "Retiring Mandatory Retirement," February 21, 2008, www.cbc.ca/news/background/retirement/mandatory_retirement.html, retrieved October 20, 2008.
25. Canadian Human Rights Commission, "Fact Sheet: Duty to Accommodate," January 2006, p. 2.
26. "Anti-Harassment Policies for the Workplace: An Employer's Guide," p. 4, www.chrc-ccdp.ca/publications, retrieved February 26, 2004.
27. "Seneca Policies," p. 1, www.senecac.on/ca/about_seneca/policies/discrimination.cfm, retrieved July 13, 2004.
28. "Anti-Harassment Policies for the Workplace: An Employer's Guide."
29. Bernard Warner, "European Law Puts Employees on Hook for E-Mail Porn," *Financial Post,* April 28, 2004, p. FP14.
30. B. Carton, "At Jenny Craig, Men Are Ones Who Claim Sex Discrimination," *The Wall Street Journal,* November 29, 1995, p. A1; "Male-on-Male Harassment Suit Won," *Houston Chronicle,* August 12, 1995, p. 21A.
31. Gerry Bellett, "Harassed Woman Awarded $950,000," *Leader-Post,* January 24, 2006, p. A3.
32. Patrick White, "Bullying a Serious Job Hazard," *The Globe and Mail,* March 10, 2008, http://www.theglobeandmail.com/servlet/story/RTGAM.20080310.wlbullying10/BNStory/lifeWork/home?cid=al_gam_mostview, retrieved October 20, 2008.
33. Virginia Galt, "Cracking Down on Workplace Harassment," *The Globe and Mail,* October 5, 2007, www.theglobeandmail.com/servlet/Page/document/v5/content/subscribe?user_URL=http://www.theglobeandmail.com%2Fservlet%2Fstory%2FLAC.20071006.RCOACH06%2FTPStory%2FBusiness&ord=22120745&brand=theglobeandmail&force_login=true, retrieved October 20, 2008.
34. "Canada's Best Diversity Employers," www.canadastop100.com/diversity, retrieved April 16, 2008.
35. Shannon Klie, "Lots of Talk, Not Much Action on Diversity," *Canadian HR Reporter,* January 15, 2008, p. 1.
36. Mary P. Rowe, "Fostering Diversity: Some Major Hurdles Remain," http://aad.english.ucsb.edu/docs/Change6.html, retrieved April 18, 2008; Eric L. Hinton, "Microinequities: When Small Slights Lead to Huge Problems in the Workplace," *Diversity Inc.,* www.magazine.org/content/files/microinequities.pdf, retrieved April 18, 2008.
37. "2003 Employment Equity Annual Report," p. 24, www.hrsdc.gc.ca/en, retrieved July 13, 2004.
38. "Diversity as a Way of Life," Wal-Mart Stores website, www.walmart.com, retrieved February 13, 2002.

39. "Business Results Through Health and Safety," Ontario Workplace Safety and Insurance Board website, www .wsib.on.ca/wsib/website.nsf, retrieved April 19, 2004.

40. www.ccohs.ca/oshanswers/legisl/ire.htm, retrieved February 25, 2004.

Chapter 3

1. "HR Leaders Talk," *Canadian HR Reporter*, January 28, 2008, pp. 11–12.

2. "Business Results Through Health and Safety," Ontario Workplace Safety and Insurance Board, www.wsib .on.ca/wsib/website.nsf, retrieved April 19, 2004.

3. www.ccohs.ca/oshanswers/legisl/ire.htm, retrieved February 25, 2004.

4. "Information on Occupational Health and Safety," Government of Canada website, http://info.load-otea .hrdc-drhc.gc.ca/publications/ohs/committees.pdf, retrieved February 25, 2004.

5. Mark Rogers, "Supporting Our Supervisors," p. 4, www.hrpao.org/Knowledge_Centre/kc_s04120403.asp, retrieved April 12, 2004.

6. Russel Zinn, "Driving Under Influence—of a Cell-phone," *Canadian HR Reporter*, February 25, 2008, p. 5.

7. Ibid.

8. "Initiative Puts Driver Safety First," *Canadian Occupational Health and Safety News*, August 2, 2004, www .ohscanada.com/article.asp?id=33374&issue=08032004, retrieved August 3, 2004.

9. "More Ontario Health and Safety Enforcers," *Canadian HR Reporter*, August 9, 2004, p. 2.

10. "Nova Scotia Gives Occupational Health and Safety Officers New Enforcement Tool," *Canadian HR Reporter*, February 2, 2004, www.hrreporter.com, retrieved February 5, 2004.

11. Ann Perry, "Workplace Safety Gets a Boost," *Toronto Star*, March 27, 2004, p. D10.

12. "Occupational Health and Safety: Labour Operations," http://info.load-otea.hrdc-drhc.gc.ca/~oshweb/homeen .shtml, retrieved February 26, 2004.

13. Uyen Vu, "Right to Refuse Dangerous Work Expands," *Canadian HR Reporter*, August 9, 2004, pp. 1, 2.

14. Andy Shaw, "Slow Evolution from WHMIS to GHS," *Canadian HR Reporter*, March 10, 2008, p. 11.

15. Ibid.

16. "The Globally Harmonized System of Classification and Labelling of Chemicals (GHS)," *Health Canada*, www.hc-sc.gc.ca/ahc-asc/intactiv/ghs-sgh/index_e.html, retrieved May 29, 2008.

17. Association of Workers' Compensation Boards of Canada, "Number of Fatalities, by Jurisdiction, 1993–2006," Table 14, www.awcbc.org, retrieved May 29, 2008.

18. J. Roughton, "Managing a Safety Program Through Job Hazard Analysis," *Professional Safety* 37 (1992), pp. 28–31.

19. M. A. Verespec, "OSHA Reform Fails Again," *Industry Week*, November 2, 1992, p. 36.

20. Roughton, ibid.

21. R. G. Hallock and D. A. Weaver, "Controlling Losses and Enhancing Management Systems with TOR Analysis," *Professional Safety* 35 (1990), pp. 24–26.

22. H. Herbstman, "Controlling Losses the Burger King Way," *Risk Management* 37 (1990), pp. 22–30.

23. "Young Worker Awareness Program," www.young worker.ca/English/index.htm, retrieved August 18, 2004.

24. T. Markus, "How to Set Up a Safety Awareness Program," *Supervision* 51 (1990), pp. 14–16.

25. J. Agnew and A. J. Saruda, "Age and Fatal Work-Related Falls," *Human Factors* 35, no. 4 (1994), pp. 731–736.

26. Todd Humber, "WCBs Lawmakers Tackle Rising Death Toll," *Canadian HR Reporter*, April 19, 2004, p. 19.

27. R. King, "Active Safety Programs, Education Can Help Prevent Back Injuries," *Occupational Health and Safety* 60 (1991), pp. 49–52.

28. T. W. Turriff, "NSPB Suggests 10-Step Program to Prevent Eye Injury," *Occupational Health and Safety* 60 (1991), pp. 62–66.

29. "BC Firm Receives Safety Award," *Canadian Health and Safety News*, www.ohscanada.com/article.asp, retrieved August 13, 2004.

30. M. Janssens, J. M. Brett, and E J. Smith, "Confirmatory Cross-Cultural Research: Testing the Viability of a Corporation-wide Safety Policy," *Academy of Management Journal* 38 (1995), pp. 364–82.

31. D. J. Hoekstra, "Workplace Searches: A Legal Overview," *Labor Law Journal* 47, no. 2 (February 1996), pp. 127–38.

32. T. A. Judge, C. J. Thoresen, J. E. Bono, and G. K. Patton, "The Job Satisfaction–Job Performance Relationship: A Qualitative and Quantitative Review," *Psychological Bulletin* 127 (2001), pp. 376–407; R. A. Katzell, D. E. Thompson, and R. A. Guzzo, "How Job Satisfaction and Job Performance Are and Are Not Linked," *Job Satisfaction*, ed. C. J. Cranny, P. C. Smith, and E. E. Stone (New York: Lexington Books, 1992), pp. 195–217.

33. C. Ostroff, "The Relationship Between Satisfaction, Attitudes, and Performance," *Journal of Applied Psychology* 77, no. 6 (1992), pp. 963–74.

34. Watson Wyatt Worldwide, *WorkUSA 2002: Weathering the Storm* (New York: Watson Wyatt, October 2002), www.humancapitalonline.com.

35. Frances Horibe, "What If HR Has No Effect?," *Canadian HR Reporter*, October 11, 2004, p. 19.

36. Hewitt Associates, "The Link Between Employee Engagement and Business Results," http://was4.hewitt .com/hewitt/resource/rptpubs/hewitcmagazine/vol6, retrieved November 29, 2004.

37. Ibid.

38. R. P. Quinn and G. L. Staines, *The 1977 Quality of Employment Survey* (Ann Arbor, MI: Survey Research Center, Institute for Social Research, University of Michigan, 1979).

39. T. Judge and T. Welbourne, "A Confirmatory Investigation of the Dimensionality of the Pay Satisfaction Questionnaire," *Journal of Applied Psychology* 79 (1994), pp. 461–66.

40. Suzanne Wintrob, "Reward a Job Well Done," *Financial Post*, May 10, 2004, p. FP7.

41. John Thackray, "Feedback for Real," March 15, 2001, http://gmj.gallup.com/content/default.asp?ci=811, retrieved November 28, 2004.

42. Ibid.

43. Theresa Minton-Eversole, "Less Engagement, Less Profit, Research Finds," *HR Magazine*, December 2007, p. 20.

44. Ibid.

45. J. Applegaste, "Plan an Exit Interview," *CNN-Money.com*, November 13, 2000, pp. 1–2.

46. H. E. Allerton, "Can Teach Old Dogs New Tricks," *Training & Development*, November 2000, Find Articles.com.

47. "Stay Interviews," www.bcjobs.ca/re/hr-centre/interview-techniques/human-resource-advice/stay-interviews, retrieved April 24, 2008.

48. Paula Kettler, "What's the Big Deal About Employee Engagement?," *T+D*, January 2008, p. 45.

49. Uyen Vu, "What's the Real Cost of Turnover?," *Canadian HR Reporter*, July 14, 2008, www.hrreporter.com, retrieved July 14, 2008.

50. "Wrongful Dismissal Law in Canada," Duhaime's Employment and Labour Law Centre, www.duhaime.orgf Employment/ca-wd.aspx, retrieved March 28, 2005.

51. Ontario Ministry of Labour, "Termination of Employment and Severance Pay," www.gov.on.ca/LAB/english/es/factssheets/fs_termination.html, retrieved March 24, 2005.

52. A. Q. Nomani, "Women Likelier to Face Violence in the Workplace," *The Wall Street Journal*, October 31, 1995, p. A16.

53. Uyen Vu, "Off-Duty Behaviour Cases," *Canadian HR Reporter*, June 14, 2004, www.hrreporter.com, retrieved March 25, 2005.

54. Kettler, ibid.

55. Government of Canada, "Corporate Social Responsibility: An Implementation Guide for Canadian Business," 2006, p. 5, www.commdev.org/content/document/detail/1468.

56. Paul Tsaparis, "Social Responsibility Gives Canadian Firms an Edge," *Canadian HR Reporter*, May 23, 2005, p. 18.

57. Ibid.

58. Anthony Watanabe, "From Brown to Green," *HR Professional*, February/March 2008, p. 49.

59. Uyen Vu, "Climate Change Sparks Attitude Shift," *Canadian HR Reporter*, March 26, 2007, p. 11.

60. Adrienne Fox, "Get in the Business of Being Green," *HR Magazine*, June 2008, p. 45.

61. Shannon Klie, "Credit Union Aims to Be CO_2-Neutral by 2010," *Canadian HR Reporter*, March 26, 2007, p. 12; www.vancity.com, retrieved June 3, 2008.

62. Klie, ibid.

63. Beth Tyndall, "Charitable Giving ROI," *HR Professional*, April/May 2007, p. 34.

64. Adine Mees and Jamie Bonham, "Corporate Social Responsibility Belongs with HR," *Canadian HR Reporter*, April 5, 2004, p. 11.

65. Andrew Wahl et al., "The Best Work Places in Canada 2007," *Canadian Business*, April 23, 2007.

66. Ibid.

67. Judith MacBride-King, "Governments, Start Your Recruitment Campaigns," *Canadian HR Reporter*, October 8, 2007, p. 18.

68. Fox, ibid.

69. K. Maher, "Wanted: Ethical Employer," *The Wall Street Journal*, July 9, 2002, pp. B1, B8.

70. Ibid.

71. Maher, ibid.

72. www.cibc.com/ca/inside-cibc/governance/governance practices/code-of-conduct.html, retrieved October 22, 2004.

73. www.cibc.com/ca/pdf/about/code-ethic-dir.pdf, retrieved October 22, 2004.

74. COMPAS, "Corporate Ethics: CIBC-Style Programs Work; Focus Above All on Account and Senior Executive Fraud," BDO Dunwoody/Chamber Weekly CEO/Business Leader Poll in the *Financial Post* for publication March 1, 2004, www.compas/ca/poll/040301-BLCorpEthics-PB.htm, retrieved May 4, 2004.

Chapter 4

1. David Brown, "Trouble with Assessing IT Skills, Bad News as Demand Heats Up," *Canadian HR Reporter*, December 6, 2004, p. 1; www.ictc-ctic.ca.

2. D. Little, "Even the Supervisor Is Expendable: The Internet Allows Factories to Be Managed from Anywhere," *BusinessWeek*, July 23, 2001, p. 78.

3. D. Shook, "Why Nike Is Dragging Its Feet," *BusinessWeek Online*, March 19, 2001; A. Bernstein, "Backlash: Behind the Anxiety over Globalization," *BusinessWeek*, April 20, 2000, pp. 38–43; A. Bernstein, "Low Skilled Jobs: Do They Have to Move?," *BusinessWeek*, February 26, 2001.

4. J. R. Hollenbeck, H. Moon, A. Ellis, et al., "Structural Contingency Theory and Individual Differences: Examination of External and Internal Person-Team Fit," *Journal of Applied Psychology* 87 (2002), pp. 599–606.

5. C. Joinson, "Refocusing Job Descriptions," *HR Magazine*, January 2001, Findarticles.com.

6. www.managers-gestionnaires.gc.ca/career_development, retrieved December 14, 2004.

7. G. Koretz, "Perils of the Graveyard Shift: Poor Health and Low Productivity," *BusinessWeek*, March 10, 1997, p. 22; C. R. Maiwald, J. L. Pierce, and J. W. Newstrom,

"Workin' 8 P.M. to 8 A.M. and Lovin' Every Minute of It," *Workforce*, July 1997, pp. 30–36.

8. A. O'Reilly, "Skill Requirements: Supervisor–Subordinate Conflict," *Personnel Psychology* 26 (1973), pp. 75–80; J. Hazel, J. Madden, and R. Christal, "Agreement Between Worker–Supervisor Descriptions of the Worker's Job," *Journal of Industrial Psychology* 2 (1964), pp. 71–79.

9. *PAQ Newsletter*, August 1989.

10. E. Primhoff, *How to Prepare and Conduct Job Element Examinations* (Washington, DC: U.S. Government Printing Office, 1975).

11. E. Fleishman and M. Reilly, *Handbook of Human Abilities* (Palo Alto, CA: Consulting Psychologists Press, 1992); E. Fleishman and M. Mumford, "The Ability Requirements Scales," in *The Job Analysis Handbook for Business, Industry, and Government*, ed. S. Gael (New York: Wiley), pp. 917–35.

12. W. Cascio, *Applied Psychology in Personnel Management*, 4th ed. (Englewood Cliffs, NJ: Prentice Hall, 1991).

13. P. Wright and K. Wexley, "How to Choose the Kind of Job Analysis You Really Need," *Personnel*, May 1985, pp. 51–55.

14. www.rcmp-learning.org/howtouse.htm, retrieved March 11, 2004.

15. Canadian Human Rights Commission website, www.ccrc-ccdp.ca/discrimination/barrier_free-en.asp, retrieved April 3, 2004.

16. M. K. Lindell, C. S. Clause, C. J. Brandt, and R. S. Landis, "Relationship Between Organizational Context and Job Analysis Ratings," *Journal of Applied Psychology* 83 (1998), pp. 769–76.

17. S. Caudron, "Jobs Disappear when Work Becomes More Important," *Workforce*, January 2000, pp. 30–32.

18. P. Gogoi, "Going to the Head of the Class," *Business-Week*, December 10, 2001, pp. 53–54.

19. R. Hackman and G. Oldham, *Work Redesign* (Boston: Addison-Wesley, 1980).

20. M. A. Campion, G. J. Medsker, and A. C. Higgs, "Relations Between Work Group Characteristics and Effectiveness: Implications for Designing Effective Work Groups," *Personnel Psychology* 46 (1993), pp. 823–50.

21. "A Few Facts About Distributed Work," *Canadian HR Reporter*, August 14, 2006, p. 21.

22. Uyen Vu, "A Variety of Options Gives Boost to Remote Work," *Canadian HR Reporter*, August 14, 2006, p. 15.

23. Ernest B. Akyeampong, "Working at Home: An Update," *Perspectives*, June 2007, p. 16 (Statistics Canada, Catalogue No. 75-001-XIE).

24. "Evolution of the Workplace: The Growing Demand for Distributed Work," *SuiteWorks*, www.suiteworks.ca/pdfs/Revolution@Work%20SuiteWorks.pdf, retrieved March 23, 2008.

25. Kevin Marron, "Remote Access System Lets Health Care Professionals Make More Accurate Off-Site Diagnoses," special to *The Globe and Mail*, Telework, March 4, 2004, www.globeandmail.com, retrieved April 22, 2004.

26. D. May and C. Schwoerer, "Employee Health by Design: Using Employee Involvement Teams in Ergonomic Job Redesign," *Personnel Psychology* 47 (1994), pp. 861–86.

27. S. F. Brown, "International's Better Way to Build Trucks," *Fortune*, February 19, 2001, pp. 210k–210v.

28. C. Haddad, "OSHA's New Regs Will Ease the Pain for Everybody," *BusinessWeek*, December 4, 2000, pp. 90–94.

29. Canadian Centre for Occupational Health and Safety website, www.ccohs.ca/oshanswers/ergonommics, retrieved April 28, 2004.

30. Peter Budnick and Rachel Michael, "What Is Cognitive Ergonomics?," *Ergonomics Today*, www.ergoweb.com/news/detail.cfm?id=352, retrieved March 25, 2008.

31. "Email Marketing: Despite Significant Increases in Email Spam, Canadian's Willingness to Subscribe to Permission Based Email Continues," June 26, 2007, www.ipsos.com, retrieved March 21, 2008.

32. E. Weinstein, "Rising Flood of Office E-Mail Messages Threatens to Drown the Unorganized," *The Wall Street Journal*, Interactive Edition, January 10, 2002; "With Mountain of Junk Mail Set to Grow, Companies Promote Tools to Reduce 'Spam," *The Wall Street Journal*, Interactive Edition, December 17, 2001.

33. "The Office of the Future Isn't Paperless. It's Wireless. And It's Wherever You Are," December 19, 2006, www.ipsos.com, retrieved March 21, 2008.

Chapter 5

1. "Skilled Workers and Professionals: Who Can Apply—Six Selection Factors and Pass Mark," Citizenship and Immigration website, www.cic.gc.ca/english/immigrate/skilled/apply-factors.asp, retrieved March 29, 2008.

2. Pinoo Bindhani, "Internships a Win for Immigrants, Firms," *Canadian HR Reporter* 20, no. 10 (May 21, 2007), p. 22; www.careerbridge.ca.

3. D. Welch, "A Contract the Big Three Can Take to the Bank," *BusinessWeek*, September 29, 2003, p. 46.

4. M. Conlin, "Savaged by the Slowdown," *BusinessWeek*, September 17, 2001, pp. 74–77.

5. "Nortel in Talks to Sell Off Factories," *Information Week*, January 22, 2004, www.informationweek.com, retrieved May 10, 2004.

6. W. E Cascio, "Whither Industrial and Organizational Psychology in a Changing World of Work?," *American Psychologist* 50 (1995), pp. 928–39.

7. "Nortel in Talks to Sell Off Factories," *Information Week*, January 22, 2004, www.informationweek.com, retrieved May 10, 2004.

8. Allan Swift and Kevin Restivo, "Montreal Loses More Tech Jobs Overseas," *Financial Post*, April 7, 2004, p. FP6.

9. K. P. DeMeuse, P. A. Vanderheiden, and T. J. Bergmann, "Announced Layoffs: Their Effect on Corporate Financial Performance," *Human Resource Management* 33 (1994), pp. 509–30.

10. P. P. Shaw, "Network Destruction: The Structural Implications of Downsizing," *Academy of Management Journal* 43 (2000), pp. 101–12.

11. R. T. King, "Is Job Cutting by Drug Makers Bad Medicine?," *The Wall Street Journal*, August 23, 1995, pp. B1–B3.

12. W. E Cascio, "Downsizing: What Do We Know? What Have We Learned?," *Academy of Management Executive* 7 (1993), pp. 95–104.

13. J. Schu, "Internet Helps Keep Goodwill of Downsized Employees," *Workforce*, July 2001, p. 15.

14. D. Skatlicki, J. H. Ellard, and B. R. C. Kellin, "Third Party Perceptions of a Layoff: Procedural, Derogation, and Retributive Aspects of Justice," *Journal of Applied Psychology* 83 (1998), pp. 119–27.

15. R. Folger and D. P. Skarlicki, "When Tough Times Make Tough Bosses: Managerial Distancing as a Function of Layoff Blame," *Academy of Management Journal* 41 (1998), pp. 79–87.

16. R. Stodghill, "The Coming Job Bottleneck," *Business-Week*, March 24, 1997, pp. 184–85.

17. S. Kim and D. Feldman, "Healthy, Wealthy, or Wise: Predicting Actual Acceptances of Early Retirement Incentives at Three Points in Time," *Personnel Psychology* 51 (1998), pp. 623–42.

18. D. Fandray, "Gray Matters," *Workforce*, July 2000, pp. 27–32.

19. www.adecco.com/Channels/adecco/press+office/corporate, retrieved May 14, 2004.

20. www.adecco.com/Channels/adecco/investor+relaations, retrieved March 4, 2004.

21. G. Flynn, "Contingent Staffing Requires Serious Strategy," *Personnel Journal*, April 1995, pp. 50–58.

22. Irwin Speizer, "Going to Ground," *Workforce Management*, December 2004, pp. 39–44.

23. Ibid.; Monica Langley, "Drivers Deliver Trouble to FedEx by Seeking Employee Benefits," *The Wall Street Journal*, January 7, 2005, pp. A1, A8.

24. Daniel Lublin, "Rule of Employment Must Be Kept," *Canadian HR Reporter*, May 21, 2007, www.canadianhrreporter.com, retrieved March 29, 2008.

25. Nurjehan Mawani, "The Federal Public Service: Opportunities for All Canadians," June 1, 2003, http://globeandmail.workopolis.com, retrieved February 17, 2004.

26. G. Koretz, "Overtime versus New Factories," *Business-Week*, May 4, 1998, p. 34.

27. "Employment Equity in the Public Service of Canada 2005–2006: Annual Report to Parliament," *Canada Public Service Agency*, www.psagency- agencefp.gc.ca, retrieved March 18, 2008.

28. A. E. Barber, *Recruiting Employees* (Thousand Oaks, CA: Sage, 1998).

29. J. D. Olian and S. L. Rynes, "Organizational Staffing: Integrating Practice with Strategy," *Industrial Relations* 23 (1984), pp. 170–83.

30. "Employers Take Recruiting Seriously," http://globeandmail.workopolis.com, retrieved March 16, 2004.

31. Rifka Rosenwein; "Help (Still) Wanted," *Inc.*, April 2001, pp. 51–52, 54–55.

32. G. T. Milkovich and J. M. Newman, *Compensation* (Homewood, IL: Richard D. Irwin, 1990).

33. S. J. Marks, "After School," *Human Resources Executive*, June 15, 2001, pp. 49–51.

34. J. Kaufman, "A McDonald's Owner Becomes a Role Model for Black Teenagers," *The Wall Street Journal*, August 23, 1995, p. A1.

35. K. Clark, "Reasons to Worry About Rising Wages," *Fortune*, July 7, 1997, pp. 31–32.

36. www.recruiting.forces.gc.ca, retrieved May 15, 2004.

37. Uyen Vu, "The Drug Sector's Staffing Remedies," *Canadian HR Reporter*, February 10, 2003, p. 1.

38. Carolyn Brandon, "Truth in Recruitment Branding," *HR Magazine* 50, no. 11 (November 2005), pp. 89–96.

39. Kim Peters, "Employment Branding Best Way to Reach Untapped Talent," *HR Voice*, November 1, 2007, www.hrvoice.org/story, retrieved March 18, 2008.

40. Kim Peters, "Passive Jobseekers Solution to Labour Woes," *Canadian HR Reporter*, July 16, 2007, p. 18.

41. Carolyn Brandon, "Truth in Recruitment Branding," *HR Magazine* 50, no. 11 (November 2005), pp. 89–96.

42. Patrick J. Kiger, "Burnishing Your Employment Brand," *Workforce Management*, October 22, 2007, http://web.eboscost.com, retrieved March 18, 2008.

43. Peters, "Passive Jobseekers," p. 18.

44. Judith MacBride-King, "Governments, Start Your Recruitment Campaigns," *Canadian HR Reporter*, October 8, 2007, p. 18.

45. S. L. Rynes and A. E. Barber, "Applicant Attraction Strategies: An Organizational Perspective," *Academy of Management Review* 15 (1990), pp. 286–310; J. A. Breaugh, *Recruitment: Science and Practice* (Boston: PWS-Kent, 1992), p. 34.

46. www.recruiting.forces.gc.ca, retrieved May 15, 2004.

47. D. M. Cable, L. Aiman-Smith, P. Mulvey, and J. R. I Edwards, "The Sources and Accuracy of Job Applicants' Beliefs About Organizational Culture," *Academy of Management Journal* 43 (2000), pp. 1076–85.

48. M. A. Conrad and S. D. Ashworth, "Recruiting Source Effectiveness: A Meta-Analysis and Reexamination of Two Rival Hypotheses," paper presented at annual meeting of Society of Industrial/Organizational Psychology, Chicago, 1986.

49. Breaugh, *Recruitment*.

50. Susan Singh, "Looking Inside for Leaders at CCL, Alliance Atlantis," *Canadian HR Reporter*, January 12, 2004, www.hrreporter.com, retrieved February 17, 2004.

51. Breaugh, *Recruitment*, pp. 113–114.

52. R. S. Schuler and S. E. Jackson, "Linking Competitive Strategies with Human Resource Management Practices," *Academy of Management Executive* 1 (1987), pp. 207–19.

53. "Quebec Targets Health Care Workers in France, Switzerland," *Canadian HR Reporter*, November 20, 2003, www.hrreporter.com, retrieved January 23, 2004.

54. Jessica Mintz, "Large Firms Increasingly Rely on Employees for Job Referrals," *The Wall Street Journal*, March 1, 2005, p. B4.

55. C. R. Wanberg, R. Kanfer, and J. T. Banas, "Predictors and Outcomes of Networking Intensity Among Job Seekers," *Journal of Applied Psychology* 85 (2000), pp. 491–503.

56. Breaugh, *Recruitment*, p. 87.

57. Steve Jones, "You've Come a Long Way Baby: What the Industry Offers Today," *Canadian HR Reporter*, November 5, 2001, www.hrreporter.com, retrieved May 16, 2004.

58. http://globeandmail.workopolis.com, retrieved February 17, 2004.

59. J. Reingold, "Casting for a Different Set of Characters," *BusinessWeek*, December 8, 1997, pp. 38–39.

60. J. Greenwald, "Invasion of the Body Snatchers," *Time*, April 23, 1984, p. 41.

61. P. Smith, "Sources Used by Employers When Hiring College Grads," *Personnel Journal*, February 1995, p. 25.

62. J. W. Boudreau and S. L. Rynes, "Role of Recruitment in Staffing Utility Analysis," *Journal of Applied Psychology* 70 (1985), pp. 354–66.

63. D. Anfuso, "3M's Staffing Strategy Promotes Productivity and Pride," *Personnel Journal*, February 1995, pp. 28–34.

64. www.rim.net, retrieved May 15, 2004.

65. http://client.njoyn.com/cl/xweb/XWeb.asp, retrieved December 12, 2004.

66. "Half of Résumés Coming by E-Mail," *Canadian HR Reporter*, February 23, 2004, p. 2.

67. J. Smith, "Is Online Recruiting Getting Easier?," *Workforce*, September 2, 2001, p. 1.

68. A. Salkever, "A Better Way to Float Your Résumé," *BusinessWeek Online*, October 9, 2000, pp. 1–2.

69. "Ernst & Young Becomes First Employer to Use Facebook," *CollegeRecruiter.com*, www.collegerecruiter.com, retrieved March 18, 2008.

70. Kris Maher, "Blogs Catch On as Online Tool for Job Seekers and Recruiters," *The Wall Street Journal*, September 28, 2004, p. B10.

71. Antonio Da Luz, "Video Enhances Online Job Ads," *Canadian HR Reporter*, February 11, 2008, p. 16.

72. Alice Snell, "Myth Dispelled: Executives Actually Search for Jobs Online," *Canadian HR Reporter*, May 21, 2007, p. 27.

73. R. Hawk, *The Recruitment Function* (New York: American Management Association, 1967).

74. C. K. Stevens, "Effects of Preinterview Beliefs on Applicants' Reactions to Campus Interviews," *Academy of Management Journal* 40 (1997), pp. 947–66.

Chapter 6

1. Jim Middlemiss, "Didn't You Check?," *National Post*, January 31, 2007, p. WK3; "Background Screening: Past, Present, and Future," *National Association of Background Checkers*, www.napbs.com/images/pdf/HistoryBackgroundScreening.pdf, retrieved April 6, 2008; www.backcheck.ca.

2. "Intelligence Officers" and "Stages in the 10 Recruitment Process," www.csis-scrs.gc.ca, retrieved June 23, 2004.

3. J. C. Nunnally, *Psychometric Theory* (New York: McGraw-Hill, 1978).

4. N. Schmitt, R. Z. Gooding, R. A. Noe, and M. Kirsch, "Meta-Analysis of Validity Studies Published Between 1964 and 1982 and the Investigation of Study Characteristics," *Personnel Psychology* 37 (1984), pp. 407–22.

5. C. H. Lawshe, "Inferences from Personnel Tests and Their Validity," *Journal of Applied Psychology* 70 (1985), pp. 237–38.

6. D. D. Robinson, "Content-Oriented Personnel Selection in a Small Business Setting," *Personnel Psychology* 34 (1981), pp. 77–87.

7. F. L. Schmidt and J. E. Hunter, "The Future of Criterion-Related Validity," *Personnel Psychology* 33 (1980), pp. 41–60; F. L. Schmidt, J. E. Hunter, and K. Pearlman, "Task Differences as Moderators of Aptitude Test Validity: A Red Herring," *Journal of Applied Psychology* 66 (1982), pp. 166–85; R. L. Gutenberg, R. D. Arvey, H. G. Osburn, and R. P. Jeanneret, "Moderating Effects of Decision-Making/Information Processing Dimensions on Test Validities," *Journal of Applied Psychology* 68 (1983), pp. 600–8.

8. Canadian Human Rights Commission, "A Guide to Screening and Selection in Employment," www.chrcen.asp, retrieved April 3, 2004.

9. Middlemiss, ibid.

10. T. W. Dougherty, D. B. Turban, and J. C. Callender, "Confirming First Impressions in the Employment Interview: A Field Study of Interviewer Behavior," *Journal of Applied Psychology* 79 (1994), pp. 659–65.

11. Alice Snell, "Using Technology in Sourcing Talent," *Canadian HR Reporter*, January 20, 2007, www.hrreporter.com, retrieved April 6, 2008.

12. J. B. Copeland, "Revenge of the Fired," *Newsweek*, February 16, 1987, pp. 46–47.

13. S. Greengard, "Are You Well Armed to Screen Applicants?," *Personnel Journal*, December 1995, pp. 84–95.

14. A. Ryan and M. Lasek, "Negligent Hiring and Defamation: Areas of Liability Related to Preemployment Inquiries," *Personnel Psychology* 44 (1991), pp. 293–319.

15. A. Long, "Addressing the Cloud over Employee References: A Survey of Recently Enacted State Legislation," *William and Mary Law Review* 39 (October 1997), pp. 177–228.

16. Lynne Van Buskirk "Can I Get a Reference?," *Canadian HR Reporter*, March 10, 2008, www.hrreporter.com, retrieved April 3, 2008.

17. Ann Zimmerman, "Wal-Mart to Probe Job Applicants," *The Wall Street Journal*, August 12, 2004, pp. A3, A6.

18. "Companies Step Up Checks as Applicants Turn to Fraud," *The Globe and Mail*, March 24, 2004, p. CS.

19. Shannon Klie, "Weeding Out the Fakes," *Canadian HR Reporter*, May 7, 2007, www.hrreporter.com, retrieved April 6, 2008.

20. *PRSI Screening News*, November 2002, p. 1, www.prsinet.com/newsletter, retrieved February 13, 2004.

21. Public Service Commission of Canada, "Office Skills Test," July 7, 2007, www.psc-cfp.gc.ca/ppc/assessment_pg2_ba_e.htm, retrieved April 6, 2008.

22. "RCMP Fact Sheets—Recruitment," www.rcmp-grc.gc.ca/factsheets/fact_recruit_e.htm, retrieved April 6, 2008.

23. L. C. Buffardi, E. A. Fleishman, R. A. Morath, and P. M. McCarthy, "Relationships Between Ability Requirements and Human Errors in Job Tasks," *Journal of Applied Psychology* 85 (2000), pp. 551–64; J. Hogan, "Structure of Physical Performance in Occupational Tasks," *Journal of Applied Psychology* 76 (1991), pp. 495–507.

24. www.psc-cfp.gc.ca/ppc/assessment, retrieved February 13, 2004.

25. M. J. Ree, J. A. Earles, and M. S. Teachout, "Predicting Job Performance: Not Much More Than *g*," *Journal of Applied Psychology* 79 (1994), pp. 518–24; L. S. Gottfredson, "The *g* Factor in Employment," *Journal of Vocational Behavior* 29 (1986), pp. 293–96; J. E. Hunter and R. H. Hunter, "Validity and Utility of Alternative Predictors of Job Performance," *Psychological Bulletin* 96 (1984), pp. 72–98; Gutenberg et al., "Moderating Effects"; F. L. Schmidt, J. G. Berner, and J. E. Hunter, "Racial Differences in Validity of Employment Tests: Reality or Illusion," *Journal of Applied Psychology* 58 (1974), pp. 5–6; J. A. LePine, J. A. Colquitt, and A. Erez, "Adaptability to Changing Task Contexts: Effects of General Cognitive Ability, Conscientiousness, and Openness to Experience," *Personnel Psychology* 53 (2000), pp. 563–93.

26. F. L. Schmidt and J. E. Hunter, "The Validity and Utility of Selection Methods in Personnel Psychology: Practical and Theoretical Implications of 85 Years of Research Findings," *Psychological Bulletin* 124 (1998), pp. 262–74.

27. W. Arthur, E. A. Day, T. L. McNelly, and P. S. Edens, "Meta-Analysis of the Criterion-Related Validity of Assessment Center Dimensions," *Personnel Psychology* 56 (2003), pp. 125–54; C. E. Lance, T. A. Lambert, A. G. Gewin, F. Lievens, and J. M. Conway, "Revised Estimates of Dimension and Exercise Variance Components in Assessment Center Postexercise Dimension Ratings," *Journal of Applied Psychology* 89 (2004), pp. 377–85.

28. W. S. Dunn, M. K. Mount, M. R. Barrick, and D. S. Ones, "Relative Importance of Personality and General Mental Ability on Managers' Judgments of Applicant Qualifications," *Journal of Applied Psychology* 79 (1995), pp. 500–9; P. M. Wright, K. M. Kacmar, G. C. McMahan, and K. Deleeuw, "P = f(M × A): Cognitive Ability as a Moderator of the Relationship Between Personality and Job Performance," *Journal of Management* 21 (1995), pp. 1129–39.

29. M. Mount, M. R. Barrick, and J. P. Strauss, "Validity of Observer Ratings of the Big Five Personality Factors," *Journal of Applied Psychology* 79 (1994), pp. 272–80.

30. "Looking for a Good Fit," *Canadian HR Reporter*, November 28, 2006, www.hrreporter.com, retrieved April 3, 2008.

31. Todd Humber, "Psychometric Testing Often Misused in Recruitment," *Canadian HR Reporter*, May 17, 2004, p. G5.

32. Saul Hansell, "Google Answer to Filling Jobs Is an Algorithm," *The New York Times*, January 3, 2007, www.nytimes.com/2007/01/03/technology/03google.html, retrieved April 3, 2008.

33. D. S. One, C. Viswesvaran, and E. L. Schmidt, "Comprehensive Meta-Analysis of Integrity Test Validities: Findings and Implications for Personnel Selection and Theories of Job Performance," *Journal of Applied Psychology* 78 (1993), pp. 679–703; H. J. Bernardin and D. K. Cooke, "Validity of an Honesty Test in Predicting Theft Among Convenience Store Employees," *Academy of Management Journal* 36 (1993), pp. 1079–1106.

34. www.chrc-ccdp.caflegislation, retrieved May 31, 2004.

35. Todd Humber, "Pre-employment Drug Tests Dealt Blow," *Canadian HR Reporter*, July 17, 2006, www.hrreporter.com, retrieved April 8, 2008.

36. Canadian Human Rights Commission website, www.chrc-ccdp.ca/legislation_policies/policies-en.asp, retrieved April 6, 2008.

37. M. A. McDaniel, E. P. Morgeson, E. G. Finnegan, M. A. Campion, and E. P. Braverman, "Use of Situational Judgment Tests to Predict Job Performance: A Clarification of the Literature," *Journal of Applied Psychology* 86 (2001), pp. 730–40; J. Clavenger, G. M. Perreira, D. Weichmann, N. Schmitt, and V. S. Harvey, "Incremental Validity of Situational Judgment Tests," *Journal of Applied Psychology* 86 (2001), pp. 410–17.

38. M. A. Campion, J. E. Campion, and J. P. Hudson, "Structured Interviewing: A Note of Incremental Validity and Alternative Question Types," *Journal of Applied Psychology* 79 (1994), pp. 998–1002; E. D. Pulakos and N. Schmitt, "Experience-Based and Situational Interview Questions: Studies of Validity," *Personnel Psychology* 48 (1995), pp. 289–308.

39. J. Cleaver, "What Kind of Question Is That?," *Chicago Tribune*, April 24, 2002, sec. 6, pp. 1, 4.

40. Todd Humber, "How BMO Financial Selects Employees," *Canadian HR Reporter*, December 6, 2004, p. G2.

41. N. Schmitt, F. L. Oswald, B. H. Kim, M. A. Gillespie, L. J. Ramsey, and T. Y Yoo, "The Impact of Elaboration on Socially Desirable Responding and the Validity of Biodata Measures," *Journal of Applied Psychology* 88 (2003), pp. 979–88; N. Schmitt and C. Kunce, "The Effects of Required Elaboration of Answers to Biodata Questions," *Personnel Psychology* 55 (2002), pp. 569–87.

42. Hunter and Hunter, "Validity and Utility of Alternative Predictors of Job Performance."

43. R. Pingitore, B. L. Dugoni, R. S. Tindale, and B. Spring, "Bias Against Overweight Job Applicants in a Simulated Interview," *Journal of Applied Psychology* 79 (1994), pp. 184–90.

44. M. A. McDaniel, D. L. Whetzel, F. L. Schmidt, and S. D. Maurer, "The Validity of Employment Interviews: A Comprehensive Review and Meta-Analysis," *Journal of Applied Psychology* 79 (1994), pp. 599–616; A. I. Huffcutt and W. A. Arthur, "Hunter and Hunter (1984) Revisited: Interview Validity for Entry-Level Jobs," *Journal of Applied Psychology* 79 (1994), pp. 184–90.

45. Y. Ganzach, A. N. Kluger, and N. Klayman, "Making Decisions from an Interview: Expert Measurement and Mechanical Combination," *Personnel Psychology* 53(2000), pp. 1–21; G. Stasser and W. Titus, "Effects of Information Load and Percentage of Shared Information on the Dissemination of Unshared Information During Group Discussion," *Journal of Personality and Social Psychology* 53 (1987), pp. 81–93.

46. C. H. Middendorf and T. H. Macan, "Note-Taking in the Interview: Effects on Recall and Judgments," *Journal of Applied Psychology* 87 (2002), pp. 293–303.

Chapter 7

1. www.pcl.com/Careers/CollegeofConstruction.aspx, retrieved May 22, 2008; www.engineering.ualberta.ca, retrieved February 7, 2005; www.pcl.com, retrieved May 22, 2008.

2. "Developing Skills in the Canadian Workplace," *Canadian Workplace Gazette* 2, no. 1, p. 98, http://labour-travail.hrdc-drhc.gc.ca.

3. Jon Younger, Norm Smallwood, and Dave Ulrich, "Developing Your Organization's Brand as a Talent Developer," *HR: Human Resource Planning* 30, no. 2 (2007), p. 21.

4. P. Derek Hughes and Michael Grant, "Learning and Development Outlook 2007" (Ottawa: Conference Board of Canada, April 23, 2007), p. 10.

5. Ibid., p. 19.

6. Ibid., p. i.

7. Ibid., p. 14.

8. I. L. Goldstein, E. P. Braverman, and H. Goldstein, "Needs Assessment," in *Developing Human Resources*, ed. K. N. Wexley (Washington, DC: Bureau of National Affairs, 1991), pp. 5-35–5-75.

9. J. Z. Rouillier and I. L. Goldstein, "Determinants of the Climate for Transfer of Training" (presented at Society of Industrial/Organizational Psychology meetings, St. Louis, MO, 1991); J. S. Russell, J. R. Terborg, and M. L. Powers, "Organizational Performance and Organizational Level Training and Support," *Personnel Psychology* 38 (1985), pp. 849–63; H. Baumgartel, G. J. Sullivan, and L. E. Dunn, "How Organizational Climate and Personality Affect the Payoff from Advanced Management Training Sessions," *Kansas Business Review* 5 (1978), pp. 1–10.

10. R. A. Noe, "Trainees' Attributes and Attitudes: Neglected Influences on Training Effectiveness," *Academy of Management Review* 11 (1986), pp. 736–49; T. T. Baldwin, R. T. Magjuka, and B. T. Loher, "The Perils of Participation: Effects of Choice on Trainee Motivation and Learning," *Personnel Psychology* 44 (1991), pp. 51–66; S. L Tannenbaum, J. E. Mathieu, E. Salas, and J. A. Cannon-Bowers, "Meeting Trainees' Expectations: The Influence of Training Fulfillment on the Development of Commitment, Self-Efficacy, and Motivation," *Journal of Applied Psychology* 76 (1991), pp. 759–69.

11. L. H. Peters, E. J. O'Connor, and J. R. Eulberg, "Situational Constraints: Sources, Consequences, and Future Considerations," in *Research in Personnel and Human Resource Management*, ed. K. M. Rowland and G. R. Ferris (Greenwich, CT: JAI Press, 1985), vol. 3, pp. 79–114; E. J. O'Connor, L. H. Peters, A. Pooyan, J. Weekley, B. Frank, and B. Erenkranz, "Situational Constraints' Effects on Performance, Affective Reactions, and Turnover: A Field Replication and Extension," *Journal of Applied Psychology* 69 (1984), pp. 663–72; D. J. Cohen, "What Motivates Trainees?," *Training and Development Journal*, November 1990, pp. 91–93; Russell, Terborg, and Powers, "Organizational Performance."

12. B. Mager, *Preparing Instructional Objectives*, 2nd ed. (Belmont, CA: Lake Publishing, 1984); B. J. Smith and B. L. Delahaye, *How to Be an Effective Trainer*, 2nd ed. (New York: Wiley, 1987).

13. "Community Report 2003: NAIT/Bring on the Future," www.nait.ab.ca, retrieved March 1, 2004.

14. G. Yohe, "The Best of Both?," *Human Resource Executive*, March 6, 2002, pp. 35, 38–39.

15. G. Stevens and E. Stevens, "The Truth About EPSS," *Training and Development* 50 (1996), pp. 59–61.

16. "More About DiscoverU," *Corporate Reports*, February 6, 2005, www.vancity.com/Community/AboutUs/CorporateReports, retrieved February 6, 2005.

17. R. W. Glever, *Apprenticeship Lessons from Abroad* (Columbus, OH: National Center for Research in Vocational Education, 1986).

18. Red Seal Program, Human Resources Development Canada, www.red-seal.ca/English/redseal_e.shtml, retrieved March 21, 2004.

19. Ibid.

20. www.sauder.ubc.ca/ccc/employers/mba_internships.cfm, retrieved March 9, 2004.

21. www.uregina.ca/coop/students/current/handbook.shtml, retrieved March 11, 2004.

22. W. J. Rothwell and H. C. Kanzanas, "Planned OJT Is Productive OJT," *Training and Development Journal,* October 1990, pp. 53–56.

23. CATSA News, April 2007, p. 6 www.catsa-acsta.gc.ca/english/media/bulletin/2007-04.pdf, retrieved May 23, 2008.

24. N. Adams, "Lessons from the Virtual World," *Training,* June 1995, pp. 45–48.

25. Pat Galagan, "Second That," *T+D,* February 2008, pp. 4, 34–37.

26. www.stratxsimulations.com/markstrat_online_home.aspx, retrieved May 23, 2008.

27. G. P. Latham and L. M. Saari, "Application of Social Learning Theory to Training Supervisors Through Behavior Modeling," *Journal of Applied Psychology* 64 (1979), pp. 239–46.

28. Manual London and Valerie I. Sessa, "How Groups Learn, Continuously," *Human Resource Management,* Winter 2007, p. 651.

29. D. Brown and D. Harvey, *An Experiential Approach to Organizational Development* (Englewood Cliffs, NJ: Prentice Hall, 2000); and J. Schettler, "Learning by Doing," *Training,* April 2002, pp. 38–43.

30. Kim Willsher, "French Firms Drop Bungee for Bouillon," *Guardian Unlimited,* February 25, 2005, www.guardian.co.uk.

31. C. Clements, R. J. Wagner, C. C. Roland, "The Ins and Outs of Experiential Training," *Training and Development,* February 1995, pp. 52–56.

32. Lesley Young, "All in the Family at Toronto Hydro," *Canadian HR Reporter,* March 24, 2008, p. 16.

33. P. Froiland, "Action Learning," *Training,* January 1994, pp. 27–34.

34. C. E. Schneier, "Training and Development Programs: What Learning Theory and Research Have to Offer," *Personnel Journal,* April 1974, pp. 288–93; M. Knowles, "Adult Learning," in *Training and Development Handbook,* 3rd ed., ed. R. L. Craig (New York: McGraw-Hill, 1987), pp. 168–79; R. Zemke and S. Zemke, "30 Things We Know for Sure About Adult Learning," *Training,* June 1981, pp. 45–52; B. J. Smith and B. L. Delahaye, *How to Be an Effective Trainer,* 2nd ed. (New York: Wiley, 1987).

35. K. A. Smith-Jentsch, F. G. Jentsch, S. C. Payne, and E. Salas, "Can Pretraining Experiences Explain Individual Differences in Learning?," *Journal of Applied Psychology* 81 (1996), pp. 110–16.

36. W. McGehee and P. W. Thayer, *Training in Business and Industry* (New York: Wiley, 1961).

37. R. M. Gagne and K. L. Medsker, *The Condition of Learning* (Fort Worth, TX: Harcourt-Brace, 1996).

38. J. C. Naylor and G. D. Briggs, "The Effects of Task Complexity and Task Organization on the Relative Efficiency of Part and Whole Training Methods," *Journal of Experimental Psychology* 65 (1963), pp. 217–24.

39. "1998 Workplace Literacy Best Practices Reader," www.conferenceboard.ca/education/pdf/Awards/litread.pdf, retrieved October 21, 2008.

40. Asha Tomlinson, "Math, Reading Skills Holding Employees Back," *Canadian HR Reporter,* October 21, 2002, www.hrreporter.com, retrieved February 11, 2005.

41. Conference Board of Canada, "Awards for Excellence in Workplace Literacy Large Business Winner, 2002 Palliser Furniture: Case Study December 2002," www.conferenceboard.ca, retrieved February 28, 2004.

42. Levels of training evaluation by Janice Cooney and Allison Cowan, "The Conference Board of Canada: Training and Development Outlook 2003: Canadian Organizations Continue to Under-Invest," May 2003, pp. 15, 16, 0070979863 0-88763-584-9.

43. Ibid.

44. K. Mantyla, *Blended E-Learning* (Alexandria, VA: ASTD, 2001).

45. Adapted from "Measurement Standards: Training Evaluation and Effectiveness Reporting," copyright 2003 TO Bank Financial Group Learning and Development Measurement 2003, www.cstd.ca/nettworks/Eva/sampleTD.doc, retrieved March 10, 2004.

46. M. R. Louis, "Surprise and Sense Making: What Newcomers Experience in Entering Unfamiliar Organizational Settings," *Administrative Science Quarterly* 25 (1980), pp. 226–51.

47. Kira Vermond, "Rolling Out the Welcome Mat," *The Globe and Mail,* April 26, 2008, www.theglobeandmail.com, retrieved April 28, 2008.

48. Ibid.

49. Ibid.

50. Danielle Harder, "Diversity Takes Flight at Air Canada," *Canadian HR Reporter,* May 5, 2008, www.hrreporter.com, retrieved May 23, 2008.

51. S. Rynes and B. Rosen, "What Makes Diversity Programs Work?," *HR Magazine,* October 1994, pp. 67–73; Rynes and Rosen, A Field Survey of Factors Affecting the Adoption and Perceived Success of Diversity Training," *Personnel Psychology* 48, no. 2 (1995), pp. 247–271; J. Gordon, "Different from What? Diversity as a Performance Issue," *Training,* May 1995, pp. 25–33.

52. Tavia Grant, "Diversity: Easier Said Than Done, but with Tenacity, It Can Be Done," *The Globe and Mail,* April 25, 2008, www.theglobeandmail.com, retrieved April 28, 2008.

53. M. London, *Managing the Training Enterprise* (San Francisco: Jossey-Bass, 1989).

54. R. W. Pace, P. C. Smith, and G. E. Mills, *Human Resource Development* (Englewood Cliffs, NJ: Prentice Hall, 1991); W. Fitzgerald, "Training versus Development," *Training and Development Journal,* May 1992, pp. 81–84; R. A. Noe, S. L. Wilk, E. J. Mullen, and J. E. Wanek, "Employee Development: Issues in Construct Definition and Investigation of Antecedents," in

Improving Training Effectiveness in Work Organizations, ed. J. K. Ford (Mahwah, NJ: Lawrence Erlbaum, 1997), pp. 153–89.

55. J. H. Greenhaus and G. A. Callanan, *Career Management,* 2nd ed. (Fort Worth, TX: Dryden Press, 1994).

56. R. J. Campbell, "HR Development Strategies," in *Developing Human Resources,* ed. K. N. Wexley (Washington, DC: BNA Books, 1991), pp. 5-1–5-34; M. A. Sheppeck and C. A. Rhodes, "Management Development: Revised Thinking in Light of New Events of Strategic Importance," *Human Resource Planning* 11 (1988), pp. 159–72; B. Keys and J. Wolf, "Management Education: Current Issues and Emerging Trends," *Journal of Management* 14 (1988), pp. 205–29; L. M. Saari, T. R. Johnson, S. D. McLaughlin, and D. Zimmerle, "A Survey of Management Training and Education Practices in U.S. Companies," *Personnel Psychology* 41 (1988), pp. 731–44.

57. "CEOs Talk—Leadership Development," *Canadian HR Reporter,* December 1, 2003, pp. 1, 2, www.hrreporter .com, retrieved February 17, 2004.

58. David Brown, "Banking on Leadership Development," *Canadian HR Reporter,* January 27, 2005, p. 7.

59. A. Howard and D. W. Bray, *Managerial Lives in Transition: Advancing Age and Changing Times* (New York: Guilford, 1988); J. Bolt, *Executive Development* (New York: Harper Business, 1989); J. R. Hintichs and G. P. Hollenbeck, "Leadership Development," in *Developing Human Resources,* pp. 5-221–5-237.

60. Joyce Rowlands, "Soft Skills Give Hard Edge," *The Globe and Mail,* June 9, 2004, p. C8.

61. Ibid.

62. C. D. McCauley, M. M. Lombardo, and C. J. Usher, "Diagnosing Management Development Needs: An Instrument Based on How Managers Develop," *Journal of Management* 15 (1989), pp. 389–403.

63. B. Pfau and I. Kay, "Does 360-Degree Feedback Negatively Affect Company Performance?," *HR Magazine* 47 (2002), pp. 54–59; J. F. Brett and L. E. Atwater, "360-Degree Feedback: Accuracy, Reactions, and Perceptions of Usefulness," *Journal of Applied Psychology* 86 (2001), pp. 930–42.

64. M. W. McCall Jr., *High Flyers* (Boston: Harvard Business School Press, 1998).

65. R. S. Snell, "Congenial Ways of Learning: So Near yet So Far," *Journal of Management Development* 9 (1990), pp. 17–23.

66. M. McCall, M. Lombardo, and A. Morrison, *Lessons of Experience* (Lexington, MA: Lexington Books, 1988); M. W. McCall, "Developing Executives Through Work Experiences," *Human Resource Planning* 11 (1988), pp. 1–11; M. N. Ruderman, P. J. Ohlott, and C. D. McCauley, "Assessing Opportunities for Leadership Development," in *Measures of Leadership,* pp. 547–62; C. D. McCauley, L. J. Esttman, and P. J. Ohlott, "Linking Management Selection and Development Through Stretch Assignments," *Human Resource Management* 34 (1995), pp. 93–115.

67. C. D. McCauley, M. N. Ruderman, P. J. Ohlott, and J. E. Morrow, "Assessing the Developmental Components of Managerial Jobs," *Journal of Applied Psychology* 79 (1994), pp. 544–60.

68. Sue Nador, "Don't Let Strengths Go to Waste," *Canadian HR Reporter,* June 14, 2004, p. 13.

69. Andrew Wahl, "Leaders Wanted," *Canadian Business,* March 1–14, 2004, pp. 33, 34.

70. M. London, *Developing Managers* (San Francisco: Jossey-Bass, 1985); M. A. Camion, L. Cheraskin, and M. J. Stevens, "Career-Related Antecedents and Outcomes of Job Rotation," *Academy of Management Journal* 37 (1994), pp. 1518–42; London, *Managing the Training Enterprise.*

71. Wahl, ibid.

72. Ibid.

73. L. Cheraskin and M. Campion, "Study Clarifies Job Rotation Benefits," *Personnel Journal,* November 1996, pp. 31–38.

74. R. A. Noe, B. D. Steffy, and A. E. Barber, "An Investigation of the Factors Influencing Employees' Willingness to Accept Mobility Opportunities," *Personnel Psychology* 41 (1988), pp. 559–80; S. Gould and L. E. Penley, "A Study of the Correlates of Willingness to Relocate," *Academy of Management Journal* 28 (1984), pp. 472–78; J. Landau and T. H. Hammer, "Clerical Employees' Perceptions of Intraorganizational Career Opportunities," *Academy of Management Journal* 29 (1986), pp. 385–405; J. M. Brett and A. H. Reilly, "On the Road Again: Predicting the Job Transfer Decision," *Journal of Applied Psychology* 73 (1988), pp. 614–20.

75. R. E. Silverman, "Mercer Tries to Keep Employees Through Its 'Externship' Program," *The Wall Street Journal,* November 7, 2000, p. B18.

76. B. Bounds, "Give Me a Break," *The Wall Street Journal,* May 5, 2000, pp. W1, W4.

77. D. B. Turban and T. W. Dougherty, "Role of Protégé Personality in Receipt of Mentoring and Career Success," *Academy of Management Journal* 37 (1994), pp. 688–702; E. A. Fagenson, "Mentoring: Who Needs It? A Comparison of Protégés' and Non-Protégés' Needs for Power, Achievement, Affiliation, and Autonomy," *Journal of Vocational Behavior* 41 (1992), pp. 48–60.

78. A. H. Geiger, "Measures for Mentors," *Training and Development Journal,* February 1992, pp. 65–67.

79. K. E. Kram, *Mentoring at Work: Developmental Relationships in Organizational Life* (Glenview, IL: Scott, Foresman, 1985); L. L. Phillips-Jones, "Establishing a Formalized Mentoring Program," *Training and Development Journal* 2 (1983), pp. 38–42; K. Kram, "Phases of the Mentoring Relationship," *Academy of Management Journal* 26 (1983), pp. 608–25; G. T. Chao, P. M. Walz, and P. D. Gardner, "Formal and Informal Mentorships: A Comparison of Mentoring Functions and Contrasts with Nonmentored Counterparts," *Personnel Psychology* 45 (1992), pp. 619–36.

80. Keynote presented by Nancy Nazer, Consultant Bell Canada-Mentoring Connections National Conference, www.mentorcanada/ca/en/en_keynote/nnazer .ppt, retrieved March 29, 2004.

81. R. A. Noe, D. Greenberger, and S. Wang, "Mentoring: What We Know and Where We Might Go," in *Research in Personnel and Human Resources Management*, vol. 21, ed. G. R. Ferris and J. J. Martocchio (Oxford: Elsevier Science, 2002), pp. 129–73.

82. D. B. Peterson and M. D. Hicks, *Leader as Coach* (Minneapolis: Personnel Decisions, 1996).

83. David Brown, "Mentoring Boosts Retention, T&D. But It's a Long-Term Game," *Canadian HR Reporter*, July 12, 2004, p. 7.

84. J. S. Lublin, "Building a Better CEO," *The Wall Street Journal*, April 14, 2000, pp. B1, B4.

85. B. Baumann, J. Duncan, S. E. Former, and Z. Leibowitz, "Amoco Primes the Talent Pump," *Personnel Journal*, February 1996, pp. 79–84.

86. Cooney and Cowan, "Training and Development Outlook 2003," p. 16.

87. Claudine Kapel and Catherine Shepherd, "Career Ladders Create Common Language for Defining Jobs," *Canadian HR Reporter*, June 14, 2004, p. 15.

88. Mary Teresa Bitti, "Online Career Branding," *The National Post*, November 21, 2007, http://digital .nationalpost.com, retrieved November 21, 2007.

89. "Women in Management in Canada," July 2008, www.catalyst.org/publications/247/women-in-management-in-Canada, retrieved July 28, 2008.

90. Alice H. Eagly and Linda L. Carli, "Women and the Labyrinth of Leadership," *Harvard Business Review*, September 2007, pp. 63–71.

91. L. A. Mainiero, "Getting Anointed for Advancement: The Case of Executive Women," *Academy of Management Executive* 8 (1994), pp. 53–67; J. S. Lublin, "Women at Top Still Are Distant from CEO Jobs," *The Wall Street Journal*, February 28, 1995, pp. B1, B5; P. Tharenov, S. Latimer, and D. Conroy, "How Do You Make It to the Top? An Examination of Influences on Women's and Men's Managerial Advancements," *Academy of Management Journal* 37 (1994), pp. 899–931.

92. U.S. Department of Labor, *A Report on the Glass Ceiling Initiative* (Washington, DC: Labor Department, 1991); R. A. Noe, "Women and Mentoring: A Review and Research Agenda," *Academy of Management Review* 13 (1988), pp. 65–78; B. R. Ragins and J. L. Cotton, "Easier Said Than Done: Gender Differences in Perceived Barriers to Gaining a Mentor," *Academy of Management Journal* 34 (1991), pp. 939–51.

93. D. McCracken, "Winning the Talent War for Women," *Harvard Business Review*, November/December 2000, pp. 159–67.

94. Wahl, ibid., p. 33.

95. W. J. Rothwell, *Effective Succession Planning*, 2nd ed. (New York: AMACOM, 2001).

96. B. E. Dowell, "Succession Planning," in *Implementing Organizational Interventions*, ed. J. Hedge and E. D. Pulakos (San Francisco: Jossey-Bass, 2002), pp. 78–109.

97. C. B. Derr, C. Jones, and E. L. Toomey, "Managing High-Potential Employees: Current Practices in Thirty-Three U.S. Corporations," *Human Resource Management* 27 (1988), pp. 273–90; K. M. Nowack, "The Secrets of Succession," *Training and Development* 48 (1994), pp. 49–54; J. S. Lublin, "An Overseas Stint Can Be a Ticket to the Top," *The Wall Street Journal*, January 29, 1996, pp. B1, B2.

Chapter 8

1. "Wardrop Engineering: People, Passion, Performance," *Achieving Business Excellence*, February, 2008, www .bus-ex.com/index.php?view+article&id=422, retrieved July 30, 2008; "Canada's Top 100 Employers: Wardrop Engineering Inc.," www.eluta.ca/work_at_wardrop, retrieved July 30, 2008; www.wardrop.com.

2. C. Lee, "Performance Appraisal: Can We Manage Away the Curse?," *Training*, May 1996, pp. 44–49.

3. Stephen Clarke, "Compensation Planning Outlook 2008" (Ottawa: Conference Board of Canada, October 2007), p. 17.

4. Ibid., p. 16.

5. "Measuring People Power," *Fortune*, October 2, 2000.

6. Wallace Immen, "Handling the First 100 Days on the Job," *The Globe and Mail*, March 14, 2008, p. C2.

7. G. Bylinsky, "How Companies Spy on Employees," Fortune, November 4, 1991, pp. 131–40; T. L. Griffith, "Teaching Big Brother to Be a Team Player: Computer Monitoring and Quality," *Academy of Management Executive* (1993), pp. 73–80.

8. Karen Williams and Caroline Beach, "Laborious Task of Tracking Skills and Performance Streamlined by Technology," *Canadian HR Reporter*, May 3, 2004, p. 12.

9. www.performancereview.com/pfasp/main.asp, retrieved May 24, 2004.

10. Mike Moralis, "Trainers Morph Into New Role," *Canadian HR Reporter*, November 22, 2004, www .hrreporter.com, retrieved February 15, 2005.

11. Claudine Kapel and Catherine Shepherd, "Four Keys to Goals and Performance," *Canadian HR Reporter*, February 23, 2004, www.hrreporter.com, retrieved February 15, 2005.

12. David Brown, "Performance Management Elusive for Public-Sector HR," *Canadian HR Reporter*, February 23, 2004, www.hrreporter, retrieved February 15, 2005.

13. Stephen Clarke, "Compensation Planning Outlook 2008," The Conference Board of Canada, p. 17.

14. Uyen Vu, "Marking Staff on a Bell Curve," *Canadian HR Reporter*, July 14, 2003, www.hrreporter.com, retrieved March 5, 2004.

15. P. Smith and L. Kendall, "Retranslation of Expectations: An Approach to the Construction of Unambiguous

Anchors for Rating Scales," *Journal of Applied Psychology* 47 (1963), pp. 149–55.

16. K. Murphy and J. Constans, "Behavioral Anchors as a Source of Bias in Rating," *Journal of Applied Psychology* 72 (1987), pp. 573–77; M. Piotrowski, J. Bames-Farrel, and F. Estig, "Behaviorally Anchored Bias: A Replication and Extension of Murphy and Constans," *Journal of Applied Psychology* 74 (1989), pp. 823–26.

17. G. Latham and K. Wexley, *Increasing Productivity Through Performance Appraisal* (Boston: Addison-Wesley, 1981).

18. U. Wiersma and G. Latham, "The Practicality of Behavioral Observation Scales, Behavioral Expectation Scales, and Trait Scales," *Personnel Psychology* 39 (1986), pp. 619–28.

19. D. C. Anderson, C. Crowell, J. Sucec, K. Gilligan, and M. Wikoff, "Behavior Management of Client Contacts in a Real Estate Brokerage: Getting Agents to Sell More," *Journal of Organizational Behavior Management* 4 (2001), pp. 580–90; F. Luthans and R. Kreitner, *Organizational Behavior Modification and Beyond* (Glenview, IL: Scott, Foresman, 1975).

20. K. L. Langeland, C. M. Jones, and T. C. Mawhinney, "Improving Staff Performance in a Community Mental Health Setting: Job Analysis, Training, Goal Setting, Feedback, and Years of Data," *Journal of Organizational Behavior Management* 18 (1998), pp. 21–43.

21. J. Komaki, R. Collins, and P. Penn, "The Role of Performance Antecedents and Consequences in Work Motivation," *Journal of Applied Psychology* 67 (1982), pp. 334–40.

22. S. Snell, "Control Theory in Strategic Human Resource Management: The Mediating Effect of Administrative Information," *Academy of Management Journal* 35 (1992), pp. 292–327.

23. R. Pritchard, S. Jones, P. Roth, K. Stuebing, and S. Ekeberg, "The Evaluation of an Integrated Approach to Measuring Organizational Productivity," *Personnel Psychology* 42 (1989), pp. 69–115.

24. G. Odiorne, *MBO II: A System of Managerial Leadership for the 80's* (Belmont, CA: Pitman Publishers, 1986).

25. R. Rodgers and J. Hunter, "Impact of Management by Objectives on Organizational Productivity," *Journal of Applied Psychology* 76 (1991), pp. 322–26.

26. P. Wright, J. George, S. Farnsworth, and G. McMahan, "Productivity and Extra-Role Behavior: The Effects of Goals and Incentives on Spontaneous Helping," *Journal of Applied Psychology* 78, no. 3 (1993), pp. 374–81.

27. G. Latham and K. Wexley, *Increasing Productivity Through Performance Appraisal* (Boston: Addison-Wesley, 1981).

28. "What Is a Balanced Scorecard?," www.2gc.co/UK/pdf/2GC-FAQ1.pdf, retrieved July 14, 2004.

29. Cam Scholey, "Alignment—Has Your Organization Got It?," *CMA Management* 81, no. 6, pp. 16–18.

30. Mehrdad Derayeh and Stephane Brutus, "Learning from Others' 360-Degree Experiences," *Canadian HR Reporter*, February 10, 2003, www.hrreporter.com, retrieved February 15, 2005.

31. R. Heneman, K. Wexley, and M. Moore, "Performance Rating Accuracy: A Critical Review," *Journal of Business Research* 15 (1987), pp. 431–48.

32. T. Becker and R. Klimoski, "A Field Study of the Relationship Between the Organizational Feedback Environment and Performance," *Personnel Psychology* 42 (1989), pp. 343–58; H. M. Findley, W. F. Giles, K. W. Mossholder, "Performance Appraisal and Systems Facets: Relationships with Contextual Performance," *Journal of Applied Psychology* 85 (2000), pp. 634–40.

33. K. Wexley and R. Klimoski, "Performance Appraisal: An Update," in *Research in Personnel and Human Resource Management*, vol. 2, ed. K. Rowland and G. Ferris (Greenwich, CT: JAI Press, 1984).

34. F. Landy and J. Farr, *The Measurement of Work Performance: Methods, Theory, and Applications* (New York: Academic Press, 1983).

35. G. McEvoy and P. Buller, "User Acceptance of Peer Appraisals in an Industrial Setting," *Personnel Psychology* 40 (1987), pp. 785–97.

36. D. Antonioni, "The Effects of Feedback Accountability on Upward Appraisal Ratings," *Personnel Psychology* 47 (1994), pp. 349–56.

37. John Kiska, "Do an Employee Self-Assessment," *HR Professional Magazine*, February/March 2004, www.hrpao.org/knowledge_Centre/HR_Professional/2003_issues, retrieved May 28, 2004.

38. R. Steel and N. Ovalle, "Self-Appraisal Based on Supervisor Feedback," *Personnel Psychology* 37 (1984), pp. 667–85; L. E. Atwater, "The Advantages and Pitfalls of Self-Assessment in Organizations," in *Performance Appraisal: State of the Art in Practice*, ed. J. W. Smither (San Francisco: Jossey-Bass, 1998), pp. 331–65.

39. Geoff Kirbyson, "Market Research Firm Lands Major Contract, *Winnipeg Free Press*, July 19, 2004, p. 07.

40. J. Bernardin, C. Hagan, J. Kane, and P. Villanova, "Effective Performance Management: A Focus on Precision, Customers, and Situational Constraints," in *Performance Appraisal: State of the Art in Practice*, pp. 3–48.

41. K. Wexley and W. Nemeroff, "Effects of Racial Prejudice, Race of Applicant, and Biographical Similarity on Interviewer Evaluations of Job Applicants," *Journal of Social and Behavioral Sciences* 20 (1974), pp. 66–78.

42. Phillip L. Hunsaker and Dale Dilamarter, *Training in Management Skills*, Cdn. ed. (Toronto: Pearson Education Canada Inc., 2004), p. 330.

43. Ibid.

44. D. Smith, "Training Programs for Performance Appraisal: A Review," *Academy of Management Review* 11 (1986), pp. 22–40.

45. G. Latham, K. Wexley, and E. Pursell, "Training Managers to Minimize Rating Errors in the Observation of

Behavior," *Journal of Applied Psychology* 60 (1975), pp. 550–55.

46. E. Pulakos, "A Comparison of Rater Training Programs: Error Training and Accuracy Training," *Journal of Applied Psychology* 69 (1984), pp. 581–88.

47. S. W. Gilliland and J. C. Langdon, "Creating Performance Management Systems That Promote Perceptions of Fairness," in *Performance Appraisal: State of the Art in Practice*, pp. 209–43.

48. S. W. J. Kozlowski, G. T. Chao, and R. F. Morrison, "Games Raters Play: Politics, Strategies, and Impression Management in Performance Appraisal," in *Performance Appraisal: State of the Art in Practice*, pp. 163–205.

49. Malcolm Gabriel and Pierre Robitaille, "Sustaining High Performance with Generation-Y Employees," *Canadian HR Reporter*, January 14, 2008, p. 13.

50. K. Wexley, V. Singh, and G. Yukl, "Subordinate Participation in Three Types of Appraisal Interviews," *Journal of Applied Psychology* 58 (1973), pp. 54–57; K. Wexley, "Appraisal Interview," in *Performance Assessment*, ed. R. A. Berk (Baltimore: Johns Hopkins University Press, 1986), pp. 167–85.

51. D. Cederblom, "The Performance Appraisal Interview: A Review, Implications, and Suggestions," *Academy of Management Review* 7 (1982), pp. 219–27; B. D. Cawley, L. M. Keeping, and P. E. Levy, "Participation in the Performance Appraisal Process and Employee Reactions: A Meta-analytic Review of Field Investigations," *Journal of Applied Psychology* 83, no. 3 (1998), pp. 615–63; W. Giles and K. Mossholder, "Employee Reactions to Contextual and Session Components of Performance Appraisal," *Journal of Applied Psychology* 75 (1990), pp. 371–77.

52. Bill Curry, "Health Canada Fires Three Whistleblowers," *Winnipeg Free Press*, July 15, 2004, p. A1.

53. James Heeney, "Personal Harassment Liability Always a Danger for Employers," *Canadian HR Reporter*, October 22, 2007, p. B15.

54. S. E. Forrer and Z. B. Leibowitz, *Using Computers in Human Resources* (San Francisco: Jossey-Bass, 1991).

55. Lauren Chesney, "HR by the Numbers," *Canadian HR Reporter*, January 15, 2007, p. 4.

56. Kristina Dell, "A Spy in Every Pocket," *Time*, March 27, 2006, p. 31; http://trackingtheworld.com/gps-asset-tracking.html, retrieved April 24, 2008.

57. Uyen Vu, "Privacy Law Working Well: Commissioner," *Canadian HR Reporter*, December 18, 2006, p. 1, 13.

Chapter 9

1. David Brown, "Soft Side of Rewards Has Hard Impact," *Canadian HR Reporter*, April 5, 2004, pp. 5, 7. Copyright *Canadian HR Reporter*, April 5, 2004, by Carswell, Toronto, Ontario, 1-800-387-5164, www.hrreporter.com.

2. "WorldatWork Total Rewards Model," www.worldatwork.org/waw/aboutus/html/aboutus-whatis.html#model, retrieved October 22, 2008.

3. "Strategic Rewards in Canada: Building the Optimal Reward Plan—Watson Wyatt's 2004 Survey of Canadian Strategic Rewards and Pay Practices," in "Why Firms Develop a Total Rewards Strategy," *Canadian HR Reporter*, February 14, 2005, p. R5.

4. "What Is Total Rewards?," www.worldatwork.org/waw/aboutus/html/aboutus-whatis.html, retrieved October 22, 2008.

5. "Cost Containment in the Works for Compensation," *InsideEdge, Newsletter of the Conference Board of Canada*, Winter 2004, p. 8, www.conferenceboard.ca, retrieved March 10, 2004.

6. B. Gerhart and G. T. Milkovich, "Organizational Differences in Managerial Compensation and Financial Performance," *Academy of Management Journal* 33 (1990), pp. 663–91; E. L. Groshen, "Why Do Wages Vary among Employers?," *Economic Review* 24 (1988), pp. 19–38.

7. J. S. Adams, "Inequity in Social Exchange," in *Advances in Experimental Social Psychology*, ed. L. Berkowitz (New York: Academic Press, 1965); P. S. Goodman, "An Examination of Referents Used in the Evaluation of Pay," *Organizational Behavior and Human Performance* 12 (1974), pp. 170–95; J. B. Miner," *Theories of Organizational Behavior* (Hinsdale, IL: Dryden Press, 1980).

8. J. P. Pfeffer and A. Davis-Blake, "Understanding Organizational Wage Structures: A Resource Dependence Approach," *Academy of Management Journal* 30 (1987), pp. 437–55.

9. This section draws freely on B. Gerhart and R. D. Bretz, "Employee Compensation," in *Organization and Management of Advanced Manufacturing*, ed. W. Karwowski and G. Salvendy (New York: Wiley, 1994), pp. 81–101.

10. E. E. Lawler III, *Strategic Pay* (San Francisco: Jossey-Bass, 1990); G. Ledford, "3 Cases on Skill-Based Pay: An Overview," *Compensation and Benefits Review*, March/April 1991, pp. 11–23; G. E. Ledford, "Paying for the Skills, Knowledge, Competencies of Knowledge Workers," *Compensation and Benefits Review*, July/August 1995, p. 55.

11. B. C. Murray and B. Gerhart, "An Empirical Analysis of a Skill-Based Pay Program and Plant Performance Outcomes," *Academy of Management Journal* 41, no. 1 (1998), pp. 68–78; N. Gupta, D. Jenkins, and W. Curington, "Paying for Knowledge: Myths and Realities," *National Productivity Review*, Spring 1986, pp. 107–23.

12. B. Gerhart and G. T. Milkovich, "Organizational Differences in Managerial Compensation and Financial Performance," *Academy of Management Journal* 33 (1990), pp. 663–91.

13. Stephen Clarke, "Compensation Planning Outlook 2008" (Ottawa: Conference Board of Canada, October 2007), p. 6.

14. G. T. Milkovich and A. K. Wigdor, *Pay for Performance* (Washington, DC: National Academy Press, 1991);

Gerhart and Bretz, "Employee Compensation";
C. Trevor, B. Gerhart, and J. W. Boudreau, "Voluntary
Turnover and Job Performance: Curvilinearity and the
Moderating Influences of Salary Growth and Promo-
tions," *Journal of Applied Psychology* 82 (1997),
pp. 44–61.

15. Kathy Chu, "What's Good Work Worth These Days?,"
Financial Post, June 16, 2004, p. FP14.

16. Shannon Klie, "New Challenges in Pay for Performance," *Canadian HR Reporter*, April 23, 2007, p. 9.

17. R. D. Bretz, R. A. Ash, and G. F. Dreher, "Do People
Make the Place? An Examination of the Attraction-
Selection-Attrition Hypothesis," *Personnel Psychology*
42 (1989), pp. 561–81; T. A. Judge and R. D. Bretz,
"Effect of Values on Job Choice Decisions," *Journal
of Applied Psychology* 77 (1992), pp. 261–71; D. M.
Cable and T. A. Judge, "Pay Performance and Job
Search Decisions: A Person–Organization Fit
Perspective," *Personnel Psychology* 47 (1994),
pp. 317–48.

18. Gerhart and Bretz, "Employee Compensation."

19. R. D. Bretz, G. T. Milkovich, and W. Read, "The
Current State of Performance Appraisal Research
and Practice," *Journal of Management* 18 (1992),
pp. 321–52; R. L. Heneman, "Merit Pay Research,"
Research in Personnel and Human Resource Management
8 (1990), pp. 203–63; Milkovich and Wigdor, *Pay for
Performance*.

20. Bretz et al., "The Current State of Performance
Appraisal Research and Practice."

21. J. Bennett, "A Career on Commission Can Be a Hard
Sell," *Chicago Tribune*, March 24, 2002, sec. 5, p. 5.

22. T. L. Ross and R. A. Ross, "Gainsharing: Sharing Improved Performance," in *The Compensation Handbook*,
3rd ed., ed. M. L. Rock and L. A. Berger (New York:
McGraw-Hill, 1991).

23. Leah Janzen, "Huge Payday for Brick Staff," *Winnipeg
Free Press*, July 17, 2004, p. A3.

24. T. M. Welbourne and L. R. Gomez-Mejia, "Team Incentives in the Workplace," in Rock and Berger.

25. L. R. Gomez-Mejia and D. B. Balkin, *Compensation,
Organizational Strategy, and Firm Performance*
(Cincinnati: South-Western, 1992).

26. This idea has been referred to as the "share economy."
See M. L. Weitzman, "The Simple Macroeconomics of
Profit Sharing," *American Economic Review* 75 (1985),
pp. 937–53. For supportive research, see the following
studies: J. Chelius and R. S. Smith, "Profit Sharing
and Employment Stability," *Industrial and Labor Rela-
tions Review* 43 (1990), pp. 256S–73S; B. Gerhart and
L. O. Trevor, "Employment Stability Under Different
Managerial Compensation Systems," working paper,
Cornell University Center for Advanced Human Re-
source Studies, 1995; D. L. Kruse, "Profit Sharing and
Employment Variability: Microeconomic Evidence on
the Weitzman Theory," *Industrial and Labor Relations
Review* 44 (1991), pp. 437–53.

27. Erick Schonfeld, "Counting the Google Millionaires,"
www.techcrunch.com/2007/11/12/counting-the-google-
millionaires, retrieved May 6, 2008.

28. Gerhart and Milkovich, "Organizational Differences in
Managerial Compensation."

29. Steve Maich, "Nortel's Final Victim," August 2, 2004,
www.macleans.ca/topstories/business, retrieved
September 20, 2004.

30. http://c3dsp.westjet.com/intemet/sky/jobs/whywestjet
Template.jsp, retrieved February 28, 2005.

31. M. A. Conte and J. Svejnar, "The Performance
Effects of Employee Ownership Plans," in *Paying for
Productivity*, pp. 245–94.

32. R. T. Kaufman, "The Effects of Improshare on Produc-
tivity," *Industrial and Labor Relations Review* 45 (1992),
pp. 311–22; M. H. Schuster, "The Scanlon Plan: A
Longitudinal Analysis," *Journal of Applied Behavioral
Science* 20 (1984), pp. 23–28; J. A. Wagner III,
P. Rubin, and T. J. Callahan, "Incentive Payment and
Nonmanagerial Productivity: An Interrupted Time
Series Analysis of Magnitude and Trend," *Organiza-
tional Behavior and Human Decision Processes* 42 (1988),
pp. 47–74.

33. C. R. Gowen III and S. A. Jennings, "The Effects of
Changes in Participation and Group Size on Gainshar-
ing Success: A Case Study," *Journal of Organizational
Behavior Management* 11 (1991), pp. 147–69.

34. D. I. Levine and L. D. Tyson, "Participation, Productivity,
and the Firm's Environment," in *Paying for Productivity*.

35. T. Welbourne, D. Balkin, and L. Gomez-Mejia, "Gain-
sharing and Mutual Monitoring: A Combined Agency–
Organizational Justice Interpretation," *Academy of
Management Journal* 38 (1995), pp. 881–99.

36. "Benefits—United States," Hewitt Associates website,
http://was.hewitt.com, retrieved August 27, 2002.

37. B. Gerhart and G. T. Milkovich, "Employee Compensation: Research and Practice," in *Handbook of Industrial
and Organizational Psychology*, vol. 3, 2nd ed., ed. M. D.
Dunnette and L. M. Hough (Palo Alto, CA: Consulting
Psychologists Press, 1992).

38. "Canadian Employers Rate Health Plans over Cash,"
The Globe and Mail, May 12, 2004, p. C2.

39. "2008 Top Five Total Rewards Priorities Survey,"
Deloitte website, www.deloitte.com/dtt/article/
0,1002,cid%253D196315,00.html, retrieved May 7, 2008.

40. www.hrsdc.gc.ca/en/isp/statistics/rates/aprjun08
.shtml#topic1, retrieved May 7, 2008.

41. J. V. Nackley, *Primer on Workers' Compensation*
(Washington, DC: Bureau of National Affairs, 1989);
T. Thomason, T. P. Schmidle, and J. F. Burton,
Workers' Compensation (Kalamazoo, MI: Upjohn
Institute, 2001).

42. Sarah Beech, "Lifestyle Choices," *Benefits Canada*,
March 2008, p. 45.

43. Mary Teresa Bitti, "Alternative Health Plan Benefits
Small Firms," *National Post*, March 8, 2004,
pp. FE1, FE4.

44. Shannon Klie, "Do Incentives Help Change Behaviour?," *Canadian HR Reporter,* April 21, 2008, www.hrreporter.com, retrieved May 7, 2008.

45. Nikki Pavlov, "A Healthy Workplace Means Recognizing Stress Is the Enemy," *Canadian HR Reporter,* April 9, 2001, www.hrreporter.com, retrieved September 29, 2004.

46. J. C. Erfurt, A. Foote, and M. A. Heirich, "The Cost-Effectiveness of Work Site Wellness Programs for Hypertension Control, Weight Loss, Smoking Cessation and Exercise," *Personnel Psychology* 45 (1992), pp. 5–27.

47. Brian Lindenberg, "Choosing the right EAP," *Canadian HR Reporter,* March 24, 2008, pp. 22, 27.

48. D. Wessel, "Enron and a Bigger Ill: Americans Don't Save," *The Wall Street Journal Online,* March 7, 2002, http://online.wsj.com.

49. "Long-Term View of Pensions Improves, but Concerns Remain—Findings from the 2007 Survey on Pension Risk" (Ottawa: The Conference Board of Canada, July 2007), p. i, www.conferenceboard.ca/documents.asp?rnext=2077, retrieved October 22, 2008.

50. "Phased Retirement: Aligning Employer Programs with Worker Preferences—2004 Survey Report," www.watsonwyatt.com/research/resrender.asp, retrieved April 21, 2004.

51. Deborah McMillan, "Redefining Retirement," *Benefits Canada,* August 2007, pp. 13, 15, 17.

52. Richard W. Yerema, "Canada's Top 100 Employers 2004" (Toronto: MediaCorp Canada Inc., ISBN 1-894450-17-5, 2004), p. 353.

53. Ibid, p. 131.

54. Statistics Canada, "Study: The Sandwich Generation," *The Daily,* September 28, 2004, www.statcan.ca/Daily/English/040928/d040928b.htm, retrieved October 22, 2008.

55. Government of Canada, "Part-Time Work and Family-Friendly Practices in Canadian Workplaces—June 2003," p. 1, www.hrsdc.gc.ca/en/cs/sp/sdc/pkrf/publications/research/2003-000183/page00.shtml, retrieved October 22, 2008.

56. Kira Vermond, "So Good They Can Help Your Math Skills," *Globe and Mail Update,* October 26, 2007, www.theglobeandmail.com, retrieved November 8, 2007.

57. "Chapter from Canada's Top 100 Employers 2007: Hill & Knowlton Canada," www.eluta.ca, retrieved May 7, 2008.

58. R. Broderick and B. Gerhart, "Nonwage Compensation," in *The Human Resource Management Handbook,* ed. D. Lewin, D.J.B. Mitchell, and M. A. Zadi (San Francisco: JAI Press, 1996).

59. Todd Humber, "Perquisites No Longer a Prerequisite," *Canadian HR Reporter,* February 10, 2003, pp. G7, G9.

60. Ibid.

61. www.intuit.com/canada/carrers_benefits.shtml, retrieved October 1, 2004.

62. B. T. Beam Jr. and J. J. McFadden, *Employee Benefits,* 6th ed. (Chicago: Real Estate Education Co., 2001).

63. Cathy O'Bright, "Flex Benefits Drive Culture Change, Contain Costs at Superior Propane," *Canadian HR Reporter,* September 8, 2003, www.hrreporter.com, retrieved March 21, 2004.

64. David Johnston, "Poorly Communicated Plans Worse Than None at All," *Canadian HR Reporter,* February 14, 2005, p. R7.

65. "Salary Surveys 101," *Canadian HR Reporter,* September 9, 2004, www.hrreporter.com, retrieved September 29, 2004.

66. M. Wilson, G. B. Northcraft, and M. A. Neale, "The Perceived Value of Fringe Benefits," *Personnel Psychology* 38 (1985), pp. 309–20; H. W. Hennessey, P. L. Perrewe, and W. A. Hochwarter, "Impact of Benefit Awareness on Employee and Organizational Outcomes: A Longitudinal Field Experiment," *Benefits Quarterly* 8, no. 2 (1992), pp. 90–96.

67. Todd Humber, "The Power to Change," Supplement to *Canadian HR Reporter,* May 31, 2004, pp. G1, G10.

68. Sinclair Steward, "Godsoe's Nest Egg Worth $122 Million," *The Globe and Mail,* January 31, 2004, pp. B1, B6.

69. Hugh Mackenzie "The Great CEO Pay Race: Over Before It Begins," December 2007, www.growinggap.ca/files/CEO%20Pay%20Study%20FINAL.pdf, retrieved October 22, 2008.

70. Ibid.

71. "Canadian Companies Reward High-Performing CEOs Better Than Low-Performing CEOs," October 27, 2003, www.watsonwyatt.com/Canada-english/news/press, retrieved February 19, 2004.

72. Ibid.

73. Duncan Mavin, "TD Chief Clark's $14.2M Pay Is Biggest of Any Bank Executive," *The Financial Post,* February 22, 2008, www.canada.com/ottawacitizen/news/business/story.html, retrieved May 8, 2008.

74. Gerhart and Milkovich, "Organizational Differences in Managerial Compensation."

75. "Canadian Companies Rewarded High-Performing CEOs Better Than Low-Performing CEOs," October 27, 2003, www.watsonwyatt.com/Canada-english/news/press, retrieved February 19, 2004.

76. "Canadian Companies Rewarded High-Performing CEOs Better Than Low-Performing CEOs."

77. Colin Campbell, "Special Report: If You Want to Win the Talent War, Great Perks Are a Must," *Maclean's,* October 15, 2007, www.macleans.ca/homepage/magazine/article, retrieved May 1, 2008.

Chapter 10

1. Chris Vander Doelen, "Windsor Modules Makes Most of Magna Deal," *The Windsor Star*, November 13, 2007, p. B1; Sonja Puzic, "Magna Workers Back New Deal: Windsor Modules Employees First to Adopt Groundbreaking Pact," *The Windsor Star*, November 8, 2007, p. A1; Lesley Young, "Unlikely Allies Team Up," *Canadian HR Reporter*, November 5, 2007, p. 1; Todd Humber, "Frank and Buzz: The New Felix and Oscar," *Canadian HR Reporter*, November 5, 2007, p. 30.

2. Hollie Shaw, "Wal-Mart Closes First Union Store in Quebec," *Financial Post*, February 10, 2005, pp. A1, A9. Material reprinted with permission of The National Post Company, a CanWest Partnership.

3. See A. M. Glassman and T. G. Cummings, *Industrial Relations: A Multidimensional View* (Glenview, IL: Scott, Foresman, 1985); W. H. Holley Jr. and K. M. Jennings, *The Labor Relations Process* (Chicago: Dryden Press, 1984).

4. T. A. Kochan, *Collective Bargaining and Industrial Relations* (Homewood, IL: Richard D. Irwin, 1980), p. 25; H. C. Katz and T. A. Kochan, *An Introduction to Collective Bargaining and Industrial Relations* (New York: McGraw-Hill, 1992), p. 10.

5. Whether the time the union steward spends on union business is paid for by the employer, the union, or a combination is a matter of negotiation between the employer and the union.

6. "History of Unions in Canada," www.mapleleafweb .com/old/education/spotlight/issue_51/history .html?q=education/spotlight/issue_51/history.html, retrieved October 22, 2008.

7. Suzanne Payette, "Yesterday and Today: Union Membership," excerpt from the *Workplace Gazette* 5, no. 3 (Fall 2002), www.rhdcc.gc.ca, retrieved November 5, 2004.

8. Human Resources and Social Development Canada, "Table 1: Union Membership in Canada, 1997–2007," *Union Membership in Canada—2007*, www.hrsdc.gc.ca/ en/lp/wid/union_membership.shtml, retrieved October 22, 2008.

9. Ibid.

10. Katz and Kochan, *An Introduction to Collective Bargaining*, building on J. Fiorito and C. L. Maranto, "The Contemporary Decline of Union Strength," *Contemporary Policy Issues* 3 (1987), pp. 12–27; G. N. Chaison and J. Rose, "The Macrodeterminants of Union Growth and Decline," in *The State of the Unions*, ed. G. Strauss et al. (Madison, WI: Industrial Relations Research Association, 1991).

11. T. A. Kochan, R. B. McKersie, and J. Chalykoff, "The Effects of Corporate Strategy and Workplace Innovations in Union Representation," *Industrial and Labor Relations Review* 39 (1986), pp. 487–501; Chaison and Rose, "The Macrodeterminants of Union Growth and Decline"; J. Barbash, *Practice of Unionism* (New York: Harper, 1956), p. 210; W. N.Cooke and D. G. Meyer, "Structural and Market Predictors of Corporate Labor Relations Strategies," *Industrial and Labor Relations Review* 43 (1990), pp. 280–93; T. A. Kochan and P. Capelli, "The Transformation of the Industrial Relations and Personnel Function," in *Internal Labor Markets*, ed. P. Osterman (Cambridge, MA: MIT Press, 1984).

12. Shannon Klie, "Women Outnumber Men in Canadian Unions," *Canadian HR Reporter*, September 24, 2007, www.hrreporter.com, retrieved May 13, 2008.

13. "Study: The Union Movement in Transition," *The Daily*, August 31, 2004, www.statcan.ca/Daily/English/040831/ d040831b.htm, retrieved November 6, 2004.

14. Charlotte Yates, "Unions Going After Private Service Sector," *Canadian HR Reporter*, October 6, 2003, www.canadianhrreporter.com, retrieved January 23, 2004.

15. "FAQ #2 May 2008: Getting to the Table," OPSEU Ontario Public Service Employees Union, www .opseu.org/caat/parttime/faq.htm, retrieved October 22, 2008.

16. "Unionization—Table 1: Union Membership and Coverage by Selected Characteristics," *Perspectives on Labour and Income-Statistics Canada*, August 2007, p. 3, www.statcan.ca/english/freepub/75-001-XIE/ comm/fact_2.pdf, retrieved May 14, 2008.

17. Christopher Hallamore, "Industrial Relations Outlook 2008" (Ottawa: Conference Board of Canada, January 2008), p. 20.

18. Ibid., p. 21.

19. www.cupe.ca/environment/enviroguide, retrieved May 14, 2008; "News Briefs," *Canadian HR Reporter*, December 3, 2007, www.hrreporter.com.

20. C. Brewster, "Levels of Analysis in Strategic HRM: Questions Raised by Comparative Research," Conference on Research and Theory in HRM, Cornell University, October 1997.

21. J. T. Addison and B. T. Hirsch, "Union Effects on Productivity, Profits, and Growth: Has the Long Run Arrived?," *Journal of Labor Economics* 7 (1989), pp. 72–105; R. B. Freeman and J. L. Medoff, "The Two Faces of Unionism," *Public Interest* 57 (Fall 1979), pp. 69–93.

22. L. Mishel and P. Voos, *Unions and Economic Competitiveness* (Armonk, NY: M. E. Sharpe, 1991); Freeman and Medoff, "Two Faces"; S. Slichter, J. Healy, and E. R. Livernash, *The Impact of Collective Bargaining on Management* (Washington, DC: Brookings Institution, 1960).

23. A. O. Hirschman, *Exit, Voice, and Loyalty* (Cambridge, MA: Harvard University Press, 1970); R. Batt, A. J. S. Colvin, and J. Keefe, "Employee Voice, Human

Resource Practices, and Quit Rates: Evidence from the Telecommunications Industry," *Industrial and Labor Relations Review* 55 (1970), pp. 573–94.

24. R. B. Freeman and J. L. Medoff, *What Do Unions Do?* (New York: Basic Books, 1984); E. E. Herman, J. L. Schwatz, and A. Kuhn, *Collective Bargaining and Labor Relations* (Englewood Cliffs, NJ: Prentice Hall, 1992); Addison and Hirsch, "Union Effects on Productivity"; Katz and Kochan, *An Introduction to Collective Bargaining*; P. D. Lineman, M. L. Wachter, and W. H. Carter, "Evaluating the Evidence on Union Employment and Wages," *Industrial and Labor Relations Review* 44 (1990), pp. 34–53.

25. B. E. Becker and C. A. Olson, "Unions and Firm Profits," *Industrial Relations* 31, no. 3 (1992), pp. 395–415; B. T. Hirsch and B. A. Morgan, "Shareholder Risks and Returns in Union and Nonunion Firms," *Industrial and Labor Relations Review* 47, no. 2 (1994), pp. 302–18.

26. "Eighth Biennial National Labor–Management Conference," *Monthly Labor Review*, January 1999, pp. 29–45; "Companies Breaking Records in Hard Times," *Milwaukee Journal Sentinel*, October 13, 2001.

27. "Perspectives on Labour and Income," August 31, 2004, www.statcan.ca/Daily/English/04031/b040831a .htm, retrieved November 6, 2004.

28. "History and Development of Unions in Canada: The Rand Formula," www.law-faqs.org/nat/un-ran.htm, retrieved October 22, 2008.

29. S. Webb and B. Webb, *Industrial Democracy* (London: Longmans, Green, 1987); J. R. Commons, *Institutional Economics* (New York: Macmillan, 1934).

30. "Sweeping Labour Law Changes in Ontario," *Canadian HR Reporter*, November 4, 2004, www.hrreporter.com, retrieved November 5, 2004.

31. Hallamore, p. 11.

32. "Frequently Asked Questions," Canada Industrial Relations Board website, www.cirb-ccrLgc.ca/fqu/ index_ e.asp, retrieved November 5, 2004.

33. "Trade Union Application for Certification," www .sdc.gc.ca, retrieved November 1, 2004.

34. Kris Maher and Janet Adamy, "Do Hot Coffee and 'Wobblies' Go Together?," *The Wall Street Journal*, www.starbucksunion.org/node/756, retrieved May 8, 2008.

35. R. B. Freeman and M. M. Kleiner, "Employer Behavior in the Face of Union Organizing Drives," *Industrial and Labor Relations Review* 43, no. 4 (April 1990), pp. 351–65.

36. Freeman and Medoff, *What Do Unions Do?*; National Labor Relations Board annual reports for 1980s and 1990s.

37. J. A. Fossum, *Labor Relations*, 5th ed. (Homewood, IL: Richard D. Irwin, 1992), p. 149.

38. Department of Justice Canada website, http://laws .justice.gc.ca/en/L-2/16931.html, retrieved November 6, 2004.

39. Labour Relations Board British Columbia website, www.lrb.bc.ca/mediation/new_cert.htm, retrieved November 8, 2004.

40. Fossum, *Labor Relations*, p. 262.

41. R. E. Walton and R. B. McKersie, *A Behavioral Theory of Negotiations* (New York: McGraw-Hill, 1965).

42. C. M. Steven, *Strategy and Collective Bargaining Negotiations* (New York: McGraw-Hill, 1963): Katz and Kochan, *An Introduction to Collective Bargaining*.

43. Statistics Canada, "Perspectives on Labour and Income," Table 4, August 2007, p. 8.

44. Kochan, *Collective Bargaining and Industrial Relations*, p. 272.

45. Katz and Kochan, *An Introduction to Collective Bargaining*.

46. T. A. Kochan, H. C. Katz, and R. B. McKersie, *The Transformation of American Industrial Relations* (New York: Basic Books, 1986), chap. 6; E. Appelbaum, T. Bailey, and P. Berg, *Manufacturing Advantage: Why High-Performance Work Systems Pay Off* (Ithaca, NY: Cornell University Press, 2000).

47. L. W. Hunter, J. P. MacDuffie, and L. Doucet, "What Makes Teams Take? Employee Reactions to Work Reforms," *Industrial and Labor Relations Review* 55 (2002), pp. 448–472.

48. J. B. Arthur, "The Link Between Business Strategy and Industrial Relations Systems in American Steel Minimills," *Industrial and Labor Relations Review* 45 (1992), pp. 488–506; M. Schuster, "Union Management Cooperation," in *Employee and Labor Relations*, ed. J. A. Fossum (Washington, DC: Bureau of National Affairs, 1990); E. Cohen-Rosenthal and C. Burton, *Mutual Gains: A Guide to Union–Management Cooperation*, 2nd ed. (Ithaca, NY: ILR Press, 1993); T. A. Kochan and P. Osterman, *The Mutual Gains Enterprise* (Boston: Harvard Business School Press, 1994); E. Applebaum and R. Batt, *The New American Workplace* (Ithaca, NY: ILR Press, 1994).

49. Eric Beauchesne, "Public Unions in Volatile Mood," *Financial Post*, December 17, 2004, p. FP2.

50. Allan Swift, "Bombardier, Union Reach Deal," *The Globe and Mail*, March 3, 2005, p. B6.

51. Frederic Tomesco and Theo Argitis, "Bombardier Workers Agree to New Contract," *The Globe and Mail*, March 7, 2005, p. B5.

52. A. E. Eaton, "Factors Contributing to the Survival of Employee Participation Programs in Unionized Settings," *Industrial and Labor Relations Review* 47, no. 3 (1994), pp. 371–89.

53. "Preventive Mediation: Nova Scotia Industrial Relations Conciliation Services," www.gov.ns.ca/enla/ conciliation/prevbro.htm, retrieved March 5, 2005.

54. Judith Lendvay-Zwicki, "The Canadian Industrial Relations System: Current Challenges and Future Options" (Ottawa: Conference Board of Canada, April 2004), www.conferenceboard.ca, retrieved April 19, 2004.

Chapter 11

1. Research in Motion website, www.rim.com, and www .rim.com/careers, retrieved June 7, 2008.

2. Towers Perrin, *Priorities for Competitive Advantage: A Worldwide Human Resource Study* (Valhalla, NY: Towers Perrin, 1991).

3. Vladimir Pucik, "Human Resources in the Future: An Obstacle or a Champion of Globalization," *Tomorrow's HR Management*, ed. Dave Ulrich, Michael R. Losey, and Gerry Lake (John Wiley & Sons, Inc. New York, 1997), pp. 326–327.

4. Lesley Young, "Attracting, Keeping Employees Overseas," *Canadian HR Reporter*, April 7, 2008, www.hrreporter.com, retrieved May 26, 2008.

5. "Hewitt Associates Study Highlights Global Sourcing Trends and Outcomes," March 2, 2004, http://was4 .hewitt.com/resource/newsroom/presrel, retrieved March 3, 2004.

6. S. Moffett, "Separation Anxiety," *The Wall Street Journal*, September 27, 2004, p. R11; A. Browne, "Chinese Recruit Top Executives Trained Abroad," *The Wall Street Journal*, November 30, 2004, pp. B1, B8.

7. Loewen website, www.loewen.com, retrieved June 7, 2008.

8. "Canadian Tire to Open Office in Shanghai," *The Globe and Mail*, June 26, 2004, p. B4.

9. "CN Rail Opens Offices in China," *Leader-Post*, October 23, 2004, p. D6.

10. "Bank of Nova Scotia Buys Fourth Largest Bank in Central America," *Leader-Post*, October 23, 2004, p. D9.

11. BP Global website, www.bp.com, retrieved June 7, 2008.

12. N. Adler and S. Bartholomew, "Managing Globally Competent People," *The Executive* 6 (1992), pp. 52–65.

13. V. Sathe, *Culture and Related Corporate Realities* (Homewood, IL: Richard D. Irwin, 1985); M. Rokeach, *Beliefs, Attitudes, and Values* (San Francisco: Jossey-Bass, 1968).

14. N. Adler, *International Dimensions of Organizational Behavior*, 2nd ed. (Boston: PWS-Kent, 1991).

15. G. Hofstede, "Dimensions of National Cultures in Fifty Countries and Three Regions," in *Expectations in Cross-Cultural Psychology*, ed. J. Deregowski, S. Dziurawiec, and R. C. Annis (Lisse, Netherlands: Swets and Zeitlinger, 1983); G. Hofstede, "Cultural Constraints in Management Theories," *Academy of Management Executive* 7 (1993), pp. 81–90.

16. Hofstede, "Cultural Constraints in Management Theories."

17. W. A. Randolph and M. Sashkin, "Can Organizational Empowerment Work in Multinational Settings?," *Academy of Management Executive* 16, no. 1 (2002), pp. 102–115.

18. Lesley Young, "Attracting, Keeping Employees Overseas," *Canadian HR Reporter*, April 7, 2008, www .hrreporter.com, retrieved May 26, 2008.

19. Randolph and Sashkin, pp. 102–115.

20. National Center for Education Statistics (NCES), "International Comparisons of Education," *Digest of Education Statistics, 2000*, chap. 6, NCES website, http://nces.ed.gov, retrieved September 23, 2002.

21. Adler and Bartholomew, "Managing Globally Competent People."

22. P. Conrad and R. Peiper, "Human Resource Management in the Federal Republic of Germany," in *Human Resource Management: An International Comparison*, ed. R. Peiper (Berlin: Walter de Gruyter, 1990).

23. "Saskatchewan Looking to Lure Nurses from Philippines," February 21, 2008, www.cbc.ca/canada/ saskatchewan/story/2008/02/21/nurses-philippines .html, retrieved June 7, 2008.

24. L. M. Kunii, "Under the Knife," *BusinessWeek*, September 10, 2001, p. 62; C. Dawson, "Saying Sayonara," *BusinessWeek*, September 24, 2001, pp. 108–9; L M. Kunii, "Japan's Jobless Need More Than a Handout," *BusinessWeek*, September 24, 2001, p. 110.

25. B. Ettore, "Let's Hear It for Local Talent," *Management Review*, October 1994, p. 9; S. Franklin, "A New World Order for Business Strategy," *Chicago Tribune*, May 15, 1994, sec. 19, pp. 7–8.

26. Lawrence A. West Jr. and Walter A. Bogumil Jr., "Foreign Knowledge Workers as a Strategic Staffing Option," *The Academy of Management Executive*, November 2000.

27. W. A. Arthur Jr. and W. Bennett Jr., "The International Assignee: The Relative Importance of Factors Perceived to Contribute to Success," *Personnel Psychology* 48 (1995), pp. 99–114; G. M. Spreitzer, M. W. McCall Jr., and J. D. Mahoney, "Early Identification of International Executive Potential," *Journal of Applied Psychology* 82 (1997), pp. 6–29.

28. J. S. Black and J. K. Stephens, "The Influence of the Spouse on American Expatriate Adjustment and Intent to Stay in Pacific Rim Overseas Assignments," *Journal of Management* 15 (1989), pp. 529–44.

29. P. Caligiuri, "The Big Five Personality Characteristics as Predictors of Expatriates' Desire to Terminate the Assignment and Supervisor-Rated Performance," *Personnel Psychology* 53 (2000), pp. 67–88.

30. J. Flynn, "E-mail, Cell Phones, and Frequent-Flier Miles Let 'Virtual' Expats Work Abroad but Live at Home," *The Wall Street Journal*, October 25, 1999, p. A26.

31. Liam Dixon and Margaret Sim, "Short-Term Assignments Growing in Popularity," *Canadian HR Reporter*, March 10, 2008, p. 17.

32. Ibid.

33. D. M. Gayeski, C. Sanchirico, and J. Anderson, "Designing Training for Global Environments: Knowing What Questions to Ask," *Performance Improvement Quarterly* 15, no. 2 (2002), pp. 15–31.

34. B. Filipczak, "Think Locally, Train Globally," *Training* (January 1997), pp. 41–48.

35. "Explore," *The Schlumberger Campus Magazine*, November 2006, p. 7, www.slb.com, retrieved June 10, 2008.

36. J. S. Black and M. Mendenhall, "A Practical but Theory-Based Framework for Selecting Cross-Cultural Training Methods," in *Readings and Cases in International Human Resource Management*, ed. M. Mendenhall and G. Oddou (Boston: PWS-Kent, 1991), pp. 177–204.

37. C. Lachnit, "Low-Cost Tips for Successful Inpatriation," *Workforce*, August 2001, pp. 42–44, 46–47.

38. D. D. Davis, "International Performance Measurement and Management," in *Performance Appraisal: State of the Art in Practice*, ed. J. W. Smither (San Francisco: Jossey-Bass, 1998), pp. 95–131.

39. M. Gowan, S. Ibarreche, and C. Lackey, "Doing the Right Things in Mexico," *Academy of Management Executive* 10 (1996), pp. 74–81.

40. L. S. Chee, "Singapore Airlines: Strategic Human Resource Initiatives," in *International Human Resource Management: Think Globally, Act Locally*, e d. D. Torrington (Upper Saddle River, NJ: Prentice Hall, 1994), pp. 143–59.

41. D. D. Davis, "International Performance Measurement and Management," in *Performance Appraisal: State of the Art in Practice*, ed. J. W. Smither (San Francisco: Jossey-Bass, 1998), pp. 95–131.

42. C. Sparks, T. Bikoi, and L. Moglia, "A Perspective on U.S. and Foreign Compensation Costs in Manufacturing," *Monthly Labor Review* 125 (June 2002).

43. See, for example, A. E. Cobet, and G. A. Wilson, "Comparing 50 Years of Labor Productivity in U.S. and Foreign Manufacturing," *Monthly Labor Review*, June 2002, pp. 51–63.

44. "China's Graduates Want Share of the Boom," *NZ Herald*, www.nzherald.co.nz/section/2/story.cfm?c_id=2&objectid=10514898, retrieved June 10, 2008.

45. P. Wonacott, "China's Secret Weapon: Smart, Cheap Labor for High-Tech Goods," *The Wall Street Journal*, March 14, 2002, pp. A1, A6.

46. "Mexican Labour Relationship," www.solutions-abroad.com/d_mexicanlaborlaws.asp.

47. The European Commission, "Taxation of European Stock Options," *Europa: The European Union On-Line*, June 26, 2001, http://europa.eu.int; D. Woodruff, "Europe: A Latecomer, Embraces Options Even as Market Swoons," *The Wall Street Journal*, May 15, 2001, www.wsj.com; "Eager Europeans Press Their Noses to the Glass," *BusinessWeek Online*, April 19, 1999, www.businessweek.com.

48. Ann Macaulay, "Scouting the Danger Online," *Canadian HR Reporter*, September 24, 2007, p. 13.

49. "Employers Compensating Employees in High-Risk Areas," August 5, 2003, www.hrreporter.com, retrieved January 23, 2004.

50. Macaulay, ibid.

51. Craig Malcolm, "Protecting Employees in Danger Zones," *Canadian HR Reporter*, September 24, 2007, p. 9.

52. Paul Glader and Kris Maher, "Unions Look for Cross-Border Allies," *The Globe and Mail*, March 15, 2005, p. B17.

53. P. J. Dowling, D. E. Welch, and R. S. Schuler, *International Human Resource Management*, 3rd ed. (Cincinnati: South-Western, 1999), pp. 235–36.

54. Ibid.; J. La Palombara and S. Blank, *Multinational Corporations and National Elites: A Study of Tensions* (New York: Conference Board, 1976); A. B. Sim, "Decentralized Management of Subsidiaries and Their Performance: A Comparative Study of American, British and Japanese Subsidiaries in Malaysia," *Management International Review* 17, no. 2 (1977), pp. 45–51; Y. K. Shetty, "Managing the Multinational Corporation: European and American Styles," *Management International Review* 19, no. 3 (1979), pp. 39–48; J. Hamill, "Labor Relations Decision-Making Within Multinational Corporations," *Industrial Relations Journal* 15, no. 2 (1984), pp. 30–34.

55. Dowling, Welch, and Schuler, p. 231.

56. P. Wonacott, "PetroChina Unit, After Job Cuts, Is Besieged by Protesters," *The Wall Street Journal*, March 14, 2002, pp. A9, A12.

57. J. K. Sebenius, "The Hidden Challenge of Cross-Border Negotiations," *Harvard Business Review*, March 2002, pp. 76–85.

58. Ibid.

59. Stephen Cryne, "Avoiding the Perils of Foreign Assignments," *Canadian HR Reporter*, March 12, 2007, p. 14.

60. Margaret Sim and Liam Dixon, "Number of Women Expats Increasing," *Canadian HR Reporter*, May 21, 2007, p. 14.

61. R. Tung, "Selection and Training Procedures of U.S., European, and Japanese Multinational Corporations," *California Management Review* 25, no. 1 (1982), pp. 57–71.

62. L. Copeland and L. Griggs, *Going International* (New York: Random House, 1985).

63. E. Krell, "Evaluating Returns on Expatriates," *HR Magazine*, March 2005, http://web5.infotrac.galegroup.com.

64. Ibid.; M. Harvey and M. M. Novicevic, "Selecting Expatriates for Increasingly Complex Global Assignments," *Career Development International* 6, no. 2 (2001), pp. 69–86.

65. M. Mendenhall and G. Oddou, "The Dimensions of Expatriate Acculturation," *Academy of Management Review* 10 (1985), pp. 39–47.

66. Arthur and Bennett, "The International Assignee."

67. J. I. Sanchez, P. E. Spector, and C. L. Cooper, "Adapting to a Boundaryless World: A Developmental

Expatriate Model," *Academy of Management Executive* 14, no. 2 (2000), pp. 96–106.

68. "Work Week," *The Wall Street Journal*, September 5, 1995, p. AI.

69. "Ten Years of Global Relocation Trends: 1993–2004," GMAC Global Relocation Services website, October 2004, www.gmacglobalrelocation.com/insight_support/grts/10-year_GRTS.pdf, retrieved October 22, 2008.

70. P. Dowling and R. Schuler, *International Dimensions of Human Resource Management* (Boston: PWS-Kent, 1990).

71. Sanchez, Spector, and Cooper, "Adapting to a Boundaryless World."

72. Ibid.; Lachnit, "Low-Cost Tips for Successful Inpatriation."

73. P. Evans, V. Pucik, and J.-L. Barsoux, *The Global Challenge: Frameworks for International Human Resource Management* (New York: McGraw-Hill/Irwin, 2002), p. 131; F. Higgins, "Survey on Expatriate Compensation and Benefits, 1996," cited in B. Fitzgerald-Turner, "Myths of Expatriate Life," *HR Magazine* 42, no. 6 (June 1997), pp. 65–74.

74. Lynne Molmar, "Addressing Expatriate Tax Issues," *Canadian HR Reporter*, March 13, 2006, p. 15.

75. Sim and Dixon, ibid.

76. J. Flynn, "Multinationals Help Career Couples Deal with Strains Affecting Expatriates," *The Wall Street Journal*, August 8, 2000, p. A19; C. Solomon, "The World Stops Shrinking," *Workforce*, January 2000, pp. 48–51; C. Solomon, "Unhappy Trails," *Workforce*, August 2000, pp. 36–41.

77. Amy Maingault, Lesa Albright, and Vicki Neal, "Policy Tips, Repatriation, Safe Harbor Rules," *HR Magazine*, March 2008, p. 34.

78. "Ten Years of Global Relocation Trends: 1993–2004."

79. "Minimizing Expatriate Turnover," *Workforce Management Online*, August 2004, www.workforce.com/section/09/article/23/81/28.html, retrieved March 22, 2005.

80. Adler, *International Dimensions of Organizational Behavior*.

81. L. G. Klaff, "The Right Way to Bring Expats Home," *Workforce*, July 2002, pp. 40–44.

Chapter 12

1. "Do Something Extraordinary for Canada and the World," *Financial Post*, April 14, 2004, p. FP13. Reprinted with permission of the Vancouver Organizing Committee for the 2010 Olympic and Paralympic Winter Games.

2. "Business Plan and Games Budget: Appendix #5: Human Resources Plan," Vancouver 2010 Organizing Committee, www.vancouver2010.com/resources/PDFs/07_05_08_VANOC_Business_Plan_EN_e_appendices.pdf and www.vancouver2010.com/en/OrganizingCommittee/AboutOrganizingCommittee/ExecutiveTeam/DonnaWilson, retrieved June 10, 2008.

3. S. Snell and J. Dean, "Integrated Manufacturing and Human Resource Management: A Human Capital Perspective," *Academy of Management Journal* 35 (1992), pp. 467–504.

4. M. A. Huselid, "The Impact of Human Resource Management Practices on Turnover, Productivity, and Corporate Financial Performance," *Academy of Management Journal* 38 (1995), pp. 635–72; U.S. Department of Labor, *High-Performance Work Practices and Firm Performance* (Washington, DC: U.S. Government Printing Office, 1993).

5. R. N. Ashkenas, "Beyond the Fads: How Leaders Drive Change with Results," *Human Resource Planning* 17 (1994), pp. 25–44.

6. "Client Testimonials," SGCI website, www.sgcicom.com, retrieved March 26, 2005.

7. SGCI correspondence with author received in an email from Judy Ells on April 4, 2005.

8. J. Arthur, "The Link Between Business Strategy and Industrial Relations Systems in American Steel Mini-Mills," *Industrial and Labor Relations Review* 45 (1992), pp. 488–506.

9. Wallace Immen, "Managers Hold Key to Keep Staff Happy," *The Globe and Mail*, June 16, 2004, p. C3.

10. D. McCann and C. Margerison, "Managing High-Performance Teams," *Training and Development Journal*, November 1989, pp. 52–60; S. Sheman, "Secrets of HP's 'Muddled' Team," *Fortune*, March 18, 1996, pp. 116–20.

11. Virginia Galt "Running Away from the Big Bad Boss," *The Globe and Mail*, November 5, 2007, www.theglobeandmail.com, retrieved November 8, 2007.

12. D. Senge, "The Learning Organization Made Plain and Simple," *Training and Development Journal*, October 1991, pp. 37–44.

13. T. T. Baldwin, C. Danielson, and W. Wiggenhorn, "The Evolution of Learning Strategies in Organizations: From Employee Development to Business Redefinition," *Academy of Management Executive* 11 (1997), pp. 47–58; J. J. Martocchio and T. T. Baldwin, "The Evolution of Strategic Organizational Training," in *Research in Personnel and Human Resource Management* 15, ed. G. R. Ferris (Greenwich, CT: JAI Press, 1997), pp. 1–46.

14. T. Stewart, "The House That Knowledge Built," *Fortune*, October 2, 2000, pp. 278–80; Viant website, www.viant.com.

15. T. A. Judge, C. J. Thoresen, J. E. Bono, and G. K. Patton, "The Job Satisfaction-Job Performance Relationship: A Qualitative and Quantitative Review," *Psychological Bulletin* 127 (2001), pp. 376–407; R. A. Katzell, D. E. Thompson, and R. A. Guzzo, "How Job

Satisfaction and Job Performance Are and Are Not Linked," *Job Satisfaction*, ed. C. J. Cranny, P. C. Smith, and E. F. Stone (New York: Lexington Books, 1992), pp. 195–217.

16. Monster Worldwide, "61 Percent of Americans Consider Themselves Overworked and 86 Percent Are Not Satisfied with Their Job, According to Monster's 2004 Work/Life Balance Survey," news release, August 3, 2004, http://pr.monsterworldwide.com.

17. P. E. Boverie and M. Kroth, *Transforming Work: The Five Keys to Achieving Trust, Commitment, and Passion in the Workplace* (Cambridge, MA: Perseus, 2001), pp. 71–72, 79.

18. R. P. Gephart Jr., "Introduction to the Brave New Workplace: Organizational Behavior in the Electronic Age," *Journal of Organizational Behavior* 23 (2002), pp. 327–44.

19. Neil Crawford, "Leading by Example," *HR Professional*, June/July 2008, pp. 32–32.

20. W. F. Cascio, *Costing Human Resources: The Financial Impact of Behavior in Organizations*, 3rd ed. (Boston: PWS-Kent, 1991); Watson Wyatt Worldwide, *Watson Wyatt's Human Capital Index: Human Capital as a Lead Indicator of Shareholder Value*, 2001/2002 survey report, October 2002, www.humancapitalonline.com.

21. Watson Wyatt Worldwide, *Watson Wyatt's Human Capital Index*.

22. B. Becker and M. A. Huselid, "High-Performance Work Systems and Firm Performance: A Synthesis of Research and Managerial Implications," in *Research in Personnel and Human Resource Management* 16, ed. G. R. Ferris (Stamford, CT: JAI Press, 1998), pp. 53–101.

23. B. Becker and B. Gerhart, "The Impact of Human Resource Management on Organizational Performance: Progress and Prospects," *Academy of Management Journal* 39 (1996), pp. 779–801.

24. B. Wysocki Jr., "To Fix Health Care, Hospitals Take Tips from Factory Floor," *The Wall Street Journal*, April 9, 2004, pp. A1, A6.

25. "Leadership: Ripe for Change," interview with Randall MacDonald, *Human Resource Executive*, 2002, pp. 60, 62+.

26. Sarah Dobson, "Project Connects Dots Between T&D, Profit," *Canadian HR Reporter*, April 21, 2008, p. 3.

27. G. Flynn, "HR Leaders Stay Close to the Line" *Workforce*, February 1997, p. 53; GE Fanuc website, "World Class Excellence," www.ge.com/gemis/gefanuc.

28. C. M. Solomon, "HR's Push for Productivity," *Workforce*, August 2002, pp. 28–33.

29. H. J. Bernardin, C. M. Hagan, J. S. Kane, and P. Villanova, "Effective Performance Management: A Focus on Precision, Customers, and Situational Constraints," in *Performance Appraisal: State of the Art in Practice*, ed. J. W. Smither (San Francisco: Jossey-Bass, 1998), p. 56.

30. J. Bailey, "Entrepreneurs Share Their Tips to Boost a Firm's Productivity," *The Wall Street Journal*, July 9, 2002, p. B4.

31. L. R. Gomez-Mejia and D. B. Balkin, *Compensation, Organizational Strategy, and Firm Performance* (Cincinnati: South-Western, 1992); G. D. Jenkins and E. E. Lawler III, "Impact of Employee Participation in Pay Plan Development," *Organizational Behavior and Human Performance* 28 (1981), pp. 111–28.

32. Gwyn Morgan, "'Merger of Equals' Pitch Created EnCana, but It Would Flop Today," *The Globe and Mail*, April 30, 2007, p. B2.

33. Uyen Vu, "HR's Role in Mergers, Acquisitions," *Canadian HR Reporter*, December 4, 2006, p. 17, 21.

34. "Involve HR Early in M&As for Success, Survey Shows," *The Globe and Mail*, December 17, 2004, p. C3.

35. Uyen Vu, ibid.

36. Ibid.

37. Ibid.

38. S. Shrivastava and J. Shaw, "Liberating HR Through Technology," *Human Resource Management* 42, no. 3 (2003), pp. 201–17.

39. R. Broderick and J. W. Boudreau, "Human Resource Management, Information Technology, and the Competitive Edge," *Academy of Management Executive* 6 (1992), pp. 7–17.

40. L. Baird and I. Meshoulam, "Managing Two Fits of Strategic Human Resource Management," *Academy of Management Review* 13, no. 1 (1988), pp. 116–128.

41. "Towers Perrin Survey Shows Companies Making Major Strides in Implementing and Streamlining HR Technology Systems," August 29, 2007, www.towersperrin.com, retrieved June 10, 2008.

42. "What's on the Horizon in HR Technology," *Canadian HR Reporter*, September 22, 2003, www.hrreporter.com, retrieved January 23, 2004.

43. Solomon, p. 31.

44. R. P. Gephart, "Introduction to the Brave New Workplace: Organizational Behavior in the Electronic Age," *Journal of Organizational Behavior* 23 (2002), pp. 327–344.

45. "Hot HR Issues for the Next Two Years" (Ottawa: Conference Board of Canada, September 2004).

46. "CFOs Showing More Interest in HR," *Canadian HR Reporter*, October 25, 2004, p. 4.

47. David Brown, "Measuring Human Capital Crucial, ROI Isn't, Says New Think-Tank Paper," *Canadian HR Reporter*, October 25, 2004, p. 4.

48. Ibid.

49. Jeff Sanford, "Value for the Money," *Canadian Business*, February 18, 2008, pp. 31–32.

50. "As Pressure to Reduce Costs Continues, HR Works to Save, but Struggles to Measure, According to Hewitt," press release, Hewitt Associates, February 17, 2004, http://was4.hewitt.com/hewitt/resource/ newsroom/ presrel/2004, retrieved February 24, 2004.

51. R. F. Stolz, "CEOs Who 'Get It,'" *Human Resource Executive*, March 16, 2005, pp. 1, 18–25.

52. D. E. Bailey and N. B. Kurland, "A Review of Telework Research: Findings, New Directions, and Lessons for the Study of Modern Work," *Journal of Organizational Behavior* 23 (2002), pp. 383–400.

Photo Credits

Name/Company Index

Titles of specific books or pubications and names of specific acts of legislation or legal cases can be found in the SUBJECT INDEX.

See also SUBJECT INDEX

Subject Index

Names of government agencies, institutions, organizations, and publications will be found in the NAME/COMPANY INDEX

See also NAME/COMPANY INDEX